Intangible Property Rights
in Ireland

To my Mother
and
In Memory of my Father

Intangible Property Rights in Ireland

Albert Power

BCL, LLM, PhD, Solicitor
Republic of Ireland, Northern Ireland

Print on Demand Edition

Published by
Tottel Publishing Ltd
Maxwelton House
41-43 Boltro Road
Haywards Heath
West Sussex
RH16 1BJ

Tottel Publishing Ltd
Fitzwarren Business Centre
26 Upper Pembroke Street
Dublin 2
Ireland

ISBN 13: 978-1-84592-551-2
ISBN 10: 1-84592-551-3
© Albert Power 2003
Formerly published by LexisNexis Butterworths

Reprinted by Tottel Publishing Ltd 2007

British Library Cataloguing-in-Publication Data
A catalogue record for this book is available from the British Library

Typeset by Marlex Editorial Services Ltd, Dublin
Printed and bound in Great Britain by
CPI Antony Rowe Limited, Chippenham, Wiltshire

Preface

The text which follows is a treatment of that aspect of the law of property which deals with rights in relation to land other than ownership or possession. In particular, it addresses the use or enjoyment of land in the context of the ownership or occupation of *other* land. Easements, profits *à prendre* appurtenant, and covenants that run with land, all fall into this category. Profits *à prendre* in gross and licences, though not linked to the ownership of land by the party entitled to the enjoyment, are in the same family, so to speak – and hence are also covered. A licence, indeed, represents something of a hybrid species: on the one hand, a mere enjoyment, less than an easement, conferring limited proprietary rights, if any; on the other hand, of a nature sometimes resembling a lease, and often confused with it. As shall be seen, a 'right of residence' – which is a variety of licence – enjoys a curious jurisprudence, reaching back into the middle of the nineteenth century, and has had something of a vogue, in the courts of both parts of Ireland, in recent years.

While I have endeavoured to explain and elaborate the relevant law, the approach taken resembles more the narrative than the lexicon. A fundamental tenet is that, though the judge-made law in Ireland has progressed in parallel with developments in England, in large measure it has developed separately and distinctly. In the case of easements, this individual development can largely be ascribed to the related causes, of the 26-year delay in enacting the Prescription Act 1832 in Ireland, and the historic preponderance of leasehold over freehold titles throughout the island. The judges of the nineteenth century deserve credit for having hewn, where they could, an independent course, with an assiduity not always believed of them from the wry modern perspective of a wholly different world.

By reason of the island's greater size and its far larger population, there is more of a plenitude of case law in Great Britain than in Ireland. A writer, in consequence, is presented with alternative approaches. He or she can unfurl the complex fabric of the law, mainly woven in Great Britain, with suitable embroidery for this side of the Irish Sea. Or an author can present the Irish law as a primary source, with developments in Britain being deployed to 'plug the gap', as it were. The approach adopted here is more consistent with the second style. It is suggested that this leaves the reader – be they scholar or practitioner – with a clearer idea of the options available in Ireland, rather than a dulled comprehension of deeming the law developed in England as the law to be applied here with mere minor modifications.

It is in the realm of covenants, that there is the greatest need for 'plugging of gaps'. The development of equity, to permit the enforceability of covenants in an estate scheme, is principally a product of the English courts. The same can be said of the so-called notions of 'annexation' and 'assignment' for the running of the benefit of restrictive covenants. Coverage of the law governing the enforceability of covenants, by and against successors, without reference to these, would be noticeably scant.

Of course, since 1922 there have been two jurisdictions in Ireland, with the potential for marked diversity of statute and judge-made law. Inevitably, the reader in Northern Ireland must approach this work with some circumspection, as it does not purport – nor could it – to offer a précis of the law of the United Kingdom. However, the continuing applicability, in both parts of the island, of the Landlord and Tenant Law Amendment, Ireland, Act ('Deasy's Act') 1860, and the immunity of each from Great Britain's Law of Property Act 1925, it is suggested, offer sound reasons why such caution should not run deep. Additionally, and significantly, the preponderance of judge-made law considered in this work derives from a time when the entire island was constituent in the United Kingdom, and so forms a rich common law inheritance for both parts of Ireland.

Where the law in Northern Ireland is clearly distinct from that in Great Britain and the Republic of Ireland, it is separately treated of. The most obvious example of this is the Property (Northern Ireland) Order 1997. Where judicial decisions in Northern Ireland and the Republic of Ireland are demonstrably consistent, I have not hesitated to refer to them interchangeably.

Were one to hazard a philosophical comment, it must be to remark the wealth of property law issues considered, and the abundance of legal learning displayed, in the decisions of the courts in Ireland in the years before 1922. A cursory inspection of many of the cases reviewed discloses a profusion of issues involving small tenant farmers, tradespersons, publicans and shopkeepers being litigated in the superior courts, often involving not one, but two, appeals (even to the House of Lords), with a minimum of intermission between the hearings in one court and in the next. In the late nineteenth century it was not uncommon to have whole law reports scattered with a miscellany of property law matters. This is not so today. The 1990s show some resurgence of incorporeal property disputes before the courts. It is to be hoped, for the development of the law, that this trend continues.

There are certain peculiarities in the work which justify comment. The rule in *Wheeldon v Burrows* and s 6 of the Conveyancing Act 1881 are often twinned, in textual treatment, through the relevance to both of the concept of 'continuous and apparent' enjoyment. I regard s 6 of the Conveyancing Act 1881 as a type of legislative implication: so it features in the chapter on easements passing by implication. On the other hand, the rule in *Wheeldon v Burrows* has always struck me as a modified form of an easement of necessity, and this is reflected in my treatment. The devotion of no fewer than four chapters to easements arising otherwise than by express grant may cause eyebrows to lift. Indeed, if I am felt to fashion a multi-movement symphonic suite from the subtle strains of implied grant, or to exalt the embattled history of presumed lost grant into a kind of odyssey, it is important for the reader to recall that these are facilities which pertain in Ireland – at least, at one time did, and may once more. This is, indeed, one of the prime purposes of the offered work – to prompt an awareness of future potential through perusal of the jurisprudence from ages past. I hope that the perseverance of the reader will be rewarded by these discoveries.

Albert Power
October 2003

Acknowledgments

Some few words of tribute are due, which I now gladly pay: to the late Professor James C Brady, who, as supervisor of the PhD thesis which was the progenitor of much (but not all) of what follows, staunchly recommended me to refine and reshape the text for publication; to Professor Andrew Lyall and Professor John Wylie, learned giants in the world of property law, than whom one could have sought no more rigorous PhD examiners, and whose seal of approval was an immense gratification; to Butterworths for undertaking the work of publication, and Louise Leavy, the managing editor in law, for her constant support and advice; to Margaret Byrne and the staff of the library of the Law Society of Ireland; and, ultimately and most warmly, to my family for their unremitting and ever cheerful encouragement.

Contents

Chapter 23 Conacre and Agistment

Table of Cases

A

C

D

E

F

G

M

T

Table of Statutes

Chapter 1

Definition and Types of Easement

Introduction

[1.01] Land is the most solid and enduring entity we know or can imagine. The ownership of land is the most evanescent form of owning. Unlike a chattel, which can be consumed or at least palpably possessed, the owner of land – no matter in what estate – has a transitory term or mode of enjoyment, following the fulfilment of which the land alone, and that which it covers or accommodates, remains. The enjoyment and the one enjoying are alike delimited by finite life. A chattel will disintegrate in time. Land may be littered with buildings, tilled, harvested, extensively mined, its surface lowered; but when the enjoyment of it has been exhausted, in some shape or form the land itself endures. As it cannot be consumed, the modes of enjoyment of land are as manifold as the diversities of interest capable of being recognised. This state of things is acknowledged, if not articulated, by the law. Emerging from feudal society's notions of tenure, the concept of land ownership over recent centuries has been laced with a network of estates, all potentially capable of co-existing. None can enjoy the land in quite the same way at precisely the same time. A life tenant's enjoyment is markedly different from that of the fee simple owner entitled in remainder or reversion. Possession by a lessee entails corresponding non-possession by a lessor. Indeed, most types of interest can be differentiated, in non-legal language, by the notions of occupation and expectation. Even occupation, as will be shown, is a vestment of varying hues.

Amidst this myriad of multiple enjoyments a unique place is occupied by that category of rights in relation to land which involve enjoyment of the fruits or facilities of land without actual ownership of it. In non-legal terms this category can be characterised as enjoyment merely. The law distinguishes between the right to draw off, or to use, the produce of the land – known as a profit *à prendre* – and a right to derive benefit from land in the context of the ownership of other land and for the overall benefit of that other land: this is known as an easement.

[1.02] An easement, accordingly, is the entitlement by an owner of land, either to exercise enjoyment rights over other land for the benefit of the land owned by him, or to oblige the owner of that other land to submit to some diminution in the enjoyment rights over his own land so as to augment the facilities enjoyed by the first owner's land. The essence of an easement is that the rights it creates are proprietorial, not personal, and that two parcels of land must be involved – the one with its enjoyment rights augmented, the other with its enjoyment rights, actually or potentially, diminished; with the purpose of this respective enhancement and curtailment being to benefit one property and burden the other one.

[1.03] Long established in Roman law, and accordingly in the legal systems on the continent of Europe, the type of easement with which we are concerned is that

1

recognised under the common law system, with some civil law accretions. The land or real property law of Ireland, though founded, as with all branches of private law, on the common law system incorporated over centuries of English administration, has been zealous in its reflection of the Irish social milieu in its many changes through as many epochs. Judges applying the law of real property in Ireland have striven to match the principles of the common law, or the interpretation of statute, to the exigencies of the peculiar situations presented to them for decision – situations begotten by the cultural and social climate of the island – or else bridled against their inability to do so.[1]

As will emerge, in many cases the law of easements affords a compelling instance of this uneasy judicial equipoise – a deft balancing of the need to apply the law as established and stated by the courts in England with a desire to effect justice in circumstances no doubt scarcely contemplated by the judges of the English courts.

---

[1] See generally, Wylie 'The "Irishness" of Irish Land Law' (1995) 46 NILQ 332. Professor Wylie states at 333, with becoming diffidence, that 'although there is little which is unique, there is much which is distinctive and which requires careful study.' There is a case for robust assertion that Irish developments in the law of easements present sufficient distinctive features warranting 'careful study'.

Definitions

In Ireland

[1.04] It is perhaps not surprising that the Irish judiciary has rarely articulated a precise definition of an easement. One striking instance appears in the judgment of Monahan CJ, in 1870, in *Hamilton v Musgrove*[1] where he described an easement thus:

> 'For the exercise of an easement, properly speaking, there must be two tenements, a dominant and a servient tenement. An easement is an incorporeal right which may be defined to be a privilege, not conferring any right to a participation in the profits of the land over which it is exercised, which the owner of one tenement has over the neighbouring tenement, by which the owner of the servient tenement is obliged to suffer something to be done, or to refrain from doing something, on his own land for the advantage of the dominant tenement. It must be imposed for the benefit of corporeal property, and imposed upon corporeal property.'

---

[1] *Hamilton v Musgrove* (1870) IR 6 CL 129 at 137.

[1.05] This definition was considered by Porter MR in *Ingham v Mackey*,[1] in the somewhat complicated context of the difference between an eel weir and a submerged cistern for the storage of eels. In 1896 the plaintiff had bought a certain portion of the bed and soil of the river Shannon in County Limerick out to the middle of the river. The deed of assurance to the plaintiff contained an exception and reservation of a number of eel weirs. The use of a weir is a common method of fishing for eels. The defendants were lessees of the weirs. In addition, the defendants retained on the river bed a number of perforated tanks or cisterns in which the caught eels were stored alive until they could be transported to England for the English market. The plaintiff sought an injunction to restrain the defendants from continuing to maintain these cisterns, on the basis that they had not been included in the exception and reservation described in the conveyance, and so were attached to the soil of the river which was owned by the plaintiff. Porter MR observed:

> 'What they [the defendants] claim is an incorporeal hereditament: the right of the owner of one tenement to use or exercise rights over the land of another. Whether the right is claimed as appurtenant to the eel weirs and fishing, or as a part of the fishing of the weirs themselves and existing ex vi termini by an exception of the latter, it is in either case an easement.'[2]

---

[1]   *Ingham v Mackey* [1898] 1 IR 272.

[2]   [1898] 1 IR 272 at 277. Porter MR awarded an injunction to the plaintiff to restrain the trespass by the defendants occasioned by the continued storage of the cisterns on the river bed. The purchase by the plaintiff had been by way of a Landed Estates Court conveyance which had extinguished all easements.

[1.06] In *Smiths (Harcourt Street) Ltd v Hardwicke Ltd*,[1] O'Keeffe P noted, in the case of a dispute over whether an easement of a right of way could be included as part of commercial properties being valued for the purpose of the acquisition of the fee simple under s 3 of the Landlord and Tenant (Ground Rents) Act 1967, that 'land' in this section was to be construed in accordance with the Interpretation Act 1937 where 'land' is described as including messuages, hereditaments and tenements. This clearly also includes an easement of a right of way, being an incorporeal hereditament. On the other hand, in a Circuit Court case, *Associated Properties Ltd v The Representatives of Timothy Nolan*,[2] the court refused to grant a decree for ejectment under the Landlord and Tenant Law Amendment, Ireland, Act 1860, for non-payment of rent in respect of a right of way appurtenant to lands held under lease, on the basis that the execution of the necessary *habere* would be impracticable in the case of an easement.

---

[1]   *Smiths (Harcourt Street) Ltd v Hardwicke Ltd* (30 July 1971, unreported) HC.

[2]   *Associated Properties Ltd v The Representatives of Timothy Nolan* (1951) 85 ILTR 86.

In England

[1.07] The precise formulation of the requisite ingredients of an easement, enunciated by Evershed MR in *Re Ellenborough Park*,[1] is cited as authoritative by most textbooks on the subject. This formulation requires that, in order for a right over land to qualify as an easement:

   (i)   there must be a dominant and servient tenement;

   (ii)   the easement must accommodate the servient tenement;

   (iii) the dominant and servient owners must be different persons;

   (iv) the right must be capable of forming the subject-matter of a grant.

The separate existence of a tenement to be benefited and of a tenement to be burdened is axiomatic: each must be clearly identified, failing which an easement will not be found to exist.[2] The requirement of accommodation is bound up with the principle that it is the tenement which is to be benefited, and not merely the owner of it in a separate capacity.[3] The test appears to be whether the benefit conferred is connected with the normal use and enjoyment of the property benefited.[4] If so, even though the benefit conferred may be a commercial one, an easement is likely to be held to exist. The two properties need not be contiguous, but it is unlikely that, save in the case of an easement of light, or in certain instances a right of way, there can be any sustainable accommodation of one property by another one, if both properties are a considerable distance apart.

---

[1]   *Re Ellenborough Park* [1956] Ch 131, adapting their proposition in Cheshire *The Modern Law of Real Property* (7th edn, 1954).

[2]   In *Woodman v Pwllbach Colliery Co Ltd* [1915] AC 634 it was held that a right to disperse coal dust over an indefinite area could not be deemed an easement in the absence of a clearly defined servient tenement to be subjected to the right.

[3]   Such as in *Hill v Tupper* (1863) 2 H & C 121, where the lessee of land adjacent to a canal, who had also been given an exclusive licence to hire out pleasure boats on the canal, failed in an action for damages against an adjoining landowner whose premises also abutted the canal and who also let out pleasure boats, on the basis that his entitlement derived from a personal licence between the canal company and himself, and was accordingly not an interest in land and did not bind a third party. In appropriate cases nowadays, the application of the principle of non-derogation from grant might result in a different outcome. See para **[2.29]** ff.

[4]   This was the situation held to obtain in *Re Ellenborough Park*, that the use of an ornamental park by the owners of adjacent properties was sufficiently concerned with the use and enjoyment of the properties, by analogy with the concept of a communal garden; it was on this basis too that Evershed MR explained and distinguished *Hill v Tupper*.

[1.08] The principle that the dominant and servient owners must be different persons is recognition of the fact that an individual cannot enjoy rights over land owned by him other than as an incident of his actual ownership of that land. If the owner of one parcel of land also owns adjacent land, and walks by a regular route from one parcel to the other one, it cannot in any meaningful sense be urged that this is being done in exercise of a right of way over one parcel of land in favour of the other, but from the fact that both lands are in common ownership.[1] In certain instances, where land formerly in common ownership is disposed of in two parts, or one part is disposed of and one part retained, rights earlier enjoyed in respect of one part over the other part as an incident of the ownership of the whole can be enlarged into easements.[2] Such rights have come to be known as 'quasi-easements'. Their deemed existence is not automatic, but depends upon the intention and user in each individual case.

In Ireland, having regard to the once higher incidence of landlord and tenant relationships in agricultural land, and the fact that an easement can be granted by a landlord to a tenant,[3] and in certain cases acquired by prescription (or on the basis of long enjoyment) between tenants of different properties under the same landlord,[4] it would be more prudent rather than to assert that, for an easement to exist, the dominant and servient *owners* must be different persons, to require that the dominant and servient tenements be in different beneficial occupation.

---

1   *Roe v Siddons* (1888) 22 QBD 224.
2   Through the application of what has come to be known as the rule in *Wheeldon v Burrows*. See para **[3.14]** ff.
3   Having regard to the informality of the relationship and the fact that since the Landlord and Tenant Law Amendment, Ireland, Act 1860 it is deemed to be founded upon contract rather than tenure, such easements are often deemed to be granted by implication rather than expressly.
4   Under the doctrine of presumed lost grant, where the development of the law in relation to lessors and lessees has diverged considerably from the decisions of the English courts, considered in ch 4.

[1.09] The fourth requirement articulated by Evershed MR in *Re Ellenborough Park*,[1] that the right must be capable of forming the subject-matter of a grant, is sometimes regarded in the nature of a 'catch-all' category, adding little.[2] It has also provoked analysis[3] in relation to whether an alleged easement can fail to qualify either as a result of its being too wide and vague or in the nature of a mere recreational facility not conferring any benefit on a particular property. The latter requirement is demonstrably a restatement of the principle that a specific dominant tenement must be identified and benefited; the former a facet of the pervasive precept of real property law that any new right being created over land must be clear, specific and capable of precise articulation in an instrument defining and imparting it.

A right of mere recreation, ambulatory and directionless in its nature,[4] and generally destitute of a dominant tenement, is sometimes described as a *jus spatiendi*: it is not an easement, but more in the nature of a local customary right.[5]

---

1   *Re Ellenborough Park* [1956] Ch 131.
2   *Gale on Easements* (16th edn, 1997) Sweet and Maxwell, pp 23–24, but then the editors, Gaunt and Morgan, expend several pages in consideration of the caselaw.
3   Not least in the course of the judgment of Evershed MR in *Re Ellenborough Park* itself and his consideration of the dicta of Farwell J in the cases of *International Tea Stores Co v Hobbs* [1903] 2 Ch 165 and *A-G v Antrobus* [1905] 2 Ch 188.
4   Laconically termed in Bland *The Law of Easements and Profits à Prendre* (1997) Sweet & Maxwell, p 24, '… a right to stray, as opposed to a right of way.'
5   In which capacity it will be considered further in ch 10 below.

[1.10] Easements are sometimes divided into positive easements and negative easements.[1] A positive easement is a right to do something for the benefit of land over other land – such as a right of way to and from, or a right of access to extract the subject matter of a profit *à prendre*. A negative easement is a right to prevent something being done on neighbouring land – such as a right of light, which precludes the owner of the servient land from so utilising it as significantly to delimit the access of light over his land to a defined aperture on the dominant land. The opinion has been expressed that negative easements should be reviewed with circumspection, as representing an unwarrantable interference with the right of a landowner to enjoy the fruits of his ownership.[2] Another view has emerged that, on the basis that many easements are acquired through prescription deriving from long enjoyment, rather than by express grant, a species of enjoyment ought not to be ranked as an easement if it seems incapable of being acquired by prescription.[3]

It is suggested that it is more logical to define an easement with reference to the character of the enjoyment rather than from the ease or difficulty of its acquisition otherwise than by express grant. It should be noted that a right incapable of taking effect as an easement, due either to its vagueness or too pervasive character, such as a right of prospect, or a right not to have percolating water drained off from beneath land, or a right to the non-obstruction or non-interruption of light or air, can be enforced if drafted as a restrictive covenant.[4] A restrictive covenant, if properly drafted, is capable of attaching to land and, in effect, running with it, in the same way as an easement, and will bind all subsequent purchasers of the land other than one who takes for value and without notice.[5]

---

[1] For example, *Gale on Easements*, pp 23–26, Bland *The Law of Easements and Profits à Prendre* pp 16–17.

[2] Lord Denning MR in *Phipps v Pears* [1965] 1 QB 76 at 83–84.

[3] Most probably on the basis of inability by the putative servient owner to prevent their enjoyment, such as the unrestricted flow of air over an open area, or an ongoing entitlement to the use of percolating sub-surface water: Anderson, 'Easements and Prescription – Changing Perspectives in Classification' (1975) 38 MLR 640; Bland *The Law of Easements and Profits à Prendre* pp 17, 19.

[4] *Moore v Rawson* (1824) 3 B & C 332 at 340, per Littledale J; see also Bodkin 'Easements and Uncertainty' (1971) 35 Conv 324.

[5] See discussion in ch 16.

Instances of Easements

[1.11] Decisions of the Irish courts are more prolific in example than definition. Many of the more novel instances are indigenous to the countryside rather than the city. A right to the watering of cattle has been held to be an easement in *Re The Estate of George Harding*[1] and in *Re Tibbotstown and Cloneen Water Arbitration*.[2] In *Barry v Lowry*[3] a right to draw water from a well was acknowledged as an easement. *Tubridy v Walsh*[4] is authority for the proposition that a right of way can have attached to it as an incident of the right the obligation on the part of the dominant owner to close a gate to prevent cattle owned by the servient owner from straying on to the road.

In *Clancy v Whelan and Considine*[5] it was held by Dixon J that a right to collect seaweed was an easement inhering in the owners of a particular holding which also conferred on them the right to eke payment from those whom they licensed to gather the seaweed. *Representative Church Body v Crawford; Crawford v Bradley*[6] concerned an action for trespass for the erection of a railing around a grave; Judge Moonan in the Circuit Court held that:

'… the right in the burial plot is … only in the nature of an easement and gives no cause of action for trespass to the grave itself, although there may be one for removal of a coffin …

The position then is that although an exclusive right to burial in a particular plot ... may be acquired by prescription such right gives no title to the soil that would support an action for trespass to the grave itself.'[7]

---

[1]   *Re The Estate of George Harding* (1874) IR 8 Eq 620.
[2]   *Re Tibbotstown and Cloneen Water Arbitration* (1897) 31 ILT 380.
[3]   *Barry v Lowry* (1877) IR 11 CL 483.
[4]   *Tubridy v Walsh* (1901) 35 ILT 321.
[5]   *Clancy v Whelan and Considine* (1957) 92 ILTR 39.
[6]   *Representative Church Body v Crawford; Crawford v Bradley* (1939–40) 74 ILTR 49.
[7]   See also Dowling 'Exclusive Rights of Burial' (1992) 43 NILQ 288.

[1.12] In *Calders v Murtagh*[1] Murnaghan J experienced some difficulty in determining the right of a tenant of a shoeing forge to enter upon the defendant's land to use a shoeing stone which had been standing on it, but which the defendant had prior to the action removed in order to build on his land.

> 'A man cannot have a right to use a shoeing stone and go around the country whenever he likes and then go back to shoe on the stone. The right must be annexed to the use of some land; and if it is a convenience to the use of the land, it can be established in law if the proper evidence is forthcoming.'

In finding that there was an easement, Murnaghan J deemed it relevant that the plaintiff had no entitlement to allow any other blacksmith the use of the shoeing stone, nor could he himself use it excessively. Excessive user, according to the judge, would not destroy the right but could be restrained by injunction.[2]

---

[1]   *Calders v Murtagh* (1939) 5 Ir Jur Rep 19.
[2]   See para **[6.16]** ff.

[1.13] In *Jeffers v Odeon (Ireland) Ltd*[1] a right by the lessee of a cinema confectionery shop to use the toilet across the corridor, for herself and her staff, and also to take water from a tap in the toilets for the purpose of making tea, was held to be an easement.[2]

---

[1]   *Jeffers v Odeon (Ireland) Ltd* (1953) 87 ILTR 187.
[2]   See also *Miller v Emcer Products* [1956] Ch 304, a case with similar facts, of which Romer LJ observed that 'during the times when the dominant owner exercised the right the owner of the servient tenement would be excluded, but [that] this in greater or less degree is a common feature of many easements (for example, rights of way) and does not amount to such ouster of the servient owner's right as was held by Upjohn J to be incompatible with a legal easement in *Copeland v Greenhalf*.'

Discommoding of owner of servient tenement

[1.14] In *Middleton v Clarence*[1] May CJ stated:

> '... the right of throwing the spoil, arising from the working of the quarry, on the adjoining lands ... is in the nature of an easement or servitude.'

So also was held to be the right to dump lime and manure on the land of another, in *Redmond v Hayes*.[2] In this latter case the actual location of the dumping and the amount of the manure dumped varied depending on the availability of manure and on the convenience of the owner of the right. The easement had been established to dump manure and lime over half an acre of the servient owner's land with the acknowledged result that the servient owner would not be able to use his own lands for some time afterwards in those places where the lime had been dumped.

Although Kenny J cited with approval the judgment of Upjohn J in the English case of *Copeland v Greenhalf*,[3] it is arguable that that learned judge would have demurred to the extent of the right contended for in *Redmond v Hayes* as usurping the right to possession of his own land by the servient owner. In *Copeland v Greenhalf* Upjohn J had been of opinion that the unlimited right to deposit motor vehicles for repair on a narrow stretch of land effectively amounted to a claim of joint user by the dominant owner, which would prohibit the recognition of the right as an easement:

> 'It is virtually a claim to possession of the servient tenement, if necessary to the exclusion of the owner; or, at any rate, to a joint user, and no authority has been cited to me which would justify the conclusion that a right of this wide and undefined nature can be the proper subject-matter of an easement.'[4]

---

[1]   *Middleton v Clarence* (1877) IR 11 CL 499.

[2]   *Redmond v Hayes* (7 October 1974, unreported) HC. Kenny J observed: 'The advice of the Privy Council in *A-G of Southern Nigeria v Holt* [1915] AC 599 and the decision of Mr Justice Upjohn in *Copeland v Greenhalf* [1952] 1 All ER 809 establish that the right to dump or deposit material on the lands of another is an easement recognised by our law.'

[3]   *Copeland v Greenhalf* [1952] 1 All ER 809, [1952] Ch 488.

[4]   [1952] ch 488 at 498.

[1.15] In *Kilduff v Keenaghan*[1] the plaintiff was held to have acquired a right of way by prescription over a forecourt owned by the defendant adjacent to the plaintiff's garage premises 'with or without vehicles (including petrol tankers) for the purpose of delivering supplies.' It was acknowledged by O'Hanlon J, in the form of his order, that the exercise of this right would in certain cases cause inconvenience to the owners of agricultural land behind the garage who also had a right to pass over the forecourt. The order provided that the exercise of the plaintiff's right was 'not to obstruct in an unreasonable manner or to an unreasonable degree the exercise of the *residual rights* '[2] either of the owner of the land over which the right was being exercised or of the owners of agricultural properties behind the site who also had a right of passage over it. The fact of some obstruction being occasioned to the servient owner and others entitled to a right of way was manifestly deemed not to be inconsistent with the finding that the plaintiff was entitled to an easement.

---

[1]   *Kilduff v Keenaghan* (6 November 1992, unreported) HC.

[2]   Italics supplied, for the purpose of emphasising the extent to which O'Hanlon J was prepared to recognise this particular claimed easement, the plaintiff's right of way acquired by prescription,

as being in the nature of a primary right, with the right of the owner of the land and those entitled to other rights of way as, in effect, secondary ('residual') rights.

The moving man sign post

[1.16] A somewhat unusual easement was successfully contended for in *Henry Ltd v McGlade*[1] in the Northern Ireland Court of Appeal. The defendants, who had the lease of a restaurant off Donegall Place in Belfast, for over a quarter of a century, since 1899, claimed as a right the facility exercised by them to have a man bearing an advertisement stand at a reasonably fixed point on the premises owned at the time of the action by the plaintiff. The man would stand stationary or move within modest limits bearing a pole with a signboard on top of it advertising the defendants' business.

Before Andrews LJ it was urged on behalf of the plaintiff that this was a *jus spatiendi*,[2] or a mere right to wander about, and not known to the law. The plaintiff had been aware of the moving man signpost arrangement when it took over the servient premises in 1919, so that the only issue was whether a claimed right 'involving the existence of a mobile human element' could be recognised by the courts. Andrews LJ acknowledged that there would have been no difficulty if the right claimed had simply been to have an advertisement carried on a pole fixed firmly in the ground. 'The *jus spatiendi* means or implies a right of walking about, spreading out, or expanding. The right which is claimed ... is, in my opinion, rather a *jus morandi* or *a jus manendi*.'[3]

The judge, however, declined to hold that the man would have the right to walk up and down the arcade and cause obstructions. It would be impossible to fix his location exactly, but, since his purpose was to advertise the defendants' restaurant to people going into the arcade, his location would have to be somewhere convenient around the environs of the mouth of it, which was sufficiently fixed and discernible for the easement to be established.[4]

---

[1] *Henry Ltd v McGlade* [1926] NI 144, 60 ILTR 17.
[2] In which capacity it will be considered further in ch 10 below.
[3] [1926] NI 144 at 151–152.
[4] On the issue of *ius spatiendi* see further *International Tea Stores Co v Hobbs* [1903] 2 Ch 165; *A-G v Antrobus* [1905] 2 Ch 188; *Re Ellenborough Park* [1956] Ch 131; Peel 'What Is An Easement?' (1964) 28 Conv (NS) 450; Bland *The Law of Easements and Profits à Prendre* pp 24–26.

Not an easement

[1.17] Despite the apparent flexibility of the ingredients of an easement, there have been certain alleged rights found not to constitute easements. In *Cochrane v Verner*[1] Porter MR held that there was no such easement known to the law as a right of shade and shelter for cattle. In *Giltrap v Busby*[2] Gibson J, in the High Court of Northern Ireland, held, where a semi-detached house had been demolished with resultant damage to the interior of the adjoining house in consequence of exposure to the elements, that there was no easement to be protected from the weather by one's neighbour's house; further, it being a natural and reasonable use of land to demolish an ancient building when its utility had ended, an actionable nuisance did not arise if rainwater thereby percolated through the wall of an adjoining house causing damage.

However, in *Tapson v Northern Ireland Housing Executive*,[3] Carswell J found it possible to distinguish *Giltrap v Busby*, in a case involving the seepage of damp from the defendant's premises to the plaintiff's premises as a result of the defendant's failure to take steps to repair bomb damage over 10 years earlier. Carswell J treated the issue as one that properly fell to be considered under the law in relation to negligence, regarding as his 'sheet anchor' the advice of the Judicial Committee of the Privy Council in *Goldman v Hargrave*[4] and the decision of the English Court of Appeal in *Leakey v National Trust for Places of Historical Interest or Natural Beauty*.[5] Each of these, according to Carswell J, was consistent with the proposition that, regardless of the strict liability criteria that govern causes of action in nuisance, a landowner may become liable to his neighbour if he fails to take such steps as he reasonably can take to prevent the encroachment on to the land of his neighbour of a naturally occurring hazard. In *Goldman v Hargrave* the defendant was found liable, for having done nothing, when a tree on his land was struck by lightning and the fire spread to his neighbour's land causing damage. In *Leakey v National Trust for Places of Historical Interest or Natural Beauty*, ostensibly a decision in nuisance, a landowner was held liable to his neighbour for damage resulting from a landfall that was deemed to be both easily foreseeable and reasonably preventable. Accordingly, Carswell J found the defendant liable for taking no steps, in 10 years, to redress the bomb damage, with the result that 'there was an invasion of moisture through the defendant's property'.[6] This was a case in which the onward march of the law in pursuit of justice pulled it away from strictly academic adherence to the traditional principles of nuisance. Carswell J observed:

> 'The pervasive criterion of reasonable care has supplanted the concept of strict liability in the law of nuisance, heedless of the protests of savants …'[7]

---

[1] *Cochrane v Verner* (1895) 29 ILT 571 cited and followed by Lord Denning MR in *Phipps v Pears* [1965] 1 QB 76: 'There is no such easement known to the law as an easement to be protected from the weather.'

[2] *Giltrap v Busby* [1970] 5 NIJB 1, following the decision of the English Court of Appeal in *Phipps v Pears*.

[3] *Tapson v Northern Ireland Housing Executive* [1992] NI 264.

[4] *Goldman v Hargrave* [1966] 2 All ER 989.

[5] *Leakey v National Trust for Places of Historical Interest or Natural Beauty* [1980] 1 All ER 17.

[6] [1992] NI 264 at 266.

[7] [1992] NI 264 at 267.

[1.18] Similarly, in *Treacy v Dublin Corpn*,[1] Finlay CJ held that, even though there could not be an easement of protection from wind and weather, nevertheless, in a case where external support had been removed from an old semi-detached house by the demolition of its neighbour, the provision of a substitute support requisite to buttress the house in any sort of durable fashion would in all likelihood indirectly produce some measure of insulation against the elements. According to the Chief Justice, '… it is unreal to limit the requirement of giving back support to putting up some form of shoring or buttress which would leave a wall, having regard to the age of the house, likely in a very short time by wind and weather to become unstable …'.[2] Any form of insulation that failed to give adequate protection from the elements would be equally unlikely to last, and thereby would be an inadequate physical support.

---

[1] *Treacy v Dublin Corpn* [1993] 1 IR 305.
[2] [1993] 1 IR 305 at 313.

[1.19] In *Cronin v O'Shea*[1] Bird CJ held that there could be no such thing as an easement to create a nuisance by allowing water from the plaintiff's yard to flow through the defendant's yard, even though the defendant's house was connected to the sewer and the plaintiff's was not. The plaintiff was held not entitled to any relief when his yard became flooded due to the defendant's obstructing the flow of water from it into his own. This case, however, must be contrasted with the decision of Teevan J in *Hobson v Fitzgerald*.[2] In this the defendants were the trustees of a golf club on the other side of the road from the plaintiff's piggery, effluent from the drains of which regularly seeped on to the golf course. Several expedients were adopted by the defendants to block up the access from the plaintiff's drains to the golf course. One such expedient succeeded so well that a subsequent rainstorm caused serious flooding to the plaintiff's piggery with resultant loss of stock after the drowning of several pigs. The defendants were held liable and damages of £500 awarded.

Even so, there cannot be an absolute right to discharge effluence on to the land of a neighbour. In *Callan v McAvinue*[3] it was held that the nature of the easement found to exist in favour of the defendant was 'to discharge properly treated effluence from his lands which was not of such a nature as to cause offensive smells on the plaintiff's lands, in other words it was not an easement to create a nuisance on the plaintiff's premises.'[4]

---

[1] *Cronin v O'Shea* (1896) 30 ILT 436.
[2] *Hobson v Fitzgerald* (31 July 1968, unreported) HC.
[3] *Callan v McAvinue* (11 May 1973, unreported) HC.
[4] (11 May 1973, unreported) HC at p 7, per Pringle J.

Whether an Easement or a Licence

[1.20] The question often arises whether any right claimed is an easement or merely a licence personal to the parties involved. In *Calders v Murtagh*,[1] for example, Murnaghan J clearly identified the right of access to, and use of, the shoeing stone as being ancillary to the use by the plaintiff of his own shoeing forge and was not a right personal to himself. Equally, his entitlement to use the shoeing stone was a right of use only and did not confer on him any ownership of the specific spot on which it was located. In *Jeffers v Odeon (Ireland) Ltd*[2] it had been argued that the right to use the toilet in the cinema and the tap water for the making of tea was a mere revocable licence, but it was held in fact to be an easement.

11

---

[1] *Calders v Murtagh* (1939) 5 Ir Jur Rep 19.
[2] *Jeffers v Odeon (Ireland) Ltd* (1953) 87 ILTR 187.

Distinction wholly dependent on circumstances

[1.21] The question of whether a particular right to draw water from a well was an easement or a licence was crucial to the decision in *Whelan v Leonard*.[1] The plaintiff and defendant were tenants of the same landlord. Their dispute was over a right alleged by the defendant to draw water from a well on the plaintiff's farm. The plaintiff held the land on which the well was sited under a lease which had excepted from the demise all waters and watercourses. The principal issue for decision was whether the exception in the lease operated to except the well in the phrase 'all waters and watercourses'. The effect of the exception's being deemed to include the well would have been to render the right to draw water of both the plaintiff and the defendant equally permissive, as the well would have not formed part of the demise to the plaintiff.

Gibson J, at first instance, found that the well had not been excepted by the words of the lease. He based his construction on the discernible purpose of the lease to the plaintiff. These lands were grazing land and so would require flowing water for home and dairy purposes. To interpret the exception as giving the well to the landlord, thereby inhibiting his needed use of it by the lessee, would offend against the purpose of the lease. Gibson J also found that, even if the well could be construed as excepted to the lessor, there was an implied release of it to the lessee, evidenced by his continuous and unbroken user, and the fact that he regularly locked the well, so demonstrating that the user of the well by the defendant and others, but not his own user, was permissive.

---

[1] *Whelan v Leonard* [1917] 2 IR 323.

[1.22] This finding was reversed on appeal, both by the Court of King's Bench and the Court of Appeal. However, the reasoning in both courts was kindred to that of Gibson J, being based upon the presumed purpose of the lease to the plaintiff as manifested by the surrounding circumstances.

In the opinion of O'Brien C, the well had been excepted in the lease to the plaintiff, on the basis that this was the only drinking water supply for most of the tenants on the demesne, and that it was more likely that the landlord had wanted to benefit all his tenants, if only by way of licence, rather than one particular tenant whose rent did not justify the inference that he was especially favoured in terms of right to use the well. In this scenario, the locking of the well by the plaintiff was simply designed to prevent against general trespass and did not in any way affect the right of the licensees of the landlord to draw water. Hence, the plaintiff, like the defendant and the other adjoining tenants, had a valid licence to use the well, and there was no easement. According to Ronan LJ, the effect of the exception of the well to the landlord in the demise to the plaintiff permitted the licensees of the use of the well, in obtaining access to it, commit what otherwise would have been a trespass on the lands of the plaintiff.

[1.23] It is clear that the question of construction in this case was principally governed by the ostensible purpose of the lease to the plaintiff, vis-à-vis both the plaintiff's needs and those of the neighbouring tenants, and the extent to which this might be rendered nugatory by opting for one construction over the other. The ingredients were present for the creation of an easement, with the farm of the plaintiff constituted as the servient tenement and the farm of the defendant the dominant tenement. The wording of the exception could have been consistent either with a lease or a licence.[1] It was the *intention* on the part of the lessor actually to *create* an easement in this instance that was lacking.

---

[1]   Just as in the case of *Ingham v Mackey* [1898] 1 IR 272. See para **[1.05]**.

[1.24] Indeed, there is some authority to support the proposition that the nature of the right enjoyed can vary depending on developing vicissitudes over time in the same case. In *Pullan v The Roughfort Bleaching and Dyeing Co (Ltd)*,[1] a complicated case involving multiple watercourses, Chatterton V-C had to consider the significance of the exception and reservation of various watercourses in several leases despite the continued enjoyment of the watercourses by the tenants. It was significant, according to the Vice-Chancellor, that there had been no change in the enjoyment of the historic rights despite the execution of the leases. The landlord had neither interfered with, nor expressed his intention to interfere with, the rights enjoyed by the tenants:

> 'He is, and has been, capable of giving his license [sic] to the respective occupiers to enjoy these rights as theretofore. Such license, if followed by expenditure on the faith of it, may be irrevocable. Even if revocable, it would be operative till revoked. ... The landlord stands by, and remains neutral, and leaves the respective parties in the possession of the premises, and the enjoyment of the easements they and their predecessors in title had previously held and enjoyed. I am of opinion that the rights of the parties *inter se* remain unaffected, and that they must be given effect to, unless and until the landlord steps in and sweeps them all away – if, indeed, he has any right, under the circumstances, to do so.'[2]

The idea of a licence, accompanied by expenditure, becoming irrevocable – particularly where the rights being claimed have been expressly excepted and reserved to their landlord in a lease to the parties claiming them – strongly suggests that the protection those rights would enjoy is at least as great as would be available if the enjoyment were by way of easement rather than of licence. Although Chatterton V-C does not expressly so state, it is nevertheless inferable from his judgment that the lessor could well be estopped from denying the greater right, or at least from denying the benefits appropriate to it, where a mere licensee has expended money on the enjoyment of the licence.[3]

---

[1]   *Pullan v The Roughfort Bleaching and Dyeing Co (Ltd)* (1888) 21 LR Ir 73.

[2]   (1888) 21 LR Ir 73 at 89. It is comments such as this, presumably, which prompted Peter Bland to observe, in *The Law of Easements and Profits à Prendre*, that certain 'decisions have resulted in the recognition of licences with all the characteristics of easements', leading him at

liii, to conclude that uncertainty as to whether a revocable licence or an irrevocable interest existed would 'inevitably result in litigation'.

[3]   Refer to *Blood v Keller* (1860) 11 ICLR 124 and see para **[19.11]**.

___

Permissive occupation

[1.25] If it can be demonstrated that enjoyment, even over a long period and in a case where the conditions for the existence of an easement would otherwise apply, has been permissive only, such enjoyment will be held referable rather to a licence than an easement. In *Barry v Lowry*[1] enjoyment by the defendant of a right to draw water from a well between 1833 and 1874 was held not to create an easement, because the plaintiff reversioner, after entering into possession in 1865, had put a lock on an already existing gate and this was acquiesced in by the defendant during seven years prior to the taking of the action. Although the case mainly centres upon the presence of permission to vitiate the establishing of a statutory prescription, on the basis that the user throughout the necessary term has not been 'as of right',[2] the result of the decision is that the same user by the defendant became reduced from a possible prescriptive easement to a mere licence by reason of the defendant's acquiescence in the placing by the plaintiff of a lock on his gate.

In *Telecom Eireann v Commissioner of Valuation*[3] Barrington J, in the Supreme Court, held that a right to install wall-affixed public telephones in a shopping centre complex did not result in an incorporeal hereditament for rating purposes, and so was not an easement. The plaintiff was entitled merely to place its personal property at a certain point in the shopping centre but could not be regarded as in physical occupation of any defined part of the shopping centre.

> 'They are licensees at will. They can enter only with the permission of the owners of the shopping centre. Their licence is not exclusive and may be terminated at any time. I doubt if they could be said to be in physical occupation of any portion of the shopping centre but, certainly, there is no portion of the shopping centre of which they could be said to be in paramount occupation.'[4]

Barrington J also acknowledged that, just as in the instant case, a licence rather than an easement would be created in the cases of the right to install a bubblegum vending machine in a shop or the right to install a cigarette or other vending machine in public toilets. Interestingly, the judgment appears to have proceeded primarily on the nature of the right involved rather than relying on the absence of a dominant tenement, an obvious and relevant consideration.

___

[1]   *Barry v Lowry* (1877) IR 11 CL 483.

[2]   If the user has not been 'as of right' – that is, in the absence of permission – it does not give rise to an easement either through the doctrine of presumed lost grant or through prescription: see the Prescription (Ireland) Act 1858, s 5 and the judgment of Fitzgibbon LJ in *Hanna v Pollock* [1900] 2 IR 664. See para **[4.36]** ff and para **[5.05]**.

[3]   *Telecom Éireann v Commissioner of Valuation* [1998] 1 ILRM 64.

[4]   [1998] 1 ILRM 64 at 69.

___

Easement or Ownership

[1.26] In certain instances the question whether a particular enjoyment is on foot of an easement or ownership of the fee simple arises, especially where it is argued that the right claimed is unsustainable on the basis that it is not an easement.

In *White v Baylor*[1] a grant of a right to exercise troops on land was held not to be an easement, but rather the grant of a fee simple. In *Gill v Hogg*[2] the defendant had become the registered owner of a plot of land in the centre of which was a lime-kiln used by the plaintiff and his predecessors in title. The plaintiff claimed title to the lime-kiln on the basis of adverse possession and sought rectification of the folio. Johnston J relied significantly upon a dictum of Lopes LJ in *Reilly v Booth*,[3] to the effect that the exclusive and unrestricted use of a piece of land indubitably passed the ownership in that land, and there was no easement known to the law giving exclusive and unrestricted use of a piece of land. On this basis, the plaintiff was entitled to an easement only. The lime-kiln was merely a structure on the land which the plaintiff had a right to use whenever he needed it. His use was not excessive, nor did he attempt to secure the lime-kiln when not using it himself. Hence, his right was not to ownership of the land, but an easement to go on to the land and make use of the lime-kiln when needed:[4]

> 'I am at a loss to understand how a person by resorting at intervals – even at frequent intervals – to a particular place on another person's land, to carry out such a natural process, could acquire an estate in fee in the particular small portion of land on which he burned the limestone from time to time ... I am of opinion that the prescriptive right that the plaintiff has established in respect of the lime-kiln is an easement and not an estate in fee – an easement appurtenant to the holding that he occupies in close proximity to the lime-kiln. It differs in no essential respect from the right that might be acquired by long user to take water from an artificially made well on the lands of another.'[5]

---

[1]   *White v Baylor* (1846) 10 Ir Eq 43.
[2]   *Gill v Hogg* (1926) 60 ILTR 97.
[3]   *Reilly v Booth* (1890) 44 ChD 12.
[4]   In relation to the similarities of enjoyment in cases of prescription and adverse possession, see *A-G of Southern Nigeria v Holt* [1915] AC 599; Goodman 'Adverse Possession or Prescription? Problems of Conflict.' [1968] Conv 270; Bland *The Law of Easements and Profits à Prendre* pp 265–270.
[5]   (1926) 60 ILTR 97 at 99.

[1.27] Similarly, in *Calders v Murtagh*[1] the plaintiff was held by Murnaghan J not to have any entitlement to ownership of the spot on which the shoeing stone rested, but rather a right to insist that it be put in a reasonable and convenient place and to have reasonable access to that place. It is perhaps indicative of a more pragmatic than technical approach to the law relating to easements, that in this case there was no specific allusion to an easement, nor indeed to a dominant or servient tenement.

---

[1]   *Calders v Murtagh* (1939) 5 Ir Jur Rep 19.

Which right defers to which?

[1.28] Where corporeal and incorporeal rights are enjoyed by different parties over the same piece of land, it is by no means the case that the incorporeal right must defer to the corporeal. In *Tennent v Clancy*[1] the plaintiff and the defendant owned separate portions of what had once been the same estate in Connemara. The dispute related to the enjoyment of a lake on the estate. The plaintiff had a grant of fishing rights over the lake, and the defendant ran an outdoor education centre which involved canoeing. The canoeing operation interfered with the plaintiff's fishing rights. In an application for an injunction by the plaintiff, the defendant urged that the principal issue for decision was whether he, who also owned the bed and soil of that part of the lake bordering his lands, was merely making reasonable use of his rights of ownership.

Costello J cited with approval the English case of *Rawson v Peters*[2] in which the plaintiff who had a grant of fishing rights, but did not own any part of the bed or bank of the waters fished in, had obtained an injunction to restrain canoeing in the waters. Lord Denning MR had held that, even though the fishing rights were an incorporeal hereditament, an action could be brought to prevent their being interfered with by the owner of a corporeal hereditament in the same property, without proof of special damage. Nor did it vitiate the entitlement of the owner of the fishing rights to redress that no one was actually fishing at the time that the canoeing took place.

Having considered *Rawson v Peters*, Costello J observed:

> ' ... it is well established that even where the riparian owner owns the soil of a river or lake to a median line out from his land, he cannot act so as to interfere substantially with the incorporeal fishing rights in the river or lake ... the court's task is not ... to inquire as to whether the defendant exercised in a reasonable manner his rights as riparian owner, but to ascertain whether there has been a substantial interference with the plaintiff's right to fish in the waters of the lakes and river.'

Accordingly, he granted an injunction to restrain canoeing during the fishing season and the spawning season, being the times when the 'substantial interference' was most likely to occur.[3]

---

[1] *Tennent v Clancy* [1987] IR 15.
[2] *Rawson v Peters* (1972) 116 SJ 884.
[3] See also *Cronin v Connor* [1913] 2 IR 119. See para **[12.19]**.

Chapter 2

Easements Passing by Implication

Introduction

[2.01] An express grant of an easement must be by deed. This is usually, but not necessarily, at the same time as the passing of an interest in corporeal property. As has been seen, one of the principal ingredients of an easement in the formulation adopted by the English courts, is that it is capable of forming the subject-matter of a grant – in effect, that it is capable of precise definition and of being imparted by a legal instrument.[1] Where an easement is specifically granted, or reserved, by deed the primary issue for consideration, if any, is one of interpretation of the meaning and extent of the words.

---

[1]   *Re Ellenborough Park* [1956] Ch 131. See para **[1.07]**.

Express Grant and Implied Grant Generally

[2.02] An easement may be either granted or reserved upon the disposal of real property by one party to another. This will most often be in a context where the owner of land is disposing of part only and retaining the other part. A grant of an easement will normally arise where the transferor of property intends the transferee to have some right over the property being retained by the transferor. In such case care must be taken to use appropriate words of limitation, in order to ensure that the full estate which the transferor is capable of passing in the easement in fact passes. It is also crucial that the exact nature of the right be clearly specified, including any limitations to which it may be subject. In the case of a right of way, for example, it is wise to specify the purpose for which it may be used, the times when it may be used, and whether it is to be confined to foot passage only or can also include conveyance by vehicle. The principle of construction applied is that any ambiguity in a grant is construed against the grantor.

[2.03] A reservation of an easement also usually arises where the transferor of property is disposing of part only and retaining the other part. The need for the reservation stems from a desire by the transferor to preserve some right over the property granted in favour of the property being retained. At common law a reservation of an easement presented a conceptual difficulty, because the item reserved had to exist at the time of the disposition of the land from which it was being withheld. If the thing existed and was tangible, such as a mine or a quarry, the correct practice was to except it from the property granted. The effect of this was that the property granted did not include the thing excepted, the title to which remained in the transferor. The common law allowed a limited number of technical reservations, on the basis that such things were either carved out of the land

17

granted, so to speak – such as the payment of a rentcharge – or were in the nature of a personal service from the grantee to the grantor. Otherwise, the principle was that there could not be a reservation in favour of the grantor, only in favour of a third party.

The way in which these common law strictures were obviated was to regard a reservation of an easement as, in effect, a specific grant of the easement back to the grantor from the land granted to the grantee – in other words, a regrant. This necessitated the deed of assurance to be executed both by the transferor (in order to pass the land to the transferee) and also by the transferee (in order to pass the 'reserved' easement to the transferor). Inevitably, the effect of this is that the so-called reservation of the easement is construed against the grantee of the land, as that person is the grantor of the easement. However, this double application of what is known as the *contra proferentem* rule has proven bewildering in practice, and the prudent course is to assume that, as the party disposing of the land usually has the principal negotiating strength, and is probably also the party charged with drafting the instrument of disposition, it is for the transferor to ensure that the purported reservation of an easement over the property disposed of is suitably drafted to accommodate his needs.

The danger of an easement, reserved to a grantor by way of regrant, being construed against a grantee of land, does not arise if an alternative method of securing it to the grantor is resorted to: this is the execution of a use under the Statute of Uses 1634. The procedure is that the land is granted to a specific feoffee to uses, to the use that the transferor should have the easement, and, subject to this, to the use of the transferee. This has the effect of executing the use so that the transferor is given a grant of the easement and the transferee is given a grant of the land. Prior to the enactment of the Conveyancing Act 1881 this device was not available, as the feoffee to uses needed to be seized of the land in order for the use to be executed, and he could not have been so seized of the easement which itself was being created by the disposition that also created the use. However, s 62(1) of the Conveyancing Act 1881 provides that a conveyance of land to the use that a named individual will enjoy an easement will have the effect of passing to that person the same estate in the easement as passed in the land under the instrument creating the use.

In practice, the method of reservation by re-grant is more frequently used, notwithstanding the difficulties of construction to which it can, in theory, give rise.

[2.04] It is important that an exception (a withholding of a physical portion of the land) and a reservation (the reserving of an incorporeal right) are not confused, where the same words might be used to describe either a physical or an intangible thing. For example, the exception of a 'way' will have the effect of not passing to the transferee a path or a lane over the property that might be understood by both parties to be a way. On the other hand, the reservation of a 'way' will be a right of way only. This distinction is important insofar as the practice of many conveyancers is to use the words 'Excepting and Reserving' in conjunction rather than separately.

[2.05] It frequently happens, in the case of corporeal property, where title is passed by way of written instrument, that intangible rights of easement are *subsequently* enjoyed, and the question then arises whether such claimed easements were in fact enjoyed prior to the grant and ought to have been implied as part of it.

Special considerations apply where property formerly held in common ownership is disposed of in separate parts with concomitant questions arising as to the enjoyment of rights over the divided property once enjoyed as an incident of the ownership of the whole. This situation often gives rise to what are termed 'easements of necessity', and, in certain cases, easements of 'qualified necessity' or easements for the 'necessary convenience' of property. These latter types of easement are usually deemed to arise from the application of what is called the rule in *Wheeldon v Burrows*,[1] after the case in which their application was first most clearly stated. A related category of easement that does not appear on the face of an instrument is presented by s 6 of the Conveyancing Act 1881, which enables formerly inchoate or precarious rights to be enlarged into easements following a disposal of the real property to which they are appurtenant.[2]

Although certain textbook writers offer the rule in *Wheeldon v Burrows* and the application of s 6 of the Conveyancing Act 1881 as virtually obverse sides of the same coin, the intention in this work is to consider s 6 in the current chapter as an easement by 'statutory implication', while easements arising under the rule in *Wheeldon v Burrows*, or easements of 'qualified necessity' or 'necessary dependence' will be reviewed in Chapter 3, treating of necessity generally.

For the purpose of this chapter the concern is principally with the implication of easements based on user[3] and, more recently, the implication of easements deriving from the principles of estoppel.

In quite a different category altogether is the concept of what is known as a presumed lost grant. This is, in essence, a prescriptive device designed for quiet enjoyment on the basis of prolonged usage: though allusions will be made to it when considering the authorities on implied grant, a fuller discussion of the concept of presumed lost grant will be undertaken in Chapter 4.

---

[1]   *Wheeldon v Burrows* (1879) 12 ChD 31. See para **[3.14]**.

[2]   See Jackson 'Easements and General Words' (1966) 30 Conv 340; Smith 'Centre Point: Faulty Towers with Shaky Foundations' [1978] Conv 449.

[3]   In *Ingham v Mackey* [1898] 1 IR 272, Porter MR observed that implied grant was to be derived from actual user. See para **[1.05]**.

Grant Accompanied by Evidence of User

[2.06] An easement may be deemed to exist by implication from the fact of a grant of corporeal property, and sometimes the words used in such grant, together with subsequent user of the property demonstrating an intention that an easement was to have been granted. This type of implication, which is primarily based on evidence of the user of the property, is to be distinguished from an easement deemed to arise by inference from the general words adopted in a deed of grant of corporeal property.[1]

The phenomenon of implied easements was criticised in 1913 by Dodd J in *Flynn v Harte*[2] as a poor substitute for an easement arising by statutory prescription or presumed lost grant. In the opinion of Dodd J, the implied grant was a vehicle for avoiding the possible determination of tenancies by the landlord's agent who, until the enactment of the Landlord and Tenant (Ireland) Act 1870, could determine, with impunity, the tenancies of those who did not abide by his rulings. Subsequent to the 1870 Act compensation was payable to a tenant whose tenancy was determined prior to its natural term.[3] Whatever might be the truth of this, it is suggested that the concept of the implied easement has been soundly established in Irish jurisprudence, and there is no reason for ignoring it merely because other modes of acquisition might seem either tidier or more appropriate.

---

[1]   See *Bayley v Great Western Railway Co* (1883) 26 ChD 534; Elliott 'Non-Derogation from Grant' (1964) 80 LQR 224; *Gale on Easements* (eds, Gaunt and Morgan, 16th edn, 1997) Sweet & Maxwell.
[2]   *Flynn v Harte* [1913] 2 IR 322.
[3]   This is a thesis taken up in Bland *The Law of Easements and Profits à Prendre* (1997) Sweet & Maxwell, p 261.

[2.07] An early instance in Ireland of the implication of an easement based on the words used in a grant allied to user of the property is afforded by *Geoghegan v Fegan*.[1] Marcella Walsh was a lessee of premises at numbers 34 and 35 Dorset Street, Dublin. Through two separate sub-leases she demised both premises to one George Colvin. At the time of these sub-leases each premises had its own outdoor toilet and ash pit, and there was a wall between them. Colvin demolished the outdoor toilet of number 34 Dorset Street, but divided that of 35 Dorset Street in two, and made a passage through the wall so that the occupants of number 34 could use the toilet of number 35.

After Colvin had been ejected from both premises for non-payment of rent, Marcella Walsh in January 1871 sub-let number 34 to the plaintiff 'together with all buildings, easements and appurtenances', the instrument of demise containing a covenant on the part of the plaintiff sub-lessee to permit the occupiers of number 35 (now the only one of the two houses with an outdoor toilet) to pass through the back yard of number 34 into Dorset Lane at least four times a year in order to empty out the natural waste.

In March 1871 Marcella Walsh sub-let number 35 to the defendant and included the outdoor toilet and the ash pit in the description of the premises. The defendant demolished these a few months later. In an action by the plaintiff asserting an easement of a right to use the toilet, it was urged that, even though the only reference to the toilet in the demise to the plaintiff, was a covenant to permit the spoil from the toilet to be transported over his back yard four times a year, this had effect as an easement, and passed, either under the general words used in the lease, or by implication from the ongoing and obvious user of the outdoor toilet. Pigot CB, in a terse judgment, held that the covenant accurately defined the right to remove the refuse from the toilet, so that the right to the use of the toilet and ash pit by the occupant of number 34 was treated as part and parcel of the demised premises and passed under the sub-lease of January 1871.

---

[1]   *Geoghegan v Fegan* (1872) IR 6 CL 139.

[2.08] A seminal authority on the implication of a grant is the poorly reported decision of Palles CB in *Conlan v Gavin*.[1] The plaintiff and the defendant were adjoining yearly tenants who held under a common landlord. The plaintiff claimed a right of way over the defendant's holding, and asserted that he had enjoyed it for more than 20 years. On the evidence Palles CB held that the way either was one of necessity or else that the common landlord, at the time of the creation of the tenancies, had reserved the right of way in favour of the dominant tenement as being reasonably necessary for its enjoyment. Since such reservation clearly had not been by way of deed, its finding to exist in this case was by way of implication.

---

[1] *Conlan v Gavin* (1875) 9 ILTR 198.

[2.09] This decision of Palles CB was referred to in the later case of *Clancy v Byrne*.[1] The plaintiff's grandfather had formerly been a yearly tenant from the common landlord of the lands at the time of the action held respectively by the plaintiff and the defendant. The plaintiff and the defendant were both yearly tenants, the defendant's tenancy having commenced only two years prior to the action. The plaintiff claimed the use of a passage over the defendant's lands to the main road, on the basis that this was the principal access to the main road from the plaintiff's land both at the time of, and prior to, the original letting to his grandfather.

Lawson J confirmed that a tenant could not acquire a right of way by user over the lands of his own landlord. Neither could there be a presumption of lost grant, because, even if the right of way had existed at some time in the past, it would have been extinguished by the unity of title and possession in the landlord, as both properties had been in the landlord's possession prior to the letting of the alleged dominant tenement to the plaintiff's grandfather.

However, Lawson J held that the evidence also established that prior to the letting, there had been a usual and accustomed access from the plaintiff's lands over the defendant's lands. In such situation, he held, an easement would pass on the granting of the letting because the right of way was necessary to the 'convenient enjoyment' of the dominant tenement:

> 'If, at the time the landlord laid out this farm for letting, there was a usual and accustomed way of access from it to the high road through other lands of the landlord, and if he demised it with the appurtenances and with all easements, &c, usually enjoyed with it, it is clear, upon the authorities, that the way would pass.'[2]

This would happen even though the way was not one of necessity, and despite the fact that the letting was by way of parol, as in this case, rather than by deed. The operative ingredient was that the particular road had been consistently used by the tenant from the time of the commencement of the tenancy and that it was necessary for the convenient enjoyment of the farm:

> 'The evidence of user is to be applied, not to show that the tenant, after the commencement of his tenancy, began to use this way; but that, anterior to his tenancy, it was the usual way, and, as such, has been since enjoyed.'[3]

---

[1] *Clancy v Byrne* (1877) IR 11 CL 355.
[2] (1877) IR 11 CL 355 at 358.

21

³   (1877) IR 11 CL 355 at 359. See also *Fahey v Dwyer* (1879) 4 LR Ir 271, in which Lawson J, in a right of way dispute between the tenants of lands adjoining a laneway holding under a common landlord, held that it would have been apt for a jury to hold that from an early period the two farms could have been demised with the way between them to benefit each of the farms, in which case 'it was a way necessary for the convenience of the farms'.

[2.10] A further instance of the consideration of an implied easement appears in the case of *Lord MacNaghten v Baird*.[1] There were two holdings, on either side of a road, both in the possession of Lord MacNaghten prior to 1875. In that year one of these holdings, the alleged dominant tenement, was let to Gilfillan, who at the time of the action, in 1903, had become a judicial tenant under the Land Act 1881. In 1883 the defendant Baird became a 'cottier tenant'[2] of the alleged dominant tenement.

The Court of King's Bench found that, since 1878 the cottier tenants had used the waters in the well on the alleged servient tenement, then also held by a cottier tenant, on the other side of the road, continuously and as of right; and that, even prior to 1875, when Lord MacNaghten had been in possession of the holdings, the cottier tenants on what later became Gilfillan's holding, the alleged dominant tenement, had been in the habit of taking water from the well.

¹   *Lord MacNaghten v Baird* [1903] 2 IR 731. This case is also an important authority on the doctrine of presumed lost grant (see para **[4.44]–[4.45]**) but its consideration at this point is confined to the issue of implied easement.
²   A cottier tenant is one holding under a letting, for not more than month to month, of a house or cottage either without any land or land under half an acre: the Landlord and Tenant Law Amendment Ireland Act 1860, s 81, Wylie *Irish Land Law* (3rd edn, 1997) Butterworths, pp 955–956.

[2.11] The basic question was whether the user of the well could properly be ascribed to a lawful origin. The court held that there could not be a presumed lost grant since all relevant parties were tenants of Lord MacNaghten and it was not permissible for a tenant to prescribe against his own landlord,[1] but the majority held that there could be deemed to be an implied grant from the plaintiff Lord MacNaghten to Gilfillan, the judicial tenant of the alleged dominant tenement, that his sub-tenants should be allowed to use the well. Barton J dissented on the basis that, in his view, such an implied grant could only arise 'unless there was a finding, or unless we could find, that such a right was necessary for the reasonable use of Gilfillan's holding, or, in other words, that Gilfillan's holding could not be conveniently enjoyed without it.' In the opinion of Barton J, this had not been established.

¹   In *Gayford v Moffat* (1868) 4 Ch App 133, it had been held that a tenant, since he was holding essentially in the right of the landlord, could not be permitted to acquire a right over his landlord by prescription.

[2.12] The decision of the majority was overturned on appeal to the Court of Appeal. Although Fitzgibbon LJ did not deal specifically with the issue of an implied grant, he attached importance to the fact that the alleged dominant tenement had had a house constructed on it as recently as 1878: before that there had only been a barn on the land, which would not have had need of access to a well on the far side of the road.

Walker LJ held that the alleged easement, in order to be valid, would have to have been granted by deed. He added:

> 'An implied grant would be the affirmation of an existing right through user creating an easement; no such user for Gilfillan and future tenants did or could exist. If there be an apparent and continuing easement existing by user, and a landlord lets to a tenant, making a division of the tenement, there will be an implied grant of the easement, as well as of the subject of the grant to which it is attached.'[1]

In the opinion of Walker LJ, the finding of an easement in this case could not be limited to providing water for the dwellinghouse occupied by the defendant, but to any number of dwellinghouses that the judicial tenant might subsequently choose to build. Such could never have been in contemplation at the time of the original lettings in 1875. Holmes LJ stated that a grant of an easement could not be implied, as the user of the well had manifestly commenced *after* the letting of 1875. He added that if the user in question had actually begun *with* the tenancy and continued without interruption, then it might have been inferred that the right contended for had been included in the demise.

It seems clear from the foregoing that the principal reason the Court of Appeal found it not possible to imply an easement was based on their finding that, unlike in the case of *Clancy v Byrne*, the right contended for by the defendant could not, on the basis of the established history of the user of the well, have existed at the time of the original demise of the alleged servient tenement.

---

[1]   [1903] 2 IR 731 at 744–745.

[2.13] In *Head v Meara*[1] Ross J held that a right to the use of an adjacent metalled road passed by implication without the necessity of interpreting a conveyance from the Land Judge in which a mansion house at Derrylahan, Co Tipperary had been sold to the plaintiff 'with the appurtenances'.[2] The metalled avenue, which debouched on the county road to Birr, was on the adjoining lands of the defendant. There was another avenue on the plaintiff's lands, also leading to the county road, so that the right claimed was not one of necessity. However, the road the subject of the action had been used continuously for the benefit of the residence at Derrylahan for more than 30 years.

---

[1]   *Head v Meara* [1912] 1 IR 262.
[2]   Towards the end of his judgment Ross J held, following *Thomas v Owen* (1888) 20 QBD 225, that the right of way would pass due to the use of the word 'appurtenances'. However, it is clear that the *ratio* of his decision is based on implied grant.

Implied easement under implied negative covenant

[2.14] An implied easement, in the form of an implied negative covenant, was found to exist in *Gogarty v Hoskins*.[1] In 1876 the predecessor in title of the plaintiff had taken a lease of two adjacent plots of land in Glasnevin, with a space 38 feet in width between them, from the predecessor in title of the defendant. The parcels clause in the lease referred to the two plots being intersected by an 'intended road' or 'intended lane', which was expressly excepted to the lessor. Though the lease was not a building lease, it contained a covenant by the lessee that any buildings thereafter erected would be maintained as private dwellinghouses. There was also an estate map of the lessor showing the plots of land being leased, and other of the lessor's land, set out as a building estate. The plaintiff's predecessor in title constructed several houses on both plots, all of which enjoyed access from their back gardens onto a lane which gave upon the 38 foot wide laneway or roadway and from there to the main road. This access was enjoyed for 30 years subsequently. There was no case for an easement of necessity, because both plots of land fronted the Glasnevin Road and so could have had access to it along the lane, rather than over the 38 foot wide roadway at the back. The original lessor never pursued his scheme of development. The plaintiff sought an injunction when the defendant proposed to sell the 38 foot wide roadway as a building plot subject to leaving a space 10 feet wide to connect with the public road.

The plaintiff argued that the defendant was not entitled to use this laneway for any purpose inconsistent with the intention declared in the original lease and that simply because the road was no longer of use to the defendant did not mean he could escape the binding obligation imposed on him by the lease. Barton J noted with sympathy the urgings of plaintiff's counsel:

'... the descriptive words in this lease should be construed as involving an implied grant to the lessee of an easement over this intersecting space, and as imposing an obligation on the lessor not to use it in any way that would be inconsistent with the intention declared in the lease. No formal words are necessary in a deed in order to constitute an implied grant or covenant, if the intention is clear.'[2]

---

[1]   *Gogarty v Hoskins* [1906] 1 IR 173.
[2]   [1906] 1 IR 173 at 181.

[2.15] Barton J held that the case turned upon the intention which could reasonably be inferred from the wording of the lease. In the view of Barton J, it was clear that the 'intended road' was more than merely descriptive and was 'much more definite and circumstantial' in its character of an intersecting road between the two plots of land, to which all the houses had access by dint of a lane running along the length of each terrace. The reference to the 'intended road' and 'to be' was consistent with the actual user over the following 30 years and seemed calculated to affect the value of the premises. Accordingly, in the view of Barton J the words used in the lease involved an implied grant of an easement and amounted to a binding promise not to use the space of 38 feet 'otherwise than in accordance with the intention so definitely and circumstantially declared.'[1]

---

[1]   Barton J decided the case on the ground of contract rather than estoppel, accepting the submission of counsel for the defendant that *Jordan v Money* (1845) 5 HL Cas 185 had established that the doctrine of estoppel could only apply to a representation of existing facts and not of mere intention, so that future promises must bind in contract or not at all: hence,

reference to an intended road could not create an estoppel. Although deciding the case on the basis of an implied contractual term in the form of a negative covenant, Barton J yet noted with approval the decision in *Furness Railway Co v Cumberland Co-Operative Building Society* (1884) 52 LT 144, in which Lord Selborne had interpreted an allusion to an 'intended road' as a representation that the road did not yet exist, then affirmed that the doctrine of estoppel would apply to ensure that the relevant land would ultimately be used as a road.

[2.16] *Gogarty v Hoskins* is strikingly similar, both in facts and outcome, to the English case of *Rudd v Bowles*,[1] decided six years later. In this, four new houses were constructed with their back gardens giving upon a strip of ground, in each case by way of a gate which opened on to it. The houses were held under lease by four different owners and the strip behind them was owned by the lessor. The strip of land was not mentioned in the lease but had been shown as coloured in a map annexed to it. The only method of obtaining access to each garden, other than through the gates, was from the houses. It was held that, interpreting the leases in light of the surrounding circumstances, each lease contained an implied right of way over the strip.

---

[1] *Rudd v Bowles* [1912] 2 Ch 60.

More modern pronouncements on implied grant

[2.17] Such judicial references as have been made to implied easements in more recent years have tended, for the most part, to eschew technical justifications. In *Kennedy v Elkinson*[1] Judge Davitt in the Circuit Court held that a tenant, who had had a letting of a basement flat for two years, was entitled to damages from his former landlord after he had moved accommodation, on the basis that the landlord had constructed two villas nearby which had seriously impaired the plaintiff's lights while a tenant. It was acknowledged that the lights were not ancient lights, so that there was no prescriptive right to their protection, and the defendant had not executed a covenant for quiet enjoyment. Even so, Judge Davitt held that the plaintiff 'was entitled to light as against his landlord, who had no right to obstruct the access of light to the plaintiff's windows by building on a portion of the property retained in the landlord's possession'.[2]

---

[1] *Kennedy v Elkinson* (1937) 71 ILTR 153.

[2] The rationale for this decision, though not articulated, was clearly based on the urging of counsel for the plaintiff that a person cannot derogate from his grant and also that there was an implied continuation of all the amenities at the date of the letting.

[2.18] In *Tallon v Ennis*[1] Gavan Duffy J held, following the decisions of *Conlan v Gavin*, *Clancy v Byrne* and *Flynn v Harte*,[2] that a weekly tenant of Dublin Corporation of a cottage at Baldoyle had a right of way to transport sanitary waste out from the back of her cottage and over a yard which had been leased to the defendant. For over 40 years the plaintiff and her predecessors in title had used this yard at the back of the cottage for the purpose of removing sanitary waste which in the alternative would have to have been transported through the house.[3] The defendant had been granted a building lease from the Corporation and had begun to build houses, thereby preventing the removal of the waste over the accustomed way. Gavan Duffy J observed:

> 'But the defendant has the temerity to urge that a weekly tenant, suing without joining her landlord, cannot establish a right of way against another tenant of the same landlord. In my opinion the defendant comes too late, for the contrary is now firmly established in Ireland, where a tenant from year to year is concerned, and a weekly tenant of long standing, like the plaintiff, can on principle, be in no worse position, for her demise may be treated as having been made for the period that it has in fact covered during her father's occupation, her mother's and her own.'[4]

Gavan Duffy J concluded that, at the time of the original parol letting to the plaintiff's father, there had been an implied grant of a limited way, which had been modified, in 1900 or thereabouts, to include the use of a horse and cart. The judge ordered, not that the original right of way be restored, which would have obliged the knocking down of the houses, but that the parties should agree a deviation of the right, and awarded the plaintiff two-thirds the cost of the action.[5]

---

[1]   *Tallon v Ennis* [1937] IR 549.

[2]   *Conlan v Gavin* (1875) 9 ILTR 198 (see para **[2.08]**); *Clancy v Byrne* (1877) IR 11 CL 355 (see para **[2.09]**) and *Flynn v Harte* [1913] 2 IR 322.

[3]   Gavan Duffy J at 553 articulated, in colourful terms, a dainty advertence that would have gladdened the heart of the lavatory-less plaintiff in *Geoghegan v Fegan* (see para 2.07): 'Primitive as were the notions current a generation or two ago in the domain of public health, it can hardly be suggested that a sailor, like plaintiff's father, living in a little cottage at Baldoyle forty years ago would complacently have carried or caused to be carried away through his house the remains of a year's filth from his outdoor closet, when there was no necessity whatever for this nuisance; in fact, the evidence is that since 1900 the removal of the ordures required a horse and cart, using the way now in question, on those somewhat rare occasions when depuration of the colluvies was thought necessary.'

[4]   [1937] IR 549 at 553.

[5]   On the issue of implied easements see also *Donnelly v Adams* [1905] 1 IR 154, 39 ILTR 1; *Maguire v Browne* [1921] 1 IR 148, 159, 55 ILTR 149 and [1922] 1 IR 23, 56 ILTR 5 at 17; also *McDonagh v Mulholland* [1931] IR 110. These cases, however, are primarily concerned with easements of necessity or qualified necessity and are more fully considered in ch 3. However, see also *Wilson v Stanley* (1861) 12 ICLR 345 in which Pigot CB held that the words 'as now in the occupation of the said Thomas Twigg' were descriptive of the boundaries of the property only and did not incorporate any alleged rights that might have been created between a certain number of sub-tenants but which could not have bound the grantor.

[2.19] Mindful that the defendant in *Tallon v Ennis* had taken a building lease from the Corporation, one is tempted to wonder at the commercial fairness of the order in view of the fact that the occupants of the houses being built would have had to submit to sanitary filth from a nearby artisan cottage being transported over whatever way was ultimately agreed between the parties, which would of necessity be contiguous to all or some of the houses. It is submitted that this might have been a better case for the award of damages, particularly in the light of Gavan Duffy J's comments about the improvement in sanitary standards over the years.[1]

[1] Bland in *The Law of Easements and Profits à Prendre* also criticises the judgment of Gavan Duffy J as being 'more eccentric than authoritative' (p 216) and describes the judge's order in providing for an alternative right of way to be agreed between the parties as 'undoubtedly bad' (p 333). One could argue that the judgment reflects a healthy and defensible pragmatism, albeit less than ideal from the perspective of the defendant. It is instructive that Gavan Duffy J found there to have been an implied easement at the time of the original demise, notwithstanding that an easement by prescription had been pleaded. See also Bland at p 316.

Easements of common intention

[2.20] The concept of an easement of common intention, as opposed to an implied easement derived from user that gleans the unspoken intention of the parties at the time of a grant of property, was aired in the English case of *Pwllbach Colliery Co Ltd v Woodman*.[1] In this Lord Parker stated that the law will imply either the grant or reservation of an easement where this is necessary to give effect to the common intention of the parties. It is important that this is not regarded as the mere application of the principles of implied term established in contract law: an easement arising from an implied common intention will not be confined to the parties to whom the intention is imputed, but comprises an interest in land.[2]

The concept of an easement of common intention was noted with approval by Shanley J in *Redfont Ltd and Wright's Fisherman's Wharf Ltd v Custom House Dock Management Ltd and Hardwicke Property Management Ltd*.[3] However, this case turned upon the identification of a right, for users of a restaurant and seafood bistro, to park along an access road, as an ancillary to a right of way over the road, having regard to the known user of the plaintiffs' premises at the time of the granting of the leases of them, which also included the right of way. An easement of common intention is one of the rare instances in which an easement can be reserved by implication, other than in cases of strict necessity.[4]

[1] *Pwllbach Colliery Co Ltd v Woodman* [1919] AC 634.
[2] *Peckham v Ellison* (1998) 79 P & CR 276, per Cazalet J. See Fox 'Implied Reservation of Easements' [1999] Conv 353.
[3] *Redfont Ltd and Wright's Fisherman's Wharf Ltd v Custom House Dock Management Ltd and Hardwicke Property Management Ltd* (31 March 1998, unreported) HC.
[4] Such as, for instance, arose in *Dwyer Nolan Developments Ltd v Kingscroft Developments Ltd* [1999] 1 ILRM 141, See para **[3.12]**.

[2.21] As a matter of practical pleading, it is recommended that, in a case where the requisite ingredients to establish an easement, on the basis either of statutory or common law prescription, or under the doctrine of presumed lost grant, present difficulties of proof, the greater flexibility disclosed by the principles enunciated in the decided cases on implied easements may furnish more fruitful and potent alternatives for argument. Where an easement has been found to have arisen by implication, it is neither necessary nor meet that an easement by presumed grant or prescription be considered.[1]

[1] *Close v Cairns* [1997] NIJB 70 at 72, per Girvan J.

Easement Arising Under the Doctrine of Estoppel

[2.22] The modern application of the principles of estoppel is a phenomenon more familiar in the domain of licences where the personal nature of the right makes the invocation of discretionary remedies demonstrably more apt.[1] However, a noticeable application of estoppel in an Irish easement case occurred in *Annally Hotel Ltd v Bergin*,[2] a decision of Teevan J from 1966. In this Teevan J applied the principles of estoppel to grant the plaintiffs an easement of light to the windows of their hotel. The plaintiffs maintained that the father of the defendant had agreed that they should have a right to light when building their hotel in the early 1950s. The defendant's father, whose lands adjoined those of the hotel, had seen the plans relating to the windows and had made certain stipulations in relation to them, which were implemented. The action was prompted by the defendant's erecting, within inches of the plaintiffs' windows in his back yard, 'barricades' consisting of sheets of galvanised iron attached to upright poles, which had the effect of making considerable noise and also of blocking the passage of light and air.

---

[1]   A significant exception is the English Court of Appeal decision in *Crabb v Arun District Council* [1976] Ch 179, in which an easement of a right of access was held to arise in equity by reason of representations made by the defendant to the plaintiff during a course of dealing which it was subsequently estopped from denying.

[2]   *Annally Hotel Ltd v Bergin* (1967) 104 ILTR 65.

[2.23] Teevan J observed:

> 'Mere standing by while one's neighbour constructs work depending on easement over an intending servient tenement, particularly when this is done at great expense and in attendant circumstances displaying acquiescence on the part of the occupier of the other land, may have the effect of creating the easement.'[1]

But this can only be so, according to the judge, if there is first discussion and agreement followed by the incurring of expense. If the plaintiffs had just built the hotel, then they would not have acquired an easement of light, notwithstanding mere acquiescence or standing by on the part of their neighbours. No right of the neighbours would have been breached, so there would be no cause to object, and the absence of objection on their part could not prejudice them. However:

> 'Where, however, there is an agreement, however informal, to allow a right of light and on the faith of such agreement the person later claiming the easement proceeds, without deed of grant, to plan, erect and expend money on, his building which, to be serviceable, must have the claimed light, and the person stands by and allows all this to be done, and particularly if he acquiesces for a considerable time, he will not be permitted to deny the right or rely on the absence of solemn grant.'[2]

---

[1]   (1967) 104 ILTR 65 at 65–66.

[2]   (1967) 104 ILTR 65 at 66.

[2.24] Although there was no written agreement, Teevan J was satisfied that the plaintiffs had sought to have their understanding reduced to writing but that the defendant's father had refused this. It was clear that the plaintiffs would not have proceeded with the building of the hotel unless they were going to have a right to light through the windows, and that they proceeded with the building on the basis that they believed they were going to get that right.[1] Notwithstanding that the primary nuisance complained of by the plaintiffs was the 'unearthly' noise occasioned by the barricades in high wind, the remedy they were granted was an injunction, on the basis of an implied grant of an easement of light (and apparently light only) arising through estoppel.

---

[1] Teevan J noted that the defendant had only erected the barricades because of the last stage of the hotel's development to which he objected, and which had caused one of his garden walls to collapse. Accordingly, Teevan J granted an injunction restraining the defendant from erecting the hoardings to block the plaintiffs' windows except in relation to the final phase of the expansion of the hotel.

[2.25] The application of estoppel was considered, albeit *obiter* but significantly, in *Smiths (Harcourt Street) Ltd v Hardwicke Ltd*.[1] The plaintiff held lands under a lease for 21 years which it sought to have enlarged into a fee simple in accordance with s 3 of the Landlord and Tenant (Ground Rents) Act 1967. At the time of the application to purchase the fee simple the lands under lease were covered with multi-storey buildings erected by the plaintiff, their value considerably enhanced by a right of way over an access road which had been granted with the original lease.

The defendant contested the entitlement to acquire the fee simple, and so the matter was referred, as the act provides, to the County Registrar who held that the plaintiff was entitled to the fee simple and recommended that the valuers for each party would negotiate a sale price. This was done on the basis that both valuers, having regard to the physical location and arrangement of the property, were assuming that the premises included the right of way, and they valued accordingly. The valuer for the defendant was not made aware that the defendant's legal advisers intended at a later stage to contend that the plaintiff had no right to procure the fee simple over the right of way. Accordingly, the County Registrar was permitted to fix a price far in excess of what the properties would have warranted if there was no access to them.

O'Keeffe P decided that the Landlord and Tenant (Ground Rents) Act 1967 permitted the acquisition of the fee simple of an easement. In response, however, to an allegation by the defendant that the plaintiff had not described the lands so as to include the right of way in the statutory notice of intention to acquire the fee simple, O'Keeffe P held that the description had been sufficiently clear for the defendant to understand that the right of way was being included; and that, in any event, the defendant could not now be heard to say that the statutory contract was for the sale of anything other than the land together with the right of way. The defendant's valuer had been allowed negotiate with the plaintiff's valuer on the basis that the right of way was included. Hence, the defendant was not entitled at a later stage to assert that the statutory contract was other than that which the plaintiff had thought it to be.[2]

1   *Smiths (Harcourt Street) Ltd v Hardwicke Ltd* (30 July 1971, unreported) HC.

2   Applying the principles established in *Clayton Love and Sons (Dublin) Ltd v British and Irish Steam Packet Co Ltd* (1970) 104 ILTR 157 in relation to the conduct of parties in the negotiation of a contract and the reasonable inferences which can be drawn by one party from the manner of doing business of the other.

[2.26] O'Keeffe P refused an application by the plaintiff to amend its pleadings to include an estoppel argument on the grounds that an estoppel was not necessary to decide the case. He added, however, that had it been necessary to rely on estoppel, the plaintiff should have succeeded. In response to a suggestion by the defendant that the plaintiff had not in fact worsened its position as a result of the representation, because it could easily serve notice to withdraw from the purchase, O'Keeffe P noted that, under s 10 of the Landlord and Tenant (Ground Rents) Act 1967, the plaintiff, in order to withdraw the original notice, would have to pay to the defendant its costs up to the time of the serving of the notice of withdrawal. Hence, the plaintiff would be obliged, either to withdraw subject to paying the defendant's costs or, in the alternative, to purchase the property including the right of way at an artificially high price. In the view of the President of the High Court, had it been necessary to decide, the defendant would have been estopped from maintaining that position.

[2.27] Estoppel was also pleaded, unsuccessfully, in *Dunne v Molloy*.[1] In this the plaintiff alleged a right of way over lands of the defendant on the basis either of prescription or lost grant. There had not been evidence of user for a sufficient period to warrant prescription, and the only people who could have made a grant were actually in court, so that a grant could not be presumed from those in a position to deny it. The plaintiff pleaded estoppel on the basis that the defendant had been aware that the plaintiff was exercising a right over his lands. Gannon J decided that, since there was no evidence that the plaintiff had incurred any expenditure or had in any way acted to his detriment on the basis of any encouragement from, or even to the knowledge of, the defendant, an estoppel could not arise.[2]

1   *Dunne v Molloy* [1976–1977] ILRM 266.

2   Gannon J cited with approval the principles governing proprietary estoppel set out by Fry J in *Willmott v Barber* (1880) 15 ChD 96 and Scarman LJ in *Crabb v Arun District Council* [1976] Ch 179. These, however, have been superseded, in England, by a broader principle governing conscionability, articulated by Oliver J in *Taylors Fashions Ltd v Liverpool Victoria Trustees Co Ltd* [1981] QB 133 at 151, as being based upon 'ascertaining whether, in particular individual circumstances, it would be unconscionable for a party to be permitted to deny that which, knowingly, or unknowingly, he has allowed or encouraged another to assume to his detriment. ...'. A formulation of this breadth has yet to be adapted in Ireland.

[2.28] In *Callan v McAvinue*[1] Pringle J held that an easement could arise from an equitable or constructive grant under the doctrine of acquiescence. The plaintiff had a leasehold interest in premises, mostly surrounded by water, in Co Louth. She had bought the property from one Farrell in 1958. At that time the defendant's lands were owned by

Camon, who had bought them in 1950 from the same Farrell as sold the plaintiff's property to her in 1958. Shortly after purchasing his lands, Camon proceeded to build a septic tank, through which passed all the effluent and sewage from his house, from there to a soak pit, and from there under the boundary of his property until it reached a concrete outlet from which it discharged itself into a stream on the northern boundary of the property later bought by the plaintiff. While Camon had been constructing the septic tank and outlet, Farrell had been clearly aware of what he was doing and raised no objection. Relations between the two men were friendly.[2]

In 1966 the defendant purchased from the successor to Camon. In 1967 the stream that flowed past the north of the plaintiff's property became silted up, with the result that effluent from the defendant's property lay stagnant on the plaintiff's land causing offensive smells. In an action, some years later, by the plaintiff for nuisance, Pringle J held, applying the doctrine of acquiescence enunciated in the cases of *Dann v Spurrier* and *Beaufort v Patrick*,[3] that there had been an equitable or constructive grant from Farrell (the former owner of the plaintiff's land) to Camon to discharge properly treated effluent through the septic tank and through the concrete outlet on to the plaintiff's land; the plaintiff would have been put on inquiry, by reason of the existence of the concrete outflow when she purchased in 1958, and so took with constructive notice of the equitable easement, and was bound by it.[4] However, Pringle J also held that the constructive easement enjoyed by the defendant was for the discharge of properly treated effluent only and that it could not be of such a nature as would cause offensive smells on the plaintiff's land. In short, it was not an easement to create what would otherwise have been an actionable nuisance.

---

[1]   *Callan v McAvinue* (11 May 1973, unreported) HC.

[2]   The judgment does not record whether there had been any verbal understanding between the two men such as was established in *Annally Hotel Ltd v Bergin* (1967) 104 ILTR 65. Significantly, that case was not alluded to by Pringle J in the course of his judgment, and the printed report does not record the submissions of counsel.

[3]   *Dann v Spurrier* (1802) 7 Ves 235, per Lord Eldon LC: 'The Court will not permit a man knowingly, though but passively, to encourage another to lay out money under an erroneous opinion of title and the circumstance of looking on is in many cases as strong as using terms of encouragement.' *Beaufort v Patrick* (1853) 7 Beav 74, per Lord Romilly MR: 'He who stands by and encourages an act cannot afterwards complain of it, or interfere with the enjoyment of that which he has permitted to be done.'

[4]   See also *Ward v Kirkland* [1967] Ch 194 and *Ives Investments Ltd v High* [1967] 2 QB 379. It could be argued, in *Callan v McAvinue*, that an estoppel, if found to have arisen between Farrell, the predecessor of the plaintiff, and Camon, the predecessor of the defendant, ought not to have bound the plaintiff since the equity would not have been raised against her personally. See Bland *The Law of Easements and Profits à Prendre* p 276. The equitable easement bound her as she was held to have purchased with notice of it. Furthermore, the case was not technically decided on the basis of an estoppel.

The Doctrine of Non-derogation from Grant

[2.29] An implied easement, as has been shown, arises principally in cases where the court is obliged to infer the intention of the original parties to a transaction that had not involved the express grant of an easement. In many cases the original grant has been by parol and the inferences derived entirely from user at the time of the grant and continued subsequently. Where a deed or agreement has actually been executed, subsequent user can assist in the interpretation of words or phrases otherwise doubtful.[1]

---

[1]   Such as in the case of *Geoghegan v Fegan* (1872) IR 6 CL 139 where words of covenant in a letting were deemed, in the light of subsequent user, to confer an easement of access to a toilet; also the case of *Wilson v Stanley* (1861) 12 ICLR 345 where, despite arguments based on user by sub-tenants, the words 'as now in the occupation of' were held to be descriptive of the property only and not to create an easement.

[2.30] The doctrine of non-derogation from grant is kindred to the concept of implied easement. However, its primary thrust is to prevent the grantor denying to the grantee the fruits of the subject-matter of the grant; hence it serves more as a doctrine of conscience than a principle of pure contract law.[1] However, it can also have the effect of binding successors in title.

An example of non-derogation from grant being found to bind the successor of a grantor is afforded by the English case of *Cable v Bryant*.[2] An adjacent stable and yard were owned in fee simple by the one person. This person had granted a lease of the yard. He then granted a lease of the stable to the plaintiff. Subsequently, he conveyed the fee simple in the yard to the defendant, the lessee of the yard surrendering the lease. The plaintiff succeeded in obtaining an injunction against the defendant for erecting hoardings in the yard which blocked the access of light and air to the stable. Notwithstanding that the vendor had not been in possession of the yard when he gave the lease of the stable, Neville J held that he was under an obligation not to prevent the reasonable use of the stable for the purpose for which it was intended, and that this obligation bound a successor in title, even without notice.

---

[1]   See Elliott 'Non-Derogation from Grant' (1964) 80 LQR 244; Lyall 'Non-Derogation from a Grant' (1988) 6 ILT 143.

[2]   *Cable v Bryant* [1908] 1 Ch 259.

[2.31] There have been very few articulations of this doctrine in the Irish case law on easements. One of the earliest is the confusingly reported case of *Nugent v Cooper*.[1] This was primarily concerned with an alleged easement of necessity, in which context it will be considered more fully in chapter 3.[2] In outline, the case involved what might best be described as a square of land at Kinsealy, Co Dublin, with on the north running from east to west the main road from Dublin to Malahide, access to which was the issue under dispute. Perpendicular to this main road, on the eastern side of the square, and running from north to south, was another road that led to the railway, called the Watery lane. The case principally concerned lands lying to the south of an imaginary line drawn parallel to the Dublin-Malahide Road bisecting the square of land, and the access from these lower lands to the outside world.

Prior to 1790 the owner in fee of the southern lands used the Watery lane for his access to the Dublin-Malahide Road. Then, the owner in fee made a lease to one

Gorman of the south-western lands (those furthest away from the Watery lane), but did not grant a right of way to the Watery lane. Even so, the effect of the grant was held by Monahan CJ to confer a right of way, regardless of whether it was expressed. In any event, Gorman used it. Next, the owner in fee granted a lease of the south-eastern lands to another party but did not reserve a right of way to the Watery lane in favour of Gorman. Monahan CJ held that the law forbade the owner in fee to derogate from his original grant to Gorman and that Gorman was entitled to a right of way over the south-eastern lands to the Watery lane, even though it had not been expressly granted to him initially, or expressly reserved to him later in a lease of the south-eastern lands to another.[3]

---

[1]   *Nugent v Cooper* (1855) 7 Ir Jur (OS) 112.
[2]   See para **[3.08]** ff.
[3]   The principal issue in this case, considered in ch 3, para **[3.08]** ff, derived from the subsequent sale by the fee simple owner, to another party, of all the lands excepting the south-western portion. The question then arose regarding the nature of the right, if any, which the occupier of the south-western portion enjoyed, particularly when the lessee of that portion of the lands also took over the lease of the south-eastern portion, was subsequently evicted for non-payment of rent, and the defendant became the occupier of the south-western lands, but not of the south-eastern lands. The doctrine of non-derogation from grant was alluded to approvingly, in the context of a right of support, in *Green v Belfast Tramways Co* (1887) 20 LR Ir 35, considered more fully in ch 9, para **[9.28]** ff.

[2.32] In *Head v Meara*,[1] in which the purchaser of a mansion house at Derrylahan, Co Tipperary, successfully claimed a right of way over an avenue running through his neighbour's land which connected with the county road to Birr, the doctrine of non-derogation from grant was touched on briefly. It was found that at the time the avenue under dispute was built the lands of the respective parties to the action had been in common ownership. Ross J held that there was an implied grant of a right of way and observed:

> 'If there are two adjacent properties belonging to the same owner, and over one of them there is a formed and constructed road, which has been, and is, in fact, used for the purposes of the other, when the other is conveyed, a right of way over the road will pass to the grantee. ... All this doctrine is founded on the principle that a man must not derogate from his own grant. If a man sells a house with windows, and retains the surrounding land, he must not the next day block up the windows.'[2]

In *Geoghegan v Henry*,[3] O'Connor MR held that it was not a derogation of a grant of a right of way for the servient owner to put fencing around his house and erect a gate to which dominant owner was allowed freedom of access on the basis that he would close the gate after him. The servient owner was entitled to take steps to prevent his livestock from straying, and it was reasonable for him to insist that the dominant owner close the gate after him as it would be irksome for the servient owner to have to close the gate himself every time the dominant owner left it open.

In *Griffin v Keane*[4] the plaintiff had bought a house and farm from the defendant, together with a right of way over a mile-long avenue leading from the main road through the defendant's land to the house. The grant of the right of way expressly provided that the defendant would not be responsible for the upkeep of the avenue nor would be liable for any failure to maintain it. The defendant had a sawmill operation, and had recently cut down so many trees and carted them away over the avenue that the avenue itself had become almost impassable. It was held that, even though the plaintiff had been aware of the defendant's timber-cutting proclivities at the time of the purchase, this user was excessive, constituting a derogation from the defendant's grant. If the defendant had wished to have an immunity against damaging the avenue on account of his sawmilling activities, he ought to have provided specifically for it in the deed. An award of damages was made, however, rather than the injunction which the plaintiff had sought.

---

1   *Head v Meara* [1912] 1 IR 262.
2   [1912] 1 IR 262 at 264–265. This adumbration closely resembles the rule in *Wheeldon v Burrows* (1879) 12 ChD 31, discussed in ch 3. See also *Browne v Flower* [1911] 1 Ch 219 and *Lyme Valley Squash Club Ltd v Newcastle-under-Lyme Borough Council* [1985] 2 All ER 405.
3   *Geoghegan v Henry* [1922] 2 IR 1.
4   *Griffin v Keane* (1927) 61 ILTR 177.

[2.33] The doctrine of non-derogation from grant was fully considered by Barron J in *Connell v O'Malley*.[1] The defendant was the owner of 90 acres of farm land in Co Meath. In 1973 he treated for the sale to the plaintiff of a site comprising 5 acres together with outline planning permission for the construction of five dwellinghouses. The site was linked to the main road by a private laneway in the ownership of the defendant which, from the point where it joined the main road, passed first through the grounds of a convent, then alongside the defendant's farm and the site under sale, and so on up to the entrance gate to the defendant's house.

Full planning permission was granted later in 1973, a condition of which was that the access road would be taken in charge by the local authority. The parties executed contracts for sale in November 1975. Disagreements ensued. The defendant erected a gate across the laneway and, after an injunction had been granted against this, constructed a gate and a cattle grid at a different part of the lane. Meath County Council in 1979 wrote to the plaintiff advising that the laneway would not be taken in charge if either there was a gate or a cattle grid on it. Finally, the defendant executed a deed of transfer but refused to remove either the gate or the cattle grid. The plaintiff instituted proceedings, seeking an injunction and punitive damages on the basis of derogation from grant.

It was common case that the existence of the gate was responsible for the refusal by Meath County Council to take the laneway in charge and that this refusal had occasioned damage to the plaintiff by reason of his inability to develop his site. The plaintiff claimed that the defendant had derogated from his grant, that the site had been sold for a particular purpose, with an implied obligation on the defendant not to do anything which would prevent the access route being taken in charge by the local authority. The defendant's case was that his was merely the lawful and legitimate use of his own property, and that if the plaintiff had wanted a gate not to be erected, he should have stipulated for a clause to that effect in the contract for sale.

Barron J observed of the doctrine of non-derogation from grant that it tended to impose obligations on the owner of land who disposes of one part while retaining the remainder. Usually, but not invariably, it arises in the context of an easement. The implied obligations depend upon the particular nature of the transaction and arise from the presumed intention of the parties.

---

¹   *Connell v O'Malley* (28 July 1983, unreported) HC; also discussed in Lyall 'Non-Derogation from a Grant' (1988) 6 ILT 143.

[2.34] Barron J adopted the reasoning of Parker J in *Browne v Flower*¹ where Parker J had held that the doctrine of non-derogation from grant did not stop short with easements or with the implication of easements specifically known to the law, but that, in the case of the grant of land for a particular purpose, the grantor came under an obligation not to use the land retained by him in such a way as to render the land granted 'materially less fit for the particular purpose for which the grant' had been made. Equally, it could not be inferred that the grantor was covenanting not to use the land retained by him as he was entitled to, merely because by so doing he might 'affect the amenities' of the property sold. In such a case the onus was on the purchaser to protect himself by extracting a covenant.²

In *Browne v Flower* it had been held that mere inconvenience was not adequate to invoke the doctrine. The plaintiff's privacy had been compromised by dint of a stairs to a first floor flat being erected between the windows of her apartment. Parker J found that this was an issue of privacy and comfort and did not make her flat significantly less habitable, so that there had been no derogation from grant.

Barron J summarised the parameters of the doctrine thus:

'Since it depends on the presumed intention of the parties it cannot apply to a situation which could not have been anticipated. While the grantor must have knowledge of the particular purpose for which the property is acquired, before any obligation arises, nevertheless he cannot have imputed to him more than ordinary knowledge of what such purpose involves.'³

---

¹   *Browne v Flower* [1911] 1 Ch 219.
²   In a commentary on *Browne v Flower*, Merritt in 'Rights of Light and Air' (1972) 36 Conv 15 at 19, observed that the concept of being materially less fit fell somewhere between definite fitness and definite unfitness; precisely 'where the line is to be drawn can only depend on the facts of the particular case. How many stones make a heap?'
³   (28 July 1983, unreported) HC at p 17.

[2.35] By way of illustration Barron J cited *Robinson v Kilvert*¹ where, property having been let to the plaintiff as a paper warehouse, the fact that a certain kind of paper would be damaged if the temperature rose, and was so damaged by heat rising from the cellar retained by the defendant, could not reasonably have been within the knowledge of the defendant. If the plaintiff had wanted special protection, as clearly he did, then the plaintiff should have negotiated for it. Barron J added that, the obligation imposed on the grantor being not to use the land retained by him in such a way as to render the land granted unfit or materially less fit for the particular purpose for which it was acquired, the extent of that obligation depended on the extent of the knowledge which could be imputed to the grantor of the conditions required to render the land fit to be so used.

Accordingly, Barron J concluded that there were two tests to be satisfied:

(a) whether the property granted has been rendered materially less fit for the purpose for which it was acquired; and, if so,

(b) whether the grantor ought to have anticipated from what he knows, or could have had imputed to his knowledge, that this result would accrue.[2]

---

[1] *Robinson v Kilvert* (1889) 41 Ch D 88.

[2] See also Bland *The Law of Easements and Profits à Prendre* pp 211–212.

[2.36] In the context of this second requirement, Barron J considered the judgment of the Court of Appeal in *Harmer v Jumbil (Nigeria) Tin Areas Ltd*.[1] Premises had been leased for use as an explosives warehouse which required a particular licence. It was a condition of the licence that buildings would not be erected within a certain distance of the magazine. Later the lessor gave a licence to the defendant to open up some mine workings. The defendant erected buildings, which thereby put the plaintiffs in breach of their licence and it was revoked. The Court of Appeal held that there had been a derogation from grant. Although the premises were still physically capable of being used as an explosives magazine, they were not legally capable of being so used as a result of an act of the defendant; this was no less a derogation from grant than if the defendant had physically interfered with the utility of the premises.

The Court of Appeal held that certain knowledge could be imputed to the lessor: that an explosives magazine needed a licence, that the licence would have certain conditions attached to it, and that breach of any of them could result in forfeiture of the licence. The lessor could not be expected to know all the terms of the licence or all the provisions of the relevant legislation. However, he could be expected to know – and knowledge to this effect would be imputed to him – that the licence would prohibit the erection of buildings within a reasonable distance of the magazine.

---

[1] *Harmer v Jumbil (Nigeria) Tin Areas Ltd* [1921] 1 Ch 200. In this case also the doctrine of non-derogation from grant was held to apply to a successor in title of the grantor.

[2.37] In *Connell v O'Malley*,[1] although the dwellinghouses could be constructed whether the access road were taken in charge or not, fewer houses would be likely to be sold if the access were strictly private. Were the laneway not to be taken in charge, it would be an uneconomical proposition to construct five dwellinghouses. Accordingly, the plaintiff was deemed to satisfy the first test posited by Barron J. Since the defendant was found to have known that the site was intended for development, that it was reasonably necessary for this development that the access road be taken in charge, and that this would not be likely to happen if there were any obstruction on the road, the second test was deemed to be satisfied as well. Hence, an injunction was granted to enable the plaintiff to comply with the planning permission and to enable the local authority take the laneway in charge.[2]

1 *Connell v O'Malley* (28 July 1983, unreported) HC.
2 There was also an award of damages, but not the punitive damages sought by the plaintiff. Barron J assessed damages on the basis of the cost to the plaintiff of having to finance the purchase of the site during the period of delay up to the time of actually developing the site.

[2.38] The view has been expressed that the obligation not to derogate from a grant is in effect a promise as to future conduct, which, in cases involving property rights, also becomes binding on successors to the original contracting parties.[1] It would appear that the principle of non-derogation from grant is as close as the law of easements comes to approximating to the principles governing the enforceability of restrictive covenants.[2]

1 Lyall 'Non-Derogation from a Grant' (1988) 6 ILT 143 at 144.
2 See ch 16.

Easements Passing by Implication from Words in a Grant

[2.39] In certain cases an easement has been deemed to pass by implication as a result of the form of words used in the grant of corporeal property. In *Kavanagh v Coal Mining Co of Ireland*[1] the Court of Queen's Bench held that a grant of a lease of a store, together with 'appurtenances', though the lease did not contain the usual form of words 'therewith usually held and enjoyed',[2] was sufficient to pass a right of way which had previously been enjoyed by the lessee on foot of an agreement for lease entered into some 40 years earlier.[3]

As has already been seen, the case of *Geoghegan v Fegan*[4] decided that a grant of property, 'together with all buildings, easements and appurtenances', which had contained a covenant by the grantee to allow the occupiers of the adjacent property empty the spoil from an outdoor toilet in their back yard through the grantee's back yard, operated as the grant of an easement to the grantee to the use of the toilet in the adjacent property. This was held to arise alternatively by way of implication or on the basis of the general words used in the operative part of the deed. Likewise, in *Head v Meara*,[5] where a conveyance was granted 'with the appurtenances', it was held to pass a right of way formerly enjoyed by the owner of the property even though such a right had never been expressly granted. Ross J observed: 'Does it make any difference if there are no apt general words? I think not, but there are adequate general words in this conveyance.'

1 *Kavanagh v Coal Mining Co of Ireland* (1861) 14 ICLR 82.
2 Prior to the Conveyancing Act 1881, s 6 it was standard practice, in a conveyance of property intending to pass all easements attaching to the property to the purchaser, to include a clause containing the words 'together with all rights used or enjoyed' or words to similar effect. This clause became known as the 'general words'. One of the intended purposes of the Conveyancing Act 1881, s 6 was to render such a devise unnecessary.
3 This case was also partially decided on the basis that the right of way was necessary for the reasonable use and enjoyment of the store.
4 *Geoghegan v Fegan* (1872) IR 6 CL 139, see para **[2.07]**.
5 *Head v Meara* [1912] 1 IR 262.

[2.40] In *Renwick v Daly*[1] premises had been demised in September 1874 to a lessee for a term of 400 years, 'together with the right to use the walls on the north side of the said plot for building purposes.' Later that same month this lessee sub-demised the premises to the defendant. In December 1874 the head-lessor demised to the plaintiff the adjoining premises of which the walls referred to in the earlier lease were part. The plaintiff, in an action by him for trespass, after the defendant had knocked holes in his wall and built a roofed shed up against it, (relying upon the right conferred in the first lease of September 1874), urged that the right to use the north wall for building purposes did not pass from the original lessee to the defendant, because the inclusion in the demise of 'the rights, members and appurtenances thereto belonging or in anywise appertaining' had not been in the operative part of the sub-lease, but the habendum only.

Counsel for the defendant contended that reference in a habendum to a right already granted is sufficient to transfer it and cited the dictum of Bayley B in *Canham v Fisk*:[2] 'By selling the house I sell the easement also ... the conveyance passes the land with the easement existing at the time.'[3] Morris CJ, dismissing the action by the plaintiff, held that the lands in the first lease of September 1874 were 'specifically stamped and impressed' with the right to use the walls for building purposes, and continued to be so 'stamped and impressed' in the later sub-lease of September 1874.

---

[1] *Renwick v Daly* (1877) IR 11 CL 126.

[2] *Canham v Fisk* (1851) 2 Cr & J 126.

[3] Counsel for the defendant also relied on the Irish case of *Dobbyn v Somers* (1860) 13 ICLR 293 which had held that the use of the word 'appurtenances' in the habendum is adequate to pass the right to them, even though the operative part of the deed itself might be silent.

[2.41] The taking over of a covenant for quiet enjoyment can serve to resuscitate an easement which otherwise might have been extinguished through languishment. In *Solomon v Red Bank Restaurant Ltd*[1] the defendants in the course of construction work obstructed the right of way to a particular chute which gave access to the plaintiff's enclosed yard. The plaintiff had not used the chute for some 40 years, and it had been shut up on the plaintiff's side. However, the defendants had purchased the freehold reversion of the plaintiff's property and had thereby taken over a covenant for quiet enjoyment entered into by the original lessor with the plaintiff.

Johnston J adopted the principle enunciated in *Andrews v Paradise*,[2] that a lessor who disturbs his lessee's use of a right of way appurtenant to the demised premises can be liable for breach of covenant. Since the defendants were on notice of the covenant for quiet enjoyment when they purchased the freehold reversion, according to Johnston J they were liable to the plaintiff for obstructing the use of the passageway, despite his non-use of it. In view of the fact that the plaintiff had clearly no real use for the chute, and had proven to be a somewhat avaricious negotiator, Johnston J awarded damages rather than an injunction to restrain the blocking of the chute.[3]

---

[1] *Solomon v Red Bank Restaurant Ltd* [1938] IR 793.

[2] *Andrews v Paradise* (1734) 8 Mod 318.

3   Johnston J held that the defendants had acted honestly, not appreciating their liability on the covenant for quiet enjoyment (even though they were on notice of it), and not believing that their current building plans would discommode the plaintiff since he had not used the chute for a very long time. In light of this, it is submitted as being all the more surprising that Johnston J did not find that the right of way had been abandoned on account of the prolonged non-use of it and the shutting up of the chute. See para **[6.07]**.

[2.42] Where a right depends on an exception and reservation for its validity in a lease, and the lease has not been executed by the lessee, the exception and reservation cannot take effect as a regrant to the grantor and the easement is therefore void. In *Corcor v Payne and Mackenzie*,[1] a lease of 1711 had contained an exception and reservation in favour of the lessor of all royalties, 'in particular the fishing, with a pathway for the fishermen'. The defendant, acting as a licensee of the fee simple owner in reversion, was successfully sued in trespass on his use of the pathway, since the lease had not been executed by the grantee of 1711, so that the exception and reservation of the easement did not take effect.

1   *Corcor v Payne and Mackenzie* (1870) IR 4 CL 380. See also para **[2.03]**.

Section 6 of the Conveyancing Act 1881

[2.43] In principle, the need for the use of appropriate words in a lease or conveyance in order to pass to a purchaser, as easements, rights exercised over the property has been rendered nugatory by s 6 of the Conveyancing Act 1881. It is a debatable point whether the application of this provision operates as an extension of the actual words of an express grant[1] or by way of what might be termed legislative implication.[2] The approach being taken in the present work is to regard easements arising under s 6 of the Conveyancing Act 1881 as being created by implication through the intervention of statute. There can be no doubt that its purpose is to serve as a kind of conveyancing shorthand, as is manifest from the terms of the section.[3]

1   A view preferred by Professor JCW Wylie in *Irish Land Law* (3rd edn, 1997) Butterworths, p 379; also Coughlan *Property Law* (2nd edn, 1998) Gill and Macmillan, p 249. In *Gregg v Richards* [1926] Ch 521, Sargant LJ affirmed that the section operated by way of express grant and not by way of implied grant. See also *Broomfield v Williams* [1897] 1 Ch 602 at 610, per Lindley LJ and at p 615, per Rigby LJ. However, see *Gale on Easements* (16th edn, 1997) London, Sweet and Maxwell p 167 for the proposition that the deemed existence of easements arising from 'the general words imported' by s 6 can often be contrary to the intention of the grantor.

2   For example, the section is discussed in Bland *The Law of Easements and Profits à Prendre* in a chapter titled 'Acquisition by Implication of Law.'

3   The statute came into effect on 1 January 1882. One of its acknowledged limitations is that it only applies to conveyances (as defined) executed after 31 December 1881: sub-s 6.

[2.44] Section 6(1) of the 1881 Act provides:

> 'A conveyance of land shall be deemed to include and shall by virtue of this Act operate to convey, with the land, all buildings, erections, fixtures, commons, hedges, ditches, fences, ways, waters, watercourses, liberties, privileges, easements, rights, and advantages whatsoever, appertaining or reputed to appertain to the land, or any part thereof, or at the time of conveyance demised, occupied, or enjoyed with, or reputed or known as part or parcel of or appurtenant to the land or any part thereof.'

Section 6(2) deals specifically with buildings:

> 'A conveyance of land, having houses or other buildings thereon, shall be deemed to include and shall by virtue of this Act operate to convey, with the land, houses, or other buildings, all outhouses, erections, fixtures, cellars, areas, courts, courtyards, cisterns, sewers, gutters, drains, ways, passages, lights, watercourses, liberties, privileges, easements, rights, and advantages whatsoever, appertaining or reputed to appertain to the land, houses, or other buildings conveyed, or any of them, or any part thereof, or at the time of conveyance, demised, occupied, or enjoyed with, or reputed or known as part or parcel of or appurtenant to, the land, houses, or other buildings conveyed, or any of them, or any part thereof.'

Section 6(4) provides that the section 'applies only if and as far as a contrary intention is not expressed in the conveyance, and shall have effect subject to the terms of the conveyance and to the provisions therein contained.'

Section 6(5) provides that a person cannot receive any better title to a right passing under the section than the title which the conveyance itself gives to the property conveyed and that such person cannot be granted by the section any right greater than that which could actually have been granted in the conveyance.

[2.45] It is clear that the section cannot enlarge upon rights capable of being granted in the first place and that the rights must exist, as defined in the section, at the time of the making of the grant to which the section is deemed to apply. Its primary effect is to shorten the wording of conveyances[1] and the extent to which the section has been resorted to in Irish case law on easements is noticeably slight.[2]

---

[1]   Jackson 'Easements and General Words' (1966) 30 Conv 340.

[2]   *Henry Ltd v McGlade* [1926] NI 144, 60 ILTR 17; *Jeffers v Odeon (Ireland) Ltd* (1953) 87 ILTR 187 at 189, per Judge Shannon: 'By virtue of section 6 of the Conveyancing Act 1881, the applicant became entitled to all rights appertaining to the premises enjoyed by the former tenant ... There was no mention of the rights in question in any tenancy agreement between the parties; the said rights form part thereof by implication.' Also *Corr v Bradshaw* (18 July 1967, unreported) SC: benefit of a right of way passed to a sub–lessee under s 6; *Redfont Ltd and Wright's Fisherman's Wharf Ltd v Custom House Dock Management Ltd and Hardwicke Property Management Ltd* (31 March 1998, unreported) HC: s 6 held not to apply because the claimed rights were not in existence at the time of the granting of the plaintiffs' leases.

The controversy over diversity of ownership and occupation

[2.46] The question whether rights enjoyed by a landowner over different parts of his own property can be converted into an easement, upon the sale of one part and the retention of the other part or upon the simultaneous disposal of both parts, though never tested in Ireland, has been judicially considered in England with varying results that have evoked vigorous academic controversy. In an attempt to anticipate just how such a question might be answered by the Irish courts in an appropriate case, it is instructive to consider briefly the essence of this debate.

[2.47] A convenient point from which to start is the decision of the Court of Appeal in *Broomfield v Williams*.[1] On the face of it, this decision is unexceptional enough. A developer built a house on portion of his land and sold the house to the plaintiff. At the time of the conveyance the remainder of the land had not been developed and no other houses had been built. The conveyance to the plaintiff described the defendant's retained land as 'building land' but the defendant did not reserve any right to build on his own land so as to reduce significantly the light entering the windows to the plaintiff's house. The action arose from the defendant's constructing houses on his own land which were so close to the boundary with the plaintiff's land as to diminish the natural light entering the windows of his house.

The Court of Appeal unanimously held that the defendant was not entitled to build so as to diminish the plaintiff's natural light. Smith LJ founded his decision on the principle of non-derogation from grant. The only wrongdoing of the defendant was to build closer to the plaintiff's house than the plaintiff had reasonably expected. Both Lindley and Rigby LJJ held that the reference to 'building land' in the conveyance was not sufficient expression of a contrary intention as to displace the application of s 6 of the Conveyancing Act 1881, on foot of which the plaintiff was deemed to be entitled to a continuance of the same level of natural light to his house as at the time he bought it. In the opinion of Rigby LJ, '... the numerous cases ... in which the quasi-easement has been treated as enjoyed with what becomes on severance the dominant tenement govern this case.'[2]

---

[1]   *Broomfield v Williams* [1897] 1 Ch 602.

[2]   [1897] 1 Ch 602 at 617. 'Quasi-easements' have been variously defined as 'rights habitually exercised by a man over part of his own land which, if the part in question were owned and occupied by another would be easements' – Megarry and Wade *Law of Real Property* (4th edn) and 'by definition inchoate 'rights' waiting to be converted by the division of the tenements into proper rights' – Sparkes 'Establishing Easements against Leaseholds' [1992] Conv 167 at 178.

[2.48] *Long v Gowlett*[1] is quite a different case entirely. In this the common owner of two plots of land, through both of which ran a watercourse, sold each part contemporaneously to the plaintiff (Lot 2) and the defendant (Lot 1). The defendant sought to enter upon the land owned by the plaintiff to repair the banks of a watercourse and cut weeds so as to ease the passage of the water through that part of the watercourse on his own land. The defendant's alleged entitlement to do this was that the vendor, when the common owner of both plots, had been accustomed, as necessary, to proceed from the south bank within Lot 1 (the defendant's land) to repair the south bank and cut the weeds within Lot 2 (the plaintiff's land), and that a right to do this passed to the defendant under s 6(2) of the Conveyancing Act 1881.

This argument was rejected by Sargant J, on the basis that evidence had not been adduced that the former common owner of both plots had ever done any work on Lot 2 other than in the context of his ownership of Lot 2; that, in effect, such work as he had done on Lot 2 was not demonstrably in the context of a 'privilege, easement or advantage'[2] for the benefit of Lot 1.

Sargant J expressed the philosophical argument thus:

'The common owner and occupier of Whiteacre and Blackacre may in fact use Blackacre as an alternative and more convenient method of communicating between Whiteacre and the neighbouring village ... it seems to me, in order that there may be a 'privilege, easement or advantage' enjoyed with Whiteacre over Blackacre so as to pass under the statute, there must be something done on Blackacre not due to or comprehended within the general rights of an occupying owner of Blackacre, but of such a nature that it is attributable to a privilege, easement, right or advantage, however, precarious, which arises out of the ownership or occupation of Whiteacre, altogether apart from the ownership or occupation of Blackacre.'[3]

---

[1] *Long v Gowlett* [1923] 2 Ch 177.

[2] Borrowing the *ipsissima verba* of sub–ss 1 and 2, but, noticeably, omitting the word 'rights' which also appears at this point. See also the observations of Wylie *Irish Land Law* (3rd edn, 1997) p 381, para 6.067).

[3] [1923] 2 Ch 177 at 200.

[2.49] Sargant J went on to observe how it would be difficult, in a case of common ownership, to find such a relationship between the two plots of land 'apart from the case of continuous and apparent easements[1] or that of a way of necessity'. In order for s 6 of the Conveyancing Act 1881 to apply, in the opinion of Sargant J

' ... *it would seem*[2] that there must be some diversity of ownership or occupation of the two closes sufficient to refer the act or acts relied on not to mere occupying ownership, but to some advantage or privilege (however far short of a legal right) attaching to the owner or occupier of Whiteacre as such and de facto exercised over Blackacre.'[3]

The defendant argued that *Broomfield v Williams* covered the case, but this was distinguished by Sargant J, on the basis that 'the access of light to a window over adjoining land is a physical fact plainly visible to any one buying a house.'[4] As such, the access of light is wholly differentiable from 'imperceptible rights or advantages, corresponding with intermittent practice or user as between two tenements of the common owner and occupier of both.'[5] Were the situation to be otherwise, according to Sargant J, a purchaser of any property forming part of a larger property formerly in common ownership, would be obliged to inquire how the common owner had been accustomed to make use of each part in connection with each other part.[6]

---

[1] Borrowing from the language of Thesiger LJ in *Wheeldon v Burrows* (1879) 12 Ch D 31, considered at para **[3.14]** ff, ch 3, but which, it is submitted, is not conclusive of the character of the right which can pass as an easement under s 6 of the Conveyancing Act 1881.

2 Italics supplied, in order to demonstrate that Sargent J was not asserting absolute conviction. In the later case of *Sovmots Investments Ltd v Secretary of State for the Environment* [1977] 2 WLR 951, this dictum was replicated in cast-iron terms.

3 [1923] 2 Ch 177 at 201.

4 [1923] 2 Ch 177 at 202.

5 [1923] 2 Ch 177 at 203.

6 A point taken up by Harpum in '*Long v Gowlett:* A Strong Fortress' [1979] Conv 113, where he laments that the view that s 6 can transform into easements rights other than those which are continuous and apparent, or which accrue from a diversity of ownership and occupation of the two parcels of land, would result in the irksome lengthening of conveyances due to the welter of exclusions which would have to be set out. 'This would lengthen conveyances and defeat the whole point of the section.' [1979] Conv 113 at 122.

[2.50] In an article published in 1966,[1] Jackson interpreted the decision in *Long v Gowlett* as being based on the fact that the common owner had not demonstrably, in exercising rights of ownership over one plot, done so for the benefit of the other plot.[2] Jackson approved the explanation of *Long v Gowlett* by Ungoed-Thomas J in *Ward v Kirkland*,[3] as turning upon the 'distinction between enjoyment exclusively for the purposes of the alleged dominant tenement or enjoyment of an advantage which might be attributable to the possession and ownership of the alleged servient tenement.' The thrust of Jackson's argument is that diversity of occupation and ownership of both parcels of land is not a prerequisite to the operation of s 6 of the Conveyancing Act 1881,[4] although he acknowledged that in most modern cases there had in fact been such diversity of occupation prior to the conveyances under dispute. Jackson also maintained that the concept of being continuous and apparent was not applicable to easements deriving from s 6 of the Conveyancing Act 1881.[5]

1 'Easements and General Words' (1966) 30 Conv 340.

2 (1966) 30 Conv 340 at 345.

3 *Ward v Kirkland* [1966] 1 All ER 609.

4 Re-enacted in Great Britain as the Law of Property Act 1925, s 62.

5 In essence, that there was a tendency to confuse the ingredients of the rule in *Wheeldon v Burrows* with those relevant to the Conveyancing Act 1881, s 6, a criticism which, it is submitted, is entirely valid.

[2.51] The matter might there have rested, confined to a textual analysis of the extent to which the decision in *Long v Gowlett* could be considered unique to its own facts, were it not for the House of Lords decision in *Sovmots Investments Ltd v Secretary of State for the Environment*.[1]

This concerned a local authority compulsory order to acquire a number of newly constructed and unoccupied maisonettes and the failure in the order to reserve certain ancillary rights in the complex, including a right of support from the building below the maisonettes and rights of passage for gas, electricity and other facilities through pipes servicing the maisonettes. It was accepted that if the ancillary rights could not be acquired, the compulsory purchase order would have to be quashed. Arguments that these ancillary rights could be attached to the compulsory purchase order by implication, under the rule in *Wheeldon v Burrows*, or s 6 of the Conveyancing Act 1881,[2] did not succeed either before Forbes J at first instance or the Court of Appeal. On further appeal to the House of Lords, these arguments were virtually abandoned,[3] but the issues arising from them were still deemed by their Lordships to be pertinent to other arguments under consideration.[4]

In the view of Lord Wilberforce, s 6 of the Conveyancing Act 1881 quite simply did not fit the case.

> 'The reason is that when land is under one ownership one cannot speak in any intelligible sense of rights, or privileges, or easements being exercised over one part for the benefit of another.[5] Whatever the owner does, he does as owner and, until a separation occurs, of ownership or at least of occupation, the condition for the exercise of rights, etc, does not exist.'[6]

Lord Edmund-Davies resorted to a narrow interpretation of *Long v Gowlett*, maintaining that s 6 of the Conveyancing Act 1881 could not apply unless there had been some diversity of ownership or occupation of the quasi-dominant and quasi-servient tenements prior to the instrument of disposition to which the section was invited to apply.[7]

---

[1] *Sovmots Investments Ltd v Secretary of State for the Environment* [1977] 2 WLR 951.

[2] For convenience, it is proposed to continue to allude to the Conveyancing Act 1881, s 6. Naturally, the section under review in the *Sovmots* case was the Law of Property Act 1925, s 62.

[3] A circumstance emphasised by Smith in 'Centre Point: Faulty Towers with Shaky Foundations' [1978] Conv 449. Since their Lordships did not have the benefit of argument from counsel, their analysis of s 6 could be deemed somewhat perfunctory. It would have been open to the House of Lords to have determined that, as a compulsory purchase order cannot give rise to a voluntary conveyance, arguments based on implied grant are meaningless. It is submitted that this consideration attenuates much of the strength otherwise attaching to a pronouncement issuing from so eminent a judicial authority as the House of Lords.

[4] [1977] 2 WLR 951 at 958–959, per Lord Wilberforce.

[5] It is significant that his Lordship made no reference to 'advantages' which are also comprehended by the section.

[6] [1977] 2 WLR 951 at 958.

[7] [1977] 2 WLR 951 at 965. The immediate aftermath to the *Sovmots* case, in England, was an inconclusive duel of words waged in the pages of the Conveyancer on the extent to which it was now an absolute prerequisite for the application of the Conveyancing Act 1881, s 6 that there should have been a diversity of ownership and occupation of the premises under sale: Harpum 'Easements and Centre Point: Old Problems Resolved in a Novel Setting' (1977) 41 Conv 415; Smith 'Centre Point: Faulty Towers with Shaky Foundations' [1978] Conv 449, Harpum '*Long v Gowlett*: A Strong Fortress' [1979] Conv 113.

[2.52] Prior to the decision of Shanley J in *Redfont Ltd and Wright's Fisherman's Wharf Ltd v Custom House Dock Management Ltd and Hardwicke Property Management Ltd,*[1] it could have been argued that the absolute assertion by the House of Lords in *Sovmots Investments Ltd v Secretary of State for the Environment,*[2] that in order for s 6 of the Conveyancing Act 1881 to apply there must have been prior diversity of ownership and occupation of the premises in sale, would not be followed by the Irish courts.

(a) The *Sovmots* case centred upon a compulsory purchase order. Arguably, s 6 of the Conveyancing Act 1881 was irrelevant, as noted by Lord Keith who observed, both of the rule in *Wheeldon v Burrows* and also of s 6 that:

> '[t]hese rules, applicable to voluntary conveyances of land and to contracts for the sale of land, have no place in compulsory purchase. They are founded on the principle that a grantor may not derogate from his grant, for which there is no room where the acquisition is compulsory.'[3]

(b) The pronouncements of Lord Wilberforce and Lord Edmund-Davies in relation to s 6 did not have the benefit of submissions from counsel as the arguments concerning s 6 had been abandoned on appeal.

(c) The dicta of Sargant J in *Long v Gowlett* were, arguably, taken out of context and translated into more imperative terms than had actually been employed in *Long v Gowlett* itself. Primarily, what Sargant J had said was, that in the case of common ownership of land subsequently sold in two lots, it seemed that there would need to be a diversity of occupation for it to be apparent that the enjoyment of any particular right was had other than in the context of the enjoyment of the land as a whole.

(d) Such commentary as has been made in Irish cases to s 6 of the Conveyancing Act 1881 has been – to apply an apt, if inelegant, expression – off-hand. In those cases where the section has been mentioned it has not received detailed consideration.[4] Arguably, the positive facet of such an off-hand approach is a disinclination to be fettered by overly technical argument. Hence, it is suggested, if the exercise of the right or privilege is discernible, such that a prospective purchaser can have actual or constructive notice of it, it will pass as an easement under s 6 of the Conveyancing Act 1881.

(e) In *Head v Meara*,[5] although s 6 of the Conveyancing Act 1881 was not specifically mentioned, Ross J evinced a view that the primary consideration is that the exercise of the right should have been manifest, rather than that there had to be diversity of occupation and ownership as a precondition of the right passing as an easement to the purchaser.[6]

---

[1] *Redfont Ltd and Wright's Fisherman's Wharf Ltd v Custom House Dock Management Ltd and Hardwicke Property Management Ltd* (31 March 1998, unreported) HC.

[2] *Sovmots Investments Ltd v Secretary of State for the Environment* [1977] 2 WLR 951.

[3] [1977] 2 WLR 951 at 972.

[4] For example, *Gaw v Coras Iompair Éireann* (1952) 89 ILTR 124; *Jeffers v Odeon (Ireland) Ltd* (1953) 87 ILTR 187; *Corr v Bradshaw* (18 July 1967, unreported) SC; *Redfont Ltd and Wright's Fisherman's Wharf Ltd v Custom House Dock Management Ltd and Hardwicke Property Management Ltd* (31 March 1998, unreported) HC.

[5] *Head v Meara* [1912] 1 IR 262.

[6] [1912] 1 IR 262 at 264–265.

[2.53] However, in *Redfont Ltd and Wright's Fisherman's Wharf Ltd v Custom House Dock Management Ltd and Hardwicke Property Management Ltd*,[1] Shanley J held that the section could not apply where there had not been diversity of ownership and occupation prior to the disposal of the property, but also found that the claimed right had not existed prior to disposal in any event. Shanley J instead held that the claimed right of parking arose as ancillary to a granted right of way. It is suggested that, notwithstanding the clear pronouncement by Shanley J that diversity of ownership and occupation is a prerequisite to the application of s 6, the actual *ratio* of the case arguably still leaves the issue open in Ireland as to whether the section would apply, if the right were found to have existed, but there had not been diversity of ownership and occupation.

---

[1] *Redfont Ltd and Wright's Fisherman's Wharf Ltd v Custom House Dock Management Ltd and Hardwicke Property Management Ltd* (31 March 1998, unreported) HC.

Permissive and reputed rights

[2.54] There is no doubt that s 6(2) of the 1881 Act can elevate into the status of an easement rights which were previously 'precarious' or enjoyed with permission.[1] If a vendor wishes to ensure that such rights are not enlarged into easements he will have to make this fact abundantly clear in the conveyance of the property.[2] The intention not to transfer the right or privilege must be expressly stated in the conveyance: it is not sufficient that a contrary intention should appear, or be urged as inferable, from the words used.[3] In the particular case of the renewal of a lease, great care must be taken to ensure that privileges conferred during an initial term are not deemed to be converted into easements upon a renewal;[4] if necessary, continued user of the privilege must be physically prevented.[5] Section 6(2) will also pass privileges or advantages that do not amount to an easement, provided that such privileges or advantages are not in the nature of services supplied under personal contract.[6] Also passed are rights reputed to appertain to property, provided that such reputation is not wholly historic and is evidenced over time by a pattern of regular usage.[7]

---

[1] *International Tea Stores v Hobbs* [1903] 2 Ch 165, *Wright v Macadam* [1949] 2 KB 744, Jackson 'Easements and General Words' (1966) 30 Conv 340 at 341–342. See discussion on parking in ch 9.

[2] Jackson 'Easements and General Words' (1966) 30 Conv 340 at 349 ff; Smith 'Centre Point: Faulty Towers with Shaky Foundations' [1978] Conv 449 at 453; Cooney 'Public Policy, Necessity and a Right of Access' (1979) 14 Ir Jur 334 at 339; Bland *The Law of Easements and Profits à Prendre* p 221.

[3] *Broomfield v Williams* [1897] 1 Ch 602; *Gregg v Richards* [1926] Ch 521; *Green v Ashco Horticulturist Ltd* [1966] 2 All ER 232; Jackson 'Easements and General Words' (1966) 30 Conv 340 at 350–351.

[4] An example appears in *Jeffers v Odeon (Ireland) Ltd* (1953) 87 ILTR 187.

[5] Jackson 'Easements and General Words' (1966) 30 Conv 340 at 352–353.

[6] Such as the provision of hot water or central heating: *Regis Property Co Ltd v Redman* [1956] 2 QB 612.

[7] *Green v Ashco Horticulturist Ltd* [1966] 2 All ER 232.

Expression of contrary intention

[2.55] Section 6(4) of the Conveyancing Act 1881 provides that the section 'applies only if and as far as a contrary intention is not expressed in the conveyance'. Such contrary intention requires to be clearly stated rather than inferred from silence or from an allusion to other rights but not to the right being claimed.

In *Steele v Morrow*[1] the plaintiff and the defendant were sub-lessees of two adjoining houses, in a row of three, in Marino, Co Down. The sub-lease to each contained grants and reservations of two rights of way, but did not grant an interconnecting right of way which was claimed by the plaintiff over the defendant's property. Both the plaintiff and the defendant had taken their respective sub-leases in 1918, the defendant in January, and the plaintiff in March. Prior to that, in 1915, the plaintiff had been a tenant from year to year and the evidence established that the plaintiff had enjoyed the interconnecting right of way while a yearly tenant. Counsel for the plaintiff urged that the absence of specific reference to the right of way in the deed to the defendant (which was two months earlier than that to the plaintiff) was not prejudicial to the plaintiff's claim, because, the lessor not being in possession, she could not grant a sub-lease to the defendant free of the right of way without derogating from her own grant to the plaintiff as a yearly tenant.[2]

---

1. *Steele v Morrow* (1923) 57 ILTR 89.
2. Counsel for the plaintiff supported his argument by reference to *Thomas v Owen* (1888) 20 QBD 225, in which a plaintiff successfully claimed a right of way over land of an adjoining landowner which had not been expressly reserved when the lease to the adjoining landowner was made. The plaintiff had enjoyed the disputed way while a yearly tenant, and was subsequently granted a longer lease, but this longer lease was granted to him some five years after the lease to the adjoining landowner. Neither lease alluded to the right of way. This case can, arguably, be distinguished on its own facts and the particular character of the claimed right of way, but the decision in *Thomas v Owen* has prompted both confusion and criticism. See *Re Flanagan and McGarvey and Thompson's Contract* [1945] NI 32 at 43, per Black J, see para **[3.31]** ff; *Gale on Easements* (eds, Gaunt and Morgan, 16th edn, 1997) Sweet and Maxwell, p 146.

[2.56] Andrews LJ, in the Northern Ireland Court of Appeal, considered the principal issue to be whether the existing easement passed under s 6(2) of the Conveyancing Act 1881 or whether there could be deemed to be a contrary intention – by referring to other easements but not to this one – expressed in the deed, as per s 6(4). The judge attached importance to the use of the word 'expressed' appearing in the sub-section and compared it with s 24 of the Wills Act 1837 where there is reference to a contrary intention which 'shall appear by the will.'

'Can the absence of all reference in the deed to the alleged right, coupled with a specific reference to other rights, amount to an expression of a contrary intention, so as so preclude the implication of a grant of such right under section 6(2)? In my opinion it cannot ... The necessity, by the terms of section 6(4), for the expression of a contrary intention, prevents the possibility of such contrary intention being deduced by mere inference.'[1]

Andrews LJ noted with approval the decision of Russell J in *Hansford v Jago*[2] where the use of the word 'appurtenances' in a grant, and the specific reference to certain rights, was held not sufficient to deem other claimed rights to have been excluded. In short, the specific reference in a deed to the grant of one or a number of rights does not prevent the court from implying the grant of other rights under s 6(2) of the Conveyancing Act 1881.

---

[1]   (1923) 57 ILTR 89 at 90.

[2]   *Hansford v Jago* [1921] 1 Ch 322. But Russell J went on to hold, that if his interpretation of the Conveyancing Act 1881, s 6(4) were incorrect, the claimed right of way would still pass by implication.

Chapter 3

Easements of Necessity and Qualified Necessity

Introduction

[3.01] The premise underlying an easement of necessity is that, in a case where property formerly held as one unit is divided, one part passing to another and one part being retained by the grantor, either one part or the other cannot be enjoyed without the granting or reserving, as the case may be, of the easement in respect of which the necessity is claimed. In the strict sense an easement of necessity arises by implication because it is not express, but this is an implication deriving, neither from the form of words or a history of user evidencing presumed intention, nor from statutory interpolation, but from a legal principle that an easement will be inferred in order that either one property or the other can be enjoyed.[1] Inevitably, given the principles that a grant is usually construed against a grantor and that a grantor cannot derogate from his grant,[2] the imputation of an easement of necessity is more strictly regarded when the easement claimed is by way of reservation rather than grant, although the application of the concept is the same in each case.[3] Furthermore, an easement arising by necessity is perforce limited to the relieving of the necessity urged, its extent closely defined by the extent of the necessity itself. An easement of necessity is most likely to arise in the context of access, and thereby manifest itself as a right of way.

---

[1]   However, easements of necessity are not infrequently pleaded as alternatives to, or facets of, implied easements or easements arising by prescription. Indeed, the subject of easements is so closely knit in its treatment in the decided cases that it is often difficult to differentiate the grounds of decision in terms of one category of origin as opposed to another. See *Clancy v Byrne* (1877) IR 11 CL 355; *Head v Meara* [1912] 1 IR 262; *Maguire v Brown* [1921] 1 IR 148, [1922] 1 IR 23 (in particular the judgment of Ronan LJ); *Tallon v Ennis* [1937] IR 549; *Dwyer Nolan Developments Ltd v Kingscroft Developments Ltd* [1999] 1 ILRM 141, where Kinlen J observed at 153, that 'the question of necessity has been brought in under the umbrella of implied easement ...'.

[2]   Wylie *Irish Land Law* (3rd edn, 1997) Butterworths, p 375.

[3]   See discussion on this point in *Maude v Thornton* [1929] IR 454 at para **[3.02]**.

The Nature and Extent of an Easement of Necessity

General

[3.02] The case of *Maude v Thornton*[1] is authority for the proposition that the principles governing the implication of an easement of necessity are the same for a grantor as for a grantee. The plaintiffs were the owners of the Meldrum Wood which, by reason of a lease made by their predecessors in title in 1877, both of the wood itself and of lands

49

between it and the public road, without reservation of a right of way, was at the time of the action completely landlocked. The plaintiffs' claim was for a right of way, over a defined passage to the public road, from Meldrum Wood across the intervening lands at the time of the action owned by the defendant.

Meredith J observed of rights of necessity:

'It is clear on the authorities that, although the principle of non-derogation from a grant only operates, of course, in favour of the grantee, the implication of a way of necessity is reciprocal, and arises as well for the benefit of a grantor as for the benefit of a grantee.'[2]

Meredith J added that the wood was no less landlocked because surrounded by lands held under determinable yearly tenancies, and that there was no valid distinction between the right of necessity required by a grantor and that required by a grantee:

'In the case of the grantor's necessity, having regard to the different foundation of the implied right, it might have been held to be only a licence, to be implied by law and irrevocable so long as the necessity continued. But such a view is now impossible, having regard to the course of the authorities. The position is now the same both for a grantor and a grantee.'[3]

The above dictum is also consistent with the proposition that a right of necessity once established continues, and does not stand to be extinguished when the occasion for the necessity has passed.[4]

---

[1]   *Maude v Thornton* [1929] IR 454.
[2]   [1929] IR 454 at 457.
[3]   [1929] IR 454 at 458.
[4]   *Holmes v Goring* (1824) 2 Bing 233 is sometimes cited as supportive of the opposite proposition, but the authority of this has been doubted: see *Gale on Easements* (eds, Gaunt and Morgan, 16th edn, 1997) Sweet & Maxwell, p 153; Bland *The Law of Easements and Profits à Prendre* (1997) Sweet & Maxwell, p 225.

[3.03] An easement of necessity can only be claimed on the basis that without it the property cannot be enjoyed at all, or cannot be effectually enjoyed: it is not adequate that it is merely necessary to the reasonable enjoyment of that property.[1] A right of access along a path over neighbouring land to the back door of a cottage may be very convenient and 'almost necessary for the comfortable enjoyment' of the cottage, but it cannot be asserted that without the right the cottage is wholly incapable of being enjoyed.[2]

---

[1]   In *Geraghty v McCann* (1872) IR 6 CL 411, the Court of Common Pleas held that, as between lessor and lessee, the existence of a right of way of necessity depended on whether, at the time of the making of the lease, the easement was necessary for the fair and reasonable enjoyment of the demised premises. This view is not generally regarded as being correct. In *Donnelly v Adams* [1905] 1 IR 154 at 161, Barton J noted that the distinction between ways of necessity and ways of convenience was 'well marked and well settled'. Also Bland *The Law of Easements and Profits à Prendre* p 223.
[2]   *Re Flanagan and McGarvey and Thompson's Contract* [1945] NI 32 at 42, per Black J.

Necessity to be measured at time of grant

[3.04] A right of necessity must be measured by the user at the time of the deed the omission in which to grant or reserve the right created the necessity. In *Maguire v Brown*,[1] the defendant had purchased from the trustees of Lord Erne a hill in Co Fermanagh comprising approximately three acres which was covered with trees and constituted what is known as a 'rath'.[2] This area had no access to the main road except over a road that ran through lands recently bought by the plaintiff from the trustees of Lord Erne, and over which there was a right of way for foot passage only to and from the rath. This way was bounded by a stone wall. When the defendant purchased the rath in 1919 he proceeded to cut down the trees with a view to selling them commercially. He then began to cart them along the way claiming that there was a right of way of necessity to do so, having regard to the status of the hill as an agricultural property. In order to get the cut trees along the way he had to knock part of the stone wall. The plaintiff, through whose lands the way ran, sued for trespass. Powell J, at first instance, experienced little difficulty in determining that there was a right of necessity. The issue for decision was its extent:

> 'There does not seem to be any doubt that the right to a way of necessity to and from a land-locked close over the surrounding land is not a general right of way for all purposes, but is limited to such a right of way as was suitable or necessary for the enjoyment of the close in the condition in which it happened to be at the time that the right first arose.'[3]

---

[1] *Maguire v Brown* [1921] 1 IR 148; [1922] 1 IR 23.

[2] A circular hill covered with trees to which folk culture attaches malevolent supernatural properties usually only invoked when the rath is disturbed.

[3] [1921] 1 IR 148 at 154.

[3.05] Powell J adopted the view articulated by Jessel MR in *Corporation of London v Riggs*,[1] that a right of necessity arises by way of implication, and is limited to enabling the party alleging the necessity enjoy the property as it had been at the time of the grant.[2] In the case of *Corporation of London v Riggs* the land in question was agricultural, and the grantor had wanted a right of way so that he could build a tea-room on the land retained. The Court of Appeal refused to hold with such an alleged right of necessity. Jessel MR stated the law thus:

> 'The object of implying the re-grant, as stated by the older Judges, was that if you did not give the owner of the reserved close some right of way or other, he could neither use or occupy the reserved close nor derive any benefit from it. But what is the extent of the benefit he is to have? Is he entitled to say, I have reserved to myself more than that which enables me to enjoy it as it is at the time of the grant? And if that is the true rule, that he is not to have more than necessity requires, as distinguished from what convenience may require, it appears to me that the right of way must be limited to that which is necessary at the time of the grant – that is, he is supposed to take a re-grant to himself of such right of way as will enable him to enjoy the reserved thing as it is. That appears to me to be the meaning of a right of way of necessity. If you imply more you reserve to him not only that which enables him to enjoy the thing reserved as it is, but that which enables him to enjoy it in the same way and to the same extent as if he reserved a general right of way for all purposes. ...'[3]

---

¹   *Corporation of London v Riggs* (1880) 13 Ch D 798.
²   The view of Megarry V-C in *Nickerson v Barraclough* [1980] Ch 325, that an easement of necessity was based on public policy, did not find favour with the Court of Appeal [1981] Ch 426, which restated that an easement of necessity was based on presumed intention. Despite an observation of Meredith J in *Maude v Thornton* [1929] IR 454, that an easement of necessity 'was for the public good', and notwithstanding advocacy by Cooney 'Public Policy, Necessity and a Right of Access' (1979) 14 Ir Jur 334 and Bland *The Law of Easements and Profits à Prendre* pp 223–224, there is no suggestion in Irish law that an easement of necessity is anything other than a variant of an implied easement arising in the special circumstances of the necessity in any one case. See also *Dwyer Nolan Developments Ltd v Kingscroft Developments Ltd* [1999] 1 ILRM 141.
³   (1880) 13 ChD 798 at 806–807. See also Simonton 'Ways of Necessity' (1925) 25 Col L Rev 57; Grundes 'Rights of Way: Ways of Necessity' (1939) 3 Conv 425; Garner 'Ways of Necessity' (1960) 24 Conv 205; *Gale on Easements* pp 151–154.

[3.06] According to Powell J, Lord Erne would not have been entitled to put houses upon the hill, but he would have been allowed to use it for agricultural purposes, which, in the view of Powell J, included transporting felled trees along the way.

On appeal to the Court of Appeal this decision was overturned, primarily on the basis of the antiquarian and quasi-religious character of a rath and the evidence of previous user during the ownership of Lord Erne.

Campbell C expressed the view that raths were traditionally regarded with a degree of reverence, and that the previous owner would probably have esteemed the cutting down of the trees and the selling of them for profit as an act of desecration. He agreed with the law as adumbrated by Powell J and accepted that a right of way of necessity must be implied, 'limited to such a way as was suitable or necessary for the enjoyment of the close in the condition in which it happened to be at the date of the original severance.'¹ This is established by the 'previous and continuous user' of the property, which since time immemorial, in the view of Campbell C, had been by foot only, and had never been intended for the haulage of timber by horses and carts.

---

¹   [1921] 1 IR 148 at 163. This follows an expression of support for the statement of the law by Jessel MR in *Corporation of London v Riggs* (1880) 13 Ch D 798 at 806–807, see para 3.05 as cited by Powell J. In *Dwyer Nolan Developments Ltd v Kingscroft Developments Ltd* [1999] 1 ILRM 141, a perception emerged that there was a divergence between Irish law and English law on this topic. With respect to Kinlen J and the submissions of counsel, this appears to have been based upon a misconstruing of the decision of the Court of Appeal in *Maguire v Brown* [1921] 1 IR 148, from p 161.

[3.07] O'Connor LJ stated that a right of necessity must be confined to the actual agreement or intention of the parties at the time the premises were severed, insofar as this can be determined. The court could not approach the issue on the basis of what it would deem a reasonable right of way, because that would be, effectively, to manufacture an agreement rather than to interpret one: '... in the absence of very strong indications to the contrary, it would be unsafe to infer a right more extensive or more generous than that actually exercised.'¹

In the opinion of Ronan LJ, there was no necessity at all, as it had not been established in evidence that the plaintiff's land was the last to have been disposed of by the Erne estate, nor that there was no alternative way of access from the defendant's land to the road through other of the surrounding lands still owned by the Erne estate. A similar view was evinced by the House of Lords, dismissing the appeal. According to Lord Buckmaster, as long as any part of the estate connecting the forested hill with the main road remained in the possession of Lord Erne, there could not be implied an easement of necessity over portions of the estate with which he had already parted.[2]

---

1   [1921] 1 IR 148 at 170.
2   [1922] 1 IR 23 at 24–25.

Necessity need not be immediately apparent

[3.08] It seems that an easement of necessity can be implied even where the necessity was not immediate at the time of the relevant grant but foreseeable. This emerges from the decision in *Nugent v Cooper*.[1] It will be recalled[2] that this case concerned a square of land at Kinsealy, Co Dublin, with on the north running from east to west the main road from Dublin to Malahide, access to which was the issue under dispute. Perpendicular to this, at the eastern extremity of the square of lands in question, and running from north to south, was another road that led to the railway, called the Watery lane.

In 1848 the fee simple owners of all the lands, who, however, were not in possession, sold the lands to one Captain Wills, excepting the south-western lands which had no direct access either to the Dublin-Malahide Road or to the Watery lane, other than, in the case of the latter, over the south-eastern lands which debouched upon the Watery lane. The lands were sold without reserving a right of way either in favour of the fee simple owners themselves or any of their tenants. At that time one Gorman had a lease over the south-western lands without having been expressly granted a right of way over the south-eastern lands to the Watery lane. Subsequently the fee simple owners had granted a lease of the south-eastern lands to another party but without subjecting them to a right of way in favour of Gorman.[3]

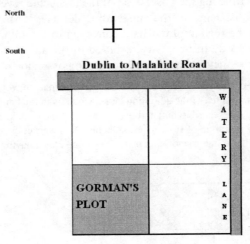

Later, Gorman took over the lease of the south-eastern lands also. He then entered into an accommodation with the tenants of the northern lands to give him a direct right of passage over their lands to the Dublin-Malahide Road. In 1850 (two years after the entire lands had been sold to Captain Wills excepting the south-western part) Gorman was evicted for nonpayment of rent from the south-eastern lands. In 1853 Gorman was evicted for non-payment of rent from his original holding, the south-western lands. At this point, the defendant became the occupier of the south-western lands and continued to use the right of way which had been negotiated over the northern lands to the Dublin-Malahide Road. However, in 1850, after Gorman's eviction from the south-eastern lands, the new owner, Captain Wills, blocked up the access to the Watery lane, thereby leaving the south-western lands potentially landlocked in the event that the permissive arrangement for the south-western occupier to traverse the northern lands to the Dublin-Malahide Road were discontinued. After the death of Captain Wills, his estate passed to the plaintiff.

---

[1] *Nugent v Cooper* (1855) 7 Ir Jur OS 112.

[2] See para **[2.31]**.

[3] On this issue, as has been shown at para **[2.31]**, Monahan CJ held that a right of way had been reserved to Gorman, regardless of the terms of the second lease, on the grounds that the fee simple owners could not derogate from their grant to Gorman in their later lease of the south-eastern lands.

[3.09] Counsel for the plaintiff argued that a right of way by necessity could not arise, since that must result from an implied grant and there could not be an implied grant for a necessity which may arise at some time in the future. At the time of the conveyance to Captain Wills, in 1848, there was no necessity: first, because there was an alternative right of way to the railway road through the Watery lane, and, secondly, because the grantors had only a reversionary interest, and, not being in actual possession, could not claim a necessity. 'That the way of necessity being one by implied grant a man cannot be held to have impliedly granted that which he had no right to at the time of such grant, namely, an easement affecting the possession of the lands, the reversion in which alone was his during the subsistence of the outstanding demises.'[1] Monahan J rejected the argument that when the fee simple owners conveyed to Captain Wills in 1848 there could not have been a way of necessity reserved in favour of the lands still held by Gorman simply because they did not have an estate in possession of them at the time:

> 'There is no case expressly on this point, viz. whether if a man conveys in fee to another a close, he being owner in fee of the adjoining close, which is in the hands of tenants, a right of way of necessity is reserved to him and his tenants. But the principle which decides that if a man, being owner in fee of two closes, sells one, he reserves a right of way from the other, applies equally to the case of a man who sells one close, having the unsold close in the hands of tenants.'[2]

---

[1] (1855) 7 Ir Jur OS 112 at 114.

[2] (1855) 7 Ir Jur OS 112 at 115.

[3.10] The question remained as to which was the right of way – that to the Dublin-Malahide Road over the northern lands or that to the Watery lane over the south-eastern lands. Since the way that led directly to the Dublin-Malahide Road was 'the most convenient way for ordinary farm purposes', accordingly, in the judgment of Monahan CJ, as it was the most convenient, the law deemed it to have been reserved as a way of necessity. '... the way of necessity is created by present use and not by the abstract right of the occupier, independent of use.'[1]

---

[1] (1855) 7 Ir Jur OS 112 at 115.

[3.11] *Nugent v Cooper*,[1] in its featuring of a right of way the apparent necessity for which had not arisen at the time of the disposal of either the dominant or the servient tenements, bears comparison with the English case of *Wong v Beaumont Property Trust Ltd*,[2] often cited in textbooks as a rare instance of an easement arising by way of necessity other than in the context of access. In this, the plaintiff successfully claimed a right to construct a ventilation shaft connecting with a duct on the outer wall, which was owned by his landlord, in order to comply with a covenant in his lease to eliminate all smells emanating from his restaurant. The necessity to construct a ventilation system connecting with an external duct had not been appreciated by either party at the time of the granting of the lease, but the English Court of Appeal still held that a right to connect to the duct was necessary in order that the business of the restaurant could legally be carried out. As Lord Denning MR explained, even though there had not been awareness by the parties of the necessity at the time of the demise, the necessity existed from the start.[3]

---

[1] *Nugent v Cooper* (1855) 7 Ir Jur OS 112.
[2] *Wong v Beaumont Property Trust Ltd* [1965] 1 QB 173.
[3] [1965] 1 QB 173 at 181.

[3.12] In *Dwyer Nolan Developments Ltd v Kingscroft Developments Ltd*[1] an easement of necessity was claimed by the owner of retained property over property he had sold, arising from a dilemma not apparent at the time of the sale. Both plaintiff and defendant were builders and developers. The lands sold were for the purpose of development, and it was found as a fact by Kinlen J that both parties might reasonably have expected that the retained lands would also be intended for development. At the time of the purchase, the plans submitted to the local authority, for planning permission purposes, in respect of the sold area, featured two numbered roads that ended where the site bordered the property retained by the plaintiff. However, these plans were amended and the planning permission eventually granted was based on a proposed arrangement of houses that would have left the plaintiff's retained land landlocked. The plaintiff claimed a right of way of necessity. A difficulty was disclosed by the fact that the plaintiff's retained lands had not been used for development purposes at the time of the sale, and the claimed necessity arose from such an intended use. The judgment of Kinlen J is somewhat diffuse, purporting (it would appear) to recognise an easement of necessity, but more probably finding an implied reservation through the common intention of the parties. According to Kinlen J, the case turned upon the fact that both parties were builders and each had a clear idea what the other proposed to do with his lands:

> 'You look at what each of the parties knew and you look at all the contract terms about all the development conditions relating to those and you look at the area itself. These were not two farmers. These were builders. Both knew what they were at. It was so obvious that this was development land.'[2]

To suggest that two builders could 'do a deal over a piece of land' and not know what either might do with the land 'is to live in a world of unreality.'[3]

---

[1] *Dwyer Nolan Developments Ltd v Kingscroft Developments Ltd* [1999] 1 ILRM 141.
[2] [1999] 1 ILRM 141 at 153.
[3] [1999] 1 ILRM 141 at 153–154.

[3.13] It is regrettable that the judgment at several points demonstrates a misunderstanding of *Maguire v Brown*[1] – even of the fact that the judgment of Powell J was reported at all, although it is an over-reliance on this judgment that appears to be at the root of the misunderstanding. To the extent that the *ratio* is founded on an easement of necessity, it is arguably defensible as an easement of necessity of a kind similar to that in *Nugent v Cooper*[2] – a necessity that at all times existed, but was not foreseen. Alternatively – and, it is suggested, preferably – the judgment is a classic instance of an implied reservation, even to the point of being interpreted as a regrant by the grantee to the grantor.

---

[1] *Maguire v Brown* [1921] 1 IR 148, [1922] 1 IR 23.
[2] *Nugent v Cooper* (1855) 7 Ir Jur OS 112.

Easements of Qualified Necessity

The rule in Wheeldon v Burrows

[3.14] An easement of qualified necessity is sometimes known as a quasi-easement and sometimes as an easement of necessary dependence. It arises when the owner of property transfers part of it without expressly granting as an easement in favour of the part granted a right over the part retained which had previously been exercised as an incident of the original owner's ownership of the whole. The implication of an easement in such circumstances, except in situations of strict necessity, falls under what has come to be known as the rule in *Wheeldon v Burrows*.[1] At the outset it should be noted that the requirement that the exercise of the easement be continuous and apparent, already considered in the context of s 6 of the Conveyancing Act 1881,[2] is fundamental to the operation of the rule in *Wheeldon v Burrows*.

---

[1] *Wheeldon v Burrows* (1879) 12 ChD 31. The rule in *Wheeldon v Burrows* is sometimes regarded as yet another application of the principle that a person may not derogate from their

grant. *Sovmots Investments Ltd v Secretary of State for the Environment* [1979] 2 WLR 951, at
p 958, per Lord Wilberforce, at p 964, per Lord Edmund-Davies and at p 972, per Lord Keith.
2   See para **[2.43]** ff.

[3.15] The facts of *Wheeldon v Burrows* concerned the disposal of a property in two
parts by its common owner. A workshop and adjoining piece of land were sold in the
following order to different parties: first, the piece of land, and subsequently the
workshop. The workshop had windows which overlooked and derived their light from
the piece of land sold. In an action by the purchaser of the workshop to prevent the
purchaser of the land building in such a way as to obstruct the light coming to his
windows, it was held, both by Bacon V-C at first instance and by the Court of Appeal,
that the vendor ought to have reserved to himself a right to light when disposing of the
plot of land, and that, since he had not done this, an action could not lie to prevent the
purchaser of the land from doing what he liked with it.

The judgment of the Court of Appeal was delivered by Thesiger LJ who observed:

> 'I think that two propositions may be stated as what I may call the general rules governing
> cases of this kind. The first of these rules is, that on the grant by the owner of a tenement
> of part of that tenement as it is then used and enjoyed, there will pass to the grantee all
> those continuous and apparent easements (by which, of course, I mean quasi-easements),
> or, in other words, all those easements which are necessary to the reasonable enjoyment of
> the property granted, and which have been and are at the time of the grant used by the
> owners of the entirety for the benefit of the part granted. The second proposition is that, if
> the grantor intends to reserve any right over the tenement granted, it is his duty to reserve
> it expressly in the grant. Those are the general rules governing cases of this kind, but the
> second of those rules is subject to certain exceptions. One of those exceptions is the well-
> known exception which attaches to cases of what are called ways of necessity …'.[1]

After reviewing the case law, Thesiger LJ summarised as follows:

> '[Y]ou may imply a grant of such continuous and apparent easements or such easements
> as are necessary to the reasonable enjoyment of the property conveyed, and have in fact
> been enjoyed during the unity of ownership, but [that], with the exception which I have
> referred to of easements of necessity, you cannot imply a similar reservation in favour of
> the grantor of land.'[2]

---

1   *Wheeldon v Burrows* (1879) 12 ChD 31 at 49.
2   (1879) 12 ChD 31 at 58–59.

[3.16] The Irish courts have not involved themselves in the controversy sometimes aired
in the English courts as to whether the requirement, for the rule in *Wheeldon v Burrows*
to apply, that the easement be 'continuous and apparent', and the requirement that it be
'necessary to the reasonable enjoyment of the property conveyed', are alternative or
cumulative.[1] It has been suggested that the articulation by Thesiger LJ of the need for an
easement to be 'continuous and apparent', in order for it to be implied as being
necessary for the reasonable enjoyment of the property which it affects, is an artificial
incorporation from the French *code civile* that made its debut in the first edition of Gale
on Easements in 1839[2] and culminated in the Court of Appeal decision in *Wheeldon v*

Burrows, 'where this French idea of the continuous and apparent quasi-easement was grafted on to the English doctrine of non-derogation from grant.'[3]

---

[1] See *Ward v Kirkland* [1967] Ch 194 at 224–226, per Ungoed-Thomas J, for the suggestion that they are alternative requirements; *Wheeler v JJ Saunders Ltd* [1995] 2 All ER 697 at 707, per Peter Gibson LJ, for the proposition that the two requirements are synonymous, as evidenced by the words 'or, in other words' in the passage from Thesiger LJ above cited; Lord Wilberforce and Lord Edmund-Davies in *Sovmots Investments Ltd v Secretary of State for the Environment* [1977] 2 WLR 951, as interpreted by Harpum 'Easements and Centre Point: Old Problems Resolved in a Novel Setting' (1977) 41 Conv 415 at 421–422 for the proposition that the requirements are cumulative.

[2] Simpson 'The Rule in *Wheeldon v Burrows* and the Code Civile' (1967) 83 LQR 240; Bland *The Law of Easements and Profits à Prendre* pp 213–214.

[3] Harpum '*Long v Gowlett*: A Strong Fortress' [1979] Conv 113, inclining the learned author to conclude that 'the concept of the continuous and apparent quasi-easement has nothing to do with the doctrine of non-derogation from grant ...'.

The Irish version

[3.17] As with many legal principles ascribed to the names of decided cases, the significance of *Wheeldon v Burrows* is rather the clearer adumbration than before of the principle as a distinct and separate principle than the formulation of a novel rule. Language similar to that adopted by Thesiger LJ appears in certain Irish cases decided both prior to, and after, *Wheeldon v Burrows*.

In *Kavanagh v Coal Mining Co of Ireland*[1] the Court of Queen's Bench determined that a right of way enjoyed by a parol lessee of a store since 1821 passed on a formal grant of a lease in 1848, even though the appropriate form of words had not been used. The court noted that the evidence established '... the great importance and utility of this right of way to the occupiers of the store ... [so that it is] yet necessary for the beneficial enjoyment of the demised premises in the condition in which they were at the time of the lease of 1848.' It is clear that this was not an easement of necessity in the strict sense. Neither was there an easement of necessity in *Clancy v Byrne*.[2] In this Lawson J found that a right of way passed by implication under a letting, which '...was not a strictly legal way of necessity, but a way the use of which was essential to the convenient enjoyment of the farm ... it was the usual and recognised way of approach, without which the farm could not be conveniently enjoyed.'

---

[1] *Kavanagh v Coal Mining Co of Ireland* (1861) 14 ICLR 82.
[2] *Clancy v Byrne* (1877) IR 11 CL 355.

[3.18] Ross J made a similar finding in *Head v Meara*,[1] observing that if two separate properties belonged to the same owner, and a formed road ran over one of them, which had been used for the benefit of the other, then on a disposal of that other property a right of way over the formed road would pass with it. The language adopted by Ross J represents something of a gloss on the dictum of Thesiger LJ in *Wheeldon v Burrows*:

'In the case of a severance of two properties it is presumed that everything in the nature of an easement, everything that is reasonably necessary for the enjoyment and use of the land granted, every reasonable adjunct that is continuous in use and apparent to the eye must be taken to pass with the property granted.'[2]

In *Connell v O'Malley*,[3] Barron J reiterated the rule in *Wheeldon v Burrows*, without specifically so describing it, in synopsis: a grantee of land does not need to contract specifically to retain a quasi-easement because the passing of it to him is implied in the deed of grant, but if a grantor wishes to preserve a quasi-easement for the benefit of the land retained he must specifically reserve it. If the grantor could not reasonably anticipate that the purchaser would require any specific right of an easement, other than that which would pass by implication on a division of the property, then it is for the purchaser to make specific provision for such additional right by contract.

---

[1]   *Head v Meara* [1912] 1 IR 262.
[2]   [1912] 1 IR 262 at 264–265.
[3]   *Connell v O'Malley* (28 July 1983, unreported) HC.

[3.19] The rule in *Wheeldon v Burrows* has not received frequent judicial commentary from the Irish Courts, and a number of cases whose facts would otherwise seem to invoke its application, have in fact been decided on the basis of a grant of an easement implied at the time of the grant of the corporeal property to which the easement is appurtenant.[1] In the section of his *The Law of Easements and Profits à Prendre* treating of the rule in *Wheeldon v Burrows*,[2] Peter Bland reserves harsh words for the judgment of Gavan Duffy J in *Tallon v Ennis*.[3] The essence of the author's criticism was that Gavan Duffy J found a right of way to exist even though the user of it, to remove the spoil from a toilet, was seriously intermittent, exercised 'at distant intervals of more than a year', and that there had been no track marking out the right of way, a fact which Gavan Duffy J found to be 'immaterial'. These are *indicia* which fly in the face of the dictum, previously cited, of Thesiger LJ in *Wheeldon v Burrows* which, in fact, is the statement of the rule itself. However, it is suggested that the principal significance of *Tallon v Ennis* was that such a right of way was found to have been implied as an incident of the original tenancy. The case of *Wheeldon v Burrows* was not once referred to by Gavan Duffy J and, on the basis of the judgment as reported, was not even pleaded by counsel.

---

[1]   Including a number of the cases reviewed at the beginning of ch 2: *Conlan v Gavin* (1875) 9 ILTR 198; *Clancy v Byrne* (1877) IR 11 CL 355; *Fahey v Dwyer* (1879) 4 LR Ir 271.
[2]   (Pages 212–217.
[3]   *Tallon v Ennis* [1937] IR 549. See para **[2.18]**.

[3.20] It seems, on the authority of the Court of Appeal decision in *Donnelly v Adams*,[1] that on a division of property formerly held in common ownership evidence need not be adduced of persistent user of a right of way from one part over the other in order for such a right to pass, provided that the circumstances surrounding the transfer made it reasonably clear that such a right could be expected to be exercised, and that it had in fact been exercised. In *Donnelly v Adams* the defendant was the owner of building land in Dublin between Adelaide Road and the Grand Canal. In 1888 he granted a long lease of a dwelling house and garden, 19 Harcourt Terrace, to the father of the plaintiff. At the back of this premises there was a door which led into waste-land belonging to the defendant, at either end of the further side of which were two gates leading on to the public road. There was no formed or defined way in this waste area, and no right of way given to the plaintiff's father. However, the defendant allowed him, and subsequently the plaintiff, bring coal across the waste-land from the public road and through the door into their garden. The defendant retained the key to the door but relinquished it whenever the plaintiff, or her father before her, needed to bring in coal, and occasionally furniture.

In 1902 the house was untenanted and the caretaker's children trespassed on the defendant's land through the doorway and invaded his cabbage patch. The defendant padlocked the door. The plaintiff's brother climbed over the wall and removed the padlock, whereon the defendant constructed a wall on the waste land in front of the door, thereby blocking it. The plaintiff sued for derogation of an implied grant of a right of way, arising as a continuous and apparent quasi-easement intended for the convenient enjoyment of 19 Harcourt Terrace, the demised premises.

---

[1]   *Donnelly v Adams* [1905] 1 IR 154.

[3.21] Barton J, at first instance, observed that this was not a case of an easement of necessity. He noted that there had not been any formed or marked path leading from the door to either of the gates on the defendant's land at the time of the lease of 1888. Neither was there any opening or connection from the coal shed into the adjoining lands, nor evidence of anything existing on the alleged servient tenement at the date of the demise intended for the use of the alleged dominant tenement:

> 'The authorities seem to show that the Courts will not, as a rule, imply a right of way when there was no visible way on the servient tenement at the date of the demise. This requirement of a visible way upon the servient tenement at the date of the demise is not a technical or a fanciful requirement. It is a question of principle; because what the Court is asked to infer is the implied demise of an apparent quasi-easement.'[1]

Barton J noted, following the analysis by Lord Blackburn in *Dalton v Angus*,[2] that the principles which had developed in relation to continuous and apparent easements had since been extended to quasi-easements that were not continuous and apparent in the strict sense: such as to covered drains, which are by no means apparent but could be held to be continuous because 'there is a necessary and permanent dependence of the house upon the drain for its enjoyment as a house'; and also rights of way, which are not, in the most technical sense, continuous, as they are not incessantly used. Barton J concluded that the authorities mainly involved the construction of words in a deed of grant in relation to a way formerly enjoyed or turned upon circumstances involving earlier enjoyment. Where there was no evidence of prior enjoyment and the applicant was resting his case almost exclusively upon the physical appearance of the property at the time of its disposal, and upon evidence of subsequent user, then the way should be a defined or a marked one.[3] Barton J held that it was reasonable to assume that, in the absence of any visible sign upon the defendant's premises, if such a right as this had been contemplated by the original contracting parties, it would have been by express agreement, and declined to find that there was an easement of a right of way.

---

[1]   *Donnelly v Adams* [1905] 1 IR 154 at 165.

[2]   *Dalton v Angus* (1881) 6 App Cas 740 at 821.

[3]   For this proposition Barton J relied, *inter alia*, on the judgment of Lawson J in *Clancy v Byrne* (1877) IR 11 CL 355.

[3.22] This decision was overturned on appeal to the Court of Appeal, principally on the interpretation of the agreement between the defendant and the plaintiff's father at the time of the lease in 1888.

Lord Ashbourne LC said of an easement of qualified necessity, that:

> '... the law recognises such a thing as a way of qualified necessity – a way which, though not physically a necessity, is necessary for the comfortable and beneficial enjoyment of the premises for the purpose for which they were let ... the right to such a way may be conferred by implication.'[1]

The Lord Chancellor attached importance to the fact that, at the time the defendant himself had acquired the property, plans submitted to Dublin Corporation provided for the construction of a row of houses, all of them with access through a lane on the field under dispute, and from there to the public road. The locating of the receptacle for coals at the back of the house was consistent with this scheme. It also appeared to the Lord Chancellor that the arrangement between the plaintiff's father and the defendant that coals could be brought in by the back door was not permissive merely. Notwithstanding that the way had not been marked out, the Lord Chancellor felt that it had been identified with sufficient clearness, since each party knew the manner of using the right and the points of entrance and exit, and, in any event, it would be competent for the defendant to direct a variation of the route, or to limit the access point to either one or other of the two gates, from time to time as his convenience should require.

---

[1]   *Donnelly v Adams* [1905] 1 IR 154 at 178.

[3.23] Fitzgibbon LJ rested his decision in contract: the actions of the parties and the user of the premises were consistent with a 'qualified necessity', so warranting the inference that it was an implied contractual term, collateral to the lease and covered by the same consideration, that the lessee should be entitled to bring coals across the field to his back door, the precise line of the right of way depending on the particular requirements at any one time of the servient owner. Walker LJ implied a right of way from the covenant by the plaintiff to use the premises as a private dwellinghouse: in order conveniently to comply with this covenant the coals would have to be brought in through the back door. In the opinion of Holmes LJ, the evidence established that the defendant had always intended that there should be a lane behind the plaintiff's premises, thereby justifying the inference, not of a general right of way, but a right to bring in coal through the field behind the house.

[3.24] The principles delineated in *Donnelly v Adams*[1] are not susceptible to indefinite extension, and the mere fact of a gate or door, belonging to one property, giving upon a lane or road which belongs to another property, both properties having at one time been in common ownership, will not invariably give rise to an inference of a right of way or access.

---

[1] *Donnelly v Adams* [1905] 1 IR 154.

[3.25] This was demonstrated in the Supreme Court decision in *McDonagh v Mulholland*.[1] The plaintiff was the fee simple owner of 25 Dunville Avenue, Ranelagh. This was one of six similarly circumstanced houses, sited side by side with gardens at the front and back. The land on which they and 26 Dunville Avenue were situated had been bought by a developer in 1864, and the six houses built by him, together with 26 Dunville Avenue, a larger house that enjoyed an avenue leading up to it along one side of number 25. The defendant was the owner of number 26. A side door in the garden wall of number 25 opened on to a short path that connected with the avenue to the defendant's house. The two houses had been in common ownership prior to 1919, when following the death of the owner, they were sold separately. The conditions of sale of 25 Dunville Avenue stated that there was no right of way in its favour. However, in 1925 this property was sold to the plaintiff who formerly had held it under a yearly tenancy at which time he *did* enjoy a right of way. The plaintiff now asserted a right of way over the avenue as far as the side door in his rear wall, for the purpose of carrying in coal and other commodities and for bringing in his bicycle. The basis of his claim was an alleged continuous and apparent right of way which passed by implication due to the necessary dependence of the two properties, after the severing of the unity of ownership in 1919 and the sale of each of them separately.

---

[1] *McDonagh v Mulholland* [1931] IR 110.

[3.26] The Circuit Court judge held that the plaintiff, while a yearly tenant, had had a right of way, which had passed by implication when the premises were bequeathed to different parties in 1919, and then sold. This was an easement appurtenant to the plaintiff's tenancy and was unaffected by the special condition in the sale of 1919 to the effect that there was no right of way. However, the Circuit Court judge also held that the plaintiff, being a purchaser of the fee simple from the person who had bought it in 1919, was estopped from denying the special condition as it applied to the fee simple, but that since the tenancy had not merged with the fee simple, the appurtenant easement remained intact for the time being. The Circuit Court judge held that there was a limited easement to pass on foot for the bringing in of coal and manure and the plaintiff's bicycle. The matter was referred to the Supreme Court by way of case stated.

[3.27] Kennedy CJ noted that the case was not, nor could have been, for an easement of necessity. According to the Chief Justice, in order to maintain a grant of a right of way by implication, the owner of 25 Dunville Avenue would have to show that there was a necessary dependence between the two properties,[1] 'or that there was then existing a continuous and apparent easement (ie quasi-easement up to severance), necessary to the reasonable enjoyment of the property granted, over the property retained.' He added: 'Mere proof of the existence of a door or gate in a boundary wall of a tenement is not of itself sufficient to establish a right of way.[2]

The Chief Justice noted that none of the other houses in the row of six had a second access point to the main road and that the plaintiff's situation might have been different in law if the access along the avenue led to another road and were to give on to a mews or stables, rather than to an eminent residence. The rateable valuation of 25 Dunville Avenue did not suggest it to be the kind of house which could reasonably expect a tradesman's entrance, particularly when the alleged servient tenement was a far more valuable property. Evidence had not been given as to the location of the coal cellar for the alleged dominant tenement, so that a case could not be made for an easement based on the necessary convenience of carrying coals through the side entrance.

---

[1]   *Pearson v Spencer* (1861) 3 B & S 761.
[2]   *McDonagh v Mulholland* [1931] IR 110 at 120.

[3.28] Fitzgibbon J had difficulty in accepting that there was any right at all. If there were to be an easement inferable from the circumstances, it ought to have been for foot passengers only, but the case argued by the plaintiff was more for lorries and trucks to deliver coal and manure. There was no facility on the avenue for lorries and trucks to turn, so they would have to have remained stationery while delivering goods, thereby blocking the only means of access to the supposed servient tenement, which the avenue had been designed to benefit in the first place. Such a broad easement could not be inferred from the mere fact of the existence of the side door:

> 'If there is to be an easement at all, I fail to see why it is to be confined to the introduction of coal, manure and bicycles … How is a right to carry in coal or a bicycle through this door more apparent or necessary than a right to go in or out on foot? … The extent of an apparent easement must be taken from that which appears; user becomes material when the easement has been acquired by prescription or implied grant.'[1]

In the opinion of Fitzgibbon J, it was more probable that, as the several tenancies in 25 Dunville Avenue were easily determinable, and since the landlord could without difficulty have prevented an easement arising by prescription through evicting any particular tenant, the landlord simply did not object to the occasional use of the avenue so long as it did not inconvenience him. Hence, the user was permissive rather than of right. *Donnelly v Adams*[2] could be distinguished, according to Fitzgibbon J, on the basis that, in that case, the facility to carry in coal was necessary to the administration of the household, and because the Court of Appeal had held that the original contracting parties had agreed that this should be allowed, the only lack of certainty being the actual boundaries of the way and through which of two access gates it should give upon the main road.

---

[1]   *McDonagh v Mulholland* [1931] IR 110 at 128.
[2]   *Donnelly v Adams* [1905] 1 IR 154.

[3.29] Murnaghan J dissented on the basis that, in his view, the evidence established that the plaintiff had been entitled to an easement under his original contract of tenancy, and that this easement then passed by implication under the will of the original common owner after whose death the two properties became divided.[1]

---

[1] *McDonagh v Mulholland* [1931] IR 110 at 132. Murnaghan J differed from the Circuit Court judge on the issue of estoppel. Although the same person had been the vendor of both numbers 25 and 26 in 1919, yet, under the will of their common owner, number 25 was held in trust for a minor beneficiary and number 26 had been bequeathed absolutely. Hence, according to Murnaghan J, that person could not be regarded as a common vendor of both properties because he was dealing with each of them in a different capacity. In such circumstances an estoppel could not be created through the purchaser of number 25.

Commentary

[3.30] Peter Bland in *The Law of Easements and Profits à Prendre* has hailed the Supreme Court decision in *McDonagh v Mulholland* as representing the 'deconstruction' of the Court of Appeal decision in *Donnelly v Adams*.[1] However, it is inferable from the judgments that the absence of any history of user of the alleged right of way in *McDonagh v Mulholland*, and the difficulty thereby of confining the nature of the user of any such right, furnished the primary basis of the majority decision of the Supreme Court. It is true that both Kennedy CJ and Fitzgibbon J regarded the grounds of the decision of the Court of Appeal in *Donnelly v Adams* as a prior agreement between the parties, and that Fitzgibbon J stated that 'quasi-easements not continuous and apparent in their nature, such as an ordinary right of way, not being one strictly of necessity, do not pass on severance of an estate, unless there is some formed or defined road over the quasi-servient tenement *to evidence their existence*',[2] adding that, in his view, the avenue leading up to 26 Dunville Avenue was neither formed nor defined. With respect to Fitzgerald J, if there had been found to be a right of way, the definition of it would surely have been clear from the physical characteristics of the two premises – along the avenue leading to 26 from the main road, as far as that point where it intersected with the short path leading to the garden door of 25. It is difficult to avoid the conclusion that the majority of the Supreme Court in *McDonagh v Mulholland* was exercised by the difficulty of implying a right of way other than for all purposes required by the plaintiff and by the fact that the alleged dominant tenement, being inherently less valuable than the alleged servient tenement, could not be seen to be allowed an advantage which might discommode the larger house. It is submitted that the course adopted by the Circuit Court judge, of allowing a limited easement to pass on foot for the bringing in of coal and manure and for the plaintiff's bicycle, was equally open to the Supreme Court. Perhaps the decision is best explained on the basis that the judges palpably had a problem in finding that the evidence submitted was consistent with the existence of any right at all.

---

[1] Bland *The Law of Easements and Profits à Prendre* p 217.

[2] *McDonagh v Mulholland* [1931] IR 110 at 130–131. Italics added, to illustrate from the context in which Fitzgibbon J made this observation, that his primary concern that the way be formed

or defined was to demonstrate that the right actually existed, not as a precondition of its validity. Arguably, if the right could be shown to exist on the basis of the character and frequency of the user, there would not be an additional need that the way be formed or defined.

Wheeldon v Burrows in Northern Ireland

[3.31] The rule in *Wheeldon v Burrows* fell to be considered by the High Court of Northern Ireland in *Re Flanagan and McGarvey and Thompson's Contract*.[1] Flanagan was the owner, under long leases, of two adjacent premises fronting on to the Armagh Road. One of these, called Aughavanagh, he occupied himself. After his death his personal representatives, a namesake Flanagan and one McGarvey, purported to sell Aughavanagh to one Thompson. The contract for sale was prepared in the absence of all the title documents which had been retained by a building society. The adjacent property had been held by Flanagan under a lease for 989 years from July 1920 and had been let by him, on a quarterly tenancy, to one Bell. Bell's house had a back door which he used for taking in coal and taking out ashes and other rubbish. Access to this was obtained by a path leading across part of the grounds of Aughavanagh. There had never been any express grant of a right of way to Bell, nor was there any reference to it in the contract between Flanagan and McGarvey with Thompson. Having since received the title deeds, the vendors sought to have an exception and reservation of a right of way included in the assignment to the purchaser for the entire residue of the term in the lease.

---

1   *Re Flanagan and McGarvey and Thompson's Contract* [1945] NI 32.

[3.32] Black J distinguished, on the one hand, between the issue of the existence of the right of way claimed on behalf of Bell, and on the other hand, the question whether it should be included as a reservation in the assignment to Thompson, the purchaser of the supposed servient tenement. The judge was satisfied that Bell had a clear entitlement to the right of way as an incident of his quarterly tenancy, and that, furthermore, he would also be entitled to continue to use the path in the event of any statutory renewal of his tenancy. Since the right of way was vested in a third party (Bell), it could not be destroyed by any contract between the vendors and the purchaser, which accordingly had to be read subject to the right of way.

[3.33] Counsel for the vendors had argued that the principle established by the rule in *Wheeldon v Burrows* entitled them to include the right of way as a reservation in the assignment of the lease. Black J summarised the rule thus:

> '... where the same person owns two adjoining tenements A and B, and has used a path over A for the more convenient occupation and enjoyment of B then if he sells and conveys tenement A to a purchaser he will *prima facie* not be entitled to contend that any reservation of a right of way over the path is to be implied for the benefit of tenement B which he retains.'[1]

In the view of Black J, the rule in *Wheeldon v Burrows* did not apply to the instant case which concerned, not the interpretation of rights passing with an assurance already executed, but the possible contents of an assurance yet to be made in terms of the reservation of a right in favour of retained property. If the contention of the vendors were to succeed, according to Black J, then they would be entitled to include in the assignment a reservation of a right of way for the entire duration of the lease for 989 years out of which the quarterly tenancy had been carved. It was hard to accept that the mere fact of there being a quarterly tenancy should so completely alter the contractual relations assumed by the vendors and the purchaser as to make the purchased property subject to an easement for the whole residue of the term of 989 years.[2]

---

1   *Re Flanagan and McGarvey and Thompson's Contract* [1945] NI 32 at 39. This is, in effect, the second rule in *Wheeldon v Burrows*: that any reservation of a right by the grantor must be express or arise from necessity.

2   Black J cited with approval the observation of Scrutton LJ in *Liddiard v Waldron* [1934] 1 KB 435: 'I confess that the idea of a weekly tenant wandering about with a series of easements when he can be got rid of by a week's notice is a thing of which the law will not take much notice.'

[3.34] Black J declined to follow the English case of *Thomas v Owen*.[1] In this the dominant and servient owners had originally been yearly tenants of their respective farms under a common landlord. The issue concerned a right of way over a lane which led through the servient tenement and appeared to serve no useful purpose other than to give access from the main road to the dominant tenement. A right of way was never expressly reserved. While the yearly tenancies were still running, the common landlord granted, first a lease of the servient tenement, and five years later a lease of the dominant tenement. Before the Court of Appeal the lessee of the dominant tenement successfully claimed a right of way over the lane. The *ratio* of this case has been found confusing. *Gale on Easements*[2] suggests that *Thomas v Owen* should be regarded as an isolated case and that the proper principle is that a lease of a dominant tenement followed by a disposal of the servient tenement, without express reservation of a right, subjects the servient tenement to the easement throughout the duration of the lease of the servient tenement and for no longer than the duration of the lease of the dominant tenement. In light of the decision of Black J in *Re Flanagan and McGarvey and Thompson's Contract*,[3] this must be modified to read that the servient tenement will also be bound for the term of any statutory renewals of the lease of the dominant tenement.

---

1   *Thomas v Owen* (1888) 20 QBD 225.
2   *Gale on Easements* p 146.
3   *Re Flanagan and McGarvey and Thompson's Contract* [1945] NI 32.

[3.35] Professor Lyall has suggested, in *Land Law in Ireland*,[1] that an alternative ground for the decision of Black J, was that the right of way originally enjoyed by Flanagan, when the common owner and occupier of both premises, was a quasi-easement that became enlarged into a full easement upon the granting of a tenancy to Bell, so binding a subsequent purchaser of what was in effect the servient tenement.

Professor Lyall's suggestion enjoys the undeniable merit that it does not involve a violation of the principles relating either to non-derogation from grant or to the rule in *Wheeldon v Burrows*. In Professor Lyall's formulation, the rule in *Wheeldon v Burrows* would have been irrelevant, since the easement would already have existed, 'fully blown' so to speak, prior to the entering into of the contract for sale. In the alternative, an easement could be deemed to have been granted by implication at the time of the first letting to Bell. Arguably, *Re Flanagan and McGarvey and Thompson's Contract*[2] is capable of comparatively straightforward analysis, as concerning an implied easement that arose as an incident of a short-term tenancy, and does not involve the application of the rule in *Wheeldon v Burrows* at all.

---

[1]   Lyall *Land Law in Ireland* (2nd edn, 2000) Sweet & Maxwell, pp 737–738.
[2]   *Re Flanagan and McGarvey and Thompson's Contract* [1945] NI 32.

[3.36] A more obvious application of the rule in *Wheeldon v Burrows* in Northern Ireland appears in *Close v Cairns*.[1] The plaintiff's father had been the registered owner of agricultural lands in Co Down. After his death, part of these lands passed to the plaintiff and part to the defendant. The lands of the plaintiff abutted upon the lands of the defendant through a gateway, which led along a lane on the defendant's lands and so to the Hillsborough Road. The plaintiff sought an order restraining the defendant from blocking up the gateway and a declaration that she was entitled to a right of way for all purposes along the lane. The County Court judge granted the declaration sought, on the basis of prescription. Girvan J, in the High Court, modified the order of the County Court, holding that the plaintiff was entitled to a right of way, on the basis not of prescription, but the rule in *Wheeldon v Burrows*. The plaintiff's father, while the owner of both the plaintiff's and the defendant's lands, had been wont to use the lane as an access route to the lands now owned by the plaintiff, for the transportation of pigs and also farm machinery. This user, in the opinion of Girvan J, had constituted a quasi-easement on the part of the plaintiff's father, which at the time of his death was necessary for the reasonable enjoyment of the land that passed to the plaintiff.

[3.37] In reviewing the rule in *Wheeldon v Burrows*, Girvan J held:

(a)   that the rule also applies where the grantor, rather than retaining land, makes simultaneous disposals of it to two or more parties, with the effect that each party obtains the same easements over the land of the other as he would have obtained if the grantor had retained that other's land.

(b)   the rule applies equally to wills as to gifts by deed;

(c)   the absence of valuable consideration is not relevant;

(d)   in a case where an easement is found to arise under the rule in *Wheeldon v Burrows*, it is neither necessary or appropriate to consider an easement by prescription: '... there is no question of presuming a grant since a grant can actually be established by the evidence.'[2]

---

[1]   *Close v Cairns* [1997] NIJB 70.
[2]   [1997] NIJB 70 at 72.

[3.38] In implying a grant of a right of way over the lane, under the rule in *Wheeldon v Burrows*, regard had to be had to the circumstances prevailing at the time of the plaintiff's father's death (which was the effective date of the implied grant), in order to determine the nature, extent and purpose of the right. In this regard, the actual character and usage of the way is crucial. Applying this test, the plaintiff was entitled to a right of access to and from her own lands for agricultural purposes, both on foot and with or without farm animals, together with such agricultural equipment and vehicles as would have fitted within the width of the lane as it existed at the time of the plaintiff's father's death. Even though the defendant, through the removal of a hedge, had widened the lane, the order of Girvan J confined the right of the plaintiff to such vehicles as would have passed (albeit barely) along the lane, as it was at the time her father died.

Chapter 4

Common Law Prescription and Presumed Lost Grant

General

Introduction and basic characteristics

[4.01] Prescription is the doctrine whereby rights in the nature of easements – that is to say, rights which would be easements if they had been granted – that have been enjoyed for a long period, but without a grant, either express or implied, can be recognised as easements in the course of litigation and made enforceable. It proceeds on the basis that the enjoyment, having been exercised continuously for a long time, bears the following characteristics:

(a)   it has been exercised as of right;

(b)   it has been exercised without specific licence or permission of the alleged servient owner;

(c)   it has been exercised openly, that is to say, in such a way that the alleged servient owner would have been aware of its exercise and in a position to seek to prevent it;

(d)   and has been exercised without force, without encountering objection or resistance from the alleged servient owner.

This is often expressed through the Latin adage – *Longus usus, nec per vi, nec clam, nec precario.*[1]

---

[1]   Coke on Littleton at 113b. The Report of the Law Reform Commission *The Acquisition of Easements and Profits à Prendre by Prescription* (LRC66–2002) sensibly recommends abolition of the Latin jingle, so that enjoyment will be as of right if it is 'without force, secrecy or permission.' The Law Reform Commission also recommends the absolute abolition of the facility to acquire an easement both at common law and by presumed lost grant. It is, respectfully, suggested that thereby much of value would be lost.

[4.02] The underlying principle is that the alleged servient owner is in a position to object to the enjoyment of the right – and thereby avert its eventual pullulation as an easement – but that he does not do so. Rights exercised furtively, or in secret, or under cover of darkness (*clam*), and rights which the intended servient owner is intimidated or bullied into tolerating (*vi*) are antithetical to that degree of consent requisite to transform the enjoyed right into an easement acquired by prescription. In consequence, such enjoyments can never burgeon into a prescriptive easement.

Somewhat more subtle is the requirement that the right not have been enjoyed 'precariously' or by permission (*precario*). In essence, this ingredient is bound up with the need for the claimed right to partake of the character of an easement – that it is a proprietorial entitlement and not a mere personal privilege. The same enjoyment can be consistent either with an easement or a licence.[1] If the enjoyment is demonstrably with the permission of the party designated as the servient tenant, then such enjoyment is a licence and not an easement. Consent enables an enjoyed right in the nature of an easement blossom into an easement acquired by prescription. Permission condemns it to the rank of licence. Acquiescence is the key that opens the door of opportunity to an easement by prescription. Permission bolts that door and secures it shut.

---

[1]   For example, *Whelan v Leonard* [1917] 2 IR 323 see para **[1.21]** ff.

[4.03] There are three methods by which an easement may be acquired by prescription:

(a)   prescription at common law;

(b)   prescription through the concept known as presumed lost grant;

(c)   prescription under the Prescription Act 1832, enacted in Ireland as the Prescription (Ireland) Act 1858. For convenience, reference throughout this work to the statute applicable in Ireland will be to the Prescription Act.

The requisites of the appropriate enjoyment needed to sustain an easement by prescription are as described above and apply to each of the three methods of acquisition. Particular refinements, especially in relation to the need for continuous enjoyment, have been introduced by the Prescription Act. The right to light is also treated differently from other easements in the Prescription Act. Partly by reason of dicta emerging from the English courts in the 26-year gap between the introduction of statutory prescription in England and in Ireland, and partly by reason of the nineteenth century prevalence of leasehold interests in Ireland, the doctrine of presumed lost grant has developed differently in the two jurisdictions, and a rich body of influential precedent concerning presumed lost grant has been amassed in the Irish courts.

Prescription and adverse possession

[4.04] Prescription, though kindred in its incidents to the concept of adverse possession in relation to corporeal property, should be distinguished from it as a principle. Primarily, adverse possession extinguishes the title of an owner of land on the basis of possession by a particular occupant for the period specified in the Statute of Limitations 1957. It does not transfer the extinguished title to the adverse possessor, unlike prescription which has the effect of establishing a right to the easement by the party who has enjoyed it. In addition, although both prescription and adverse possession have emerged from the principle of enabling right to title be acquired by long enjoyment, adverse possession, as its name suggests, is adverse, or hostile, to the ownership of the party whose land is being occupied. A prescriptive easement proceeds on the basis that it is with the consent, but not the permission, of the prospective servient tenant. That person's ownership of their land is not brought into question, but is confronted by the prospect of being burdened with the easement once acquired. In short, a prescriptive easement is enjoyed 'as of right', whereas enjoyment of land, through occupation on the basis of adverse possession is, by definition, not 'as of right' against the true owner.

[4.05] A claim to ownership of real property on the basis of adverse possession and a claim to an easement or a profit *à prendre* by prescription are inconsistent alternatives.[1] A prudent course is to regard them each as mutually exclusive. Otherwise, failure to sustain a claim for adverse possession will fetter an alternative claim to a prescriptive easement: the essence of an easement is that ownership of the land subject to the easement is in *another party*, who is thus constituted the servient tenant. A person laying claim to a right cannot, in logic, from one perspective be entitled to enforce an enjoyment against the owner of other land, and from another perspective assert that they themselves, through prolonged occupation, have dispossessed that other owner.

---

[1] *A-G for Southern Nigeria v John Holt and Co Ltd* [1915] AC 599. For an apparent judicial blurring of the distinction, see *Kilduff v Keenaghan* (6 November 1992, unreported) HC. See generally, Goodman 'Adverse Possession or Prescription? Problems of Conflict' [1968] Conv 270; Bland *The Law of Easements and Profits à Prendre* (1997) Sweet & Maxwell, pp 265–268.

Prescription at Common Law

[4.06] Originally, at common law, a right to an easement by prescription might be established if it could be shown that user had been enjoyed since the beginning of legal memory. Under the Statute of Westminster 1275 legal memory has been set at 1189, the beginning of the reign of King Richard I. However, the courts have frequently held a title by prescription to have been established at common law where there has been continuous user within living memory.[1] Even so, the common law doctrine is subject to the limitation that if it can be conclusively established that the right could not have been so long enjoyed, due to the known nonexistence of the alleged servient tenement at a particular time, or due to the unity of ownership of the dominant and servient tenements at any time during the prescriptive period, then the acquisition of the right can be defeated. Unity of ownership of the dominant and servient tenements would clearly have the effect of transforming any enjoyment otherwise resembling an easement into an incident of the ownership of the entire parcel of land.

---

[1] See *Angus v Dalton* (1877) 3 QBD 85, per Lush J; also *Aynsley v Glover* (1875) 10 Ch App 283; *Clancy v Whelan and Considine* (1957) 92 ILTR 39; *Daly v Cullen* (1957) 92 ILTR 127; *RCP Holdings Ltd v Rogers* [1953] 1 All ER 1029 at 1031, per Harman J.

[4.07] Prescription at common law can only bind an estate which is capable of extending as far back as the commencement of legal memory. The only estate capable of so being bound is a fee simple. According to Walker LJ, in the landmark case of *Hanna v Pollock*,[1] prescription at common law necessarily involves absolute estates and historic usage. Neither a life estate nor a leasehold interest could sustain prescription at common law, because these inherently commenced within the memory of man. Only a fee simple estate is capable of being as long as legal memory. As will be shown, a considerable number of cases on prescription in Ireland involve leasehold properties, with the result that the application of prescription at common law by the Irish courts has been rare.

---

1   [1900] 2 IR 664 at 693–694.

Presumed Lost Grant

[4.08] In order to compensate for the ostensible rigours of the common law doctrine, in the eighteenth century the courts devised the fiction of a lost modern grant,[1] the derivation of which, as stated by Lord Mansfield in *Eldridge v Knott*,[2] was 'from a principle of quieting the possession.' In the case of *Flynn v Harte*[3] Dodd J, in reviewing the history of prescription, observed that at common law an easement could be acquired both by prescription and by grant. Prescription, which was deemed to run from time immemorial, bound all parties, including the fee simple owner. Enjoyment for a lesser term than the fee simple could only be enjoyed by a grant; hence the fiction of a lost modern grant. 'The Judges of the eighteenth century, recognising enjoyment of a lengthened period, but not such as would establish a prescriptive right, and being desirous of having a legal origin for a well-established user, resorted to the legal fiction of a lost grant. At first juries were told that they might presume a deed between such parties as were to be bound, from continued enjoyment. The judges later told juries that such grant might be presumed, even though no such grant ever existed. And later still they told the jurors they ought to find so, in accordance with the user, and twenty years was somehow fixed upon.'[4] It is significant that Dodd J is effectively saying that the original purpose of the presumed lost grant was to legitimise an easement based on user against a leasehold property. In the case of *Bright v Walker*,[5] decided only two years after the introduction of the English statute, Parke B held that with the passing of the Prescription Act 1832, the doctrine of presumed lost grant could no longer be invoked to secure a prescriptive enjoyment which did not bind the fee simple. As will be seen, this idea never gained currency in Ireland. It is inferable from the judgment of Dodd J that prescription and presumed lost grant are in fact wholly differentiable concepts rather than the latter merely being a category of the former as is commonly believed.

---

1   For a general history of the origin of the doctrine of presumed lost grant, see Delany 'Lessees and the Doctrine of Lost Grant' (1958) 74 LQR 82 at 83–85.
2   *Eldridge v Knott* (1777) 1 Cowp 214.
3   *Flynn v Harte* [1913] 2 IR 322.
4   [1913] 2 IR 322 at 323.
5   *Bright v Walker* (1834) 1 CM & R 211.

[4.09] The Prescription Act 1832, enacted in Ireland as the Prescription (Ireland) Act 1858 which came into effect on 1 January 1859, was designed to shorten the time for acquiring title by prescription. However, given the prevalence of titles still held under long lease in Ireland, and the fact that one of the earliest cases decided under the Prescription Act 1832 – *Bright v Walker*[1] – had held that a right to an easement could not be acquired under the act if it did not bind all interests including the fee simple, the doctrine of presumed lost grant has continued to enjoy judicial popularity in Ireland and is still a live method of acquiring title to an easement other than by express or implied grant.

Many of the principles applicable to the acquisition of an easement by prescription, enunciated by the Irish courts, have emerged from cases in which an alleged entitlement to an easement arising from presumed lost grant fell to be decided. In consequence, a voyage through the rocky archipelago of decisions of the Irish courts on presumed lost grant will illuminate much that is necessary to an understanding of prescriptive easements generally.

Upon such a tortuous voyage, therefore, we must now embark.

---

[1] *Bright v Walker* (1834) 1 CM & R 211.

Knowledge and acquiescence of the freehold servient owner

[4.10] Prior to the enacting of the Prescription (Ireland) Act 1858, the principal judicial concern in Ireland, in cases of presumed lost grant, was with the extent of the knowledge of, and presumed acquiescence by, the owner in reversion of a servient tenement under lease. If the owner of the reversion were found not to be capable of being aware of the enjoyment alleged by the party claiming the presumed grant, then a jury could not be directed to presume that a grant of the easement, now lost, had been executed.[1] The doctrine was expressed succinctly in the dissenting judgment of Fitzgerald B in the case of *Deeble v Linehan*, decided the year after the coming into effect of the Prescription (Ireland) Act 1858:[2]

> 'The enjoyment of an easement over the land of another, uninterruptedly for a period of twenty years, is strong presumptive evidence that the enjoyment had a legal origin; and where, in such cases, there could be no legal origin without a grant, juries were, in such cases, before the Prescriptive Act told that they might, or that they ought to, presume a grant, without which the title, of which there was such evidence, could not exist. This presumption of title was founded on the acquiescence of the owner of the land on which the easement was enjoyed; the co-existence of a possession of the land, with the enjoyment of a privilege abridging the enjoyment of possession being prima facie inexplicable, except on the supposition of title: and, in such cases, it appears to me that it was not considered necessary that the jury should be satisfied that a grant in fact was made, though it was only through their finding of a grant that effect could be given to the title evidenced by enjoyment. But however strong this evidence was, as between the occupants of the land and the parties who enjoyed the easement, the foundation of it failed as between the owners of the land not in possession, and the party enjoying the easement; and, in order to make the enjoyment evidence of title as against a reversioner, there must have been evidence against him of acquiescence, distinct from the mere enjoyment of the easement, co-existing with the possession of the land which was not in the owner.'[3]

---

[1] See Chua 'Easements: Termors in Prescription in Ireland' (1964) 15 NILQ 489 at 490.
[2] *Deeble v Linehan* (1860) 12 ICLR 1.
[3] (1860) 12 ICLR 1 at 15–16.

[4.11] In *Hanks v Cribbin*,[1] decided shortly before the passing of the 1858 Act, the issue was whether the public character of the claimed enjoyment ought to have put the servient freehold owner on notice that an easement was in the process of being acquired, where the servient freehold owner had not been in possession throughout the entire term of the purportedly prescriptive enjoyment.

---

[1] *Hanks v Cribbin* (1857) 7 ICLR 489, judgment of Monahan CJ; (1857) 9 ICLR 312, judgments of Ball and Jackson JJ.

[4.12] The plaintiff had a right to the supply of water through a watercourse to his mill. More than 40 years prior to the action, this had become silted up, and a new cut had been established through the lands of the defendant which from then on supplied water to the plaintiff's mill. The defendant's lands had been held under a lease for several lives until 1841 when the last *cestui que vie* died. In 1843, the reversionary owner, the Duke of Leinster, demised these lands to the defendant for 21 years, a term that was still running at the time of the action. Accordingly, throughout the period of 40 years prior to the action, there had been only 2 years when the alleged servient tenement was not under lease. The plaintiff's action was for the unlawful diversion of his water, after the defendant, maintaining that the substituted watercourse was wrongfully claimed over his land, and furthermore that it had caused flooding, lowered the channel of the original watercourse that had been silted up over 40 years earlier, thereby diverting the water out of the new watercourse back into the old one.

[4.13] Monahan CJ held that if the making of the new cut 40 years before had been with the knowledge and acquiescence of the Duke of Leinster, then the water had been rightfully flowing through the land of the defendant and a grant of a right to the use of the watercourse could be presumed. On behalf of the defendant it was argued that the fact that the rent had been collected by a middleman was inconsistent with the alleged knowledge and acquiescence. Monahan CJ disagreed, concluding that the evidence warranted referring the case to a jury to presume a grant, on the basis of:

> '... the length of time since the act was done, and, not only that, but the nature as well of the act as the thing itself, which were both of a public character. A watercourse is cut in a place open to the observation of everyone, creating an alteration in the course of a stream from an ancient mearing, to very near the centre of a farm; it supplies a mill at a considerable distance, and has the effect of choking up the channel which formed the old mearing. It also appears that in the meantime there was a change of tenancy: and the presumption is, that persons will look after their own, it being their interest and duty so to do.'[1]

Since the servient tenement was the Duke of Leinster's property, in the view of Monahan CJ it could have been reasonably assumed that his agent would have seen what had been happening and accordingly reported to his principal.[2]

---

[1] (1857) 7 ICLR 489 at 497.

[2] A view that has not commended itself to the courts in England. See *Diment v Foot (NH)* [1974] 1 WLR 1427, per Pennycuick V-C. However, constructive notice of its enjoyment, as opposed to actual notice, will prevent the owner of an alleged servient tenement from denying a right to

an easement by prescription: *Lloyds Bank v Dalton* [1942] Ch 466. See also *Pugh v Savage* [1970] 2 QB 373, where it was suggested that a reversioner may be powerless to intervene, and so should not invariably be bound, where a tenancy was already in existence at the commencement of the prescriptive period; Bland *The Law of Easements and Profits à Prendre* pp 255–257.

[4.14] Jackson J concurred in the decision of the Chief Justice, primarily on the basis that the mill being an edifice well known publicly in the neighbourhood, and the old mill-stream being on the boundary of the Duke's property, it was unlikely that he would have been unaware of what had been taking place, from which circumstance his acquiescence could have been inferred and a lost grant presumed. Jackson J added, however, that mere length of time alone would not have been sufficient to raise a presumption of knowledge and assent by the alleged servient owner. Ball J, while also concurring, expressed misgivings as to whether there was anything in the plaintiff's case other than length of enjoyment, noting that the Duke of Leinster had never been in possession and that the diverting of the watercourse had taken place across lands under tenancy, which would not therefore have been in public view. In the opinion of Ball J, the English authorities had established that actual knowledge was required.[1]

---

[1] In particular *Gray v Bond* (1821) 2 Brod & Bing 671; *Daniel v North* (1809) 11 East 372 and *Davis v Stephens* (1836) 7 C & P 570, in which latter case Lord Denman had observed: '… what must have been known to the public at large was not likely to have been unknown to the owner of the land on which the acts of user had taken place.' The basic point made by Ball J was that the diversion of the watercourse had not been done in circumstances such that the public would have known about it.

[4.15] It should be noted that, in *Hanks v Cribben*,[1] the only party capable of being bound was the Duke of Leinster, as the fee simple reversioner. By the time the case had come on for hearing, in 1857, the defendant, a lessee for 21 years, had been in occupation for only 14 years. Twenty years was the minimum period of enjoyment which attracted the presumption of lost grant.[2] Between 1841 and 1843 the alleged servient tenement had not been under lease. There could have been no question of a presumed lost grant being made by the defendant lessee.

---

[1] *Hanks v Cribben* (1857) 7 ICLR 489.
[2] *Price v Lewis* (1761) 2 Wms Saund 175; *Read v Brookman* (1789) TR 151; *Penwarden v Ching* (1829) Moo & Mal 400; Delaney 'Lessees and the Doctrine of Lost Grant' (1958) 74 LQR 82 at 84; *Gale on Easements* (eds, Gaunt and Morgan, 16th edn, 1997) Sweet & Maxwell, p 172.

[4.16] The principles governing the presumption of a lost grant, and in particular the significance of the state of knowledge of an agent of the reversionary owner of the alleged servient tenement, were next and amply considered in *Linehan v Deeble*.[1] The defendant was the reversionary owner of a mill outside Cork City which, from the early years of the eighteenth century, had been supplied by a watercourse running through the lands of the plaintiff. The plaintiff's lands were held under a renewable lease from the

See of Cork which had been many times renewed. In 1797 a sub-lease was granted out of the bishop's lease containing a covenant that any compensation paid, in the event that a new public road then being contemplated were constructed upon the premises, would be for the benefit of both the sub-lessor and sub-lessee.

In 1824 a new road was constructed on the site of the old watercourse, and the tenant in possession under the 1797 sub-lease was paid compensation of £200. In 1827 the defendant cut a new watercourse through another portion of the plaintiff's land. At this time the defendant's lands were also in the possession of a tenant. A renewal of the 1797 sub-lease, granted in 1829, omitted any reference to the provision of compensation, as this had already been paid.

Prior to 1841 the plaintiff lived in Mallow, and a barrister relation of his, who when practising on the Munster Circuit used to take lodgings in a house near the site of the watercourse, collected the rents. The plaintiff only took up possession in 1851 following an ejectment of the tenant holding under the renewal of the 1797 sub-lease. In 1853 the plaintiff stopped the watercourse. In 1858 the defendant's tenant took out a lease of the watercourse from the plaintiff and started to pay rent. The defendant ejected his tenant and discontinued the payment of rent for the use of the watercourse, whereon the plaintiff blocked it up. The defendant's entering upon the plaintiff's land in order to remove the obstruction, prompted the current action for trespass.

A jury had found that there was no evidence on which to found a lost grant from the plaintiff to the defendant, a finding upheld by Monahan CJ on appeal to the Court of Common Pleas.[2] The owner of the watercourse (the plaintiff) had been out of possession until 1851, following which he had immediately asserted his right not to permit user of the watercourse until he was paid rent which the defendant's tenant eventually agreed to do. The Chief Justice held that the fact of payment of rent by the defendant's tenant would not in itself debar the defendant's claim of right if the right to the watercourse had actually existed at the time, but it rebutted any presumption of acquiescence on the part of the plaintiff as reversioner. Since the plaintiff reversioner had not actually been in possession, he would not have been obliged to bring an action for any injury to the reversion as a result of the cutting of the new watercourse.

---

[1]   *Linehan v Deeble* (1859) 9 ICLR 309.

[2]   At the original trial Greene B had directed the jury that, in order to return a verdict for the defendant, they had to find as a fact that a deed had been executed: (1860) 12 ICLR 1 at 5–6; Delany 'Lessees and the Doctrine of Lost Grant' (1958) 74 LQR 82 at 92.

[4.17] A further appeal was taken to the Court of Exchequer Chamber: *Deeble v Linehan*.[1] This Court, by a majority of five[2] to one, overturned the decision of the Court of Common Pleas and the finding of the jury.

Hughes B attached importance to the fact that when in 1824 the new road was constructed, compensation had been paid to the tenant under the 1797 sub-lease. In 1829 a new lease was given which made no reference to any payment of compensation. From this it could reasonably be inferred that the plaintiff's barrister relation had known and approved of the substitution of the new watercourse for the old watercourse, since the road in respect of which compensation had been paid was on the site of the old watercourse; and that if he had received any part of the compensation payment, and had acquiesced in the enjoyment of the new watercourse by those holding under the defendant, it could be further assumed that such knowledge bound the plaintiff, and that a case could be put to the jury that a grant had been executed by plaintiff, for the use and enjoyment of the new watercourse.

---

1   *Deeble v Linehan* (1860) 12 ICLR 1. For the purposes of convenience this summary continues to describe the parties respectively as plaintiff (Linehan) and defendant (Deeble) following their respective positions in the Court of Common Pleas.
2   Although the judgment of Lefroy CJ demonstrates considerable doubt in the matter.

[4.18] Hayes J distinguished between the presumption of a grant in cases involving an owner in possession and an owner who is a reversioner. In the case of an owner in possession a grant could be presumed on the basis of 20 years enjoyment to the knowledge of the alleged servient owner. In the case of a reversioner, not only must he have knowledge of the user, but he must in some way have acquiesced in it. Hayes J went on to observe that, in certain cases, the enjoyment of the right would not be inherently adverse to the interests of the reversion, and that, in such circumstances, failure by the reversioner to take any action did not warrant the imputation of acquiescence.

'But if the matter be of such a permanent character that it must fairly be presumed in its nature to be injurious to the reversion ... then if a reversioner, or those under whom he derives, be aware for twenty years of the existence of that enjoyment, and does not remonstrate against it, but permits the party to enjoy quietly and of right, he may fairly be said to acquiesce in it; and thus, as against him, the presumption of a grant may be raised, unless some circumstance of disability be shown, which would render such a grant in fact impossible.'[1]

According to Hayes J, the jury had, not only a power, but a duty to presume that a grant has been made, in circumstances warranting it, in order to quiet the possession. In the opinion of O'Brien J, it was not necessary in every case to give direct and positive evidence of acquiescence by the reversioner. In the instant case, the involvement of the barrister relative, and the omission in renewals of the sub-lease of the land containing the watercourse after 1827 of any reference to the payment of compensation, justified the inference, that there was a recognition by all relevant parties that the defendant and his predecessors were entitled to the use of the new watercourse to service the mill.[2] Pigot CB noted that the presumption of execution of a grant was rebuttable and could be displaced by contrary evidence, but found that this did not arise.

---

1   (1860) 12 ICLR 1 at 17–18.
2   O'Brien J expressed the view that the present was an even stronger case for warranting the inference of acquiescence on the part of the reversioner than *Hanks v Cribbin* (1857) 7 ICLR 489, since, in the earlier case, there was no actual evidence that the Duke had ever been on the alleged servient lands, or resided near them, or had ever been involved in the collecting of rent.

[4.19] Lefroy CJ expressed considerable misgivings about the level of knowledge and acquiescence deemed necessary to bind a reversioner. In particular, Lefroy CJ felt that it would be difficult to hold that a reversioner had acquiesced merely because he had done nothing. It might not have been necessary or desirable that anything be done. Acquiescence could be inferred if the reversioner had taken no action in a case involving waste, but the making of a watercourse was not an act of waste and it was difficult to determine what step the reversioner could have taken.[1] The dissenting judgment of Fitzgerald B was based upon the fact that throughout the entire period of user the respective tenements had been held under tenancies and that, as soon as the plaintiff entered possession in 1851, he had taken immediate steps to assert his right by blocking the watercourse. Furthermore, the interest of the person in occupation of the defendant's premises at the time of the construction of the substituted watercourse was the same interest as the person in possession at the time the plaintiff took up possession of his own lands, who effectively acknowledged that he had no right to the new watercourse by paying rent for it. According to Fitzgerald B, since that particular occupant clearly had not acquired the right, neither could the defendant acquire it through that occupant's enjoyment.

---

[1] (1860) 12 ICLR 1 at 33, per Lefroy CJ: 'I should, therefore, in such a case, require evidence of something more than mere knowledge on the part of the reversioner; and it is only of late that length of time and mere knowledge have been attempted to be set up as a ground of acquiescence in cases of this kind.'

Some reflections

[4.20] It has been suggested, that the effect of the decision in *Deeble v Linehan*[1] was that, although the doctrine of presumed lost grant applied in Ireland prior to the enacting of the Prescription (Ireland) Act 1858, it could only apply where there was evidence of knowledge of, and acquiescence in, the enjoyment of the right by the owner of the reversion in the alleged servient tenement; and that subsequent decisions of the Irish courts, during the late nineteenth century, which found a presumption of lost grant pertaining between tenants, without evidence of such knowledge of and acquiescence by the reversioner, are inconsistent with *Deeble v Linehan*.[2] A closer examination of the facts in *Deeble v Linehan* demonstrates certain flaws in this reasoning:

(a)   in *Deeble v Linehan*, the action was taken against the freehold owner of the dominant tenement, for trespass, after he had removed an obstruction placed on the watercourse by the owner of the servient tenement. The tenancy of the dominant tenement and the mesne tenancy of the servient tenement had both been determined. Any suggestion that the doctrine of presumed lost grant might have applied against the mesne lessee of the servient tenement for the duration of his tenancy could not arise because by the time of the action there was no such tenancy. This is a markedly different scenario from that prevailing in later Irish cases which involved both tenements under tenancies;

(b)   the plaintiff servient owner himself held under a renewable lease from the See of Cork. It does not appear from the judgments that this had been enlarged into a fee farm grant under the Renewable Leasehold Conversion Act 1849. Accordingly, the fee simple in the servient tenement remained in the See of

Cork, and there was no suggestion that the presumed lost grant was binding against it;[3]

(c) the reversioner whose knowledge and acquiescence was deemed relevant was himself in possession at the time of the action, and was, in fact, the party bringing the action. This circumstance is quite at variance with the facts in most of the cases decided later in the nineteenth century, which usually involved both tenements being under tenancy at the time of the action.

---

[1] *Deeble v Linehan* (1860) 12 ICLR 1.
[2] Chua 'Easements: Termors in Prescription in Ireland' (1964) 15 NILQ 489.
[3] A point taken up by Palles CB in *Timmons v Hewitt* (1888) 22 LR Ir 627 at 639–640, also noted by Delany 'Lessees and the Doctrine of Lost Grant' (1958) 74 LQR 82 at 92, 94.

[4.21] *Deeble v Linehan*[1] was the last case concerning presumed lost grant decided in Ireland prior to the coming into effect of the Prescription (Ireland) Act 1858 on 1 January 1859.[2] It is tempting to speculate that, had the Irish statute not been enacted some 26 years subsequent to the English Prescription Act 1832, with the interim accretion of a considerable body of interpretative English case law, the Irish courts might have continued to apply, with fewer inhibitions, the pragmatic approach already demonstrated by them in the presumption of lost grant. As it was, certain of the judgments of the Irish courts after 1859 display a discernible enthusiasm to square their decisions within the parameters set down by the English decisions on the Prescription Act since 1832, an enthusiasm only vitiated by the continued survival as an independent concept of the doctrine of presumed lost grant.

---

[1] *Deeble v Linehan* (1860) 12 ICLR 1.
[2] As was noted by Fitzgibbon LJ in *Hanna v Pollock* [1900] 2 IR 664, the case of *Deeble v Linehan* was in fact decided after the coming into effect of the Prescription (Ireland) Act but the action which it adjudicated had been instituted prior to the enacting of that statute.

Problems with the Prescription Act regarding tenancies

[4.22] An early example of this judicial straining is disclosed by the first prescription case in Ireland after the coming into effect of the Prescription (Ireland) Act 1858 – *Wilson v Stanley*.[1] This involved yet another action for the diversion of a watercourse. Lands in Co Tyrone were demised for a lease for one life in 1775. The cestui que vie died in 1840. During the currency of this lease for life a mill was built on part of the lands, which successive tenants of it operated through a flow of water from a lake elsewhere on the same lands. In 1836 the reversioner appointed to his son, for his son's life, that portion of the lands where the lake – the alleged servient tenement – was located. In 1841 the son granted a lease for a term of years of the land that included the lake, and this was in due course assigned to the defendant. In short – other than between 1840, when the cestui que vie died, and 1841, when the reversioner's son granted the lease – from the time of the construction of the mill up to the time of the action, in 1861, the land on which the lake was situated was under tenancy. In 1840, following the death of the cestui que vie, the reversioner came into possession of that part of the lands which bore the mill. In 1843 he granted a lease of the mill, which was assigned to the plaintiff. The current action arose when the defendant blocked the access of water from the lake to the watercourse.

---

[1] *Wilson v Stanley* (1861) 12 ICLR 345.

[4.23] Pigot CB observed that the purpose of the Prescription Act, then just enacted in Ireland, seemed to have been to give additional rights to those claiming easements on the basis of long user, not to take them away,[1] but added that this had not been the result of certain judicial decisions in England. According to Pigot CB, the statute could conveniently either have retained the old principle of inferring lost grants from long user 'with its occasional acknowledged inconveniences', or else abolished that entirely and replaced it with a rule of law which would give to a long enjoyment 'the force of presumptive title'.[2]

---

[1] This is the central thesis urged by Delany in 'Lessees and the Doctrine of Lost Grant' (1958) 74 LQR 82.
[2] *Wilson v Stanley* (1861) 12 ICLR 345 at 350, 351.

[4.24] The decision of the English Court of Exchequer in *Bright v Walker*[1] had failed to elect for either alternative, hewing instead a middle course entirely less than satisfactory in the context of the Irish experience of long leases. It decided that following the Prescription Act:

> ' ... first, presumptive title, founded on a presumed grant, cannot now be established at all by proof of long uninterrupted enjoyment alone; and, secondly, the prescriptive title, which the statute has given the means of establishing, can only be applied where the enjoyment has been such as to bind all estates, comprising the whole fee simple, in the servient tenement.'[2]

This case involved a claim of a right of way where there had been clear enjoyment for at least 20 years, but when both the dominant and servient tenements were held under leases for lives from a common lessor. Noting that under s 8 of the Prescription Act, continuous enjoyment as of right for 40 years could be defeated within 3 years after the expiry of any lease under which it was held,[3] Parke B observed that enjoyment for the shorter prescriptive period of 20 years[4] must be liable to be similarly defeated; that the statute could not be construed as creating different categories of rights in different situations: '[T]he statute nowhere contains any intimation that there may be different classes of rights, qualified and absolute – valid as to some persons and invalid as to others.'[5]

---

[1] *Bright v Walker* (1834) 1 Cr M & R 216.
[2] *Wilson v Stanley* (1861) 12 ICLR 345 at 351, per Pigot CB.
[3] See para **[5.07]**, **[5.27]** ff.
[4] Prescription Act, s 2.
[5] (1834) 1 Cr M & R 216 at 221.

[4.25] To this observation rejoinder might be made, that neither does the Prescription Act state the reverse.[1] Nor does it commend itself to common sense, that if a lessee is capable of making an express grant to another lessee, a presumed grant cannot be inferred in appropriate circumstances.[2] In *Bright v Walker*[3] Parke B acknowledged that, prior to the Prescription Act, the facts might have warranted the presumption of a lost grant, but that this course, subsequent to the passing of the Act was no longer open, as the grant would be incapable of binding the fee simple, both tenements being under lease.

---

1   Delany 'Lessees and the Doctrine of Lost Grant' (1958) 74 LQR 82 at 89: '... it is difficult to see why legislation which was intended to facilitate the acquisition of titles by prescription should be deemed to have impeded their acquisition by lost grant, a title which was necessarily of a qualified character and which was not inconsistent with a title by prescription, either at common law or under the statute.'

2   Kiralfy 'The Position of the Leaseholder in the Law of Easements' (1948) 13 Conv 104 at 107–108; see also Sparkes 'Establishing Easements Against Leaseholds' [1992] Conv 167 at 173.

3   *Bright v Walker* (1834) 1 Cr M & R 216.

[4.26] Pigot CB commented that it would have been preferable to construe the Prescription Act as validating easements on the basis of long enjoyment, not only against the owner of the fee, but also against the owners of derivative interests: in many cases there might be little practical difference, in terms of enjoyment or value, between a long lease and a fee simple.

> 'Between an estate for lives renewable for ever, or an estate for the residue of 999 years, created a century ago, and an estate in fee, the difference in substantial value is small, and has sometimes been treated as little more than nominal. This is the more important because, in other respects the statute, as expounded by several decisions, has considerably abridged the means of establishing incorporeal rights by proof of long enjoyment.'[1]

Pigot CB stated that it would not have been inconsistent with the obvious purpose of the Prescription Act, to continue to allow the presumption of a lost grant to apply in cases where prescription was not possible. He acknowledged, however, that this had been ruled out by *Bright v Walker*[2] which as, 'sitting in a Court of co-ordinate jurisdiction,' he regarded as binding on him.

---

1   (1861) 12 ICLR 345 at 356, per Pigot CB. See also the somewhat rueful (and highly reminiscent) observations of Fox LJ in the recent English case of *Simmons v Dobson* [1991] 1 WLR 720 at 724: 'In terms of practicalities, it is difficult to see if one were starting from scratch that there is serious objection to leaseholders prescribing against each other for the duration of their limited interests (but it has to be said that to introduce such a rule retrospectively now could affect what were hitherto bought and sold as clear titles). ... in a modern, urban situation it is hard to see how two householders on one side of the street should be able to prescribe for easements against each other's land because each holds in fee simple while on the other side of the street one leaseholder under the residue of a 999-year lease can for 20 years or more walk along a path at the back of his neighbour's garden (also held on a long lease) without acquiring any rights in respect thereof. That, however, is the way the law has gone in England.' Also, reviewing *Simmons v Dobson* in the context of the law on

presumed lost grant generally, Sparkes 'Establishing Easements Against Leaseholds' [1992] Conv 167.

2 *Bright v Walker* (1834) 1 Cr M & R 216.

[4.27] Applying these principles to the facts of *Wilson v Stanley*, prescription under the Prescription Act could not have arisen prior to 1840 when the named life in the lease of 1775 had died, because prior to that each tenement had been in the occupation of tenants the enjoyment of neither of whom could have been 'as of right' against his landlord. Since 1840 there had been uninterrupted enjoyment for more than 20 years, but the reversioner had been in possession of the putative dominant tenement for only a three-year period from 1840 to 1843, and at the time of the action, both tenements were held under leases then still current. Reluctantly, Pigot CB was driven to conclude that the interpretation of the Prescription Act in *Bright v Walker*[1] precluded its being applied, and also the doctrine of presumed lost grant, in the instant case.

> 'There was, therefore, what would have been plainly a state of things warranting the presumption of a grant before the statute. But the case is, in effect, precisely that in which the Court decided, in *Bright v Walker*, that the presumption was taken away, and to which the Court there also held that the prescriptive rights, given by the statute, did not apply. There was, in each case, a reversionary estate which prevented the acquisition of the right given by the statute in lieu of that which it took away.'[2]

---

1 *Bright v Walker* (1834) 1 Cr M & R 216.
2 *Wilson v Stanley* (1861) 12 ICLR 345 at 359.

Short-term lettings

[4.28] In the latter part of the nineteenth century prescription cases concerning leases mainly involved parol and periodic lettings where both tenements were under lease, not infrequently from a common landlord. In such circumstances prescription under the Prescription Act would have been impossible, due to the principle articulated by Lord Cairns in *Gayford v Moffatt*,[1] that it was a violation of one of the first principles of the relationship of landlord and tenant that a tenant through occupation could acquire an easement over other property of his landlord also held under lease.

As has been shown, the case of *Clancy v Byrne*[2] resolved the problem of a claimed right of way, in a case of both tenements held under tenancy from a common landlord, by holding that prior to the creation of either tenancy the common landlord had provided a usual and accustomed access for the dominant tenement which became appurtenant to it and passed with it as an easement. It is significant that, in relation to the presumption of lost grant in that case, Lawson J merely observed that, since there had been unity of ownership and possession prior to the creation of the tenancies, any right existing earlier would have been extinguished. With respect to Lawson J, it is suggested that this observation is more appropriate to a claim for prescription at common law or under the Prescription Act. Arguably, following the principles enunciated in *Deeble v Linehan*[3] (prior to the decision in *Wilson v Stanley*)[4], it would have been competent for the court, or for a jury, to have presumed a lost grant during the period of the tenancies, on the basis of the clearly found knowledge of, and acquiescence by, the common landlord.[5]

---

1   *Gayford v Moffatt* (1868) 4 Ch App 133, quoted with approval by Palles CB in *Timmons v Hewitt* (1888) 22 LR Ir 627 at 635. This does not apply to 40 years user under the Prescription Act, s 8: *Beggan v McDonald* (1878) 2 LR Ir 560. See para **[5.28]** ff.
2   *Clancy v Byrne* (1877) IR 11 CL 355. See para **[2.09]**.
3   *Deeble v Linehan* (1860) 12 ICLR 1.
4   *Wilson v Stanley* (1861) 12 ICLR 345.
5   In *Fahey v Dwyer* (1879) 4 LR Ir 271, Lawson J, following *Beggan v McDonald*, held that a right of way, which had been enjoyed for 40 years, was capable of binding two tenants under a common landlord, but not the landlord himself. Hence, it seems clear that this case cannot be cited in support of a proposition that in Ireland it is possible for a tenant to acquire an easement under the Prescription Act against his own landlord, as is suggested by Chua 'Easements: Termors in Prescription in Ireland' (1964) 15 NILQ 489 at 499, and by Wylie 'The 'Irishness' of Irish Land Law' (1995) 46 NILQ 332 at 344. For the contrary view, see *Lord MacNaghten v Baird* [1903] 2 IR 731.

Tenants of a common landlord

[4.29] The principles of presumed lost grant in the context of a parol annual letting, where both tenements were held under a common landlord, were considered by Palles CB in the seminal case of *Timmons v Hewitt*.[1] This was an action for the interruption of a right of way alleged to have been enjoyed for upwards of 40 years. Both the dominant and servient tenants held under parol lettings from year to year from a common landlord. The plaintiff dominant tenant had been in occupation for 23 years, the defendant servient tenant for 20 years. Each had come into their respective holdings, following the death of relatives who had earlier had the holdings during approximately concurrent terms. The plaintiff dominant tenant and her predecessors had throughout their successive tenancies used a way, passing over the defendant servient tenant's lands, which connected with the county road from Armagh to Portadown, for the purpose of transporting animals and goods. Holmes J, at first instance, directed a jury which found that the plaintiff dominant tenant and her predecessors had enjoyed the way as of right and without interruption for 40 years before the action, and also that the landlord when creating the defendant's tenancy had reserved the right of way in favour of the plaintiff's holding.

---

1   *Timmons v Hewitt* (1888) 22 LR Ir 627.

[4.30] On appeal to the Court of Exchequer, Palles CB held that the jury had been correctly directed and that their finding was consistent with the facts. Noting that the Prescription Act could not apply because each of the tenements was held under tenancy, neither of whom could enjoy any alleged easement 'as of right', Palles CB nevertheless considered that it was open to a jury to have found a presumed lost grant from one tenant to the other for the duration of the tenancy and not binding the fee. The language used by the Chief Baron is consistent either with a presumed lost grant between the tenants or an implied easement based on user at the time of the original letting:

'I am of opinion that where two parcels of land are held under a common landlord by tenancies, each of which has existed for upwards of twenty years, it is competent for the jury to infer, from twenty years' enjoyment, as of right and without interruption, of an easement claimed by the owner of one of the tenements over the land of the other tenement, a grant by deed from one tenant to the other tenant of such easement. I am also of opinion that where, as here, those tenancies have not been created by writing, and the user is proved to have existed as far back as the memories of the witnesses can go, a jury may infer that the alleged dominant tenement was such dominant tenement when originally demised by the landlord – that is, that it consisted not of the land merely, but of the land, with a right of way as appurtenant. Such a demise could be made at law, even by parol, provided the right of way existed as an appurtenant to the lands in the hands of the landlord immediately before he made the demise.'[1]

---

1. (1888) 22 LR Ir 627 at 637. A dictum scarcely 'vague and imprecise' as suggested by Chua in 'Easements, Termors in Prescription in Ireland' (1964) 15 NILQ 489 at 502. Nor is it consistent with Chua's interpretation at 503, that for a presumed lost grant to apply between tenants there must be evidence of knowledge of and acquiescence by the landlord. Indeed, the language of Palles CB seems redolent of the requirement for a quasi-easement to be 'continuous and apparent' for it to blossom into a full easement upon a disposal of the property in parts. See para **[3.14]**. See also, *Head v Meara* [1912] 1 IR 262. See para **[2.13]** and para **[3.18]**.

[4.31] In reviewing the case of *Deeble v Linehan*,[1] Palles CB noted that all of the judges in the Court of Exchequer Chamber had been agreed, that if the freehold owner of the dominant tenement (the mill) had been in possession for 20 years prior to the action, rather than a tenant, a grant might have been inferred from 20 years uninterrupted user as of right. In addition, Palles CB noted a point which, had it occurred to Pigot CB in *Wilson v Stanley*,[2] might have enabled him avoid the overwhelming authority of *Bright v Walker*:[3] that the presumption of lost grant in *Deeble v Linehan* was, in fact, a grant from a lessee holding under a bishop's lease, such being the extent of the servient owner's interest in that case, and therefore did not bind, nor could have bound, the fee simple reversion.[4]

---

1. *Deeble v Linehan* (1860) 12 ICLR 1.
2. *Wilson v Stanley* (1861) 12 ICLR 345.
3. *Bright v Walker* (1834) 1 Cr M & R 216.
4. A further appeal to the Court of Appeal, unreported save in outline, was dismissed on the basis that there had been sufficient evidence to support both findings of the jury; namely, that there had been continuous beneficial enjoyment by the plaintiff and her predecessors in title of the way for 40 years before the action, and, that the landlord had reserved the right of way in favour of the plaintiff's holding prior to the letting. The Court of Appeal did not comment on the views expressed by Palles CB in relation to presumed lost grant and the Prescription Act. This enabled Fitzgibbon LJ (dissenting) to discount the views of Palles CB in *Hanna v Pollock* [1900] 2 IR 664 at 673.

[4.32] A similar issue arose for decision in *O'Kane v O'Kane*.[1] The plaintiff and the defendant were tenants from year to year under holdings created more than 40 years before by a common landlord. The plaintiff claimed a right of way over the defendant's lands which, at first instance, was held by a jury to have been enjoyed, as of right, for more than 20 years, but less than 40 years. O'Brien CJ, in the Court of Queen's Bench, noted with approval the observation of Lawson J in *Tennent v Neill*,[2] to the effect that there was no need for the jury to believe as a matter of fact that a lost deed had ever been actually executed, and added:

> 'We do not formally decide whether one tenant can or cannot confer upon another such a right of way by grant, but we do not see why a tenant from year to year should not be able to grant such a right as long as his tenancy lasted. He could, in my opinion, confer by express grant such a right as long as his tenancy subsisted; and as to the doctrine of lost grant I consider it a very useful one, and I think this case is an example of the salutary effects of this fiction of a lost grant by which a state of things which has existed uninterruptedly for a long series of years can be validated.'[3]

---

[1] (1891) 30 LR Ir 489.

[2] (1870) IR 5 CL 418. The Court of Exchequer Chamber had held, in a case where there was a covenant to execute certain improvements by a specific date, or in the alternative an additional rent would be chargeable, and where the stated improvements had not been carried out, but other more expensive ones were, and an additional rent was never charged or paid, that a jury could be instructed to regard themselves as at liberty to infer the execution of a release of the covenant. The Court decided that where there was evidence of long and continuous non-observance, a jury could presume a release of the covenant to have been executed in circumstances where a release might have been executed before the accrual of the breach.

[3] The decision of O'Brien CJ was criticised by Chua in 'Easements, Termors in Prescription in Ireland' (1964) 15 NILQ 489 at 502, precisely because it made it possible for a presumed lost grant to apply between tenants of a common landlord for the duration of the tenancy of the servient tenement.

[4.33] By the end of the nineteenth century, despite the restrictive decision in *Wilson v Stanley*,[1] the judges of the Irish courts had striven to restore to the doctrine of presumed lost grant the crucial significance it had formerly enjoyed before the enactment of the Prescription (Ireland) Act 1858. By the end of the nineteenth century also, as is manifest from the decisions reviewed above, the primary character of landholding in Ireland had changed markedly from that of 60 years earlier: leases for lives with their complicating accretions of subordinate life estates, marriage settlements and myriad sub-leases had developed into a less formal, but equally intricate, system of landholding, based on leases for terms of years, or sometimes mere annual lettings created by verbal agreement. This would be further transformed by the facility for tenant farmers to purchase the freehold of their lands under a succession of enabling statutes now collectively designated the Land Purchase Acts. Perhaps inevitably, against a background of such dramatic changes in the agrarian landscape, the entire phenomenon of the acquisition of easements by prescription and presumed lost grant would again attract comprehensive judicial scrutiny. This took place in the pivotal *fin de siècle* decision of the Court of Appeal in *Hanna v Pollock*.[2]

[1] *Wilson v Stanley* (1861) 12 ICLR 345.
[2] *Hanna v Pollock* [1900] 2 IR 664.

The decision in Hanna v Pollock (1898–1900)

[4.34] In 1861, the predecessor of the plaintiff, a tenant farmer with a holding near Ballycastle, Co Antrim, in order the better to water his lands, constructed a drain through them to the nearby river, the Killaggan. On this drain he also constructed a weir and a conduit, that led off some of the surplus water through the defendant's adjoining farm, in the process supplying a tank placed there by the defendant, before emptying itself into the Killaggan lower down. The two lands were contiguous, both plaintiff and defendant holding under the same landlord. In 1894, they each purchased the freehold of their respective holdings under the Land Purchase Acts. In 1896, the plaintiff altered the drainage and removed the conduit. This resulted in cutting off the water supply to the defendant's tank. The defendant entered upon the plaintiff's holding to restore the conduit, and the plaintiff sued for damages.

The jury in the Court of Exchequer found that there had been a lost grant. On appeal to the Court of Queen's Bench,[1] Andrews J[2] held that the law had been correctly stated by Palles CB in *Timmons v Hewitt:*[3] that there can be prescription on the basis of presumed lost grant between tenants of the same landlord where they have held for upwards of 20 years, without interruption, 'as of right'. He added, however, that it was vital that the enjoyment should have been as of right. In this case any enjoyment by the defendant could have been no more than permissive, since the watercourse constructed by the plaintiff was temporary, designed for his own use and benefit only, and liable to be removed if he found a more satisfactory method of draining his lands. To infer a grant of an easement in such a case would be to prevent a landowner from developing his land merely to enable an adjoining landowner continue to derive a benefit which he had enjoyed as a by-product of the original temporary watercourse.

[1] *Hanna v Pollock* [1898] 2 IR 532.
[2] With whom Madden and Boyd JJ concurred.
[3] *Timmons v Hewitt* (1888) 22 LR Ir 627.

Merger or surrender

[4.35] Kenny J dissented on the basis that he believed the watercourse to have been permanent. However, he also addressed the question of the fate of a presumed lost grant between lessees where the servient tenement is either surrendered or merges with the freehold. Accordingly to Kenny J, the easement continues. An implied grant, he said, just like an actual grant, is capable of binding an estate for its natural duration, so that it is not to be defeated by surrender or other voluntary act on the part of the servient owner. In the case of either a voluntary merger or a surrender an easement cannot be rendered nugatory by a servient owner who is a lessee:

'… whether the easement rests on an actual existing deed, or on a deed presumed to have been executed but now lost, it subsists during the term for which the servient tenancy is held, and [that] it cannot be determined by assignment, surrender or by what I may designate a voluntary merger.'[1]

---

[1]   *Hanna v Pollock* [1898] 2 IR 532 at 541.

A thorough review of presumed lost grant

[4.36] On a further appeal to the Court of Appeal,[1] the judges exhaustively reviewed the then current case law on presumed lost grant.[2] Regarding the specific issue of whether the interrupted artificial watercourse could be deemed to be permanent or temporary, Fitzgibbon and Walker LJJ constituted a majority to hold, that the enjoyment by the appellant had been permissive only, and so not as of right; the watercourse being a temporary convenience for the party who had constructed it, while Holmes LJ, dissenting, was of the view that the watercourse was permanent, conferring reciprocal easements on both parties to the action.

In relation to presumed lost grant, a different majority, of Walker and Holmes LJJ, held that it was now settled law, that the presumption of lost grant could operate, where the dominant tenement and the servient tenement were both held under leases from a common landlord, and the aspiring easement had been enjoyed as of right for no less than 20 years.

Fitzgibbon LJ disagreed, believing that there had not been any clear Irish decision on the issue of whether one lessee can prescribe against another for an easement based on enjoyment of less than 40 years user. It had not been decided in *Timmons v Hewitt*,[3] because that case had been disposed of on its facts, by the jury in the court below, leaving the comments of Palles CB on presumed lost grant technically *obiter*. In *O'Kane v O'Kane*[4] Palles CB had put to the jury the possibility of finding a presumption of grant from one tenant to another where there had been only 20 years user. However, O'Brien CJ, on appeal, had left undecided the crucial question whether the case of *Deeble v Linehan*,[5] the judgment of Pigot CB in which he cited with approval, could still be deemed to be an authority, as the action which it had decided had been instituted prior to the coming into effect of the Prescription (Ireland) Act 1858. In the opinion of Fitzgibbon LJ, subsequent to the enactment of this statute, an easement could only be acquired between lessees of a common landlord on the basis of a presumed lost grant in circumstances where acquiescence by the owner in fee of the servient tenement could reasonably be inferred and the enjoyment would also bind the fee.

---

[1]   *Hanna v Pollock* [1900] 2 IR 664.
[2]   In the case of Fitzgibbon LJ this was done with some reluctance, he holding that since the user in this case had clearly been permissive, and the appellant's case failed on the facts, a detailed review of the law was unnecessary.
[3]   *Timmons v Hewitt* (1888) 22 LR Ir 627. The jury had found that there had been 40 years' enjoyment, as of right and without interruption, and also that the right had been reserved by the common lessor at the time of the letting of the servient tenement. See para **[4.29]**.
[4]   *O'Kane v O'Kane* (1891) 30 LR Ir 489.
[5]   *Deeble v Linehan* (1860) 12 ICLR 1.

[4.37] Walker LJ was in no doubt as to the importance of final resolution of this matter:

'In this country, where long leases are so common, and even tenancies from year to year have become almost perpetuities, the importance of a decision adverse to the possible existence of such a right cannot be exaggerated.'[1]

While sharing the view expressed by Fitzgibbon LJ on the distinguishable features of both *Timmons v Hewitt*[2] and *O'Kane v O'Kane*[3] and their limited value as precedents, Walker LJ nevertheless held that, to the extent that the English case of *Bright v Walker*[4] was inconsistent with dicta in the two later cases, he preferred to accept the pronouncements in the Irish authorities.

---

[1]   [1900] 2 IR 664 at 690. This is a resounding echo of the observations of Pigot CB in *Wilson v Stanley* (1861) 12 ICLR 345 at 356. The development of the land purchase laws between 1861 and 1900 should be noted in the points of contrast between the observations of Pigot CB and Walker LJ, in particular where Walker LJ comments on annual tenancies having become virtual perpetuities. In remarking on the judgment of Pigot CB, Holmes LJ in *Hanna v Pollock* observed that the views expressed by the chief baron had since become all the more cogent due to the land purchase legislation which had ensured that agricultural tenants, though still holding under lease, practically enjoyed fixity of tenure.

[2]   *Timmons v Hewitt* (1888) 22 LR Ir 627.

[3]   *O'Kane v O'Kane* (1891) 30 LR Ir 489.

[4]   *Bright v Walker* (1834) 1 CM & R 211.

[4.38] According to Walker LJ, prescription and presumed lost grant were different concepts. The notion of presuming a lost grant had been devised in order to support a title established by analogy with the Statutes of Limitations in cases which would not satisfy the requirements of common law prescription. 'The principle was to quiet a possession had against another, and attribute to it for that purpose a lawful origin, the analogy of which would apply to a grant from termor to termor.'[1] Even *Bright v Walker*[2] demonstrated that prior to the Prescription Act, 20 years enjoyment as of right between termors or lessees would have been adequate to presume a grant, while the decisions in *Deeble v Linehan*[3] and *Wilson v Stanley*[4] had established that this was still so in Ireland.[5]

---

[1]   *Hanna v Pollock* [1900] 2 IR 664 at 694.

[2]   *Bright v Walker* (1834) 1 CM & R 211.

[3]   *Deeble v Linehan* (1860) 12 ICLR 1.

[4]   *Wilson v Stanley* (1861) 12 ICLR 345.

[5]   Walker LJ derived some support from more recent English authorities; in particular, *Angus v Dalton* (1877) 3 QBD 85 at 118, where Cockburn CJ had said that the presumption of lost grant still applied to claims involving 20 years enjoyment, and that in this regard the Prescription Act changed nothing; also *Aynsley v Glover* (1875) LR 10 Ch 283, in which Mellish LJ had said that the presumption of lost grant was still necessary to protect claims which would otherwise be defeated by the statute, as where evidence of user does not go right down to the time of taking the action, or where there has been at some stage an interruption. Noting that the decision of the Court of Appeal in *Wheaton v Maple* [1893] 3 Ch 48 was against the continued application of the presumption of lost grant in leasehold cases, Walker LJ stated that the Irish

cases of *Deeble v Linehan* (1860) 12 ICLR 1 and *Beggan v McDonald* (1877) IR 11 CL 362, (1878) 2 LR Ir 560, with which it was inconsistent, were binding on him.

[4.39] In the estimation of Walker LJ, since prescription at common law was stated to be in theory from time immemorial, it was always intended to bind the fee simple, and there was no reason to suppose why this should not continue to be the case following the Prescription Act.

> 'But it seems strange that the making of prescriptive title easier by shortening the duration of the necessary user to twenty years should be held to take away the qualified right which existed before it, the presumed grant from termor to termor which I assume to have existed before ... I can conceive no reason for saying that a statute which was intended to facilitate title by enjoyment should be held to take away a class of title by enjoyment which existed before it and which from its qualified character does not interfere with, and is not inconsistent with, title by prescription in its old character from user from time immemorial against the fee, or its statutory character of twenty years against the fee.'[1]

Therefore, if the presumption of lost grant survived the passing of the Prescription Act, it would fly in the face of sense and reason that the right should not have survived with all its attributions, one of which was that one termor or lessee might be presumed to have granted to another one. The conventional concept of prescription could not apply in the case of two tenants holding under the same landlord, since that would have the effect of a reversioner acquiring a right against himself. But it was not inconsistent with the doctrine of presumed lost grant that it could apply to lessees holding either under a common landlord or under two different landlords for the duration of their respective terms of lease, even if the enjoyment had been for not more than 20 years.

---

[1]   *Hanna v Pollock* [1900] 2 IR 664 at 697. Also Delany 'Lessees and the Doctrine of Lost Grant' (1958) 74 LQR 82 at 86–90.

[4.40] Holmes LJ was satisfied that the courts in the eighteenth century had devised the fiction of a presumed lost grant to cater for cases where all the conditions for common law prescription could be met, except that the enjoyment had begun within human memory. Enjoyment, throughout a 20 year period, of the same character[1] as that which, if it had lasted during legal memory, would have established an easement by prescription at common law, gave grounds for presuming that it had originated in a grant later lost:

> 'It was never necessary to have evidence of a grant in fact. In most cases, it was recognised that the grant was purely imaginary. Formerly Judges were in the habit of advising juries that they were at liberty to presume it without actually directing them to do so; but in later times it has been laid down that it is the duty of juries to make the presumption, if they are satisfied that there has been what is called 'user as of right' for twenty years.'[2]

According to Holmes LJ, there was nothing to prevent a fee simple owner being bound by a presumed lost grant which, if it had actually existed, could not have existed longer ago than 30 years; likewise, neither was there anything to prevent a lessee being bound by a presumed lost grant during the residue of his term.[3] In the view of Holmes LJ, prescription and the doctrine of lost modern grant differed in 'their origin, character, and incidents.'

Prescription is a common law doctrine, presupposing a historic grant, which, once established, is absolute and indefeasible. The doctrine of lost modern grant was designed to give a legal basis to rights which prescription would not protect, rights which 'might have been conditional on the continuance, or limited to the duration, of particular estates in lands over which they were to be exercised.'[4]

---

[1]   See para **[4.02]**.

[2]   *Hanna v Pollock* [1900] 2 IR 664 at 701.

[3]   Also Kiralfy 'The Position of the Leaseholder in the Law of Easements' (1948) 13 Conv 104 at 107–108.

[4]   [1900] 2 IR 664 at 702.

[4.41] Both common law prescription and presumed lost grant, according to Holmes LJ, depend on fiction. Common law prescription is based on the fiction of user since the beginning of legal memory, whereas presumption of lost grant supposes that a grant which never existed has been lost. Once a fiction has been adopted by the law, stated Holmes LJ, it ceases to be a fiction and becomes the formal mode of expressing the reality. The title of the Prescription Act states that its purpose is to shorten 'the Time of Prescription in certain Cases'. In the opinion of Holmes LJ, this asserted purpose ruled out the application of the Prescription Act to cases of presumed lost grant, since the period of enjoyment for presuming a lost grant is 20 years, itself the shortest prescriptive period provided for in the statute. According to Holmes LJ, the Prescription Act left intact all the remedies a litigant would have had prior to its enactment, for establishing a right on the basis of user, while also giving additional facilities. He added that 'the statute is confined to amending the common law of prescription, and [that] this is done by giving a statutory mode of prescription in addition to the methods then existing for establishing rights by evidence of enjoyment.'[1]

---

[1]   [1900] 2 IR 664 at 704. Holmes LJ was dismissive of *Bright v Walker*: 'I am compelled to reject Baron Parke's reasoning as founded on an assumption that cannot be supported, and as repugnant to the canons of construction applicable to statutes dealing with private rights. Such rights are not to be abridged by legislation relating to a different subject-matter, unless the intention to do so appears either expressly or by clear intendment, and I can find in the Prescription Act neither the one nor other.' [1900] 2 IR 664 at 711. Holmes LJ commented that throughout his own career at the Bar, the lack of satisfaction with the dicta in *Bright v Walker* had resulted in cases being unduly protracted, in an attempt by judges to avoid having to decide cases on the basis of *Bright v Walker*, and directions not being given to the jury even though the issue would be clear if *Bright v Walker* were strictly applied.

[4.42] As a result of *Hanna v Pollock*[1] it is now settled that an easement can be acquired by presumed lost grant between lessees holding under a common landlord where there has been continuous enjoyment of the alleged easement as of right for not less than 20 years.[2]

1　*Hanna v Pollock* [1900] 2 IR 664.

2　Not all commentators were supportive of the articulation in *Hanna v Pollock*: 'Right of Way or Water Claimed by One Tenant Against Another' (1902) 36 ILTSJ 249. *Hanna v Pollock* was applied, with manifest approval of the principle espoused by the majority in that case, by Dodd J in *Flynn v Harte* [1913] 2 IR 322 and by Kingsmill Moore J in the High Court in *Tisdall v McArthur and Co (Steel and Metal) Ltd and Mossop* [1951] IR 228.

Presumed lost grant must have capable grantor

[4.43] Although the lost grant is clearly a fiction, it cannot be presumed if the party alleged to have executed the grant is incapable of executing it: *McEvoy v The Great Northern Railway Co.*[1] In this case it was held that the defendant, on account of its statutory duty to provide for the safety of a railway line through the installation of suitable drainage arrangements, could not be presumed to have granted a right to a neighbouring landowner to the use of a temporary watercourse constructed by the defendant railway company and used by it for almost 50 years.[2]

1　*McEvoy v The Great Northern Railway Co* [1900] 2 IR 325 at 334, per Palles CB: 'It is well settled that, though a presumption of grant is not now necessary to find a prescriptive right, still there cannot be a prescription if the owner of the servient tenement be so restrained by statute, or by the common law, as to be incapable of granting the easement in question.'

2　Despite the fact that the temporary watercourse had been supplied from a diversion of an underground stream formerly enjoyed by the plaintiff and his predecessors. See para **[8.30]** ff.

Presumed lost grant by landlord

[4.44] In *Lord MacNaghten v Baird*[1] the possibility of a presumed lost grant binding the fee simple in favour of a tenant fell to be considered. The plaintiff was the reversionary owner in fee of both the alleged dominant and servient tenements, each of which was under tenancy. The two tenements were on opposite sides of a road. The claim was for the use of a well on the servient tenement for a cottage on the dominant tenement that had been constructed 3 years after the letting of the dominant tenement. The Court of King's Bench held unanimously that there could not be a presumed lost grant by the tenant of the servient tenement, as the servient tenement had been under lease for only 17 years. Furthermore, Barton J observed that, as the claim of easement was being made by a mere cottier tenant[2] of the supposed dominant tenement, not in his own right, but through the judicial tenant (whose holding was superior), this was tantamount to a claim being made through the plaintiff, Lord MacNaghten himself, the fee simple reversioner. In such circumstance a lost grant could not be presumed because this would have the effect of binding the fee in favour of a tenant:

> '... in my opinion it is not possible in law to presume a lost grant of that kind from a landlord to his tenant. Such an easement must bind the fee ... and it is repugnant to our law to suppose that a tenant of a holding under a landlord can acquire by user an easement attached to his holding as against his landlord over the lands of his own landlord.'[3]

1   *Lord MacNaghten v Baird* [1903] 2 IR 731.

2   See para **[2.10]**.

3   [1903] 2 IR 731 at 738. For this proposition Barton J relied on the judgment of Lord Cairns in *Gayford v Moffat* (1868) 4 Ch App 133 who described such a supposition as '... an utter violation of the first principles which regulate the relationship of landlord and tenant.'

[4.45] On appeal to the Court of Appeal, Fitzgibbon LJ held that, had the lease of the servient tenement endured for 20 years, then, following the authority of *Hanna v Pollock*,[1] it would have been possible to presume a lost grant for the term of the tenancy of the servient tenement only. If, however, Lord MacNaghten himself had been in occupation an easement could not have been raised against him, Fitzgibbon LJ interpreting the decisions in *Timmons v Hewitt*[2] and *Hanna v Pollock* as affirmative of the proposition that a grant cannot be presumed by a tenant against the owner in fee.

However, Fitzgibbon LJ acknowledged that there was a dearth of logic in the potential ramifications of this. Where there is continuous user as of right for 20 years, a lessee can seek to presume a lost grant from another lessee of the same landlord for the duration of that lease, without binding the fee simple owner, even though, had there been a grant actually executed, the fee simple owner would have been the person most likely to have made it. From this flowed the incongruous consequence that a servient tenant could allow the enjoyment of a right over his land which, though it could not ultimately bind the landlord after the lease had expired, the landlord would not have permitted him to allow if he could have stopped it. Disastrous consequences would follow if the tenancy in the servient tenement were enlarged into a fee simple:

> 'If the tenancy subsequently became a perpetuity – by conversion into a judicial tenancy, or by purchase of the fee by the occupying tenant, or possibly even on surrender – the land would be burdened for ever with an easement which could not have bound, or existed against, the original owner in fee, and which, therefore, could not affect the value of his interest, or the price payable to him, in respect either of the dominant or the servient tenement.'[3]

Holmes LJ cautioned that the principles enunciated in *Hanna v Pollock* ought not to be extended further, noting that since it was the possession given by the landlord of the servient tenement which alone made the user possible, that user could not be relied upon so as to establish a right against him.

1   *Hanna v Pollock* [1900] 2 IR 664.

2   *Timmons v Hewitt* (1888) 22 LR Ir 627.

3   [1903] 2 IR 731 at 743–744. Even so, this was pretty much the situation that obtained in *Hanna v Pollock* [1900] 2 IR 664, where both parties, originally tenants, had since become freeholders through the statutory land purchase scheme, and the doctrine of grant might well have applied there, had the user of the watercourse not been found to be permissive, without the fateful outcome dreaded by Fitzgibbon LJ in the later case.

Unity of ownership and possession

[4.46] The continuing significance of the doctrine of presumed lost grant derives mainly from the inability to make title by prescription, either at common law or under statute, in cases where there has been, or may have been, at any time unity of ownership of both the dominant and the servient tenements.[1] This was the principal point under review in *Tisdall v McArthur and Co (Steel and Metal) Ltd and Mossop*.[2] The dominant and servient tenements were adjacent premises on Merchant's Quay, Dublin. The dominant tenement overlooked a yard belonging to the servient tenement which for many years had been open to the direct sunlight. In 1919 the then owner of the servient tenement constructed a roof, partially of glass, over the yard. This resulted in some diminution in light, but still left sufficient for the purpose of the business carried on in the dominant tenement. In 1948 the defendant servient owners, in order to reduce the premium of their fire assurance, erected concrete blocks in front of the windows of the dominant tenement, then owned by the plaintiff. The plaintiff sought an injunction. This was resisted by the defendants, on the basis that there could be no prescriptive right to receive indirect or refracted light, so that any title being acquired by the plaintiff by prescription had been interrupted and broken once the glass roof had been constructed in 1919.

---

[1] For example, in *Whelan v Leonard* [1917] 2 IR 323, the alleged dominant tenement was held under lease but the putative dominant owner had not been in possession between 1884 and 1886. During this time the lands had vested in the landlord and Gibson J held that this automatically precluded the operation of the Prescription Act.

[2] *Tisdall v McArthur and Co (Steel and Metal) Ltd and Mossop* [1951] IR 228, 84 ILTR 173.

[4.47] Kingsmill Moore J, in the High Court, disposed of the light issue, by holding that refracted light was no less light than direct sunlight, and that a right to it could be acquired. He then proceeded to consider the possibility of a presumed lost grant – since there had been no evidence as to whether there had ever been unity of possession of the dominant and servient tenements, a claim based upon the Prescription Act could perhaps be defeated on that ground.[1] Following a comprehensive review of the caselaw, Kingsmill Moore J concluded that it was still possible to acquire a right to light by presumed lost grant rather than by prescription. The House of Lords decision in *Tapling v Jones*,[2] in which Lord Westbury had said that the acquisition of an easement of light now depended upon positive enactment rather than any presumption of grant or fiction, Kingsmill Moore J distinguished on the basis that a lost grant had not been raised in the pleadings, and that the learned law lord's dictum had application only to a claimed easement of light under s 3 of the Prescription Act. In the opinion of Kingsmill Moore J, since s 4 of the Prescription Act required the requisite period of enjoyment to have taken place immediately prior to an action to establish the alleged easement, it could be argued that '... the Prescription Act which was passed to facilitate the proof of claims of long user, should not be interpreted as abolishing a mode of proof which was in some ways more convenient than the mode of proof provided by the Prescription Act inasmuch as the user need not have extended to the point of time immediately before an action.'[3]

Kingsmill Moore J also considered the decision of the Court of Appeal in *Hanna v Pollock*.[4] Although this had involved a claimed right over a watercourse, Kingsmill Moore J had no difficulty in finding that the judgments were also applicable to an easement of light, and expressed himself of the view, that the law in Ireland, since *Hanna v Pollock*, was that any easement could properly be claimed on the basis of a lost modern grant. The decision of Kingsmill Moore J was upheld on an appeal to the Supreme Court, though the four judges avoided commenting on the principles of lost grant reviewed by Kingsmill Moore J, preferring to rest their decisions on s 3 of the Prescription Act.[5]

---

[1] This was a concern not shared by any members of the Supreme Court all of whom felt they could rely on s 3 of the Prescription Act which deals specifically with the acquisition of a right to light.

[2] *Tapling v Jones* (1865) 11 HL Cas 290.

[3] *Tisdall v McArthur and Co (Steel and Metal) Ltd and Mossop* (1951) 84 ILTR 173 at 178. On this point Kingsmill Moore J derived succour from the judgment of Mellish LJ in *Aynsley v Glover* (1875) 10 Ch App 283, especially where Mellish LJ had observed at 284–285: 'There are no negative words in the statute to take away rights existing independently of it. ... Indeed, as the statute requires, the twenty years or forty years (as the case may be), the enjoyment during which confers a right, to be the twenty years or forty years next immediately before some suit or action is brought with respect to the easement, there would be a variety of valuable easements which would be altogether destroyed if a plaintiff was not entitled to resort to the proof which he could have resorted to before the Act was passed.'

[4] *Hanna v Pollock* [1900] 2 IR 664.

[5] Maguire CJ indicated that he thought it unnecessary to decide whether the easement arose on the basis of a presumed lost grant. See also 'Acquisition of the Right to Light: Does the Prescription Act 1832 Oust the Doctrine of Lost Modern Grant?' (1947) 15 Ir Jur 15.

[4.48] In *Cullen v Dublin Corpn*[1] Kingsmill Moore J, then in the Supreme Court, had his own opportunity to consider a presumed lost grant in the context of an artificial watercourse. This watercourse, which ran through the lands of the plaintiff, had been first constructed in the thirteenth century as the principal supply of water to the city of Dublin. Kingsmill Moore J rejected a suggestion that because the watercourse was artificial and its origin known, it was not permissible in law to presume a lost grant.[2] He was sustained in this view by the provisions of a statute of the Irish parliament from 1719, which provided for the payment of compensation to the owners of lands through which the watercourse passed, as a result of their being prohibited from carrying out various trades that would have the effect of polluting the water. Since certain of these milling businesses had only recently been established in 1719, the payment of compensation to their owners 'as if legal rights had been interfered with' implied a recognition that the owners of land through which the watercourse passed had an ongoing entitlement to its use, which '... would support the presumption of lost grant conferring such rights.'[3]

---

[1] *Cullen v Dublin Corpn* (22 July 1960, unreported) SC.

2   *Cullen v Dublin Corpn* '... the law will always presume a legal origin for rights which have been exercised long and openly. This is indeed one of the most fundamental and far reaching of legal principles.' (22 July 1960, unreported) SC at p 10.

3   *Cullen v Dublin Corpn* (22 July 1960, unreported) SC at p 14.

[4.49] The doctrine of presumed lost grant has been pleaded more recently in *Dunne v Molloy*[1] and *Flanagan v Mulhall*.[2] In each case the easement claimed was a right of way, and in each case also the claim failed. In *Dunne v Molloy* Gannon J, in the High Court, noted that, since the only parties who could have executed a grant were in court, a lost grant could not be presumed, thereby limiting the doctrine to cases where it was not shown conclusively that a grant either could not be, or had not been, executed. In *Flanagan v Mulhall* the servient owner during the preceding 30 years had been both out of possession and of unsound mind.

To the extent that it was alleged that the servient owner's agent had been aware of the user by the plaintiff, O'Hanlon J, in the High Court, held that the onus of establishing actual knowledge by the servient owner's agent rested on the person alleging it, and that this onus had not been discharged.[3]

---

1   *Dunne v Molloy* [1976–1977] ILRM 266.

2   *Flanagan v Mulhall* [1985] ILRM 134.

3   This decision has been criticised in Bland *The Law of Easements and Profits à Prendre* pp 256–257 on the basis that the judgments in *Hanks v Cribben* (1857) 7 ICLR 489 had not been considered. However, it is arguable that there is a clear difference between the circumstances prevailing in *Hanks v Cribben*, where the Duke of Leinster had been unaware of a watercourse cut on his own property, and those in *Flanagan v Mulhall*, where the owner of the alleged servient tenement had been bereft of reason.

[4.50] It seems clear that with the greater preponderance of freehold ownership nowadays, than in the years before 1900, the more subtle aspects of the doctrine of presumed lost grant will, with the increasing passage of time, continue to diminish.[1] As in the case of *Hanks v Cribbin*,[2] the principal relevant issue will become once more the knowledge of the alleged servient owner and the extent to which he can be said to have acquiesced in the enjoyment of the alleged easement as of right. Even so, the possibility of unity of ownership of the dominant and servient tenements at some time in the past, and the fact that the period of user for claims under the Prescription Act must be immediately prior to the instituting of a claim, will still present serious impediments to the application of the statute in all cases. It is likely that common law prescription, statutory prescription, and presumed lost grant will continue to be alternative pleadings in most actions involving the establishment of an easement.[3] Indeed, perhaps the single greatest threat to the ongoing importance of presumed lost grant as a mechanism for the acquisition of easements through long enjoyment resides, not in any objection or prohibition of principle, but in its indiscriminate confusing with statutory and common law prescription by the courts in modern times.

1   As, for example, in *Kilduff v Keenaghan* (6 November 1992, unreported) HC, where the acquisition of a right of way by presumed lost grant and by prescription and the acquisition of ownership by adverse possession were considered by O'Hanlon J virtually interchangeably. This is not a happy development.

2   *Hanks v Cribbin* (1857) 7 ICLR 489 and 9 ICLR 312.

3   The usual order of pleading being, the Prescription Act, prescription at common law, presumed lost grant: Wylie *Irish Land Law* (3rd edn, 1997) Butterworths, p 387.

Chapter 5

Statutory Prescription

Introduction and General Summary

[5.01] The Prescription Act 1832[1] was enacted into Irish law, in its entirety, without modification, by the Prescription (Ireland) Act 1858.[2] It came into effect on 1 January 1859. Its short title describes it as 'an Act for Shortening the Time of Prescription in certain cases.' The Prescription Act has not had the benefit of a popular or a complimentary press: strenuously criticised for its obliquity in drafting,[3] even its overall purpose has been considered speculative.[4] As Holmes LJ observed slightingly in *Hanna v Pollock*, the Prescription Act had neglected the opportunity to settle definitively the nature and extent of rights acquired by prescription, and thus was of little practical value; he concluded that '... it does not purport to be a code, and only deals with a comparatively small portion of the law of easements.'[5] In Ireland the Prescription Act has come a poor second to presumed lost grant as a judicially applied vehicle for giving legal right to claimed easements enjoyed continuously over a long period.

---

[1]   2 & 3 Wm 1V c 72.

[2]   21 & 22 Vict c 42.

[3]   English Law Reform Committee's 14th Report *Acquisition of Easements and Profits by Prescription* (1966; Cmnd 3100) para 40; Report of the Irish Republic's Law Reform Commission, *The Acquisition of Easements and Profits à Prendre by Prescription* (LRC66-2002) at 24 para 2.26: 'The legislation is cumbersome and unclear.' Wylie *Irish Land Law* (3rd edn, 1997) p 390.

[4]   *Gale on Easements* (eds, Gaunt and Morgan, 16th edn, 1997) Sweet & Maxwell, p 179.

[5]   *Hanna v Pollock* [1900] 2 IR 664 at 703; also Delany 'Lessees and the Doctrine of Lost Grant' (1958) 74 LQR 82 at 85–86.

[5.02] The essential characteristics of enjoyment requisite to acquire an easement by common law prescription or presumed lost grant continue to apply to an easement claimed under the Prescription Act. Enjoyment must be continuous, and as of right, openly, peacefully, and with the consent, but not the permission, of the alleged servient owner.[1] A noted exception is an easement of light, separately dealt with under s 3, where the prerequisite of being 'as of right', applicable to enjoyment of all other easements, and also of profits *à prendre*, is not contained. For the most part, the Prescription Act proceeds by giving two different categories of legal protection – one tenuous, one definitive – to enjoyments of different duration, while also providing for the subtraction of certain terms from the periods of enjoyment in specified cases. The chart below describes in broad outline the provisions of the act.

Claimed Right	Enjoyment	Effect
Easements other than light	20 years	Not to be defeated by showing enjoyment only for 20 years or more
Easements other than light	20 years	Periods of infancy, life tenancy, prosecution of suit until death of litigant, and unsound mind to be deducted from calculation [but not terms of years]
Rights of way and water [probably all easements other than light]	40 years	Absolute and indefeasible unless in writing
Rights of way and water [probably all easements other than light]	40 years	Leases for lives and leases for more than 3 years to be deducted from calculation but only if reversioner so applies not more than 3 years after expiry of lease
Profits à *Prendre*	30 years	Not to be defeated by showing enjoyment only for 30 years or more
Profits à *Prendre*	30 years	Periods of infancy, life tenancy, prosecution of suit until death of litigant, and unsound mind to be deducted from calculation [but not terms of years]
Profits à *Prendre*	60 years	Absolute and indefeasible unless in writing
Rights of Light	20 years	Absolute and indefeasible unless in writing

It now behoves us briefly to consider the provisions of the Prescription Act, following which we will review the relevant case law on the several sections, taking related sections together.

---

[1] See para [4.02].

Summary of the statute

[5.03] Section 1 of the Prescription Act provides that a common law claim to any right of common, or other profit or benefit, which has been actually enjoyed by the person claiming right to it, without interruption, for a full period of 30 years, cannot be defeated simply on the basis of its being established that the enjoyment first commenced some time more than 30 years earlier, but that the claim remains liable to be defeated by any other method which, at common law prior to the enactment of the statute, could have defeated it. If the right has been enjoyed, by the person claiming entitlement to it, without interruption, for a full period of 60 years, the right will become 'absolute and indefeasible' unless it can be established that the enjoyment was based on a consent or agreement given in writing expressly for that purpose.

[5.04] Section 2 of the Prescription Act provides that a common law claim to any right of way or water, or other easement, which has been actually enjoyed by the person claiming right to it, without interruption, for a full period of 20 years, cannot be defeated simply on the basis of its being established that the enjoyment first commenced some time more than 20 years earlier, but that the claim remains liable to be defeated by any other method which, at common law prior to the enactment of the statute, could have defeated it. If the right has been enjoyed, by the person claiming entitlement to it, without interruption, for a full period of 40 years, the right will become 'absolute and indefeasible' unless it can be established that the enjoyment was based on a consent or agreement given in writing expressly for that purpose.

[5.05] Section 5 of the Prescription Act, which is principally concerned with amendment to the forms of pleadings previously current, provides that it must be established that the enjoyment was 'as of right by the occupiers of the tenement in respect whereof the same is claimed'. From this it is evident that the benefits of the Prescription Act can only be invoked in respect of a profit *à prendre* that is appurtenant to a tenement. A profit *à prendre* in gross cannot be claimed by statutory prescription.

[5.06] Section 4 of the Prescription Act states that the period of enjoyment necessary to acquire an easement or profit under the Act must have occurred immediately before an action or suit is instituted to establish the right. It is important to note that an easement or profit cannot be acquired by prescription except in the context of the initiation or defence of legal proceedings. Section 4 adds that an interruption of the period of enjoyment (which ss 1 and 2 state must be 'without interruption for the full period') will not be deemed to be such unless the person claiming the right has submitted to the interruption, or acquiesced in it, for a year after he shall have had notice of the fact of the interruption and of the identity of the person causing or authorising it. Section 6 states that in cases for which the act provides, no presumption will be allowed on the basis of enjoyment for any number of years less than those specified.

[5.07] Sections 7 and 8 of the Prescription Act provide for deductions from the period of enjoyment in certain cases. These deductions will defeat the establishment of a right, if the effect of them is to reduce the term of calculable enjoyment below the minimum necessary to secure statutory recognition. Section 7 provides that in cases where the alleged servient tenant was under a disability, such as being an infant, a tenant for life, or of unsound mind, or where a suit had been actively prosecuted until a party to it had died, the period of such disability will be deducted in all cases except where the statute provides that the right is to be absolute and indefeasible; in short, except in cases of profits enjoyed for 60 years under s 1, easements enjoyed for 40 years under s 2, and rights of light enjoyed for 20 years under s 3. Expressed another way, s 7 only applies in the cases of profits enjoyed for 30 years and easements (other than light) enjoyed for 20 years.

Section 8 provides that in the cases of rights of way and water, where the enjoyment has been for 40 years, and where the servient tenement during that period has been held under a lease for life, or under a lease for a term of years exceeding 3 years, such period shall be excluded in the computation of the term of enjoyment, *provided* that the party entitled to the reversion on the expiry or earlier determination of the term shall resist the acquisition of title within 3 years of such determination. Section 8 does not apply to profits *à prendre*. Neither does it apply to rights of light.

[5.08] Section 3 of the Prescription Act is peculiar to easements of light, and enjoys the additional uniqueness that it does not oblige the enjoyment to have been 'as of right': it states that where access of light to a premises has been enjoyed, without interruption, for a full period of 20 years, such right will be absolute and indefeasible unless established that it was enjoyed pursuant to a consent or agreement given in writing expressly for that purpose.

[5.09] As has been shown, the doctrine of presumed lost grant has enjoyed a continued currency in Ireland, largely due to the late nineteenth century phenomenon of periodic tenants, with statutory security of tenure, holding under a common landlord and enjoying rights over each other's land. To this extent there are fewer judicial decisions specific to the Prescription Act than one might suppose.

Sections 1, 2 and 5: Continuous Enjoyment as of Right

[5.10] *Wilson v Stanley*[1] was the first decision in Ireland to consider the newly enacted Prescription Act. In this, the dominant and servient tenements had both been held under a lease for one life between 1775 and 1840. Prior to the expiry of the lease for life, the enjoyment of the watercourse had been by a sub-tenant of the dominant tenement. During the currency of the lease for life, according to Pigot CB, there could not have been any enjoyment 'as of right' under the Prescription Act, because the lessee could not acquire an easement in the lands both of which he occupied. Similarly, as against the reversioner, the sub-tenant of the lessee could not have acquired any such right or easement by enjoyment.[2] Subsequent to 1840, after the expiry of the lease for life, the dominant tenement and the servient tenement were held under different leases. Although there had been uninterrupted enjoyment for more than 20 years since 1840, Pigot CB felt constrained to follow the decision of the English Court of Exchequer in *Bright v Walker*,[3] which had held that an easement could not be acquired under the Prescription Act where both dominant and servient tenements were in the possession of lessees holding under a common landlord who had occupied their respective lands for more than 20 years and fewer than 40 years.

---

[1]   *Wilson v Stanley* (1861) 12 ICLR 345. See para **[4.22]** ff.

[2]   The principle that a tenant cannot prescribe against his own landlord, or against another tenant of his own landlord in such a way as to bind the landlord, is firmly enshrined in Irish law. See Palles CB in *Timmons v Hewitt* (1888) 22 LR Ir 627 at 635: 'It is a user by a termor, who if he acquire the right, must acquire it as incident to the land of which he is termor, and thus for the benefit of his reversioner. Such user cannot be as of right, unless a reversioner can in law by user acquire a right against himself.' See also O'Brien C in *Whelan v Leonard* [1917] 2 IR 323.

[3]   *Bright v Walker* (1834) 1 CM & R 211.

[5.11] Uninterrupted enjoyment will not be as of right if it can be attributed to an agreement in writing made before the commencement of the longer prescriptive period, even if by a tenant for life only of the servient tenement: *Lowry v Crothers*.[1]

---

¹   *Lowry v Crothers* (1871) IR 5 CL 98. This involved a right to cut turf: the principle applies equally to easements.

Servient tenant must know right is being exercised

[5.12] In order for the enjoyment to be as of right the alleged servient owner must know that the right is being built up and the right must be such as adversely to affect his land. Mere user of a facility which from time to time may affect the servient land is not enough. In any event, such user would fail to qualify as a prescriptive easement on the grounds that it is not continuous. In *O'Brien v Enright*,¹ the plaintiff owned lands adjacent to a river. The defendant owned a mill further up-river, and for more than 20 years had enjoyed the use of a weir and mill dam. A recent rare incidence of flooding of the river near the plaintiff's land prompted proceedings. The defendant pleaded an established right to occasion such flooding, under the Prescription Act, on the basis of 20 years' continuous user. Whiteside CJ, in the Court of Queen's Bench, reduced the defendant's argument to the basic proposition that, the defendant, having enjoyed the use of a weir for over 20 years without any adverse consequences to the plaintiff's lands, the plaintiff, by reason of such user, is disentitled to complain once his lands are affected for the first time.

Whiteside CJ, following Lord Ellenborough in *Daniel v North*,² maintained that the defendant could not succeed in this defence unless he could show knowledge on the part of the servient owner; that, in effect, until the plaintiff had sustained some damage from the defendant's use, no prescriptive right against him could even begin to be established.

> 'What is the right the defendant must insist upon? The right to place the water upon the lands of the plaintiff. How does he aver that? By averring simply that he was in the habit of penning back water, and nothing more. But if he penned back water for a century without ever touching or injuriously affecting the land of the plaintiff, what of it? In my opinion, the right asserted by the defendant over the land of the plaintiff can only be co-extensive with the user; and the measure of the user is the measure of the right.'³

O'Brien J held that the defendant could not succeed because he had not maintained that the right claimed by him, even where enjoyment had been continuous over the requisite period, was responsible for the grievance suffered by the plaintiff.

---

¹   *O'Brien v Enright* (1867) IR 1 CL 718.
²   *Daniel v North* (1809) 11 East 393, per Lord Ellenborough: 'The foundation of presuming a grant against any party is, that the exercise of the adverse right on which such presumption is founded was against the party capable of making the grant; and that cannot be presumed against him, unless there were some probable means of knowing what was done against him.'
³   (1867) IR 1 CL 718 at 728, per Whiteside CJ.

[5.13] On the other hand, in the curious case of *Donnelly v Murray*,¹ in which the defendant enjoyed a way through an underground passage, part of which led beneath the plaintiff's land, the fact that the plaintiff servient owner (who only became lessee of the servient property the year before the action) had been unaware of the user, was held not to defeat the defendant's claim to an easement of passage, on the basis that the user had lasted for more than 20 years and otherwise satisfied the conditions necessary to establish a prescriptive right. The fact that the passage was underground did not, in itself, present a problem, the Court of Exchequer holding that the user was as 'open and notorious' as the nature of the tenement allowed; also that it had been 'as of right and not stealthily, and that the owners of the servient tenement knew of the existence and use of the passage and acquiesced in it'[2] and that the plaintiff servient owner derived his title from them. Much of this is unexceptionable. However, the decision of the court was to the effect, that if user has lasted for more than 20 years, and satisfies the necessary conditions of being continuous, open and without permission, the party disputing the claimed right, if adducing lack of knowledge, must demonstrate that this endured throughout the entirety of the prescriptive period. It is highly questionable whether such an approach would be followed today, since the corollary is that if the alleged servient owner had had knowledge of the user for a fraction only of the requisite 20-year period, but not for the rest of it, he would be unable to resist a claim. It is clear from the wording of the statute that the conditions necessary to satisfy a prescriptive right must persist throughout the entirety of the term.

Indeed, in *Donnelly v Murray* itself, the servient lessee, having entered into possession in April 1864, took steps to interfere with the defendant's user as soon as he discovered it in August the same year. This was done by the removal of a wall in the passage which precluded entry to it from the plaintiff's property, even though part of the tunnel passed beneath it. In April 1865 (less than a year later) the defendant re-instated the wall. This prompted the plaintiff's action for trespass, which came up for trial in October 1865. The evidence disclosed that the defendant's user of the tunnel had endured for in excess of 20 years.

It is suggested that the proper ground of decision would have been to invoke s 4 of the Prescription Act, since the user had been open and notorious, and permitted and *known*, for well in excess of 20 years, and the purported interruption of it by the plaintiff had lasted for less than a year until resisted by the claiming dominant owner, which had then resulted in an action being taken to dispute the right.

---

[1]   *Donnelly v Murray* (1865) 11 Ir Jur (NS) 159.
[2]   (1865) 11 Ir Jur (NS) 159 at 161.

Servient tenement must be competent to be prescribed against

[5.14] Where a lease for lives renewable forever has been converted into a fee farm grant under the Renewable Leasehold Conversion Act 1849, continuous user against the tenement formerly under lease must start again from the time of its conversion, in order to acquire a right under the Prescription Act.

In *Re The Estate of George Harding*,[1] Flanagan J refused to find that a claimed easement for watering cattle had been established by prescription where the applicant had exercised the right for over 30 years prior to 1873 against a property which had been held under a lease for lives renewable for ever, but was converted into a fee farm grant in 1865 under the Renewable Leasehold Conversion Act. Prior to 1865, following the authority of *Bright v Walker* Flanagan J held that user could not have given the applicant a prescriptive right against the fee simple reversioner. The question for decision was whether, when the nature of the estate has changed, 'she can make use of the right which she exercised against the old estate as against the new estate in the same owner.'[2] Flanagan J held that the case would be different if there had been user for 20 years after the conversion of the estate, but that, because there had not been, the principle of *Bright v Walker*, as applied by Pigot CB in *Wilson v Stanley*, provided that user for a term of 20 years was not capable of binding a leasehold interest unless it could also bind the fee simple, and that prior to the enlargement of the leasehold into a fee farm grant it was not capable of doing that.[3]

---

[1]   *Re The Estate of George Harding* (1874) IR 8 Eq 620.
[2]   (1874) IR 8 Eq 620 at 621.
[3]   See the reservations expressed by Fitzgibbon LJ in *Lord MacNaghten v Baird* [1903] 2 IR 731 on the enlargement of a tenancy subject to a prescriptive easement into a perpetuity, see ch 4, para **[4.45]**. *In re George Harding's Estate* does not appear to have been considered in the later case. See also the contrary opinion of Kenny J in the Court of Queen's Bench in *Hanna v Pollock* [1898] 2 IR 532.

[5.15] Similarly, in *Traill v McAllister*[1] it was held that, where a user had formerly suffered from a statutory illegality, the prescriptive term could only start to run from the time that the prior illegality had been statutorily lifted. The action was for pollution of a stream flowing past the plaintiff's lands, from which he grazed his cattle. The defendants steeped flax in another stream that joined the affected stream further up, thereby contaminating it. The steeping of flax had been rendered illegal by a statute of Elizabeth I, but this statute had been repealed by the Statute Law Revision (Ireland) Act 1878, which also provided that its passing would not affect the validity or invalidity of any act already done or of any right or title already accrued. The defendants alleged in defence to the plaintiff's action a prescriptive right, based on user, to create dams in the stream, and to steep flax in them and then discharge the water, after the flax had been steeped, into the stream.

Chatterton V-C observed that the general rule of law was that when a statute had been absolutely repealed, it was to be regarded as if it had not been passed. However, this did not signify that acts previously prohibited could confer rights retrospectively as if they had never been illegal. He gave as an example, user during the currency of the statute which had lasted for 20 years less one day. It would be unfair on the alleged servient owner if as soon as the statute was repealed the previous user would be retrospectively validated, thereby denying to the person who ought to have the power to complain, any opportunity to resist the accretion of a right against his estate which would thereafter bind it.

---

[1]   *Traill v McAllister* (1890) 25 LR Ir 524.

[5.16] In the opinion of Chatterton V-C, since the theory of prescription depended upon the presumption of a grant having been made,[1] if it could be shown that no grant could legally have been made then prescription could not arise. Regardless of whether the illegality derived from common law or statute, the illegality would prevent a grant from being lawfully made, and an easement by prescription, based on the user deriving from an illegal source, could not be established.[2]

---

1   Quoting Cockburn CJ in *Angus v Dalton* (1877) 3 QBD 85.

2   Chatterton V-C also cited in support the decision of Lord Westbury in *Staffordshire and Worcestershire Canal Navigation v Birmingham Canal Navigations* (1866) LR 1 HL 254, that if an applicant is relying on the Prescription Act he must establish that the right based on the claim of user could have been lawfully granted at the beginning of, or during, the period of user; if it could not have been lawfully granted, then prescription cannot apply.

Tenant cannot prescribe against his own landlord

[5.17] The decided cases demonstrate it to be axiomatic that a tenant cannot prescribe against his own landlord. The question whether a tenant can assert a claim under the Prescription Act against another tenant of his landlord was considered in a very short judgment by Lawson J in *Fahey v Dwyer*.[1] The plaintiff and the defendant held lands adjoining each side of a laneway as tenants under a common landlord. The plaintiff had acquired his farm as assignee under a lease for 21 years in 1851, which expired in 1872, after which he remained in possession at the same rent. The plaintiff's action against the defendant was for an alleged trespass comprising the use of the laneway between the two holdings and breaking down a gate that the plaintiff had erected across it. The defendant pleaded a right of way by prescription.

It was found as a fact that the way had been enjoyed as of right by the defendant for 40 years. Lawson J noted that, ever since the decision in *Beggan v McDonald*,[2] the Prescription Act had been held capable of applying between tenants, without binding the landlord. Lawson J failed, however, to comment on a significant distinguishing feature, which is that *Beggan v McDonald* was concerned with a claim between tenants of different landlords, thereby ensuring that the prescription would not be indirectly against the landlord of the claiming tenant.

---

1   *Fahey v Dwyer* (1879) 4 LR Ir 271.

2   *Beggan v McDonald* 1877) IR 11 CL 362, (1878) 2 LR Ir 560. See para **[5.28]** ff.

[5.18] Counsel for the plaintiff had urged that the Prescription Act could not apply to the defendant's user by reason of the plaintiff's tenancy having expired, that there could not be prescription against mere possession which was the true nature of the plaintiff's enjoyment, and that after 1872 the landlord would have been entitled to possession freed from the alleged right of way. Lawson J declined to accept this, adding that a jury would have been entitled to hold that from an early period the two farms had been demised, together with the way between them for the benefit of each of the farms, so that, accordingly, 'it was a way necessary for the convenience of the farms.' This language borrows heavily from the case of *Clancy v Byrne*,[1] also a decision of Lawson J, which had held that in a dispute between two tenants of the same landlord over a way enjoyed for many years, if there was evidence that prior to either letting the common landlord had provided the way as an accustomed access for one of the tenancies, an easement could arise by implication on a subsequent demise of the tenement.

Demonstrably, this is the correct rationale of the decision in *Fahey v Dwyer*, thereby leaving intact the proposition that a tenant cannot prescribe against another tenant of the same landlord, but must rely, if possible, on the doctrine of presumed lost grant, as elaborated in *Timmons v Hewitt*[2] and *Lord MacNaghten v Baird*.[3]

---

[1] *Clancy v Byrne* (1877) IR 11 CL 355. See para **[2.09]**.

[2] *Timmons v Hewitt* (1888) 22 LR Ir 627. See also *Whelan v Leonard* [1917] 2 IR 323.

[3] *Lord MacNaghten v Baird* [1903] 2 IR 731. The case of *Tallon v Ennis* [1937] IR 549 is also concerned with a claimed right of way between the tenants of the same landlord, in this instance Dublin Corporation. Although counsel for the plaintiff referred to *Timmons v Hewitt* (1888) 22 LR Ir 627 and *Fahey v Dwyer* (1879) 4 LR Ir 271, and Gavan Duffy J held that the plaintiff was entitled to the right of way claimed, yet he did not rest his decision clearly on any one doctrine, and seems implicitly to have proceeded on the basis of an implied grant from the Corporation to the father of the plaintiff. See also 'User of Right of Way as Affecting the Term of the Reversioner' (1877) 11 ILTSJ 599 and 'Prescriptive Claims by Tenants Under a Common Landlord' (1904) 38 ILTSJ 229. One is inclined to concur with the author of the earlier note, to the effect that '... rights of way, claimed and disputed as they are with an obstinacy which is often out of all proportion to their actual value, yet, the law as to rights of way is not only rendered doubtful by statutes not very easy of explication, but is still further complicated by decisions which it is not easy, nor indeed possible, to reconcile.'

Section 4: the Bringing of a Claim and Interruption

[5.19] This section has received comparatively little commentary in Irish decisions, primarily because the fact and significance of intermissions in user do not appear to have been argued with specific reference to it. A good example is *Barry v Lowry*.[1] In this the defendant claimed a right, enjoyed for over 40 years, to take water from a well on land held under lease between 1801 and 1862. In 1862 the plaintiff took over the reversion of the land where the well was, entering into possession in 1865. Shortly after taking up possession the plaintiff put a lock on an already existing gate, although he occasionally gave the defendant the key. The Court of Exchequer held that the locking of the gate by the plaintiff evinced a denial of any right of access to the well on the part of the defendant whose user was accordingly deemed to be permissive. No reference was made to s 4 of the Prescription Act, even though the facts present an ideal instance for its application.

---

[1] *Barry v Lowry* (1877) IR 11 CL 483.

[5.20] In *Wilson v Stanley*,[1] Pigot CB conceded that the facility to establish a right to an easement or a profit on the basis of long enjoyment had been attenuated by interpretations of the Prescription Act by the English courts. Noting that the period of enjoyment had to be computed backwards 'not from the obstruction complained of, but from the bringing of the action', Pigot CB accepted that 'it has been laid down, by high authority, that there must be some act of user and enjoyment within the year next preceding the bringing of the action'.[2] From this it followed that 'the delay of a year in asserting the right by action causes a forfeiture of the benefit of all the antecedent enjoyment, however prolonged.'[3]

This seems, arguably, a somewhat strained reading of s 4, which is primarily concerned with identifying the period of relevant user for the purpose of calculating potential entitlement to statutory protection. This period 'shall be deemed and taken to be the Period next before some Suit or Action wherein the Claim or Matter to which such Period may relate shall have been or shall be brought into question.' In other words, the relevant period of uninterrupted enjoyment is that before an action brought in which the alleged right is asserted or resisted. The section goes on to provide that an act apparently constituting an interruption of the enjoyment will not be deemed to be such unless it has been submitted to, or acquiesced in, by the party claiming the right 'for One Year after the Party interrupted shall have had or shall have Notice thereof, and of the Person making or authorising the same to be made.' On a literal interpretation of the section, it seems rather that there must not be a demonstrable interruption of the enjoyment for a whole year prior to an action being brought, than that there must be evidence of actual enjoyment during that year. If there is no evidence, or insufficient evidence, of enjoyment, then the alleged right will fail to qualify on the fundamental and obvious ground of absence of enjoyment without interruption.

---

[1]   *Wilson v Stanley* (1861) 12 ICLR 345.
[2]   Pigot CB alluded specifically to the judgment of Parke B in *Lowe v Carpenter* (1851) 6 Exch 825.
[3]   (1861) 12 ICLR 345 at 356.

[5.21] There is a clear difference between actual interruption for a period of a year, which has the effect of breaking the period of user under s 4, and basic absence of evidence of any enjoyment of a right, which defeats an easement by prescription under s 2, the section setting out the relevant periods of enjoyment. The difference is basically, that between submitting to an interruption of enjoyment, and not in any real sense enjoying the asserted right at all.

[5.22] In real terms, enjoyment for marginally over 19 years, which is only at that stage interrupted on a continuous basis, will probably qualify for statutory protection, provided that the party alleging right institutes proceedings to protect it as soon as the 20 years are up and before the interruption has lasted for a full year. To proceed before the 20 years are up will fail to sustain the right because there will not have been enjoyment for the minimum period specified by the Act. To delay too long after the 20 years has passed will, in the example given, result in the right being defeated because the interruption will have lasted for a full year. If the interruption commences shortly before the expiry of 19 years' enjoyment, and continues for a full year, then notwithstanding the period of enjoyment, a statutory right will not be able to be sustained at all.

[5.23] Evidence of a pragmatic approach, shorn of technical complexity, is disclosed by the decision of Kenny J, in the High Court, in *Redmond v Hayes*.[1] The defendant in 1966 bought a farm in Co Wexford comprising 65 acres and alleged a right to dump lime and manure on the adjacent farm lands of the plaintiff which comprised a little over three acres. The plaintiff had recently built a bungalow on his lands. The defendant established that from the 1930s onwards, between November and April each year, manure had been dumped on the plaintiff's lands, in varying locations, as also had been quantities of lime or limestone for use as fertiliser. The defendant likewise, since purchasing the lands in 1966, had dumped manure and limestone each year between November and April. He was held to have an easement.

Kenny J did not specifically refer, either to common law or statutory prescription, or to presumed lost grant. Nor was it clear from the judgment that the dumping had taken place every year, but that it had commenced in the 1930s and had been engaged in every year by the plaintiff since he bought his farm in 1966.[2]

---

1   *Redmond v Hayes* (7 October 1974, unreported) HC.
2   See also *Kilduff v Keenaghan* (6 November 1992, unreported) HC, where prescription and lost grant and adverse possession are considered without manifest differentiation between them; Bland *The Law of Easements and Profits à Prendre* (1997) Sweet & Maxwell, p 267.

Section 6: Prohibition of Presumption for Less than the Minimum Term

[5.24] At one time, principally by reason of the judgment of Parke B in *Bright v Walker*,[1] s 6 was construed as precluding any claim to an easement, whether by prescription or presumed lost grant, where the period of enjoyment had been for a lesser time than the minimum of 20 years specified in the Act.

---

1   *Bright v Walker* (1834) 1 Cr M & R 216, as applied in Ireland by *Wilson v Stanley* (1861) 12 ICLR 345.

[5.25] Palles CB in *Beggan v McDonald*[1] was of the view that s 6 of the Prescription Act also applied to presumed lost grant, but only to the extent that there could not be a presumption of lost grant where enjoyment for less than the minimum statutory period was unaccompanied by other circumstances that might assist the presumption. It is inferable that the chief baron was alluding to acquiescence being established against the holder of a superior estate not in actual possession. This view was endorsed by Fitzgibbon LJ in *Hanna v Pollock*,[2] where he observed that if the evidence of right were being established by mere user alone, a presumption could not be made unless the user were for the statutory minimum period. In the opinion of Fitzgibbon LJ, this was 'quite consistent with retaining the right to make the presumption of the lost grant from evidence, or from circumstances other than mere user with which alone the Act is conversant.'[3]

As has been seen,[4] the majority judgments of Walker and Holmes LJJ decided that the Prescription Act did not apply to presumed lost grant at all. Accordingly, the prohibition under s 6 against drawing presumptions from user for less than the statutorily prescribed time can now be of no significance except to statutory prescription itself. This conclusion is supported by the express language of the section. It begins with the words,

'And be it further enacted, That in the several Cases mentioned in and provided for by this Act, no Presumption shall be allowed or made ...' thereby, it is suggested, making it manifest that its ambit is confined to claims of entitlement arising under the statute only.

---

1   *Beggan v McDonald* (1877) IR 11 CL 362.
2   *Hanna v Pollock* [1900] 2 IR 664.
3   [1900] 2 IR 664 at 686, per Fitzgibbon LJ. See Delany 'Lessees and the Doctrine of Lost Grant' (1958) 74 LQR 82 at 95–96. It is suggested that the absence of a comma after the words 'mere user' quoted above establishes that, in the estimation of Fitzgibbon LJ, the Prescription Act is only concerned with issues of user, and not with background or ancillary circumstances, such as the state of knowledge or inclination of a reversionary owner not in possession.
4   See para [4.36] ff.

Sections 7 and 8: Deductions from the Prescriptive Period

[5.26] Section 7 provides that, except in cases where the right is stated to be absolute and indefeasible – that is to say, where the enjoyment is *not* one of the following:

(a)   an easement other than light for 40 years;

(b)   a profit *à prendre* for 60 years;

(c)   a right of light for 20 years,

any time when the person entitled to resist was under a legal disability, specifically 'an Infant, Idiot, Non compos mentis, Feme Covert[1], or Tenant for Life,' or during which an action had been pending and had been vigorously prosecuted until either party to it had died, shall be deducted from the computation.[2] It should be noted that a term of years is not deducted from the computation of the term of enjoyment in s 7.

---

1   'Married Woman', a now obsolete impediment.
2   The attempted distinction drawn by Palles CB in *Beggan v McDonald* (1877) IR 11 CL 362 between s 7 on the basis that the limited owner referred to in it is holding *part of* the fee and s 8 which treats of a lessee holding *under* the fee is of doubtful assistance.

[5.27] By reason of the difficulties of interpretation to which it has given rise, s 8 merits being quoted in full:

> 'Provided always, and be it further enacted, That when any Land or Water upon, over, or from which any such Way or other convenient Watercourse or Use of Water shall have been or shall be enjoyed or derived hath been or shall be held under or by virtue of any Term of Life, or any Term of Years exceeding Three Years from the granting thereof, the Time of the Enjoyment of any such Way or other Matter as herein last before mentioned, during the Continuance of such Term, shall be excluded in the Computation of the said Period of Forty Years, in case the claim shall within Three Years next after the End or sooner Determination of such Term be resisted by any Person entitled to any Reversion expectant on the Determination thereof.'

[5.28] The status of the claimed right, after the passing of the statutory maximum term of 40 years, but before the expiry of a lease for longer than 3 years, fell to be considered in *Beggan v McDonald*.[1] In this the defendant, a lessee, claimed a right of way by prescription, on the basis of both 40 years' user and 20 years' user, over the land of the plaintiff, who had been a lessee for in excess of 40 years, but of a different landlord to that of the defendant. There was no evidence of any acquiescence on the part of the plaintiff's landlord. In the Court of Exchequer, Deasy and Fitzgerald BB, constituting a majority, held that the defendant could not establish a prescriptive right against the plaintiff unless he could also establish the right against the plaintiff's landlord, which s 8 of the Prescription Act prohibited him from doing.

---

[1] *Beggan v McDonald* (1877) IR 11 CL 362.

[5.29] According to Deasy B, this was the result of the English Court of Exchequer decision in *Bright v Walker*,[1] approved of by the Irish Court of Exchequer in *Wilson v Stanley*,[2] which, even though confined to a case of 20 years' user, laid down a general doctrine, applicable also to 40 years' user, that if a good title was not acquired against the fee simple it did not bind anybody. Fitzgerald B, concurring, believed it to be inherently unreasonable that, in the example of a case of a lease of 60 years, user as of right having been enjoyed for 40 of them, a landlord taking an action after 50 years would have judgment against him, on the basis that he ought to have proceeded within 3 years following the expiry of the 60 years, and not before.

---

[1] *Bright v Walker* (1834) 1 CM & R 211.
[2] *Wilson v Stanley* (1861) 12 ICLR 345.

[5.30] Dowse B and Palles CB were of a different view.

In the opinion of Dowse B, the proper construction of s 8 of the Prescription Act, taken in conjunction with s 2, was that the right is to be deemed absolute and indefeasible unless and until it has been resisted not later than three years after expiry of the lease by the reversioner. The term of the lease is not to be excluded otherwise. Any other construction would go against the express words of the statute, and would exclude the term of the lease before the time had come for any action to be taken. The only person entitled to take any action is the reversioner, who has to wait until his estate becomes vested in possession. To that limited extent, the easement must bind the fee. The tenant has the burden of it imposed on him during his lease, the landlord till he 'puts it off.'

Dowse B was able to rationalise the conclusion at which he had arrived in the context of the decision in *Bright v Walker*.[1] *Bright v Walker* had decided that 20 years' user only could not sustain the acquisition of an easement by prescription against the landlord. This made eminent sense, because otherwise the landlord would be entirely unable to rid himself of the easement, as the liberty to object to the accruing of a prescriptive right within three years of the expiry of a lease applies to 40 years' user under s 8 only.

> 'If we were to hold here that the landlord is bound, he is bound without any possible way of freeing himself from the obligation; and this anomalous state of the law would be established, that the landlord could free himself when he was bound for forty years and he

could not free himself when he was bound for twenty years ... an enjoyment of twenty years, if it give not a good title against all, gives no good title at all.'[2]

---

[1] *Bright v Walker* (1834) 1 CM & R 211.

[2] (1877) IR 11 CL 362 at 369. This is not necessarily inconsistent with the views of the majority of the Court of Appeal in *Hanna v Pollock* [1900] 2 IR 664 and can be distinguished from them on the basis that Dowse B is clearly talking about a claim under the Prescription Act only, whereas the thrust of the decisions of Walker and Holmes LJJ was that the case of *Bright v Walker*, and *a fortiori* the terms of the Prescription Act, did not apply to a presumed lost grant where user by a termor could bind the tenancy of another termor but not the fee simple reversion.

The new notion of the defeasible right

[5.31] According to Palles CB, it would be entirely wrong if, in the common case of a lease for 999 years, a claim to a prescriptive easement, arising from enjoyment, would remain inchoate and unable to become an enforceable easement throughout the entirety of the residue of the term and for 3 years afterwards. 'A strange effect, I venture to think, of an Act for *shortening* the time of prescription.' Palles CB held that on a strict and grammatical interpretation of the word 'excluded' in s 8, the right is one which is defeasible only in the event of resistance during the 3 years after the expiry of the lease by the reversioner.

Hence, the primary purpose of the Prescription Act had been to obviate the necessity for juries presuming, on the basis of mere enjoyment, a lost grant from the lessee of a servient tenement, and so put the parties in the same position as the presumption of lost grant would have done before the act – both in cases where user of 40 years would have bound the fee, and where it would not but would have bound a lesser interest. In order to achieve this latter result, the statute had to devise a concept unknown to the common law, namely a defeasible right:

'The result of the old presumption was that the easement bound the term, but, unless there were circumstances evidencing the acquiescence of the owner of the reversion, not the fee. The result of the statute is that, in cases to which it applies, the enjoyment binds the term absolutely during the term, and, until resistance, binds the fee, but it binds it *sub modo* only. The reversioner has an opportunity (by resistance at any time within three years after the term) of preventing his estate being affected by the user during the term. The statute gives to the absence of resistance by the reversioner within three years from the expiration of the term the same effect which juries previously attributed to his acquiescence.'[1]

---

[1] *Beggan v McDonald* (1877) IR 11 CL 362 at 388–389.

[5.32] The Court of Appeal upheld the views of Palles CB and Dowse B.[1] May CJ maintained that the Prescription Act, despite the limited purpose expressed in its preamble, *had* succeeded in creating a novel right – the concept of a 'defeasible, inchoate right' which fell into different classes 'qualified and absolute, valid as to some persons and invalid as to others.' Accordingly, a court had no business not giving effect to the obvious meaning of the statute merely 'because the result may not altogether harmonise with ideas which prevailed previous to its enactment.'[2] Ball C observed that the opportunity under the Prescription Act, of enabling enjoyment without interruption for 40 years blossom into an absolute and indefeasible right, was to use 'the strongest words that can be used to denote the character of a right when acquired.'[3] Such enjoyment conferred a right to an easement enforceable against the whole world, liable only to be defeated by the intervention of the reversioner not more than 3 years after the determination of the intervening lease.

---

[1]   *Beggan v McDonald* (1878) 2 LR Ir 560.
[2]   (1878) 2 LR Ir 560 at 572. In *Timmons v Hewitt* (1888) 22 LR Ir 627 this decision was cited with approval, but the case distinguished on the basis that there could not be prescription under the Act between termors holding under a common landlord, such a possibility being in breach of the primary principles of landlord and tenant law.
[3]   (1878) 2 LR Ir 560 at 567.

Defeasible concept does not apply to profits à prendre

[5.33] May CJ expressed the view that s 8 only applied to watercourses and rights of way, believing that the word 'convenient' could not be enlarged to include a right to light or a profit *à prendre*.[1] He contrasted this section, taken alone, with a combination of ss 1, 7 and 8, and noted that if a profit *à prendre* had been enjoyed for 60 years, and the land over which it was enjoyed during that time was subject to a tenancy, whether for life or years, or the owner was either abroad or suffering under some disability, the right was still rendered absolute and indefeasible. Section 7 only applied to the shorter prescriptive period, of 30 years, and s 8 only applied to rights becoming absolute and indefeasible after 40 years which did not include profits *à prendre*. In such circumstance it was clear to May CJ, that the meaning of s 8 is that the right to a way or watercourse after 40 years becomes absolute and indefeasible, subject only to having the term of lease deducted if the reversioner so applies not more than 3 years after the determination of the lease, otherwise becoming absolute and indefeasible without condition. If the lease is current after 40 years, as in the instant case, then the right is already absolute and indefeasible as regards the lessee of the servient tenement, but can still be challenged and defeated by the reversioner if he applies in time at the appropriate time.

---

[1]   In *Wright v Williams* (1836) 1 M & W 77, Parke B observed that the word 'convenient' was more likely than not a drafting error, and that the word 'easement' was what was intended. May CJ either seems to have been unaware of this view or else did not accept it. The point was noted by Porter MR in *Ingham v Mackey* [1898] 1 IR 272 but he refrained from pronouncing an opinion. See Wylie *Irish Land Law* p 394 (fn 404), Bland *The Law of Easements and Profits à Prendre* p 241.

Not a remainderman

[5.34] The provisions of s 8 must be construed strictly, so that the right given to a reversioner to resist no more than 3 years after the expiry of a lease cannot be extended to give a similar right to a remainderman: *Ingham v Mackey.*[1]

---

1 *Ingham v Mackey* [1898] 1 IR 272 at 282, per Porter MR: '... the saving in s 8 of the [Prescription Act] – whether or not the word "convenient" is to be read as merely a mistake for "easement", or as an equivalent for "convenience", and so including easements – only enures for the benefit of a person entitled to the "reversion" expectant upon the determination of the life estate; and the word *reversion* is to be strictly construed in this context, and will not include a remainder.'

Section 3: Rights of Light

[5.35] A right to light is the easiest easement to acquire under the Prescription Act, since s 3 provides that once the access of light to a building 'shall have been actually enjoyed therewith for the full Period of Twenty Years without Interruption, the Right thereto shall be deemed absolute and indefeasible' unless the enjoyment was based on a consent or agreement given in writing expressly for that purpose. Unlike ss 1 and 2, s 3 does not provide that the enjoyment shall have been by a person 'claiming right thereto'; in short, it does not have to be, to use the language of s 5, 'as of right'.[1] It has been held that, under s 3 of the Prescription Act, a tenant can acquire a right to light against his own landlord[2] and also against a tenant holding under the same landlord as himself, and so bind the freehold.[3] However, there is no Irish judicial pronouncement on this point.

---

1 Although Professor Wylie suggests some doubt in the matter: *Irish Land Law* p 396 (fn 414).
2 *Frewen v Phillips* (1861) 11 CB (NS) 449.
3 *Morgan v Fear* [1907] AC 425. See 'Acquisition of Right to Light by One Tenant Against Another Tenant Holding Under the Same Landlord' (1907) 41 ILTSJ 269.

No agreement in writing

[5.36] The existence or otherwise of a consent or agreement in writing was fundamental to the decision of Keogh J in *Judge v Lowe.*[1] The plaintiff and the defendant were adjoining householders. The plaintiff's action was for obstruction of light and air coming through a window in the party wall between his premises and the premises of the defendant, by the defendant's erecting on his premises a wall and roof which blocked the passage of light and air. The defendant alleged that when their respective fathers had occupied the respective premises, the father of the plaintiff, not then having any windows, had obtained verbal permission from the father of the defendant to construct a window, subject to a further verbal agreement that the defendant's father and his successors could at any time build a wall adjacent to the premises and so block the aperture, notwithstanding the construction of the window.

The plaintiff rejoined that the access of air and light had been enjoyed without interruption and as of right for 20 years before the bringing of the action and that the agreement alluded to was not by deed or in writing. This was met by further argument from the defendant, that the parol agreement was not effective to confer an easement of light, which would require to have been in writing; but that it *had* given to the defendant's father a licence to obstruct the access of light and air to the plaintiff's father's windows. This licence, while executory, remained revocable, but when acted upon became irrevocable. Being wholly inconsistent with the alleged easement of light granted by parol, the licence once executed extinguished the easement.

---

[1]   *Judge v Lowe* (1873) IR 7 CL 291.

[5.37] Keogh J gave no credence to the defendant's sophistries. The licence to obstruct, contended for by the defendant, was unenforceable, as the death of the parties to it, while unexecuted, effected its revocation. Keogh J held that the right to light, having been exercised continuously for over 20 years, and not pursuant to a written agreement, had become absolute and indefeasible, in accordance with s 3 of the Prescription Act.

[5.38] It is instructive to note, in *Judge v Lowe*,[1] that despite the plaintiff's contention that he had a right to light, the enjoyment was manifestly *not* 'as of right', since it was on foot of a parol agreement that, effectively, gave a residual right to its grantor at any time to destroy it. It is suggested that any other easement (s 2) or a profit *à prendre* (s 1) would not have qualified for statutory protection, if enjoyed under an agreement similar to that in *Judge v Lowe*, since it would not have been enjoyed, as s 5 requires, 'as of right'. A right to light is unique in this regard.

---

[1]   *Judge v Lowe* (1873) IR 7 CL 291.

Refracted light

[5.39] Light which is refracted by passing through a glass roof is still light that can be acquired under s 3 of the Prescription Act. Nor is the right to light extinguished by reason of the dominant owner's acquiescing in the construction of a glass roof, which refracts and partly curtails the access of light, but still leaves sufficient for the legitimate uses of the dominant tenement.[1] In such a situation, it would be an absurd outcome if, in order not to lose the entirety of his right to ancient lights, under s 4 of the Prescription Act, a householder were compelled to institute proceedings to seek to prevent his neighbour constructing a partially transparent roof, to which the householder might not otherwise object and which might be of great value to the neighbour.[2]

---

[1]   *Tisdall v McArthur and Co (Steel and Metal) Ltd and Mossop* (1951) 84 ILTR 173.

[2]   (1951) 84 ILTR 173 at 177, per Kingsmill Moore J: 'In the absence of any authority or any convincing argument, I refuse to be the first to lay down a proposition which seems to me not required by principle and calculated to work great inconvenience in practice.'

Crown and State property

[5.40] The failure to include land owned by the Crown in s 3, unlike in ss 1 and 2, means that a right to light cannot be acquired by the Prescription Act over land owned by the Crown in Northern Ireland.[1] This used to be perceived as also the case in relation to property owned by the State in the Republic of Ireland. However, it has now been established that the omission of specific reference to the State in a statute does not imply that the State will not be bound by the provisions of that statute.[2]

It remains technically possible for a right to light to be obtained over land owned by the Crown in Northern Ireland, either through common law prescription or presumed lost grant. A claim for a right to light by prescription at common law would be most unlikely of success, since it would require acceptance that an aperture in a building had existed since 1189.

---

[1] See Stroud 'Rights of Light Over Crown Land' (1942) 58 LQR 495. Also, *Wheaton v Maple and Co* [1893] 3 Ch 48.

[2] *Howard v Commissioners of Public Works* [1994] 1 IR 122.

Rights of Light Act (Northern Ireland) 1961

[5.41] In Northern Ireland, the accruing of a right to light, pursuant to s 3 of the Prescription Act, can be prevented otherwise than through the physical interposition of an obstacle in the path of the light gaining access to the aspirant dominant tenement, provided that the apprehending servient owner takes action prior to the expiry of 19 years from when the access of light commenced to be enjoyed.

This is provided for by the Rights of Light Act (Northern Ireland) 1961.[1] Following the cessation of hostilities in the Second World War, numerous edifices and structures throughout the United Kingdom lay demolished or in ruins, in the wake of enemy aerial bombardments throughout the years of conflict. Buildings left standing but in ruins, were more often knocked down than reconstructed. Depressed economic conditions and a variety of building regulations resulted in the derelict condition of many properties persisting for close on 20 years after the war had ended. The eventual outcome of this enduring stasis would have been the burgeoning of statutory entitlement to access of light on the part of properties contiguous to sites left derelict since the end of the war. Throughout the 1950s, the grim expedient to prevent this, adopted by several owners of derelict properties, was to construct large unlovely hoardings that would block out the light from adjacent buildings, to the same extent as effected by the structures that formerly stood there. Several of these hoardings, still extant in the early 1960s, in particular besmirched the aspect of the city of Belfast.

---

[1] c 18 of 1961, through a combination of the provisions of s 2(3) and s 2(4).

[5.42] In 1961, the parliament of Northern Ireland,[1] introduced legislation which obviated the need for the ongoing erection, and maintaining erect, of physical obstructions to prevent the accrual of a right to light. Similar legislation had been enacted in Great Britain two years earlier. A short-lived expedient was the temporary extension of the prescriptive period of 20 years, under s 3 of the Prescription Act, to 27 years in respect of actions commenced by not later than 31 December 1962.[2] This effectively precluded, until the commencement of 1963, the taking of any action in relation to a right to light acquired by statutory prescription as a result of the bombing campaign during the Second World War.

---

[1] Pursuant to a power conferred in the Rights of Light Act 1959, s 6.
[2] Prescription Act, s 3, repealed in 1976.

[5.43] The principal provisions of the Rights of Light Act (Northern Ireland) 1961,[1] which are still extant and still relevant – from the effects of terrorist bombing campaigns that marred the last three decades of the twentieth century[2] – enable the prevention of the accruing of a right to light through the registration, in the Statutory Charges Register,[3] of a light obstruction notice.[4]

The act provides that '[f]or the purpose of preventing the access and use of light from being taken to be enjoyed without interruption'[5] the owner of a servient tenement over which light passes to a dominant building, defined as 'a dwellinghouse, workshop or other building'[6] can register a notice:

> '... intended to be equivalent to the obstruction of the access of light to the dominant building across the servient land which would be caused by the erection, in such position on the servient land as is specified in the application, of one, and not more than one, opaque structure of unlimited height.'[7]

Notice of the intended registration must be given to all parties likely to be affected by it[8] and must also be published in a local newspaper.[9] The application for registration must clearly identify both the servient land and the dominant building in a map attached to the application[10] and also the identities and addresses of the parties most liable to be affected by the application.[11]

---

[1] These came into effect on 1 March 1962. See Obayan *The Rights of Light Act (Northern Ireland) 1961* (1964) 15 NILQ 248.
[2] Although nowhere in the statute is it stated that a designated servient tenement requires to be a derelict or bomb-destroyed site.
[3] Established by the Statutory Charges Register (Northern Ireland) Act 1951.
[4] Wylie *Irish Land Law* p 398.
[5] Borrowing the exact words of s 3 of the Prescription Act.
[6] Rights of Light Act (Northern Ireland) 1961, s 1(1).
[7] Section 1(3)(f).
[8] Section 1(4)(a).
[9] Section 1(4)(b).
[10] Section 1(3)(c).
[11] Section 1(3)(e).

[5.44] Once the notice has been registered, it has the same effect, in relation to the acquisition of a right to light, as if an actual opaque structure of unlimited height, had been erected on the identified servient tenement, by the applicant, on the date of registration of the notice,[1] and remained there for the period of a year or until the registration is earlier cancelled.[2] If nothing is done by the owner of any dominant tenement affected by the notice, then after the expiry of a year from the date of registration, the enjoyment of the right to light will be deemed to have been interrupted for a full period of one year as provided in s 4 of the Prescription Act.[3] The bringing of an action by an interested party, during the period that the notice remains registered, counters the presumption of acquiescence in the interruption that commences from the date of registration of the notice.[4] From the date that any action is brought, a party is no longer deemed to be acquiescing in the obstruction.[5] However, if the court holds against any claim made by a dominant owner, then the fact of bringing of the action is disregarded, and the acquiescence is deemed to have endured from the date of registration of the notice.[6]

---

[1] Rights of Light Act (Northern Ireland) 1961, s 2(1)(a).
[2] Sections 2(1)(b) and 2(2).
[3] Section 2(6)(a).
[4] Section 2(6)(a) and (b).
[5] Section 2(6)(c).
[6] Section 2(6).

[5.45] Any party on whom a notice has been served, and who would have had a right to light, now effectively obstructed by the registration of the notice, is entitled to a right of action, on foot of the registration, provided an action is initiated while the notice is still current.[1] In any action taken, the plaintiff shall be entitled to 'such declaration as the court may consider appropriate in the circumstances', including an order directing the notice to be cancelled or varied.[2] There is special provision for affected parties whose right to light would have accrued during the year for which the notice is registered: such a person is deemed to have commenced their continuous enjoyment of a right to light a year earlier than they in fact commenced it,[3] so that their right to take an action during the currency of the notice is not negatived by the deemed interruption's occurring in the final year of the 20 years' prescriptive enjoyment, which otherwise would deprive them of any statutory redress.

---

[1] Rights of Light Act (Northern Ireland) 1961, s 2(3).
[2] Section 2(5).
[3] Section 2(4).

[5.46] The saving against acquiring a right to light by prescription over land owned by the Crown, in s 3 of the Prescription Act, is preserved, but the acquisition of a right to light on behalf of Crown land can be resisted through the registering of an obstruction notice as provided by the act.[1] Crown land includes land owned, or beneficially enjoyed by, a department of the government of Northern Ireland.[2]

---

[1] Rights of Light Act (Northern Ireland) 1961, s 4(1) and (2).
[2] Section 4(3).

Chapter 6

Extinguishment and Abandonment

Introduction

[6.01] For the purpose of this chapter, the word 'extinguishment' will be used to describe a situation where an easement is automatically obliterated, from the legal consequence of a particular act or state of affairs: such as, where excessive user by the dominant owner destroys the easement, or where there is unity of ownership and possession of the dominant and servient tenements, with the result that ongoing enjoyment is no longer in the nature of an intangible right involving two properties.

The word 'abandonment' will be taken as a virtual synonym for implied release – as where the dominant owner fails to use the easement for such a significant period, and in such circumstances, that the abandonment of the easement may reasonably be inferred; or where the dominant owner by his actions manifests an intention never to use the easement again, nor to assign a right to its enjoyment to any other party.[1]

---

[1] *Tehidy Minerals Ltd v Norman* [1971] 2 QB 528; *Gotobed v Pridmore* (1970) 115 SJ 78; *Williams v Usherwood* (1983) 45 P & CR 235, to the effect that an easement can only be deemed to be abandoned where the conduct of the dominant owner makes it clear that he does not intend to use the easement again or to transfer it to someone else; approved by O'Hanlon J in *Carroll v Sheridan and Sheehan* [1984] ILRM 451 at 459.

[6.02] An easement can be released, just as it can be created, expressly. This must be by deed. However, similarly as with the claimed creation of an easement, the preponderance of issues that fall to be litigated on its demise, involve circumstances where there has not been an express release of an easement, and the fact of its being either destroyed or impliedly released is in contention.

Extinguishment by Statute

[6.03] An easement can be extinguished by the express or implied operation of statute. Throughout the eighteenth century and the early nineteenth century the vast number of private inclosure acts, enacted in Great Britain and Ireland, invariably provided for the stopping up and extinguishing of a myriad rights of way. In more modern times, the most frequently encountered statutory extinguishment of easements is in the guise of compulsory purchase legislation.

[6.04] In Ireland the Land Purchase Acts of the late nineteenth century, principally through the Landed Estates Court (Ireland) Act 1858, have had the effect of passing title to statutory purchasers freed and discharged from all liabilities, including easements, which are not expressly provided for, or in respect of which a purchaser is not reasonably put on notice. The Landed Estates Court (Ireland) Act 1858 has been interpreted as only passing by way of deed such rights as are expressed or referred to in the deed, but otherwise freed from all equities, charges and easements.[1] The presumption is that prior to the conveyance all possible easements have been looked into and all adjoining landowners invited to set out such claims as they believe they possess.[2]

On the other hand, where a statutory conveyance of the fee simple is made subject to all leases and tenancies listed in a schedule,[3] if the reference to a lease in such schedule merely describes the land itself, its quantity and the particulars of the lease, but does not in any way elaborate the lease's terms, then the lease itself must be consulted in order to ascertain the terms thereby incorporated into the statutory conveyance. Where the lease has to be so consulted, rights unalluded to which are incidental to easements set out in the lease will also be preserved.[4] Otherwise the elaborating of the terms of the lease in the schedule is deemed to describe such terms conclusively, and any rights contained in terms not so set out are extinguished.[5]

---

[1] In *Re Tottenham's Estate* (1869) Ir 3 Eq 528.

[2] *Ingham v Mackey* [1898] 1 IR 272. In this case the conveyance had been made subject to rights of way. The easement being contended for was a right to store eels in perforated tanks at the bottom of the Shannon and it was held that this had been extinguished by the statutory conveyance.

[3] Landed Estates Court (Ireland) Act 1858, s 54.

[4] *Middleton v Clarence* (1877) IR 11 CL 499. In this a right to throw quarry spoil on adjoining lands was deemed a necessary incident to the grant of a right to quarry by lease. May CJ held that 'this incidental accessorial right or easement' was not extinguished by a Landed Estates Court conveyance in the schedule to which the terms of the relevant lease had not been set out.

[5] Landed Estates Court (Ireland) Act 1858, s 61, as interpreted by *De Vesci v O'Kelly* (1869) IR 4 CL 269.

[6.05] Although the reservation of a right of way for foot passage only in a Landed Estates Court conveyance does not entitle the dominant owner to any enlargement of the easement so described, yet the right of way thus limited to foot passage only is not extinguished merely because the dominant owner may bring proceedings alleging that a challenged obstruction now renders the right of way more difficult for the rolling of trucks and the carrying of burdens.[1]

---

[1] *Austin v Scottish Widows' Assurance Society* (1881) 8 LR Ir 197, 385.

[6.06] The Property (Northern Ireland) Order 1978[1] contains specific provision for the extinguishment of easements, and also of profits *à prendre* appurtenant and profits *à prendre* in gross, upon the application of any interested party to the Lands Tribunal, where the effect of such easement or profit is found unreasonably to inhibit the enjoyment of land. The principal application of the Property Order 1978, in the context of this work, is to the extinguishment of covenants, in which regard it will be considered more fully.

---

[1]   1978 No 459 (NI 4). See para **[18.03]** ff.

Implied Abandonment Due to Non-user

Acts necessary to evidence abandonment

[6.07] Non-user of an easement for a considerable period, accompanied by circumstances that evince an intention never to use it again, will warrant an inference that the easement has been abandoned. There is no specific minimum time established to support the implication of abandonment, although it seems as if, by analogy with statutory prescription and presumed lost grant, exceptional circumstances will be required to warrant the conclusion of abandonment where there has been non-user for no more than twenty years. The decided cases also demonstrate that some additional act or circumstance, apart from mere non-user, is required to establish conclusively an intention to abandon.

It will be recalled that one of the indicia of an easement is that it accommodates the dominant tenement.[1] If a particular easement is judicially found no longer to accommodate the dominant tenement, because the dominant tenant has evinced, through prolonged desuetude and kindred behaviour, that the accommodation is neither required nor used, then the erstwhile easement will cease to partake of the character necessary to remain one. Accordingly, it will be deemed to have been abandoned. The law frowns upon the perpetuation of nugatory burdens on property.[2]

---

[1]   See para **[1.04]**, **[1.07]**.
[2]   See discussion in *Gale on Easements* (eds, Gaunt and Morgan, 16th edn, 1997) Sweet & Maxwell, p 429.

[6.08] In *Mulville v Fallon*[1] the plaintiff had taken a lease of lands, containing a covenant to erect a dwellinghouse, subject to a right of passage in favour of another premises. In time he discovered that the reserved right of passage would have been inconvenient for the dwellinghouse he proposed to build, in accordance with the covenant, and so entered into a parol agreement with the lessor to change the site of the passage reserved by him. Between 1844 and 1871 any person entitled to use the passage reserved under the lease, made use of the substituted one, and no claim was ever made to the original until 1872, and then not by the lessor. Chatterton V-C held that the original passage had been abandoned. Intermittent user was not abandonment of an easement; but, held the Vice Chancellor, where a way was substituted through parol agreement by another one, subsequent non-user of the original way accompanied by acts warranting the inference that it was intended to release the existing right, also warranted the conclusion that the original way could not be resumed. The primary test is one of intention:

> 'The extinguishment of easements, however created, may be by either actual or implied release; the latter will be sufficiently proved by a cessation of user, coupled with any act clearly indicative of an intention to abandon the right; and if such intention be thus shown, the duration of the cesser need not be for twenty years or any other defined period.'[2]

[1]   *Mulville v Fallon* (1872) IR 6 Eq 458.
[2]   (1872) IR 6 Eq 458 at 463. See also 'Extinguishment of Easements by Abandonment' (1942) 76 ILTSJ 189; Dowling 'Once a Highway Always a Highway' (1994) 45 NILQ 403.

Alternative arrangements by dominant owner

[6.09] It seems, however, that the mere fact of using an alternative right of way to the original does not necessarily justify the implication of abandonment. In *Stevenson v Parke*,[1] the dominant owner had a right of way to another part of his own land through the adjoining land of the servient owner. When the servient owner perceived that the dominant owner was no longer using the right of way, but instead had discovered a different way of access to his other lands and had even had it surfaced, he erected posts and fences on that part of his lands through which the dominant owner's right had run. An action by the servient owner for trespass when the dominant owner took the posts and fences down failed. The High Court held, that there was no evidence of abandonment, merely that the way had not been used for a considerable time; that non-user alone was not proof of abandonment; and that the dominant owner had only used the alternative way because it was more convenient.

[1]   *Stevenson v Parke* [1932] LJ Ir 228. It should be noted that this case has been most scantly reported, and any seeming incompatibility between it and other cases on the issue of implied abandonment arising from non-user are perhaps ascribable to this reporting deficiency.

[6.10] However, if the dominant owner seems to acquiesce in the blocking up of a right of way, inaction by him until many years afterwards will be sufficient to infer an intention to abandon. In *Haugh v Heskin*,[1] a lease for lives of December 1828 had reserved a right of way over the demised property. In 1947 a door leading from an adjacent road to the reserved right of way was built up with concrete blocks, to the full knowledge of the person entitled to the right. An action taken by the same person less than 20 years later failed to revive the right. According to Kenny J, as the dominant owner had acquiesced in the building of the wall, he was deemed to have abandoned any right he may have had.

In *Solomon v Red Bank Restaurant Ltd*,[2] a right of way to a chute giving access to the plaintiff's enclosed yard had not been used by him for 40 years and had in fact been shut up on the plaintiff's side. Johnston J held that the easement would have been extinguished were it not for the fact that the defendants, who disturbed it, had bought the freehold reversion of the property, and thereby taken over a covenant for quiet enjoyment by which they were bound.

[1]   *Haugh v Heskin* (2 October 1967, unreported) HC.
[2]   *Solomon v Red Bank Restaurant Ltd* [1938] IR 793.

Alternative arrangements by servient owner

[6.11] Alternative user of the former servient tenement, and the absence of objection to this by the dominant owner, is another circumstance from which an intention to abandon may be inferred, even though the former dominant owner may at some future time wish to resume the easement.

[6.12] In *O'Gara v Murray*[1] the plaintiff and the defendant were adjoining property owners in Connolly Street, Sligo. The defendant – the putative dominant tenant – owned a licensed premises. On account of the recent blocking of commercial access at the front of his premises, he had taken to using a way at the back. The defendant did not have clear title to the way, although a gap in the rear boundary of his property, that appeared on a map annexed to a lease of 1912, suggested that some sort of way had been intended for access. McCarthy J found that there had, in fact, been such a way, and that it had been used by the then owner of the defendant's licensed premises until the early 1950s. After that it had become overgrown, and was cultivated as a vegetable garden by the plaintiff who also built a wall where the gap had been. Part of the area was used as a public dumping ground. When the defendant discovered the need for access to the rear of his premises, he knocked down the wall and opened an entrance road.

The plaintiff secured an injunction and damages. In relation to the abandonment of a right of way,[2] McCarthy J observed:

> 'A right-of-way or other easement may be released expressly or impliedly; such implied release may arise where it is established that there was an intention on the part of the owner of the easement to abandon it. Mere cesser of user may not be enough; cesser of user coupled with incidents indicating abandonment may well be enough.'[3]

The proven alternative user of the servient tenement since the 1950s sustained a finding that the right of way had 'long since been released by cesser of use and surrounding circumstances.'[4]

---

[1] *O'Gara v Murray* (10 November 1988, unreported) HC.

[2] Adapting the statement of the law by O'Hanlon J, in *Carroll v Sheridan and Sheehan* [1984] ILRM 451 at 459: 'With regard to a private right of way, the authorities appear to establish that mere evidence of non-user is not sufficient to bring about the extinction of rights of way or other 'discontinuous' easements.' Referring to the decision of the Court of Appeal in *Tehidy Minerals v Norman* [1971] 2 QB 528, O'Hanlon J noted that abandonment can only arise where the person entitled 'has demonstrated a fixed intention not at any time thereafter to assert the right himself or to attempt to transmit it to anyone else.' See also *Peilow v ffrench O'Carroll* (1972) 106 ILTR 29, and the discussion in Bland *The Law of Easements and Profits à Prendre* (1997) Sweet & Maxwell, pp 287–288.

[3] (10 November 1988, unreported) HC at p 2.

[4] (10 November 1988, unreported) HC at p 2.

Disuse

[6.13] In *Cullen v Dublin Corpn*,[1] Kingsmill Moore J, in the Supreme Court, held that merely because a mill adjacent to a watercourse had fallen into a ruinous state, having not been used from 1884 to 1960, was no justification for inferring an abandonment, especially as all the other facilities to operate the mill were in working order and the installation of appropriate machinery would also have enabled the production of electrical power. 'Disuse ... is not abandonment. There can be no abandonment without an intention to abandon and though long disuse may raise the presumption of such an intention the circumstances of the disuse must be considered to see if such an intention should be implied.'[2] The fact that a lessee took no steps to embark on repair work did not justify imputing an intention to abandon. Even if there were a case that it should, the owner in fee would have to be found to have acquiesced in the abandonment by his lessee in order for a similar intention to abandon to be imputed to him.[3] It is clear that Kingsmill Moore J was influenced by the seeming absurdity of an intention being imputed to the owner of a valuable right to abandon that right which could significantly enhance the sale value of his lands. This makes eminent sense. The owner of a valuable, if intangible, adjunct to his land, ought not to be imagined as forsaking it lightly. The mere fact that it might not be required at one time, cannot be construed as implying that it will never be required at another time.

---

[1]   *Cullen v Dublin Corpn* (22 July 1960, unreported) SC.
[2]   (22nd July 1960, unreported) SC at p 23.
[3]   (22nd July 1960, unreported) SC at p 24.

Delay in enforcement

[6.14] Where, upon the purchase of land stated to be subject to rights of watercourses running through the land, the purchaser inadvertently blocks up the outflow of a neighbour's watercourse, a delay by that neighbour in clearing the gap is not sufficient discontinuance of user to evince an intention to abandon the watercourse.[1]

---

[1]   *Craig v McCance* (1910) 44 ILTR 90.

Partial non-user

[6.15] Mere non-user by the dominant owner of the easement for part of the purpose for which it was created does not give rise to an abandonment either whole or partial. In *Corr v Bradshaw*,[1] the owners of a right of way at Ulverton Road in Dalkey, Co Dublin, from the Harbour Road to the back of their premises over other premises, were jointly responsible for the surfacing and maintenance of the way. They agreed to reduce the size of a gateway across the way on the basis that all rights heretofore enjoyed would be preserved. Evidence was adduced that when the right had originally been granted there had been occasional use of the way by both the dominant and servient owners for the passage of motor vehicles, but less so in the recent past. Fitzgerald J, in the Supreme Court, held that there was nothing from which to infer an intention to abandon any part of the right of way, adding:

'... there is no legal basis upon which it could be held that the grantee of an easement can abandon portion of his right while retaining another portion of it.'[2]

1   *Corr v Bradshaw* (18 July 1967, unreported) SC.
2   (18 July 1967, unreported) SC at pp 3–4.

Extinguishment Due to Excessive User

[6.16] An easement will be extinguished by operation of law if the user exerted upon the servient tenement becomes so excessive that it is tantamount to changing the character of the servitude altogether. The test was succinctly stated by Grove LJ, in the English Court of Appeal, in *Harvey v Walters*,[1] quoted with approval by Barton J in *Craig v McCance*,[2] '... that there must be an additional or different servitude, and the change must be material either in the nature or the quantum of the servitude imposed ...' in order for the easement to be destroyed.

1   *Harvey v Walters* (1872) LR 8 CP 162.
2   *Craig v McCance* (1910) 44 ILTR 90.

[6.17] In *Craig v McCance*[1] the plaintiff in 1905 had purchased a small piece of land near Donaghadee, Co Down, subject to all existing rights over the streams and watercourses that ran through it. The plaintiff's land comprised a downward sloping hill with a stream at its bottom. Above the plaintiff's land ran a small road, with the defendant's field above that again. The drains from the defendant's land led under the road and discharged into a watercourse on the plaintiff's land and so on down to the stream. The defendant's drains had been unscoured for a long time, so that they had become overgrown and did not work freely. The defendant's eventual scouring of his drains prompted the plaintiff to sue, on the basis that the flow of water had significantly increased and was placing an unreasonably greater burden on the plaintiff's lands. Barton J was satisfied that the defendant had not deepened the drains. The increased flow of water which resulted from the scouring was not such an additional burden as the plaintiff could complain of. Neither the nature or the quantity of the servitude had been appreciably increased. Indeed, it was more probable, according to Barton J, that the servient owner might have good cause to complain, if the drains continued not to be scoured and he were anxious to maintain a normal flow of water. Scouring merely restored the drains to their normal condition.

In the course of his judgment, Barton J distinguished the English case of *Cawkswell v Russell*,[2] in which the easement had effectively been transformed by user, from a right to discharge clean water to a right to discharge dirty water, thereby fundamentally altering its character. In that case, since it was not possible to sever the lawful user from the excessive user, the servient owner was allowed prevent the entire discharge.[3]

1   *Craig v McCance* (1910) 44 ILTR 90.
2   *Cawkswell v Russell* (1856) 26 LJ Ex 34.
3   In distinguishing *Cawkswell v Russell*, Barton J commented that his decision might have been different if the right to discharge water had been specifically with reference to the size of the culvert or if the defendant dominant owner had alleged that his easement was to discharge all

'surface drainage water within the limits of ordinary and reasonable husbandry.' The principal issue was whether the burden of the easement had been materially increased.

Severance of additional user

[6.18] Where additional user is of a kind that alters the nature of the easement, imposing an unreasonable extra burden on the servient tenement, and is capable of being identified and severed, the courts will prevent such additional user from being continued, but the authorised user will be preserved. Where it is not possible to decouple the permitted from the unreasonable additional user, the easement will be extinguished. Accordingly, excessive user which is capable of being specifically identified and restrained does not itself destroy the easement, but will be restrained.[1]

---

[1]   *Calders v Murtagh* (1939) 5 Ir Jur Rep 19.

[6.19] However, the mere fact that the dominant tenement may be sold to a purchaser who is likely to increase the burden on the servient tenement by excessive user does not give rise to a cause of action until such excessive user has taken place:

> 'The nature and extent of such additional burden must necessarily depend upon the purpose for which the purchaser or lessee uses the lands and the volume and nature of the traffic which might seek to use the passage in exercise of the right. Whether the right-of-way is or has been excessively used is a question which cannot be determined until [there is] evidence as to the extent of the user, actual or prospective, by the purchaser or lessee ... has been established.'

per Fitzgerald J in *Corr v Bradshaw*.[1]

---

[1]   *Corr v Bradshaw* (18 July 1967, unreported) SC at p 4.

Change of user of dominant tenement

[6.20] The fact of change of user of the dominant tenement does not necessarily destroy the easement provided the burden on the servient tenement has not been increased. In *Pullan v The Roughfort Bleaching and Dyeing Co (Ltd)*,[1] a case involving a right to use a watercourse, the servient tenant alleged that a scutch-mill formerly operated by the dominant tenant's predecessor had not been used since his death, and that the dominant tenant had set up a bleachworks which was an entirely new operation.[2] Chatterton V-C held that there was nothing to suggest that it had ever been intended to abandon the supply of water to the scutch-mill and that the mill stream had continued to supply water to it until the servient tenants changed their pipes and so caused a diminution in the water coming to the dominant tenant's mill:

> 'The bleachworks were substituted for the dairy and carpentry works previously existing, and the same supply of water theretofore used for the latter was applied to the working of the former ... I am of opinion that he was justified in applying it in any way that was not more onerous to the servient tenement.'[3]

---

¹ *Pullan v The Roughfort Bleaching and Dyeing Co (Ltd)* (1888) 21 LR Ir 73.
² See *Luttrel's Case* (1601) 4 Rep 86a, in which it was held by the English Court of Exchequer Chamber that conversion from a fulling mill to a grist mill was one of quality, and not of substance.
³ (1888) 21 LR Ir 73 at 90.

Change of method of user of dominant tenement

[6.21] An additional burden, potentially rendering the easement unenforceable, can be imposed on the servient tenement where the method only, and not the nature, of the user is changed: McDermott J, in the Northern Ireland Court of King's Bench, in *West v Great Northern Railway (Ireland)*:[1]

> '... the burden of an easement may be increased by more than a change of purpose. The same purpose may be pursued more intensively or the vehicles or implements used in the enjoyment of the easement may have so altered as to increase the burden by their physical effect or presence on the servient tenement.'[2]

---

¹ *West v Great Northern Railway (Ireland)* [1946] NI 55. See also Abbott, 'Extinguishment of Easements by Impossibility of User' (1913) 13 Col L Rev 409.
² [1946] NI 55 at 61.

[6.22] In *West v Great Northern Railway (Ireland)*, the plaintiff was the owner of a farm bisected by the defendant's railway line. In accordance with the Railway Clauses Consolidation Act 1845, the defendant was obliged to make and maintain 'convenient passages' over the railway line, to accommodate the owners of land traversed by it. This had been done in the present case by devising a crossing of loose ballast which comprised broken stones, up to two inches in diameter, placed between the metals and on either side of the tracks. An accident occurred when a tractor and connected rake owned by the plaintiff got stuck in trying to cross the track and were hit by a train. It was found that the stones had not been tightly compacted, and that more of the side surface of the rails was exposed than was necessary for the rolling of the trains. The combination of needlessly exposed rail and comparatively soft filling made it likely that the tractor's wheels would sink.

The authorities considered by McDermott J demonstrated that the extent of the statutory duty to provide the accommodation must be related to the use of the lands at the time of its provision, or to any alteration or extension of that use then reasonably within the contemplation of the parties. Furthermore, the landowner receiving the accommodation was not entitled to use it so as substantially to increase the burden of the easement by altering or enlarging its character, nature or extent as enjoyed at the time of construction.

[6.23] The principal issue was whether the implements in use at the time of the accident, specifically the tractor which would not have been invented at the time of the original accommodation, so increased the burden on the servient tenement as to remove liability from the defendant for failure to maintain the accommodation at a satisfactory standard.

McDermott J held that the burden had not been increased and that the defendant was liable. The wheels which had caught the rail were of iron, but no heavier necessarily than other wheels might have been, and no more prone to sink. 'This whole question does not turn on new methods, but on the results of new methods.' The accident which had befallen the tractor and rake could as easily have happened to a horse-drawn wagon.

[6.24] An increase in trade by the dominant owner, designed to compensate for adverse changes in market trends, as where the owner of licensed premises opens an additional lounge bar in her public house in order to prevent traditional custom wending elsewhere, does not in law increase the burden on the servient tenement, merely because the anticipated swell of customers will pass over a right of way through a side entrance beneath it.[1] In *Connell v Porter*, Teevan J, in the High Court, observed: '... mere increase of custom in the same trade cannot in law adversely affect the plaintiff's rights if these be no more than rights over private property of another.'[2]

---

[1]   *Connell v Porter* (21 December 1967, unreported) HC, (18 December 1972, unreported) SC.

[2]   (21 December 1967, unreported) HC at p 20. In the appeal to the Supreme Court (18 December 1972, unreported) SC, Ó Dálaigh CJ at 4, noted that the differences between a lounge bar and an 'old-time bar', though of some cultural significance, were superficial in legal terms. Customers, of whatever sex or social class, in either form of imbibing emporium are there to have a drink. Accordingly, the introduction of a lounge bar did not constitute an alteration in user; nor could an analogy be drawn between this and the conversion of flats into a women's club, as in *Keith v Twentieth Century Club Ltd* (1904) 73 LJ Ch 545. See also Bland *The Law of Easements and Profits à Prendre* p 293.

Extinguishment Due to Unity of Ownership and Possession

[6.25] Where the dominant and servient tenements become vested in ownership and possession in one person an easement is normally extinguished, because the subsequent enjoyment of what was formerly an intangible right, over one property for the benefit of another property, is now an incident of the ownership of one property only. Where the unity of ownership, however, is of the freehold of the dominant tenement and a lease of the servient tenement, an easement is suspended during the unified ownership and resumes after the expiry of the lease of the servient tenement.[1]

---

[1]   *Nugent v Cooper* (1855) 7 Ir Jur OS 112.

[6.26] There is at the very least some doubt as to whether a short-lived unity of ownership and possession of the fee simple, between the expiry of a yearly tenancy and the granting of a new tenancy, will extinguish an easement where the easement was originally created by implication as being necessary for the beneficial enjoyment of the demised premises.[1] In *Kavanagh v Coal Mining Co of Ireland*,[2] a yearly tenancy had been enjoyed pursuant to an agreement for lease of 1802 which was never executed. This parol yearly tenancy determined upon the execution of a formal lease in 1848. The fee simple owner of the store was also the fee simple owner of the land over which the claimed right of way passed. O'Brien J held that there had not in fact been unity of possession, but, on the question of the possible extinguishment of the right of way, observed:

> 'It is moreover difficult to see how this question of extinguishment, by unity of possession, can arise with reference to a right or easement which is claimed ... upon the ground of its being necessary for the convenient enjoyment of the premises demised by a lease as in their then condition, and where the lessor is also owner in fee of the land over which such right or easement is claimed. The very fact of his being owner, both of the demised premises and of the land over which the easement is claimed, is a reason why he should not be allowed to interrupt that easement, when it is necessary for the reasonable and convenient enjoyment of the demised premises in their then condition.'[3]

---

[1]   In *Pheysey v Vicary* (1847) 16 M & W 484 Alderson B observed that an easement of absolute necessity to the dominant tenement would not be extinguished by unity of ownership of both tenements.

[2]   *Kavanagh v Coal Mining Co of Ireland* (1861) 14 ICLR 82.

[3]   (1861) 14 ICLR 82 at 95.

[6.27] A landlord of lands comprising both the dominant and servient tenements, if he accepts the surrender of lands to which a right of way is appurtenant, can demise them again by parol with the benefit of the right of way. So too if such a landlord demise a dominant tenement to which a right of way is appurtenant, at a time when the servient tenement is vacant or occupied by the landlord himself; then regardless of how many subsequent tenancies there are of either tenement, the easement originally created will continue to have legal effect.[1] The mere fact of enlargement of the dominant owner's interest from sub-lessee to fee simple owner does not extinguish any easement held by the dominant owner on foot of the sublease which has since merged with the freehold.[2]

---

[1]   *Timmons v Hewitt* (1888) 22 LR Ir 627 at 640, per Palles CB.

[2]   In *Corr v Bradshaw* (18 July 1967, unreported) SC, an application by the defendants to amend their defence to include this very argument was refused.

Extinguishment by Positive Act of Servient Owner Inconsistent with Easement

[6.28] An easement, as has been shown, can be deemed to be abandoned due to non-user by the dominant owner, when accompanied by circumstances demonstrating an inferable intention to abandon. In certain instances, a like inference can be drawn from the actions of the servient owner and a failure to respond, or delay in responding, by the dominant owner.

[6.29] In *Tottenham v Byrne*,[1] the servient owner, through whose lands ran a laneway which had been reserved to his lessor in a lease of the lands in 1805, and over which another party also had a right of way, knocked down the fences bounding the laneway and erected a wall in front of a well at the end of it. An action brought over 20 years later by the successor-in-title of the original lessor failed. On account of the reservation of the laneway to the lessor, the primary issue in this case was the application of a limitation statute and not simply the extinguishment of a right of way. According to Deasy B, however, the principles underlying each are the same:

'... there must be not only a cessation or discontinuance of possession by one person, but an acquisition of possession by another ... possession is evidenced by user; and there is here, I think, a user which indicates an assumption or taking of possession by the defendant, as well as a discontinuance of possession by the plaintiff.'[2]

---

[1]   *Tottenham v Byrne* (1861) 12 ICLR 376.
[2]   (1861) 12 ICLR 376 at 385.

[6.30] Where the alleged servient tenement, despite being used at one time by the dominant owner, is then subsequently used for a different purpose by a next door neighbour, without demur by the dominant owner who ceases to use the servient tenement at all, an action over 30 years later by the dominant owner to reinstate his former user as of right because it then suits him will not succeed.[1]

---

[1]   *O'Gara v Murray* (10 November 1988, unreported) HC.

Acquiescence and encouragement of expenditure

[6.31] Where a right of way originally provided for by deed is not used but is substituted by parol by another way, in the laying out of which the servient owner incurs considerable expense, having been led to believe that the original way would be discontinued, after almost 30 years of non-user the original way cannot be reinstated.

[6.32] This is demonstrated in *Mulville v Fallon*.[1] In 1844 the plaintiff had taken a lease of building land in Gort, Co Galway from Lord Gort, subject to a right of passage leading from the Bridge House in Queen Street, which was owned by an order of nuns, to adjoining premises. The plaintiff covenanted in his lease to erect a dwellinghouse, but found that the reserved right of passage would have been inconvenient for his planned dwellinghouse, and, accordingly, entered into an arrangement with Lord Gort, his lessor, to change the site of the passage. This was done, and the plaintiff then built the house covenanted for, into which he subsequently moved to live. The plaintiff's boundary wall ran across the grounds of the originally proposed passage.

In 1851 Lord Gort's estate was sold in the Encumbered Estates Court. Between 1844 and 1871 anyone entitled to use the passage described in the lease to the plaintiff, used the substituted one, and no claim was ever made to use the original. In 1869 the plaintiff applied to the Landed Estates Court to sell his Gort premises, but neglected to tell his solicitor about the substituted right of passage, so that the abstract of title lodged by the solicitors referred to the old right of passage in the lease of 1844. The nuns in the Bridge House Convent (the property in favour of which the right of passage had originally been reserved) expressed an interest in purchasing the plaintiff's property, but negotiations for the sale fell through. The nuns subsequently bought other property in Queen Street, which they turned into schools; and since these were opposite the location of the original right of passage, of which they had, seemingly, only become aware through reading the documentation for the proposed sale of the plaintiff's property, they knocked down portion of the plaintiff's wall which covered the original passage, and also broke open a gate.

The plaintiff sought an injunction to compel the nuns (the defendant was the Superioress of the convent) to rebuild the wall, and sued for damages.

---

1   *Mulville v Fallon* (1872) IR 6 Eq 458.

[6.33] Counsel for the defendant urged that the plaintiff was merely a parol licensee of the right to use the substituted passage, and that an easement, except where it arose by presumed lost grant or prescription, could only be created and discharged by deed. Chatterton V-C declined to hold with this contention, maintaining that the original easement had been abandoned by non-user of the reserved way and the substitution of an alternative one. While accepting that the primary test is one of intention, Chatterton V-C observed that in the instant case one had also to consider the significance of a licensee, with the approval of the licensor, having expended money on the faith of the licence. Lord Gort had given the plaintiff a licence to close up the passage, and the plaintiff, with the approval of Lord Gort, had expended money on the construction of the new passage and deprived himself of the right to use the old one.

In such circumstances, the plaintiff was held entitled to equitable redress in the form of a perpetual injunction. This case being decided some years prior to the passing of the Supreme Court of Judicature (Ireland) Act 1877, Chatterton V-C also held that, on the balance of convenience, the plaintiff ought not to be put to the trouble of establishing his case at law before any relief could be granted to him.[1]

---

1   Quite clearly, Chatterton V-C was unimpressed with the high-handed conduct of the nuns and believed himself bound to intervene at the earliest possible opportunity, to 'prevent the continuance of acts which constitute a case of trespass under the colour of title.' See also *Winter v Brockwell* (1807) 8 East 308; *Liggins v Inge* (1831) 7 Bing 682. Davis in 'Abandonment of an Easement: Is It a Question of Intention Only?' [1995] Conv 291 at 293, makes the case that if a licence, inconsistent with an easement, is acted upon by the licensee who is also the servient owner, then the easement will be extinguished. 'It seems that the act permitted must not only cause a permanent and continuing interference with the easement, but must have involved expense so that the servient owner would suffer loss if the licence could be revoked.'

[6.34] The decision in *Mulville v Fallon*[1] is consistent with that in the English case of *Crossley and Sons Ltd v Lightowler*[2] decided some six years earlier. This involved the fouling of a watercourse by the refuse from a dye-works which had been discontinued and dismantled in 1839, and only re-opened in 1864. In the intervening years the plaintiff carpet manufacturers, who required pure water for their operation, had carried on their business availing of the selfsame watercourse. In finding that the facts warranted an inference of abandonment, Page Wood V-C held that the question of whether abandonment had taken place or not, depended not only on the length of time intervening, but also on the 'whole of the circumstances of the case'. He added:

> '… a person in possession of a certain right, and leaving the right wholly unused for a long period of time, and having given so far an encouragement to others to lay out their money, on the assumption of that right not being used, should not be allowed at any period of time to resume his former right, to the damage and injury of those who themselves have acquired a right of user, which the recurrence to this long disused easement will interfere with.'[2]

---

[1]   *Mulville v Fallon* (1872) IR 6 Eq 458.
[2]   *Crossley and Sons Ltd v Lightowler* (1866) LR 3 Eq 279.
[3]   (1866) LR 3 Eq 279 at 292–293. Upheld on appeal to the House of Lords, (1867) 2 Ch App 478. See also, for contrasting facts and outcome, *Cook v Mayor and Corporation of Bath* (1868) LR 6 Eq 177; *Gale on Easements* (16th edn, 1997) pp 449, 457.

[6.35] It is instructive, however, that in *Crossley and Sons Ltd v Lightowler* the supposed dominant owner was the party impliedly encouraging the expenditure; whereas in *Mulville v Fallon* it was the servient owner's lessor who had verbally permitted the substituted passage and thereby encouraged the expenditure. However, it seems clear from the judgment that the overall behaviour of the nuns, as much as the preliminary encouragement of Lord Gort, wrought upon Chatterton V-C in arriving at his finding.

[6.36] It is arguable that where an easement is granted by parol, with a corresponding parol licence reserved to the grantor to do an act inconsistent with the easement, the easement itself is extinguished if the licence is acted upon, but not otherwise.[1]

---

[1]   This was the point made by counsel for the party disputing the easement in *Judge v Lowe* (1873) IR 7 CL 291, see para **[5.36]** ff. The argument was not expressly rejected by Keogh J, who based his decision on the fact that a right of light had been enjoyed for more than 20 years *without* a consent or agreement in writing, and had thereby been acquired under s 3 of the Prescription Act.

[6.37] The mere fact that the owner of the dominant tenement, over 30 years before bringing an action, had acquiesced in the covering by a glass roof of the servient tenement, which was a courtyard adjacent to his premises, through which natural light had once passed, does not amount to an abandonment of the easement of light, where the owner of the dominant tenement was still able to receive adequate natural light – if less than before – through the glass roof.[1]

---

[1]   *Tisdall v McArthur and Co (Steel and Metal) Ltd and Mossop* (1951) 84 ILTR 173.

Full enjoyment by servient owner consistent with easement

[6.38] The owner of the servient tenement is entitled to the full use and enjoyment of his property consistently with any easement to which it is subject. In *Grainger v Finlay*,[1] the owner of land through which there was a right of way kept a vicious dog on his premises which put the owner of the dominant tenement in terror of using the right of way. Lefroy CJ held that an action could only be sustainable if it was clearly maintained that the dog was dangerous, and liable to cause injury either to the plaintiff or his family. This had not been sufficiently established in the pleadings. Hence, it was not illegal for the defendant to keep the dog, and nothing short of an illegal action by the defendant on his own land would give the plaintiff a cause of action. There was no illegality in keeping the dog on the defendant's land simply because a right of way passed through it.

> 'Now the defendant has as good a right to the enjoyment of his lands, in every way consistent with the law, as the plaintiff has to the right of way; and in order to deprive him of it, the plaintiff must show that the defendant has been using the land illegally, and to the prejudice of the enjoyment by the plaintiff of his right of way.'[2]

---

1   *Grainger v Finlay (*1858) 7 ICLR 417.
2   (1858) 7 ICLR 417 at 422. Just as the actions of the owner of the alleged servient tenement can have the effect of strengthening the inference of abandonment, so too such actions can prevent the acquisition of an easement by prescription in the first place, even though the enjoyment by the owner of the alleged dominant tenement has been constant throughout: *Barry v Lowry* (1877) IR 11 CL 483, para **[5.19]**.

Chapter 7

Rights of Light

Introduction

[7.01] An easement of light is a right to the lateral or horizontal access of sunlight through an aperture on the dominant tenement designed for the receiving of sunlight, after having passed unobstructed over the servient tenement. The easement subsists, not so much in the access of the light through a particular aperture, as the right to keep the channel of access over the servient tenement open and unencumbered so that the light can be admitted to the dominant tenement.[1] The right to light as an incident of property ownership itself is confined to vertically descending light.[2] The right to light other than that descending vertically necessarily entails that light passing over other land, and the easement arises in cases where that land belongs to another.[3] Unlike a right of way, or a right of access by persons, which depend on human action for their use, and hence are sometimes called discontinuous easements, a right to light does not require any positive act by the dominant owner for its enjoyment, and is sometimes known as a continuous easement. Furthermore, its effect on the owner of the servient tenement is purely negative: it prevents him from enjoying his property in any way which curtails the access of such light as the law will protect. To that extent, it is also unlike a right of way where the principle is that the servient owner is entitled to enjoy his property to the maximum extent that does not actually interfere with the easement.

---

[1] See *National Provincial Plate Glass Insurance Co v Prudential Assurance Co* (1877) 6 ChD 757; *Scott v Pape* (1886) 31 ChD 554; and *Andrews v Waite* [1907] 2 Ch 500 at 509, per Neville J: 'I think the real test is … identity of light and not identity of aperture, or entrance for the light.'

[2] Correctly stated by the author of 'Ancient Lights' (1955) 89 ILTSJ 175, thus: 'There is no natural right to light; the owner of land at common law has no right to light except in so far as ownership of lands is deemed to extend even to the heavens. He is only entitled to so much light as falls perpendicularly on his property.'

[3] A right to light can only be acquired in respect of a dominant tenement which is a building: s 3 of the Prescription (Ireland) Act 1858. This seems also to have been the previous position at common law: *Roberts v Macord* (1832) 1 Mood & R 232; *Harris v De Pinna* (1886) 33 ChD 238.

[7.02] It is perhaps not surprising that rights of light are rarely granted by deed and arise more frequently by implication or prescription. As has already been demonstrated,[1] the Prescription Act indirectly acknowledges the peculiar status of the enjoyment of light, by not obliging that its enjoyment be shown to have been as of right, providing its protection after enjoyment for the shortest period for which the statute provides.[2]

---

1   See para **[5.08]**.
2   20 years.

[7.03] Disputes concerning the access of light primarily relate to the purpose for which the premises are used and the extent to which light of a particular intensity or distribution is required. On the other hand, there are frequent dicta on the significance of the quality of light, with reference, for example, to the direction of origin of the light, the interposition of obstructive buildings and possible fluctuations in intensity throughout the day. It is intended to consider the case law on the subject by distinguishing between the amount of light and quality of light, and also noting consistent considerations which seem unique to easements of this kind. Finally, given the extent to which an easement of light can hamper the owner of the servient tenement in what otherwise would be the legitimate enjoyment of his or her property, some attention will be devoted to the attitude of the courts on the issue of redress.

Amount of Light and User of Premises

[7.04] The basic principles governing the protection of the access of light were enunciated, in 1877, by Christian LJ in *Mackey v Scottish Widows' Assurance Society*.[1] There is no greater liberty to obstruct ancient lights[2] in the city than in the country. Once the enjoyment of light has become 'ancient', the right to it becomes 'absolute and indefeasible', no matter where it is located.

> '... the amount and degree of light to which that character of ancientness can attach will generally, from the very nature of things, be less in the city than it would in the country. But once that character has been acquired, whatever be its amount, it will be entitled to the protection of law in the town as in the country, and indeed will need it more.'[3]

---

1   *Mackey v Scottish Widows' Assurance Society* (1877) IR 11 Eq 541.
2   'Ancient lights' is the term given to access of light which has the status of an easement and can therefore be protected at law. Access of light, right to which has not been granted either expressly or by implication, or which has not yet acquired the character of an easement by prescription, is unenforceable. *Higgins v Betts* [1905] 2 Ch 210.
3   (1877) IR 11 Eq 541 at 561.

[7.05] Once the easement of light has been acquired, and the right to it become absolute and indefeasible, its enjoyment will be protected regardless of the purpose for which the light is used. Neither is it open to a servient owner to allege that the acts complained of have left the dominant owner with sufficient light for his present purposes without also leaving him enough for whatever purposes it may reasonably be anticipated he might want to use the light.[1] If a person at any time does not use the full quota of light which can be protected at law, he does not thereby lose his entitlement to continue to have it protected, except in cases where an intention to abandon the right can be inferred.[2]

---

1   Per Cockburn CJ in *Moore v Hall* (1878) 3 QBD 178, per Lord Davey and Lord Lindley in
    Colls v Home and Colonial Stores Ltd [1904] AC 179.
2   See para **[6.07]** ff.

[7.06] In *Mackey v Scottish Widows' Assurance Society*[1] the plaintiff was the lessee of premises in Westmoreland Street, Dublin, where he operated the business of seed merchant. The defendant was an insurance company which had purchased the adjacent building and carried out significant structural changes which, it was alleged, sufficiently darkened and obstructed the ancient windows of the plaintiff's house – in particular, a back drawing room window facing east – as to render it difficult for the plaintiff to carry out his business. The room in question was used as a store-room and communicated directly with the shop. In this room the seeds were deposited in bags bearing labels with the names of the seeds written on them, usually in small handwriting. Here also the seeds were sifted and examined before being transferred to drawers in the shop. It was an issue in the case that, although light had been admitted through these windows for over 20 years, thereby constituting them as 'ancient lights', the plaintiff had only been in occupation for 17 years and the premises had not previously been used for the business of a seed merchant.

According to Christian LJ, it did not matter that the room had been used for the inspecting and storing of seeds for 17 and not 20 years. Since the light itself had been admitted to the room for more than 20 years, it was an ancient light and so entitled to protection. While acknowledging that the possible extent to which such a doctrine could be pushed might have to be tested in the House of Lords, it was still clear to Christian LJ that:

> '... a window being ancient, if the owner of it has made an actual appropriation of the light coming through it for a particular business, although such particular appropriation may have lasted for less than twenty years, he is entitled to be protected in his enjoyment of it for that purpose, though the quantity of light thereby actually consumed (so to speak) be considerably greater than was required for the earlier use of the room....'

It cannot now be asserted that this bare proposition is good law, following the decision of the House of Lords, in 1904, in *Colls v Home and Colonial Stores Ltd.*[2] This definitively established that a cause of action could only arise in the case of deprivation of lights where the diminution was such as to be actionable in nuisance, on the basis that the degree of light to which one is entitled is that required for the ordinary use of the building – be it residential or business – according to the ordinary notions of mankind. On the other hand, if the nature and extent of the user of the *light*, as opposed to the user of the *room*, were the same for the entire prescriptive period of 20 years as during the 17 year period when the room was used for the storage of seed-bags, and the owner of the servient tenement were aware of that user, it is arguable that access of the light required for the purpose of storing seedbags would still be protected.[3]

---

1   *Mackey v Scottish Widows' Assurance Society* (1877) IR 11 Eq 541.
2   *Colls v Home and Colonial Stores Ltd* [1904] AC 179. See also *Higgins v Betts* [1905] 2 Ch
    210; *Lyme Valley Squash Club Ltd v Newcastle-under-Lyme Borough Council* [1985] 2 All ER

405. The *Colls* formulation has been adopted in a number of Irish cases: *O'Connor v Walsh* (1906) 42 ILTR 20; *Smyth v Dublin Theatre Co Ltd* [1936] IR 692; *Gannon v Hughes* [1937] IR 284; *McGrath v Munster and Leinster Bank Ltd* [1959] IR 313; *Loughney v Byrne* (7 October 1974, unreported) HC. See also Bland *The Law of Easements and Profits à Prendre* (1997) Sweet & Maxwell, pp 81–82, 91–92.

3   This would appear to be the effect of the decision in *Allen v Greenwood* [1980] Ch 119.

[7.07] Ball LC, though of a similar view to Christian LJ, expressed it in more moderate terms, adopting the statement of the law by Jessel MR in *Aynsley v Glover*,[1] that, in order for there to be a right of action, '… there must be a substantial privation of light, sufficient to render the occupation of the house uncomfortable, or to prevent the plaintiff from carrying on his accustomed business on the premises as beneficially as he had formerly done.'[2] In consequence, the Prescription Act had not protected every scintilla of light which had formerly been admitted, but allowed a cause of action where the comfort of the house had been diminished by the reduction in light or alternatively, if the house were a business premises, where the business could not be carried on as beneficially as it had previously.

---

1   *Aynsley v Glover* (1874) LR 18 Eq 544 at 552, itself adapted from *Back v Stacey* (1826) 2 C & P 465; subsequently affirmed by the Court of Appeal in (1875) 10 Ch App 283.

2   *Mackey v Scottish Widows' Assurance Society* (1877) IR 11 Eq 541 at 555.

[7.08] A similar point had arisen in the earlier case of *Manning v The Gresham Hotel Co*[1] in relation to the legitimacy of the alleged right to light vis-à-vis the history of the user of the premises. The plaintiff had claimed a diminution in the light to a wareroom, used by him in his trade as a silk mercer, by the defendant's building upon the back of their hotel to a height above the level of a dome the light through which had previously illuminated the plaintiff's wareroom. The defendant's premises had been raised by an additional 26 feet, which served to exclude from the plaintiff's southern windows a quantity of direct southern light. The plaintiff, however, had only taken a lease of his premises 10 years earlier, in 1857, prior to which his lessor had used it for 26 years as a picture gallery, prior to which again it had been used for the purposes of the book trade.

This factor, according to O'Brien J, did not vitiate the plaintiff's claim. Rather the case to be put to the jury was whether the obstruction 'would materially and sensibly diminish the quantity of light which had previously flowed into the wareroom – whether he should use it for his present business, or … for any other purpose for which it was heretofore used or might hereafter be used in its present condition, and without changing its character.'[2] It did not matter that the diminution might be insignificant while the wareroom was used for its present purpose, provided that it would be significant if the user of the premises, but not its character, were to be changed at some future time.

---

1   *Manning v The Gresham Hotel Co* (1867) IR 1 CL 115.

2   (1867) IR 1 CL 115 at 122.

Extraordinary quantity of light

[7.09] However, by the time of the decision in *Mackey v Scottish Widows' Assurance Society*,[1] a dictum of Mallins V-C in *Lanfranchi v Mackenzie*[2] had suggested, that where the user of premises required an 'extraordinary quantity of light', that quantity of light must have been specifically enjoyed for 20 years. Ball LC in *Mackey* considered the significance of the words 'Access and Use of Light' in s 3 of the Prescription Act and held that Mallins V-C's dictum effectively placed a forced and unnatural construction on the word 'Use'. According to Ball LC, the significance of the word 'Use' was that the light should actually enter the building, rather than that it should necessarily be used for a specific purpose *having* entered the building. The word 'Access' alone would merely have obliged that the light reach the building. '... there was no intention of prescribing that any particular user, either in kind or degree, should have existed. The object was to give title to relief, but not to define its extent.'[3] Christian LJ expressed the view that the employment by Mallins V-C of the words 'ordinary' and 'extraordinary' in the context of light was misleading, and that his dictum should be confined to the narrower proposition that the enjoyment of any light cannot be protected where that enjoyment had endured for less than 20 years.

Mallins V-C had actually said:

> 'If a man cannot establish a right within 20 years to an ordinary quantity of light, how can he establish in a less period the right to an extraordinary? All he can establish is the right to the quantity of light he would be entitled to for ordinary purposes. If he has been in the enjoyment of an extraordinary user for 20 years, that would establish the right against all persons who had reasonable knowledge of it.'[4]

---

[1] *Mackey v Scottish Widows' Assurance Society* (1877) IR 11 Eq 541.

[2] *Lanfranchi v Mackenzie* (1867) LR 4 Eq 421.

[3] (1877) LR 11 Eq 541 at 559.

[4] (1867) LR 4 Eq 421 at 430.

[7.10] This last sentence formed the focus of a consideration of the case by the English Court of Appeal in *Allen v Greenwood*[1] which established that a right to an exceptional amount of light can be acquired, either by prescription or presumed lost grant, where that amount of light has been enjoyed for 20 years to the knowledge of the owner of the alleged servient tenement, and provided that such exceptional light, 'according to ordinary notions', is reasonably required by the use to which the dominant tenement has been put.

---

[1] *Allen v Greenwood* [1980] Ch 119; also *Price v Hilditch* [1930] 1 Ch 500, in which it was stated that the internal arrangements of a building are not the measure by which the quantity of legally protectible light coming through an aperture is to be gauged; *Scott v Pape* (1886) 31 ChD 554 where it was held that an alteration of the purpose for which the dominant tenement is used does not in itself result in the extinguishment of an acquired right to light.

Extent of diminution in light prohibited

[7.11] In different cases the principle is differently, but consistently, stated. In *Maguire v Grattan*[1] the lessee of a public house in Hammonds Court, Belfast was confronted with the likely reduction of two-thirds of the current sunlight passing to his premises by reason of the defendant's reconstructing the outer wall of their hotel from a height of 30 feet to 60 feet. This diminution in the plaintiff's lights was held excessive on the basis that there was here more than mere interference, in fact a 'substantial injury'. According to Walsh MR, in order to secure an injunction there had to be a substantial injury caused, rather than a mere interference with the plaintiff's ancient lights.

The plaintiff in *Mercer, Rice and Co v Ritchie, Hart and Co*[2] was a shirt manufacturer in Vulcan Street, Belfast, with whose ancient lights a newly constructed building was held by Porter MR to constitute a substantial interference, causing significant damage to his business. In such a case one had to take the attitude of 'persons of ordinary sense and judgment' and look to the reasonable use of the house or business. On the other hand, in *Sankey v Gunn*,[3] where the erection by the defendant of a bathroom onto his house at Merrion Square, Dublin interfered with the direct sunlight coming to his neighbour's dining room, with the result that the dining room was darkened for a quarter of an hour each day, it was held that this disturbance was too trifling, and its duration too brief, to warrant redress.

---

[1] *Maguire v Grattan* (1868) IR 2 Eq 246.
[2] *Mercer, Rice and Co v Ritchie, Hart and Co* (1903) 3 NIJR 123.
[3] *Sankey v Gunn* (1894) 28 ILTR 128.

[7.12] In *Gannon v Hughes*,[1] Johnston J, following the decision of the House of Lords in *Colls v Home and Colonial Stories*,[2] observed that in order to secure redress the obstruction complained of must be a nuisance, interfering seriously with the plaintiff's accustomed business so that he would not be able to carry it on as beneficially as before. In order to determine the fact of nuisance one had to look to the quantity of light which had been enjoyed in the past and the proximity of the premises complained of.[3]

---

[1] *Gannon v Hughes* [1937] IR 284.
[2] *Colls v Home and Colonial Stories* [1904] AC 179.
[3] See also Dixon J in *McGrath v The Munster and Leinster Bank Ltd* [1959] IR 313 and Murnaghan J in *Loughney v Byrne* (7 October 1974, unreported) HC, in both cases borrowing heavily from *Colls v Home and Colonial Stores Ltd* [1904] AC 179; also *Smyth v The Dublin Theatre Co Ltd* [1936] IR 692.

[7.13] In *McGrath v The Munster and Leinster Bank Ltd*,[1] Dixon J observed that the owner of the dominant tenement could not be prejudiced by reason of the fact that from time to time only the premises might be as well lighted as they had formerly been. In this case, involving the diminution in the access of sunlight to a solicitor's office due to the defendant bank's rebuilding portion of its adjoining premises to a greater height than before, Dixon J held that 'the value of the light' coming to the dominant owner's office 'in relation to the normal hours of office work and over the year as a whole ... [had] been materially depreciated.'

---

[1] *McGrath v The Munster and Leinster Bank Ltd* [1959] IR 313.

Light coming through glass and other apertures than windows

[7.14] Light which passes through a glass covering on the servient tenement is capable of conferring an easement, either under s 3 of the Prescription Act or the doctrine of presumed lost grant, and can be protected by way of injunction.[1] An easement of light by prescription can only be made out where the aperture through which the right to light is claimed has been used for the purposes of admitting light, rather than as a door, for the entirety of the prescriptive period.

---

[1] *Tisdall v McArthur and Co (Steel and Metal) Ltd and Mossop* [1951] IR 228.

[7.15] In *Walsh v Goulding*,[1] the plaintiff in 1959 had purchased a mews which she subsequently converted into a residence. In an action by her to protect her ancient lights, when the defendants constructed a large office block across the road from her that substantially diminished the access of light, the question arose whether apertures, which up to 1959 had been the door of a coachhouse and the door of a hayloft respectively, could have the light passing through them protected since they had not been used primarily for the access of light for a full 20 years. Teevan J endorsed the doubts expressed by Peterson J in *Levet v Gaslight and Coke Co*[2] about the difficulty in determining the measure of light which had been enjoyed by a doorway possessing a door that was opened and shut as the occasion might require. Concerning s 3 of the Prescription Act, Peterson J had said:

> '... the section applies to windows or apertures in the nature of windows and not to apertures with doors in them, which were primarily constructed for the purpose of being closed and thus excluding light.'[3]

Teevan J noted that the crucial factor was the distinction between a doorway and a door, and that apertures which had not had a door, and which in addition to providing a doorway also seemed designed to admit light, should be protected on the basis that light now passing through them partook of the character of ancient lights.[4]

---

[1] *Walsh v Goulding* (31 July 1968, unreported) HC.

[2] *Levet v Gaslight and Coke Co* [1919] 1 Ch 24.

[3] [1919] 1 Ch 24 at 27.

[4] Teevan J went on to hold, however, that in the assessment of damages the total light deprivation, through all lights in the same wall plane, ancient as well as modern, should be taken into account. On an appeal to the Supreme Court, *sub nom Scott v Goulding Properties Ltd* [1973] IR 200, a majority held that damages must be confined to the results of the deprivation of

ancient lights only. In neither court was it felt that an injunction should be granted on account of the hardship it would wreak on the defendants.

The Nature and Character of Light

[7.16] It is clear from a consideration of certain of the Irish cases that the question whether the access of light, having been enjoyed for the prescriptive period, warrants protection is not wholly dependent on the amount of light gaining access or the purpose to which it is put, but is also bound up with such less tangible factors as the nature and character of the light, including the origin of the light, the manner in which it falls into a room and the extent to which its distribution is affected by the existence or otherwise of obstructions on the servient tenement lying within the path of the light but not diminishing its access.[1] Not infrequently also, judicial identification of these considerations is linked to an unease about the strictures of certain types of technical evidence, the import of which is to seek to limit the right to light gaining ingress to the dominant tenement to that light only which conforms to certain strict scientific principles.[2]

[1]　See Bodkin 'The Acquisition of Rights of Light for Badly Lighted Premises' (1974) 38 Conv 4 at 7.
[2]　For example, *Smyth v The Dublin Theatre Co* [1936] IR 692 at 705, per Meredith J.

Reflected light

[7.17] In *Manning v The Gresham Hotel Co*,[1] counsel for the defendant had argued that, since the only obstruction was of reflected rather than direct light, such light did not warrant protection. This was uniformly rejected by the Court of Queen's Bench, the test being stated as whether there had been 'sensible and material' interference with the light regardless of whether the light itself was direct or otherwise. George J observed that a jury would probably have been confused by the attempted distinction, and added, '... no such distinction can be maintained: the question ought to have been, whether any sensible diminution of light – whether direct or refracted – had taken place.'[2] However, in *Sankey v Gunn*,[3] while Chatterton V-C held that a case for the diminution of diffused light had not been made out by the plaintiff, it seems clear that such diminution, if sustained and substantial, would have been restrained.

[1]　*Manning v The Gresham Hotel Co* (1867) IR 1 CL 115.
[2]　(1867) IR 1 CL 115 at 124.
[3]　*Sankey v Gunn* (1894) 28 ILTR 128.

Origin of light

[7.18] In certain cases, particularly those involving the inspection of goods and apparel, importance has been attached to the origin of the light. In *Mercer, Rice and Co v Ritchie, Hart and Co*,[1] the Belfast manufacturer of collars and shirts used a downstairs room for the examination of linen, which Barton J recognised as a highly delicate job requiring skill and application. The examination was done along a bench in front of the windows and was accepted by Barton J as requiring a good and steady light, not necessarily a strong light, and certainly not a fluctuating one or one coming from different directions.[2] In *Black v Scottish Temperance Life Assurance Co*,[3] Barton J held that a Belfast manufacturer of ready-made clothing, particularly boys' suits, the windows on whose three-storey building faced north and south, required a good light coming from the north. This was most evident in the examining room where the plaintiff's employees checked the finished product for defects and where prospective purchasers inspected the range of finished products from which they might then choose to place an order.

The case was made, and accepted by Barton J, that a northern light was needed to examine the cloth and check the matching of colours. This was not accepted in the Court of Appeal, both Fitzgibbon LJ and Holmes LJ expressing the view that the alleged requirement for northern light had been much exaggerated, and Holmes LJ observing that the garments manufactured by the plaintiff tended to be made from a cheap woollen fabric usually blue in colour. A further appeal to the House of Lords reinstated the injunction and level of damages awarded by Barton J, although the law lords refrained from commenting on the relevance of northern light.

---

[1] *Mercer, Rice and Co v Ritchie, Hart and Co* (1903) 3 NIJR 123.

[2] In this case it had also been argued that the angle of light resulting from the new building erected by the servient owner was less than 45 degrees. Barton J held that this made no difference, because there was no such thing as a 45 degree rule. He noted that the suggestion of a rule derived from the Metropolitan Buildings Act in England, and was not a rule, as such. In fact, this was the Metropolis Management Amendment Act 1862 and the non-existence of a 45 degree rule was clearly stated by the House of Lords in *Colls v Home and Colonial Stores Ltd* [1904] AC 179.

[3] *Black v Scottish Temperance Life Assurance Co* [1908] 1 IR 541.

Where light most naturally falls

[7.19] In *Smyth v The Dublin Theatre Co Ltd*,[1] the specific portion of the room in which the light most naturally falls was deemed a vital consideration. The plaintiffs had for many years run the business of the manufacture and repair of cotton and jute bags and the colour printing of them. In 1934 the defendants demolished their old theatre, the Theatre Royal, and built a new one which was considerably higher and had the effect of diminishing the plaintiffs' lights. Meredith J held that the plaintiffs' colour printing process required only ordinary light and that the principal trouble had resulted from the diminution in direct lighting available in the vicinity of the window.

According to Meredith J, the plaintiffs' case largely depended on the use to which the room was put in the location where the light most naturally fell. Most rooms laterally lighted, he observed, have an uneven distribution of light. Ordinary light must mean more than just the general lighting of the room and be 'concerned in any case with the amount of direct light obtainable in parts of the room where such light might be expected to be obtainable.'[2] He gave as an example a wine merchant, who might be satisfied if he had a greater preponderance of light near the window if this was where he worked out the customer's accounts, but that if there were less light at the counter where the customer signed the cheque, then 'artificial light is supplied without a murmur and it never occurs to the merchant to suggest waiting for a brighter day.'[3]

---

[1]   *Smyth v The Dublin Theatre Co Ltd* [1936] IR 692.
[2]   [1936] IR 692 at 703.
[3]   [1936] IR 692 at 704.

[7.20] There had been detailed submission on, and analysis of, such technical terms as 'daylight factor', 'sill ratio', and 'grumble point', with some complex and comprehensive technical charts offered in evidence. Meredith J found the technical evidence difficult to accept on account of its theoretical character which took no heed of the exigencies of a particular situation or the nuances inherent in any one case. He said:

> 'The practical minimum tolerable is different from the theoretical minimum tolerable of the experts, and differs for different parts of the room in which different ordinary purposes are customarily satisfied. There is nothing special, peculiar or extraordinary in requiring a reasonable amount of direct light near the window of a room laterally lighted. In the vast majority of cases of rooms lighted laterally in which evidence is given of a nuisance caused by the obstruction of light I apprehend that the evidence offered would be directed to the altered position quite near the window – that is, at a point at which the light would probably be in fact well above the theoretical "grumble point".
>
> 'In several of the decided cases that were cited the court stressed the point that the evidence of the experts is not as safe a guide as the evidence of those accustomed to use the room in question. The wearer of the shoe is the one best qualified to say if and where it pinches. The attention of those who use a room is at once directed to what is of practical concern, whereas that is a matter frequently overlooked by the experts who for the most part only concern themselves with what is of general application and can readily be illustrated by charts of a general type'.[1]

Johnston J in *Gannon v Hughes*[2] equally found the concepts of 'daylight factor' and 'grumble point' unhelpful, while in *McGrath v The Munster and Leinster Bank Ltd*,[3] Dixon J observed that the problem with all technical calculations was that, though accurate in a certain scientific sense, they assumed a uniform distribution of natural light, even when there was no direct sunlight, an assumption which the realities of life did not justify.[4] In the case of the solicitor's office darkened by the enlargement of the bank, variations affecting the use of the office at critical times during the day were taken into account, and particular importance was attached to the greater darkening effect in the afternoon due to the impact of the newly constructed building on light coming from the west. These considerations, held Dixon J, and also the direction of the new obstruction relative to the windows of the plaintiff's office, were of considerable significance but were also ones of which the 'grumble line' or 'sky factor contour' could take no account. Accordingly, '... in the absence of any available scientific method, one has to fall back on the admittedly faulty but less limited method of human observation.'[5]

[1]   *Smyth v The Dublin Theatre Co Ltd* [1936] IR 692 at 704–705. Meredith J concluded that the flexibility of the principle enunciated in *Colls v Home and Colonial Stores* [1904] AC 179 required that 'ordinary light' be interpreted in a common-sense manner.

[2]   *Gannon v Hughes* [1937] IR 284.

[3]   *McGrath v The Munster and Leinster Bank Ltd* [1959] IR 313.

[4]   Dixon J stated at 325, that the reason he found the scientific evidence comparatively unhelpful was 'not by reason of any lack of precision in that evidence but solely because I regard the methods adopted as being inherently inadequate to give a sufficiently comprehensive result.'

[5]   [1959] IR 313 at 325.

Psychological effects

[7.21] In *McGrath v The Munster and Leinster Bank Ltd*[1] Dixon J expressed the view that account should be taken of what he termed the 'shadow effect' – specifically, the consciousness of an exterior building shutting out the light or an awareness that shadows have deepened. He accepted that this was largely a psychological reaction, but added that one also had to note the effect of reduced light on the solicitor's clients, even on days when the light seemed quite adequate for the solicitor, and that this too should be adverted to in determining whether the beneficial user of the office through the curtailed access of natural light had been impaired. Likewise, in *Loughney v Byrne*[2] Murnaghan J took account of the adverse psychological reaction that would probably be occasioned by an unsightly wall extension constructed by the defendant, which also effected a significant diminution in the plaintiff's light.

[1]   *McGrath v The Munster and Leinster Bank Ltd* [1959] IR 313.

[2]   *Loughney v Byrne* (7 October 1974, unreported) HC.

[7.22] Notions of comfort have doubtless expanded and improved over the centuries. In 1752, Lord Hardwicke LC, in *Fishmongers' Co v East India Co*[1] declined to grant an injunction in a case of an interference with ancient lights on the grounds that the obstruction complained of did not constitute an actionable nuisance. Notwithstanding this, he noted that 'the value of the plaintiff's house may be reduced by rendering the prospect less pleasant, but that is no reason to hinder a man from building on his own ground.'[2] This decision should be contrasted with *Kine v Jolly,*[3] in which an actionable nuisance was held to have occurred when a diminution in the light entering a morning room constituted 'a large interference with the cheerfulness of the room.'

[1]   *Fishmongers' Co v East India Co* (1752) 1 Dick 163.

[2]   (1752) 1 Dick 163 at 165.

[3]   *Kine v Jolly* [1905] 1 Ch 480, affirmed at [1907] AC 1.

The Special Case of Poorly Lit Premises

[7.23] Special account is taken in the Irish courts of the extent to which the dominant tenement might already be poorly lit, in determining whether any interference with the access of light is actionable. In most cases the fact of the premises being poorly lit, though adverted to as a consideration, is not specifically identified in the grounds of the decision.[1]

---

1   The fact that the premises had already been poorly lit was identified as relevant in *Maguire v Grattan* (1868) IR 2 Eq 246; *Mackey v Scottish Widows' Fund Assurance Society* (1877) IR 11 Eq 541, per Barton J; *Gannon v Hughes* [1937] IR 284; *McGrath v The Munster and Leinster Bank Ltd* [1959] IR 313; *Walsh v Goulding* (31 July 1968, unreported) HC, and in *Loughney v Byrne* (7 October 1974, unreported) HC.

[7.24] However, in *O'Connor v Walsh*,[1] the prior illumination of the premises was specifically addressed in the judgment of Meredith MR. The plaintiff was a tailor carrying on business in St Andrew Street, Dublin. The skylight and windows to his cutting-room and fitting-room respectively were illuminated by lateral light coming through a high narrow alley directly outside. Some diffused light also came over the top of the wall of the alley, but was held to be insignificant. The defendant owned the premises on the other side of the alley, and had recently constructed a toilet that jutted out into it and was almost 8 feet high. The Master of the Rolls found that the light coming into the plaintiff's premises had never at the best of times been considerable, and that its actual diminution by reason of the construction of the defendant's toilet was in the order of one-third to one-half.

During the course of the hearing Meredith MR himself had visited the plaintiff's fitting-room[2] and was of the view that even prior to the construction of the toilet '… there was, owing to the surrounding buildings, as little light as was compatible with the comfortable carrying on of any business in the back portion of the plaintiff's shop according to the ordinary notions of mankind …' He posited the test to be applied as follows:

> 'Has that source of supply been affected to such a real, appreciable and substantial extent – to such an extent as to materially lessen the enjoyment and use of the house that the owner previously had, so as to leave it substantially neither comfortable nor fit for occupation according to the ordinary requirements of mankind?'[3]

Meredith MR concluded that, such had been the minimal level of light earlier enjoyed, due to the arrangement of the surrounding buildings, virtually any structure erected in the gap would affect the light in the fitting room. An injunction was granted, on the basis that the plaintiff's only alternative would be to use artificial light which Meredith MR deemed to be a very poor substitute in a shop in St Andrew Street. The Master of the Rolls noted that this case was one which might not have given a cause of action under the principle laid down in *Colls v Home and Colonial Stores*.[4] From this one can conclude that, even in cases where the requirement is only to what might be termed 'ordinary light', if the effect of any abridgement is substantial because of the already poorly lit status of the dominant tenement, a cause of action arises regardless of whether the servient owner was aware of the effect of his building works on the dominant owner's lights.[5] Expressed another way, the amount of light whose access attracts legal protection depends upon the essential character of the dominant tenement[6] and the extent to which it is already adequately lit.

---

1   *O'Connor v Walsh* (1906) 42 ILTR 20.
2   A soundly sensible exercise it is suggested, a view concurred in by Lord Denning MR in *Ough v King* [1967] 1 WLR 1547 at 1552.
3   (1906) 42 ILTR 20 at 21.
4   *Colls v Home and Colonial Stores* [1904] AC 179.
5   Aptly and succinctly expressed in Bland, *The Law of Easements and Profits à Prendre* at p 93: '… the servient owner has to take the plaintiff's premises as they are.' See generally, Bodkin, 'The Acquisition of Rights of Light for Badly Lighted Premises' (1974) 38 Conv 4.
6   See *Manning v The Gresham Hotel Co* (1867) IR 1 CL 115, per O'Brien J.

[7.25] In *Colls v Home and Colonial Stores*,[1] Lord Robertson had stated that the owner of the servient tenement ought not to be liable if the owner of the dominant tenement had supplied himself with less lighting than was adequate and if the level of lighting which actually reached the dominant tenement would not have been adversely affected by the obstruction complained of. After *O'Connor v Walsh*,[2] this cannot be stated as being the law in Ireland. However, one possible construction of the speech of Lord Robertson is that the owner of the dominant tenement can only blame himself if he provides his premises with inadequate lighting. From the facts in *O'Connor v Walsh* it is obvious that the owner of the dominant tenement had little control over the amount of light available to him.[3] It can be argued that in England the owner of an inadequately lighted premises is now more likely to be able to prescribe for adequate light, following the decision of the Court of Appeal in *Allen v Greenwood*,[4] provided that the dominant owner's need for exceptional light – which, by contrast with the existing inadequate level of lighting, ordinary adequate lighting would be – is known to the servient owner.

---

1   *Colls v Home and Colonial Stores* [1904] AC 179.
2   *O'Connor v Walsh* (1906) 42 ILTR 20.
3   Hudson has suggested in 'Ancient Lights for an Office' (1960) 24 Conv 424, that Lord Robertson's observation ought to be confined to the person who had originally erected the defective dominant tenement, since that person can, presumably, remedy the problem themselves by opening more windows.
4   *Allen v Greenwood* [1980] Ch 119.

Dominant Owner Need Not Take Precautions

[7.26] Contrary to the usual principle that the plaintiff in a civil action is obliged to try and mitigate his loss, in actions arising from obstruction of light a dominant owner is not bound to take curative measures himself, or to submit to remedial steps proposed by the owner of the servient tenement which themselves would not give rise to a right to compel their continuance. This principle was established by Christian LJ in *Mackey v*

Scottish Widows' Assurance Society.[1] He asserted[2] that it could be no answer to the interruption of a person's 'ancient lights' to urge that there are remedies which he can procure for himself, such as by changing the use of his house or of parts of it, or that the servient owner can provide a substitute remedy like erecting glazed tiles or mirrors. The dominant owner would have no right to oblige the indefinite persistence of these facilities. Neither would a covenant to maintain them be able to run with the land.[3] The owner of a servient tenement, said Christian LJ, cannot claim the right to damage his neighbour on condition of providing a remedy of his own choosing. In such cases, a dominant owner quite properly stands on his rights and will decline to rely on such consideration as his offending neighbour may show him from time to time.

In the instant case much of the light which the plaintiff dominant owner needed came from the south-east. This had been partly compensated for by the removal by the defendant of a projection which obstructed the light coming from the east. However, the plaintiff had no right to prevent the reinstatement of this obstruction. In 10 years time, according to Christian LJ, if it were reinstated, he would not have acquired sufficient right by prescription to prevent a new obstruction, and his old easement of light might have been deemed abandoned.

---

[1] *Mackey v Scottish Widows' Assurance Society* (1877) IR 11 Eq 541.
[2] Following the judgment of Wood V-C in *Dent v The Auction Mart Co* (1866) LR 2 Eq 238.
[3] See para [14.25] ff.

[7.27] In *Carson v McKenzie*[1] the plaintiffs operated the business of general merchants, grocers and wine merchants at premises in Corn Market, Belfast, and also at a smaller premises abutting on a lane at the rear of Corn Market, between Corn Market and High Street, called Hodgson's Entry. These latter premises were lighted by two windows, which had existed since 1819, and by a glass door, a feature since 1835. The only air and natural light came through these apertures, and it was in this premises, of necessity assisted by natural light, that articles, such as tea, sugar, flour and wine were inspected for their quality. Colour was a vital determinant of quality and frequently the articles had to be compared with other specimens of known value.

In 1864 the defendant, who owned premises on the other side of Hodgson's Entry, had these premises demolished and constructed new ones to a much higher altitude and width, thereby cutting off the natural light and so precluding the inspection of commodities in the plaintiffs' premises for which natural light was so necessary. In an action by the plaintiffs for an injunction and damages, the defendant responded that the plaintiffs could enhance the quality of their own light by replacing the 'muffed glass' at present in the windows with transparent glass. Brady LC declined to hold with this contention, and, having found that the plaintiffs' ancient lights, which were necessary for the running of their business, had been substantially impaired, granted an injunction to remove the offending structure.

Similarly in the case of *Mercer, Rice and Co v Ritchie, Hart and Co*,[2] the plaintiff manufacturer of collars and cuffs on Vulcan Street, Belfast, used a downstairs room for the delicate operation of examining the linen, the examination being carried out by employees along a bench in front of the window. The defendant had alleged that the plaintiff did not place great store by the light he received through the ground floor windows because ground glass was used in the lower parts of the windows. However, Porter MR held that this was partly designed to prevent the employees being distracted by people from outside looking into the room, even though the ground glass would probably also cause the light to fluctuate, thereby impeding work. In any event, he added, the plaintiffs did not destroy their right to light simply because the access of some of the light was denied.

> 'If he does not use the whole of it and obstructs part of it, that does not prevent him from maintaining an action for the residue of the light ... A man does not lose his right by using curtains or blinds.'[3]

---

[1]   *Carson v McKenzie* (1865) 18 Ir Jur 337.

[2]   *Mercer, Rice and Co v Ritchie, Hart and Co* (1903) 3 NIJR 123.

[3]   (1903) 3 NIJR 123 at 127. See also Lord Lindley in *Colls v Home and Colonial Stores* [1904] AC 179 at 211; Maugham J in *Price v Hilditch* [1930] 1 Ch 500 at 508.

[7.28] It can be difficult to determine whether or not preventative measures adopted by the owner of the servient tenement should be accepted in lieu of redress at law, particularly when these are embarked upon to try and settle an action during the course of it. In *Black v Scottish Temperance Life Assurance Co*,[1] the Belfast boys' suits haberdasher found the defendant's newly constructed premises especially detrimental to his light on account of the walls being constructed of red brick which reflected a reddish hue making it difficult to distinguish the colours in the cloth. In a preliminary hearing, Barton J decided not to enforce an injunction order (having found that there was a substantial interference with the plaintiff's ancient lights) until the defendant had had the opportunity to face the red brick with a white brick called verapal to see if this could abate the nuisance sufficiently for damages to be an adequate remedy. This experiment was undertaken, but according to Barton J did not sufficiently improve matters in the instance of the examination of woollens. Hence, since both the red brick and the white brick constituted a nuisance, he awarded an injunction and damages. Barton J also noted that, even if the white tiles had redressed the problem, the plaintiff still had no prescriptive right to the light reflected from them.

This decision was overturned by the Court of Appeal, Fitzgibbon LJ observing, that since steps had been taken to see if the nuisance could be abated, the court was now confronted 'with a much mitigated injury, and that it has been mitigated is a strong corroboration of the justice of holding that compensation is now the proper and adequate remedy.'[2] The corollary of this logic, however, would have rendered the plaintiff worse off for having allowed the action to be deferred while the white tiling was tested, even though the results of it from his point of view were far from satisfactory. A further appeal to the House of Lords reinstated the decision of Barton J, Lord Robertson stating that the court would not 'have been warranted in holding that an actionable obstruction of ancient lights could be justified by the substitution of light reflected from a white surface, when the injured owner had no legal right to the continuance of these newly created conditions.'[3]

---

[1]   *Black v Scottish Temperance Life Assurance Co* [1908] 1 IR 541.
[2]   [1908] 1 IR 541 at 571.
[3]   [1908] 1 IR 541, at 579. This view was also evinced by Johnston J in *Gannon v Hughes* [1937] IR 284 who refused to take into account any possible benefit to the plaintiff resulting from reflected light off the new building which otherwise had the effect of substantially darkening the plaintiff's pharmacy.

[7.29] In *McGrath v The Munster and Leinster Bank Ltd*,[1] Dixon J stated that any benefits of reflected light from the elevated bank wall were not to be considered in mitigation of the plaintiff's case, because the defendant could not be obliged to maintain its walls in any particular colour or to any specific degree of cleanliness, while the plaintiff, on the other hand, could not be tied down to a single scheme of decoration. He held, furthermore, that the plaintiff ought to be allowed to be the best judge in the matter of the appointment and arrangement of her office and could not legitimately be criticised for the way in which she effected this.

---

[1]   *McGrath v The Munster and Leinster Bank Ltd* [1959] IR 313.

Character of the Dominant Tenement and its Locality

[7.30] It is, arguably, a corollary of the principle that the owner of the dominant tenement is not expected to take remedial measures on his own account that neither should he be worse off if his premises are a less than glamorous specimen in a respectable and developing neighbourhood. Christian LJ, when speaking of the equal entitlement to protect ancient lights in the country as in the city, in *Mackey v Scottish Widows' Assurance Society*,[1] commented that if the legal protection of the right to ancient lights were seen to get in the way of architectural embellishment and sanitary improvement in great towns, then those who want to build imposing structures 'must bear in mind that the law requires them to have careful regard to the rights to light and air of their more old-fashioned and less ambitious neighbours.'

---

[1]   *Mackey v Scottish Widows' Assurance Society* (1877) IR 11 Eq 541 at 561.

[7.31] Nevertheless, the counter argument is often made.[1] In *Maguire v Grattan*,[2] where the plaintiff publican stood to lose two-thirds of his ancient lights by reason of the projected reconstruction of the defendant's hotel, counsel for the defendant argued that since the plaintiff's windows gave upon inferior rooms of little value they were incapable of being seriously injured by the diminution in light. Walsh MR, however, held that the evidence sustained the conclusion that substantial injury would be done to that part of the dominant tenement which *was* of value, a circumstance which warranted intervention from the court.[3]

Perhaps not surprisingly, this controversy was also aired in the twice appealed case of *Black v Scottish Temperance Life Assurance Society*.[4] In the Court of Appeal, Fitzgibbon

LJ felt that the character of the locality was important to the determining of redress and that the award of a mandatory injunction would enable the plaintiff compel the defendant to purchase the plaintiff's premises at a vastly exaggerated price in order to defeat the injunction. He commented that the plaintiff's premises properly belonged to a bygone era and that it was likely to be rebuilt in the near future so as to become worthy of the new and better appearance of Belfast.

Holmes LJ went so far as to intimate that the award of a mandatory injunction in this case could give rise to a kind of 'legalised blackmail' and that, in any event, it would be a dangerous remedy when, in the course of a city development, someone builds a beautiful edifice which, without bad faith, causes injury to his neighbour.

These views found no favour in the House of Lords, Lord Robertson observing that from the vantage of remedy it made no difference that the locality was on the verge of being improved and that the plaintiff's property was old-fashioned by comparison:

> 'It is the existing condition that determines the measure of the inhabitant's rights; and the fact that his neighbours have recently built better houses than his own does not force him to elect between conformity to their standard and forfeiture of his rights.'[5]

---

1   See Bodkin 'Local Standard of Light' (1926) 42 LQR 443; Bland *The Law of Easements and Profits à Prendre* pp 85–86.

2   *Maguire v Grattan* (1868) IR 2 Eq 246.

3   It is inferable from the language used by Walsh MR that he experienced some sympathy with the argument being made by defendant. This is demonstrated by his expression of regret in awarding a prohibitory injunction, on the grounds that he feared the principal value of such an injunction would be the power it gave the plaintiff of controlling his neighbours, presumably by giving him the whip hand in a bid to compel the defendant to buy him out.

4   *Black v Scottish Temperance Life Assurance Society* [1908] 1 IR 541.

5   [1908] 1 IR 541 at 581, per Lord Robertson.

Redress: Damages or Injunction

[7.32] Since the removal of an obstruction to ancient lights necessarily involves either the cessation of building, or the demolition of a structure already raised on the servient tenement, or both, the granting of an injunction in disputes over lights is regarded circumspectly by the courts.[1] Even so, certainly in the nineteenth century, the judicial view was that the right to access of natural light was just as much an incident of property as a person's house and equally entitled to protection. Where the interference was of such a kind as seriously to inconvenience a person in the enjoyment of his house, or to prevent him carrying on his business with the same convenience as before, this right could be protected by way of mandatory injunction.

The attitude was that a person ought to be restored to the enjoyment of his property *in specie*, not obliged to accept money in lieu of it at the behest of the party interrupting his lights.[2] In consequence, the construction of premises higher than those existing before, which impaired the carrying on of his business by a grocer and wine merchant in Belfast, resulted in an injunction directing that the offending buildings were not to be erected above the original height of the previous buildings, nor suffered to remain at their greater height: in short, the injunction was both mandatory and prohibitory.[3]

---

[1] See *Walsh v Goulding* (31 July 1968, unreported) HC and the same case on appeal, *Scott v Goulding Properties Ltd* [1973] IR 200.
[2] Kindersley V-C in *Martin v Headon* (1866) LR 2 Eq 425 and Lord Hatherley in *Dent v Auction Mart Co* (1866) LR 2 Eq 238, quoted and considered with approval by Christian LJ in *Mackey v Scottish Widows' Assurance Society* (1877) IR 11 Eq 541.
[3] *Carson v McKenzie* (1865) 18 Ir Jur 337.

[7.33] An injunction could be awarded because the dominant owner's business cannot be carried on except by the use of artificial light, which, depending on the circumstances, may be a very poor substitute.[1] Similarly where it became necessary to turn on the gaslight three-quarters of an hour early,[2] or where the dominant owner might be obliged to examine his linen on a different floor, perhaps taking longer to do it, and having to pay higher salaries or employ additional staff.[3] An injunction was granted where the light reaching the dominant owner's pharmacy was substantially reduced, even though the servient owner was only trying to do the best for his large family by erecting a two-storey extension in the first place.[4]

---

[1] *O'Connor v Walsh* (1906) 42 ILTR 20, where Meredith MR held that artificial light would be a very poor substitute for shops in St Andrew Street, Dublin and deemed it 'a new departure to hold that because the injury might be mitigated by the use of artificial light damages would be a sufficient compensation.'
[2] *Black v Scottish Temperance Life Assurance Co* [1908] 1 IR 541, per Barton J.
[3] *Mercer, Rice and Co v Ritchie, Hart and Co* (1903) 3 NIJR 123.
[4] *Gannon v Hughes* [1937] IR 284.

[7.34] Nevertheless, there are dangers attached to the granting of injunctions in ancient lights disputes, particularly in cases of urban development. In *Carson v McKenzie*,[1] counsel for the defendant protested strongly against the granting of an injunction in such a case, 'for then no vacant piece of ground could be built upon in a city ... this injunction ... will have the effect of preventing, in nine cases out of ten, in towns, the building of opposite houses in a street or lane.'[2]

There is also the risk that in cases where the dominant tenement is significantly less valuable than both the servient tenement and the surrounding property, the grant of a mandatory injunction could confer an extortionate advantage on the dominant owner in possibly persuading the servient owner to buy him out in lieu of complying with the injunction.[3]

---

[1] *Carson v McKenzie* (1865) 18 Ir Jur 337 at 340.
[2] A concern also identified by Lord Hardwicke LC in *Fishmongers' Co v East India Co* (1752) 1 Dick 163, although in that case the Lord Chancellor also held that the obstruction did not constitute a legal nuisance.

3   A fear expressed by Walsh MR in *Maguire v Grattan* (1868) IR 2 Eq 246, in which he regretted granting a mandatory injunction, 'the price of which is to be measured not so much by the good it does as by the good it may prevent.' See also Fitzgibbon LJ and Holmes LJ in *Black v Scottish Temperance Life Assurance Co* [1908] 1 IR 541; Bland *The Law of Easements and Profits à Prendre* pp 327–328.

[7.35] At one time it used to be thought, in a case of obstruction of ancient lights, that an injunction could only be awarded if the alternative remedy would have been substantial damages.[1] The current view is that the amount of damages should not affect whether an injunction is granted or not.[2]

1   Per Jessel MR in *Aynsley v Glover* (1875) 10 Ch App 283, following *Back v Stacey* (1826) 2 C & P 465, quoted with approval by Ball LC in *Mackey v Scottish Widows' Assurance Society* (1877) IR 11 Eq 541.
2   *McGrath v Munster and Leinster Bank Ltd* [1959] IR 313.

Behaviour of the parties

[7.36] It seems, however, that where the dominant owner protests in advance against the anticipated obstruction, and the servient owner proceeds to erect it in flagrant disregard of the dominant owner's rights, a stronger case can be made for an injunction.[1] In *Black v Scottish Temperance Life Assurance Society*,[2] this point was vigorously debated in three different courts, Barton J in the High Court observing:

> ' ... the seriousness of the injury is an important element in the case. There is also the deliberation and the full knowledge with which the defendants acted. To refuse an injunction in this case would be to recognise that the defendants had a right to compulsorily inflict this serious nuisance upon the plaintiff, upon terms of compensation to be fixed by the court. That is a proceeding which, in my opinion, the law, as it stands at present, does not permit.'[3]

Both Barton J, and later Lord Loreburn and Lord Robertson in the House of Lords, noted that when the plaintiff originally protested his lights, the defendants had replied that they had an indemnity against suit under the lease from their vendor to which, if necessary, they would take recourse. This was a point not taken up by the Court of Appeal which held that there had been no element of high-handedness in the defendants' conduct, and that they had acted in good faith, relying on professional advice from their architect. Fitzgibbon LJ observed that if the award were to include any element derived from a perception of high-handed behaviour, this would savour of 'vindictive damages'.[4]

Lord Loreburn on appeal, reinstating the injunction, believed that the defendants had 'deliberately, and after repeated warning, inflicted a substantial wrong upon another man, knowing that it is a wrong, with a view simply to their own advantage, and in contempt of their neighbour's lawful rights.'[5] Lord Robertson, noting that not all infringements of lights were actionable as a nuisance, observed that when a person in fact causes an obstruction to his neighbour's lights, 'he backs his luck, and must be held to have foreseen and intended to violate his neighbour's rights, if, in the sequel, this is found to have occurred.'[6] It is clear from the quoted comments of the law lords that the manner of proceeding by the defendants contributed strongly to the inference of intention on their part, with the resultant award of an injunction and additional damages.

---

1   *Black v Scottish Temperance Life Assurance Society* [1908] 1 IR 541; *Scott v Goulding Properties Ltd* [1973] IR 200; *Loughney v Byrne* (7 October 1974, unreported) HC. In this latter case, the extension had been erected without planning permission, which would have warranted its being knocked down in any event, unless a retention order had been sought and secured.

2   *Black v Scottish Temperance Life Assurance Society* [1908] 1 IR 541.

3   [1908] 1 IR 541 at 560.

4   But see the concluding portion of the judgment of Kingsmill Moore J in *Tisdall v McArthur and Co (Steel and Metal) Ltd and Mossop* [1951] IR 228, in which he observed that he was unable to award damages 'in spite of the unduly assertive action of the defendants' on the basis that damages had not been claimed.

5   [1908] 1 IR 541 at 578.

6   [1908] 1 IR 541 at 580.

[7.37] Conversely, where there is a genuine legal question as to whether there has been an obstruction or not, and the servient owner has acted in a spirit of good neighbourliness, damages, as opposed to an injunction, ought to be awarded.[1]

---

1   Per Dixon J in *McGrath v The Munster and Leinster Bank Ltd* [1959] IR 313.

Redress only to protect ancient lights

[7.38] The case of *Walsh v Goulding*[1] in the High Court, which became *Scott v Goulding Properties Ltd*[2] on appeal to the Supreme Court, affirmed that an injunction would not be awarded where the effect of it would be likely to wreak undue hardship on the owner of the servient tenement, in particular where he would be obliged to pull down an entire building. Both Teevan J in the High Court and Walsh J, dissenting, in the Supreme Court held that where damages were awarded they ought to be assessed on the deprivation of all the dominant owner's lights, including modern lights which would not have acquired a prescriptive right to their protection.

Walsh J proceeded on the basis of the principle that an injury which is not actionable in its own right could be redressed, if it is in the nature of an additional injury resulting from the same cause as that which has occasioned an injury that *is* actionable, and is an injury of the same kind:[3]

> ' ... the damages are damages for the injury to the hereditament which enjoys the easement which is the direct result of the unlawful act, not just damages for the particular quantity of light interfered with coming through the windows which were protected by a right enforceable at law. Once the defendant by his wrongful act has directly caused the damage complained of, he cannot seek to segregate one part of it from another where the whole of the damage resulting from his act was known and foreseeable by him. In such a case it would be completely contrary to legal principle that he should be permitted by an unlawful act to cause damage with impunity to another.'[4]

In the opinion of Walsh J, a litigant should not be worse off because he sought damages rather than an injunction: an injunction would manifestly have restored both ancient and modern lights.[5]

---

1   *Walsh v Goulding* (31 July 1968, unreported) HC.
2   *Scott v Goulding Properties Ltd* [1973] IR 200.
3   In substantial reliance upon *Campbell v Paddington Corpn* [1911] 1 KB 869 and *Griffith v Richard Clay and Sons Ltd* [1912] 2 Ch 291.
4   [1973] IR 200 at 212.
5   Hudson in 'Parasitic Damages for Loss of Light' (1975) 39 Conv 116 suggested that the fears expressed by Fitzgerald J on the potentially extreme effect of an award of parasitic damages could be countered if the scope of a possible injunction were to be the yardstick by which parasitic damages were measured. See also Bland *The Law of Easements and Profits à Prendre* pp 336–337.

[7.39] Fitzgerald J, with whose judgment McLoughlin J concurred, held that there was no legal justification for the protection of modern lights on the same basis as ancient lights. He adduced the example of a one-storey building with one window constituting an ancient light being replaced by a new building of 10 or 15 storeys with hundreds of windows; if damages could be awarded for the obstruction of modern lights on the same basis as for ancient lights, this new building would be entitled to have damages assessed in respect of the obstruction to those hundreds of windows, even though only one window had originally been an ancient light, if a neighbouring owner in the course of building on his property were to cause an obstruction to all the windows.[1] Clearly this would be inequitable to the owner of the servient tenement.

---

1   The illustration chosen by Fitzgerald J, to be effective in law, would also require that the dominant owner not so have confused his ancient and his modern lights as to be held to have extinguished his ancient lights; and, that the obstruction occasioned by the servient owner to the modern lights could not have been caused without also obstructing the ancient lights: *Tapling v Jones* (1865) 11 HLC 290; *Frechette v La Compagnie Manufactiere de St Hyacinthe* (1883) 9 App Cas 170; *Ankerson v Connolly* [1906] 2 Ch 544, [1907] 1 Ch 678; *News of the World Ltd v Allen Fairhead and Sons Ltd* [1931] 2 Ch 402.

[7.40] In each court the judges agreed that the award of damages should contain specific ingredients for depreciation in value and loss of amenity.[1] Teevan J in the High Court had noted that in cases of light there was not so much a discernible damage to the property, which could be gauged by the diminution in sale value, as an impairment in the enjoyment of the property. In this latter situation the owner-occupier would be in a better position as regards the measurement of compensation than a non-owning occupier or a non-occupying owner. Compensation could not be limited to a prospective loss of sale value, because there might be no intention to sell. Likewise, unless some proportion of damages awarded were ascribed to loss of amenity, the dominant owner would have no effective remedy, should there be a sudden market fluctuation causing the property, even after the nuisance, to become more valuable than it had been before.

In the Supreme Court Fitzgerald J also held that the damages had to include ingredients both of loss of amenity and depreciation, while Walsh J cautioned that the respective ingredients in the award of damages had to be balanced carefully:

> '...[B]earing in mind the possibility of duplication if the relative positions of depreciation in value and loss of amenity are not kept in proper perspective, one fixes a figure to cover the situation which will include both of these to the extent to which they exist or may exist.'[2]

---

[1]   Bland *The Law of Easements and Profits à Prendre* pp 333–336.
[2]   *Scott v Goulding Properties Ltd* [1973] IR 200 at 215.

Right to Air

[7.41] A right to the passage of air over the servient tenement through an aperture on the dominant tenement is, technically, capable of existing as an easement, although such a right, if urged as being over an unlimited area of the servient tenement, rather than through a defined course or channel, is likely to fail on the grounds of being vague, uncertain, and incapable of interruption by any reasonable means. There is no decision regarding claims to a right of air in the canon of the Irish law reports, although both in pleadings, and also in certain of the decisions, rights to light and air are sometimes twinned as though they were kindred concepts. They are not. The special status of a right to light, for the purposes of long enjoyment, is catered for by s 3 of the Prescription (Ireland) Act 1858. A right to air, like all other easements, is catered for under s 2. Neither can a judicial interpretation concerning an aperture to which the right of an access of light has been found warrant the inference that a right to the access of air through the same aperture has been determined.

[7.42] Such decisions of the English courts as have treated of a claimed right to air, by prescription, other than through a specific aperture on the dominant tenement or along a specific channel on the servient tenement, have held against the alleged right on the basis that in most cases it would be virtually impossible for the servient owner to be able to do anything to prevent the enjoyment of it.[1] While the courts tend to seek to prevent acts by the owner of the alleged servient tenement that impede the adequate ventilation of the dominant owner's property,[2] and 'have interfered to prevent the total obstruction of all circulation of air',[3] the judicial preference appears to be to strive to vindicate rights to air through the discovery or implication of a covenant to the appropriate effect. In cases where the disposal of property by the owner of a contiguous property is done in the knowledge of the intended user of that property by the purchaser, then the doctrine of non-derogation from grant may be invoked to prevent the vendor undertaking activities on his retained property which would have the effect of limiting or interrupting the passage of air to the purchaser's property in such a way as to interfere with the known purpose to which the purchaser intended to put the property.[4]

---

[1]   *Webb v Bird* (1862) 13 CB (NS) 841 is the best known of these.
[2]   *Gale v Abbott* (1862) 8 Jur (NS) 987; *Dent v Auction Mart Co* (1866) LR 2 Eq 238.

3 *Dent v Auction Mart Co* (1866) LR 2 Eq 238 at 252, per Page Wood V-C.
4 See para [2.29] ff.

[7.43] A cause of action can lie in nuisance where foul or impure air is imparted by the owner of one property to property owned by another: the right not to receive air in a contaminated state from a neighbouring property is one of the natural incidents of ownership. It does not depend for its authenticity on the grant of easement, actual, implied or imputed. Ideally, particular requirements regarding the passage of air between adjoining landowners should be dealt with by grant or covenant. Given the inherent, if paradoxical, intangibility of the atmosphere in which we live and breathe, there is an inevitable limit on the extent to which controversies of this sort can be resolved by intervention from the courts.

Chapter 8

Watercourses and Rights of Water

Natural and Acquired Rights in Relation to Water

Introduction and general principles

[8.01] A riparian owner is one who owns land, either through which, or on the boundary of which, naturally flowing water passes in a defined channel. Such a channel is known as a watercourse. A riparian owner has the following rights:

(a) to receive such of the water as any upper riparian owner does not reasonably require for the ordinary and primary uses of his property;

(b) to receive the water in a pure state;

(c) to use the water for the ordinary and primary purposes of his own property;

(d) to have the water flow through his land and so on to the property of a riparian owner or owners further down.

The rights of a riparian owner are subject to a corresponding duty to permit to pass on to riparian owners further downstream such of the water, in its natural state, as any particular riparian owner does not reasonably require. Where the water passes through land by means of a drain, the right can be expressed as one to discharge the flow of the water on to lower-lying riparian lands.[1] The water itself is not owned until sequestered. The right inheres in the flow of the water through the channel and the use and enjoyment of the water. This also includes a right to ply vessels upon the water.

The general nature of the right was set out by Palles CB in *Ewart v Belfast Poor-Law Guardians*:[2]

> 'As to surface streams, it is now perfectly settled that every riparian proprietor has *ex jure naturae*, as a natural incident to the right to the soil itself, a right to the use of the water of the stream as it flows past his lands. ... The right depends on the mode in which the stream was accustomed to flow. If this mode were incapable of being known or ascertained, the measure of the right should itself be uncertain.'

---

1 *Craig v McCance* (1910) 44 ILTR 90; *Doona and Kissane v O'Donoghue* (1957) Ir Jur 85.
2 *Ewart v Belfast Poor-Law Guardians* (1881) 9 LR Ir 172 at 185.

[8.02] Unlike the access to laterally directed light – that is to say, light flowing across a servient tenement and entering through some aperture on the dominant tenement designed for the receiving of light – a right to the user and flow of water running in a defined channel is a natural right inhering in ownership of the adjacent or penetrated land. Such a right is not an easement. A right to the use of running water becomes an easement if granted by a riparian owner to one who is not a riparian owner, provided that it is appurtenant to some dominant estate of the grantee and is not a mere personal licence;[1] or if a riparian owner increases the level of his own enjoyment beyond that inhering as a natural right and so acquires a right to it by prescription. Like all easements, a grant of water rights can be express or implied, and can be acquired by presumed lost grant and prescription.

---

[1]   See Montrose 'Registered and Unregistered Easements – Natural and Artificial Watercourses' (1938) 2 NILQ 142. Such a person then becomes the dominant owner of an easement. They do not themselves become a riparian owner. See para **[8.14]**.

Character and extent of user

[8.03] There are three ways in which the owner of land through which a river or stream runs can use the water to which his ownership gives him access:[1]

(a)   he can use it for ordinary or primary purposes, in which case there are no limitations and the water can be entirely exhausted;

(b)   he can use it for extraordinary or secondary purposes, which are nevertheless incident to, or connected with, the land, and this is subject to conditions:

'The use must be reasonable. The purposes of (sic) which the water is taken must be connected with the tenement, and he is bound to restore the water which he takes and uses for those purposes substantially undiminished in volume and unaltered in character.'[2]

(c)   the water can be enjoyed for some purpose foreign to, or unconnected with, the riparian tenement, and this is not allowed at all.

---

[1]   Derived from the speech of Lord MacNaghten in *McCartney v Londonderry and Lough Swilly Railway Co* [1904] AC 301; also (1904) 38 ILTR 143.

[2]   (1904) 38 ILTR 143 at 146.

[8.04] It was this latter type of user which was being contended for in *McCartney v Londonderry and Lough Swilly Railway Co*.[1] The respondent railway company owned land through part of which ran a stream. Their intention was to construct a three-inch-wide pipe to siphon off water from the stream and use it to fill their ten locomotive engines with water. These were stationed half a mile away and the respondent company had 40 miles of tracks plus the right to ride over the tracks of other railway companies. The water thus siphoned off was to be used by the boilers of the locomotive engines in the course of their journeys. The appellant lower riparian owner, who owned a mill, had taken up the respondents' pipe, which it was accepted he was entitled to do if the respondents had no right to extract the water.

The evidence established that if the respondents used the full 15,000 gallons a day, which the pipe could siphon off, the appellant's mill would be stopped for less than three minutes a day. However, it was urged that the respondents would only use 5,000 gallons of water a day thereby causing a daily stoppage in dry weather of less than a minute.

---

[1] *McCartney v Londonderry and Lough Swilly Railway Co* [1904] AC 301; also (1904) 38 ILTR 143.

[8.05] Lord Halsbury LC, while observing that the primary issue for determination was, not so much the quantity of water used as the purpose for which it was being used,[1] held that the quantity of water abstracted was unreasonable; that, in effect, a small stream passing through a small area of riparian land was being used to service 40 miles of railway line and all the exigencies of the railway service. The Lord Chancellor cited in support the decision of Lord Cairns in *The Swindon Waterworks Co v The Berkshire Canal Navigation Co*[2] which he regarded as codifying the law on riparian rights. In that case Lord Cairns had stated:

> '... the use which they claim the right to make of it, is not for the purpose of their tenements at all, but is a use which virtually amounts to a complete diversification of the stream. ... it is a confiscation of the rights of the lower owner.'[3]

---

[1] It seems clear that where the purpose is not in issue, there is no cause of action if the diminution of water is not substantial: *Cooper v Owens* (1858) 3 Ir Jur NS 434; *Embrey v Owen* (1851) 6 Exch 353.

[2] *The Swindon Waterworks Co v The Berkshire Canal Navigation Co* (1875) LR 7 HL Cas 697.

[3] (1875) LR 7 HL Cas 697 at 704–705.

[8.06] According to Lord MacNaghten, the purpose proposed for the siphoned water was entirely alien to the ordinary use of the riparian tenement and was one which the law did not allow. In his Lordship's view, 'they [the respondents] mean to efface and blot out as it were that portion of the stream which they propose to extract.' The whole enterprise was solely undertaken for gain by the respondents; they would be unable to return the water extracted; and, as far as the lower riparian proprietors were concerned, the activity was tantamount virtually to enabling the respondents to sell the water. It could not be maintained that all the railway lines of the respondent company, or all the railway lines of other companies over which they had running powers, constituted one riparian tenement; or that the railway company, by reason of that one single contact with a stream, possessed throughout all their own lines, and all the lines over which they had permission to run, rights 'analogous to those possessed by persons who dwell on the banks of a river in respect of their riverside property.'[1]

---

[1] *McCartney v Londonderry and Lough Swilly Railway Co* (1904) 38 ILTR 143 at 147.

[8.07] Lord Lindley held that, even though, in terms of the overall quantity of water lost, the infringement of the lower riparian owner's right was not especially significant, yet, if uninterrupted and suffered to persist for 20 years, the railway company could acquire a right to it by prescription – a circumstance that the court would interfere to prevent happening:

'The railway company in this case became riparian owners simply by having a small strip of land crossed by the stream. They thereby acquired the water rights, whatever they were, of the owner of the land so bought, but they acquired no greater rights than he could give them in respect of that land. These rights did not include the right to take water from the stream for consumption off the land, the possession of which conferred his rights. He could not lawfully take water from the stream in any appreciable quantity and sell it for use miles away, or, indeed, use it himself at a distance from his riparian tenement without returning it to the stream. Such a user is unreasonable, and can only be justified by a grant from lower riparian owners or by prescription.'[1]

---

[1]   *McCartney v Londonderry and Lough Swilly Railway Co* (1904) 38 ILTR 143 at 148.

Ancillary rights of riparian owners

[8.08] The owner of land which is drained by a gullet or channel is entitled to clean his drains by scouring the base of them provided he does not deepen them. Even though the scouring may have the effect of increasing the flow of water through the drain, and thereby increasing the flow of water through a servient owner's lands, that does not extinguish the right to use the drain.[1] Neither will the right to use a mill be extinguished by reason of changing the purpose of the use provided that the resultant user is not more onerous on the servient tenement.[2]

Where the owner of land which is at a higher elevation than that of his neighbour constructs a new drain or gullet in lieu of an old one which had become obstructed, a cause of action does not arise if the easier throughput of drainage water causes intermittent and serious flooding on the lower lands of his neighbour simply because it happens to fill a watercourse which also runs through the neighbour's land: this is because the drainage by a landowner of his own land is the ordinary and natural use of it and does not give rise to a cause of action.[3]

---

[1]   *Craig v McCance* (1910) 44 ILTR 90.

[2]   *Pullan v The Roughfort Bleaching and Dyeing Co (Ltd)* (1888) 21 LR Ir 73.

[3]   *Doona and Kissane v O'Donoghue* (1956) 23 Ir Jur Rep 85. In this case Judge Barra O'Briain in the Circuit Court relied upon the decision in *Shine v The Irish Land Commission and Roscommon County Council* (1946) 81 ILTR 100, where the plaintiff's lands had been flooded by reason of the defendant's cutting a bog on his land and it was held that the flooding thereby occasioned was not actionable, since the drainage of a bog was the ordinary and natural use of land of this kind. However, the proposition that drainage activity confers total immunity stands to be qualified by the emergence of recent developments in the law of negligence and nuisance. See para [9.37] ff and paras [12.14]–[12.15].

[8.09] The owner of a drain which passes over his neighbour's land and discharges itself into a river on the far side of the neighbour's land is entitled to enter upon the neighbour's land to clear the drain, but is not entitled to insist that the neighbour clean his own drain; however, if prevented from entering, and in particular if he has to incur expense as a result of this, he will be entitled to an injunction and damages.[1]

[1]   *Kelly v Dea* (1955) 100 ILTR 1.

Preservation of prescriptively acquired rights

[8.10] If prescriptive rights have been acquired to the use of a particular drain or watercourse, they cannot be varied unilaterally by the servient owner, nor can the watercourse be blocked up. In *Claxton v Claxton*,[1] the plaintiff and the defendant were neighbouring tenants who for 55 years had used a covered drain which carried surface water off the plaintiff's land and through the defendant's land. In 1872 the defendant filled in the drain passing through his land and constructed a new channel which met the drain above the obstruction, thus continuing to drain off the water from the plaintiff's land. The Court of Exchequer held that the defendant was not entitled to do this, Dowse B maintaining that the plaintiff would not have the continuity of enjoyment requisite to confer a prescriptive right in the new channel; while Fitzgerald B held that the plaintiff's right was to have the water carried off his own land in a regular channel through the defendant's land, and that the defendant had no entitlement to interrupt that right, even though damage might not be caused thereby.

[1]   (1873) IR 7 CL 23. See also *Hanks v Cribbin* (1857) 7 ICLR 489, 9 ICLR 312, see ch 4, para **[4.11]**.

[8.11] In *Callaghan v Callaghan*,[1] a stream had flowed out from the defendant's lands, through two gullets in a public road, from which it entered the plaintiff's land. The defendant constructed a new gullet, blocked up the old ones, and thereby diverted the water from the plaintiff's land. Murphy J held that since the plaintiff had never acquiesced in this, and had enjoyed user of the flow of water for over 20 years, he had acquired a right to the flow of the stream from the public road through the two gullets.

[1]   *Callaghan v Callaghan* (1897) 3 ILT 418. Generally, a diminution in the right to take water from the land of another must be material in order for a non-riparian owner to have a cause of action in damages. 'Easements in Respect of Water. Non-Riparian Owners of Land' (1951) 85 ILTSJ 95.

Quality of water

[8.12] A riparian owner is entitled to have the water continue to flow past his lands 'without a substantial alteration in its character or in its quality': Kenny J in *Raymond Kerin v Bord na Mona*.[1] The plaintiff owned lands in Co Offaly bounded by the River Blackwater which flooded annually. In 1960 the defendant started working on the Blackwater Bog a mile and a half upstream with the purpose of securing milled peat for the generation of electricity. One consequence of these works was that the flooding of the Blackwater was increased and large deposits of black silt, resulting from turf dust floating downstream from the defendant's works, were deposited on the plaintiff's lands, permanently ruining 58 acres which had been used for agricultural purposes. Kenny J awarded damages for the loss occasioned by the interference by the defendant with the plaintiff's riparian rights.[2]

---

[1]   *Raymond Kerin v Bord na Mona* (30 January 1970, unreported) HC.

[2]   Kenny J stated that he would not grant an injunction, as the injury to the plaintiff's property had already been done, and an injunction would have had the effect of compelling the defendant to cease its work on the Blackwater Bog the ultimate purpose of which was to facilitate the generation of electricity for public supply.

[8.13] The owner of land bounded on three sides by running water, and on the fourth by an inlet from a stream through which seeps effluence from a septic tank constructed by a nearby landowner, is not obliged to clean the inlet after it has silted up and the sewage, being untreated, begins to occasion a nuisance, even though the cleaning of the inlet would have the additional effect of abating the nuisance.[1]

---

[1]   *Callan v McAvinue* (11 May 1973, unreported) HC.

Rights of licensees to take water

[8.14] It appears now to be settled by the courts in England that a mere licensee of riparian rights from a riparian owner, has a cause of action only against his own grantor, and not against any other riparian owner, for diversion or pollution of the waters licensed to him, at a point higher up on the watercourse.[1] This is because the proprietorial right to the use and enjoyment of water is bound up with ownership of the land across or alongside which the water flows in a defined channel. A right granted other than as appurtenant to the land of a grantee is a licence: redress for the infraction of this lies in contract, and is subject to the principles governing and delimiting contractual liability.

---

[1]   *Stockport Waterworks Co v Potter* (1864) 3 H & C 300; *Ormerod v The Todmorden Joint Stock Mill Co Ltd* (1883) 11 QBD 155.

Defined Channel

[8.15] One of the principal considerations in determining whether a particular flow of water constitutes a watercourse, is whether it flows in what is termed a defined channel. Water which squanders itself indiscriminately over an indefinite area does not flow in a defined channel and so is not a watercourse.

[8.16] The exact meaning of a defined channel arose for decision in *Briscoe v Drought,*[1] a case before the Irish Court of Exchequer. From at least the opening years of the nineteenth century, the residents of the town of Banagher in Co Offaly had drained rainwater and effluence through culverts at the side of the main street, which ran downhill to the bottom of the town. There the culverts converged and the discharge flowed, first through a laneway owned by the defendant (for the purpose of this case the servient tenant), and then through a drain owned by the plaintiff (the dominant tenant), from which it emptied itself into the River Shannon. The plaintiff held property adjacent to the lane under a lease of 1831 (more than 20 years prior to the action) which provided that he was entitled to the benefit of the manure from the road and drain passing beside his premises. The present action arose when the defendant diverted the waters that flowed down the main street of the town, at the point where they entered his laneway, and used them for the fertilising of his own land. The evidence established that, since the defendant's laneway had a higher elevation at one side than at the other, the water coming through the town tended to collect on one side of the lane, only taking up its full expanse in times of flood.

The Court of Exchequer unanimously accepted that the people of Banagher had the right to discharge their water and effluence over the land of the defendant, Hughes B maintaining that a jury could have presumed a grant to that effect arising from long user by the townspeople. The Court, however, was divided on whether the plaintiff and the defendant, as against each other, could mutually insist that the waters continue to flow from the land of the defendant to the land of the plaintiff and be received by the plaintiff from the land of the defendant.

---

[1]   *Briscoe v Drought* (1859) 11 ICLR 250.

[8.17] Hughes B held that a grant could be presumed as between the plaintiff and the defendant, in the nature of a mutual or reciprocal easement, provided there was nothing either in the origin or character of the water and sewage to negative such a grant, on the same basis as a grant could be presumed from both the plaintiff and the defendant to the townspeople of Banagher:

> '... if the owner of the lane [the defendant] and the owner of the drain [the plaintiff] are to be presumed to have been parties to a grant conferring upon the inhabitants of the town the right I have mentioned, the owner of the land and the owner of the drain had, as between themselves, also acquired certain rights and certain liabilities. For instance, the owner of the drain would not be at liberty to close up that drain, as against the owner of the lane, and thus throw back upon the lane the street water and sewage, and keep it permanently there.'[1]

Hughes B then addressed the issue of whether the alleged watercourse had a defined channel. It had been argued that this was an 'occasional' or 'temporary' watercourse, since there was not always water flowing through it, and even when there was it did not invariably take up the full width of the lane due to the lane itself being higher at one side than the other. Hughes B distinguished between intermission resulting from natural causes, such as the absence or abundance of rain, which, he held, inherently affects all natural watercourses, and intermission resulting from the acts of individuals. He added:

> 'And the meaning I attribute to the words "temporary" and "occasional" is that, when the volume or duration is dependent on the will or convenience of individuals, it is to be considered temporary or occasional; but, if it is proved that rain-water forms itself, from the nature of the locality upon which it descends, into a visible stream, and, as far back as memory can extend, has pursued a fixed and definite channel for its discharge, in my opinion, the "volume" of the stream may be "occasional" and "temporary"; but its "course" is neither "occasional" or "temporary".'[2]

[1] *Briscoe v Drought* (1859) 11 ICLR 250 at 262.
[2] (1859) 11 ICLR 250 at 263–264.

[8.18] According to Christian J (who with Hughes B delivered the majority judgments of the Court), the inhabitants of Banagher had the right to continue the flow of water and sewage as against both the defendant and the plaintiff. As long as they chose this particular method of siphoning off their water and sewage, the upper owner of such land, namely the defendant, had the right not to have his drainage blocked off by the lower owner so as to cause flooding of the upper lands. The question to be decided, therefore, was whether the lower owner, the plaintiff, had a correlative right – that is to say, whether he could compel the continuance of the flow of water in terms of a right to receive it.

In the opinion of Christian J, such a right could not be maintained against the inhabitants of Banagher themselves, who were entitled to alter the flow of their rainwater and sewage without any suit lying with either the plaintiff or the defendant. However, despite the fact that the watercourse existed only at the whim, and for the convenience, of the townspeople of Banagher, there was no reason why its continuance could not be the subject-matter of a grant between the defendant and the plaintiff, provided that the user justified such an inference, as in this case it did. The plaintiff had had the benefit of the use of this water and sewage for more than 20 years, thereby plainly constituting it as a right to which he attached value.

[8.19] Christian J confirmed that any watercourse must contain the essential ingredients of an easement:

> '... a flow of water possessing that unity of character by which the flow on one person's land can be identified with that on his neighbour's. Water which squanders itself over an indefinite surface is not a proper subject-matter for the acquisition of a right by user.'[1]

In order to determine whether there is a watercourse or not, one must look at the *whole* stream from its source to its discharge, and not merely to one part of it. If the defendant's lane had not intervened, the watercourse would unquestionably have flowed in a defined channel from start to finish. Hence, the question had to be asked whether there was anything in the lane that would take away this character. The only relevant characteristic was that the laneway was higher at one side than at the other, so that the water tended to flow at the lower end, only taking up the entire width in times of flood. The significant factor, according to Christian J, was that the water was incapable of going beyond the width of the lane, and was therefore clearly defined. The identity of the water entering the lane was the same as that which discharged itself into the plaintiff's drain. Even if this had always been a natural stream, flowing between natural banks before it reached the defendant's lane, and once again flowing between natural banks after it had left the defendant's lane, and the intervening space had sometimes been dry and then used as a footway, but when flooded was used as a watercourse, that would not make the defendant's lane any less a watercourse.

[1] *Briscoe v Drought* (1859) 11 ICLR 250 at 271.

[8.20] According to Fitzgerald B, dissenting, the fact that the waters took up the whole width of the lane in times of flood, but not at other times, was insufficient to render the lane a defined channel for the purposes of the definition of a watercourse. Since, in the view of Fitzgerald B, the water did *not* flow in a defined channel, a presumed lost grant could not arise from its use, even if enjoyed for more than 20 years.

Fitzgerald B also felt himself bound by the case of *Rawstron v Taylor*.[1] In this marshy water regularly came to the surface on the moors near the defendant's land and flowed off, in indiscriminate courses, down a slope, and so into an old watercourse belonging to the plaintiff. There was no clear ditch through which the water flowed, and no water at all in dry weather. An action by the plaintiff when the defendant diverted the water failed. Parke B's ground of decision was that the water itself was common surface water, with a purely casual flow, in no defined channel, and that the owner of any land on which it chanced to emerge could do with it what he liked. Christian J, also alluding to this case, distinguished it, on the basis that, unlike in *Briscoe v Drought*,[2] there was there no clearly defined watercourse.

---

[1]   *Rawstron v Taylor* (1855) 11 Exch 369.
[2]   *Briscoe v Drought* (1859) 11 ICLR 250.

Irrigated channels

[8.21] Where a natural stream has been diverted to irrigate farmlands in a particular area and then rejoins its original course further on, the fact that the irrigated part of the stream is distributed in small cuts or channels at certain times of the year for irrigation purposes does not mean that the channel is any less defined for the purpose of its character as a watercourse. The permanency of the main channel continues despite the irrigation cuts and the water returns to it after its distribution.[1]

---

[1]   *Powell v Butler* (1871) IR 5 CL 309.

Artificial Watercourses

Definition and basic principles

[8.22] An artificial watercourse is one which is man-made, such as a canal or weir or a channel constructed to discharge products from a mine, rather than one which arises through operation of nature. The right to the use of water flowing in a natural watercourse is a natural right incidental to the ownership of the property through which the watercourse flows; the right to the use of water flowing in an artificial watercourse is an easement, depending upon grant, actual or presumed.[1] The extent to which the rights governing artificial watercourses can be assimilated to those applicable to natural watercourses depends on the purpose for which the watercourse was constructed and whether it was intended to be permanent or temporary. The law on the subject was set out by Chatterton V-C in *Blackburn v Somers*:[2]

'It appears to be settled that riparian rights identical with those attaching to natural streams may be acquired by prescription in artificial watercourses of a permanent character. Those rights must depend upon the character of the watercourse, and the purposes for which it was constructed. If the watercourse was of a permanent nature, and constructed for lasting purposes, and especially for the general benefit of the parties in its vicinity, and not merely with the temporary and private object of benefiting the property of those by whom it was constructed, such as draining a mine, or a mining district, or the like, riparian rights may be acquired in its water, just as in a natural stream.'

---

1   See the advice of the Privy Council in *Rameshur v Koonj* (1878) 4 App Cas 121, cited with approval by Kingsmill Moore J in *Cullen v Dublin Corpn* (22 July 1960, unreported) SC. Montrose in 'Registered and Unregistered Easements – Natural and Artificial Watercourses' (1938) 2 NILQ 142 at 144, suggested that the rights of those entitled to the use of an artificial watercourse will approximate to those of a riparian owner 'when the watercourse is constructed in such a way as to be a permanent geographical feature, when in law it will be treated as if it were a natural stream, and then the grantee of the watercourse is considered to be in the same position as a riparian owner.'

2   *Blackburn v Somers* (1879) 5 LR Ir 1 at 7–8.

[8.23] In *Cullen v Dublin Corpn*[1] Kingsmill Moore J held that there was a presumed lost grant of riparian rights in an ancient artificial watercourse in favour of the owners of lands through which the watercourse passed, on the basis of the prolonged history of user evidenced by the landowners and their predecessors. The judge felt that it was 'not only natural but also inherently probable' that, in return for their permission given to Dublin Corporation to run the watercourse through their lands, the landowners would have been allowed riparian rights.

Neither were these rights inconsistent with the absolute right asserted by the Corporation to be able to dispose of the waters for consumption in the city from the point where they reached the city boundaries onwards. Kingsmill Moore J stated that he found it 'impossible to suppose that all these mills and their auxiliary works existed merely by leave and licence of the Corporation and are not attributable to rights asserted by riparian owners.'[2] He further held that, once the rights were assumed to have been granted 'in as full and ample a manner as if the watercourse were natural' they cannot be deemed to be destroyed by non-user, but like rights in a natural watercourse, being an incident of the enjoyment of the property, could only be disposed of by an express alienation.[3]

---

1   *Cullen v Dublin Corpn* (22 July 1960, unreported) SC.
2   (22 July 1960, unreported) SC at p 17.
3   (22 July 1960, unreported) SC at p 8, following the decisions in *Roberts v Richards* (1881) 50 LJ Ch 297 and *Sampson v Hoddinott* (1857) 1 CB (NS) 611.

Rights of lower riparian owner against upper riparian owner creating watercourse

[8.24] The rationale behind the legal differentiation between natural and artificial watercourses was articulated by Lord Abinger in the English Court of Exchequer in

Arkwright v Gell.[1] This case concerned a claim by lower riparian owners to compel the owners of a mine to continue a discharge of water arising from the draining of the mine, which the lower riparian owners had enjoyed for over 20 years. Lord Abinger held that such a right could not enure in the lower riparian owners, because the sole purpose of the watercourse was to facilitate the draining of the mine; in all likelihood, the watercourse was meant to be discontinued once the mineral ore had been exhausted. To hold otherwise would be to prevent the mine owners from working their mine in the ordinary way after draining operations had been completed and to compel the retention – for the sole purpose of benefiting those who had accidentally enjoyed the water – of an artificial watercourse for which the mine owners would no longer have any use.[2]

Lord Abinger further observed that the mine-owners would be unable to take an action to prevent the lower riparian owners enjoying the use of the water, nor would they be able physically to stop it, short of siphoning off the water further down from the mine before it reached the land of others – an expensive and inconvenient expedient.[3]

In relation to the then newly enacted Prescription Act, Lord Abinger observed that, as the claim had to be based on enjoyment without interruption against someone capable of resisting the claim, the enjoyment in this case was not of such a kind, since the mine owners would have been incapable of preventing the enjoyment until – as in the instant case – the lower riparian owner asserted a right. On this account also, the enjoyment would not have been 'as of right' and thus failed to satisfy the conditions of the statute.[4]

---

[1] *Arkwright v Gell* (1839) 5 M & W 203.

[2] A like argument prevailed in the Irish case of *Hanna v Pollock* [1898] 2 IR 532, per Andrews J; [1900] 2 IR 664, per Fitzgibbon LJ and Walker LJ. See para **[4.34]**.

[3] It will be recalled that a similar consideration has disinclined the courts in England to find as an easement a right to the passage of air over an unlimited area or other than through a defined course or channel. See para **[7.41]**.

[4] Anderson in 'Easement and Prescription – Changing Perspectives in Classification' (1975) 38 MLR 641 has suggested that a number of nineteenth century cases treating of easements were more concerned with whether any particular right was one which could be prescribed for, rather than with the nature of the right itself, thereby limiting the value of such cases as precedents.

Rights of lower riparian owner against upper riparian owner not creating watercourses

[8.25] Similar reasoning to that applied in *Arkwright v Gell*[1] prevailed again, 10 years later, in *Wood v Waud*,[2] in which the English Court of Exchequer held that a right could not be asserted by a lower riparian owner against an upper riparian owner, not the author of the discharge, who diverted the water for his own purposes. This case also involved the draining of a mining operation. Pollock CB, in delivering the judgment of the Court, observed:

'These [mine] owners merely get rid of a nuisance to their works by discharging the water into the sough, and cannot be considered as giving it to one more than another of the proprietors of the land through which that sough is constructed; each may take and use what passes through his land, and the proprietor of the land below has no right to any part of that water until it has reached his own land – he has no right to compel the owners above to permit the water to flow through their lands for his benefit; and, consequently, he has no right of action if they refuse to do so.'[3]

---

[1] *Arkwright v Gell* (1839) 5 M & W 203.
[2] *Wood v Waud* (1849) 3 Exch 748.
[3] (1849) 3 Exch 748 at 779–780.

[8.26] It should be noted that in Ireland, the case of *Briscoe v Drought*[1] has diverged from the articulation in *Wood v Waud*,[2] insofar as concerns the mutual rights between lower riparian owners in the context of an artificial watercourse intended for public waste. In *Briscoe v Drought*, Christian J, having considered with approval both *Arkwright v Gell*[3] and *Wood v Waud*, interpreted the latter to apply only to natural rights and not to cases arising from a grant, whether actual or presumed; and held that each of the lower riparian owners had rights, as against each other, respectively to pass on and receive the water flowing through the watercourse, but had not such rights against the citizens of the town, at whose will, and for whose convenience, the watercourse had been constructed. These had the right to alter the method of discharging their waste without any right of action lying against them by either of the lower riparian owners.[4]

---

[1] *Briscoe v Drought* (1859) 11 ICLR 250.
[2] *Wood v Waud* (1849) 3 Exch 748.
[3] *Arkwright v Gell* (1839) 5 M & W 203.
[4] Christian J also noted that the enjoyment by the plaintiff in *Wood v Waud* of the water flowing through the artificial watercourse had been for less than 20 years, so that a grant of a right to its use could not be presumed. This point of distinction further demonstrates the willingness of the Irish courts in the middle of the nineteenth century to consider the application of a presumed lost grant between the owners of contiguous properties.

Partially or intermittently artificial watercourses

[8.27] In Ireland, due to the absence of a significant industrial culture and the more muted impact of the Industrial Revolution, disputes involving watercourses are usually of a different kind from those encountered in *Arkwright v Gell*[1] and *Wood v Waud*.[2] Frequently, only part of the watercourse is alleged to be artificial and the question arises whether the rights governing natural watercourses are to apply to such watercourse in its entirety.

---

[1] *Arkwright v Gell* (1839) 5 M & W 203.
[2] *Wood v Waud* (1849) 3 Exch 748.

[8.28] Hence, in *Powell v Butler*,[1] where a natural watercourse was diverted through part of its course for the purpose of irrigating adjacent farmlands in Co Tipperary, an obstruction by an upper riparian owner was successfully resisted by a lower riparian owner, both owners holding in the diverted portion. Monahan CJ stated that a right can be acquired by user in an artificial watercourse and in this case had been so acquired, as the diversion of the stream had taken place over 30 years earlier and the plaintiff lower riparian owner had enjoyed the irrigation for at least 20 of those. Furthermore, the evidence had established that the watercourse had been diverted for the benefit of all the tenants through whose farmlands the waters ran and not for some of them only.

---

[1]   *Powell v Butler* (1871) IR 5 CL 309.

[8.29] Where a watercourse started out as a stream, was briefly diverted in order to accommodate the construction of a new road, then resumed its natural course before discharging into a river, it is not an artificial watercourse in the legal sense, as the artificial portion of it would have been intended to have had permanent effect for the purpose of providing a permanent convenience: *Blackburn v Somers*.[1] In this case, which was an action for pollution rather than diversion of water, Chatterton V-C observed that it would be too wide a proposition to assert that rights to watercourses arising from enjoyment were under all circumstances identical, regardless of whether the watercourse was natural or artificial; but that, in the case of an artificial watercourse, much depended upon whether it was temporary or permanent in nature and the circumstances under which it was created. By way of illustration the Vice Chancellor adduced the example of enjoyment for 20 years of a stream penned up by permanent embankments, which he suggested was on a different footing from enjoyment of a flow of water resulting from a temporary alteration in the use of a person's property. He went on to hold, relying largely on the judgment of Erle CJ in *Gaved v Martyn*,[2] that the question of the status of a watercourse, whether natural or artificial, can depend on whether the origin of the stream is natural: '... if the stream flows at its source by the operation of nature, it is a natural stream; if it flows at its source by the operation of man, it is an artificial stream.'[3]

---

[1]   *Blackburn v Somers* (1879) 5 LR Ir 1.
[2]   *Gaved v Martyn* (1865) 19 CB (NS) 732.
[3]   (1879) 5 LR Ir 1 at 10. Chatterton V-C supported this proposition with reference to the decision of Monahan CJ in *Powell v Butler* (1871) IR 5 CL 309. See also *Hanna v Pollock* [1898] 2 IR 532, para **[4.34]** ff.

Diversion of hidden waters above source of natural spring

[8.30] The case of *McEvoy v The Great Northern Railway Co*[1] is authority for the proposition, that where a natural stream fed by percolating or underground waters, is interfered with at a point higher up than its natural head, by diversion of the hidden source waters, the landowners who had previously enjoyed the waters in the natural stream have no right to compel the continuance of an artificial watercourse into which the diverted waters have been channelled, even where they enjoy the use of that watercourse for nearly 50 years – if it is manifest that the artificial watercourse is not intended to be permanent. The predecessors of the plaintiff had prior to 1849 the right to take water from a natural stream flowing near their holdings. In 1849, while the defendant railway company was in the process of constructing a railway line, the course of a subterranean stream, which eventually fed into the natural stream, was tapped and the water found its way to a cutting of the defendant's new railway line. The defendant conveyed this water alongside its railway line in an artificially constructed channel, so as to drain it away and prevent its being a safety hazard on the line. Only in 1898 did the defendant start to make use of the water in this artificial channel for its own purposes, and the plaintiff who had been enjoying the water for domestic purposes since 1849 took an action for disturbance of an alleged prescriptive right.

---

[1] *McEvoy v The Great Northern Railway Co* [1900] 2 IR 325.

[8.31] Palles CB adumbrated the general law applicable to rights over water flowing in an artificial watercourse:

> 'It is settled law that the rights to the water flowing in an artificial watercourse constructed by a particular person upon his own land and for his own benefit are not regulated by the law applicable to natural water-courses, but are to be ascertained by a view of the purpose for which the original structure was built ... as a general rule, circumstances which are sufficient to create an easement in favour of a particular person, do not necessarily subject the land of that person to the servitude of continuing to maintain in existence, for the benefit of the servient tenement, the works constructed by him for the purposes only of that easement. In other words, the existence of an easement does not carry with it any presumption of the creation or existence of a counter-easement in the owner of the servient tenement against the owner of the dominant tenement.'[1]

---

[1] *McEvoy v The Great Northern Railway Co* [1900] 2 IR 325 at 333.

[8.32] It is clear that the Court of Queen's Bench was principally concerned with the dangers to a railway company if compelled to preserve in perpetuity an artificial watercourse intended only for the purposes of safety while other scientifically more sophisticated methods of hazard prevention were not available to it. Palles CB derived comfort from the obligations and limitations imposed by the defendant's corporate status and suggested that, since the defendant had a duty extending into the future to maintain the safety of the railway line, it must be allowed an absolute discretion as to how this should be effected, and that, accordingly, any agreement, whether implied or otherwise, to confer an absolute right to the preservation of the watercourse would be illegal and void.[1]

---

[1] According to O'Brien J, there was an actual agreement that the plaintiff would not seek compensation for the diversion of the subterranean source of the natural stream, on the basis that its waters were to be conducted into an artificial watercourse constructed by the defendant which the plaintiff was to be allowed to use; but this agreement was incapable of binding the defendant, as being in excess of its corporate authority. It is evident that O'Brien J was ill at ease about the decision he felt compelled to give, believing that there was an inequality of bargaining power between the railway company and the plaintiff's predecessor, which had constrained the latter to undue deference.

Percolating and Underground Water

[8.33] The enjoyment of underground water, to the extent that such water does not flow in a known or defined channel, or the enjoyment of water percolating through land, is on a different footing from the enjoyment of water which flows in either a natural or a permanent artificial watercourse: neither gives rise to any right which can be defended at law.

Known and defined channel

[8.34] In *Ewart v Belfast Poor-Law Guardians*[1] Palles CB thus stated the law:

> '...the principle of the decisions regulating the flow of surface-water in a well-defined channel seems ... to be applicable to all water flowing in a certain and defined course, whether in an open visible stream, or in a known subterranean channel. ... the principles which apply to water flowing in streams are wholly inapplicable to water percolating through underground strata which has no certain course, no defined limits, but which oozes through the soil in every direction in which the rain penetrates.'[2]

The plaintiff and Andrew Clements were the respective owners of two adjacent plots of land on the side of Cavehill in Co Antrim. The plaintiff's land was below that of Andrew Clements and formerly enjoyed the benefit of a clear spring of water, whose source was in his own land and which flowed along a defined surface channel. The defendant, a local sanitary authority, was licensed by Andrew Clements to bore holes in his land for the purpose of pumping out a sufficient water supply for a nearby village. This resulted in the inadvertent diverting of the underground source of the plaintiff's spring. The plaintiff sought an injunction.

---

[1] *Ewart v Belfast Poor-Law Guardians* (1881) 9 LR Ir 172.
[2] (1881) 9 LR Ir 172 at 186.

[8.35] Palles CB regarded the case as mid-way between a known and defined watercourse and percolating water: the water was 'flowing in a course which, in a sense, may be said to be certain and defined, but which is not an open, visible stream, nor a known subterranean channel.' It was a channel incapable of being ascertained by the exercise of reasonable diligence. The flow of the water through it depended on the geological formation of underground strata, requiring for its verification deep excavations on Clements's land, which the plaintiff would have been unable to undertake short of Clements's express permission or through committing an act of trespass. Palles CB concluded that, in the absence of firm scientific evidence, a continuous and defined channel could be held to exist, but not a known one.

Continuing right to ordinary and reasonable use of land

[8.36] In the course of his judgment in *Ewart v Belfast Poor-Law Guardians*[1] Palles CB considered the English case of *Acton v Blundell*,[2] one of the bedrock authorities on subterranean water. In this the defendant had sunk coal-pits on his land which had the effect of draining off subterraneous water that otherwise would have percolated through to the plaintiff's land. The decision of Tindal CJ is, not so much to the effect that the owner of land through which water flows in a subterraneous channel has no right to its continuance, but rather that the owner of lands beneath which for the time being there is underground water is entitled to the ordinary and reasonable use of his own lands, and that the sinking of coal-pits is such a reasonable use.[3] Palles CB cited with approval Abinger CJ's identification of the potentially unfair consequences of applying the law uniformly to both types of water. The owner of land through which subterranean water passes may, all inadvertently, cause serious injury to his neighbour, the extent of that injury being virtually a matter of chance and entirely unpredictable.

> '... the advantage on one side and the detriment on the other may bear no proportion. The well may be sunk to supply a cottage, or a drinking-place for cattle, whilst the owner of the adjoining land may be prevented from winning metals and minerals of inestimable value. Lastly, there is no limit of space within which the claim of right to an underground spring can be confined. In the present case, the nearest coal-pit is at a distance of half a mile from the well. It is obvious that the law must apply equally if there is an interval of many miles.'[4]

---

[1]   *Ewart v Belfast Poor-Law Guardians* (1881) 9 LR Ir 172.

[2]   *Acton v Blundell* (1843) 12 M & W 324.

[3]   Though not itself referred to in *Ewart v Belfast Poor-Law Guardians*, the case of *Acton v Blundell* was cited with approval in *Galgay v The Great Southern and Western Railway Co* (1854) 4 ICLR. The submission by counsel that *Acton v Blundell* '... held that the owner of land through which water flows in a subterranean course has no right or interest in it which will enable him to maintain an action against a landowner who, in carrying on mining operations in his own land in the usual manner, draws away the water, and makes his well dry' was accepted by Lefroy CJ, who added that if the injury were 'occasioned only by the exercise of the right of property over the defendants' own land, and in the lawful enjoyment and use of it', a cause of action could not be sustained. See also *Cooper v Owens* (1858) 3 Ir Jur NS 434.

[4]   (1843) 12 M & W 324 at 352.

[8.37] The case of *Chasemore v Richards*,[1] also considered by Palles CB, held that a claimed right to the continued flow of percolating water was irreconcilable with the natural and ordinary rights of landowners and could not be sustained. According to Wightman J, it would be impossible to set any reasonable limits to the exercise of such a right and it would interfere with, if not prevent, the draining of land by the owner of that land.[2] Lord Cranworth noted that percolating water is an invisible process of nature, which will usually require scientific evidence to establish it.

Approbating these principles, Palles CB observed that if the contrary proposition were to be held good:

> '...we would have the startling doctrine, that an action at law would lie against a man, without any limit to the damages that could be recovered, for doing an act which, as far as he knows, or as far as can be known by reasonable inquiry, is a lawful act and the unlawfulness of which would depend upon the fact that, by some newly discovered method of examination being resorted to, it was ascertained that the water flowed in a defined channel – a fact which but for that method being resorted to would have remained for all ages unknown. That would be a monstrous doctrine.'[3]

1   *Chasemore v Richards* (1859) 7 HL Cas 349.
2   In the view of Wightman J, a grant could not be presumed to a right to the use or flow of percolating water, itself dependent upon unpredictable and unascertainable natural forces, such as the level of rainfall and the natural moisture of the soil, which the owner of the alleged servient tenement would not, in any event, be able to prevent.
3   (1881) 9 LR Ir 172 at 194–195.

Defined channel to be defined by human knowledge

[8.38] An appeal to the Court of Appeal in *Ewart v Belfast Poor-Law Guardians*[1] affirmed the decision of Chatterton V-C. In the opinion of Deasy LJ, the rights of a landowner beneath whose land flow percolating waters, fall within the principle that a person owns all the soil and land beneath his property[2] and can effectively do with them what he pleases, without giving any cause of action to his neighbour merely because he might thereby draw off the water in his neighbour's well.

Fitzgibbon LJ noted that part of the underground course of the water was 'in a definite, that is, a contracted and bounded channel and stream, but [that] its course was unknown, invisible, and *undefined by human knowledge*. This, to my mind, is the only sense in which the words "defined channel" can be used in deciding upon rights.'[3] In the judgment of Fitzgibbon LJ, the case urged by the plaintiff could not be conceded without having to hold that the defendant was prohibited from embarking on an exceptional use of the land licensed to it if that would interfere with unknown streams below; in short, that the lands would have to be subjected to an easement identical to that applying in the case of an ordinary surface watercourse. This was an unsustainable contention.

1   *Ewart v Belfast Poor-Law Guardians* (1881) 9 LR Ir 172.
2   The maxim 'cujus est solum ejus est usque ad infernos'.
3   (1881) 9 LR Ir 172 at 205.

Further consideration of a known channel

[8.39] In *Black v Ballymena Commissioners*[1] it fell to Chatterton V-C to consider the legal significance of an underground channel being 'known' as well as 'defined', the meaning of 'known' having been less fully considered than 'defined' in *Ewart v Belfast Poor-Law Guardians*.[2]

The plaintiff was a lower riparian owner of lands watered by the Quolie River. Robert McTurk was an upper riparian owner, who had granted the defendants a licence to cut a trench, lay pipes, and divert water for the supply of the town of Ballymena in Co Antrim. The plaintiff alleged that the defendants were diverting the waters of a subterranean stream that connected with the Quolie River, which had once flowed above ground for a greater distance than it currently did, and were thereby interfering with his riparian rights. He sought and secured an injunction. Chatterton V-C found that there had at one time been an overground stream, whose source was upland of Quolie River near an old thorn tree, which had then coursed through a defined and open channel, past McTurk's well, and so on into the river. More recently, the channel between the thorn tree and

McTurk's well had been covered over by falling stones and soil, but Chatterton V-C found that the channel still pursued its erstwhile course, though underground. He held that it should not make a difference that the channel was covered over by natural means, rather than through the construction of masonry: in the latter case there would have been no doubt but that the channel continued and that riparian rights arising from it would be preserved. Neither was it inconsistent with the continuation of the known and defined channel underground that sometimes water appeared at another point, either through percolation or from the water's bursting up due to lack of room in the subterranean channel.

The Vice Chancellor summarised the law:

'... it is now well established that no riparian rights exist as to [subterranean waters], unless they are shown to flow in defined and known channels. In all cases of percolation, or soakage, or oozing of water through the subsoil, the law of riparian rights cannot exist, for the plain reason that *ripae* can exist only in the case of watercourses or channels. The owner of the soil, under the surface of which such waters are found, has the proprietary right of digging beneath the surface for every purpose, although the effect of his underground working may be to drain his neighbours' wells or springs by intercepting, whether intentionally or unintentionally, the water which by such percolation, soakage, or oozing, would otherwise have supplied those wells or springs ... But the law is different as to underground watercourses which flow in defined and known channels, and to these the rules as to riparian rights apply.'[3]

---

[1] *Black v Ballymena Commissioners* (1886) 17 LR Ir 459. See also 'Hidden Streams Underground' (1903) 37 ILTSJ 15.

[2] *Ewart v Belfast Poor-Law Guardians* (1881) 9 LR Ir 172.

[3] (1886) 17 LR Ir 459 at 474.

[8.40] A difficulty, however, arose from the use of the word 'known', as opposed to 'defined', since the law was not clear as to the nature or extent of the knowledge necessary to establish riparian rights. On the one hand, it could not mean that the channel must be visible throughout its course, since that would be impossible by the simple fact of its being subterranean. On the other hand, it could not either mean knowledge elucidated from the excavation of the channel or through the application of abstruse scientific calculations;[1] rather must be it 'a knowledge, by reasonable inference, from existing and observed facts in the natural, or rather the pre-existing, condition of the surface of the ground.' The onus of proof lay on the party alleging the existence of the right, who must establish that 'men of ordinary powers and attainments would know, or could with reasonable diligence ascertain, that the stream, when it emerges into light, comes from and has flowed through a defined subterranean channel.'[2] In illustration of the kind of knowledge that could reasonably be inferred from appearances, Chatterton V-C adduced an overground stream, which disappears underground at a certain point, then resurfaces further on. No one can *actually* know that the stream has flowed from one point to another one through a defined channel underground, or even that it is the same stream which has re-appeared:

'... but our reason, grounded on our knowledge of ordinary natural laws, and on the impossibility or great improbability of the phenomena being otherwise accounted for, leads to an inference of fact amounting practically to knowledge, that it is the same stream, and that it has flowed underground in a defined channel.'[3]

---

1 It was on this basis that the Vice Chancellor distinguished *Ewart v Belfast Poor-Law Guardians* (1881) 9 LR Ir 172, where the channel contended for could only have become known as 'the result of *ex post facto* geological investigations', and so – for the purpose of an attempt to assimilate the law in relation to it to that applicable to a known and defined channel – had to be regarded as unknown.

2 *Black v Ballymena Commissioners* (1886) 17 LR Ir 459 at 474, 475.

3 (1886) 17 LR Ir 459 at 475.

[8.41] The cases of *Ewart v Belfast Poor Law Guardians*[1] and *Black v Ballymena Commissioners*[2] were both decided with reference to the level of geological knowledge and standard of skill current at the turn of the twentieth century. It could be argued that, in more recent times, with the advantages of more sophisticated technology and modern expertise, there should be no automatic immunity from suit by a landowner for the diverting or drying up of percolating or subterranean waters; and that liability to a neighbouring landowner whose waters of this kind are so diverted may arise in either nuisance or negligence, depending upon foreseeability.[3] It has been suggested that, in light of the forward march of science within the last hundred years, 'the right to support from percolating water is no more indefinite and unlimited (or restrictive of enjoyment) than any of the other restraints on land enjoyment imposed by the law of tort.'[4] If such a proposition is sustained, then one can anticipate a shifting of the attitude of the courts to the rights that govern underground waters flowing in channels unknown and undefined according to the standards of a hundred years and more ago, but which are, within reason, amenable to being probed and gleaned by the technological resources of the twenty-first century.

---

1 *Ewart v Belfast Poor-Law Guardians* (1881) 9 LR Ir 172.

2 *Black v Ballymena Commissioners* (1886) 17 LR Ir 459.

3 Harwood in 'Water, Water, Everywhere' [1988] Conv 175, citing in support of his proposition the cases of *Solloway v Hampshire County Council* (1981) 79 LGR 449 and *Russell v Barnett London Borough Council* (1984) 83 LGR 152, in each of which it was recognised that local authorities could be held liable to landowners whose houses subsided due to abstraction of water beneath them by the roots of trees planted on local authority land after an exceptionally hot summer (that of 1976).

4 [1988] Conv 175 at 178.

Pollution of Watercourses

[8.42] A riparian owner is entitled as an incident of such ownership to the flow of the waters past or through his land without any substantial alteration or impairment of their quality or character.[1] In a case where the waters are polluted an action lies with the riparian owner, even if such owner could have mitigated the nuisance by cleansing the watercourse and did not do so.[2] An injunction can be obtained restraining the discharge of sewage into a watercourse, as also against the discharge of industrial spoil injurious to fish life. It does not signify whether the nuisance caused is public or private. Nor will the fact that the award of an injunction might adversely affect a particular business or trade warrant the court adjusting to his detriment the natural riparian rights of a landowner through or beside whose land a watercourse passes.[3]

---

[1]   *Blackburn v Somers* (1879) 5 LR Ir 1; *Kerin v Bord na Móna* (30 January 1970, unreported) HC.
[2]   *Callan v McAvinue* (11 May 1973, unreported) HC.
[3]   *Traill v McAllister* (1890) 25 LR Ir 524.

[8.43] *Blackburn v Somers*[1] concerned an action for the pollution of a stream held either to be a natural watercourse or a permanent artificial watercourse.[2] The plaintiff owned lands at Rathfarnham, Co Dublin through which ran a watercourse called the western stream. The source of this was above the Loreto Convent in Rathfarnham. The western stream wended through the demesne of Rathfarnham, then through the plaintiff's demesne which also included Rathfarnham Castle, finally discharging into the river Dodder. The action arose as a result of the nuns at Loreto Convent emptying their sewage into the western stream at a point above where it flowed through the plaintiff's demesne, and thereby polluting his watercourse. The premises at Loreto Convent had been bought by an order of nuns in 1828 and had been significantly enlarged, with a corresponding augmentation of nuns, in 1867. This had the effect also of increasing the amount of untreated effluent discharged into the plaintiff's steam. In 1878 there was a further access in the population of nuns and a further increase in the level of sewage discharge. In 1873 the convent was successfully prosecuted under the Sanitary Acts. The defendant was the Reverend Mother of the order of nuns, who asserted a prescriptive right, for more than 40 years and 20 years respectively, to decant the convent sewage into the stream.

---

[1]   *Blackburn v Somers* (1879) 5 LR Ir 1.
[2]   The western stream had a natural origin, but had been briefly diverted along part of its course some years prior to the action, in order to accommodate the construction of a new road. According to Chatterton V-C, this circumstance did not alter the watercourse's permanent status.

[8.44] Chatterton V-C, noting that the watercourse was intended to have permanent effect, found that the plaintiff had all the rights of a riparian proprietor, 'including that of a flow of the water into his lands in its pure and natural state, but subject of course to any easement acquired in respect of it by other riparian proprietors.'[1]

He also held:

(a)   a right to foul water could be acquired either by presumed lost grant or prescription, and had often been so acquired in the cases of mines and factories;[2]

(b)   there could be no right to foul water by sewage: any such presumed grant would have been tainted with illegality, as constituting a private nuisance to the plaintiff and a threat to public health;

(c)   it was no defence that the order of nuns might not be the only parties causing pollution of the watercourse; even if others had acquired a right to pollute the stream, either by grant or user, that could not justify an aggravation of the nuisance;[3]

(d)   even if the discharge of sewage into the watercourse were not contrary to law, the user would be so fluctuating in quantity as to make it impossible to warrant presumption of a grant, or to support a claim by prescription;

(e)   even if a right to pollute the stream could have been established, it was limited to the extent of the user at the time of the commencement of the prescriptive period, when the number of nuns was fewer and the level of pollution by sewage proportionately less;

(f)   even if a limited right to pollute the stream could have been established, should it subsequently become impossible to separate the illegal excess from that degree of user to which a right had been acquired by prescription, then the wrongdoer would have no ground for redress if the outcome were a total prohibition of user.

---

[1]   *Blackburn v Somers* (1879) 5 LR Ir 1 at 13.

[2]   For example, *Wright v Williams* (1836) 1 M & W 77.

[3]   See also *Crossley and Sons Ltd v Lightowler* (1867) 2 Ch App 478.

Chapter 9

Rights of Way and Support

Rights of Way

Introduction

[9.01] Rights of way are the most readily recognised and most often contested of intangible property rights, and those that leap first to the imagination when an easement is mentioned. By a paradox, their most frequent appearance in the jurisprudence of the Irish courts is in the mode of their acquisition and the related fundamental point as to whether an easement can be deemed to exist at all or not. Accordingly, the principal incidence of rights of way appears in cases of easements of necessity and implied easements arising from continuous and apparent user.[1] A further point of potential confusion resides in the fact that, in former times, rights of way were categorised to reflect the principal intended mode of user: such as, footways, bridleways, carriageways, tramways. The better approach is to regard such rights as in the nature of a right of passage, rarely unlimited, which can be confined as to purpose, time and frequency of use, and the method of enjoyment – either on foot or by various modes of conveyance.

---

[1] See para **[3.14]** ff. A right of way can also arise through an implied negative covenant: *Gogarty v Hoskins* [1906] 1 IR 173; and by way of implied reservation: *Dwyer Nolan Developments Ltd v Kingscroft Developments Ltd* [1999] 1 ILRM 141.

Construction

[9.02] As with all easements, a right of way can be acquired by grant or prescription. A grant can be express or implied. Where a right of way is deemed to arise by implication, the nature and extent of the right falls to be determined by the individual circumstances in each case giving rise to the implication.[1] In the case of an express grant, the nature and extent of a right of way depends upon the correct construction of the instrument creating it. Where the right of way has been granted, the instrument of grant is construed against the grantor. A reservation of a right of way, which is deemed to be a regrant from the grantee of the land to the grantor, is construed against the grantee.[2] In either case, the interpretation of the grant creating the right of way will also depend on the circumstances surrounding the execution of the grant, including the physical nature of the area over which the right passes. As was stated in the authoritative pronouncement of Jessel MR in *Cannon v Villars*,[3] '... a very material circumstance is the nature of the *locus in quo* over which the right of way is granted. ... the grant of a right of way is the grant of a right of way having regard to the nature of the road over which it is granted and the purpose for which it is intended to be used.'

[1]   Such as arose in *Dwyer Nolan Developments Ltd v Kingscroft Developments Ltd* [1999] 1
      ILRM 141, and also in *Close v Cairns* [1997] NIJB 70. See para [3.12].
[2]   *Doolan v Murray* (21 December 1993, unreported) HC; Wylie *Irish Land Law* (3rd edn, 1997)
      Butterworths, pp 374–376. See para [2.02] ff.
[3]   (1878) 8 ChD 413 at 420–421, per Jessel MR; cited by Keane J in *Doolan v Murray* (21
      December 1993, unreported) HC and by Girvan J in *Close v Cairns* [1997] NIJB 70 at 73. See
      also *Redfont Ltd and Wright's Fisherman's Wharf Ltd v Custom House Dock Management Ltd
      and Hardwicke Property Management Ltd* (31 March 1998, unreported) HC.

[9.03] Even so, where the language of the grant is specific, the construction of the scope of the right will not necessarily be delimited by the physical constraints of the premises under grant at the time of the grant. In *Bulstrode v Lambert*,[1] a reservation of a right to pass over a particular passage, with or without vehicles, for the purpose of servicing an auction room, was construed to permit vehicular access that could not have been accommodated through a narrow entrance gate with overhanging bar which fronted the passage at the time of the grant. The grant was also construed to permit commercial vehicles to stop and unload produce, and to remain stationary for as long as it was necessary to transport goods to and from the auction rooms. However, the provisions of the grant in this case were 'very particular';[2] and, in general terms, a right of way is capable of taking effect within the broad parameters of a reasonable construction of the instrument creating it at the time it was made – so that a right to pass and repass, *not specifically confined to pedestrian passage*, will be construed as including the use of vehicles appropriate to the physical character of the premises.[3] Accordingly, in *Redfont Ltd and Wright's Fisherman's Wharf Ltd v Custom House Dock Management Ltd and Hardwicke Property Management Ltd*[4] Shanley J held that the grant of a right of way to a licensed restaurant and seafood bistro, in the International Financial Services Centre, in Dublin, incorporated as an ancillary right, the right of patrons of the premises to park their cars along the way, while using the restaurants, provided that they did not cause obstruction.

[1]   *Bulstrode v Lambert* [1953] 1 WLR 1064.
[2]   So described by Russell LJ in *Keefe v Amor* [1965] 1 QB 334 at 346.
[3]   *Cannon v Villars* (1878) 8 ChD 413 interpreted by Jenkins J in *Kain v Norfolk* [1949] Ch 163.
[4]   *Redfont Ltd and Wright's Fisherman's Wharf Ltd v Custom House Dock Management Ltd and
      Hardwicke Property Management Ltd* (31 March 1998, unreported) HC.

General principles

[9.04] A right of way, once established for a particular purpose and of a particular character, cannot be expanded into a different purpose and a broader character; so that, on the purchase of a property stated to be subject to a right of way by foot, an action for interference cannot sustain an additional claim that the disputed obstruction prevents the carriage of burdens and the rolling of trolleys along the way.[1]

Where a right of access to a several fishery arises by implication in the context of a grant of fishing rights, the right must 'be exercised in a manner which is as little detrimental to the riparian owners as is consistent with the full beneficial use of the right of fishing.'[2] In general, this means such a right of access as would permit an able-bodied person enjoy the beneficial use of the fishing rights, and, where this is possible by foot, the right of access is pedestrian only.[3] It will, however, include a right to maintain the access route clear of encumbering vegetation.[4]

---

[1] *Austin v Scottish Widows' Assurance Society* (1881) 8 LR Ir 197 at 385.
[2] *Gannon v Walsh* [1998] 3 IR 245 at 277, 283, per Keane J.
[3] [1998] 3 IR 245 at 284.
[4] *Caldwell v Kilkelly* [1905] 1 IR 434 at 446; *Gannon v Walsh* [1998] 3 IR 245 at 279.

[9.05] The grantee of a right of way is entitled to take such steps as are necessary to adapt the way, as may be required, for the purpose for which it was granted.[1] This includes entering upon the servient tenement in order to carry out the work.[2] But it also requires taking steps to insure that injury is not caused to the servient tenement through the use of the right; so that, if a person has the right to lay pipes over another's land, he must see to it that they are watertight.[3] Although neither the dominant owner nor the servient owner are, in theory, obliged to repair the right of way, the fact that the dominant owner has the use of it means that the primary responsibility to maintain it rests on him.[4] Certainly, the dominant owner has a right to keep the right of way in good repair and condition for whatever use he is entitled to make of it.[5] Hence, a person with a right of way over a lane connecting two public roads was held not to have engaged in excessive user by clearing off all bushes and briars, or through doubling the width of the lane and resurfacing it.[6] The dominant owner cannot so use the right of way that the right of the owner of the servient tenement to the normal enjoyment and cultivation of his property is destroyed.[7]

---

[1] *Caldwell v Kilkelly* [1905] 1 IR 434 at 443.
[2] *Newcomen v Coulson* (1877) 5 ChD 143; *Rudd v Rea* [1921] 1 IR 223 at 247.
[3] *Ingram v Morecroft* (1863) 33 Beav 49; *Rudd v Rea* [1921] 1 IR 223 at 245.
[4] *Taylor v Whitehead* (1781) 1 Wm Saunders 565; *Jones v Pritchard* [1908] 1 Ch 630.
[5] *Caldwell v Kilkelly* [1905] 1 IR 434 at 446; *Carroll v Sheridan and Sheehan* [1984] ILRM 451 at 458.
[6] *Carroll v Sheridan and Sheehan* [1984] ILRM 451. O'Hanlon J also felt that the dominant owner was entitled to widen and re-surface the lane even when he then went on to use it for the provision of access to a building development, notwithstanding that the use of the lane had previously been agricultural. However, it is clear that O'Hanlon J so held because of the public character of the lane as disclosed in the evidence.
[7] *Rudd v Rea* [1921] 1 IR 223.

[9.06] In the case of a restaurant owner who enjoyed a right to have a man carrying a placard advertising the restaurant stand outside the arcade which housed the restaurant, it was held that this easement did not include a right to walk up and down inside the arcade thereby causing obstruction. On the other hand, the placard bearer's location could not be defined to a nicety, and the right would not be unreasonably enlarged if he moved around in the general environs of the mouth of the arcade.[1] Nor is a right of way over a railway track with agricultural equipment, granted at a time when the principal access would have been by horse-drawn wagon, enlarged to the extent of placing an additional burden on the servient tenement, so as to extinguish the right, when the mode of conveyance has become a tractor pulling a rake.[2]

---

[1] *Henry Ltd v McGlade* [1926] NI 144, 60 ILTR 17.
[2] *West v Great Northern Railway (Ireland)* [1946] NI 55. McDermott J stated that the dominant owner was not entitled 'substantially to increase the burden of the easement by altering or enlarging its character, nature or extent as enjoyed or acquired at the time...' of the granting of the easement.

Burden on servient tenement

[9.07] A right of way, like any easement, represents a limitation on the enjoyment capacity of the servient tenement, and the law will be zealous to ensure that this is not availed of in such a manner as to impose an unreasonable restriction on the usage of the servient tenement.

Where a laneway led to the property of an agricultural tenant, who was deemed to have a right of way of necessity over it (because otherwise his farm would be landlocked), another party who also enjoyed a right of way over the lane was held entitled to cut turf from a bog beside the lane and draw his turf along the lane, notwithstanding that the first dominant owner would thereby occasionally be inconvenienced in the exercise of his own right of way: *Cleary v Bowen.*[1]

In *McCaw v Rynne*[2] it was held that a farmer, who had a right of way over another person's farm, could use the way to take away turf which he was entitled to cut and was in the business of selling. According to O'Byrne J, the issue of the usage of the right of way was one of degree: if an intolerable burden were placed upon the servient tenement by the enjoyment of the dominant owner, such usage could be restrained, but, in this instance, even though the exercise of the right to draw off turf inflicted 'considerable hardship', it was not excessive user and therefore permissible.

---

[1] *Cleary v Bowen* [1931] LJ Ir 148. In this case also it was held that both parties had an obligation to keep the way under repair.
[2] *McCaw v Rynne* [1941] 7 Ir Jur Rep 12.

User of servient tenement

[9.08] In the same way as a dominant owner cannot expand upon the usage or character of the right of way so as to occasion an intolerable burden to the servient tenement, similarly the owner of the servient tenement cannot so use his own lands as to render unusable the right of way. In *Griffin v Keane*[1] the defendant had sold a house and farm to the plaintiff together with a right of way over an avenue more than a mile long which led through the defendant's lands to the house purchased by the plaintiff. The grant of the right of way had expressly provided that the defendant would not be responsible for the upkeep of the avenue or be liable for any failure to maintain it. Shortly afterwards the defendant proceeded to saw down trees on his demesne and to cart them along the avenue to the open road. As a result, the right of way became virtually impassable, especially by motor car. This was held to be an excessive user by the defendant, even though the plaintiff had been aware of his vendor's timber-cutting enterprise at the time of the purchase. Regardless of whether the purchaser is responsible for the upkeep and maintenance of the avenue, the vendor cannot resort to excessive user, which in this case was held to constitute a derogation from grant.[2]

---

[1] *Griffin v Keane* (1927) 61 ILTR 177.
[2] See para **[2.29]** ff.

[9.09] Neither the owner of the dominant tenement nor the owner of the servient tenement can normally be compelled to repair a right of way.[1] Neither will the burden of a covenant to repair a lane run with freehold land, although in certain cases the benefit of it may do so.[2]

---

[1] See para **[9.05]**.
[2] See para **[14.07]** ff. See 'Rights and Duties to Repair the Subject Matter of a Right of Way' (1954) 84 ILTSJ 189, 195; also *Gaw v Coras Iompair Éireann* [1953] IR 232.

[9.10] The servient owner is entitled to the reasonable use of his own lands despite the existence of the right of way: the fact that the dominant owner is in fear of a dangerous dog kept by the servient owner, though there was no suggestion that the dog actually interfered with, or was in danger of interfering with, the way over which the right was exercisable, does not warrant a finding that the servient owner has interfered with or interrupted the right of way.[1] Neither, in the case of agricultural land, is the erection of fencing around the land, in the interests of good farm husbandry and the preservation of livestock, an interference with a right of way over the land, provided that a gate is put in the fencing so that the dominant owner can continue to use the way.[2] Similarly, a shop owner, whose premises fronts on to an arcade which he also owns, is entitled to erect a gate at the entrance from the street to the passageway for security purposes, provided that a key to the gate is provided to the owner of other premises also using the arcade; who will be obliged to lock the gate after he has used it.[3]

---

[1] *Grainger v Finlay* (1858) 7 ICLR 417.
[2] *Geoghegan v Henry* [1922] 2 IR 1.
[3] *Barrett v Dowling* (20 March 2002, unreported) HC, Kinlen J.

Right of way by implication

[9.11] Where the right of way arises by implication rather than by express grant, the extent of the right will be delimited by the character of the user warranting the implication. In *Donnelly v Adams*[1] the plaintiff, on the basis of exchanges between the parties, the history of the user and the physical location of the plaintiff's coal shed, was held by the Court of Appeal to be entitled to an implied right of way over a fallow field behind his premises belonging to the defendant, for the purpose of bringing supplies of coal to his house: it was not found to be a right of way for all purposes. In *McDonagh v Mulholland*,[2] one of the difficulties encountered by the majority of the Supreme Court in considering the contended for implied easement of way was, that the physical layout of the premises, and the possible usage of the lane over which the right was alleged, did not assist in the implication of a right: on the one hand, the layout of the premises, and a comparison between its character and rateable valuation and those of neighbouring premises, did not warrant the implication of a right; and on the other hand, it could not be said that any implied right must be limited to a right of passage on foot or by bicycle. If the right were also to include a right to have items delivered, such delivery could not be effected without, in certain instances, a large vehicle having to remain stationary for some time in the laneway, thereby blocking the only access to the servient tenement, the house originally constructed by the builder for his own occupation, which was considerably more valuable.[3]

---

[1]   *Donnelly v Adams* [1905] IR 154.

[2]   *McDonagh v Mulholland* [1931] IR 110.

[3]   [1931] IR 110 at 128, per Fitzgibbon J: 'The extent of an apparent easement must be taken from that which appears; user becomes material when the easement has been acquired by prescription or implied grant.'

[9.12] In *Maguire v Brown*[1] an easement of a right of way, arising by implication through necessity, was confined to the category of user at the time of the implied grant and could not be expanded from a right of passage by foot to a right to carry felled trees along the way by means of machinery and vehicles, even though, in broad terms, the legitimate user of the way was deemed agricultural. In *Tallon v Ennis*,[2] where the user for over 40 years was the removal of accumulated ordures through the back of the house and over the alleged way, Gavan Duffy J had little difficulty in holding that a right of way for this purpose had been granted by implication through intention, rather than necessity, at the date of the original demise.

---

[1]   *Maguire v Brown* [1921] 1 IR 148, [1922] 1 IR 23.

[2]   *Tallon v Ennis* [1937] IR 549.

[9.13] Where the right of way has been expressly granted, an auxiliary right to park cars can arise by implication. In *Redfont Ltd and Wright's Fisherman's Wharf Ltd v Custom House Dock Management Ltd and Hardwicke Property Management Ltd*[1] Shanley J held that there was an auxiliary right to park cars, by the patrons of the demised licensed premises to which the right of way had been granted appurtenant. In the opinion of Shanley J, such an implied auxiliary right was warranted by the known intended user of the demised premises, the broad language in the grant of the right of way, together with the width of the way itself, which enabled those frequenting the plaintiffs' restaurants to park without causing obstruction.

1   *Redfont Ltd and Wright's Fisherman's Wharf Ltd v Custom House Dock Management Ltd and Hardwicke Property Management Ltd* (31 March 1998, unreported) HC. Shanley J relied to a significant degree on the English cases of *Bulstrode v Lambert* [1953] 1 WLR 1064 and *McIlraith v Grady* [1968] 1 QB 468, in which a right to pass and repass along a yard with vehicles was held also to include a right to park for a reasonable period for the purpose of loading and unloading furniture and goods.

The gate – and the opening and closing thereof

[9.14] Perhaps it is symptomatic of the kind of 'folksy' attribution with which rights of way disputes in Ireland have invested themselves, that the purpose, and proper mode of use, of a gate across the way frequently feature. This most often arises in the context of the erection of a gate by the servient tenant and the refusal or failure by the dominant tenant to close it having passed through, or where a locked gate on the servient tenement threatens to obstruct the right of way.

[9.15] In *Tubridy v Walsh*[1] Judge Carton held that the obligation to close a gate, on the part of a person having a right of way through land, in order to prevent the straying of cattle, operated as a valid limitation on the right of way. In *Flynn v Harte*,[2] both parties were the tenants of the same landlord; the dominant owner, having acquired a right of way, removed a gate which the servient owner had placed across it. Dodd J held that, irrespective of the derivation of the right, it had to be exercised reasonably having regard to the legitimate use of property. According to Dodd J, the vicissitudes of agricultural use meant that the requirement for a fence could vary from season to season or from field to field.

> 'Whether a gate is or is not an obstruction of the right is a matter of fact. He who acts in a neighbourly manner may be sure he is within the law. He who acts in an unneighbourly way is breaking the law ... The question in most cases is – convenience or 'cussedness'? Convenience or 'cussedness' in putting up a gate; convenience or 'cussedness' in not closing a gate after passing through.'[3]

He concluded that the dominant owner ought not to have removed the gate.

1   *Tubridy v Walsh* (1901) 35 ILT 321.
2   *Flynn v Harte* [1913] 2 IR 322.
3   [1913] 2 IR 322 at 328–328.

[9.16] This case was followed by the Court of Appeal in *Geoghegan v Henry*.[1] Here the servient owner, anxious to improve his lands, and not intending to derogate from his own grant, put fencing around his house, but also erected a gate, so that the defendant dominant owner could still use the right of way. The dominant owner refused to close the gate. Since the gate did not interfere with the right of way, O'Connor MR held that the dominant owner should close it after passing through, as the gate was designed to prevent livestock from wandering in and out, and it would be irksome for the servient owner if he had to close it himself every time the dominant owner left it open. It being accepted that the gate was not an obstruction, it followed that the person using the right of way was bound to open and shut the gate or else 'the gate would cease to secure its legitimate purpose.'

---

[1] *Geoghegan v Henry* [1922] 2 IR 1.

[9.17] These principles of mutual reasonableness were applied by Kinlen J in *Barrett v Dowling*,[1] which involved a dispute over the locking of a gate that connected between a shopping arcade and the main street in Bray, Co Wicklow. The plaintiff was the owner of a couple of shopping units in the arcade and also of the passageway itself. For security reasons he affixed a locked gate to the entrance of the arcade from the main street. The locking by the plaintiff of the gate caused problems for the defendant, whose licensed premises also required access through the arcade to the main street, in order to comply with fire regulations. The case went to several hearings with an inveteracy that can only be described as typical of rights of way disputes. Kinlen J held that nobody but the plaintiff was entitled to obstruct the right of way through the arcade by the erection of a locked gate; that the plaintiff, if he so obstructed it (as he had a right to), must allow others with a right of way through the arcade unlock the gate or remove the obstruction; provided that they, having passed through, should then lock the gate or replace the obstruction.

---

[1] *Barrett v Dowling* (20 March 2002, unreported) HC, noted at (2002) 7 CPLJ 44.

Access

[9.18] For a right of way to be sustained, points of ingress and egress must be clearly identifiable, though it is not necessary for a specific track or path to exist between them. In *Donnelly v Adams*[1] a right of way was held to exist where the access point was through a door from the dominant tenement leading into the servient tenement, which was a waste-land, and from there through either of two gates on to the main road. The servient owner was at liberty to direct along which path the dominant owner might pass across the field and through which of the two gates he might at any time come and go.[2] The legal principle was succinctly stated by Fitzgibbon LJ:

> 'Every lawful way must be capable of identification; it must have a terminus a quo, and a terminus ad quem. But it is not essential to a way that there shall be a beaten track between its termini. The precise line which a person must follow in exercising a right of way need not always be the same; frequently the owner of the servient tenement may vary it from time to time, as where there is a right to cross a field which is sometimes in tillage. The reasonable use of the servient tenement, consistently with the servitude, may entitle the owner of it to require the dominant owner to diverge, and the easement may co-exist with the right of the owner of the servient tenement to vary the path from time to time.'[3]

---

[1] *Donnelly v Adams* [1905] 1 IR 154.
[2] [1905] 1 IR 154 at 178, per Lord Ashbourne C: '...it remained competent for the defendant to vary the route from time to time or to limit it to either outer gate.' See also *Barrett v Dowling* (20 March 2002, unreported) HC.

3   [1905] 1 IR 154 at181. For an alternative view of the current status of the Court of Appeal
    decision in *Donnelly v Adams·* see Bland *The Law of Easements and Profits à Prendre* (1997)
    Sweet & Maxwell, pp 216–217.

[9.19] In *Tallon v Ennis,*[1] the case involving the removal of accumulated ordures through
a way at the back of an artisan's cottage, Gavan Duffy J held that the existence of a track,
though valuable in terms of evidence to establish the right of way, was not absolutely
necessary. On the other hand, the absence of a clear path and the existence of a number
of different alternative termini proved fatal to the establishing of the claimed right of
way in *Flanagan v Mulhall.*[2] Here the defendant alleged a right of way by way of
counterclaim to an action for trespass. Two different possible *termini a quo* were
identified, one for a right of way on foot only, and the other for a right of way for animals
and machinery. There were three different possible *termini ad quem*. There were no clear
paths nor any decisive fencing. Furthermore, the boundaries of an alleged public right of
way[3] failed to coincide with the right of way claimed by the defendant. O'Hanlon J held
that the absence of a defined path was not fatal in itself, but 'there has always been an
insistence on a defined *terminus a quo* and *terminus ad quem*.'[4] Neither could one infer a
right where the points of entry and exit were haphazard and where there were no
discernible gates or other openings.

1   *Tallon v Ennis* [1937] IR 549. See para **[2.18]**.
2   *Flanagan v Mulhall* [1985] ILRM 134.
3   It is not inconsistent with a private right of way that a public right of way may be found to exist
    over the same track.
4   O'Hanlon J cited with approval the passage from the judgment of Fitzgibbon LJ in *Donnelly v
    Adams* [1905] 1 IR 154 quoted above.

[9.20] In *Liverpool City Council v Irwin,*[1] the House of Lords held that tenants of
premises in a high rise corporation flat enjoyed implied easements to use stairs, lifts and
rubbish chutes. By reason of the peculiar nature of the dominant tenements, it was also
held that these implied easements imported an additional responsibility by the
corporation to repair the stairs, lifts and rubbish chutes. In *Heeney v Dublin Corpn,*[2]
O'Flaherty J held, as a corollary to the constitutional right to the inviolability of a
citizen's dwelling, under Article 40.5, that there was a right to insist, by the inhabitants
of Ballymun flats, that Dublin Corporation, notwithstanding an industrial dispute, take
every step possible to ensure that the lifts would work. This implied easement is at
variance with the principle that a servient owner is not required to repair or maintain the
subject-matter of the servitude. It arises by necessary implication from the nature of the
premises themselves, and the character of the letting, and will not be of universal
application.[3] Such a right could scarcely arise by prescription.[4]

1   *Liverpool City Council v Irwin* [1977] AC 239. See discussion in Lyall *Land Law in Ireland*
    (2nd edn, 2000) Sweet & Maxwell, pp 719–721.
2   *Heeney v Dublin Corpn* (17 August 1998, unreported) SC.

3   *Miller v Hancock* [1893] 2 QB 177.
4   Bland 'Easements of Elevator and of Parking: From Ballymun to the IFSC' (1998) 3 CPLJ 80
    at 82.

Parking

[9.21] A right of parking is capable of being recognised as an easement provided that it is appurtenant to a dominant tenement.[1] A right of parking in a defined area has been held, in England, capable of constituting an easement.[2] However, a problem can arise where the right to park is dedicated to a specific parking space, because this, in effect, can oust the servient owner from his proprietary rights as owner.[3] Whether a right to park comprises an easement or not largely depends on its extent.[4] A right, in general, to park in an area in common with others is likely to be a personal licence, unless it is linked to the ownership of property on the part of those parking their cars. It has been suggested that a right to park in a dedicated place, sealed off with chain and post, would be difficult to categorise as an easement; if granted by lease it might well be considered part of the premises demised.[5] Where parking has been permissively enjoyed by tenants on an estate, the right to park is capable of being elevated into an easement, upon a further lease or assignment of the property, through s 6 of the Conveyancing Act 1881.[6]

1   See generally, Bland 'The Easement of Parking' (1997) 2 CPLJ 26.
2   *Newman v Jones* (22 March 1982, unreported) ChD, per Megarry V-C, quoted in *Handel v St
    Stephen's Close* [1994] 1 EGLR 70.
3   *London & Blenheim Estates Ltd v Ladbroke Retail Parks Ltd* [1992] 1 WLR 1278.
4   [1992] 1 WLR 1278 at 1288, per Judge Baker.
5   *Gale on Easements* (eds, Gaunt and Morgan, 16th edn, 1997) Sweet & Maxwell, p 350; *Hilton
    v James Smith and Sons (Norwood) Ltd* [1979] 2 EGLR 44.
6   *Newman v Jones* (22 March 1982, unreported) ChD, per Megarry V-C, quoted in *Handel v St
    Stephen's Close* [1994] 1 EGLR 70.

[9.22] The High Court of the Irish Republic has on two occasions found a right to park, *for a specific purpose*, to be incidental to a right of way. In *Kilduff v Keenaghan*[1] – a case confused by a claimed title by adverse possession being found to confer a right by prescription – O'Hanlon J held that the incidental right to park, which included petrol tankers, was for the purpose of delivering supplies. In *Redfont Ltd and Wright's Fisherman's Wharf Ltd v Custom House Dock Management Ltd and Hardwicke Property Management Ltd*[2] Shanley J held that the incidental right to park was for the purpose of patronising the plaintiffs' licensed restaurants, and was principally based on the known intended user of the demised premises, the language of the grant, and the physical dimensions of the way. In neither case was a right to park indefinitely, or on an overnight basis, held to exist. There should be little difficulty with this being found to constitute an easement, if granted expressly, and on the basis of occupation of property where dedicated car-parking is not provided. In many estates comprising apartments and town houses, an entitlement to park in a general parking area (often divided into parking bays) is granted by way of purported easement to the several property owners. In most cases the general parking area is owned by a management company, itself beneficially owned by the house owners through a company limited by guarantee. In this situation, there is no difficulty in principle with each house owner having a right, in common with all other house owners, to share the parking bays. The risk of ouster of the proprietary rights of the servient owner is eliminated, by reason of the fact that the servient owner is a management company, whose only utility of the area is to grant parking accommodation to the members of the management company, who are collectively the dominant owners of the benefited properties. In such cases, if the car-parking rights were not granted by way of easement, they would constitute a licence only, and so would run the risk of not being capable of being assigned by the property owner upon a disposal of his or her property. Where a particular parking space is granted to a house owner, it is difficult not to regard this as being a virtual physical adjunct to the property itself.

---

[1] *Kilduff v Keenaghan* (6 November 1992, unreported) HC. See also Bland 'The Easement of Parking' (1997) 2 CPLJ 26.

[2] *Redfont Ltd and Wright's Fisherman's Wharf Ltd v Custom House Dock Management Ltd and Hardwicke Property Management Ltd* (31 March 1998, unreported) HC. See also Bland 'Easements of Elevator and of Parking: From Ballymun to the IFSC' (1998) 3 CPLJ 80.

[9.23] A right of parking in a parking space will not arise by implication if the property expressly granted allows adequate alternative facility to park. In *Knox v AQ Properties Ltd*,[1] the lease of a commercial unit in a business park in Belfast, granted by the defendant to the plaintiff, included an extensive yard area in which car-parking was possible and lorries could load and unload goods. It did not include an additional four dedicated parking spaces which were close to the unit demised to the plaintiff. Neither were the 'common parts' in the demise clearly defined. The defendant subsequently demised an adjacent business unit to another party. This demise included the four parking spaces to which the plaintiff wanted access. In an action by the plaintiff, for negligence and breach of contract, Girvan J noted that adequate parking facility had been allotted to the plaintiff through the inclusion in the demise to it of the yard area. He added:

> 'There is however no business necessity to imply any common rights of parking in any given part of the Business Park since it could not be said that the Units were incapable of beneficial use without the implication of such parking rights. ... in the absence of agreement it could not be said that such a common parking right was necessary for the enjoyment of the property or was inevitably a matter upon which the parties would have agreed had they turned their mind to it.'[2]

Accordingly, the 'common parts', in the absence of definition, had to be given their natural meaning, and could not include any part of the business park specifically demised to a lessee.

---

[1] *Knox v AQ Properties Ltd* [1997] NIJB 51.

[2] [1997] NIJB 51 at 54.

Rights of Support

Introduction – support of land by land

[9.24] A right of support of land by land is inherently not an easement, but an incident of the ownership of land. Such a right assumes the style and attributions of an easement when the requirement for it is greater than is necessary for the sustaining of the land on its own. This most usually arises when some structure is raised on the land which increases the weight imposed upon it. In such a case the land bearing a greater weight requires additional support from the adjacent land and the right to such additional support, if acquired, comprises the easement. An easement of support can be acquired in the several ways in which an easement can normally be acquired. In the nature of things, it is unlikely to arise by express grant:

> '... [I]ndependent both of prescription and of implied grant, the ordinary right of the owner of land is to have the support of the adjoining land in its natural state, and the right by prescription is only acquired in the case of buildings where it appears that the buildings add to the weight on the land, and that but for that weight the support would have continued; but supposing that element not to exist, and the support to be taken away, damages may be recovered for the buildings that are on the land.'[1]

This latter dictum may be construed as meaning, that where the withdrawal of a support for land, on which there is a building constructed, occurs in circumstances where, if no building had been constructed, the land would still have subsided or yielded for the lack of the former support, damages may be secured in respect not only of the collapsed land, but also for the damage to the building.[2]

---

[1] *Green v Belfast Tramways Co* (1887) 20 LR Ir 35 at 40–41, per O'Brien J. See also *Wyatt v Harrison* (1832) 3 B & Ad 871; *Hanly v Shannon* (1834) Hay & Jon Rep 645.

[2] See also Wu 'The Right of Lateral Support of Buildings from the Adjoining Land' [2002] Conv 237.

[9.25] A right of support acquired by prescription must conform to the principles that govern prescriptive acquisition: it must be open, peaceable, and with consent but without permission. Ordinarily, the erection of a building where there had been no building before will put a prospective servient owner on notice that a right of additional support is being cultivated against the land owned by him. However, if the servient owner is manifestly unaware that a right of support is being acquired an easement cannot be raised against him. In *Gately v A & J Martin Ltd*,[1] Palles CB observed that knowledge 'or means of knowledge of the material facts constituting the easement' must be established on the part of the alleged servient owner.

---

[1] *Gately v A & J Martin Ltd* [1900] 2 IR 269 at 272.

Support of buildings by land

[9.26] In the case of land on which a building has been constructed the right of support, once acquired, is not necessarily confined to the land immediately adjoining. In *Latimer* *v The Official Co-Operative Society (Ltd)*[1] a right of support was held to exist in favour of a house at Harcourt Place, Dublin over the land beneath another house two doors away where all three houses adjoined each other. The house two doors away had been destroyed by fire and rebuilt by its owner, the defendant. The new house had been competently constructed, but using heavier materials, and the soil beneath it was soft. As the new house began to settle it pulled on the house next to it, with the result that this house and the plaintiff's started to separate and fissures emerged in the walls of the plaintiff's house. At first instance judgment had been entered for the defendant, on the grounds that he had not been negligent in the reconstruction of his house.

Morris CJ, in the Court of Common Pleas, rested his decision on the case of *Dalton v Angus*,[2] which he held as being authority that:

'... where there is an ancient building, which is supported by adjacent soil, it has acquired a right to such support of that soil as it immemorially enjoyed, and [that] a right of action exists against the owner of the adjacent soil if he disturbs his own land so as to take away the lateral support previously afforded.'[3]

If the intervening house had been the house affected then the case would have come squarely within the principles of *Dalton v Angus*. But the principle that the right of support is not to be interfered with still applied: the plaintiff's house had a right to support by the soil on which the defendant's house stood, and it was because the defendant had constructed a heavier building than previously existed, despite not being negligent, that the subsidence occurred. In such a case, where a right to support has been established, the fact of the injury is all that matters. Liability is strict and negligence irrelevant.[4]

---

[1] *Latimer v The Official Co-Operative Society (Ltd)* (1885) 16 LR Ir 305.

[2] *Dalton v Angus* (1881) 6 App Cas 740: a protracted *locus classicus*, contested in three different courts, and before no fewer than 18 judges, which conclusively established that a right of support for a building by adjacent land is an easement, which can be acquired either by prescription or presumed lost grant.

[3] (1885) 16 LR Ir 305 at 308.

[4] *Carroll v Kildare County Council* [1950] IR 258.

[9.27] The effect of *Dalton v Angus*,[1] as interpreted in and approved by *Latimer v The Official Co-Operative Society (Ltd)*,[2] enables an easement of support of a building to be acquired through continuous user, as of right, for not less than 20 years, on the basis of either lost grant or prescription, provided that, in the case of statutory prescription, all the other conditions of the Prescription Act are satisfactorily met.[3]

---

[1] *Dalton v Angus* (1881) 6 App Cas 740.

[2] *Latimer v The Official Co-Operative Society (Ltd)* (1885) 16 LR Ir 305.

[3] Most crucially, s 4 which provides that the enjoyment be proven for the requisite period prior to an action taken either to establish, defend or resist the alleged easement, and also allowing for possible deductions from the prescriptive period in accordance with ss 7 and 8.

Time from which support is enjoyed

[9.28] The precise time when the right of support is acquired, and whether by implication concurrently with a grant of corporeal property, or by prescription, can be crucial where the deprivation of the support derives from either one or both of the activities on two different sets of adjoining lands. The case of *Green v Belfast Tramways Co*[1] presents an interesting instance of the potential difference in outcome depending on whether the easement of support is found to have been acquired by implied grant or by prescription. The plaintiffs held two houses at Malone Place, Belfast under a fee farm grant. This grant, which had been made in 1863, contained a building covenant. Houses were constructed soon afterwards. In 1876 two of these houses were conveyed to the plaintiffs. The Belfast Central Railway, which passed close to the buildings, had been opened two years earlier, in 1874, and the former owner of the houses was paid compensation for disturbance. In 1885 the defendant bought the land adjacent to the plaintiffs' houses from the grantor of the original fee farm grant and used it for the storage of large stone blocks. These on occasion could be several tons in weight. Cracks soon started to appear in the plaintiffs' houses. At first instance a jury had held that the weight of the stones on the adjacent ground was alone responsible for the damage to the plaintiffs' houses. However, the defendant contended that the jury ought to have been invited to consider whether the cracks in the plaintiffs' houses could have been principally caused by the construction of the Belfast Central Railway and the effect of vibration from the passing trains, and only partially compounded by the defendant's storage of heavy stone sets. It was further urged that the payment of compensation had in some way vitiated the original right of support prevailing when the houses were built.

---

[1]   *Green v Belfast Tramways Co* (1887) 20 LR Ir 35.

[9.29] Accordingly, the question fell to be determined whether the right to support had been acquired by prescription, *following* the construction of the houses over 20 years prior to the action, through the enjoyment of support since then; or whether it had been acquired by implied grant, at the time of the fee farm grant in 1863, *before* the construction of the houses.

[9.30] In the view of O'Brien J, were the right being acquired by prescription, it would also be necessary to determine whether the period of relevant enjoyment ran from the change in the condition of the premises, after the railway line had been built, in which case less than 20 years had elapsed; and, in the event of the right having been acquired by implication, whether, under the fee farm grant of 1863, such right could continue to apply to the changed conditions resulting from the construction of the railway line. O'Brien J found in favour of the plaintiffs, on the basis that the right of support had been acquired by implied grant in 1863, before the houses were built, rather than afterwards, by prescription. He held that 'before the railway was made ... [the plaintiffs' property] enjoyed an absolute grant of support, and that that continued in its integrity after, as before, the compensation, the advantage of which could not be taken by a stranger.'[1] According to O'Brien J, if the right to support were to have been acquired by prescription, then the prescriptive period would have been interrupted, because the enjoyment was not the same after as before the construction of the railway. The implied grant of an easement of support, conterminously with the fee farm grant, did not stand to be affected by the payment of compensation, which was primarily for inconvenience and disturbance. Since the right of support had been vested before the construction of the railway, it could not have been diminished by anything taking place afterwards.

---

[1] *Green v Belfast Tramways Co* (1887) 20 LR Ir 35 at 39.

[9.31] Johnson J differed from the judgment of O'Brien J, on the basis that once the fee farm grantor had not actually derogated from his own grant, and did not interfere with the right of support he had granted, then he and his successors in title should be entitled to deal with their own lands in a reasonable manner. According to Johnson J, if the piling of the stone sets would not alone, without the additional vibration caused by the passage of trains on the foundations of the plaintiffs' houses, have caused the damage, the issue ought not to have been decided in the plaintiffs' favour. However, Johnson J elected to support O'Brien J in allowing judgment for the plaintiffs.[1] With respect to the diffidence evinced by Johnson J, it could be urged that more recent articulations of the principle of non-derogation from grant, in particular by the English Court of Appeal in *Harmer v Jumbil (Nigeria) Tin Areas Ltd*[2] and the Irish High Court in *Connell v O'Malley*,[3] are sufficiently pervasive to draw in the activities of the defendant. The principle of non-derogation from grant, binding the grantor's successor no less than the grantor himself, obliges that nothing be done on the land retained to render otiose the known purpose to which the land granted was to be put. This requirement is undiminished by the fact that activities on other land, not under the control of the grantor, indirectly further reduce the freedom of the grantor or his successor to apply the retained land in whatsoever manner they choose.

---

[1] There was no other judgment in the case. It had originally been argued before May CJ also, and upon his resignation the remaining judges gave the parties the option to have the case argued again before themselves and Lawson J. The parties elected to proceed without further arguments and so judgment was delivered by O'Brien J and Johnson J in favour of the plaintiffs, though each judge differed on the law.
[2] *Harmer v Jumbil (Nigeria) Tin Areas Ltd* [1921] 1 Ch 200.
[3] *Connell v O'Malley* (28 July 1983, unreported) HC. See para **[2.33]** ff.

Support of buildings by buildings

[9.32] A right of support principally applies where the support is by the servient land only. A house does not have a right to be supported by another house except where the fact of one house physically supporting the other is actually apparent to the alleged servient owner.[1] If such owner is not aware of the fact of support, then a right of support cannot be inferred at law.

Awareness of the fact of support will not be inferred where there is no evidence that the houses had been built either at the same time or by the same builder. It must be shown that enjoyment is open and known, or at least capable of being known.[2]

¹ See Bodkin 'Rights of Support for Buildings and Flats' (1962) 26 Conv 210 at 213; also Garner, 'Rights of Support' (1948) 12 Conv 280.
² *Gately v A & J Martin Ltd* [1900] 2 IR 269. See para **[9.25]**.

[9.33] Where the alleged dominant tenement, being a house, does not adjoin the alleged servient tenement, being another house, it has no right to be supported by it.¹

¹ *Solomon v Vintners' Co* (1859) 4 H & N 585, cited with approval in *Latimer v The Official Co-Operative Society (Ltd)* (1885) 16 LR Ir 305.

[9.34] Even where the houses are adjoining, the fact that the owner of one of them may demolish his house, thereby exposing the dividing wall, which was not proofed against the elements, to rainwater, with resultant damp in the other house, does not give rise to a cause of action, *for withdrawal of support*, in the owner of that other house.¹ There is no easement to be protected from the weather by a neighbour's house.² Furthermore, it is a natural and reasonable use of land to demolish a derelict house standing upon it, and the fact that rainwater might percolate through the dividing wall to the neighbouring house has not traditionally been regarded as an actionable nuisance.³ The duties of the owner of a house to another house owner whose house is supported by the first owner's house, were succinctly summarised by Greene MR in *Bond v Nottingham Corpn*:⁴ the servient owner is under no obligation to repair his property so as to maintain the support, the dominant owner having the right to enter the servient property and undertake necessary remedial work himself; but the servient owner has no right to remove the protected support without replacing it with an equivalent.

¹ But see *Tapson v Northern Ireland Housing Executive* [1992] NI 264. See para **[1.17]** and consideration of incursion from the principles of negligence at paras **[9.37]–[9.39]**.
² *Phipps v Pears* [1965] 1 QB 76, noted with uneasy approval in *Tapson v Northern Ireland Housing Executive* [1992] NI 264 at 265–266, per Carswell J.
³ *Giltrap v Busby* [1970] 5 NIJB 1.
⁴ *Bond v Nottingham Corpn* [1940] Ch 429.

[9.35] Where a local authority demolishes a derelict terraced house on the basis that it is a dangerous structure, it must provide sufficient support to the premises adjoining to ensure that this does not become a dangerous structure also; a local authority can have no greater right to remove the support to a property than would the owner of the property adjoining.¹ In *Treacy v Dublin Corpn*, Finlay CJ, while accepting that there was no easement of protection from wind and rain, observed that it would be unrealistic for the local authority to replace the removed support from the dominant tenement with buttressing that would be inadequate to withstand weathering.² It has been suggested that by this comment the Chief Justice effected an enlargement of the conventional category of easement through the device of an ancillary to a recognised easement.³ On the other hand, it could also be suggested that Finlay CJ's comments should be construed in their literal sense only – that a substituted support inadequate to withstand the action of wind and rain would be unlikely for very long to constitute an appropriate equivalent support.

---

1   *Treacy v Dublin Corpn* [1993] 1 IR 305.
2   [1993] 1 IR 305 at 312–313.
3   Bland *The Law of Easements and Profits à Prendre* p 18.

[9.36] It can be argued, that where a boundary wall has stood for a long time, such as for a hundred years or more, an easement of support should arise in respect of such a wall.[1] Where a premises is supported and enclosed by a wall which is subsequently taken down by its owner, and the premises is damaged and rendered useless, it is no defence to an action by the owner of the premises to aver that the wall was taken down with reasonable care and diligence.[2] However, once an award of damages has been made for the withdrawal of an easement of support, the mere fact that the owner of the wall does not rebuild it does not give rise to a right to continuing damages.[3]

---

1   *Kennedy v Daly* (31 November 1969, unreported) HC.
2   *Toole v Macken* (1855) 7 Ir Jur (OS) 385. On the irrelevance of due care and diligence, where an alternative structure damages the right of support enjoyed by a nearby premises over the land on which the new building has been constructed, see *Latimer v Official Co-Operative Society Ltd* (1885) 16 LR Ir 305. See para **[9.26]**.
3   *Nugent v Keady Urban District Council* (1911) 46 ILTR 221.

Negligence

[9.37] Notwithstanding the comparative straightforwardness of the law in relation to rights of support, certain developments in the law of negligence have established that the owner of land, in cases where his neighbour does not enjoy an easement of support, may yet be liable to his neighbour if foreseeable damage is caused to his neighbour's land which it would have been possible for the landowner, by the reasonable adoption of corrective measures, to prevent.[1] In *Bradburn v Lindsay*[2] the owner of a semi-detached house was held liable to his neighbour in negligence for damage done to a party wall due to dry rot, where the owner had let his house fall into decay, even though there was no right of support found to exist in the case, and ordinarily there is no duty cast upon the owner of the servient tenement to repair his property. However, this action appears to have arisen principally from the spreading of dry rot rather than from the withdrawal of support. In *Munnelly v Calcon Ltd*[3] the removal of support from a building, even where a prescriptive right to support was not held to exist, gave rise to a successful cause of action in negligence. The fact that this case was disposed of, entirely with reference to negligence, arguably reduces its value as a precedent on the law of easements.

---

1   *Goldman v Hargrave* [1966] 2 All ER 989; *Munnelly v Calcon Ltd* [1978] IR 387; *Leakey v National Trust for Places of Historical Interest or Natural Beauty* [1980] 1 All ER 17; *Bradburn v Lindsay* [1983] 2 All ER 408; *Tapson v Northern Ireland Housing Executive* [1992] NI 264; *Daly v McMullan* [1997] 2 ILRM 232; *Holbeck Hall Hotel Ltd v Scarborough Borough Council* (2 March 2000, unreported) CA; *Rees v Skerrett* [2001] 1 WLR 1541; Bland *The Law*

of Easements and Profits à Prendre pp 74–76; Report of the Law Reform Commission: *The Acquisition of Easements and Profits à Prendre by Prescription* (LRC66-2002) at 47–55, para 5.07–5.17.

²   *Bradburn v Lindsay* [1983] 2 All ER 408. See also Waite 'Developing the Law of Easements' [1987] Conv 47.

³   *Munnelly v Calcon Ltd* [1978] IR 387.

[9.38] However, in *Rees v Skerrett*,[1] another case involving percolation by rainwater after demolition of a terraced house had removed support for a party wall, the English Court of Appeal went so far as to hold that, in such circumstances, there was a duty to protect one's neighbour's house from incursion by the weather. It was considered reasonable, by the court, that a person who demolished his house had a positive duty to provide weatherproofing for a party wall that he had thereby caused to be exposed. This is similar to the 'invasion of moisture' identified by Carswell J in *Tapson v Northern Ireland Housing Executive*[2] as providing a point of distinction from *Giltrap v Busby*[3] which had affirmed the traditional line that there did not exist any easement to be protected from the elements.

Thus far, the courts in the Irish Republic have not articulated as strong a view as emerged in *Rees v Skerrett*. However, in *Daly v McMullan*,[4] Judge Buckley, following *Leakey v National Trust for Places of Historical Interest or Natural Beauty*,[5] in a case of damage by soil slippage, held that there was a duty on the owners of property to take such steps as were reasonable in the circumstances to prevent the risk of foreseeable injury to their neighbour arising from either natural or man-made hazards on their land. This duty stands to be qualified by the capacity of the owner of land on which the hazard arises to take steps to prevent its encroachment. The obligation is to take all reasonable steps under the circumstances.

¹   *Rees v Skerrett* [2001] 1 WLR 1541.

²   *Tapson v Northern Ireland Housing Executive* [1992] NI 264. See para **[1.17]**.

³   *Giltrap v Busby* [1970] 5 NIJB 1.

⁴   *Daly v McMullan* [1997] 2 ILRM 232.

⁵   *Leakey v National Trust for Places of Historical Interest or Natural Beauty* [1980] 1 All ER 17. See para **[12.14]**.

[9.39] The argument may be adduced that the easement of support represents an instance of human activity in which the precepts of the law of property should yield in course to the more flexible doctrines of the law of tort.[1] As yet, however, it is too early to say. It is suggested that the better course is to regard the withdrawal of a support, where a right to it has been acquired as an easement, as conferring no automatic entitlement other than to redress for withdrawal of the support. One could envisage this being confined to a case where the house collapses. However, where the effect of the withdrawal of support is to cause other damage in lieu of, or in addition to, the absence of basic support – such as the spread of rot or the incursion of damp – then liability may arise, either in negligence or nuisance, depending on foreseeability. In such circumstances, it could scarcely be contended, with credibility, that the 'neighbour principle' ought not to apply between parties who are neighbours. Where the withdrawal of support occasions no auxiliary or alternative loss, then liability will be confined to the infringement of the easement, provided that one has been acquired. Where an easement has not been acquired, and the withdrawal of support causes no other loss than the support itself, then a cause of action will not arise.

---

[1] Bland *The Law of Easements and Profits à Prendre* p 76. If this is so, then the law of property will become a far less fruitful ground for litigation in this area than the law of tort.

Chapter 10

Public and Local Customary Rights Resembling Easements

Public Rights of Way

Introduction

[10.01] The law recognises a number of rights in favour of the general public that resemble particular easements and profits *à prendre*. Public rights of navigation and of fishing in coastal and tidal waters will be considered in the context of fishing rights generally.[1] The public right most analogous to an easement is a public right of way. A public right of way is sometimes known as a highway. Inevitably it lacks one of the essential ingredients for an easement, the existence of a dominant tenement.

---

[1]   See para [13.03].

Dedication and acceptance

[10.02] The essence of any public right is, that it has either been granted by statute, or at some time in the distant past been dedicated to the use of the public by the fee simple owner, and the public has, by the evidence of user of the right, accepted that dedication.[1]

In *Re The Estate of Thomas Connolly*[2] Flanagan J expressed the principle thus:

> 'Rights in the public are created not by prescription but by dedication. The question is whether, having regard to the nature of the user by the public, I can assume that there was a dedication. ... Where I find this user existing from time immemorial – because we cannot go beyond the memory of living man – can I infer that there was, in point of law, a dedication, with the assent and knowledge of the owners of this property?'[3]

---

[1]   *Neill v Byrne* (1878) 2 LR Ir 287; recently affirmed in *Smeltzer v Fingal County Council* [1998] 1 IR 279, per Costello P; *Fortin v Delahunty* (15 January 1999, unreported) HC, per Quirke J.
[2]   *Re The Estate of Thomas Connolly* (1871) 5 ILTR 28.
[3]   (1871) 5 ILTR 28 at 29; also *Fitzpatrick v Robinson* (1828) 1 Hud & Br 585; *Early v Flood* [1953–1954] Ir Jur Rep 65.

[10.03] Evidence of user for the period of living memory will raise a presumption that there was a dedication of a right of way to the public at an earlier time.[1] The dedication of a right to the public must be to the whole public and not merely to a limited section of it.[2] The dedication of a right to a limited section of the public constitutes a local customary right, to which different considerations apply. If the user of the alleged public right is of such a kind that it would deprive the owner of the land through which it passes of the enjoyment appropriate to ownership, then a public right will not be deemed to exist, and any enjoyment by members of the public will be permissive only.[3]

A person exercising a public right of way is not deemed to be a licensee or invitee of the occupier of the soil. Permission given by a landowner to walk along a particular way before it became subject to the public right is extinguished in the dedication of the public right of way.[4]

---

[1]   *Browne v Dowie* (1959) 93 ILTR 179 at 183, per Judge Fox.

[2]   *Poole v Huskinson* (1843) 11 M & W 827; *Giant's Causeway Co Ltd v AG* (1898) 5 NIJR 301 at 305, per Chatterton V-C; *Abercromby v Town Commissioners of Fermoy* [1900] 1 IR 302 at 313, per Holmes LJ.

[3]   *Giant's Causeway Co Ltd v AG* (1898) 5 NIJR 301 at p 305, per Chatterton V-C, at p 311, per Fitzgibbon LJ.

[4]   *Campbell v Northern Ireland Housing Executive* [1995] NI 167.

[10.04] At one time, for a right of way to be a public right it had to join one definite place to another definite place in each of which the public had a right to be: it has now been settled that there can be a public right of way along a defined way ending in private lands the terminus of which provides the facility for viewing a natural amenity of outstanding interest or beauty, such as the Giant's Causeway.[1] In short, a cul-de-sac is capable of constituting a public right of way. Even so, a public right of way must be exercised along a definite track between definite points; there can be no right for the general public simply to wander and recreate. [2]

A public right of way must be dedicated by the owner of the fee simple, but it has been held that such a right can also be dedicated by the grantee under a fee farm grant.[3]

---

[1]   *Giant's Causeway Co Ltd v AG* (1898) 5 NIJR 301. See also Judge Fox in *Browne v Dowie* (1959) 93 ILTR 179, at p 184: 'As regards user for pleasure and recreation, I gather from the older authorities that it was difficult to establish a public right of way for these purposes, but in more recent times a more liberal view as to what are highways has been taken.' Judge Fox also cited Atkin LJ in *Moser v Ambleside Urban District Council* (1925) 89 JP 118, to the effect that '…you can have a highway leading to a place of popular resort even though when you have got to the place of popular resort which you wish to see you have to return on your tracks by the same highway.'

[2]   *Giant's Causeway Co Ltd v AG* (1898) 5 NIJR 301; *A-G v Antrobus* [1905] 2 Ch 188; *Smeltzer v Fingal County Council* [1998] 1 IR 279; *Murphy v Wicklow County Council* (19 March 1999, unreported) HC, Kearns J. See also Dawson 'The *Giant's Causeway Case*: Property Law in Ireland 1845–1995' in *One Hundred and Fifty Years of Irish Law* (eds Dawson, Greer and Ingram, 1996) Sweet & Maxwell, pp 250–253.

[3]   *Giant's Causeway Co Ltd v AG* (1898) 5 NIJR 301; *Smith v Wilson* [1903] 2 IR 45.

[10.05] In *Bruen v Murphy*[1] the law on the acquisition of a public right of way was restated and elaborated by McWilliam J:

'The only methods by which a public right of way can be established are by showing use from time immemorial, by relying on creation by statute or by proving dedication to the use of the public and acceptance of such use by the public. ... it must be emphasised that a public right of way cannot be acquired by prescription although user may provide sufficient evidence to support a presumption of dedication. The user need not be for any particular length of time but it is only evidence of dedication and must be such as to imply the assertion of the right with the knowledge and acquiescence of the owner in fee.'[2]

This case involved an alleged public right of way near Templeogue in Dublin between the back gardens of the houses on Fortfield Drive and on nearby Templeville Drive. McWilliam J held that the evidence did not support such a claimed right.

Those using the alleged right had to negotiate fields and fences, and at one point a ruined wall, on lands neither the ownership or the ordinary use of which had been given in evidence. Neither was there any suggestion of an identifiable track. The only sure fact was that the area of the alleged way fell between one public road and another one, but the sporadic and uncertain use by a varying number of people of the disputed area over a period of some 10 years was not consistent with dedication and acceptance of a public right of way. Furthermore, the development company that owned the property that in all likelihood had no real idea of what was happening to what was in effect a piece of waste ground, so that their acquiescence, even had the usage been consistent with a public right, could not have been inferred.[3]

---

[1]   *Bruen v Murphy* (11 March 1980, unreported) HC.
[2]   (11 March 1980, unreported) HC at pp 4–5.
[3]   (11 March 1980, unreported) HC at p 9: '... I cannot assume that the casual user by members of the public for dumping, rowdiness and occasional passing across it between the two roads was such that I should imply the assertion of a public right of way with the knowledge and acquiescence of [the developers].'

Demonstrable public user and maintenance

[10.06] The requirement of significant public user, together with continuing public maintenance, for a right of way to be deemed public, was a significant element, in the judgments both of the High Court and the Supreme Court, in *Connell v Porter*.[1] This concerned a dispute over a right to use a court off James Street in Dublin City called Nash's Court. Number 130 James Street was a private residence fronting on to James Street, above an archway which overhung Nash's Court. This was held by the defendant under a lease of 1900. Number 131 James Street was a public house, which enjoyed rear access on to Nash's Court. This was held by the plaintiff under a lease of 1880. The fee simple owner of both premises, when devising the licensed premises at number 131 James Street in 1880, had granted it with access to Nash's Court, but had *not* given a right of way. The action arose when the defendant erected a sheeted gate in front of Nash's Court, thereby denying access through it to the plaintiff and the patrons of her licensed premises.

In support of the existence of a public right of way, Teevan J noted that there were entries from no fewer than three public houses on to Nash's Court, with the strong suggestion that all three had enjoyed access to Nash's Court even before the lease of the plaintiff's premises in 1880. The defendant's assertion that Nash's Court was not subject to a public right meant that the lessees of the premises over the arch would always have had the right to construct a gate in the archway, a proposition inconsistent with the historic and ongoing access to it by three public houses.

---

[1] *Connell v Porter* (21 December 1967, unreported) HC, Teevan J, (8 December 1972, unreported) SC, before Ó Dálaigh CJ, Walsh and Budd JJ (judgment delivered by Ó Dálaigh CJ).

[10.07] Teevan J was of the view, that the fact of access being given from the licensed premises on to Nash's Court, together with the *absence* of a grant of a right of way, was consistent with the existence of a public right. Where a public right of way was held to exist, a private right of way would be unnecessary.[1] If the fee simple owner found it difficult to differentiate between those legitimately using the licensed premises and others, and in consequence:

> '... throws the way open to all and fails to take steps to exclude, or indicate his intention to exclude, the general public as distinct from a particular section, or particular sections of the public, or to confine user to particular times, or occasions, then it must be presumed that he intended the way to be open to everyone.'[2]

---

[1] Although there is no prohibition in principle against a public right of way and a private right of way co-existing over the same area.

[2] *Connell v Porter* (21 December 1967, unreported) HC at p 8.

[10.08] The finding of the dedication of a public right of way by the fee simple owner, and its acceptance by the public, is bolstered if there is also evidence of the way being maintained on an ongoing basis by a local authority.

> 'When in addition it is found that instead of maintaining the way himself, or imposing an obligation for its maintenance on some grantee, or grantees of easement over it, the original owner permits the local authority to expend public money in its maintenance, then the case becomes even stronger ... If a way is a public way then its maintenance should fall on the public.'[1]

There was evidence that Nash's Court had been maintained by Dublin Corporation since 1931, been publicly lighted since 1919, and that, for as long as anyone could remember, a typical urban nameplate had been placed upon it which was maintained by the Corporation. It was also regarded as a public place, from the point of view of policing and of prosecutions for infringements against public order.

---

[1] *Connell v Porter* (21 December 1967, unreported) HC at pp 8–9. This was also a relevant consideration in *The Giant's Causeway Case* (1898) 5 NIJR 301, considered by Dawson in 'The *Giant's Causeway Case*: Property Law in Ireland 1845–1995' in *One Hundred and Fifty Years of Irish Law* pp 246, 251.

[10.09] The finding by Teevan J that Nash's Court had been dedicated as a public right of way was upheld on an appeal to the Supreme Court. The judgment of the court was delivered by Ó Dálaigh CJ:

> 'Apart from statute, no highway can be created except by the dedication, express or presumed, by the owner of land, of a right of passage over it to the public at large and the acceptance of that right by the public. When there is no direct evidence as to the intention of the owner, an *animus dedicandi* may be presumed either, from the fact of public user without interruption, or from the fact that the way has been maintained and repaired by the local authority.'[1]

The Chief Justice stated that the law now was that a cul-de-sac could be a highway, the absence of separate points of entrance and exit not being fatal to its status as a public way. He added, however, that it was difficult to establish a cul-de-sac as a highway, although the expenditure of public money, in repairing or maintaining the property or in lighting it, was an important consideration; and a landowner who had permitted public money to be spent on a roadway could hardly be heard to say that it was private.

---

[1] *Connell v Porter* (8 December 1972, unreported) SC at p 5. However, the mere fact that a local authority has agreed to take certain lands, to which the public has access, 'in charge' is not in itself proof of dedication and acceptance: *Fortin v Delahunty* (15 January 1999, unreported) HC, Quirke J.

[10.10] According to Ó Dálaigh CJ, a potential difficulty arose from the fact that all the public maintaining had taken place during the tenure of several lessees. The owner of the fee simple alone would have been competent to dedicate a public right and the acquiescence of his lessees could not be deemed to bind him without proof of his awareness. However, in the view of Ó Dálaigh CJ, where the acts of user had gone on for a very long time the knowledge of the fee simple owner could be inferred. In the instant case, the public maintenance was 'such a notorious and obvious fact that it would require strong evidence on the part of the owner of the fee to displace the presumption that he must have been aware of it.'[1]

---

[1] *Connell v Porter* (8 December 1972, unreported) SC at p 8.

Public maintenance must be by consent of fee simple owner

[10.11] The taking in charge of a piece of property by a local authority can be no evidence of the dedication of that property to the public use if the local authority so acts in circumstances where the dedication of a public way by the fee simple owner cannot be inferred. This arose in *O'Connor v Sligo Corpn*.[1] In 1882, some 19 years prior to the action, Evelyn Ashley granted a lease for 99 years of a plot of ground at Abbey Street in Sligo town to John Lavin. At that time the plot was bounded on the Abbey Street side by a wall that also ran along the length of the street. When John Lavin went into possession he knocked down that part of the wall which skirted his plot and built three houses, set back about 7 feet from Abbey Street, with the intervening area left as a kind of forecourt. The forecourt eventually began to resemble the footpath adjacent to it. In time the public started to use the forecourt as a footpath and the defendant Corporation maintained it as if it were one. In 1900, John Lavin's interest vested in the plaintiff who constructed ornamental walls in front of all three houses flush with the line of the original wall, the remainder of which still ran along the street. The defendant Corporation, believing this action by the plaintiff to be in breach of the public right, passed a resolution and pulled the walls down. The plaintiff's action was for an injunction and damages.

Chatterton V-C, granting the application, held that the sole issue in the case was whether there had been a valid dedication and acceptance of the forecourt area as a right of way to the public by someone competent to dedicate it. In this instance the owner in fee was the only party competent to make the dedication. As the owner in fee had leased the property, he would have had no right to interfere in the actions of the lessee and, quite properly, had not so interfered. There was no evidence that he was even aware of the existing state of affairs in 1900 and, according to Chatterton V-C, proof of actual knowledge by the fee simple owner was necessary. Since there had not been a dedication of a public right of way, the defendant Corporation had acted wrongfully, and the plaintiff was entitled to the relief sought.

---

[1] *O'Connor v Sligo Corpn* (1901) 1 NIJR 116.

Access and termini

[10.12] A public right of way must conform to similar conditions as a private right of way, in terms of a specific entrance to and exit from the way. In *O'Connor v Sligo Corpn* Chatterton V-C observed on this point:

> 'Now, I can understand a right of way across a piece of land, from one point on one side of it to another point on the opposite or another side, but how can there be said to be a right of way across a piece of ground which is merely an inshot of the public street?'[1]

Similarly, in *Re The Estate of Thomas Connolly*[2] Flanagan J held that a right could not be sustained to traverse in all directions, as was contended for, but rather from a particular point on the strand at Bundoran, Co Donegal to a stile, so placed as to accommodate the public, and thence to another point along the strand. In *Abercromby v The Town Commissioners of Fermoy*,[3] a case involving an alleged public right of way and also a local customary right of leisure and recreation, Holmes LJ noted that the right enjoyed by the people of Fermoy, Co Cork over the Barnane Walk was, not to reach any definite point or place, but the facility to use it 'as a place of recreation – to walk, to saunter, to lounge, to chat, to meet their friends.' As such, it could not be deemed to have been dedicated as a public right of way which 'generally means a right to the public to pass from one public place to another public place.'[4]

However, the point of entrance can also be the point of exit. A cul-de-sac is capable of constituting a public way.[5]

---

[1] *O'Connor v Sligo Corpn* (1901) 1 NIJR 116 at 117.
[2] *Re The Estate of Thomas Connolly* (1871) 5 ILTR 28.
[3] *Abercromby v The Town Commissioners of Fermoy* [1900] 1 IR 302.

4   [1900] 1 IR 302 at 313–314.
5   See para **[10.04]**.

Obstruction

[10.13] An action by an individual for damage arising from an obstruction of a public right of way can only be taken with the fiat of the Attorney General who must join in the action.[1] The decision of the Attorney General not to join in such an action can only be challenged by a judicial review in the High Court.

In certain limited instances an individual can take an action for the disturbance of a public right without the fiat of the Attorney General. These were set out by Brett J in *Benjamin v Stone*[2] and applied by Judge Sheridan in *Dunne v Rattigan*:[3]

    (a)   the plaintiff must show a particular injury to himself beyond that suffered by the rest of the public;

    (b)   the injury to the individual must be a direct and not a consequential injury;

    (c)   the injury must be shown to be of a substantial character, not fleeting or evanescent.

In the case before him Judge Sheridan held that none of these conditions had been met, where the only detriment was that the blocking of the public right over the defendant's land meant that the plaintiff, who had been accustomed to drive his cattle over it, now had to use a longer route to go to his desired destination, just like the rest of the public. Judge Sheridan distinguished this from a situation in which the applicant might be so inconvenienced in the method of driving his cattle that his employees, by reason of having to drive the cattle over a far longer route, would thereby be prevented from attending to other duties to which the applicant might otherwise have directed them.[4]

1   *O'Sullivan v Cork County Council* (18 December 1969, unreported) HC; *Dunne v Rattigan* [1981] ILRM 365. In *Browne v Dowie* (1959) 93 ILTR 179, in which the defendant alleged a public right of way in defence to an action for trespass, Judge Fox held that, since the Attorney General had not been joined by the plaintiff, his only jurisdiction was to determine whether the defendant had made out a case for a public right of way to sustain his defence to the claimed trespass.
2   *Benjamin v Stone* (1874) LR 9 CP 400.
3   *Dunne v Rattigan* [1981] ILRM 365.
4   See *Smith v Wilson* [1903] 2 IR 45, in which the plaintiff was found to have sustained an injury beyond that suffered by the public and was awarded damages.

Abandonment

[10.14] It is difficult to infer an intention to abandon a public right of way. Mere non-user for a limited period, or permitting a lane used by the public frequently to become overrun by brambles and shrubbery, is not sufficient.[1] Where, however, the public had been excluded from a road for over 60 years, and an alternative road had been constructed and used, an abandonment was held to have arisen.[2] More recently, it has been held that mere discontinuation of user of a road or track as a highway is unlikely to extinguish a public right of way, although it may have the effect of rendering the way no longer subject to the public right. Even so, actual discontinuation would have to persist for a considerable time before a legal abandonment could be presumed.[3]

---

1   *Carroll v Sheridan and Sheehan* [1984] ILRM 451.
2   *Representative Church Body v Barry* [1918] 1 IR 402.
3   *O'Sullivan v Cork County Council* (18 December 1969, unreported) HC. Presumably this is because planning authorities now have the power formally to extinguish a public right of way under the Local Government (Planning and Development) Act 1963, s 76.

[10.15] This subtle point of distinction – between formal extinguishment and a way no longer being subject to the public right – was fundamental to the decision in *O'Sullivan v Cork County Council*.[1] The defendant local authority was engaged in a road-widening exercise south of Cork city following the construction of Cork Airport. The old public road, part of which ran through the land of the plaintiff, had been extremely windy, and the widening programme was also designed to straighten the road. A contract for the sale of portion of the plaintiff's land to the defendant local authority, so as to facilitate the road-widening programme, omitted the site of the old road. Although the circumstances were not such as to warrant rectification, the plaintiff only properly realised after the road-widening had been completed, that the defendant local authority had no power to accommodate a householder dispossessed by the roadwidening scheme in a new house built on the site of the old road where it had run through the plaintiff's land. Teevan J held that no part of the old road on the plaintiff's land had passed to the defendant local authority which, even though the public right had not been formally extinguished,[2] could no longer assert that the plot remained subject to the former public right. As a result, the defendant local authority had no right to relocate the dispossessed householder in a new house built there.

Neither was there any case of an estoppel, as the plaintiff had not induced the defendant to act to its detriment. Accordingly, the plaintiff was entitled to possession.[3]

---

1   *O'Sullivan v Cork County Council* (18 December 1969, unreported) HC.
2   Through the power to extinguish a public right of way accorded to a local authority under the Roads Act 1993, s 73(10). The right of way cannot effectively be extinguished until intention to extinguish has been published in the public press, and due consideration has been given to representations received: *Smeltzer v Fingal County Council* [1998] 1 IR 279.
3   In 'Once a Highway Always a Highway' (1994) 45 NILQ 403, Dowling suggests that the maxim *omnia praesumuntur rita esse acta* should apply to extinguish a public right of way in circumstances where its continuing and manifest non-use makes it fair to do so. 'It is unreasonable to expect that purchasers of land should be subjected to revival of public rights of way long disused in circumstances where neither inspection of the land nor local inquiry will reveal their existence.' (1994) 45 NILQ 403 at 407.

Local Customary Rights

Introduction

[10.16] A public right of way should not be confused with a local customary right. The rudiment of a public right is that it is open to the entire public, and not confined to a section of it. Public rights are finite: way, navigation and fishing in tidal waters. On the other hand, a local customary right, as the name implies, is limited to the inhabitants of a locality, but can be for any of a variety of purposes. A typical example is the right of people in a parish to use a dedicated path as a route to their local church, or to conduct public sports in a particular place.[1] In *Adair v Natural Trust for Places of Historical Interest or Natural Beauty*,[2] Girvan J observed:

> '... customary rights only arise where there is no common law right in existence. A custom is a particular rule which has existed either actually or presumably from time immemorial and has obtained the force of law in a particular locality although contrary to or not consistent with the general law of the realm ... A custom is in the nature of a local common law within the particular locality.'

Like a public right, a local customary right cannot arise by prescription, although it seems that, in appropriate circumstances, a lost grant can be presumed in relation to it.[3]

---

1   *Re Pews of Derry Cathedral* (1864) 8 Ir Jur (NS) 115.
2   *Adair v National Trust for Places of Historical Interest or Natural Beauty* [1998] NI 33 at 44.
3   *Briscoe v Drought* (1859) 11 ICLR 250 at 262, per Hughes B.

[10.17] A local customary right cannot arise over land owned by the Crown in Northern Ireland or by the State in the Republic of Ireland. The rationale for this, is that the existence of a right favouring a limited number only, over lands so owned, is inconsistent with the role of public trustee which the Crown or the State, as the case may be, is deemed to occupy. In *MacNamara v Higgins*,[1] which involved an alleged local customary right to remove sand and soil from a part of the seashore in Co Clare between high tide and low tide, the dichotomy was expressed thus by Lefroy CJ:

> 'If the Crown be a royal trustee of the sea shore, how can it be said to be good for the subjects of the Crown to abridge the right of the Crown by a custom, and limit the enjoyment of that right to take sand to a few; to confine the exercise of the right to the occupiers of a particular district? The reason of the thing shows there is no such distinction. ... and we see no ground for allowing such.'[2]

Another explanation for the decision in *MacNamara v Higgins* is that the courts refuse to find a local customary right in the nature of a customary profit *à prendre*, or in other words, a right to take anything off the land.[3] This is on the basis that it would be unreasonable to allow a right be exercised by a fluctuating and indeterminate body of persons, the ultimate effect of which could be to destroy the subject matter of the right itself.[4]

---

1   *MacNamara v Higgins* (1854) 4 ICLR 326.
2   (1854) 4 ICLR 326 at 332.
3   *Race v Ward* (1855) 4 E & B 702; *Hamilton v AG* (1881) 5 LR Ir 555; *Tighe v Sinnott* [1897] 1 IR 140; *Adair v National Trust for Places of Historical Interest or Natural Beauty* [1998] NI 33 at 44–45, per Girvan J.
4   See paras **[11.06]**, **[11.16]**.

[10.18] In the case of registered land, a local customary right falls among the category of burdens capable of binding such land without the necessity of being registered.[1]

---

[1] The Registration of Title Act 1964 s 72(1)(g); formerly the Local Registration of Title (Ireland) Act 1891, s 47(f).

Ambit of local customary right

[10.19] A local customary right by definition is confined to a limited part of the public. It can include a right to wander, saunter and recreate, rights which cannot be acquired by the public at large, and without being constrained by the requirements of specific *termini*, such as delimit a public right of way.[1]

> '... our law has always recognised that the people of a district – a town, a parish, or a hamlet – are capable of acquiring by dedication or custom, certain rights over land which cannot be gained by the general public ... legal principle does not require that rights of this nature should be limited to certain ancient pastimes. Popular amusement takes many shapes; and there is no outdoor recreation so general and perennial as the promenade ... those who use the walk may wander over every portion of its surface, either in groups or solitary meditation.'[2]

However, an alleged local customary right will be found not to exist where the size of the community stated to have right to enjoy it is too large. In *Giant's Causeway Co Ltd v AG*,[3] Chatterton V-C held that there could not be a local customary right to wander about the Giant's Causeway for all the inhabitants of the counties of Antrim and Londonderry.[4] Still less for anyone who might want to view the place hailing from any part of the world.[5]

---

[1] *Abercromby v The Town Commissioners of Fermoy* [1900] 1 IR 302. That part of the decision in *Smeltzer v Fingal County Council* [1998] 1 IR 279, to the effect that there can be no local customary right to wander (as opposed to a right in the public generally) is erroneous. The pronouncement was *obiter* since the case concerned a public right of way.

[2] [1900] 1 IR 302 at 314.

[3] *Giant's Causeway Co Ltd v AG* (1898) 5 NIJR 301.

[4] (1898) 5 NIJR 301 at 307: 'This is certainly a bold defence of custom, and seems to be in violation of the settled rules of law on the subject. There have been so many decisions upon claims to rights of custom that I should have supposed the law on this subject was well settled. Custom is a *lex loci*, and where it exists it displaces the common law, so that it was necessary to provide safeguards for it, and it must be restricted within due limits. It must be certain, and it must be reasonable.'

[2] (1898) 5 NIJR 301, at p 307: 'No rule on this subject is better settled than that a custom cannot be claimed for all the inhabitants of the realm, or for all persons in the world.' See also Dawson 'The *Giant's Causeway Case*: Property Law in Ireland 1845–1995' in *One Hundred and Fifty Years of Irish Law* pp 244, 247–248.

Conditions for existence of local customary right

[10.20] In *Daly v Cullen*[1] Judge Deale set out the basic principles which the law had established for the existence of a local customary right:

(a)   the custom must have existed without interruption from time immemorial; latterly, this had been satisfied by showing 20 years' uninterrupted user up to the bringing of the action, so that, in the absence of evidence to the contrary, user from time immemorial would be presumed;

(b)   the custom must be reasonable;

(c)   the custom must be certain – both in terms of its nature and in respect of the locality.[2]

(d)   although not included by Judge Deale, an accepted additional requirement is that a local customary right cannot be in the nature of a communal profit *à prendre*: there can be no collective right to take anything off the land.[3]

Daly v Cullen concerned an alleged local customary right, claimed by five Co Wexford fishermen, on behalf of all fishermen in a particular area, to use a laneway over the defendant's farm which led down to the foreshore. The right claimed was also to carry their tackle and their catches, using whatever mode of conveyance was convenient to them, down the lane and then along a detour through the defendant's lands to the foreshore, as the end of the lane was not level with the foreshore but had a fall of about three feet.

Judge Deale held that the plaintiffs' claim failed on the basic test of continuous long enjoyment. Seven years prior to the action, the defendant had erected a paling and stile at the end of the laneway which would have made it difficult to descend to the shore without trespassing on his land. Nobody had objected at the time. Although there had been evidence of user extending back 55 years, only the five plaintiffs had given evidence, and according to Judge Deale, 'such a custom would be notorious and universal in character and so could be proved by some parishioners other than the plaintiffs themselves.'[4] The mere granting of permission by the owner of the farm to various persons to traverse the lane at various times was in no way consistent with a local customary right of passage.

---

1   *Daly v Cullen* (1957) 92 ILTR 127.

2   Addendum derived from Girvan J in *Adair v National Trust for Places of Historical Interest or Natural Beauty* [1998] NI 33, who said, at p 44: 'To be valid a custom must have four essentials: (1) it must be immemorial; (2) it must be reasonable; (3) it must be certain in respect of its nature and in respect of the locality; (4) it must have continued without interruption.'

3   *Mullen v Irish Fishermen Co Ltd and Sam Henry and Partners Ltd* (9 November 1970, unreported) HC, see para **[10.23]**–**[10.26]**, *Adair v National Trust for Places of Historical Interest or Natural Beauty* [1998] NI 33.

4   (1957) 92 ILTR 127 at 131.

[10.21] Neither did the alleged right satisfy the test of reasonableness. The evidence showed that after each annual threshing the defendant farmer would leave his chaff and straw in the laneway for several days. Clearly he needed unrestricted access at all times.

This would be significantly interfered with if the plaintiffs, or any more of the local community who became fishermen, had a particularly busy run of fishing and left vehicles that would block up the laneway at its foreshore end. Even if the way were restricted to access on foot, according to Judge Deale this could still be unreasonable because the laneway was not peripheral to the defendant's land, but ran right through his farm and was not fenced off from it.

[10.22] In order for an alleged right to rank as a local customary right, the class of the public entitled to use it must be free from vagueness and uncertainty. In *Adair v National Trust for Places of Historical Interest or Natural Beauty*,[1] Girvan J was confronted with a claimed right, by an individual, to take shellfish and lugworms from the tidal waters of Strangford Lough, who asserted that it was enjoyed by members of the 'fishing community of Co Down'. Girvan J found that the claimed right was in effect a profit à prendre, which could not constitute a local customary right, on the grounds of unreasonableness as potentially destroying the subject-matter of the right. In addition, there was no evidence of a widespread customary right to take shellfish and lugworms from the Lough, and the alleged class of local community was both vague and uncertain. It was unclear, for example, whether the class included retired or unemployed fishermen, or the families of those currently or formerly engaged in fishing.[2] On account, therefore, of the unreasonableness of the claimed right, and the vagueness of the alleged class, a local customary right to extract shellfish and lugworms from the tidal waters of Strangford Lough could not be sustained.

---

[1]   *Adair v National Trust for Places of Historical Interest or Natural Beauty* [1998] NI 33.
[2]   [1998] NI 33 at 45.

Time of satisfying the requirement of reasonableness

[10.23] The issue of the time at which the test of reasonableness is to be determined was considered by Kenny J in *Mullen v Irish Fishermen Co Ltd and Sam Henry and Partners Ltd*.[1] This was a claim of a local customary right by four brothers who were fishermen of salmon and mussels in the River Boyne and who, in common with the other fishermen in the village of Mornington, near Drogheda in Co Louth, beached their boats and hung their nets on a narrow spit of land called The Crook, a wasteland useless for grazing or tillage. The Crook was bounded on three sides by sand and shingle and covered by the Boyne in high tide. Access to it was possible only from the south, through a rough track from the village of Mornington. Each fisherman's family regarded itself as enjoying a particular patch or strip into which The Crook was notionally divided. There was a long established custom that nobody infringed anybody else's right. It was asserted that the practice of beaching boats and draping fishing nets over erected poles had persisted for at least 200 years. Actual evidence was adduced of this activity being carried out openly, and in a belief of right, on the several notional strips comprising The Crook, from 1906 onwards. The construction by the defendants of a fish-processing plant on a part of The Crook that they had purchased had the effect of dispossessing the plaintiffs from their own particular patch.

¹   *Mullen v Irish Fishermen Co Ltd and Sam Henry and Partners Ltd* (9 November 1970, unreported) HC.

[10.24] Kenny J summarised the law on local customary rights:

(a)   the custom must be certain;

(b)   the custom must be reasonable;

(c)   the custom must have been exercised from time immemorial;

(d)   the custom must have been exercised continuously and without interruption;

(e)   the custom must not have given a right to take anything away from the land.

He accepted that, for practical purposes, it was impossible to demonstrate enjoyment from 1189, the year of commencement of legal memory:

'The requirement that the custom has been exercised since time immemorial involves that it must have existed before 1189 but as proof of this is impossible, evidence that it has been exercised during the period of living memory is sufficient to raise a presumption that it dates back to 1189 although the defendant may establish, if he can, that it commenced some time between that date and the beginning of legal memory.'¹

¹   *Mullen v Irish Fishermen Co Ltd and Sam Henry and Partners Ltd* (9 November 1970, unreported) HC at p 8.

[10.25] The defendants argued that the alleged local customary right was unreasonable, as being in the nature of a proprietary claim which prevented them building on the lands they had bought. Kenny J conceded that this circumstance would have made the claimed right unreasonable if the test of reasonableness had to be satisfied at the time of the action. However, in the judgment of Kenny J, the issue of reasonableness depended on what would have been reasonable at the time of commencement of the custom and the conditions then prevailing. Both in 1189, and in 1906 when the evidence first clearly established actual user, the lands comprising The Crook had been useless either for grazing or tillage, and nobody would have thought of growing or building anything there. In consequence, the custom would *then* have satisfied the test of reasonableness, and that was the time that mattered.

[10.26] Kenny J was clearly influenced by the circumstance that the claimed custom was intended to benefit a local community. Hence, it did not signify that the particular portion of The Crook under dispute benefited only the four plaintiffs themselves. Indeed, the notional division of the entire area into separately occupied strips had served the additional purpose of avoiding disputes. Neither could it be contended that the boundaries of the area covered by the alleged right were unclear: the alleged right was clearly confined to The Crook (albeit that some of its borders were dubious) and to the fishermen inhabitants of Mornington. It did not lie with the defendants to suggest that the plaintiffs might transfer their right to other areas of The Crook because of the tacit agreement with the other fishermen that each would be confined to his own patch.

The construction of the defendants' factory had obliged the plaintiffs to hang their nets and moor their boats elsewhere, for which, moreover, they required permission. Additional inconvenience and time loss was caused by the plaintiffs' need now to be ferried across the River Boyne to get at their nets and boats. Kenny J awarded damages for the infringement of the local customary right enjoyed by the plaintiffs.

Chapter 11

The Nature and Characteristics of a Profit *à Prendre*

Introduction

[11.01] A profit *à prendre* is the most tangible fruit of an intangible right. It is the right to take off land some of the natural produce of the land, such as turf, shot game, timber for fuelling, minerals, soil, and fish from rivers and lakes.[1] Its bid for inclusion in a work of this kind is that the exercise of such rights does not derive from ownership of the land over which the profit *à prendre* is enjoyed, but from a right granted *over* that land for the purpose of acquiring and removing the subject of the profit. By its very nature a profit *à prendre* must be linked with a further intangible right, so that the land (or water) can rightfully be entered in order for the subject of the right to be acquired, and, once acquired, removed. Such auxiliary right may be either a licence or an easement, according as the profit is linked to the enjoyment of land also owned by the holder of the profit, or is not so linked.[2]

---

[1] This does not include water from a well or spring, which is deemed to be an easement; the test is whether the item taken is capable of ownership before being taken: *Race v Ward* (1855) 4 E & B 702; *Alfred F Beckett Ltd v Lyons* [1969] 1 Ch 449. In this context, game, which is wild, must be killed before becoming capable of ownership. The distinction is sometimes stated as being between that which is produce of the soil and that which is 'adventitious to the soil.'

[2] See para **[20.02]**.

[11.02] Depending on its subject-matter, and depending also on the terms of enjoyment of the profit, the right to its enjoyment may be bound up with the ownership of land by the holder of the profit: in this case it is referred to as a profit appurtenant. Profits appurtenant most usually involve either fuel for a house in the form of turf (turbary) or timber (estovers). Other profits are not associated with the ownership of land by the holder of the profit, principally those granted either for pleasure (such as, shooting and fishing) or commercial gain (such as quarrying and mining). Such profits are known as 'profits in gross'.

Profits Distinguished from Easements

[11.03] A profit, being an interest in land, must be granted by instrument in writing. A profit can be the subject of a lease[1] or a licence. If conferred by licence, it is deemed to be a licence coupled with an interest, not a bare licence, and accordingly irrevocable, save in accordance with the terms of its grant.[2] It can also be claimed by prescription and by presumed lost grant.[3] The doctrine of presumed lost grant cannot be invoked to sustain the actual existence of the profit *à prendre*, merely to establish that a particular claimant is entitled to it.[4]

In order for a profit to be acquired under the Prescription (Ireland) Act 1858, it must arise in the context of a 'tenement' occupied by the person asserting right.[5] In short, a profit in gross cannot be established through statutory prescription.

---

[1]   *Bayley v Marquis of Conyngham* (1863) 15 ICLR 406.

[2]   *Radcliff v Hayes* [1907] 1 IR 101 at 112–113, per Meredith MR. In this case, however, the profit *à prendre* was held to have been granted by way of demise for 10 years.

[3]   *Little v Wingfield* (1859) 11 ICLR 63; *Dawson v McGroggan* [1903] IR 92; *Congested Districts Board v Gavaghan* (1904) 38 ILTR 228.

[4]   *Little v Wingfield* (1859) 11 ICLR 63 at 79, per O'Brien J; *Foyle and Bann Fisheries Ltd v Attorney-General* (1949) 83 ILTR 29 at 40, per Gavan Duffy P.

[5]   Prescription (Ireland) Act 1858, s 5. See also, Bland *The Law of Easements and Profits à Prendre* (1997) Sweet & Maxwell, pp 126, 234.

[11.04] In *Lowry v Crothers*[1] 60 years' actual and uninterrupted enjoyment of a right to cut turf failed as a prescriptive right, under s 1 of the Prescription (Ireland) Act 1858, where the enjoyment was referable throughout the entire period to an agreement in writing made by a tenant for life of the servient tenement who had died before the commencement of the statutory prescriptive period. The evidence demonstrated that the successors to the servient tenement had proceeded on the basis that the original consent was still current, and so the claim was defeated.

---

[1]   *Lowry v Crothers* (1871) IR 5 CL 98.

[11.05] Although a profit may be released, it is incapable of abandonment as that concept is applied to easements.[1] It seems, however, that, similarly to an easement, a profit *à prendre* can be extinguished by operation of law. For example, if the holder of a common appurtenant himself purchases part of the land over which the common is enjoyed, this act will bring to an end that holder's right of common in respect of the entire land.[2]

In *Re Bohan*,[3] a tenant farmer in Co Leitrim enjoyed a right to cut turf from a bog in the possession of his landlord, for consumption on the tenant's holding. The tenant subsequently purchased the freehold of his holding under the Land Purchase Acts. He was registered as full owner, together with his right of turbary. In due course the Land Commission compulsorily acquired these lands, under s 24(3) of the Land Act 1923, for the purpose of allotting them in portions to the holders of uneconomic holdings.

One of these was Rose Bohan, to whom the Land Commission also purported to give the former tenant's turbary right. However, the erstwhile tenant's dwellinghouse had not been on that part of the lands allotted to Rose Bohan. Nor had the Land Commission compulsorily acquired the landlord's bog.

Teevan J held that the Land Commission *had* appropriated the former tenant's turbary right, but that, since this turbary right had to be appurtenant to a building and the portion of compulsorily acquired land assigned to Rose Bohan contained no buildings, the turbary right had in effect been extinguished:

'Either they [the Land Commission] have dealt with an acquired right of turbary, in a manner which results in its being no longer accessorial to enjoyment of dominant land (and there cannot be such a right in gross) and thereby have caused its extinguishment; or they have attempted to create a new appurtenance over a supposedly servient tenement not in their ownership ...'[4]

---

1 *Neill v Duke of Devonshire* (1882) 8 App Cas 135; *Tighe v Sinnott* [1897] 1 IR 140; *O'Neill v Johnston* [1908] 1 IR 358 at 380, [1909] 1 IR 237 at 242, p 264.
2 *Wyat Wyld's case* (1609) 8 Co Rep 78b; *Hargrove v Lord Congleton* (1861) 12 ICLR 368; *White v Taylor (No 1)* [1969] 1 Ch 150 at 158.
3 *Re Bohan* [1957] IR 49.
4 [1957] IR 49 at 56–57.

[11.06] Unlike in the case of an easement, there cannot be a local customary right in the nature of a profit *à prendre*, on the principle that the boundless exercise of a right to reap the fruits of land by an unlimited and fluctuating body of people will ultimately tend to the total destruction of the thing that is enjoyed.[1] Furthermore, as explained by Barton J in *Westropp v Congested Districts Board*:[2]

'... prescription presupposes a grant to have anciently existed, and one of the tests of the legality of the origin of such a prescriptive claim is whether it can be referred to a grant from a person capable of making a grant to a person capable of taking under a grant.'[3]

A succession of residents or occupiers are not capable of being competent grantees, unless they could claim through the owner or owners of property benefited by the profit *à prendre*. Otherwise, the actual owners of the property would be unable to release the profit *à prendre*, which would forever after remain indeterminate.[4]

A claim to a profit *à prendre* by prescription is confined to the owner of the land benefited by the profit, and cannot be asserted by a group of people in the guise of a public right. This was affirmed by Chatterton V-C in *Hamilton v AG*,[5] a case involving a claim by a number of the inhabitants of Skerries, Co Dublin to take sand, seaweed and gravel from the seashore:

'Prescription for *profits a prendre* must be in the *que estate*, that is to say, it must be laid in the party claiming the right, and those whose estate he holds. It cannot be claimed by the inhabitants of a town, village, or district as such, but only in right of the particular tenement which the party claiming holds; and with the exception of the customary tenants of a manor ... it must be laid in the name of the owner in fee, and claimed in his right. This is unquestionably the law as regards land in general, and I see no ground for making any difference in the case of the sea-shore.'[6]

---

1 *Gateward's Case* (1607) 6 Co Rep 59b. See also *Murphy v Ryan* (1868) IR 2 CL 143 at 154, per O'Hagan J: 'A right of way upon the land; a right of passage upon the water....; a right for the people of a parish to dance upon a particular field – all these rights may be established by usage, because they are mere easements, which may be enjoyed consistently with the interest of the owner of the land. But no usage can establish a right to take a profit in another's soil, which

might involve the destruction of his property; and such a profit would be the taking of fish.' See also *MacNamara v Higgins* (1854) 4 ICLR 326. See para **[10.17]**.

2   *Westropp v Congested Districts Board* [1918] 1 IR 265.
3   [1918] 1 IR 265 at 268.
4   [1918] 1 IR 268 at 269–270.
5   *Hamilton v AG* (1881) 5 LR Ir 555.
6   (1881) 5 LR Ir 555 at 576.

[11.07] The holder of a profit *à prendre*, on the basis that its enjoyment carries with it a possessory right, is entitled to bring an action in trespass for infringement of the right.[1] In the case of grazing rights exercised in common, an action in trespass does not lie, but what is called an action for 'overstint' that is, an action to prevent a commoner from grazing more than his allotted number of animals.[2] The owner of an easement is confined to an action in nuisance.

1   *Holford v Bailey* (1849) 13 QB 426, cited in *Radcliff v Hayes* [1907] 1 IR 101 at 114.
2   *O'Sullivan v O'Connor* (1980) 114 ILTR 63. See para **[12.26]**.

Types and Characteristics of a Profit *à Prendre*

[11.08] Profits *à prendre* can in general be divided into those enjoyed by one or a number of people in common with the owner of the land that produces the profit, and those, whether enjoyed by one or a number of people, in respect of which the owner of the land is excluded from enjoyment of the profit. The former are known as profits in common; the latter are termed (somewhat confusingly!) sole or several profits.

Profits *à prendre* are further labelled on the basis of the fruits of the enjoyment. Broadly, these labels fall into two categories: those that accommodate need and those that serve pleasure and profit.

The following are examples of profits that accommodate need:

(a)   right to cut, dry and take away turf for fuelling (turbary);

(b)   right to cut and remove timber for domestic purposes or general utility (estovers);

(c)   right of pasturage (not to be confused with agistment, which is a licence).

The following are examples of commercial profits and profits for pleasure:

(a)   fishing rights (also known as piscary);

(b)   sporting rights (principally shooting);

(c)   quarrying and mining, and rights to extract soil.

[11.09] In addition to the above listed generic and descriptive classifications, profits *à prendre* are further divisible into four specific types, of which the latter two are for the most part of historic relevance nowadays:

Profits appurtenant: this type of profit most closely approximates to an easement, since the purpose of the profit is to accommodate property owned by the holder of the profit. Indeed, the needs of the profit holder's property determine the scope of the profit and thereby serve as a necessary limitation on the right to enjoy it. For example, a right to pasture cattle, appurtenant to property owned by the profit holder, is normally limited to the number of animals that the property is capable of housing in the winter. Hence, the notion of cattle *levant et couchant* – getting up and lying down. A right of pasture can also be limited to a specific number of cattle. A profit appurtenant of estovers is limited to the fuelling needs of the profit holder's property. Similarly, with a right of turbary, which is most often for domestic consumption of turf only. In this context, it is apt to speak (as with easements) of the servient tenement (being the property over which the profit is exercised) and the dominant tenement (being the property for the benefit of which it is exercised).

Profits in gross: these profits are enjoyed by an individual or individuals in their personal right and are not associated with the accommodation of property. They are not subject to the same degree of limitation as a profit appurtenant. Being unconnected with the ownership of a tenement, there is no inherent constraint in relation to their enjoyment. Additionally, profits appurtenant are most often held in common, so that if one of the commoners were to enjoy unrestricted usage, this might destroy the subject of the right to the detriment of other commoners.[1] This circumstance does not feature in the case of a profit in gross. Even so, there is no inherent right, in the holder of a sole or several profit, to exercise the right to such an extent that the capacity of the owner of the land to enjoy his property for its ordinary purposes is destroyed. If this were to be permissible, then the owner of the property would in effect have no rights at all.[2]

It will often be found that a sole or several profit (that is, one which excludes the owner of the land from also enjoying the right) is a profit in gross. Profits appurtenant are typically held in common. This is because profits appurtenant usually derive from the needs of one or a group of property owners or tenants, which are met from the resources of another owner of property, most often a local landlord. Turf, timber and pasture are the obvious examples. In this scenario, it is scarcely to be expected that the owner of such a community-serving property should himself be denied any right to participate in the fruits of it.

Profits appendant: a profit appendant was a feudal right of common pasturage, over waste ground owned by the lord of the manor, which the law implied into a freehold grant of arable land. The right was confined to beasts of utility and the number limited to those which the freeholder's land was capable of accommodating during the winter. The right arose through subinfeudation which was subsequently prohibited by the statute of Quia Emptores 1290.[3]

Profits *pour cause de vicinage*: this is a permissive right, begotten of custom, for cattle to stray between neighbouring unfenced commons. It is limited to

(i)   accidental straying only;

(ii)   no more cattle than any one commoner is entitled to graze on his common;

(iii)   contiguous commons.

The fencing off of the common will bring the right to an end.

---

[1] *Lord Chesterfield v Harris* [1908] 2 Ch 397 at 427, per Kennedy LJ, following *Bailey v Stephens* (1862) 12 CB (NS) 91.

[2] *Rudd v Rea* [1921] 1 IR 223 at 239–240, per Powell J.

[3] *Westropp v Congested Districts Board* [1918] 1 IR 265 at 269, per Barton J.

[11.10] There is no prohibition on any one piece of land accommodating different varieties of profit *à prendre*, although this can give rise to difficulties. For example, in *Radcliff v Hayes*,[1] a landowner demised extensive lands that included a mountain already subject to grazing rights by yearly tenants, over which he granted a ten-year lease of shooting rights to the lessees of the lands. The conflict arose when the tenants with the grazing rights, assuming that they also had the shooting, sought to interfere with the shooting rights of those to whom the landowner had demised them.[2] In *Jameson v Fahey*,[3] the extent of a right of turbary, and the location on a particular mountain where it could be cut, were largely determined by the fact that a common of pasturage had been reserved under the same lease as had reserved the common of turbary.

---

[1]   *Radcliff v Hayes* [1907] 1 IR 101.

[2]   Meredith MR found it pertinent that no-one of the yearly tenants laying claim to the shooting was possessed of a firearm. Even so, in display of an acuity to rustic custom not often believed of Irish judges in the nineteenth century, the Master of the Rolls declined to deem this factor conclusive that no game had been caught: 'When one remembers the position of the property, remote from the residence of the owner, not under the immediate control of landlord, or agent, or anybody else, anyone who knows anything of the west of Ireland would say that if a witness stated that in such circumstances there was no poaching, he would not be worthy of credit.' [1907] 1 IR 101 at 106.

[3]   *Jameson v Fahey* [1907] 1 IR 411. See paras **[12.11]–[12.12]**.

[11.11] It seems that, in Ireland, a profit *à prendre* reserved by a grantor of property can be deemed to be a 'concurrent right' enjoyed both by the grantee of the property and the grantor who had reserved the right. However, it also appears that this will only arise where the language used in the reservation is insufficient to establish an exclusive right. In *Reynolds v Moore*,[1] a lease for lives of 1792 had reserved 'free liberty' to the grantor, 'his heirs and assigns, and his and their attendants, gamekeepers, and servants, to hunt, fowl, fish, hawk, and set ...' on the demised premises. It was held that a successor of the grantor (in effect, the *grantee* of the profit) had no authority to grant a licence to another to shoot game on his own account. According to the Court of Queen's Bench, the regranted right of hunting was a profit *à prendre* in fee simple limited to the grantee of the right, his attendants, gamekeepers and servants. Even so, the exercise of a concurrent right by the grantee could not be done in such a way as to exhaust the opportunity of the grantor also to participate in the right.[2] Rather than to regard a concurrent right as a special feature of the Irish law of profits *à prendre*, it would be wiser to interpret the decision in *Reynolds v Moore* as turning fundamentally upon the words used in the reservation of 1792.[3]

---

[1]   *Reynolds v Moore* [1898] 2 IR 641.

[2]   [1898] 2 IR 641 at 648, per O'Brien J.

[3]   Andrews J stated that an exclusive sporting right would have to be expressly created. However, it has been suggested that the form of words used in *Reynolds v Moore* is commonly found in reservations of hunting and shooting rights in Ireland: Bland *The Law of Easements and Profits à Prendre* p 187.

Profits Appurtenant and the requirement of Appurtenancy and Stint

[11.12] In the same way as an easement over a servient tenement must 'accommodate' the dominant tenement, so too a profit appurtenant must bring a direct and tangible benefit to the property to which it appertains. This is sometimes expressed in the cumbrous language, that there needs to be a propriety of relation between the principal and the adjunct, which is determined by considering whether they so agree in nature and quality as to be capable of any union without incongruity.[1] To the extent that this formulation clearly connotes anything in modern times, it should be construed as requiring there to be an obvious and relevant accommodation of the property by the profit. The following succinct judicial articulation is apt:

> '... no profit to be enjoyed over or taken from land can be made appurtenant to land unless it is accessorial to the enjoyment of the land in relation to which it is claimed.'[2]

---

[1]   Note 7 to Coke on Littleton at 121b, cited with approval by Buckley J in *Hanbury v Jenkins* [1901] 2 Ch 401 and by the Irish House of Lords in *Hayes v Bridges* (1796) 1 Ridg Lef and Sch 390 at 413, itself cited as an authority by Hamilton J in *A-G v Reynolds* [1911] 2 KB 888 at 921. See also Bland *The Law of Easements and Profits à Prendre* p 124, fn 20.

[2]   *Lord Chesterfield v Harris* [1908] 2 Ch 397 at 426, per Kennedy LJ, cited with approval by Teevan J in *Re Bohan* [1957] IR 49.

[11.13] In *A-G v Reynolds*[1] it was held that the destruction of an ancient house, to which rights of common of estover and turbary were appurtenant, did not necessarily result in an extinguishment of the rights. They could be continued as appurtenant to a new house, provided that no greater burden was placed upon the servient land. Hamilton J observed that, in any case, it was a question of fact whether the new house is a continuation of the old one. Nor is it necessary that the new house be built precisely upon the foundations of the old house, although '... I daresay that any considerable remoteness in the new building, unless there were modifying circumstances, go far to destroy the continuity.'[2] For example, if a frame house made entirely of timber were moved a few feet away, it could not be argued as not being the same house merely because some of the land was not taken with it.[3]

---

[1]   *A-G v Reynolds* [1911] 2 KB 888.

[2]   [1911] 2 KB 888 at 934.

[3]   [1911] 2 KB 888 at 935.

[11.14] A turbary right is capable of becoming appurtenant to property yet to be built, provided it is clearly intended to be built.[1] Neither will a turbary right be rendered incapable of being utilised by the owners of houses yet to be built, merely because the eventual result will be the exhausting of the bog, if the language of the instrument creating it permits the wider construction.[2] The requirement of appurtenancy can also be satisfied by another incorporeal right, such as a right of way accommodating a several fishery.[3] However, a profit *à prendre* cannot be regarded as appurtenant to property if the purported profit is stated to be for the benefit of inhabitants only of a building, rather than its owners, as inhabitants are not capable of taking under a grant.[4]

If enjoyment of a profit appurtenant is decoupled from the property to which it is said to appertain, the preferred view is that the profit is extinguished rather than becomes a profit in gross.[5]

---

[1]   *Hargrove v Lord Congleton* (1861) 12 ICLR 368.

[2]   *Duggan v Carey* (1858) 8 ICLR 210 at 221–222, per Pigot CB.

[3]   *Hanbury v Jenkins* [1901] 2 Ch 401 at 423, per Buckley J: 'The one supposed incorporeal right is a right of fishing in the river. The other incorporeal right is a right to walk along the bank for the purpose of fishing in the river. What is there incongruous in the union of these two? One seems to me very clearly congruous to the other. You can scarcely enjoy the one without using the other.' But land cannot be appurtenant to land: if something is granted as appurtenant to land, it must be an incorporeal hereditament: *Knox v Earl of Mayo* (1858) 9 Ir Ch Rep 192.

[4]   *Westropp v Congested Districts Board* [1918] 1 IR 265.

[5]   *Re Bohan* [1957] IR 49 at 57. This was a turbary case, but the principle arguably applies to all appurtenant profits, notwithstanding an apparent instance to the contrary, involving common of pasture, noted by Teevan J in *Sherry v Clarke* (4 July 1968, unreported) HC. However, this factor was not central to the decision in the case: Bland *The Law of Easements and Profits à Prendre* pp 126–127.

[11.15] It has been long established that a profit appurtenant cannot be enjoyed without some kind of restriction on the scope of the enjoyment, so as to guard against the total destruction of the subject-matter of the profit.[1] This restriction is often – and invariably in the case of pasturage – described as 'stint'. A profit appurtenant is sometimes known as a profit in the *que* estate. Implicit in the notion of a *que* estate is a correlation between the needs of the estate concerned and the extent of the profit *à prendre*.[2] In *Clayton v Corby*[3] a claim by prescription to a profit *à prendre* of digging and removing clay and sand from the defendant's land for use in the plaintiff's brick kiln failed on account of its potentially unlimited character which could tend towards the destruction of the property over which it was exercised. According to Denman CJ:

> 'It is observable that, in all cases of a claim of right *in alieno solo* … such claim, in order to be valid, must be made with some limitation and restriction. In the ordinary case of common appurtenant, the right cannot be claimed for commonable cattle without stint, and to any number; but such right is measured by the capability of the tenement in question to maintain the cattle during the winter; levancy and couchancy must be averred and proved. Again, in the case of common of estovers, or a liberty of taking wood, called in the books house bote, plough bote and hay bote, such liberty is not wholly vague and indeterminate, but confined to some certain and definite use. The like of the common of piscary.'[4]

Such an alleged right would be more likely, if sustained, to be regarded as a profit in gross, which cannot be made appurtenant to land since its purpose is primarily commercial, and is not 'accessorial' to an estate.[5]

---

[1]   For example, *Clayton v Corby* (1845) 5 QB 415; *Bailey v Stephens* (1862) 12 CB (NS) 91; *Foyle and Bann Fisheries Ltd v AG* (1949) 83 ILTR 29.

2   *Lord Chesterfield v Harris* [1908] 2 Ch 397 at 410, per Kennedy LJ; cited with approval in *O'Neill v Johnston* [1909] 1 IR 237 at 256, 257.
3   *Clayton v Corby* (1845) 5 QB 415.
4   (1845) 5 QB 419 at 420.
5   *Lord Chesterfield v Harris* [1908] 2 Ch 397 at 426, per Kennedy LJ.

No Local Customary Right in a Profit *à Prendre*

[11.16] A local customary right cannot be established over a profit *à prendre*. The rationale is akin to the requirement of stint in the case of an appurtenant profit: an anxiety not to destroy the subject matter of the profit itself. This was established by *Gateward's case*,[1] which, according to Lefroy CJ in *MacNamara v Higgins*,[2] '... ever since its decision has been recognised as sound law, [and] negatives any right to a profit in the soil of another by custom.'[3]

In *Hamilton v AG*,[4] Chatterton V-C stated that a claim by prescription to a local customary right to remove sand, seaweed and gravel from the seashore, would fail on the grounds both of uncertainty and unreasonableness:

'It would be bad as uncertain; for who would be grantees to whom the grant could be presumed to have been made? The right here claimed is for an indefinite and unlimited number of persons, having neither cohesion nor continuity. It would be bad also as unreasonable, for it would be a right in all persons without limit or restriction to take and carry away the soil itself. In this respect it differs from an easement which may be claimed by custom.'[5]

1   *Gateward's case* (1607) 6 Co Rep 59b.
2   *MacNamara v Higgins* (1854) 4 ICLR 326.
3   (1854) 4 ICLR 326 at 331.
4   *Hamilton v AG* (1881) 5 LR Ir 555.
5   (1881) 5 LR Ir 555 at 576.

[11.17] An exception to the principle that a profit *à prendre* cannot be acquired as a local customary right is possible in the case of a Crown grant to a corporation, whether actual or deemed.[1] The idea of deeming a local community to be incorporated for the purpose of a presumed Crown grant does not appear to have been tested in Ireland.

1   See Bland *The Law of Easements and Profits à Prendre* pp 132–133 and the cases cited therein.

[11.18] In *Goodman v Saltash Corpn*,[1] a majority of the House of Lords employed the concept of a presumed charitable trust to validate a claimed right by 'the free inhabitants of ancient tenements in the borough of Saltash' to extract oysters from the river Tamar between Candlemas and Easter each year. The principle applied was that the defendant corporation had established, on the basis of immemorial usage as of right, a prescriptive right of fishing in the river Tamar, subject to a trust in favour of the asserting 'free inhabitants.' An advantage of regarding the trust as public or charitable was that, being in favour of a fluctuating body of private individuals, it would not offend the rule against perpetuities.[2]

---

[1]   *Goodman v Saltash Corpn* (1882) 7 App Cas 633.
[2]   A point strongly made in the speech of Lord Cairns at p 650.

[11.19] Although hailed as 'a splendid effort of equitable imagination in furtherance of justice',[1] reaction by Irish judges to the principle purportedly established by *Goodman v Saltash Corpn*[2] has been more muted. In *Tighe v Sinnott*,[3] Porter MR described it as a 'peculiar and remarkable case',[4] adding that the question whether a perpetual right of fishing for profit, not confined to those in need and independent of their means, could be established as a charity, might not be 'finally closed as to Ireland.'[5] Six years later, in 1902, in *Dawson v McGroggan*,[6] the same Master of the Rolls cited *Goodman v Saltash Corpn* as authority for the proposition that a grant in gross to the inhabitants of a townland could not be presumed, but that 'if the principle is capable of application, there is no difficulty about the form.'[7] He found it possible instead to rely upon a presumed lost grant to specific individuals, a concept applicable as much to a profit *à prendre* as to an easement.[8] In *Westropp v Congested Districts Board*,[9] Ronan LJ, stating it to be 'elementary law'[10] that a profit *à prendre* could not be claimed by custom, synopsised *Goodman v Saltash Corpn* as being a case '... where the House of Lords introduced the trust into what I may call the imaginary deed.'[11]

---

[1]   By Lord Ashbourne in *Harris v Lord Chesterfield* [1911] AC 623 at 633. However, Lord Ashbourne's was a dissenting judgment in a case that involved an alleged local customary fishing right.
[2]   *Goodman v Saltash Corpn* (1882) 7 App Cas 633.
[3]   *Tighe v Sinnott* [1897] 1 IR 140.
[4]   [1897] 1 IR 140 at 152.
[5]   [1897] 1 IR 140 at 155.
[6]   *Dawson v McGroggan* [1903] 1 IR 92.
[7]   [1903] 1 IR 92 at 100.
[8]   [1903] 1 IR 92 at 98. See para **[11.03]**.
[9]   *Westropp v Congested Districts Board* [1918] 1 IR 265.
[10] [1918] 1 IR 265 at 292.
[11] [1918] 1 IR 265 at 293.

[11.20] *Tighe v Sinnott*[1] concerned an attempt to establish a local customary right in favour of a group of fishermen from Inistioge in Co Kilkenny to fish in the river Nore. Porter MR found that the plaintiff had established a several fishery in the waters, although tidal.[2] The principal issue was whether, through application of the decision in *Goodman v Saltash Corpn*,[3] a right could be found to fish by the inhabitants of Inistioge 'either by virtue of some trust engrafted on the title of the plaintiff, or by reason of an exception legally established in favour of the class.'[4] The Master of the Rolls, with manifest lack of enthusiasm, acknowledged that the House of Lords decision in *Goodman v Saltash Corppn* 'must be taken to have conclusively established the proposition that in some way, whether by analogy to the law applicable to charities, or by way of exception from the grant' a several fishery could be held to be subject to the right of a 'fluctuating and unincorporated body of persons' to fish in the fishery for all time, even to the extent of its possible destruction.[5]

The evidence, however, in support of any such suggested local right, could most kindly be described as tenuous. Into this elegant and technical debate about the possible presuming of a charitable trust in favour of fishermen strode the fierce and falsehood-serving fervour with which the rural Irish are famed to thrash out property disputes at law. An alleged statute from Henry VIII, in 1537, purportedly granting the local right, was found not to exist – either in 1537, or in any other year during the 'disturbed times' of the reign of that monarch.[6] A meeting convened by Colonel Tighe in 1866, to assert his several fishery rights and to give permission for limited fishing to local fishermen, though copiously attended, eluded the memory of each of the defendants and their witnesses. A caretaker for the plaintiff gave evidence that he had several times routed night-time fishing. This evidence was traduced by the caretaker's son, who testified for the defendants and charged his father with perjury.[7]

The best that could be produced for the defendants was an Inquisition of 1607, which had found that a body called 'the commons of Inistioge' was 'in the habit of fishing therein'. No more. There was no suggestion that such habit was as of right or continuous. Indeed, nothing further could be asserted than that, two centuries after the Inquisition of 1607:

> '... some persons who lived in the town of Inistioge, and some others who did not, have on some occasions, more or less frequent, more or less precariously, more or less secretly, fished in the same place.'[8]

Unsurprisingly, Porter MR declined to presume a charitable trust or exception in favour of such a surreptitious and shifting community of fishermen.

---

[1]   *Tighe v Sinnott* [1897] 1 IR 140.
[2]   See para **[13.18]** ff.
[3]   *Goodman v Saltash Corpn* (1882) 7 App Cas 633.
[4]   [1897] 1 IR 140 at 152, citing the *ipsissima verba* of the pleadings by defendants' counsel.
[5]   [1897] 1 IR 140 at 155.
[6]   [1897] 1 IR 140 at 160.
[7]   [1897] 1 IR 140 at 150–151. With greater diffidence than the frustration he experienced could have inspired, Porter MR discounted the greater part of the testimony offered by the defendants, as being 'evidence, which to say the least, would need to be very largely discounted by anyone anxious to arrive at the truth.'
[8]   [1897] 1 IR 140 at 160–161.

Chapter 12

Profits *à Prendre* that Accommodate Need

Turbary and the Right to Extract Turf

Characteristics

[12.01] A profit *à prendre* of turbary is the right, usually exercised in common, to dig for, cut and remove turf from the land of another, for the purpose of fuelling the home of the profit holder. At common law, the tenant of land was entitled to cut timber growing on his land for the purpose of constructing instruments of transport and husbandry and also for necessary household fuel. This is known as 'estovers'. A tenant using timber for these purposes was not impeachable for waste: indeed, he would have so been if the repairs were not made.[1] A combination of the greater availability in Ireland of turf for fuelling than timber, together with a series of eighteenth century statutes that encouraged the planting of trees and effectively eliminated the traditional right of estovers, resulted in recognition of a right at common law for a tenant to cut turf on his land for fuelling.

This right was amply expressed, in 1859, by Pigot CB in *Howley v Jebb*:[2]

> '... In Ireland, it is a matter of common notoriety that, from the great abundance of bog, and the absence of coal fit for domestic purposes, peat (or turf, as it is called here) has been the ordinary fuel for the great mass of the population, and, in the memory of many now living, was much used by all classes, in places to which there was difficulty of access for sea-borne coal. In a country and in districts so situated, the very nature of things suggests that the principle of the law of estovers should be applied to the materials which alone exist for satisfying its requirements. If timber do not exist, or if it be so scant and precious as to be inadequate for those requirements, it would be unreasonable and absurd to restrict the law of estovers to timber alone, and to reject a cheaper, a readier and a more abundant material for fire-bote – a material too in general use for fuel.'[3]

In similar vein, a year earlier, Pigot CB, in *Duggan v Carey*,[4] suggested that, in an epoch when vast tracts of bog were available to be worked, the grant of turbary rights provided a method of guaranteeing improvement of the lands, despite the fact that the bogs would thereby one day be exhausted:

> '... in those early times, the parties, with abundance of bog in the country, and looking to the future improvement of the land demised, contemplated that improvement by means of sub-tenants, whose very existence, to some extent, must depend upon fuel, and were content voluntarily to incur the risk of a contingency so remote as that of the bog becoming exhausted in one or two centuries after the granting of the lease.'[5]

---

[1] *Howley v Jebb* (1859) 8 ICLR 435, at p 441, per Pigot CB.

[2] *Howley v Jebb* (1859) 8 ICLR 435.

[3] (1859) 8 ICLR 435 at 441–442. A year later this right was given statutory recognition by the Landlord and Tenant Law Amendment, Ireland, Act 1860, s 29, in which context a lease or

demise is deemed to include a letting from year to year: *Lord Lifford v Kearney* (1883) 17 ILTR 30. See also *Congested Districts Board v Gavaghan* (1904) 38 ILTR 228.

4   *Duggan v Carey* (1858) 8 ICLR 210.

5   (1858) 8 ICLR 210 at 222. See also the observations of O'Brien LC in *Re Scott's Estate* [1916] 1 IR 180 at 198.

[12.02] This right, however, does not include a right to cut the turf for sale.[1] For example, a tenant for life can be restrained from cutting turf otherwise than for personal use on lands demised to him that include a bog, notwithstanding that the settlor had occasionally cut and sold turf from the bog, if the settlement deed does not specifically authorise cutting turf for sale.[2] On the other hand, according to Sugden LC in *Coppinger v Gubbins*,[3] a different view could prevail '… where bog and nothing else is demised, and turf could be cut for no valuable purpose except for sale; as if it was a bog always cut for sale, and demised as such in the same manner as an open mine. Such cases depend on contract, and must be considered as standing on their own ground.'[4]

Except in such a situation, the frequently encountered covenant by a tenant to keep the property in repair and deliver it up at the end of the term militates against a construction which would confer upon a tenant a right to cut turf for sale.[5] More recently, however, it has been suggested that where a right of turbary is granted without restriction as to purpose, and the holder of the right constructs a drain in order to enhance its value, such person will be entitled to sell the turf once cut.[6]

---

1   *Lord Courtown v Ward* (1802) 1 Sch & Lef 8; *Chatterton v White* (1839) 1 IR Eq 200; *Howley v Jebb* (1859) 8 ICLR 435; *Stevenson v Moore* (1858) 7 Ir Ch Rep 462; *Dawson v McGroggan* [1903] 1 IR 92.

2   *Jones v Meaney* [1941] Ir Jur 50.

3   *Coppinger v Gubbins* (1846) 9 Ir Eq 304.

4   (1846) 9 Ir Eq 304 at 310. Followed in *Fowler v Blakely* (1862) 13 Ir Ch Rep 58.

5   (1846) 9 Ir Eq 304 at 316.

6   *Convey v Regan* [1950] IR 56.

[12.03] The right of a tenant to cut turf for consumption from a bog on his holding is liable to be displaced by prior agreement with the landlord. Such an agreement can be proven by the conduct of the parties, as where there was an established practice that the tenants had to apply for a written permit or licence to draw turf.[1]

---

1   *Lord Lifford v Kearney* (1883) 17 ILTR 30; *McGeough v McDermott* (1886) 18 LR Ir 217; *Congested Districts Board v Gavaghan* (1904) 38 ILTR 228.

[12.04] Where a right of turbary is granted, it is deemed to include such incidental rights as are necessary to secure access to the turf and extract it in useable form. A right of way is regarded as appurtenant to a right of turbary.[1] It can also arise as a way of necessity.[2]

Additionally, '[t]he right to cut must, from the nature of turbary, include the right to spread the turf and keep it on the bog for a reasonable time.'[3] In short, the turf once cut, has to be saved, and is then drawn away when saved. A turbary right incorporates a right to '… the user of the stuff – turf, peat, moss, or whatever they choose to call it – for all reasonable purposes …', including for use as manure, but does not comprehend '… a right to destroy the land for all purposes except the exercise of the right itself.'[4] The holder of the turbary right has no right in the soil once the turf has been cut away.[5]

---

[1]   *Re Hutchinson* (1883) 12 LR Ir 79.
[2]   *Reynolds v Kinsella* (1865) 11 Ir Jur Rep (NS) 308.
[3]   *Cronin v Connor* [1913] 2 IR 119 at 125, per Kenny J.
[4]   *Hutchinson v Drain* (1899) 33 ILTR 147.
[5]   *Oates v Stoney* (1882) 16 ILTR 30.

[12.05] Where a person has the right to the use of a bog owned by another for the purpose of extracting turf over a number of years, such user will not result in dispossessing the ownership of the owner of the bog, unless the owner is dispossessed of his land in its entirety for the purposes for which he would normally have used it, and there is also a demonstration of an unequivocal intention to dispossess. If the act of enjoyment can be referred either to an easement or a profit *à prendre*, then an intention to dispossess will not be presumed:[1]

> 'It is not … enough that the acts *may* have been done with the intention of asserting a claim to the soil, if they may equally have been done merely in the assertion of a right to an easement or to a profit *à prendre*. When the acts are equivocal – when they may have been done equally with either intention – who should get the benefit of the doubt, the rightful owner or the trespasser? I think it should be given to the rightful owner.'[2]

---

[1]   *Convey v Regan* [1950] IR 56.
[2]   [1950] IR 56 at 59, per Black J. See also *Egan v Greene* (12 November 1999, unreported) CC, Judge Moran, noted in (2000) 5 CPLJ 42.

[12.06] There is some authority that a right of turbary, if sought to be assigned in portions, can be preserved upon assignment provided that it remains accessorial to the enjoyment of a house or premises to which it can be proven to be appurtenant.[1]

---

[1]   *Re Bohan* [1957] IR 49 at 54–55, per Teevan J.

Words of grant

[12.07] Frequently, a landlord granted lands to a tenant, excepting from the demise all boglands, while regranting to the tenant a right of turbary over them. In many cases the language used begot confusion as to what precisely had been granted and what retained. In *Boyle v Olpherts*[1] Brady CB held that an exception from a lease by a landlord of 'bogs and turf mosses' was an exception of a portion of ground and not merely reservation of a turbary. The fact that by the same instrument the landlord had reserved a turbary right in favour of others did not diminish the exception of the bog for himself. In *Quinn v*

Shields[2] Palles CB followed *Boyle v Olpherts* to hold that an exception of 'all mosses and turbaries', apart from such as the tenant needed for his own consumption, was an exception of the land where the mosses and turbaries were to be found. In the case of doubt, according to Palles CB, it was permissible to consider the state of the subject matter at the date of the deed, and the practice of usage at that time, as an aid to construction.[3] However, even apart from authority, the chief baron was of the view that 'unless controlled by the context', the use of the words 'mosses' includes the soil:

> 'There appears to me to be more difficulty as to the meaning of the word "turbaries". No doubt, turbary in the singular would *prima facie* mean "a right of cutting turf", but I doubt whether the word "turbaries" in the plural, in a context like the present, does not more properly mean "places in which turf may be cut".'[4]

---

[1] *Boyle v Olpherts* (1841) 4 Ir Eq 241.
[2] *Quinn v Shields* (1877) IR 11 CL 254.
[3] Following the judgment of Parke B in *Lord Waterpark v Fennell* (1859) 7 HLC 650. This was a point also taken in *Knox v Earl of Mayo* (1858) 9 Ir Ch Rep 192, where it was held that, in interpreting a grant of 'turbary, furze, heath, bogs, loughs, mountains,' the question whether a corporeal or an incorporeal hereditament has passed will depend on what the words passing the interest have been understood to mean at the time of the grant, and also on the manner in which the property was enjoyed at the time of the grant.
[4] (1877) IR 11 CL 254 at 266.

[12.08] On the other hand, in *Irons v Douglas*,[1] an exception of 'turbaries', with a right granted to the tenant to cut, save and take as much turf each year as was required for fuelling, was held to pass the soil in the bog to the tenant. However, this finding seems inconsistent with the general trend, as exemplified by *Beere v Fleming*,[2] where it was held that there was no repugnancy between the grant of a bog and the reservation of a turbary, since a right of turbary is not a grant of the soil, but a profit *à prendre*. The basis for this was succinctly expressed by Fitzgerald B: '… the grant of an exclusive right of digging turves will not be a grant of the soil; and for the very reason, that the turves are not the sole profit of the soil.'[3]

---

[1] *Irons v Douglas* (1841) 3 Ir Eq 601.
[2] *Beere v Fleming* (1862) 13 ICLR 506.
[3] (1862) 13 ICLR 506 at 515.

[12.09] Accordingly, in *Earl of Shaftesbury v Doherty*,[1] an exception in a fee farm grant of all 'bogs, turf mosses, turbaries, save so much as is sufficient for consumption and shall be used on the premises' to the grantor was effective as an exception of the soil. In the opinion of Porter MR, the word 'turbary' was itself ambiguous, since it could mean either the *place* on which turf is cut or the *right* of cutting turf. He preferred to regard it as a neutral word, relying instead on the reference to bogs and turf mosses to establish that the fee simple was being excepted. Nor was the grantee's right to consumption of turf for fuelling vitiated by the fact that the grantor might also licence a similar right to others. Provided there was no derogation from grant, the fee farm grantee's rights could not exclude those of the fee farm grantor's licensees who should also be entitled to cut turf. The turbary right could not be expected to last forever.

> '… the meaning of a sufficiency of a supply of turbary for consumption and use on the premises is not that the supply is to be one which will last for ever. Something plainly was to remain with the landlord. No human ingenuity can preserve the bog for all time. It would be absurd to hold that during the continuance of the fee farm grant, which will last for ever, the right of bog is to be preserved to the tenant purchasers for ever, because the bog must come to an end at some time, while the fee farm grant will not. The meaning of the proviso must be, what is a reasonable sufficiency?'[2]

---

[1]   *Earl of Shaftesbury v Doherty* (1904) 4 NIJR 220.
[2]   (1904) 4 NIJR 220 at 221. In *Duggan v Carey* (1858) 8 ICLR 210, Pigot CB declined to hold that a proper construction of a lease of 1728 granting turbary rights to a lessee for lives precluded the right applying to houses yet to be built, notwithstanding that the entirety of the bog might thereby be exhausted.

[12.10] A lease of lands, accompanied by a covenant to grant turbary rights over an adjacent bog owned by the landlord, will be effective to grant a right of turbary:

> 'There can be no doubt that words which in form would import a covenant will operate as a grant, if such appears from the context to be the intention of the parties: and there is, in effect, no difference between declaring that the lessor shall allow the lessee and his heirs and assigns free liberty to cut turf, during the continuance of the demise, and declaring that the lessee, his heirs and assigns, shall, during the continuance of the demise, have such liberty.'[1]

---

[1]   *Duggan v Carey* (1858) 8 ICLR 210 at 216, per Pigot CB; also *Hargrove v Lord Congleton* (1861) 12 ICLR 363.

[12.11] Where necessary, both the established character of the turf cutting, and the circumstances of granting the right of turbary, can be considered to determine the area over which the right extends and the manner in which it is to be exercised. In *Jameson v Fahey*[1] a lease of 1741 reserved both a common of turbary and a common of pasturage over the surface of a mountain above the town of Clonmel, Co Tipperary. At the time of the lease the turf extracted was confined to that found in the deep bogs on the mountain and was effected through a device called a 'slane'. Indeed, the lease itself measured the turbary right of the commoners with reference to a 'slane', as being the amount of turf that could be lifted in a day by a man using such an instrument. By the early twentieth century, the deep bogs had largely disgorged their wealth of turf, and it was suggested that the peaty surface of the mountain, which was also capable of producing fuel, could be profitably scraped, and sods of peat called 'scraws' lifted, by an implement called a 'bosheen'. The evidence disclosed that a 'slane' and a 'bosheen' were quite different devices and that the quantities of turf extractable by each varied considerably.

¹ *Jameson v Fahey* [1907] 1 IR 411.

[12.12] Barton J declined to accept that under no circumstances could a right to scrape peat from a mountain surface ever be comprehended by a right of turbary.¹ However, in the instant case, it was clear that the paring of peat had not been envisaged as a method of turf extraction when the lease of 1741 had been granted. It was inconsistent both with the practice of extraction at the time and the unit of measurement specified in the lease, and was additionally irreconcilable with the reservation of a common of pasturage in the same lease. The effect of unlimited peat extraction as contemplated would be wholly to destroy the right of pasturage. Barton J also noted two relevant distinguishing features between common of pasture and turbary:

> 'In the first place, a common of pasture extends to every part of the demised premises on which there is food for cattle, or across which there is access to such food; but a common of turbary, from its nature, only extends to ground where turf is to be found. Secondly, the lease – following the rule of ancient law that there might be approvement against a right of pasturage, but not against a right of turbary – allowed the lessee to enclose the pasture lands for gardens, corn, or meadow, but not the lands the subject of the right of turbary, ie, the lands where turf was to be found.'²

This being so, it could not be reasonably supposed that the inhabitants of Clonmel had been granted a right to pare over the entire mountain and so destroy the common of pasturage; rather that the turbary right was to be confined to that part of the mountain where there was bog.

¹ Paring for peat, he noted, was quite a common method of fuel extraction in England where bogs are much rarer than in Ireland.
² *Jameson v Fahey* [1907] 1 IR 411 at 417.

Drainage

[12.13] The owner of a bog used for the extraction of turf, and over which turbary rights have been granted, has been deemed entitled to drain his bog adequately notwithstanding that this may cause occasional flooding to lower-lying land.¹ Although new drains may be dug and existing drains improved, the bog owner has no right, through the use of heavy machinery, to cause flooding on neighbouring lands greater than would be occasioned by the ordinary draining of the bog.²

In *Shine v Irish Land Commission and Roscommon County Council*³ it was held that where the owner of higher lands, for the purpose of the proper draining of them, gathers together water, that in the course of nature would duly discharge itself, without damage, on to contiguous lower-lying lands, the owner of the lower lands '... is, without the positive constitution of any servitude, bound to receive that body of water on his property.'⁴ This ought not to be construed to imply that the owner of the lower-lying lands is prohibited from taking steps to prevent his property from being injured by the drainage activities of the owner of the higher lands, provided that his preventative measures do not themselves cause damage to the higher lands.⁵

1   *Connolly v Congested Districts Board* (1918) 52 ILTSJ 52, 57.
2   *McDonnell v Turf Development Board* (1944) 78 ILTR 94.
3   *Shine v Irish Land Commission and Roscommon County Council* (1946) 81 ILTR 100.
4   (1946) 81 ILTR 100 at 101, following Lord Dunedin in *Gibbons v Lenfestey* (1915) 84 LJPC 158 at 160.
5   Bland *The Law of Easements and Profits à Prendre* (1997) Sweet & Maxwell, pp 105–106.

[12.14] Recent developments in the law of negligence and nuisance represent a serious qualification on the extent to which it can be asserted that drainage activities on the part of the owners of higher-lying land are immune from liability. In *Leakey v National Trust for Places of Historical Interest or Natural Beauty*,[1] the English Court of Appeal held that the defendant was liable to a neighbouring landowner for damage caused by the subsidence of a natural mound in Somerset called the Burrow Mump. A duty reposed on the owner of land on which there was a potential hazard to do all that was reasonable under the circumstances, but no more than that, to prevent or minimise the known risk of damage to neighbouring property.[2] The duty stands to be affected by the extent to which the risk of injury can be foreseen, the extent to which it can be prevented, and the probable cost involved.

The principles established in *Leakey* were applied, in Ireland, by Judge Buckley in *Daly v McMullan*,[3] a case involving damage from soil spillage, where the judge observed that the extent of the liability can also depend upon the means of the occupier of the property which carries the hazard, the extent to which the owner of the threatened land can take corrective measures on his own account, and the respective values of the two properties. In *Tapson v Northern Ireland Housing Executive*,[4] Carswell J applied *Leakey* to a situation where seepage of damp resulted from failure by a neighbouring landowner to repair bomb damage caused over 10 years earlier.

However, in *Holbeck Hall Hotel Ltd v Scarborough Borough Council*,[5] the English Court of Appeal held that the defendant was not liable for damage caused by subsidence, where the extent of the damage would not have been foreseeable without expensive and elaborate geological investigation. In this case, however, the potential hazard resided as much on one party's land as the other's: accordingly, the scope of the duty was limited to warning of the foreseeable risk and sharing information in relation to it.[6]

1   *Leakey v National Trust* [1980] 1 All ER 17.
2   [1980] 1 All ER 17 at 35, per Megaw LJ .
3   *Daly v McMullan* [1997] 2 ILRM 232.
4   *Tapson v Northern Ireland Housing Executive* [1992] NI 264. See para **[1.17]**.
5   *Holbeck Hall Hotel Ltd v Scarborough Borough Council* (2 March 2000, unreported) CA.
6   See O'Callaghan 'Liability for Subsidence' (2000) 5 CPLJ 10.

[12.15] Those involved in the drainage of land must consider the extent to which the actions in which they engage will cause damage to adjoining or lower-lying lands. The proposition that drainage is part of the natural and reasonable user of land now lies alongside the concept that the owners of land will be obliged to take reasonable steps to prevent foreseeable damage to their neighbour by natural or man-made acts that occur upon the land.

Whether turbary to be allocated or chosen

[12.16] Up to at least the early years of the nineteenth century, the right of a turbary holder was to dig for and cut turf on any part of the bog where turf could be found, subject to the restriction that the right could only be exercised in relation to ground capable of producing fuel.[1] In *Hargrove v Lord Congleton*[2] Pigot CB noted that the effect of a turbary right, granted by covenant in a lease of 1735, was to enable the tenant to cut and lift turf on any part of the bog, and not permit the landlord to confine the tenant to a particular part of the bog only. The right granted, he observed, was one to take turf, not to have turbary assigned: this could be explained on the basis that, in 1735, it would have been less convenient for a landlord, in remote parts of his estate to appoint someone to take charge of the bog for the purpose of assigning turf banks to particular tenants, than in 1861 when the case was heard.

This change in practice, from the early eighteenth to the mid-nineteenth centuries, adverted to by Pigot CB, tallies with the observation of Porter MR, in *Dawson v McGroggan*,[3] in 1902, a case involving a claim of a turbary right by presumed lost grant, that the evidence disclosed '...no interference with those cutting turf, save such as is always exercised by an owner in fee over whose land there is a right of turbary, that is, the power to point out the place where those who have the right may reasonably exercise it ... the right to interfere in that way has always been admitted.'[4]

---

[1] *Irons v Douglas* (1841) 3 Ir Eq 601; *Peardon v Underhill* (1850) 16 QB 120; *Jameson v Fahey* [1907] 1 IR 411 see para **[12.11]**; *Walsh v Johnston* (1913) 47 ILTSJ 231.
[2] *Hargrove v Lord Congleton* (1861) 12 ICLR 363.
[3] *Dawson v McGroggan* [1903] 1 IR 92.
[4] [1903] 1 IR 92 at 97.

[12.17] Accordingly, as greater numbers of tenants were permitted to partake of turbary rights, it became necessary for the landlord, either expressly or by implication, to reserve the right to assign 'turf banks' to the several turbary holders. In *Dawson v McGroggan*,[1] where ten parties received turbary rights on the same day, and the bog over which the rights had been granted was later assigned by the landlord, Barton J inferred that it had been contemplated, in the original grant of the turbary rights, that the owner of the bog would reserve a right to allocate turf banks. The purpose of this was primarily to preserve the bog, in order to prevent against its total destruction through indiscriminate and unregulated usage. The right of the landowner to derive commercial benefit from the bog on his land also had to be protected, but only after the turbary rights of the several holders had been satisfied. The turbary right was described as being one to enter the bog, dig and carry away sufficient fuel for consumption on the tenants' holdings in such reasonably convenient places as would not prejudice the preservation of the bog.[2]

---

[1] *Dawson v McGroggan* [1903] 1 IR 92.
[2] [1913] 1 IR 8 at 14.

[12.18] Section 5 of the Land Law (Ireland) Act 1881 permitted a landlord to give turbary rights to other of his tenants over a holding that contained a bog, in respect of which a fair rent order had been made. This enabled a balance to be preserved between the interest of the tenant of the holding, who was paying rent for more than just the bog, and also the need of other tenants who had to apply to their landlord for fuel for their holdings. It was effected through the issuing of 'bog tickets' which would set out where the turf was to be cut, and the extent to which it could be removed, so as to ensure that the turf would not be cut entirely away.[1] Where a holding on which a bog was situate had been acquired by the now defunct Land Commission, s 21 of the Land Act 1923[2] enabled the Land Commission to make comparable regulations for the protection and continuance of turbary rights.

---

[1]   *Re Scott's Estate* [1916] 1 IR 180 at 198, per O'Brien LC.

[2]   As interpreted in *Re Scott's Estate* [1916] 1 IR 180; also *Burke v Ryan* (1921) 55 ILTR 152; *Re Drummond's Estate* [1933] IR 166.

Respective rights of landowner and turbary holder

[12.19] It is inevitable that the exercise of a right of turbary will significantly interfere with the natural rights of the owner of the land where the bog is. On occasion, the landowner, whose total rights give him a greater facility for adjustment, will be obliged to defer to the rights of the holder of the profit *à prendre*. For example, in *Cronin v Connor*,[1] the plaintiff and other landowners enjoyed turbary rights over a bog on land owned by the defendant who also pastured his cattle there. The defendant's cattle wandered on to that part of the bog where the plaintiff's cut turf was being dried. On account of the fact that the plaintiff, being the owner of a profit *à prendre* merely, did not have a right to erect fences, and because the cutting and saving of turf was limited to a comparatively brief portion of the year, Kenny J held that the landowner was obliged to make some arrangement to prevent damage to the plaintiff's turbary right. It was important, in the view of Kenny J, that no additional burden was imposed upon the defendant's servient tenement, while at the same time the reasonable exercise by the servient owner of his own rights ought not to diminish the value of the profit *à prendre*.

Accordingly, the balance of relations between the parties fell to be adjusted 'only by applying the test of what seems most reasonable under the circumstances ...'[2]

---

[1]   *Cronin v Connor* [1913] 2 IR 119.

[2]   [1913] 2 IR 119 at 126.

[12.20] The landowner also has a right to reclaim the bog after the turbary rights have been exhausted, and to prevent the continuance of turf extraction once the land has been cut back to the soil.[1] A person having a profit *à prendre* of turbary has the right of cutting turf only as long as he does not render the land incapable of such reclamation as, according to its nature, it is capable of.[2] The landowner must be entitled to say when the bog has been completely cut out.[3] Nor can a turbary holder stop the landowner from giving a licence to others to cut turf simply on the basis that there is a discernible limit to the turbary life left in the bog.[4]

---

1   *Oates v Stoney* (1882) 16 ILTR 30; *Hutchinson v Drain* (1899) 33 ILTR 147; *Walsh v Johnston* (1913) 47 ILTSJ 231; *R (Keenan) v Tyrone County Court Judge* [1940] NI 108.
2   *Walsh v Johnston* (1913) 47 ILTSJ 231 at 231, per Judge Johnston.
3   *Daly v Gillman* (1897) 31 ILTSJ 429.
4   *Hutchinson v Drain* (1899) 33 ILTR 147.

Estovers and the Right to Cut Timber

[12.21] The right at common law of a tenant of land to cut timber growing on that land for the purpose of mending fences and the construction and repair of instruments of transport and husbandry, such as ploughs and carts, and for household fuel, is known as 'estovers'.[1] This derives from *estoffer*, a Norman French expression, meaning to supply with necessaries.[2] Traditionally, the Anglo-Saxon word 'bote' – meaning satisfaction or recompense – has been adopted, and is twinned as a suffix with another word denoting the purpose for which the timber is to be applied: hence, house-bote, for timber to repair the house; hedge-bote and hay-bote, for timber to repair fences; fire-bote, for fuel; and cart-bote and plough-bote, for the making and repair of carts and ploughs.[3]

---

1   See para **[12.01]**.
2   *Howley v Jebb* (1859) 8 ICLR 435 at 446.
3   *Howley v Jebb* (1859) 8 ICLR 435; *Congested Districts Board v Gavaghan* (1904) 38 ILTR 228.

[12.22] Where timber rights are granted for the purposes of domestic or agrarian utility, these are normally also styled 'estovers'. Timber cut for fuel must be appurtenant to a particular house and cannot be sold. If the house is demolished, it can be rebuilt, not necessarily on the same exact spot, provided that it is demonstrably the property intended to be benefited by the estovers and does not place a greater burden on the land which supplies the timber.[1]

However, it is generally accepted that the traditional concept of estovers as a profit *à prendre* to cut and utilise timber for domestic purposes was effectively abolished in Ireland by a series of afforestation acts passed during the reign of George III.[2]

---

1   *A-G v Reynolds* [1911] 2 KB 888.
2   In particular, 31 Geo 3, c 40: *Howley v Jebb* (1859) 8 ICLR 435, per Pigot CB at p 442, Greene B at p 444. See also Wylie *Irish Land Law* (3rd edn, 1997) Butterworths, p 263; *Galwey v Baker* (1840) 7 Cl & Fin 386; *Pentland v Somerville* (1852) 2 Ir Ch Rep 289; *Lord Mountcashel v Lord O'Neill* (1856) 4 ICLR 345; *Re Renewable Leasehold Conversion Act, ex p Armstrong* (1857) 8 Ir Ch Rep 30; *Re Moore's Estate* (1902) 36 ILTR 14.

[12.23] A right of estovers must be distinguished from a right to cut timber for commercial purposes, which is a profit *à prendre* in gross, governed by the terms of the licence or contract that grants it. Such contract can, in appropriate cases, be subject to the interpolation of implied terms by the courts.

In *Rudd v Rea*,[1] Powell J held that a prior exception of timber cutting rights for a five-year term over the demesne of Oriel Temple in Co Louth, did not, either expressly or by necessary implication, enable the licensee, in his manner of obtaining and removing the timber, wholly destroy the normal rights incident to ownership of the subsequent owner of the demesne. The licensee was entitled, as an adjunct to his profit *à prendre,* to such ancillary rights as were reasonably necessary to its enjoyment,[2] and it was inevitable that the exercise of these rights would for significant periods exclude the owner of the land from parts of his property.[3] While the licensee was entitled to reasonable access to cut and remove the trees, in the absence of express agreement such right must be subordinate to the common law right of the property owner not to have his lands, or the right to enjoy them, destroyed.[4] Since the licensee has no legal right to prevent the property owner from the normal enjoyment of his property, he cannot indirectly assume such a right through the method he adopts to reap the fruits of his licence.[5]

By analogy with the right of a dominant owner to adapt a right of way for the purposes for which it was granted, Powell J held that the licensee, if he wished to employ such ground-rupturing devices as a traction engine, steam lorry and caterpillar tractor, could only do so if he could contrive thereby not to destroy the landowner's avenues, farm roads, and drains, or render them dangerous for use.[6] On the other hand, it was reasonable for the licensee to employ a railway for the removal of the felled trees, and the landowner had no right to select the site of the line. A sawmill could also be used, provided it was not for the purpose of manufacturing implements for sale from the timber. Similar reasoning prohibited the licensee from conducting auctions on the landowner's property. However, the licensee was entitled to make additional gaps to the standard entrances in the boundaries of the demesne, subject to reinstating them once the timber had been removed.[7]

---

[1] *Rudd v Rea* [1921] 1 IR 223, affirmed on appeal [1923] 1 IR 55.

[2] *Hext v Gill* (1872) LR 7 Ch 699; *Rudd v Rea* [1921] 1 IR 223 at 226.

[3] [1921] 1 IR 223 at 230, 240.

[4] [1921] 1 IR 223 at 234.

[5] [1921] 1 IR 223 at 237.

[6] [1921] 1 IR 223 at 249.

[7] [1921] 1 IR 223 at 254.

Pasturage

[12.24] A profit of pasture is the right to graze cattle or other beasts of the field on the land of another. The right is for the cattle to crop grass and similar verdure on the land itself, not for the herbage to be cut and removed. A profit of pasture is most often held in common. It is to be distinguished from an agistment, which has been described as a letting of the grazing of the land rather than a letting of the land for grazing.[1] In one particular agistment case, the subject matter was specified as 'after grass', succinctly termed by Pigot CB as '… a demise of the grass after the hay is cut.'[2] Furthermore, a profit of pasture can be the subject of a lease or tenancy, an agistment is deemed to create no more than a licence '… for the use of the lands for certain purposes and for a certain time.'[3] The principal differences between a profit of pasture and an agistment are:

(i)   a profit of pasture is normally held in common, an agistment is a licence to graze granted to one or a few;

(ii)   a profit of pasture must be created by instrument in writing, an agistment can arise verbally;

(iii) a profit of pasture is capable of being demised by lease, an agistment cannot (notwithstanding that the words 'demise' and 'letting' are sometimes used);

(iv) a profit of pasture is normally ongoing, whereas the usual period of an agistment licence is 11 months,[4] though this is often renewed;

(v)   an agistment is usually confined to a particular area, whereas a profit of pasture permits the cattle to roam in quest of herbage across the pastureland.[5]

---

[1] *Fletcher v Hackett* (1906) 40 ILTR 37. See paras **[23.01]**, **[23.14]**–**[23.15]**.
[2] *Hickey v Cosgrave* (1861) 6 Ir Jur (NS) 251.
[3] *Plunkett v Heeney* (1904) 4 NIJR 136, per Porter MR.
[4] *Collins v O'Brien* [1981] ILRM 328 at 329, per Doyle J.
[5] *Hickey v Cosgrave* (1861) 6 Ir Jur (NS) 251.

[12.25] A right of pasture is a profit *à prendre* appurtenant to land.[1] Accordingly, where a tenant applied for a 'fair rent' order under s 8 of the Land Law (Ireland) Act 1881 the grazing rights appurtenant to his tenancy were deemed to comprise part of his 'holding'. If the tenant were to assign his holding, the profit of pasture would pass to his assignee.[2] A profit of pasture will also be deemed to include such ancillary rights as are necessary to its enjoyment: these include watering and herding the cattle. Unlike a profit of turbary, which is limited to places where turf is actually to be found, a profit of pasture will permit cattle to wander all over the pasturing territory in search of food.[3]

---

[1] *Re Hutchinson* (1883) 12 LR Ir 79, per Palles CB.
[2] *Re Hutchinson* (1883) 12 LR Ir 79, per Andrews J.
[3] *Peardon v Underhill* (1850) 16 QB 120; *Jameson v Fahey* [1907] 1 IR 411 at 417. See para **[12.12]**. Subject to the landowner's potential right of 'approvement'. See para **[12.29]**.

[12.26] Like all profits appurtenant, a profit of pasture is liable to specified restriction or 'stint'. This can be with reference either to a determined number or to the capacity of the land benefited by the profit (the dominant tenement) to accommodate cattle during the winter. This latter mode of measurement is known as cattle *levant et couchant* (rising up and lying down). Where the extent of the right of pasture is determined with reference to a specified number of cattle, this is normally based on a measurement called a 'collop'. In *O'Sullivan v O'Connor*[1] Judge Wellwood in the Circuit Court appears to have accepted, without demur, counsel's elaboration of the principle, which it would be difficult to better:

'An action for overstint is recognised by the law in the case of common pasturage. A stint is the right to common pasturage according to a fixed rate and the term thus represents a limitation in the numbers of animals, according to kind, which are allotted to each portion into which pasture or common land is divided or to each person who is entitled to the right of common pasturage. This might be for one animal or for a certain number of animals, according to type, size or capacity of eating. The extent of the stint is represented by the number of collop allotted to each grazier.

One collop represents the grass of a full-grown horse or cow for a year and this is taken as the standard or unit for grazing animals. The grass of six sheep or eighteen geese also represents a collop.'[2]

---

[1] *O'Sullivan v O'Connor* (1980) 114 ILTR 63.

[2] Gerard A Lee, a long respected authority, advocate and author on incorporeal property matters.

[12.27] Where a profit of pasture is held in common, and one of the commoners exceeds his allotted stint, the right of action against him by the other commoners lies, not in trespass, but in 'overstint', for which an injunction and damages can be awarded.[1]

---

[1] (1980) 114 ILTR 63.

[12.28] A profit of pasture held in common is sometimes called 'commonage'.[1] However, 'commonage' is a term that both statutorily[2] and popularly can include various categories of co-ownership. It can also include turbary as well as pasture. Upon application to the Department of Agriculture and Food,[3] commonage holdings can be partitioned by order. This can include an arrangement whereby land, formerly held in commonage in its entirety, continues in commonage in respect of one part, but is partitioned among a number of former commonage-holders in respect of the other part.[4]

---

[1] As, for example, in the instruments of grant in *Lord Waterpark v Fennell* (1855) 5 ICLR 120 and *O'Hare v Fahy* (1859) 10 ICLR 318.

[2] The Land Act 1939, s 24 defines commonage as involving a joint tenancy or a tenancy in common, whereas the Land Act 1953, s 23 (amending the earlier section) includes as commonage the phenomenon of two or more persons enjoying grazing or turbary.

[3] Following the dissolution of the Land Commission on 31 March 1999: the Land Commission (Dissolution) Act 1992, s 4, activated by the Irish Land Commission (Dissolution) Act (Commencement) Order 1999 (SI 75/1999).

[4] Such as occurred in *Re Commonage at Glennamaddoo* [1992] 1 IR 297.

[12.29] The owner of land over which there is a profit of pasture is entitled, at common law, to retrieve and enclose that portion of the pasture not actually required by those enjoying the right. This is known as 'approvement'[1] and is particularly valuable when, for whatever reason, there is a diminution in the numbers enjoying the common of pasture.

¹   *Jameson v Fahey* [1907] 1 IR 411 at 417.

[12.30] Where the holder of a profit of pasture *levant et couchant* purports to assign portion of his property benefited by the profit, the right of pasture *levant et couchant* is correspondingly apportioned.¹ However, the principle of appurtenancy must still apply, so that the holder of the profit could not assign the entirety of his lands and purport to retain the pasture rights for himself.² This commends itself to sense, as the essence of pasture *levant et couchant* is based on the number of cattle that the land benefited can accommodate when the animals need to be brought in for the winter. On the other hand, where the owner of the land to which the profit of pasture is appurtenant purchases any part of the property over which the pasture is enjoyed, this will bring to an end the profit of pasture insofar as concerns that owner.³

¹   *Wyat Wyld's Case* (1609) 8 Co Rep 78b; *Sacheverell v Porter* (1657) Cro Car 482; *O'Hare v Fahy* (1859) 10 ICLR 318.
²   *O'Hare v Fahy* (1859) 10 ICLR 318. But Buckley J in *White v Taylor (No 2)* [1969] 1 Ch 160 at 190, held that where the number of cattle to be pastured is determined, not on the basis of *levant et couchant,* but by a fixed amount, the owner of the property may dispose of the entirety of his property while retaining his right of pasture, so that it becomes a profit in gross. It has been suggested that this is at variance with the practice of commonage of pasture in Ireland: Bland *Easements and Profits à Prendre* p 302.
³   *White v Taylor (No 1)* [1969] 1 Ch 150, particularly per Buckley J at 158–159.

Chapter 13

Profits *à Prendre* for Pleasure and Profit

Public Rights in Tidal Waters

[13.01] At common law the sea and all tidal waters are vested in the Crown.[1] In the Republic of Ireland, under Article 10 of Bunreacht na hÉireann, such ownership now inheres in the State.[2] The Crown has been deemed to be a trustee for the natural rights of the public both in the sea, its estuaries[3] and in all tidal waters.[4] This arises as an incident of the soil over which the water flows, so that the public rights are not an incorporeal hereditament.[5] These natural or common law rights are of navigation and fishing only.[6] There is a presumption that fishing rights in the sea or arms of the sea belong to the public, and the onus of proof to establish a sole or several fishery in tidal waters rests on the person asserting it.[7] Public rights of navigation can extend beyond the tidal reach of a river, but the public right of fishing will not: there is no public right of fishing in non-tidal waters.[8] For inland water to be navigable:

> '... means that the public have the right of passing over it in ships and boats, but it does not follow that they have any other rights. A public right of way by a road does not confer the right of shooting on the road.'[9]

To the extent that a river is navigable it is deemed to be a highway.[10] However, the word 'navigable' also has a purely technical legal connotation, which limits it to tidal waters in which the public has a right to fish.[11]

---

1   *Malcolmson v O'Dea* (1863) 10 HLC 593 at 619, per Willes J; *Murphy v Ryan* (1868) IR 2 CL 143 at 154.
2   *Daly v Quigley* [1960] Ir Jur 1.
3   *Miller v Little* (1879) 4 LR Ir 302.
4   *Murphy v Ryan* (1868) IR 2 CL 143 at 149.
5   Hale *De Jure Maris* Vol 1, *Duke of Devonshire v Neill* (1877) 1 LR Ir 132 at 173.
6   *Hamilton v AG* (1881) 5 LR Ir 555.
7   *Bloomfield v Johnston* (1868) IR 8 CL 68 at 83, *Tighe v Sinnott* [1897] 1 IR 140 at 145, *Foyle & Bann Fisheries Ltd v AG* (1948) 83 ILTR 29 at 35.
8   *Williams v Willcox* (1837) 8 A & E 333, cited in *Bloomfield v Johnston* (1868) IR 8 CL 68 at 90; *Daly v Quigley* [1960] Ir Jur 1.
9   *O'Neill v Johnston* [1908] 1 IR 358 at 382, per Ross J.
10 *Murphy v Ryan* (1868) IR 2 CL 143 at 152, 153.
11 *Murphy v Ryan* (1868) IR 2 CL 143 at 148.

[13.02] Though navigable, the public does not have a right to fish in an inland, non-tidal lake, such as Lough Erne and Lough Neagh. Nor can such rights be acquired by custom.[1]

[1] *Bloomfield v Johnston* (1868) IR 8 CL 68, *Bristow v Cormican* (1875) 3 App Cas 641; *O'Neill v Johnston* [1908] 1 IR 358, [1909] 1 IR 237; *Toome Eel Fishery (Northern Ireland) Ltd v Cardwell* [1966] NI 1.

[13.03] The rights of the public over the sea and tidal waters, apart from navigation and swimming, are confined to fishing, both in the waters and on the seabed, and the extraction of objects naturally there which float. The right of the public to take floating seaweed is akin to its established right to fish.[1] The public has a right to fish for oysters and other shellfish,[2] including whelks and winkles,[3] but has no inherent right to take away sea-shells.[4] Similarly, the public has no right to take soil, sand, or gravel from the seashore.[5] Neither is there a common law right for the public to enter upon the seashore to take and carry away seaweed, whether growing upon the rocks or cast up by the tide.[6] Such right can only exist if granted by licence from the owner of the foreshore.[7]

[1] *Brew v Haren* (1877) IR 11 CL 198 at 201–202. See generally, Lee 'The Right to Take Seaweed from the Foreshore' (1967) 18 NILQ 33.
[2] *Crichton v Connor* (1871) ILTR 161.
[3] *Adair v National Trust for Places of Historical Interest or Natural Beauty* [1998] NI 33.
[4] *Bagot v Orr* (1801) 2 Bus & Pul 472.
[5] *MacNamara v Higgins* (1854) 4 ICLR 326; *Blewett v Tregonning* (1835) 3 Ad & El 554; *Hamilton v AG* (1881) 5 LR Ir 555.
[6] *Howe v Stawell* (1833) Alc & Nap 348; *Mulholland v Killen* (1874) IR 9 Eq 471; *Brew v Haren* (1877) IR 11 CL 198.
[7] *Mahoney v Neenan* [1966] IR 559 at 564–565.

[13.04] The foreshore can be defined as the ground that lies between the high-water mark and low-water mark of ordinary tides occurring between the spring tide (that which befalls twice monthly at full moon and new moon respectively) and the neap tide (ordinary tides between the times of changing of the moon).[1] The ground is identified as that alternatively covered and exposed as the tide enters and ebbs.[2] Once seaweed arrives on the foreshore, it becomes the property of the person who owns the foreshore.[3] Indeed, the entitlement to take seaweed by a landowner contiguous to the sea has often been relied on as evidence of his claimed title to the foreshore.[4]

There can be no public right to take sea-coal from the seashore.[5] Neither does the public have the right to cross the sea-shore between high water mark and low water mark for the purpose of bathing.[6]

[1] *Adair v National Trust for Places of Historical Interest or Natural Beauty* [1998] NI 33 at 37, per Girvan J; more tersely, if loosely, described as '... the bed of the shore lying between low-water mark and the highwater mark of ordinary medium tides.' *Mahoney v Neenan* [1966] IR 559 at 564, per McLoughlin J.
[2] Wylie *Irish Law Law* (3rd edn, 1997) Butterworths, p 408; Lee 'The Right to Take Seaweed from the Foreshore' (1967) 18 NILQ 33, citing Hale's *De Jure Maris*. At common law, the

foreshore in Northern Ireland is vested in the Crown. In the Republic of Ireland it is vested in the State: Foreshore Act 1933, s 3.

3   *Brew v Haren* (1877) IR 11 CL 198 at 213, per Morris CJ.

4   *Brew v Haren* (1877) IR 11 CL 198 at 214, per Morris CJ: 'It would appear to be a contradiction in terms, while exclusive user of the foreshore by the taking of the seaweed is acceptable as proof of the ownership of the soil, that, when the ownership of the soil is established, the owner of the foreshore has not the property in the seaweed. By common law, seaweed cast on the shore of the owner of the soil is an increment for his benefit.'; also per May CJ at p 216. In *Stoney v Keane* (1903) 37 ILTR 212, the payment to the plaintiff of money by those who cut seaweed from the foreshore was found by Palles CB to support the plaintiff's claim to a possessory title in it.

5   *Alfred F Beckett Ltd v Lyons* [1969] 1 Ch 449.

6   *Blundell v Catterall* (1822) 5 B & Ald 268; *Hamilton v AG* (1881) 5 LR Ir 555; *Adair v National Trust for Places of Historical Interest or Natural Beauty* [1998] NI 33.

[13.05] In *Adair v National Trust for Places of Historical Interest or Natural Beauty*,[1] an unemployed fisherman claimed a right to fish for whelks and winkles in the tidal waters of Strangford Lough, and to pick winkles from the rocks on the exposed foreshore, and also to dig for lugworms on the foreshore. Girvan J held that the plaintiff, as did all members of the public, enjoyed a right at common law to fish in tidal waters and to navigate vessels over such waters for the purpose of fishing. Although there was no right to cross the foreshore for the purpose of bathing, or to undertake any activities on the foreshore, Girvan J held that the right to fish in tidal waters imported an additional right to collect exposed shellfish from the foreshore when the tide is out.[2] Noting that the public has a right to collect seaweed that floats in the open sea, but has not a right to collect seaweed from the foreshore, Girvan J conceded that the common law, in relation to foreshore rights, has tended to develop piecemeal and not always logically.[3] The commonly held view was that the right of the public to fish in the sea extended to collecting fish, and also shellfish, on the exposed foreshore when the tide was out, and this had not been displaced by any of the arguments in the instant case. According to Girvan J, it scarcely commended itself to sense, that a member of the public could pluck shellfish from that part of a rock which lay submerged, but had to leave alone that part of the rock above water; or that the lawfulness or otherwise of lifting shellfish from a particular area depended on whether the tide had withdrawn over it, or not, at the time of lifting.[4]

However, on the basis that lugworms are not fish, the common law right to dig for them is not part of the public right to fish, but is a deemed ancillary to it, and must be directly related to the exercise of that right. Hence, it is not an unrestricted right, nor can it be exercised freely at any time or place, nor can the lugworms be lifted for any purpose and in any quantities. Girvan J stated that the plaintiff would have to have dug for the lugworms as an incident to his own personal right to fish as a member of the public, and not for the purposes of sale.[5] The implication of this observation is that the public right to fish in tidal waters, itself is confined to fishing for consumption, and not commercially.

1   *Adair v National Trust for Places of Historical Interest or Natural Beauty* [1998] NI 33.

2   [1998] NI 33 at 41.

Profit *à Prendre* of Piscary or Fishing

[13.06] A profit *à prendre* of fishing, like all profits *à prendre*, may exist as a sole or several profit or as a profit in common. A right of several fishery has been defined as an exclusive right to fish in a particular place.[1] It can be enjoyed by one or a number of people, but is exclusive of all to whom the right has not been granted.[2] A common of fishery is also sometimes known as a common of piscary. At one stage the confusing concept of 'free fishery' also entered the nomenclature, but to the extent that it means anything, it is perhaps best regarded as a widely shared common of fishery.[3]

In the case of a common of piscary or common of fishery, the profit must be appurtenant to property owned by the profit holders and the extent of it limited to the needs of that property. In short, a common of piscary cannot exist without 'stint'.[4]

The use of the word 'several' is not necessary to grant a sole or several fishery, provided that the words employed demonstrate that it is a sole or exclusive fishery which is intended to be granted.[5] It can be inferred from the grant of a weir that a right of several fishery was intended also to be granted.[6]

---

1 *Malcolmson v O'Dea* (1863) 10 HLC 593.

2 *Gannon v Walsh* [1998] 3 IR 245 at 272, 276.

3 For a flavour of the debate, see *Bloomfield v Johnston* (1868) IR 8 CL 68 at 79–88. The idea that a sole or several fishery could be designated a free fishery derives from a confusion over the concept of 'free warren'. (1868) IR 8 CL 68 at 80. A 'free warren' was described in *Allen v Donnelly* (1856) 5 Ir Ch Rep 452 as potentially being acquired by prescription as appurtenant to a manor.

4 *Lord Chesterfield v Harris* [1908] 2 Ch 397, approved in *Foyle & Bann Fisheries Ltd v AG* (1949) 83 ILTR 29. In *Lord Chesterfield v Harris* Cozens-Hardy MR noted that it had been suggested that '… a common of piscary or a right of fishing differs from all other rights, such as turbary, estovers, and pasture. But there is no foundation in principle for this distinction; and there are many dicta which treat common of piscary as governed by the same rules as other profits *à prendre*.' [1908] 2 Ch 397 at 412.

5 *Holford v Bailey* (1849) 13 QB 426; *Ashworth v Brown* (1855) 7 Ir Jur Rep 315.

6 *Hanbury v Jenkins* [1901] 2 Ch 401; *Moore v AG* [1934] IR 44.

[13.07] A right of fishing can take the following forms:

(i) a corporeal right based upon ownership of land through which a river flows;

(ii) a profit *à prendre* appurtenant to land, which most usually arises in the case of a common of piscary;

(iii) a profit *à prendre* in gross, which is what is most commonly understood by a fishing right.

A right of fishing as a corporeal right

[13.08] In *Gannon v Walsh*,[1] Keane J distinguished between a right of fishing as a profit *à prendre* and as a corporeal right derived from the ownership of waterside property. In relation to the latter Keane J observed:

> 'It is, however, perfectly possible for the right to fish to co-exist with the ownership of the bed or soil of the river. In such a case, the right is properly described as a corporeal hereditament and, apart from any other legal consequences, this will have the result that the owner of the fishery will be entitled to carry out works, such as the erection of weirs on the portion of the river bed in his ownership, provided he can do so without interfering with any other person's rights.'[2]

This is consistent with the traditional common law presumption that the owner of land bounded by a river is deemed to be the owner of the bed and soil of the river up to an imagined line in its centre running parallel to the bank – *usque ad medium filium aquae* – and to enjoy a several fishery on account of such ownership.[3] The right, in theory, is to fish in that half of the river contiguous to the owner's property, but it can also be construed as a species of tenancy in common to fish in the entire river, since fish swim from one side of the river to the other.[4]

---

[1] *Gannon v Walsh* [1998] 3 IR 245.
[2] [1998] 3 IR 245 at 273.
[3] *Murphy v Ryan* (1868) IR 2 CL 143 at 148–149; *Duke of Devonshire v Neill* (1877) 2 LR Ir 132 at 172, both strongly in reliance upon Lord Hale's *De Jure Maris*, Vol 1.
[4] *Board of Conservators of Waterford Fishery District v Connolly* (1889) 24 ILTR 7.

A right of fishing as an incorporeal right

[13.09] Where a right of fishing is granted as a profit *à prendre*, it is '… no more than a right vested in a person to kill and take away fish from a particular stretch of a river or lake.'[1] This can arise in the context of the ownership of land by the holder of the right, in which the fishing right is said to be appurtenant to land and that land can be termed the dominant tenement. It is axiomatic that the exercise of an appurtenant fishing right must be subject to predetermined limit or stint; in many cases this will be the actual requirements of the occupants of the property to which the fishing right is appurtenant. The fishing right can also be independent of the ownership by its holder of any land, in which case it is a right in gross. In such case the holder of the fishery right is entitled to derive maximum profit from it provided he does not encroach upon the legitimate rights of others.[2]

---

[1] *Gannon v Walsh* [1998] 3 IR 245 at 272, per Keane J.
[2] *Caldwell v Kilkelly* [1905] 1 IR 434 at 443, per Barton J.

[13.10] A perennially vexed question is whether the grant of a sole or several fishery carries with it by implication a grant of the soil and bed of the river. Such a presumption is patently at odds with the presumption that the owner of land adjacent to a river is deemed to be the owner of the bed and soil of the river as far out as its middle thread in consequence of that landowner's natural riparian rights. Lord Coke had favoured the view that the soil did not pass to the holder of the fishing right, largely on the basis that if, peradventure, the river ran dry, the owner of the land ought to be entitled to such fruits as might be yielded by the river bed.[1] The view has also been expressed that if a right of fishing is deemed to be an incident of the ownership of land by a river, it seems contrary to logic that a specific grant of a right of fishing should incidentally carry with it the ownership of the soil: if this were the intention, why would the landowner not merely execute a deed of grant of the riverbed, and the fishing rights would automatically follow, in the traditional manner of the lesser following the greater?[2]

However, in *Gannon v Walsh*[3] Keane J firmly accepted as a primary presumption that the holder of a several fishery is also deemed to be the owner of the soil and bed of the river.[4] This presumption displaces the presumption that otherwise arises in favour of riparian proprietors being regarded as owner of half the riverbed out to its middle thread. However, being itself a presumption, it also is liable to be displaced by evidence tending towards a conclusion that it was not intended to give any rights of ownership in the soil.

---

[1]   Coke on Littleton at 46.

[2]   *Marshall v Ulleswater Steam Navigation Co* (1863) 3 B & S 732, at p 748, per Cockburn CJ.

[3]   *Gannon v Walsh* [1998] 3 IR 245 at 273.

[4]   Keane J drew support from the decisions of the House of Lords in *A-G v Emerson* [1891] AC 647 and the Court of Appeal in *Hindson v Ashby* [1896] 2 Ch 1 and from the criticisms of *Coke on Littleton* in Moore's *History and Law of Fisheries* (1903).

[13.11] This presumption is not free from difficulties. In the case of a sole or several fishery held by a number of parties, there is the curious consequence of multiple co-ownership in the bed of the river. If the holder of a several fishery right dies, will a succession issue arise over the deemed co-ownership of the river bed? A grant of a right of fishing, generally regarded as a profit *à prendre*, in the view of Keane J will be a corporeal right if the presumption that it carries with it an ancillary grant of the soil of the river is sustained.[1] Such notion arguably seems to confuse a right of fishing that itself is incidental to ownership of waterside property and a right of fishing that is specifically appurtenant to property which may or may not be flush with a river. Where enjoyment of a fishing right is not in consequence of the ownership of riparian property, the better view is that it remains incorporeal, and that any rights over the river bed need to be specifically granted by the owner of the soil.[2] However, the effect of the decision in *Gannon v Walsh* is that the law in the Republic of Ireland is that the presumption that the holder of a fishery right is deemed to be the owner also of the soil and bed of the river has precedence over the older presumption that a riparian proprietor enjoys a several fishery in the waters that run through his land as an incident of his ownership of the land.

---

[1]   *Gannon v Walsh* [1998] 3 IR 245 at 275.

[2]   For example, in *Ingham v Mackey* [1898] 1 IR 272, a right to store eels in perforated cisterns on the river bed was the subject of grant, albeit a presumed grant.

[13.12] Some guidance as to how to interpret the clearly conflicting presumptions is suggested by the judgment of the Court of Exchequer Chamber in 1868, in *Bloomfield v Johnston*:[1]

'Though the grant of a piscary, generally, may perhaps pass the soil, yet it will not if there be any words to denote a different intention, as where one seised of a river grants a several fishery in it ... and much less will the soil pass when there is an express reservation of it.'

In *Caldwell v Kilkelly*,[2] a case of a statutory purchase of lands by a tenant under the Land Purchase Acts, with reservation of fishing rights in favour of the landlord, it was held that the proposed placing of rocks and stones on the bed of the river in order to improve the fishing was not properly incidental to the reserved right of fishing but a purported enlargement of it. In that case, Barton J stated that the landlord's exclusive right of fishing did *not* carry the right to possession of the riverbed.[3]

Regrettably, it seems unavoidable that the confusion is likely to persist.

---

[1] *Bloomfield v Johnston* (1868) IR 8 CL 68 at 78.
[2] *Caldwell v Kilkelly* [1905] 1 IR 434.
[3] [1905] 1 IR 434 at 445. This can be explained, however, on the basis of the terms of the Land Commission order that created the judicial tenancy.

[13.13] It is possible for rights in relation to different kinds of fish to exist in the same waters, so that while one party might have a right of several fishery to fish generally, another might have the right to take oysters or lampreys.[1] In *Crichton v Connor*,[2] a statutory grant of a several fishery in an estuary was deemed confined to 'floating fish' and did not displace the common law right of the public to take shell-fish from the seabed in a river estuary. The distinction, where it arises, seems primarily to be taken between 'floating fish' and 'testaceous' creatures 'adhering to rocks or other substances.'[3]

---

[1] *Ecroyd v Coulthard* [1897] 2 Ch 554.
[2] *Crichton v Connor* (1871) ILTR 161.
[3] (1871) ILTR 161 at 164.

Lakes – with particular reference to Lough Neagh

[13.14] The same principles that govern fishing rights in a river, as the natural incident of the ownership of waterside property, also apply to a lake situate on or adjacent to land. Where a number of property owners own land bordered by a lake, it can be contended that their respective rights extend from the boundaries of their properties to a notional point of convergence at the centre of the lake. The public has no automatic right of fishing in an inland lake, even if it is large enough to be navigable.[1]

---

[1] Decided in relation to Lough Erne in *Bloomfield v Johnston* (1868) IR 8 CL 68, applied to Lough Neagh in *Bristow v Cormican* (1874) LR 10 CL 398.

[13.15] Perennial problems in relation to Lough Neagh have arisen, largely on account of its sheer size, as the largest inland lake in the British Isles, and the fact of a several fishery in the entire lake having purportedly been granted by King Charles II in 1661 to Sir Arthur Chichester, Earl of Donegall. Lough Neagh is approximately 24 miles long, 10 to 12 miles wide, comprising approximately 100,000 acres, and bounded by 5 counties. It is fed by 13 rivers, but only the Lower Bann flows out of Lough Neagh, at its north-western corner, to the sea near Coleraine. For centuries local fishermen have fished in the waters of the lough, principally for eels, pollen and herring. Those claiming under the Chichester title fish extensively, for eels only, on a commercial basis, concentrating their activities around Toome Bay at the mouth of the Lower Bann where the eels, matured after nurturing in the lough, congregate before discharging themselves upriver to spawn in the open sea. For the most part the Crown-granted rights and the locally enjoyed rights have managed to co-exist, controversies arising only when the local activities are embellished in such as way as to threaten the commercial operations of those holding under the Chichester grant. In three celebrated cases, extending over the better part of a century from 1874 to 1966 – *Bristow v Cormican*,[1] *O'Neill v Johnston*[2] and *Toome Eel Fishery (Northern Ireland) Ltd v Cardwell*[2] – finality has been striven to be brought to the issues, but with limited success.

---

[1]   *Bristow v Cormican* (1874) IR 10 CL 398, (1875) 3 App Cas 641.
[2]   *O'Neill v Johnston* [1908] 1 IR 358, [1909] 1 IR 237.
[3]   *Toome Eel Fishery (Northern Ireland) Ltd v Cardwell* [1966] NI 1.

[13.16] Each of the cases has asserted that there can be no public right to fish in the waters of an inland non-tidal lake, and each has also asserted that the Crown is not 'of common right' entitled to the soil of such a lake. Accordingly, an anxiety has been demonstrated, on the one hand not to inhibit the containable operations of those who depend for their livelihood on fishing otherwise than under the Chichester grant,[1] and on the other hand not openly to impugn a purported Crown title, which at best seems debatable and at worst dubious.[2] In consequence, strenuous effort has been made, with generally credible results, to authenticate the claimed Crown title, through both an accumulation of title papers and continuous ongoing evidence of user of the several fishery, so as to offset any possible tincture by a blatantly expressed right of plantation conquest, or an exaggerated application of royal prerogative which reached its apogee in England during the troubled reigns of the Stuarts.

---

[1]   In *O'Neill v Johnston* [1908] 1 IR 358, Ross J noted that some 700 fishermen and 3,000 people in the adjoining counties depended on the fishing for a livelihood, observing also at 385, as a salutary appeal to common sense, '... we must consider the subject-matter: the enormous extent of the lough, the great expense of protecting such a sheet of water, the value of the fishing to be protected, and the small amount of injury suffered in allowing people to fish.'
[2]   In *Bristow v Cormican* (1878) 3 App Cas 641 at 658, Lord Hatherley acknowledged that there was no evidence of how the title to Lough Neagh came to vest in the Crown: 'Clearly no one has a right to say that it became vested in the Crown because it belonged to nobody else. This is an inland lake, and therefore it is not a portion of land belonging to the Crown by reason of its being on the shore of the sea, or a navigable strait or river.'

[13.17] The result, and the current state of the law, is that the validity has been firmly established of the several fishery grant from King Charles II in 1661, while the Lough Neagh fishermen continue to fish without any right at all.

The curious case of tidal waters

[13.18] At common law the right of the public to fish in tidal waters arose as an incident of the Crown's ownership of the soil over which the waters flowed.[1] The Crown was regarded as a trustee for the rights of the public to fish in tidal waters.[2] In principle, the owner of a right is at liberty to grant it to another. However, in *Malcolmson v O'Dea*,[3] chapter 16 of Magna Carta 1215 was interpreted as prohibiting the Crown from granting a several fishery over tidal waters unless it could be established that a several fishery had existed in the relevant waters prior to 1189 – the first year of the reign of King Richard I, set as the commencement of legal memory. There was no prohibition on a several fishery, that had been validly acquired prior to 1189, being granted by its holder to another after 1189, nor on a grant of a several fishery in tidal waters by the Crown after 1189, if such several fishery having been in private ownership prior to 1189, it subsequently reverted to the Crown.

---

[1] Hale *De Jure Maris* Vol 1, *Duke of Devonshire v Neill* (1877) 2 LR Ir 132 at 173.
[2] See para **[13.01]**.
[3] *Malcolmson v O'Dea* (1863) 10 HLC 593.

[13.19] Since in most cases it would be impossible to establish documentary evidence relating to a several fishery that extended back prior to 1189, 'although there may be plausible antiquarian speculation about it',[1] certain presumptions are made from prolonged user and enjoyment of the fishery. These were memorably expressed in the advice to the House of Lords by Willes J *in Malcolmson v O'Dea:*

> 'If evidence be given of long enjoyment of a fishery to the exclusion of others of such a character as to establish that it has been dealt with as of right as a distinct and separate property, and there is nothing to shew that its origin was modern; the result is, not that you say this is a usurpation, for it is not traced back to the time of Henry II, but that you presume that the fishery being reasonably shewn to have been dealt with as property, must have become such in due course of law, and therefore must have been created before legal memory.'[2]

The technical expression used is that the several fishery must have been 'put in defence' by the Crown prior to 1189, in which event either the Crown, or an individual if the Crown has granted a several fishery, will obtain a propriety exclusive of the common liberty of fishing.[3] Subject to the requirement of its first having been 'put in defence', a person can acquire a several fishery in tidal waters either by express grant or prescription,[4] or by presumed lost grant.[5] In the case of a presumed lost grant, the presumption is not to be relied upon to establish the actual existence of a several fishery in tidal waters to the exclusion of the public, but the entitlement of the party claiming right to it from the length of time that they enjoyed the exclusive fishing.[6]

¹ *Neill v Duke of Devonshire* (1882) 8 AC 135, at p 158, per Lord O'Hagan, cited in *Little v Cooper* [1937] IR 1 at 8.

² (1863) 10 HLC 593 at 618, quoted with approval in *Neill v Duke of Devonshire* (1882) 8 AC 135, at p 180, per Lord Blackburn, and in *Moore v AG* [1934] IR 44, at p 62, per Kennedy CJ.

³ Adapting the language of Hale *De Jure Maris* (1747 edn) at p 11.

⁴ *Neill v Duke of Devonshire* (1882) 8 AC 135, at p 158, per Lord O'Hagan.

⁵ *Little v Wingfield* (1859) 11 ICLR 63.

⁶ (1859) 11 ICLR 63 at 79, per O'Brien J, approved in *Foyle & Bann Fisheries Ltd v AG* (1948) 83 ILTR 29 at 40, per Gavan Duffy P.

[13.20] In *Ashworth v Brown*[1] it was held that a several fishery in tidal waters will be found to have been 'put in defence' prior to 1189 if the evidence establishes that from the earliest period the Crown had exercised rights consistent with a several fishery and with no other right less than a several fishery.

The established surrender of a several fishery to the Crown, by a monastery suppressed after the confiscations of King Henry VIII in the 1530s, is *prima facie* evidence of the several fishery having been 'put in defence' through a grant by the Crown to the particular monastery prior to 1189.[2] Where a several fishery, acknowledged as having been 'put in defence', is granted to the owners of land on opposite sides of the tidal reach of a river, their right to the several fishery in no way derives from the ownership of any land by either of them, so that their respective rights to fish remain unchanged even after the river diverts its course while continuing to be bounded by the estuary.[3]

¹ *Ashworth v Brown* (1855) 7 Ir Jur Rep 315, a case involving the Corrib.

² As in the instance of the Monastery of St Columba and the River Nore: *Tighe v Sinnott* [1897] 1 IR 140 at 145.

³ *Miller v Little* (1879) 4 LR Ir 302.

[13.21] It should not be supposed that the presumption of a several fishery in tidal waters having been 'put in defence' is virtually a foregone conclusion once prolonged user by a current claimant and his predecessors has been established and there is no obvious evidence to suggest that the enjoyment was ever otherwise. In the celebrated case of *Moore v AG*,[1] a claimed several fishery in the tidal waters of the River Erne in Co Donegal was held to fail because of the clear historical fact that English law did not effectively pervade the land of Tirconnail until 1542 at the earliest. Notwithstanding that Kennedy CJ found that 'enormous weight' should be attached to the prolonged history of evidence of enjoyment of the several fishery offered by the plaintiff, and that '… no Court could, save for the strongest and most convincing reasons, ascribe an enjoyment so long continued to an illegal origin …',[2] yet legal presumption must yield to historical fact, and the manifest impossibility of Magna Carta 1215 being applied in Tirconnail at the time of its enactment, and the fact that the Crown could not have 'put in defence' a several fishery in that region prior to 1189, proved fatal to the plaintiff's claim. A further nail in the coffin was hammered in by the preponderance of antiquarian evidence to the effect that the Brehon law system, which *did* prevail in Tirconnail in 1189, did not recognise, no more than did Roman law, private fishing rights in tidal waters.[3]

---

[1]   *Moore v AG* [1934] IR 44.
[2]   [1934] IR 44 at 65.
[3]   [1934] IR 44 at 66–68.

[13.22] It seems that the immediate aftermath of the decision in *Moore v AG* was an indiscriminate rush by eager fishing enthusiasts to the tidal waters of the west of Ireland, in total defiance of claimed private fishing rights there, on the basis of some '... broad abstract proposition that a several fishery, in an arm of the sea, is illegal, unconstitutional and impossible ...'[1] no matter how arising. Such notions were resoundingly scotched in *Little v Cooper*,[2] in which Johnston J held, that evidence of prolonged and sustained enjoyment from the early seventeenth century, allied to the historical possibility of its having been 'put in defence' prior to 1189, entitled the court to hold that a valid several fishery had been established in the estuary of the River Moy.

---

[1]   *Little v Cooper* [1937] IR 1 at 6, per Johnston J.
[2]   [1937] IR 1.

[13.23] Notwithstanding the cautionary note sounded in *Little v Cooper*,[1] in a further case involving the rivers of the north-west – *Foyle & Bann Fisheries Ltd v AG*[2] – Gavan Duffy P again ploughed the 'historical impossibility' furrow that had been dug out by the Supreme Court in *Moore v AG*. In this, the plaintiff claimed a right of several fishery in a tidal offshoot of the River Foyle in Co Donegal, on the basis both of historical long possession, and no fewer than three paper titles, including a private Act of Parliament from the reign of Queen Anne.

Perhaps with an eye on the tortuous analysis of the alleged Crown title in the Lough Neagh fishery cases, Gavan Duffy P found little persuasive strength in the charter and letters patent offered from the early seventeenth century, delivering himself of a view on Stuart assertions of title in language illustrative of an attitude to such things:

> 'But the statecraft of a resourceful age insisted upon a colourable juristic title for the expropriation of Irish property and divers royal claims were evolved to preserve a veneer of legality.'[3]

Hence, an alleged expropriation of the several fishery, on the alternate bases of an escheat for treason after the flight of the Earl of Tyrconnell, a confiscation of monastic property, and an exercise of royal prerogative through Star Chamber, were roundly repudiated. It appears from the judgment of Gavan Duffy P that the requirement for a several fishery in tidal waters to be 'put in defence' prior to 1189, in order to deny the right of the public to fish, must be more than mere possibility.

> 'It is settled law that by virtue of Magna Carta, a several fishery in waters tidal and navigable, to the exclusion of the public right, presupposes, as the condition of its validity, the existence before 1189 of an effective veto on the natural right of the public to fish those waters as an arm of the sea.'[4]

---

[1] *Little v Cooper* [1937] IR 1.
[2] *Foyle & Bann Fisheries Ltd v AG* (1948) 83 ILTR 29.
[3] (1948) 83 ILTR 29 at 33.
[4] (1948) 83 ILTR 29 at 34.

Access to a several fishery and ancillary rights

[13.24] At common law a grant of a several fishery carries with it an implied right of access to the banks of the water, unless the fishing can be carried out by boat.[1] In *Gannon v Walsh*,[2] Keane J stated that:

> '[t]he right of access to the bank must, however, be exercised in a manner which is as little detrimental to the riparian owners as is consistent with the full beneficial use of the right of fishing.'[3]

Keane J held that the right of access was a pedestrian one only, based on the requirements of an able-bodied angler of average strength and mobility. Since vehicular access had not been enjoyed by holders of the fishing rights in the days before motor cars, there was no reason why a right of driving to the bank should be allowed. Furthermore, since fishing by net was illegal,[4] the only equipment required to be carried was rod, line, and associated tackle.[5]

Keane J also found that a right of access could be derived from s 13 of the Irish Land Act 1903, which provides that, in the case of a sale of tenanted land, sporting rights – defined as including fishing rights – could be either granted or reserved, and became assigned to the Land Commission in default of agreement; in the event of a right being reserved, ss 4 provides that:

> '... there shall be attached thereto a right to enter upon the land in respect of which the first mentioned right may be exercised, and to authorise any person to do so; but any person entering upon land in pursuance of this subsection shall be liable to make reasonable amends and satisfaction for any damage done or occasioned thereby.'

---

[1] *Gannon v Walsh* [1998] 3 IR 245 at 277.
[2] [1998] 3 IR 245.
[3] [1998] 3 IR 245 at 277, 283.
[4] Under the Fisheries Act 1939, s 35.
[5] [1998] 3 IR 245 at 284.

[13.25] This section was relevant to three decisions of Barton J, at the turn of the twentieth century, regarding rights ancillary to a several fishery reserved over a river that passed through lands occupied by a judicial tenant. In *Palmer v Byrne*[1] Barton J held that the holder of the several fishery was entitled to maintain the riverbank in its reasonable and normal condition by cutting and lopping some of the sallies and thorn bushes that grew along it. Provided that the stability which the roots of these plants gave to the riverbank was not interfered with, such trimming did not adversely affect the tenant in the management of his farm.[2] The tenant could not be held liable if he permitted the sallies and thorn bushes to grow to such height as obstructed the fishing, but he would have to permit the holder of the fishing right to cut them back.[3]

Equally, the tenant is entitled to take all reasonable and proper means necessary for the management and cultivation of his farm, including the erection of fences to prevent the escape of cattle.[4] Indeed, provided he is so doing, the holder of the fishery right must be content to accept the condition of the riverbank as it may be in from time to time.[5] On the other hand, as Barton J observed in *Boyle v Holcroft*,[6] the tenant cannot do anything which unreasonably or maliciously hinders the exercise of the right of fishing, such as the placing of a barbed wire fence that renders dangerous the exercise of the fishing right and virtually obliterates it altogether.[7]

---

[1]　*Palmer v Byrne* [1906] 1 IR 373.

[2]　[1906] 1 IR 373 at 376.

[3]　[1906] 1 IR 373 at 377–378.

[4]　*Boyle v Holcroft* [1905] 1 IR 245 at 249.

[5]　[1905] 1 IR 245 at 250; *Caldwell v Kilkelly* [1905] 1 IR 434 at 447.

[6]　[1905] 1 IR 245.

[7]　[1905] 1 IR 245 at 250–251.

[13.26] In *Caldwell v Kilkelly*[1] Barton J set a limit to the ancillary rights that might reasonably be claimed by the holder of a several fishery. By analogy with the right to repair a right of way, there could be implied a right to cut down useless and injurious weeds, but not a right to cut down weeds in any part of the river.[2] In certain cases there might even be a right to repair the riverbank.[3] However, there could not be asserted a right to place large blocks or stones on the river bed, which though they might enhance the right of fishing, would obstruct the passage of cattle and also present the risk of injuring them.[4] Similarly prohibited was a proposed artificial embankment to ease the efforts of the rod fishermen. In addition to providing a further risk of injury to cattle, which run up and down the stream in hot summer weather to fend off flies, such a construction would be more akin to a luxury than a necessity in exercise of the right of fishing.[5] Care must be taken that, under the guise of exerting a legitimate ancillary right to the right of fishing, that right itself is not thereby enlarged and extended. Any such augmentations must be the subject of agreement.[6]

---

[1]　*Caldwell v Kilkelly* [1905] 1 IR 434.

[2]　[1905] 1 IR 434 at 446.

[3]　[1905] 1 IR 434 at 443.

[4]　[1905] 1 IR 434 at 445.

[5]　[1905] 1 IR 434 at 442–443. Barton J expatiated, with considerable eloquence, on the importance of the application of skill and resourcefulness in overcoming the obstacles of bed and bank, so as to give to the exercise of fishing: '... whether it be regarded as a pursuit or a sport, its peculiar zest, excitement and fascination ...'

[13.27] The foregoing paragraphs represent a distillation of the common law applicable to both public and private rights of fishing as elaborated by the courts. Although the detailed domain of statutory intervention falls outside the scope of a work that treats of intangible property rights, it must be noted that there is a comprehensive panoply of statute law and regulation, both in Northern Ireland and the Republic of Ireland, that orders and delimits many aspects of the right of fishing – not least the locations where fishing may be undertaken, the type of fish that may be caught, and the type of apparatus used in catching them – and appoints dedicated fishery officers with wide-ranging duties and powers.[1]

---

[1] For a flavour, see Bland *The Law of Easements and Profits à Prendre* (1997) Sweet & Maxwell, pp 173–177; Wylie *Irish Land Law* (3rd edn, 1997) Butterworths, pp 407–408.

Sporting Rights

[13.28] The owner of land has a natural right to kill wild animals and fowl found upon his land. While wild animals are alive they are incapable of being controlled, but when dead they are deemed to belong to the owner of the land where they are found.[1] Tame or cultivated animals while still alive are owned by the landowner, who will accordingly be liable for damage should they escape.[2] When wild animals stray, the owner of the soil from which they have wandered will not be liable for any damage that they cause: a neighbouring landowner's remedy for trespass is to shoot the wild animal.[3] A dead wild animal is deemed 'of the soil' and so the property in it attaches to the owner of the soil.[4]

---

[1] *Blades v Higgs* (1865) 11 HLC 621 at 631.
[2] As in the case of deer that occasionally wander and tend to return 'home': *Brady v Warren* [1900] 2 IR 632.
[3] As in the case of rabbits not bred or acquired by the landowner: [1900] 2 IR 632 at 663.
[4] *Brew v Haren* (1877) IR 11 CL 198 at 217.

[13.29] The right of ownership in a dead wild animal is capable of being detached from the soil and being specifically granted to others, in the form of a right to enter, hunt or shoot, then remove the killed animal. Other than fishing, a right of shooting is the sporting right most commonly found and this includes a right to take away the game when shot.[1] It is a profit *à prendre*[2] and is capable of being subject of a fee simple,[3] a lease or a licence. If granted by licence, this is deemed to be a licence coupled with an interest. Infraction of the right begets a cause of action in its holder for trespass.[4] An action can also lie in conversion.[5]

---

[1] *Radcliff v Hayes* [1907] 1 IR 101 at 112.
[2] *Reynolds v Moore* [1898] 2 IR 641 at 649, per Andrews J.
[3] A fee simple most usually arises where the right is reserved. A grant tends to be either by way of lease or licence.
[4] *Radcliff v Hayes* [1907] 1 IR 101 at 114–115.

⁵ *Blades v Higgs* (1865) 11 HLC 621. In *Toome Eel Fishery (Northern Ireland) Ltd v Cardwell* [1966] NI 1, at 29, Lord McDermott LCJ regarded the reducing into possession of stolen eels, by packing them alive in boxes and transporting them to the market, as comparable to reducing game into possession by killing and taking it, for the purpose of founding a claim in conversion.

[13.30] During the eighteenth century it was not uncommon for a grantor of a lease for lives to reserve rights of hunting and shooting when granting the lease.[1] With shorter term tenancies, such as became normal in the nineteenth century, reservations of game were infrequently made, since, prior to the enactment of the Land Act 1870, a landlord could merely determine, by giving 6 months' notice expiring on a gale day, the tenancy of any tenant who objected to his shooting.[2] However, subsequent to the Landlord and Tenant Law Amendment, Ireland, Act 1860 (better known as Deasy's Act) the grantor of a lease of lands seems invariably to have reserved the sporting rights.[3] The effect of such a reservation is a regrant in fee simple of the sporting rights, by the grantee of the lands to the grantor of the lands.[4] Under s 13(1) of the Irish Land Act 1903, sporting rights not reserved by the vendor or otherwise assigned were vested in the Land Commission.

1 *Reynolds v Moore* [1898] 2 IR 641.
2 *Radcliff v Hayes* [1907] 1 IR 101, at p 108, per Meredith MR.
3 Bland *The Law of Easements and Profits à Prendre* p 172.
4 [1898] 2 IR 641 at 649, per Andrews J; *Radcliff v Hayes* [1907] 1 IR 101 at 113, per Meredith MR.

[13.31] The holder of a sporting right is entitled to employ a gamekeeper to carry out the hunting for him, but is not required to accompany the gamekeeper. However, the gamekeeper is not entitled to kill game on his own account.[1] In the absence of express words that clearly grant a larger right, a reservation of a sporting right will not be deemed to permit its holder to licence the right to others; nor will the holder of the right be able to exclude the grantee of the fee simple from participating: this hybrid profit *à prendre* shared between the holder of the shooting right and the owner of the land has been called a 'concurrent right'.[2]

1 *Hudson v Foott* (1859) 9 ICLR 203.
2 *Reynolds v Moore* [1898] 2 IR 641.

[13.32] While the owner of land over which a sporting right has been granted or reserved is entitled to do all things reasonably necessary for the cultivation of his land, this cannot go so far as unnecessarily to interfere with the profit *à prendre*. In appropriate circumstances an injunction will be granted to restrain an excess of zeal in the cultivation efforts of the landowner. In *Fetherstonhaugh v Hagarty*,[1] a lease of lands reserved all gaming rights to the landlord. The lessee had the right to break up 40 acres for tillage. For several years he used only 16 acres, then he broke up another 7 acres in which there were a number of rabbit burrows. Fearing lest the rabbits destroy his crops, the tenant blocked all the rabbit burrows both in that field and also elsewhere on his farm. Sullivan MR held that the tenant did not have a general right to destroy the rabbit burrows outside the tilled ground and could be restrained from destroying rabbits or blocking burrows except such as were the necessary result of the proper cultivation of his farm in accordance with the terms of his lease.

The Master of the Rolls stated the applicable law thus:

'... a tenant under a lease ... where an exclusive profit *à prendre* is reserved or granted to the landlord, cannot be made answerable for acts done in the ordinary and proper cultivation of the farm, even though they result in the destruction or removal of game. The tenant in this lease has a right to break up forty acres of the farm; and if, in the honest exercise of that right, and without any collateral object, in tilling those forty acres he drives his plough through rabbit-burrows, in my opinion he cannot be made answerable for so doing at the suit of the landlord, although that landlord has the profit *à prendre* which I have described. But there, in my opinion, his right ceases and his privilege closes. If he seeks for any higher right he must contract for it.'[2]

Accordingly, the tenant would be restrained from blocking up rabbits burrows elsewhere than on the tilled land, for otherwise he could effectively block up every rabbit burrow on the entire farm and thereby annihilate the profit *à prendre* that he had granted by the reservation to his landlord.[3]

---

[1] *Fetherstonhaugh v Hagarty* (1879) 3 LR Ir 150.

[2] (1879) 3 LR Ir 150 at 158–159, following the decisions of *Jeffreys v Evans* (1865) 19 CB (NS) 246 and *Gearns v Baker* (1875) LR 10 Ch 355.

[3] (1879) 3 LR Ir 150 at 159.

[13.33] Except, however, in cases where the enterprise of the landowner tends towards the destruction of the profit, the holder of the sporting rights must take the land over which he enjoys those rights as he finds it, and cannot object to *bona fide* exercises of cultivation undertaken by the landowner, even if, for instance, the draining of swampy ground results in an exodus of snipe, or the discontinuation of the growing of turnips is followed by the disappointed departure of partridge.[1]

---

[1] *Caldwell v Kilkelly* [1905] 1 IR 434 at 447, per Barton J.

[13.34] Similarly as in the case of fishing, the exercise of sporting rights, both in Northern Ireland and the Republic of Ireland, is extensively qualified by statutes for the protection of various categories of wildlife.[1] In cases of registered land, where sporting rights (other than fishing rights) have not been exercised for a period of 12 years after the coming into effect of the Land Act 1965, they can be discharged from the folio upon application by any party interested in the land to the Registrar of Titles.[2]

---

[1] Wylie *Irish Land Law* p 409.

[2] Land Act 1965, s 18(c).

Profits *à Prendre* for Profit – Mining and Quarrying

[13.35] Although sporting and fishing rights can be exercised as much for profit as pleasure, and are certainly very lucrative, profits *à prendre* of mining and quarrying are for commercial purposes purely. They are also subject to strict controls in both parts of Ireland in terms of their potential for future private development. Subject to all estates existing in them at the time, Article 10 of Bunreacht na hÉireann vests all natural resources in the State. There are also several statutes dealing specifically with minerals development.[1] In Northern Ireland, the Mineral Development Act (Northern Ireland) 1969 vests all working mines, and most mines and minerals remaining unworked, in the Department of the Environment.

Upon a disposal of land the vendor can except from his grant either mines and quarries, or both, while reserving a right to have access to them.[2] Alternatively, he can make a specific disposal of a profit *à prendre* to undertake mining and quarrying operations. Whether in a particular case the grant or reservation is of the actual soil beneath which the minerals are to be worked and wrought, or of a *à prendre* to mine or quarry, will depend on the wording of the instrument itself.[3] Where a profit *à prendre* to mine or quarry has been granted by licence only, the traditional view is that it is a licence coupled with an interest, and accordingly irrevocable until its subject matter has been exhausted or the term for which it was granted has expired.[4] However, this is liable to be affected by the obligation or otherwise on the licensee to mine, and the ease or lack of ease with which the sought substance can be brought to the surface.[5] The preferred modern view is that the respective rights and obligations under a profit *à prendre* to mine or quarry granted by licence fall to be determined by the provisions of the contract granting or embodying the licence and such other conditions as require reasonably to be implied.[6]

---

[1] For example, Minerals Exploration and Development Company Act 1941; Minerals Development Acts 1940 and 1979; Mines and Quarries Act 1965.

[2] *Earl of Antrim v Gray* (1875) IR 9 Eq 513 at 520, per Chatterton V-C.

[3] *O'Donnell v Ryan* (1856) 4 ICLR 44.

[4] *Atkinson v King* (1877) IR 11 CL 536, (1878) 2 LR Ir 320, see ch 20, para **[20.02]** ff; but see the dissenting judgment of Christian LJ (1878) 2 LR Ir 320 at 338–362, see paras **[20.05]**–**[20.06]**

[5] As in the extraction of 'bog ore' in *Stanley v Riky* (1892) 31 LR Ir 196, see para **[20.07]** ff.

[6] *Winter Garden Theatre (London) Ltd v Millennium Productions Ltd* [1946] 1 All ER 678, [1948] AC 147, *Australian Blue Metal Ltd v Hughes* [1963] AC 74, considered and followed in *Woods v Donnelly* [1982] NI 257, see para **[20.20]** ff.

[13.36] By reason primarily of its commercial importance, a grant of a right of mining or quarrying is most often as a several profit in gross. In cases, however, where it is granted as a profit appurtenant to land, like all such profits it falls to be delimited, either by a specific modicum of 'stint' or to the reasonable needs of the occupiers of the property to which it is appurtenant.[1]

---

[1] *Clayton v Corby* (1843) 5 QB 415.

[13.37] In the middle years of the nineteenth century, there was some confusion as to whether an exception of minerals included a right to extract them by quarrying as well as by mining. The distinction between the two activities was capably expressed by Monahan CJ, in 1857, in *Brown v Chadwick*:[1]

> 'The distinction between a mine and a quarry appears to me to be this – a mine is a place where the substratum is excavated, but the surface is unbroken; whereas in a quarry the surface is opened, and the material, in the present case limestone, is exposed and raised.'[2]

In that case Monahan CJ expressed the view that a right to extract minerals, in a predominantly limestone district, could not be construed as including a right to work out every last particle of limestone through the digging of an open quarry. In a similar vein was the judgment of Brady LC in *Mansfield v Crawford*,[3] in which he granted an injunction restraining a sub-lessee for years, holding under a lease for lives renewable forever, from working an open quarry situated on the lands in the sub-demise, that had not been expressly referred to either by way of grant or exception. This tendency towards stringent technical definition was continued by Crampton J in *Listowel v Gibbings*,[4] where he held that an exception of 'all mines and minerals' did not include a right to quarry limestone, on the basis that:

> 'Usually, "mine" imports a cavern or subterranean place, containing metals or minerals, and not a quarry; and "minerals" mean ordinarily metallic fossil bodies, and not limestone …'[5]

Crampton J did, however, concede that if the intention of the parties, as embodied in the relevant instrument, seemed designed to include a right to quarry, then such a right should be deemed to pass.

---

1 *Brown v Chadwick* (1857) 7 ICLR 101.
2 (1857) 7 ICLR 101 at 108.
3 *Mansfield v Crawford* (1846) 9 Ir Eq Rep 271.
4 *Listowel v Gibbings* (1858) 9 ICLR 223.
5 (1858) 9 ICLR 223 at 232.

[13.38] The linguistic pedantry inherent in this overall approach was reversed, in 1872, by the English Court of Appeal in *Hext v Gill*,[1] which in *Fishbourne v Hamilton*[2] Lord Ashbourne C acknowledged was binding on the Irish Court of Appeal. In *Hext v Gill*, Mellish LJ had stated that:

> '…a reservation of "minerals" includes any substance which can be got from underneath the surface of the earth for the purpose of profit, unless there is something in the context, or in the nature of the transaction, to induce the Court to give it a more limited meaning.'[3]

Applying this dictum in *Fishbourne v Hamilton*, Chatterton V-C observed that the use of the word 'mines' in the instrument of grant did not restrict the 'minerals' only to those which could be accessed by mining: the mere fact that certain minerals, in the case of those won by a quarry, could not be secured without some destruction of the surface did not, *in itself*, affect the definition of a mineral, but might have the effect of preventing the owner of the mineral from taking it out, unless there were provision for the payment of compensation for damage to the owner of the surface.[4] Similarly, Chatterton V-C declined to accept that the word 'mineral' should be differently construed depending on whether or not the land is in a limestone district:

> 'It would lead to useless confusion if we had to construe a reservation of minerals according to the preponderance of particular minerals in that district. The argument would go to this, that where limestone is the formation, the word "minerals" does not include limestone, but that where it does not preponderate it does include it.'[5]

To the extent that *Brown v Chadwick*[6] and *Listowel v Gibbings*[7] held otherwise, in the view of the Vice-Chancellor they should be regarded as overruled as being inconsistent with *Hext v Gill*.

---

1   *Hext v Gill* (1872) LR 7 Ch App 699.

2   *Fishbourne v Hamilton* (1890) 25 LR Ir 483.

3   (1872) LR 7 Ch App 699 at 712; quoted by Chatterton V-C, (1890) 25 LR Ir 483 at 490.

4   Lord Ashbourne C stated that if the working of the lands, in order to secure limestone, could not be undertaken without injury to the surface of the land, '… and no justice can be rendered to the grantee or lessee by way of compensation, an injunction will go to prevent the grantor from getting the benefit of the reservation.' (1890) 25 LR Ir 483 at 500.

5   (1890) 25 LR Ir 483 at 491.

6   *Brown v Chadwick* (1857) 7 ICLR 101.

7   *Listowel v Gibbings* (1858) 9 ICLR 223.

[13.39] However, in *Staples v Young*[1] it was held that, where the topsoil largely comprised sand and some miscellaneous decayed vegetable matter, an exception of 'minerals' could not be deemed to include sand, where the effect of this would be to leave no topsoil at all. In the opinion of Fitzgibbon LJ, in determining what is meant by 'mines and minerals':

> '… evidence of the nature and character of the land at the time is admissible, and is persuasive. … "Minerals", in its widest possible meaning, includes everything capable of being dug out and taken away, having a specific character and value, and being won by mining.'[2]

According to Holmes LJ, in each case one must look to the nature of the transaction as an aid to interpretation, and while sand may be construed as a mineral in one instance, it might not be so in another.[3]

---

1   *Staples v Young* [1908] 1 IR 135.

2   [1908] 1 IR 135 at 149.

3   Perhaps the final word on this fluctuating topic is best left to the sensible enunciation of Holmes LJ: 'In truth, any attempt to lay down, in a sentence, a rule of general application to a subject-matter which in its nature is diversified and multiform can never be completely satisfactory. The formula is likely to include what ought to be excluded, and to exclude what ought to be included. Moreover, a qualification making a rule to depend upon the nature of the transaction is so far-reaching as to deprive the rule of much value as a general guide.' [1908] 1 IR 135 at 154.

[13.40] Like with all profits *à prendre*, a grant or reservation of a right of quarrying or mining is deemed to include all incidental rights reasonably necessary to secure the subject of the right.[1] Having regard to the nature of the principal rights, these can be considerable. A right of throwing excavated spoil on adjoining land has been held to be an easement accessorial to a profit of quarrying.[2] In the case of a right to mine for coal, there is an ancillary right to employ such machinery as is necessary to draw the coal from the pits, including a steam engine to work out the lower seams.[3] In *McDonnell v Kenneth*[4] it was held that the erection of a pier on a rock running out to the sea and the construction of tram lines were reasonable accessories to a right to mine, and that the implements of mining were not to be confined to those in currency at the time of the granting of the right to mine.

In *Earl of Antrim v Dobbs*[5] O'Brien J stated that the methods adopted to work the mine must be considered on the basis of a test of reasonableness:

> 'The way must be a way the reasonableness of which is to be judged at the time of the actual use ... There is no other measure of the right, where the deed is silent, but the common convenience and use of mankind. It is a right which in its nature is to attend from time to time the exercise of another right, and must therefore receive its form and measure from what is usual and proper at the time it is used. ... the customary and reasonable method of working the mines must be the test.'[6]

According to Holmes J the devices adopted to yield the produce of the mine can 'vary with the circumstances of the time and the locality', and it would be virtually impossible to extract minerals from the earth by any method 'that would not for the time being exclude the surface owner from some portion of his property ...'[7]

---

1   *Rudd v Rea* [1921] 1 IR 223 at 226, per Powell J.
2   *Middleton v Clarence* (1877) IR 11 CL 499.
3   *Dand v Kingscote* (1840) 6 M & W 174, cited with approval in *Rudd v Rea* [1921] 1 IR 223 at 230–231.
4   *McDonnell v Kenneth* (1850) 1 ICLR 113.
5   *Earl of Antrim v Dobbs* (1890) 30 LR Ir 424.
6   (1890) 30 LR Ir 424 at 428–429.
7   (1890) 25 LR Ir 424 at 432. Having regard to observations made in *Fishbourne v Hamilton* (1890) 25 LR Ir 483, see para **[13.38]**, it is instructive to note that in the instrument of grant in *Earl of Antrim v Dobbs* there was express provision for the payment of reasonable compensation to the owner of the surface for damage done.

[13.41] However, it should not be assumed that in the granting of a profit *à prendre* of mining or quarrying the owner of the surface is to be regarded as having acquiesced in the abandonment of all his rights to the soil.

> 'The surface-owner has at Common Law a right to have the surface supported by the subjacent land. It is not reasonable to suppose that the surface-owner intends to give up a right so important for the user of the surface without adequate consideration, and the Courts do not easily come to the conclusion that it is the intention of a contract to give up this right to support; and therefore, in construing a contract intended to determine the relative rights of the surface-owner and the owner of the subjacent land, it is fitting to take

into consideration, not only the words of the contract, but the nature of the right which it is sought to say that the contract intends that the surface-owner was surrendering.'[1]

The owner of the surface is deemed to grant to the holder of the profit of mining or quarrying no more than a right to effect 'temporary damage', rather than the effecting of a 'serious, continuous, and permanent injury to the surface.' If the intention is that the surface may be destroyed in gaining access to the minerals, then this must be expressed in clear language in the instrument granting the profit.[2]

1   *Rudd v Rea* [1921] 1 IR 223, at pp 233–234, per Powell J.
2   *Hext v Gill* (1872) LR 7 Ch 699 at 714, 718, per Mellish LJ, cited with approval in *Rudd v Rea* [1921] 1 IR 223 at 236–237, per Powell J.

[13.42] Similar considerations apply to a profit *à prendre* for the cutting and removal of timber for commercial purposes, previously discussed in the section on estovers.[1]

1   See para **[12.23]**.

Chapter 14

Running of Positive Covenants

Concept and Definition of a Covenant

Introduction

[14.01] A covenant is a contract or promise entered into by deed. A clause in a deed containing a promise or undertaking by one party to it can be described as a covenant. In the context of the present discussion, the kind of covenant being considered is that entered into between two parties, concerning the use or enjoyment of land. Such a covenant usually provides that one party is to do something, or to refrain from doing something, which affects the other party in the enjoyment of land owned by him. In consequence, one speaks of the 'benefit' of the covenant as being that which is enjoyed by the party in whose favour the covenant is made. That party is described as the covenantee. Similarly, the party undertaking either to do, or to refrain from doing, that which comprises the subject of the covenant is said to be liable to the 'burden' of the covenant. The person undertaking the covenant is the covenantor.

[14.02] A covenant intended to benefit the land of the covenantee can be either positive or negative. A positive covenant most often involves the undertaking of works or the payment of monies. For example, covenants to maintain, to clean, to drain, to fence, to insure, or to contribute to the cost of repairing – all these rank as positive covenants. Frequently, the performance of the duties imposed by the covenant is personal to the party undertaking them. In such circumstance, the extent to which the covenantor can assign the obligation to engage in the activity will depend on the terms of the covenant itself. Where there is no facility to assign the obligation under the covenant, the responsibility to perform remains personal to the covenantor.

There are certain positive covenants which are incident to the covenantor's ownership of a particular parcel of land. Examples of these include a covenant to erect or maintain a fence between two properties; a covenant to cut back verdure on one property overhanging another property; a covenant to maintain and repair a roof of one property which depends over a neighbouring one. In each of these cases, the essence of the covenant is the performance of acts by the covenantor, not so much in a personal capacity, but as the owner of property which in some way is associated or connected with the use or enjoyment of other property, owned by the covenantee. In these situations also, the principle is that unless the responsibility to perform the duties imposed by the covenant can be assigned by the covenantor to a subsequent owner of the covenantor's property, liability on the covenant remains with the covenantor. This is because the law, generally, does not oblige a person to undertake an act or to make a payment to which that person has not – either by deed under seal, or through a contract supported by consideration – agreed.

[14.03] A negative covenant purports to benefit the land of the covenantee through the imposition of some restraint or prohibition on the enjoyment by the covenantor of land owned by him. By its very nature, a negative covenant, commonly known as a restrictive covenant, entails the benefiting of the land of the covenantee 'at the expense', so to speak, of the land of the covenantor. Examples of negative or restrictive covenants include covenants not to build at all on the property, not to build more than to a certain extent on the property, or to maintain all or a particular part of the property in the state in which it existed at the time of a grant of it.

Whether a covenant is positive or negative depends, not on the label placed by the parties upon it, but upon the nature of the obligation it imposes on the covenantor. Hence, a covenant to preserve a property uncovered by trees or shrubbery, will be a positive covenant where the property affected has trees or shrubbery already growing on it: the essence of the covenant is to cut them down and preserve the property henceforth free of herbage. However, a covenant to preserve a property uncovered by buildings will be a negative covenant if given in the context of an open site.

Analogy with easements

[14.04] The potential range of a covenant is far greater than that afforded by the categories of easements recognised by the law. A landowner by covenant can secure the enjoyment of a higher intensity of natural light than could be acquired as an easement.[1] A right of prospect, which is not an easement, could also be provided for by an appropriately drafted covenant. Similarly, a right not to drain off water percolating in an undefined channel beneath the lands of the covenantor.[2] The reluctance evinced by the law to recognise a right to the flow of air, except in a defined channel or through a specific aperture, can be, at least conceptually, overcome through the construction of a suitably drafted covenant between the relevant parties.

---

[1]   'Restrictive Covenants' (1967) 101 ILTSJ 272 at 273.
[2]   Bodkin 'Easements and Uncertainty' (1971) 35 Conv 324.

[14.05] A further analogy with the principles governing easements is that covenants often affect both the land of the person making the covenant ('the covenantor') and invariably the land of the person benefiting from the covenant ('the covenantee'). Comparison with dominant and servient tenements in the realm of easements is apt. In this regard also, one speaks of the burden of the covenant, as being that to which the covenantor is liable, and the benefit of the covenant, which is the enjoyment accruing to the covenantee.

The enforcement of a covenant between the original contracting parties depends on the principles of contract law.[1] That with which this discussion is principally concerned is the extent to which the successors in title to the lands owned by either party can, on the one hand, enforce the benefit, and, on the other hand, be subjected to the burden, of the covenant affecting the land entered into by the original contracting parties.[2]

1 Except in the case of a covenantee who is not a party to the instrument creating the covenant whose entitlement to enforce the covenant was provided for by the Real Property Act 1845, s 5. See para **[15.11]**.

2 In Northern Ireland the traditional principles of law and equity relating to the mutual enforceability of covenants have been superseded by the Property (Northern Ireland) Order 1997 (1997 No 1179 (NI 8), Article 34). See para **[14.34]** ff.

Principles governing enforcement by and against successors

[14.06] In order to determine the mutual enforceability of covenants by or against successors to the original parties, a number of considerations are relevant:

(a) whether the property is freehold or leasehold. The extent to which the enforceability of leasehold covenants by parties other than the original lessor and original lessee has been the subject of statutory intervention justifies deferring a consideration of leasehold covenants *qua* leasehold covenants to a subsequent chapter that concentrates on statutory intervention. It is unavoidable, given the continuing high incidence of leasehold titles in both parts of Ireland, that certain of them will feature in the current chapter treating of the running of positive covenants;

(b) whether the covenant itself is positive or restrictive. To the extent that particular equitable principles[1] have been developed in relation to the enforceability of restrictive covenants, both by and against successors to the original contracting parties, a consideration of restrictive covenants as a special genus of equitable right is also deferred to a subsequent chapter;

(c) whether one is concerned with the enforcement of the burden of the covenant against a successor or assign of the original covenantor, or whether one is concerned with the enforcement of the benefit of the covenant by a successor or assign of the original covenantee. Consequently, in considering the running both of positive and restrictive covenants, separate consideration will be given to the principles governing the running of benefit and burden in each case.

1 Generally ascribed to the judgment of Lord Cottenham LC in the case of *Tulk v Moxhay* (1848) 2 Ph 774. See also the cases in which this concept is clarified and elaborated: *Haywood v The Brunswick Permanent Benefit Building Society* (1881) 8 QBD 403; *London and South Western Railway Co v Gomm* (1882) 20 ChD 562, *Austerberry v Corporation of Oldham* (1885) 29 ChD 750; Strachan 'Restrictive Covenants Affecting Land' (1930) 46 LQR 159; Bailey 'The Benefit of a Restrictive Covenant' [1938] CLJ 339; 'Restrictive Covenants' (1966) 100 ILTSJ 421; 'Equity and a Restrictive Covenant' (1966) 100 ILTSJ 146; 'Restrictive Covenants' (1967) 101 ILTSJ 153, 182, 223, 272; Robinson, 'Restrictive Covenants' (1974) 38 Conv 90; Bell '*Tulk v Moxhay* Revisited' [1981] Conv 55; Griffith, '*Tulk v Moxhay* Reclarified' [1983] Conv 29.

The Running of the Benefit

[14.07] The most thorough examination in Irish law of the running of positive covenants took place, in 1952, in the case of *Gaw v Coras Iompair Éireann*.[1] Dixon J[2] noted that there are three conditions for the running of the benefit of a positive covenant:

(a)   the successor must be in the same estate as the original covenantee;

(b)   the successor must have an interest in the subject-matter of the covenant independently of the covenant;

(c)   the covenant must touch and concern that interest. The requirement that the covenant 'touch and concern' the land of the covenantee derives from the English Court of Queen's Bench decision in *Spencer's Case*[2] which was concerned with the enforceability of covenants between an assignee of the lessor and an assignee of the lessee. The old common law principle was that only the parties to a covenant could sue or be sued upon it. This was amended to allow action by or against successors to both the lessor and the lessee by the Grantees of Reversions Act 1540, enacted in Ireland in 1634. *Spencer's Case* introduced the qualification that the covenant had to relate to either party in their capacity as lessor or lessee (or a successor or assignee of either) rather than in a purely personal capacity.[3]

---

[1]   *Gaw v Coras Iompair Éireann* (1952) 89 ILTR 124.

[2]   *Spencer's Case* (1583) 5 Co Rep 16a.

[3]   The extent to which this has been changed, insofar as concerns the ability of the lessor or his assigns to enforce a covenant against a lessee or his assigns, under the Landlord and Tenant Law Amendment, Ireland, Act 1860, s 12 (23 & 24 Vict, c 154, also known as 'Deasy's Act'), is considered in ch 15, para **[15.12]** ff.

[14.08] The facts of *Gaw v Coras Iompair Éireann* involved a written covenant of almost 100 years earlier to maintain a right of way. In January 1848, the predecessor of the defendant, a railway company, contracted to purchase lands at Dalkey, Co Dublin, between a house called Kyber Pass and the sea, from a predecessor of the plaintiff. This was for the purpose of running a railway line between Dalkey and Killiney. The agreement between the parties provided that a right of way would be transferred back to the grantor subject to the railway company's entering into a covenant for its continued maintenance. By a conveyance of February 1848 the lands were transferred to the railway company, but there was no grant of a right of way. This was rectified by a further deed, of March 1856, in which the railway company granted a right of way over the lands formerly owned by him to the predecessor of the plaintiff and also covenanted to maintain the way. One issue in the case concerned the somewhat diffuse wording of the right of way, which required decision on whether the interest granted was a licence in gross or an easement proper. Dixon J held in favour of the interest being an easement, adding that any part of the agreement which savoured unduly of a personal licence 'may be treated as surplusage or severable.'[1]

¹ *Gaw v Coras Iompair Éireann* (1952) 89 ILTR 124 at 128.

[14.09] The issue of the running of the burden of a positive covenant did not arise for decision.¹ The liability of the original railway company had passed, through a succession of railway statutes, to the defendant. Dixon J was also prepared to hold, that insofar as concerned the burden of the covenant, this was a covenant 'in gross' – that is to say, a covenant which did not require for its efficacy the ownership of any land by the covenantor – even though it was, arguably, open to him to hold that the covenant clearly 'touched and concerned', as much as the right of way itself, the land over part of which it ran, that had been acquired by the covenantor in February 1848.

¹ Dixon J endorsed the law as set out in a number of English cases commencing with *Haywood v The Brunswick Permanent Benefit Building Society* (1881) 8 QBD 403, that the burden of a freehold covenant does not run with the land at law. In this case, the parties to the action were the successors of the original covenantor and covenantee and the covenant was one to repair. Cotton LJ said of it at 409: 'The covenant to repair can only be enforced by making the owner put his hand into his pocket, and there is nothing which would justify us going that length.' This is the principal reason why the courts have refused to enforce the burden of a positive covenant against a successor of the covenantor; see also *London and South Western Railway Co v Gomm* (1882) 20 ChD 562; *Austerberry v Corporation of Oldham* (1885) 29 ChD 750; *Rhone v Stephens* [1994] 2 WLR 429. Dixon J cited *Haywood* with approval, but declined to accept that it was an authority to the effect that the *benefit* of a positive covenant could not run with the land to which it related.

[14.10] Since the covenant to maintain the right of way (as opposed to the right of way itself) had never been expressly assigned in any subsequent conveyance of the land, the sole question for decision was whether the benefit of the covenant – that is to say, the legal capacity to enforce it – ran with the land.

To determine this Dixon J turned to the leading authority on the running of covenants, *Spencer's Case*,¹ citing from the commentary on it by the editors of *Smith's Leading Cases*,² as follows:

> 'With respect to … covenants made with the owner of the land to which they relate, there seems to be no doubt that the benefit, ie the right to sue on such covenants, runs with the land to each successive transferee of it, provided that such transferee be in the same estate as the original covenantee was.'

It was clear that the covenant touched and concerned the right of way. The principal issue, accordingly, was whether this was 'land' within the meaning of the proposition derivable from *Spencer's Case*. According to Dixon J, it was. He was supported in this view by the decision in *Holmes v Buckley*,³ a case from the late seventeenth century, in which a covenant to cleanse a watercourse running through the covenantor's land was held binding on a subsequent owner of the lands in favour of a subsequent owner of the watercourse. Dixon J concurred with the interpretation of the editors of *Smith's Leading Cases* that, since both parties were assignees, in order for an action to succeed on the covenant it would have been necessary to hold that the burden of the covenant ran with the land and the benefit of it with the watercourse.

According to Dixon J, that is precisely what *Holmes v Buckley* did decide:

> 'As the covenant to cleanse the watercourse was positive in its nature, it is hardly now good law that the burden of it should run with the land, but this does not necessarily impair the authority of the case for the proposition that the benefit could run with the watercourse.'[4]

---

1 *Spencer's Case* (1583) 5 Co Rep 16a.

2 (13th edn, 1929).

3 *Holmes v Buckley* (1691) Prec in Ch 39.

4 *Gaw v Coras Iompair Éireann* (1952) 89 ILTR 124 at 135.

[14.11] Dixon J also held that, since all conveyances of the right of way, other than the initial one of March 1856, had been executed after the passing of the Conveyancing Act 1881, the benefit of the covenant to repair would have passed under that part of s 6(1) which provides that a conveyance is deemed to include all 'privileges, easements, rights and advantages whatsoever, appertaining or reputed to appertain to the land.'[1]

---

1 A proposition which has not found universal favour in the English courts: *Kumar v Denning* [1989] QB 193, *J Sainsbury plc v Enfield London Borough Council* [1989] 1 WLR 590. On the other hand, the benefit of a right of way, together with a right to enforce a covenant to maintain and resurface the way, seems to have been accepted as passing under s 6 of the Conveyancing Act 1881 in *Corr v Bradshaw* (18 July 1967, unreported) SC; also Bland *The Law of Easements and Profits à Prendre* (1997) Sweet & Maxwell, p 29.

It is instructive at this point to examine more closely the three-part test advanced by Dixon J for the running of the benefit of a positive covenant.

The successor must be in the same estate as the original covenantee

[14.12] In order for the benefit of a covenant to run with the land the party claiming entitlement to the benefit must have the same interest in the land as the original covenantee had.[1] In *Monroe and Darley v Plunket*[2] Monroe was the successor of a Land Judge who had demised lands for a term of years. Darley was a receiver. The defendants were the sureties for the rent covenanted to be paid by the tenant. Palles CB had to consider whether the covenant on the part of the sureties, not having any interest in the land, was a covenant 'relating to land', and as such enforceable by the receiver under s 5 of the Real Property Act 1845[3] even though he was not party to the lease. There was no difficulty in holding that the covenant related to the land. Did it run with the land? In the opinion of Palles CB, the concept of 'relating to land' was equivalent to the old requirement, for the benefit of a covenant to run, of 'touching and concerning land'. However, the benefit of the covenant, in the chief baron's view, could not run with the land, even though it related to it, if the party claiming benefit of the covenant had not the same interest as the original covenantee, as the receiver obviously had not.[4]

1   It is questionable whether this requirement applies any longer in England: the Law of Property Act 1925, s 78, *Smith and Snipes Hall Farm Ltd v River Douglas Catchment Board* [1949] 2 KB 500, Wylie 'Contracts and Third Parties' (1966) 17 NILQ 351 at 362.

2   *Monroe and Darley v Plunket* (1888) 23 ILTR 76.

3   Which provides that a party intended to benefit from a covenant may enforce the covenant, though not a party to the deed creating it. See para **[15.11]**.

4   (1888) 23 ILTR 76 at 77.

[14.13] A clearer example of the same principle appears from the decision of the English Court of Appeal in *Westhoughton Urban District Council v Wigan Coal and Iron Co Ltd*.[1] The owner of lands had demised a lease of the minerals beneath them to the defendants, who had covenanted for themselves and their assigns, with their lessor and his assigns, not to let down the surface, and, in the event of any actual damage done to the surface of the lands, to pay compensation. The owner of the lands then granted a lease of the surface to the plaintiff, subject to the defendants' lease. When the workings by the defendants caused actual subsidence, they refused to pay damages to the plaintiff.

Swinfen Eady MR held that this covenant was clearly for the benefit of the surface of the land retained by the lessor, and accordingly 'touched and concerned' it, and so was enforceable by the original lessor and his assigns. However, added Swinfen Eady MR, the plaintiff lessee, not being in the same estate as the original covenantee, was not entitled to sue upon a positive covenant. Furthermore, since the plaintiff was a lessee and not an assign, neither was it in a position to enforce the covenant under s 5 of the Real Property Act 1845, as a covenant with assigns could not be construed as a covenant with a lessee of the covenantee.[2]

1   *Westhoughton Urban District Council v Wigan Coal and Iron Co Ltd* [1919] 1 Ch 159.

2   Swinfen Eady MR was able to conclude, however, that the plaintiff under the terms of its own lease was entitled to the support of the surface of the lands to the extent that this had not been taken away by the lease to the defendants; the defendants were held liable to the plaintiff on that account.

[14.14] Where the covenantee and his successor are in the same estate, it is a question of construction whether the benefit of the covenant was intended to be assigned. In *Shayler v Woolf*,[1] the defendant sold to the predecessor of the plaintiff a site on which to build a bungalow and covenanted to supply water from a pump on his own adjoining land and also to keep the pump in repair. The covenant was stated to bind the defendant-covenantor's successors, but no mention was made of assigns of the covenantee. When the pump fell into disrepair the defendant sank a new shaft but did not connect the supply to the bungalow which had now been sold on to the plaintiff. According to Lord Greene MR, the question to be decided was whether a proper construction of the contract, in light of its subject matter and the surrounding circumstances, warranted the inference of an intention that the covenant should be assignable. Applying these criteria, the covenant was manifestly assignable, because otherwise the bungalow, which had no water supply to begin with, would be unable to secure a supply of water after the original covenantee had died or sold on, with resultant adverse consequences for its potential sale value.

---

1   *Shayler v Woolf* [1946] Ch 320.

There must be an interest in the subject-matter of the covenant independently of the covenant

[14.15] There are two particular aspects to this requirement:

(a)   the subject-matter to which the covenant relates must be enjoyed by the party claiming benefit other than *only* through the benefit which the covenant itself confers. In short, the benefit of the covenant must enhance the enjoyment of some property right of the covenantee, either already existing or granted to the covenantee together with the covenant. The covenant cannot be the sole source of the benefit;

(b)   the party claiming the benefit of the covenant must actually have an interest in that which the covenant is intended to benefit. This most often arises as an issue either where the party suing on the covenant has no interest in the hereditament benefited by the covenant[1] or in a case where land has been transferred from the covenantee to the covenantor and the covenantor covenants to undertake some positive act on other land owned by the covenantee, who then transfers that other land to someone else who purports to claim the benefit of the covenant.

---

1   This is the situation disclosed in the facts of *Austerberry v Corporation of Oldham* (1885) 29 ChD 750, discussed further under the rubric that the covenant must touch and concern the land of the covenantee, see para **[14.19]**.

[14.16] In *Fitzgerald v Sylver*[1] the defendant was a lessee of lands, on which there was a storehouse, in Gort, Co Galway. He had covenanted with his lessor to erect a storehouse on other lands of the lessor to substitute for the one being demised. The lessor subsequently assigned these other lands to the plaintiff who sued the defendant on foot of the covenant. Sullivan P and O'Byrne J held that this scenario was governed by the principles enunciated in *Spencer's Case*,[2] to the extent that the benefit of a covenant affecting leasehold property was only enforceable if it 'touched and concerned' the land the subject of the lease between the original contracting parties, and that, since this was a covenant to build on land not included in the original letting, it did not run with the reversion.[3]

---

1   *Fitzgerald v Sylver* (1928) 62 ILTR 51.
2   *Spencer's Case* (1583) 5 Co Rep 16a.
3   The decision of the High Court in this case has been criticised by both Wylie in *Irish Land Law* (3rd edn, 1997) Butterworths, p 944 and by Coughlan in *Property Law* (2nd edn, 1998) Gill and Macmillan, p 267, on the basis that it was open to the court to have found the covenant enforceable against the lessee under the Landlord and Tenant Law Amendment, Ireland, Act

1860, s 12. Section 1 of this statute defines a 'landlord' as including anyone entitled to the estate or interest of the original landlord 'under any Lease or other Contract of Tenancy' and 'whether he has a Reversion or not.' The case is here being considered solely in illustration of the proposition that underlay the summarily reported judgment of the High Court. See also Bready, 'Covenants Affecting Land' (1944) 6 NILQ 48, who expressed himself at 51, 'amazed on reading the report in *Fitzgerald v Sylver*' that no attempt appeared to have been made to bring the plaintiff within the Landlord and Tenant Law Amendment, Ireland, Act 1860, s 12.

[14.17] Where the covenantee is not the party primarily intended to be benefited by the covenant, and there is a fiduciary relationship between the covenantee and the party intended to be so benefited, such party can sue to enforce the covenant in his own name. This is not on the basis that the benefit of the covenant runs with the land, but derives from an equity arising in favour of the third party who is effectively in the role of a *cestui que trust*.

In *Walsh v Walsh*[1] the father of both the plaintiff and the defendant granted lands by deed to the defendant on the defendant's marriage. The plaintiff also lived on these lands The deed contained a covenant by the defendant that, in the event of any disagreement between the plaintiff and the defendant which would result in the plaintiff's having to vacate that part of the lands being assigned as he actually occupied at the date of the deed, the defendant would pay a specific sum in compensation to the plaintiff. When, after the death of the grantor-covenantee, the feared dispute took place and the plaintiff was dispossessed, Barton J held that the plaintiff was entitled to take an action on his own account for the designated compensation. Barton J, acknowledging the common law rule that a person not party to the deed could not sue on his own account, held that the court, exercising its equitable jurisdiction, could enable a third party to claim where the terms of the covenant put that third party in the position of a *cestui que trust*.

Kelly v Larkin and Carter is to like effect.[2] The brother of the plaintiff, by deed in September 1887, assigned his leasehold interest in lands to Susan Carter, her heirs, successors, assigns and administrators, subject to a covenant to pay half the annual profit rent to the plaintiff. Susan Carter died in April 1892 having bequeathed the property to the defendants as joint tenants. Andrews J, finding in favour of the plaintiff, held that the common law rule that a stranger could not sue on a covenant was subject to an exception in equity that, where the covenantee stood in a fiduciary relationship to the party intended to be benefited, thereby rendering that party a *cestui que trust*, that party was entitled to sue upon the covenant. Nor was it necessary that the original covenantee have been requested to institute proceedings and have refused: even if the covenantee himself had taken an action, it would have been his immediate duty to hand over the money to the party whom the covenant meant to benefit. Accordingly, that party was entitled to proceed in his own right.

---

[1]   *Walsh v Walsh* (1900) 1 NIJR 53.
[2]   *Kelly v Larkin and Carter* [1910] 2 IR 550.

[14.18] It is interesting to note, that in neither *Walsh v Walsh*[1] or *Kelly v Larkin and Carter*[2] was judgment given with reference to s 5 of the Real Property Act 1845, which enables a person entitled to the benefit of a covenant under an indenture executed after 1 October 1845 to enforce the covenant, even though such person has not been named as a party to the indenture.[3]

---

[1]   *Walsh v Walsh* (1900) 1 NIJR 53.

[2]   *Kelly v Larkin and Carter* [1910] 2 IR 550.

[3]   Yet another example of the tendency of the courts to resort to the comparative comfort of an established common law rule, rather than to apply the specific provisions of a statute. See para **[15.11]**.

The covenant must touch and concern the land or interest to which it relates

[14.19] In *Gaw v Coras Iompair Éireann*[1] Dixon J quoted with approval from the judgment of Cotton LJ in *Austerberry v Corporation of Oldham*:[2]

> 'In order that the benefit may run with the land, the covenant must be one which relates to or touches and concerns the land of the covenantee.'[3]

In *Austerberry v Corporation of Oldham* the owner of lands had granted a site to trustees for the construction of a road. The trustees covenanted with the landowner, his successors and assigns, that they, the trustees, and their heirs and assigns, would maintain the road constructed on the site and keep it in repair and charge a toll for its use by the public. This road was bounded by lands owned by the landowner who subsequently sold them to the plaintiff, who then sought to enforce the covenant for repair against the defendants, to whom the trustees had sold the road. Both parties had taken their respective lands with notice of the covenant to repair.

The Court of Appeal held that neither the benefit nor the burden of the covenant was enforceable by or against the respective successors to the original covenanting parties. The burden could not be enforced against the defendants, despite their taking with notice of it, because it was a positive rather than a restrictive covenant, and so did not come within the equitable principles established by *Tulk v Moxhay*[4] for the enforceability of the burden of a restrictive covenant against a successor of the covenantor.

The benefit of the covenant was held not to run because it did not touch and concern the land of the covenantee. In the opinion of Cotton LJ, this covenant did not affect the land of the covenantee at all, and seemed on its face more intended to benefit the public for whom the construction of the road had originally been undertaken. Lindley LJ noted that there might have been some prospect of the covenant to repair being held to touch and concern the covenantee's land if it had been stated as applying particularly to that part of the covenantee's land adjacent to the site on which the road had been built.

In *Smith and Snipes Hall Farm Ltd v River Douglas Catchment Board*,[5] Tucker LJ elaborated the need, for the benefit of a positive covenant to run with the land which it benefits, to 'touch and concern' that land, as also requiring that:

> '… it must either affect the land as regards mode of occupation, or it must be such as *per se*, and not merely from collateral circumstances, affects the value of the land, and it must then be shown that it was the intention of the parties that the benefit thereof should run with the land.'[6]

In the same case, Denning LJ noted that one of the historical justifications for the common law deeming the assignee of a covenantee entitled to enforce the benefit of a covenant which touched and concerned his land, was that otherwise the covenantor could breach his covenant with impunity, since the original covenantee, after having disposed of the lands to which the covenant related, would recover very little damages for its breach.[7]

---

1   *Gaw v Coras Iompair Éireann* (1952) 89 ILTR 124.
2   *Austerberry v Corporation of Oldham* (1885) 29 ChD 750.
3   (1885) 29 ChD 750 at 776; (1952) 89 ILTR 124 at 136; also quoted with approval by Kenny J in *Lyle v Smith* [1909] 2 IR 58 at 86.
4   *Tulk v Moxhay* (1848) 2 Ph 774 to be further considered in ch 16.
5   *Smith and Snipes Hall Farm Ltd v River Douglas Catchment Board* [1949] 2 KB 500.
6   [1949] 2 KB 500 at 506, adapted from the judgments of Bayley J in *Congleton Corpn v Pattison* (1808) 10 East 130 and Farwell J in *Rogers v Hosegood* [1900] 2 Ch 388. Delany in 'Restrictive Covenants – Some Basic Principles' (1957) 23 Ir Jur 1 suggested at 2, that the concept of a covenant's touching and concerning the land 'in this sense is one which, if the lands had been leaseholds, would have affected the landlord *qua* landlord, or the tenant *qua* tenant.'
7   This also is one of the reasons why the common law held that for a successor of a covenantee to sue on the benefit of a covenant, he had to be in the same estate as the original covenantee.

[14.20] The courts in Ireland have been similarly stalwart in maintaining, that for a covenant to 'touch and concern' the land of the covenantee, its connection with that land must be more than of a superficial or incidental kind. Unfortunately, however, such pronouncements are most frequently made in the context of covenants affecting land under lease, to which the provisions of ss 12 and 13 of the Landlord and Tenant Law Amendment, Ireland, Act 1860[1] would grant an easier and readier resolution, if the courts would only apply them.

---

1   Otherwise and more popularly known as Deasy's Act. See para **[15.12]** ff.

[14.21] In *Athol v Midland Great Western Railway Co*[1] a lessor demised lands that included an iron foundry. The lessor covenanted with its lessees to permit them,

> 'to make use of the overfall and conduit made and erected for conveying the waste and superfluous water, if any … and to take, use, and enjoy such waste and superfluous water (if any there shall be) for their own use.'

In an action by the plaintiff, who was the successor of the lessee-covenantees, against the successor of the lessor-covenantor, for breach of covenant by the diverting of the water, Whiteside CJ held that the making of a cut above the point from which the water was accustomed to feed the plaintiff's iron foundry was in breach of covenant, and that, furthermore, this covenant ran with the land, since 'the use of the water was a use essentially connected with the very thing demised'; that the covenants concerning the use of the water, including reciprocal covenants by the lessee about the repairing of the drains and not interfering with the flow of the water, all tended to demonstrate that the use of the water 'was a use essentially connected and enjoyed with the premises demised, and that the covenants relating thereto run with the land.' It was, in addition, a relevant consideration that the continued enforceability of the covenant would materially affect the overall value of the land at the end of the term of the lease.[2]

---

1   *Athol v Midland Great Western Railway Co* (1868) IR 3 CL 333.

2   'These circumstances relate directly to the demised premises, to the mode of their occupation and enjoyment, and to things in existence, parcel of the demised premises, and therefore run with the land, and bind the assignee of the reversion at the suit of the assignee of the lessee.'(1868) IR 3 CL 333 at 343. See also Wylie, 'Contracts and Third Parties' (1966) 17 NILQ 358, and his discussion of the 'value preserving characteristic' in relation to covenants in leases at 359 ff.

[14.22] The Chief Justice, in the *Athol* case, did not differentiate between the running of the benefit and of the burden of the covenant, and, indeed, it is clear from his judgment that both the benefit and the burden must be held to have run for the plaintiff to have been able to sustain his action and for the defendant to be liable. However, at a later point, Whiteside CJ observed, *obiter*, that he had doubt as to whether 'there is authority for saying that the burthen of a covenant will run with the land in any case, except that of landlord and tenant'.[1] Accordingly, although the Landlord and Tenant Law Amendment, Ireland, Act 1860 was not invoked to decide the case,[2] it is clear that Whiteside CJ would have had to devote more attention to the issue of the running of the *burden* of the covenant specifically, if the case had involved a freehold rather than a leasehold interest.

---

1   *Athol v Midland Great Western Railway Co* (1868) IR 3 CL 333 at 344.

2   Which it could have been, since the assignee of the lessee would have been entitled to enforce a covenant 'concerning the Lands' against the assignee of the reversion, under s 13. See also Bready 'Covenants Affecting Land' (1944) 6 NILQ 48 at 50–51; Wylie 'Contracts and Third Parties' (1966) 17 NILQ 358 at 360, fn 46.

[14.23] The case of *Lyle v Smith*[1] established that, while the connection between the covenant and its subject-matter must be close for the covenant to 'touch and concern' it, there is no need for the covenant immediately or only to affect the covenantee's property, provided it is bound up with its protection or continued survival.

The plaintiff was a lessor of a house and lands at Ballyholme in Co Down. This house was one of a row of seven whose front gardens abutted upon a road on the far side of which lay the sea. The predecessor of the plaintiff had built a seawall on the far side of the road in order to protect the road and the houses from encroachment by the sea. The defendant was the assignee of a lease of one particular property. This lease contained a covenant by the lessee to contribute proportionately to the cost of maintaining the seawall. In November 1905 there had been heavy storms which occasioned breaches in the wall, with the result that the plaintiff had had to repair it. The plaintiff sought a contribution from the defendant towards the cost of repairing the wall in accordance with the covenant. The defendant maintained that the covenant to contribute to the cost of the repairs was collateral, did not run with the land, and so was not binding on him.

Accordingly, although the issue in this case was the running of the burden of the covenant, rather than the benefit, the consideration by the Court of King's Bench of whether the covenant 'touched and concerned' the seawall is equally pertinent to the possible running of the benefit.[2] The court was unanimously of the view that the covenant to contribute to the cost of maintaining the seawall satisfied the old common law requirement that it should 'touch and concern' the property it was intended to benefit.

According to Lord O'Brien LCJ:

'... though the thing to be done is not upon parcel, nor intended to become parcel, of the subject-matter demised, yet if the thing to be done is clearly for the benefit, support, and maintenance of the subject-matter demised, the obligation to do it runs with the land.'[3]

According to Madden J, the covenant was bound up with the actual preservation of the subject-matter of the lease and, hence, touched and concerned it in a more direct way than covenants affecting the mode of user of the demised premises which, he noted, had always been held to run with the land.

---

1   *Lyle v Smith* [1909] 2 IR 58.
2   A considerable portion of the arguments before the Court of King's Bench centred on the application of the Landlord and Tenant Law Amendment, Ireland, Act 1860, s 12, and on whether the original covenantee would need to have retained an interest in the reversion in order to maintain an action on the covenant. In this context the case is further considered in ch 15.
3   [1909] 2 IR 58 at 65.

[14.24] The English Court of Appeal has held in *Smith and Snipes Hall Farm Ltd v River Douglas Catchment Board*[1] that it is not necessary, in order for the benefit of a positive covenant to run with the land of the covenantee, and be enforceable by the covenantee's assignee, that the covenantor is the owner of land also affected by the covenant. The defendant catchment board had covenanted with the owners of lands along the banks of the River Douglas that, subject to the payment of a contribution by the landowners, it would replace a defective outfall, widen and deepen the banks of portion of the river, and then maintain the work in perpetuity. One of the covenantees sold her lands to the plaintiff who sought to enforce the covenant when the river burst its banks and flooded his lands. The Court of Appeal held that:

(a)   the benefit of the covenant did not cease to be enforceable merely because the successor of the covenantee had no interest in the land at the time the covenant was entered into;[2]

(b)   neither did the covenant cease to be enforceable because the covenantor did not have any land of its own: the issue of a 'servient tenement' – land owned by the covenantor – only became relevant if there was a question of the *burden* of the covenant running with land;[3]

(c)   neither was it necessary for the covenantor to have been party to the deed by which the relevant lands had first been conveyed to the covenantees.

---

[1] *Smith and Snipes Hall Farm Ltd v River Douglas Catchment Board* [1949] 2 KB 500.

[2] Inconsistency with this reasonable proposition is another ground on which the decision of the Irish High Court in *Fitzgerald v Sylver* (1928) 62 ILTR 51 can be criticised. See para **[14.16]**.

[3] 'This is a question of the benefit running, and ever since *The Prior's Case* (1368) 1, *Smith's Leading Cases* (10th edn) 55 it has been held that the covenantor is liable because of his covenant given to the owner of the dominant tenement and not because of his relationship to any servient tenement.' [1949] 2 KB 500 at 518, per Denning LJ.

The Running of the Burden

Does not run at common law

[14.25] As has already been noted from the judgment of Dixon J in *Gaw v Coras Iompair Éireann,*[1] the burden of a positive covenant does not run with the land of the covenantor at law. This principle was articulated by the English Court of Appeal in *Haywood v The Brunswick Permanent Benefit Building Society.*[2] Land had been granted by deed to a party who entered into a covenant to repair with the grantor and also covenanted to pay a perpetual rentcharge. The covenantee conveyed his interest to the plaintiff and the covenantor assigned his lands to another party who mortgaged them to the defendant. The action was brought by the plaintiff against the defendant on foot of the covenant to repair. According to Brett LJ, the authorities had established that a covenant to build did not run with the rent in the hands of an assignee.[3] Equally, the enforceability of the burden of a covenant in equity[4] against a purchaser from the covenantor depended on that covenant's being restrictive rather than positive. In order to enforce a positive covenant against a successor of the covenantor, a new equity would have to be created. Brett LJ was not prepared to do this: if the court were to enforce the burden of a positive covenant against a party who had not covenanted, this would have the effect of compelling a landowner to expend money in order to comply with a covenant entered into by his predecessor in title.

This principle was re-affirmed, with slightly different emphasis, by Cotton LJ in *Austerberry v Corporation of Oldham,*[5] a case in which the assignee of the lands of the covenantor took them with notice of a covenant to repair:

> 'A Court of Equity ... will not enforce a covenant not running at law when it is sought to enforce that covenant in such a way as to require the successors in title of the covenantor to spend money, and in that way to undertake a burden upon themselves. The covenantor must not use the property for a purpose inconsistent with the use for which it was originally granted: but in my opinion a Court of Equity does not and ought not to enforce a covenant binding only in equity in such a way as to require the successors of the covenantor himself, they having entered into no covenant, to expend sums of money in accordance with what the original covenantor bound himself to do.'

---

[1] *Gaw v Coras Iompair Éireann* (1952) 89 ILTR 124.

[2] *Haywood v The Brunswick Permanent Benefit Building Society* (1881) 8 QBD 403. See also *London and South Western Railway Co v Gomm* (1882) 20 ChD 562; *London County Council v Allen* [1914] 3 KB 642.

3 Especially *Milnes v Branch* (1816) 5 M & S 411.

4 Following the principle enunciated by Lord Cottenham LC in *Tulk v Moxhay* (1848) 2 Ph 774. See para **[16.02]**.

5 *Austerberry v Corporation of Oldham* (1885) 29 ChD 750 at 773–774, per Cotton LJ.

[14.26] The late nineteenth century cases confirming the non-enforceability of the burden of a positive covenant against an assignee of the land owned by the covenantor were reviewed, and the principle for which they are authority strongly restated, by the House of Lords in *Rhone v Stephens*.[1] This concerned a building which in 1960 had been divided into two separate dwellings, a house and a cottage. At that time the two properties had a common owner. Part of the roof of the house overhung a bedroom in the cottage. The owner of the two properties sold the cottage, while retaining ownership of the house. In the deed of assurance, the vendor covenanted, for himself and his successors in title, with the purchaser of the cottage, to maintain the roof overhanging the bedroom in the cottage in wind and watertight condition. The plaintiffs were the current owners of the cottage on foot of a conveyance which had contained an express assignment of the covenant. The defendant was the successor of the original covenantor and the current owner of the house.

An action by the plaintiffs to enforce the covenant succeeded in the County Court, on the grounds that the maintaining of the roof also benefited the defendant's own property. This decision was overturned both by the Court of Appeal and by the House of Lords, affirming the traditional approach of the common law that the burden of a positive covenant cannot be enforced against an assignee of the lands of the covenantor. Lord Templeman, in the House of Lords, differentiated between a positive covenant and a restrictive covenant, on the basis that the essence of a restrictive covenant is that the purchaser of a property subject to it is buying the property subject to a limitation which deprives the purchaser of certain of the rights inherent in ownership. According to Lord Templeman, the issue is not whether the burden of a restrictive covenant is deemed to run with the land, but, as expressed by Lord Cottenham LC in *Tulk v Morhey*, 'whether a party shall be permitted to use the land in a manner inconsistent with the contract entered into by his vendor, and with notice of which he purchased.'[2] Hence, in the view of Lord Templeman, equity does not contradict the common law by enforcing a restrictive covenant against an assignee of the land of the covenantor, but prevents that person from exercising one of the normal rights of ownership which in fact he never acquired:

> 'Equity cannot compel an owner to comply with a positive covenant entered into by his predecessors in title without flatly contradicting the common law rule that a person cannot be made liable upon a contract unless he was party to it. Enforcement of a positive covenant lies in contract; a positive covenant compels an owner to exercise his rights. Enforcement of a negative covenant lies in property; a negative covenant deprives the owner of a right over property.'[3]

Having reviewed the case law on the running of the burden of a positive covenant, Lord Templeman concluded:

> 'For over 100 years it has been clear and accepted law that equity will enforce negative covenants against freehold land but has no power to enforce positive covenants against

successors in title of the land. To enforce a positive covenant would be to enforce a personal obligation against a person who has not covenanted. To enforce negative covenants is only to treat the land as subject to a restriction.'[4]

---

[1]   *Rhone v Stephens* [1994] 2 WLR 429.
[2]   (1848) 2 Ph 774 at 777–778.
[3]   [1994] 2 WLR 429 at 433. See also Pritchard 'Making Positive Covenants Run' (1973) 37 Conv 194; 'The Rights and Duties to Repair the Subject Matter of a Right of Way (1954) 84 ILTSJ 189, 195.
[4]   [1994] 2 WLR 429 at 435.

Approach of the Irish courts

[14.27] While, as has been shown, the approach of the English courts, to the non-enforceability of the burden of a positive covenant against the assignee of the land of the covenantor, has been endorsed, *obiter*, by Dixon J in *Gaw v Coras Iompair Éireann*,[1] the actual approach of the Irish courts has been less consistent with the adoption of this principle as definitive. To a certain extent the issue has heretofore been somewhat academic in both parts of Ireland, on account of the continuing prevalence of leasehold titles and the greater facility for the running of the benefit and burden against the lands both of the covenantee and the covenantor respectively under the Landlord and Tenant Law Amendment, Ireland, Act 1860.[2]

However, with the prohibition, in the Republic of Ireland, against granting future leaseholds of a dwelling house, contained in the Landlord and Tenant (Ground Rents) (No 1) Act 1978,[3] and the prohibition in Article 30 of The Property (Northern Ireland) Order 1997, against the granting of a lease in a dwelling house for a term of longer than 50 years, an increasing number of domestic properties are now being conveyed in fee simple, so that the issue of the running of the burden of covenants is likely to be of greater significance in the future.

---

[1]   *Gaw v Coras Iompair Éireann* (1952) 89 ILTR 124.
[2]   Specifically Landlord and Tenant (Ground Rents) (No 1) Act 1978, ss 12 and 13, to be considered in ch 15.
[3]   Landlord and Tenant (Ground Rents) (No 1) Act 1978, s 2(1). The prohibition relates to the creation of future ground rents in 'dwellings'. Exempted from the prohibition are the renewal of existing leases, local authority properties and certain types of separate and self-contained flats.

[14.28] Both in *Athol v Midland and Great Western Railway Co*[1] and in *Lyle v Smith*,[2] it was held that the burden of the covenant ran against the land of the covenantor, without exclusive reference to the statutory provisions concerning the running of leasehold covenants. In *Athol*, Whiteside CJ based his decision on the common law requirement that the covenant 'touch and concern' the land; in *Lyle v Smith*, three of the judges gave judgment on common law grounds, with s 12 of Deasy's Act as an alternative ground of decision only, while Madden J gave judgment on the common law principle alone. In each case, it should be noted, there was a degree of reciprocity between the covenantor and the covenantee, thereby establishing a strong connection between the benefit and the burden, which, it is submitted, perhaps in part explains the finding by the courts in each case that the burden of the covenant was enforceable against a successor of the covenantor. In *Athol*, the covenantee, who was entitled to siphon off superfluous water generated by the covenantor, had also covenanted not to interfere with the covenantor's sewage and drains. In *Lyle v Smith* the covenantee had undertaken the responsibility of repairing damages to the sea-wall and the covenantor's covenant was to contribute proportionately to the cost.

---

[1]   *Athol v Midland Great Western Railway Co* (1868) IR 3 CL 333.
[2]   *Lyle v Smith* [1909] 2 IR 58.

Reciprocal covenants

[14.29] The principle of reciprocal enforceability of the benefit and burden of covenants has received limited support from the English courts,[1] particularly from the judgment of Upjohn J in *Halsall v Brizell*.[2] In this, the predecessor in title of the defendants had purchased one of a number of properties fronting an access road, together with a right to the use of the access road and also the sewers, and had covenanted to pay a proportion of the maintenance costs of these facilities. The defendants subsequently refused to pay a contribution to the cost of repair of the road on the basis that the burden of the covenant did not run against them. Upjohn J acknowledged that the burden of a positive covenant did not run, but added 'that it is ancient law that a man cannot take benefit under a deed without subscribing to the obligations thereunder.'[3] In the view of Upjohn J, if the defendants wished to enjoy the benefits granted by the original conveyance, they were obliged also to comply with the burdens which it imposed.

The principle established by *Halsall v Brizell* commended itself to Megarry V-C in *Tito v Waddell (No 2)*[4] who distinguished between cases where the benefit and burden are totally independent of each other and where the enjoyment of the benefit is conditional upon compliance with the burden or where the benefit and burden are annexed to the property.

> 'A burden that has been made a condition of the benefit, or is annexed to the property, simply passes with it: if you take the benefit of the property, you must take it as it stands, with all its appendages, good or bad.'[5]

Megarry V-C also held that, where the burden is to take 'once off' effect sometime in the future, a party who has already enjoyed the related benefit cannot simply cease to accept the benefit and refuse to make good the enjoyment they have derived from it when the obligation to discharge the burden becomes due.[6]

---

[1]   Other than in the case of estates of development, where a scheme of covenants intended to be mutually enforceable among all the purchasers has been established by the developer, to which equity has supplied special principles for enforcement: considered in ch 17.
[2]   *Halsall v Brizell* [1957] Ch 169.
[3]   [1957] Ch 169 at 182.
[4]   *Tito v Waddell (No 2)* [1977] Ch 106.
[5]   [1977] Ch 106 at 302.

⁶ The decisions in *Halsall v Brizell* and *Tito v Waddell (No 2)* have received some favourable academic commentary: Garner 'Restrictive Covenants Restated' (1962) 26 Conv 298; Aughterson 'Enforcement of Positive Burdens' [1985] Conv 12; Dowling 'Your Deed Not Mine: Unilateral Execution of Multipartite Deeds' (1997) 48 NILQ 264. However, the possible danger of offending the rule against perpetuities cannot be disregarded: Delany 'Restrictive Covenants – Some Basic Principles' (1957) 23 Ir Jur 1 at 4, Aughterson [1985] Conv 12 at 22.

[14.30] In *Rhone v Stephens*[1] Lord Templeman sounded a note of caution in terms of the possible corollary of the principles established in *Halsall v Brizell* and *Tito v Waddell (No 2)*.[3] According to Lord Templeman, in *Halsall v Brizell*[2] the defendants had had the option not to enjoy the right of access to the road and the sewers and not to pay the costs of contribution to their upkeep. If the defendants had not wished to benefit from the services, then a covenant to contribute towards their maintenance should not have been enforced against them in any case. In *Rhone v Stephens*, even though the owner of the cottage had covenanted that the adjacent house could continue to be supported by the cottage, according to Lord Templeman this was wholly independent of the covenant by the owner of the house to maintain the roof. Lord Templeman warned:

> 'It does not follow that any condition can be rendered enforceable by attaching it to a right nor does it follow that every burden imposed by a conveyance may be enforced by depriving the covenantor's successor in title of every benefit which he enjoyed thereunder. The condition must be relevant to the exercise of the right.'[4]

---

1 *Rhone v Stephens* [1994] 2 WLR 429.
2 *Halsall v Brizell* [1957] Ch 169.
3 *Tito v Waddell (No 2)* [1977] Ch 106.
4 [1994] 2 WLR 429 at 437.

Can the burden of a positive covenant be made to run?

[14.31] There is, arguably, a lack of logic in the bare assertion that the benefit of a positive covenant should be enforceable by an assignee of the lands of the covenantee, while the burden of a positive covenant cannot be enforced against an assignee of the lands of the covenantor. In many cases a cogent factor must be the absence of certainty as to whether a particular covenant is, in effect, intended to be personal to the covenantor or is designed to bind the lands owned by the covenantor.[1] In many cases too, a covenant to repair, maintain, build or carry out works is, by its nature, more likely to be a covenant personal to the party undertaking it than a covenant to maintain property, or part of it, in a particular condition. But this is not invariably the case, nor need it be so.

A purchaser for value without notice of a covenant binding only in equity cannot, in any event, be compelled to comply with that covenant. Therefore, it should not be relevant whether the covenant is restrictive, or whether it involves a positive act or the expenditure of money, provided that it is uniquely linked to a particular property and is known to a purchaser of that property. The common causes of logic, good sense and consistency warrant making enforceable, against a successor to the lands of the covenantor, a covenant entered into by that covenantor which, insofar as concerns its benefit complies with the requirements for the running of the benefit; and is furthermore intended to bind the lands of the covenantor, which it directly affects; when the successor of the covenantor takes with notice of the covenant.

---

[1] On the question of whether a covenant can be construed as personal to a covenantor or may on its terms also affect other parties, see *Costello v Brice and McGinfsey* (1932) 66 ILTR 146; *Tophams Ltd v Earl of Sefton* [1967] 1 AC 50; *Williams and Co Ltd v LSD and Quinnsworth* (19 June 1970, unreported) HC; *Northern Ireland Carriers Ltd v Larne Harbour Ltd* [1981] NI 171.

[14.32] In the alternative, the only way to ensure that the burden of a positive covenant does not continue to bind the covenantor even after he has disposed of any land affected by it, is to insist on each subsequent purchaser entering into an indemnity with his vendor regarding liability under the covenant. This means that, in order for the burden of the covenant to follow the ownership of the related property, for as many times as the property is transferred from one party to another, the transferee must enter into an indemnity covenant with the transferor. A failure by any one party in the succession of ownership changes to insist on a covenant of indemnity will result in liability under the original covenant remaining with that party. As a mechanism for ensuring that the burden of a covenant passes as the land passes, the chain of indemnities is both cumbrous and unsatisfactory.

[14.33] An additional reason for the desirability of being able to enforce, without recourse to complex legal machinery, the burden of covenants affecting freehold land against successors of the covenantor, is the extent to which, from the 1960s onwards, freehold interests have been granted in premises, both residential (as in the case of flats, apartments and town houses) and commercial (as in the case of serviced office units in a single building), which form part of a multiple or larger unit, dependent for their support, access to services and continuity of maintenance on other premises above, below and beside them.[1] Otherwise, the problem might be conveniently ignored as an occasional irritant, buffeted by the traditional, but now diminishing, high incidence of transactions involving properties under lease.

---

[1] Bodkin 'Rights of Support for Buildings and Flats' (1962) 26 Conv 210; Bell 'Enforcement of Positive Covenants in Trinidad and Tobago' [1983] Conv 211.

The Property (Northern Ireland) Order 1997

[14.34] Article 34 of the Property (Northern Ireland) Order 1997, which came into effect on 10 January 2000,[1] specifically 'replaces the rules of common law and equity relating to the enforceability between the owners of estates in fee simple of covenants burdening or benefiting such estates', by statutorily rendering enforceable between successors of covenanting parties a panoply of covenants that were hitherto unenforceable by or against them.[2]

It should be noted that covenants contained in deeds, or resulting from obligations, entered into prior to the coming into effect of the order are exempt from its provisions, as are covenants for title and covenants *stated to be personal to the covenantor*.[3] Article 34 applies to covenants affecting freehold land only.

---

[1] Under Property (1997 Order) (Commencement No 2) Order (Northern Ireland) 1999 (SR 1999 No 461).

[2] Article 34(1).

[3] Article 34(2). Emphasis supplied.

[14.35] Article 34 of the Property (Northern Ireland) Order 1997 specifically covers both restrictive covenants[1] and a range of positive covenants, including:

    (i)   covenants to maintain party walls, fences and boundaries;[2]

    (ii)   covenants to carry out work on, or contribute financially to the carrying out of work on, 'the land of the covenantor for the benefit of land of the covenantee or other land';[3]

    (iii)   covenants to carry out work on, or contribute financially to the carrying out of work on, 'land of the covenantee or other land where the works benefit the land of the covenantor';[4]

    (iv)   covenants to reinstate in the event of damage or destruction;[5]

    (v)   covenants arising in estate schemes.[6]

---

[1] Article 34(4)(e), from which one must infer that the specific rules devised in equity for the running of the burden of restrictive covenants, discussed in ch 16, are also replaced by the provisions of Article 34.

[2] Article 34(4)(a).

[3] Article 34(4)(b).

[4] Article 34(4)(c).

[5] Article 34(4)(f).

[6] Article 34(6) and (7).

[14.36] There is no prohibition on parties affected by the running of covenants agreeing to execute a deed of release.[1] Neither is there a requirement that the covenants have to be registered. The Article also conclusively presumes that the benefit and burden of any covenant are deemed to apply to each and every part of the lands both of the covenantee and the covenantor respectively.[2]

Save in the case of the transfer of membership of a company established for the management of land, a person is not liable to the enforcement of the burden of a covenant against him once he has ceased to be the owner of the land so burdened, unless a breach arose while the former owner was owner of the burdened land.[3] Neither will a person be entitled to seek to enforce the benefit of a covenant after they cease to be owner of benefited land.[4]

1   Article 34(8).
2   Article 34(5). This is doubtless because of the uncertainty evinced in certain English cases whether a covenant is effectively annexed to 'all or every part of land' if words to this effect are not specifically employed in the instrument creating it. See para **[16.28]–[16.30]**.
3   Article 34(4)(f)(ii).
4   Article 34(4)(f)(i).

[14.37] Although the Article does not treat of the precise formality by which a covenant is created, nevertheless, the specific saving from its application of a covenant 'which is expressed to bind only the covenantor', and the absence of any corresponding reference to a covenant personal to the covenantee, begs the inference that once a covenant conforms to the character of a covenant defined as running with the land, the benefit of it will run with the land which it affects regardless of whether the benefit was intended to be personal only to the covenantee. In consequence, while the types of covenant described in Article 34(4) are demonstrably of a kind more calculated to benefit property than an individual, considerable care in drafting will have to be taken by property and conveyancing practitioners in order not to invite consequences, which though consistent with the order, the parties to any particular transaction might not have intended.

The future

[14.38] A possible consequence of the implementation of Article 34 of the Property (Northern Ireland) Order 1997 will be the eventual erosion, through the device of the covenant affecting land, of the traditional strictures imposed by the common law regarding the character and varieties of easements. At the commencement of this chapter it was noted that covenants affecting land had the capacity to create rights of a kind incapable at the moment of constituting easements – such as rights of prospect, percolating water, an extraordinary level of light, and the passage of air. Clearly, many of the strictures applied by the courts in relation to the running of the burden and benefit of covenants derive from a recognition of the wisdom of having a limit on the range of rights which can be created to affect land.

As long ago as 1834, Lord Brougham in *Keppell v Bailey*[1] observed:

> 'But it must not therefore be supposed that incidents of a novel kind can be devised and attached to property at the fancy or caprice of any owner … great detriment would arise and much confusion of rights if parties were allowed to invent new modes of holding and enjoying real property and to impress upon their lands and tenements a peculiar character which should follow them into all hands however remote.'

The ultimate shape of the future of the running of positive covenants even in Northern Ireland remains conjectural. However, the natural analogy of the dominant and servient tenements of an easement with the benefit and burden of covenants affecting land unavoidably suggests a certain course. One certainty which remains is that, in the absence of legislative intervention such as the Property (Northern Ireland) Order 1997 provides, the law in the Republic of Ireland, regarding the running of the burden and benefit of positive covenants, will continue to be troubled, confusing – and *uncertain*.[2]

---

1   *Keppell v Bailey* (1834) 2 My & K 535. See also Peel 'Deserted Wife's Licence and Rights of Residence' (1964) 28 Conv 253.

2   The Report of the Irish Republic's Law Reform Commission: *Land Law and Conveyancing Law: Positive Covenants Over Freehold Land and other proposals* (LRC70–2003) recommends the introduction of a statutory scheme for the running of freehold covenants that affect dominant and servient land, subject to a facility by an interested party to seek to vary or set aside a covenant that has existed for more than 20 years, which unreasonably interferes with the use or enjoyment of land. The report favours the clear statement in the Property (Northern Ireland) Order 1997 that its provisions replace the rules of common law and equity relating to the enforceability of covenants, while it is against the idea of a limited list of covenants that attract statutory protection.

Chapter 15

The Application of Statute to the Running of Covenants

Introduction

[15.01] This chapter might, with some justification, have equally been titled 'the running of leasehold covenants', since the principal thrust of statutory intervention in the realm of covenants has been in the context of the relationship of landlord and tenant. However, as has been shown, in certain cases of leasehold covenants, despite the availability of statutory redress, the courts have tended to resort to the ancient principles of common law whose proper continuing relevance is in the domain of freehold covenants only. Furthermore, the legislation regarding covenants is not confined to the traditional relationship of lessor and lessee for a limited term, but can also apply to fee farm grants, and even to the fee simple estate into which certain leases may be enlarged.

[15.02] The common law principle that only the parties to a contract could sue on foot of that contract was modified in relation to lessors and lessees by the Grantees of Reversions, Ireland, Act 1634[1] which in its preamble recited the then prevailing common law thus:

'... forasmuch by the common law of this realm no stranger to any covenant, action or condition, shall take any advantage or benefit of the same by any means or wayes in the law, but onely such as be parties or privies thereunto...'

Section 1 provides that a lessor and his assignees shall have the like action against the lessee and assignees of the lessee, arising from the breach or non-performance of covenants, agreements and conditions contained in the lease, as the original lessor would have had against the original lessee. Section 2 provides for a similar right by and on behalf of the assignees of a lessee against the original lessor and his assignees, arising from the breach of any covenant, agreement or condition contained in the lease.

The Grantees of Reversions, Ireland, Act 1634 did not remove the requirement for the lessor or his assignee to retain an interest in the reversion.

---

[1]   10 Chas 1 sess 2 c 4 which essentially enacted in Ireland the Grantees of Reversions Act 1540 (32 Hen 8 c34).

[15.03] In 1583 the English Court of Queen's Bench, in *Spencer's Case*,[1] had held that, in order for the benefit and burden of a leasehold covenant to run with the lessee's interest and bind assignees of that interest – so that the assignee of the lessee could both sue the original lessor on foot of a covenant in the lease and be sued on foot of a covenant entered into by the lessee – the covenant in question had to 'touch and concern' the land involved, rather than be merely a collateral covenant or one personal either to the lessee or the lessor. Furthermore, the lessee's assignee had to be in the same estate as the original lessee: an assignee only was affected by the decision in *Spencer's Case*, not a sub-lessee.[2]

This concept of being 'in the same estate' has come to be known as 'privity of estate'. In essence, for privity of estate to exist, the assignee must have the same interest in the land as the person by whom it had been assigned. Furthermore, the assigns of original contracting parties can have privity of estate with each other. For example, if a lessor assigns his interest in the reversion to Carmichael, there will be privity of estate between Carmichael and the lessee; if the lessor retains his interest and the lessee assigns his interest in the lease to Talbot, then there will be privity of estate between the lessor and Talbot; if the lessor assigns his reversion to Carmichael and the lessee his lease to Talbot, then there will be privity of estate between Carmichael and Talbot. A sub-lessee is not in the same estate as a lessee, so that there can be no privity of estate between a sub-lessee and a head-lessor.

---

[1] *Spencer's Case* (1583) 5 Co Rep 16a.
[2] See Bready 'Covenants Affecting Land' (1944) 6 NILQ 48 at 48–49, Wylie 'Contracts and Third Parties' (1966) 17 NILQ 351 at 358.

[15.04] The principal effect of *Spencer's Case*[1] was to interpret the Grantees of Reversions, Ireland, Act 1634 as preserving the enforceability of covenants between the assigns both of the lessor and the lessee, provided that any such covenant must 'touch and concern' the land involved.

---

[1] *Spencer's Case* (1583) 5 Co Rep 16a.

Renewable Leasehold Conversion Act 1849

[15.05] The Renewable Leasehold Conversion Act 1849,[1] which came into effect on 1 August 1849, made it possible for a lessee holding under a lease for lives renewable forever to compel his lessor to convert the lease for lives into a fee farm grant. This is a fee simple estate subject to a perpetual rent, but without a reversion. Sections 20 and 21 provided a mechanism for the former lessor, and also his assignees, to sue for the recovery of the fee farm rent. The Fee Farm Rents (Ireland) Act 1851[2] extended this remedy to other grants reserving a rent (such as a perpetual rentcharge) where the grantor did not retain a reversion.

---

[1] 12 & 13 Vict c 105. Repealed by the Property (Northern Ireland) Order 1997.
[2] 14 & 15 Vict c 20. Repealed by he Property (Northern Ireland) Order 1997.

Covenant to set off expenses against rent will not run

[15.06] Where the original fee farm grantor had entered into a covenant with the fee farm grantee to allow an abatement of, or set off against, the fee farm rent in certain cases, an assignee of the covenantor's right to receive the rent (to whom the reversion has not been assigned), is not liable on the covenant in favour of the fee farm grantee, since the burden of a covenant does not run against a right to receive the rent only: *Butler v Archer*.[1] In this case, the plaintiff was the assignee of a rentcharge reserved under a fee farm grant of 2 April 1852 between his predecessor, the fee farm grantor, and the defendant, the fee farm grantee. The original fee farm grant had included a covenant by the defendant fee farm grantee to construct a suitable dwellinghouse within seven years, and also a covenant by the fee farm grantor, on behalf of himself, his heirs and assigns, to allow to be deducted from the fee farm rent the price of slates and timber for the roofing. The defendant fee farm grantee duly built the house within seven years and incurred expense in the slating and roofing. The monies expended had not been allowed from the rent when the plaintiff took the assignment of the rentcharge with notice of the covenant. In an action by the plaintiff for recovery of arrears of rent, the defendant urged that the cost of the roofing and slating should be allowed against it.

---

1   *Butler v Archer* (1860) 12 ICLR 104.

[15.07] A majority of the Court of Queen's Bench held that the Fee Farm Rents (Ireland) Act 1851 could not be construed so as to render an assignee of the rent *only*, when seeking to recover arrears of the rent, open to suit on a covenant entered into by the original fee farm grantor, upon which, at common law, the original fee farm grantor alone would have been liable.

Lefroy CJ distinguished, in the context of the enforceability of a covenant attaching to them respectively, between a reversion and a right to the rent:

> 'Now a reversion, which, although a mere ideal thing, yet has this quality of land attaching to it; for, by its very definition, it is that estate in the land which reverts or returns to the grantor upon the determination of the particular estate. But a fee-farm rent has none of these attributes; nor is there anything in its nature consistent with the notion of its being attached, in any manner, to the land.'[1]

In the opinion of Lefroy CJ, it was clear from the recitals to both the Grantees of Reversions, Ireland, Act 1634 and its English progenitor of 1540, that at common law an assignee of the reversion had no action on the covenant against the lessee because there was no privity of contract between them. Similarly, the assignee of a rentcharge had no entitlement to the recovery of the rent, in cases other than converted fee farm grants under the Renewable Leasehold Conversion Act 1849, until the enactment of the Fee Farm Rents (Ireland) Act 1851. Accordingly, the Chief Justice was of the view that if the legislature had intended the fee farm grantee to be able to enforce a right against an assignee of the rentcharge, it would need to have done so by express enactment.[2]

---

1   (1860) 12 ICLR 104 at 126.

2   The cautionary note sounded by Lefroy CJ on the limits of legitimate statutory interpretation is one of which modern practitioners could usefully be aware: 'The function of a Court of Law is

only to construe Acts of Parliament, not to add to them. ... It is, no doubt, very desirable that, in construing Acts of Parliament, our decisions should be, as far as possible, in accordance with common sense, and broad principles of justice ... but, on the other hand, we must remember that we cannot, without plain words or necessary implication, carry the operation of an Act of Parliament beyond what the Legislature have expressed in the Act itself. When cases of injustice or hardship result from the operation of an Act of Parliament, it is for the Legislature to remedy the mischief.' (1860) 12 ICLR 104 at 128–129.

Preservation of all covenants in a lease for lives converted except for those interfering with cultivation

[15.08] Under s 10 of the Renewable Leasehold Conversion Act 1849, where a lease for lives renewable forever is enlarged into a fee farm grant, any covenant which is 'of such a Nature as that the Burden thereof doth by Law run with the Land' will continue to be enforceable against the estate into which the lease for lives has been converted; and, in relation to the interest retained by the covenantee, 'the benefit of such Covenants shall run with the Estate into which such Estate is converted under this Act and the Owner or Assignee for the Time being of the Estate created by such Conversion shall have the full Benefit of such Covenants, and be entitled to maintain Actions thereon.'[1] This is so even where the covenant has not been complied with for some considerable time.[2] Neither is s 10 constrained by the doctrine of privity of estate: covenants in a head-lease are capable of being enforced by and against a sub-lessor if the sub-lease is a lease for lives converted into a fee farm grant.

---

[1]   On the possible use of the Renewable Leasehold Conversion Act 1849, s 10 to make the burden of a covenant run with the fee simple into which the lease for lives renewable forever has been enlarged, see Lyall 'Freehold Covenants and What to Do With Them' (1991) 9 ILT (NS) 157 at 160; also Lyall *Land Law in Ireland* (2nd edn, 2000) Sweet & Maxwell. However, it must be borne in mind that a ground rent can no longer be created in respect of a 'dwelling' under the Landlord and Tenant (Ground Rents) (No 1) Act 1978, s 2(1), and, should an existing fee farm rent fall within the definition of a ground rent, under the Landlord and Tenant (Ground Rents) (No 2) Act 1978, ss 9 and 10, the fee simple can be acquired freed from the rent and the covenants – ss 28 and 78. See para **[18.11]**.

[2]   In *Smyth v Shaftesbury* (1900) 1 NIJR 34 a covenant in a lease for lives renewable forever of 1825 to plant fences and trees, which had never been complied with since the grant of the lease in 1825, was held by Chatterton V-C not to be 'obsolete' and to have been preserved upon the enlargement of the lease for lives into a fee farm grant.

[15.09] Section 3 of the Renewable Leasehold Conversion Act 1849 provides that a lessee holding under a lease for lives, who acquires a fee farm grant, in a case where 'any Right under Covenant or otherwise annexed or belonging to the Reversion or Estate from the Owner of which a Grant is required, interferes with the proper Cultivation of the Lands comprised in such Lease or Under-lease', may require that the particular right under covenant should cease; the fee farm rent is then increased by an amount equal to the value of the covenanted right – in short, the covenantee is to be compensated.

[15.10] In *Re McNaul's Estate*[1] it was held that – except in cases where the covenant had been discharged under s 3 – even a covenant which would have been repugnant, if sought *ab initio* to be attached to a fee simple, but was not repugnant in a lease, will continue to be enforceable against the fee farm grant into which a lease for lives renewable for ever is converted. A lease for lives of 1763, subsequently converted into a fee farm grant, had contained a covenant that, if the grantee disposed of the property to anyone other than a linear descendent of his own, without the consent of the grantor, an additional rent should be reserved.[2]

In the opinion of Fitzgibbon LJ:

> '...the doctrine of repugnancy applicable at common law to an estate in fee is modified, in the case of fee-farm grants founded on renewable leases, by whatever obligations are lawfully inserted in the grants. The object of the Act was to give a perpetual estate in fee, but was an estate created under the statute, which was to remain subject to all covenants and conditions which had bound the previous leasehold estate, save so far as they were got rid of in the manner provided by the Act.'[3]

Holmes LJ explained that a lease for lives with a covenant for perpetual renewal had been a form of tenure peculiar to Ireland, which in large part owed its origin to a desire to attach to the closest legal equivalent to a perpetual freehold the terms, conditions, and covenants to which leaseholds could legally be made subject:

> 'The political history of the country, taken in connexion with the peculiar tenure and the comparatively moderate amount of the rent and fines, suggests that in making these leases the lessors were not influenced solely by pecuniary considerations; and it was natural for them to secure, as far as possible, that the holdings should remain in the hands of friendly tenants.'[4]

According to Holmes LJ, this had been the purpose of the covenant in the original lease for lives, and it was preserved upon enlargement into a fee farm grant.[5]

---

1   *Re McNaul's Estate* [1902] 1 IR 114.
2   The Statute of Westminster III 1290 (18 Ed 1), otherwise known as the Statute of Quia Emptores, provided that a fee simple estate should be freely alienable.
3   [1902] 1 IR 114 at 124–125.
4   [1902] 1 IR 114 at 136.
5   With the result that, even though there had not been an alienation outside the category of persons limited by the covenant, the value of the covenant's possibly taking effect in the future had to be considered in order to determine the enhanced value of the fee farm rent upon a sale of the fee simple under the Land Purchase Acts.

Real Property Act 1845

[15.11] At common law only a party to a deed can sue to enforce the benefit of a covenant created by that deed. This was changed by s 5 of the Real Property Act 1845,[1] which provides that, in respect of an indenture executed after 1 October 1845, a person intended as a covenantee is entitled to enforce the benefit of a covenant 'respecting any Tenements or Hereditaments' created by the indenture, even though such person has not been named as a party to the indenture. There have been suggestions that, in order for a covenant to be enforceable under s 5, it must 'touch and concern' or 'relate to' land.[2] As has been shown, in cases where the covenantee under a deed creating a covenant is in a fiduciary relation to a third party intended to benefit under the covenant, that party is entitled in equity to sue to enforce the covenant.[3]

Section 5 does not purport to increase the range of those entitled to sue on foot of a covenant.[4] It is confined to cases of a deed of indenture, and not a deed poll, and is also limited to an immediate estate created by the indenture. It does not apply, no more than does the common law rule which it modifies, to personalty, to equitable interests, or to future interests.[5]

---

[1] 8 & 9 Vict c 106.
[2] *Monroe and Darley v Plunket* (1888) 23 ILTR 76. See also, *Lloyd v Byrne* (1887) 22 LR Ir 269; *Westhoughton Urban District Council v Wigan Coal and Iron Co Ltd* [1919] 1 Ch 159.
[3] *Walsh v Walsh* (1900) 1 NIJR 53; *Kelly v Larkin and Carter* [1910] 2 IR 550, see ch 14, para **[14.17]**.
[4] *Beswick v Beswick* [1968] AC 58.
[5] *White v Bijou Mansions Ltd* [1937] 1 Ch 610.

Landlord and Tenant Law Amendment, Ireland, Act 1860 ('Deasy's Act')

[15.12] The Landlord and Tenant Law Amendment, Ireland, Act 1860 (popularly known as Deasy's Act)[1] repealed the Grantees of Reversions, Ireland, Act 1634 and founded the relationship of landlord and tenant upon 'the express or implied Contract of the Parties, and not upon Tenure or Service', adding that 'a Reversion shall not be necessary to such Relation, which shall be deemed to subsist in all Cases in which there shall be an Agreement by One Party to hold Land from or under another in consideration of any Rent'.[2]

Section 12 treats of the right of the landlord, his heirs and personal representatives to sue a tenant or his assignee on foot of a covenant:

> 'Every Landlord of any Lands holden under any Lease or other Contract of Tenancy shall have the same Action and Remedy against the Tenant, and the Assignee of his Estate or Interest, or their respective Heirs, Executors or Administrators, in respect of the Agreements contained or implied in such Lease or Contract as the original Landlord might have had against the original Tenant, or his Heir or personal Representative respectively ...'

Section 13 treats of the right of the tenant, his heirs and personal representatives to sue a landlord or his assignee on foot of a covenant:

> 'Every Tenant of any Lands shall have the same Action and Remedy against the Landlord and the Assignee of his Estate or Interest, or their respective Heirs, Executors or Administrators, in respect of the Agreements contained or implied in the Lease or other Contract concerning the Lands, as the original Tenant might have had against the original Landlord, or his Heir or personal Representative respectively...'

The two sections are identical except that s 13 includes the words 'concerning the Lands' after the reference to a lease or contract, thereby inviting inference that the old common law stipulation that the benefit of a covenant must touch and concern the land of the covenantee, in order to be enforceable, still applies to a covenant sought to be enforced by a lessee or his assigns against the current holder of the lessor's estate.

---

[1]   23 & 24 Vict c 154.
[2]   Section 3.

[15.13] Regrettably, the opportunity to determine the true scope of s 13, though it arose in the case of *Borrowes v Delaney*,[1] was not availed of. A lease contained a covenant, that if the term of the lease ran its full course, a sum of £40 paid by the lessee at its commencement would be deemed to be in satisfaction of the final half year's rent. The plaintiff was the original lessor and the defendant an assignee of the lessee. It was held that the defendant was entitled to rely on the benefit of the covenant, without reference to Deasy's Act. The closest Andrews J came to alluding to s 13 was where he observed:

> 'With respect to the point that the covenant in question does not run with the land, even assuming that it does not (which I by no means decide), I think the defendant, as assignee of the lease, is entitled to the right which was incident to the tenancy by virtue of the covenant when he became assignee...'[2]

Despite its obliquity, this observation has been construed by some commentators as confirming that s 13 enables an assignee of the lessee enforce against the lessor a covenant which would not have run against the land under the common law rules.[3]

---

[1]   *Borrowes v Delaney* (1889) 24 LR Ir 503.
[2]   (1889) 24 LR Ir 503 at 517.
[3]   Bready 'Covenants Affecting Land' (1944) 6 NILQ 48 at 50; Wylie 'Contracts and Third Parties' (1966) 17 NILQ 351 at 360. However, Bready also notes of the judgment of Andrews J that 'he did not decide that the covenant in question was not one of those which runs with the land at common law.'

[15.14] Section 14 of Deasy's Act provides that the assignee of either landlord or tenant shall only be entitled to the benefit, or liable to the burden, as the case may be, of any covenant while they are an assignee, the entitlement, or liability, passing once the interest has been further assigned; except that the liability of a tenant in relation to his landlord can only be discharged following the giving of written notice by the tenant to the landlord of the particulars of the assignment.

[15.15] The application of s 12 of Deasy's Act fell to be considered by the Court of King's Bench in *Lyle v Smith*.[1] This involved an action by a lessor against an assignee of the lessee on foot of a covenant to contribute financially to the maintenance of a protective sea wall fronting a number of houses in Co Down, of which the assignee's holding was one.

Counsel for the plaintiff lessor had urged that s 12 operated to render enforceable other covenants than those which ran with land, including collateral covenants. Unfortunately, this interesting argument did not receive its due definitive consideration by the court, since each of the judges held that the covenant was one which, by its nature, touched and concerned, and so ran with, the land at common law.

---

[1]   *Lyle v Smith* [1909] 2 IR 58, see ch 14, para **[14.23]** and **[14.28]**.

[15.16] Even so, the extent to which the pre-existing law had been changed by Deasy's Act was noted by at least some of the judges in the case. Lord O'Brien LCJ evinced support for the view expressed by Lord Hatherley in *Liddy v Kennedy*,[1] that s 12 was designed to redress in Ireland some of the limitations of the Grantees of Reversions Act 1634, and that the relationship of landlord and tenant now depended on contract and not a reversion. As a result of this statutory stripping away of the old technicalities that too often had got in the way of fairness, the parties to a lease or tenancy were enabled to give proper effect to the true meaning of the contract into which they had entered.[2] Adopting these sentiments, Lord O'Brien LCJ observed that the principal effect of Deasy's Act had been to rescue the relationship of landlord and tenant from the constraints of tenure and 'privity of estate', and to render the liability of both lessor and lessee and their respective assigns, to the enforcement of covenants, subject to the contractual terms expressed in the lease or tenancy.[3]

In the opinion of Gibson J, Deasy's Act finally freed the principles governing leasehold covenants from the shackles of *Spencer's Case*,[4] leaving them instead to be determined by the principles of contract law.[5]

---

[1]   *Liddy v Kennedy* (1871) LR 5 HL 134.
[2]   (1871) LR 5 HL 134 at 143.
[3]   *Lyle v Smith* [1909] 2 IR 58 at 71. Also, Bready 'Covenants Affecting Land' (1944) 6 NILQ 48 at pp 57, 58; Delany 'Restrictive Covenants – Some Basic Principles' (1957) 23 Ir Jur 1 at 5.
[4]   *Spencer's Case* (1583) 5 Co Rep 16a.
[5]   [1909] 2 IR 58 at 76.

[15.17] The obligation by a lessor's successor to comply with the burden of a covenant under s 13 of Deasy's Act cannot be avoided merely because that party no longer has a reversionary interest, due to merger of the affected lease with the freehold: *Whelan v Cork Corporation*.[1] In 1937 a lessee holding under a reversionary lease granted a sub-lease of certain lands in which he covenanted not to erect on specified adjacent lands, also held by him under lease, premises in excess of a height of 12 feet. In 1948 this lessee (the sub-lessor in the sub-lease of 1937) granted to another party a sub-lease of the adjacent lands specified in the covenant in the sub-lease of 1937; this sub-lease of 1948 contained a covenant by the sub-lessee not to erect a premises in excess of a height of 12 feet on the lands demised to him. In 1984 the defendant local authority took an assignment of the sub-lease of 1948, in 1989 an assignment of the head-lease and a week later in 1989 a conveyance of the freehold. The defendant then embarked on the construction of a 'fly-over' road which was clearly in breach of the covenant in the sub-lease of 1948. The plaintiff was the assignee of the sub-lease of 1937.

Murphy J held that the burden of the covenant in the sub-lease of 1937 bound all parties claiming through the sub-lessor, including sub-lessees of the adjacent land subject to the burden.[2] He observed:

'A covenant in respect of the conduct of the person entitled to receive the rent payable under the 1937 underlease by virtue of his having a reversionary interest only in the lands comprised in that lease would be meaningless. Such an interest would not enable him to give a covenant in respect of adjoining lands. The terms of the 1937 underlease are intelligible only on the basis that the lessor had an estate or interest, as he did, which gave him control over a sufficient parcel of land which entitled him first to receive rent issuing out of part of it and secondly to impose burdens on other parts.'[3]

---

[1] *Whelan v Cork Corpn* [1991] ILRM 19.

[2] Following the decisions in *Holloway Brothers v Hill* [1902] 2 Ch 612 and *Ricketts v Churchwardens of the Parish of Enfield* [1909] 1 Ch 544. But see the criticism expressed in Lyall 'Freehold Covenants and What to Do with Them' (1991) 9 ILT (NS) 157 at 158; also Lyall, *Land Law in Ireland* p 665.

[3] [1991] ILRM 19 at 26.

[15.18] However, the extent to which *Whelan v Cork Corpn*[1] is an authority in relation to s 13 of Deasy's Act is diminished by Murphy J's holding, on the one hand, that the case primarily involved a restrictive covenant to which the equitable principles enunciated by *Tulk v Moxhay*[2] applied, and, on the other hand, that the covenant had been extinguished on the acquisition by the defendant of the fee simple under s 28 of the Landlord and Tenant (Ground Rents) (No 2) Act 1978.

---

[1] *Whelan v Cork Corpn* [1991] ILRM 19.

[2] *Tulk v Moxhay* (1848) 2 Ph 774.

Conveyancing and Law of Property Act 1881

[15.19] In relation to the enforceability of covenants by and against the successors and assigns of the respective parties to a lease containing covenants, certain provisions of the Conveyancing and Law of Property Act 1881 (for convenience styled the Conveyancing Act 1881) bear close resemblance to the provisions of Deasy's Act already considered.[1]

---

[1] The Conveyancing and Law of Property Act 1881 applied throughout the United Kingdom of Great Britain and Ireland. The legislative drafters may not have been conscious of the extent to which the Landlord and Tenant Law Amendment, Ireland, Act 1860 had already catered for certain of the concerns addressed by the statute of 1881. For further reflections on this point, see Wylie 'Contracts and Third Parties' (1966) 17 NILQ 351 at 360; Wylie *Irish Land Law* (3rd edn, 1997) Butterworths, pp 942–943, Coughlan *Property Law* (2nd edn, 1998) Gill and MacMillan, p 267.

[15.20] Section 10 of the Conveyancing Act 1881 provides that 'the benefit of every covenant or provision' contained in a lease and 'having reference to the subject-matter thereof',[1] which is to be performed by the lessee:

'shall be annexed and incident to and shall go with the reversionary estate in the land, or in any part thereof, immediately expectant on the term granted by the lease, notwithstanding severance of that reversionary estate...'

Section 11 provides in similar terms for the enforcement of the 'obligation of a covenant entered into by a lessor with reference to the subject-matter of the lease' which

'... shall, if and as far as the lessor has power to bind the reversionary estate immediately expectant on the term granted by the lease, be annexed and incident to and shall go with that reversionary estate, or the several parts thereof, notwithstanding severance of that reversionary estate...'

---

[1] A covenant's 'having reference to the subject-matter' of a lease has been held as equivalent to 'touching and concerning the land' in *Davis v Town Properties Investment Co Ltd* [1903] 1 Ch 797; *Breams Property Investment Co Ltd v Stroulger* [1948] 2 KB 1; *Hua Chiao Commercial Bank Ltd v Chiaphua Industries Ltd* [1987] AC 99.

[15.21] It should be noted that there are certain fundamental differences between the facility for the running of covenants introduced respectively by Deasy's Act 1860 and the Conveyancing Act 1881.

Deasy's Act 1860	Conveyancing Act 1881
Applies to all landlord and tenant relationships, including tenancies and short periodic lettings and leases for a term of years or lives	Applies to leases only
There needs to be payment of rent	No requirement for payment of rent
Covenant need not 'touch and concern' the land unless the words 'concerning the lands' in s 13 are so construed	Covenant must 'touch and concern' the land, through requirement of 'reference to the subject-matter' of the lease
Not limited to leases or tenancies made after the coming into effect of the act.	Limited to leases made after the coming into effect of the act.

[15.22] Section 58 of the Conveyancing Act 1881 enables the heirs, executors, administrators and assigns of a covenantee to sue on foot of a covenant, on the basis that:

'[a] covenant relating to land of inheritance ... shall be deemed to be made with the covenantee, his heirs and assigns, and shall have effect as if heirs and assigns were expressed.'

Section 59 provides:

'A covenant, and a contract under seal, and a bond or obligation under seal, though not expressed to bind the heirs, shall operate in law to bind the heirs and real estate, as well as the executors and administrators of the personal estate, of the person making the same, as if heirs were expressed...'

provided that a contrary intention has not been expressed in the instrument creating the covenant.

[15.23] In *Federated Homes Ltd v Mill Lodge Properties Ltd*,[1] Brightman LJ in the English Court of Appeal held that s 78 of the Law of Property Act 1925 (which had replaced s 58 of the Conveyancing Act 1881 in Great Britain) effected a statutory annexation of the benefit of a covenant to the lands which the covenant was designed to benefit where the benefit of the covenant touched and concerned those lands.

Section 78(1) of the Law of Property Act 1925 provides:

'A covenant relating to any land of the covenantee shall be deemed to be made with the covenantee and his successors in title and the persons deriving title under him or them, and shall have effect as if such successors and other persons were expressed ... 'successors in title' shall be deemed to include the owners and occupiers for the time being of the land of the covenantee intended to be benefited.'

In the opinion of Brightman LJ, the requirement that the covenant be one 'relating to any land of the covenantee' was equivalent to the old common law requirement of 'touching and concerning' the land of the covenantee; this requirement once satisfied

'... the covenant runs with the land, because *ex hypothesi* every successor in title to the land, every derivative proprietor of the land and every other owner and occupier has a right by statute to the covenant.'[2]

The implications of this decision, in terms of the possibility that s 78 of the Law of Property Act 1925 effects an automatic annexation of the benefit of a restrictive covenant, has been the subject of considerable academic controversy.[3] However, Brightman LJ's decision, arguably, is in essence based on the different language employed by s 58 of the Conveyancing Act 1881 and s 78 of the Law of Property Act 1925 respectively. It must be noted that s 58 did not include reference to the covenantee's successors in title or persons deriving title under him or them, nor to the owners or occupiers for the time being of the land of the covenantee intended to be benefited. From this one can conclude that the scope of s 58 of the Conveyancing Act 1881 was intended to be more limited.

---

[1]   *Federated Homes Ltd v Mill Lodge Properties Ltd* [1980] 1 All ER 371.
[2]   [1980] 1 All ER 371 at 379.
[3]   For a flavour of this, see Hayton 'Revolution in Restrictive Covenants Law?' (1980) 43 MLR 445; Newsom 'Universal Annexation' (1981) 97 LQR 32; Newsom 'Universal Annexation – A Postscript?' (1982) 98 LQR 202; Hurst 'Transmission of Restrictive Covenants' (1982) 2 Leg Stud 53; Todd 'Annexation after *Federated Homes*' [1985] Conv 177.

[15.24] Furthermore, in *Roake v Chadha*,[1] it was held that the implied annexation of the benefit of a covenant effected by s 78 of the Law of Property Act 1925 can be displaced by an express requirement in the deed creating the covenant, that the benefit of the covenant cannot be invoked by any subsequent owner of the covenantee's lands unless the benefit of the covenant has been expressly assigned. 'The true position ... is that, even where a covenant is deemed to be made with successors in title as section 78 requires, one still has to construe the covenant as a whole to see whether the benefit of the covenant is annexed.'[2] In *Sainsbury plc v Enfield London Borough Council*,[3] Morrit J expressed the view that s 58 of the Conveyancing Act 1881 did *not* effect an annexation of the benefit of the covenant to the land which it affects, in the absence of a declared intention so to annex:

> 'There are no words in section 58 capable by themselves of effecting annexation of the benefit of a covenant. All that section did was to deem the inclusion of words which both before and after the enactment of section 58 had ... been consistently held to be insufficient without more to effect annexation of the benefit of a covenant.'[4]

In effect, this means that, for the benefit of a covenant to run with a lease of lands, it must 'touch and concern' the lands, and s 58 operates merely as a parliamentary shorthand for the inclusion of the words 'heirs and assigns.'

---

1 *Roake v Chadha* [1983] 3 All ER 503.
2 Per Baker QC, sitting as a High Court Judge. [1983] 3 All ER 503 at 508.
3 *Sainsbury plc v Enfield London Borough Council* [1989] 1 WLR 590.
4 [1989] 1 WLR 590 at 601.

[15.25] The Irish courts have not so far determined whether, despite the difference in wording between s 58 of the Conveyancing Act 1881 and s 78 of the Law of Property Act 1925, the broader interpretation adopted in relation to s 78 by Brightman LJ in *Federated Homes Ltd v Mill Lodge Properties Ltd*[1] can be applied to the earlier statutory provision. There is no reason to expect that the Irish courts will elect for a broader interpretation.

---

1 *Federated Homes Ltd v Mill Lodge Properties Ltd* [1980] 1 All ER 371.

[15.26] Section 65 of the Conveyancing Act 1881 provides that, where there is a residue of not less than 200 years of a term which was originally for not less than 300 years, 'and without any rent, or with merely a peppercorn rent or other rent having no money value,' or where a former rent has been released, barred by lapse of time, or in any other way ceased to be payable, the person entitled to the lessee's interest has the power to declare by deed that, with effect from the date of the deed, 'the term shall be enlarged into a fee simple.'

Once that has happened, sub-s 3 provides that the former lessee will enjoy a fee simple. Subsection 4 states:

> 'The estate in fee simple so acquired by enlargement shall be subject to all the same trusts, powers, executory limitations over, rights, equities and to all the same covenants and provisions relating to user and enjoyment, and to all the same obligations of every kind, as the term would have been subject to if it had not been so enlarged.'

Section 11 of the Conveyancing Act 1882 introduced a retrospective qualification, that the term so enlarged could not be one which was liable to be determined by re-entry for condition broken, and, significantly, that the term could not be a sub-lease of a superior lease itself incapable of being enlarged into a fee simple.

[15.27] Apart altogether from the strictures imposed by s 65 (as amended) to eligibility for enlargement of the leasehold term, the section is of less use than might appear were one to seek to employ it as a device to attach the burden of positive covenants to the fee simple. This is primarily because s 28 of the Landlord and Tenant (Ground Rents) (No 2) Act 1978, as interpreted in *Whelan v Cork Corpn*,[1] provides that once the fee simple has been statutorily acquired, with few exceptions all covenants, including those in favour of third parties, subject to which the property had formerly been held, are extinguished.[2]

---

[1]   *Whelan v Cork Corpn* [1991] ILRM 19 (HC), [1994] 3 IR 367 (SC). See para **[18.12]** ff.
[2]   See Lyall *Land Law in Ireland* pp 689–690. For a more optimistic assessment of the possible application of s 65, see Lyall 'Freehold Covenants and What to Do with Them' (1991) 9 ILT (NS) 157 at 159–160.

[15.28] In *Gaw v Coras Iompair Éireann*[1] an alternative ground for the decision of Dixon J, that the benefit of a covenant that touched and concerned the land of the covenantee could be enforced by a successor of the covenantee, was that, in the case of any deed executed after the coming into effect of the Conveyancing Act 1881,[2] the benefit of such a covenant would pass under s 6(1).[3] This provides that '[a] conveyance of land shall be deemed to include and shall by virtue of this Act operate to convey, with the land, all … rights, and advantages whatsoever, appertaining or reputed to appertain to the land, or any part thereof …'

It is difficult to understand how the benefit of a covenant that touches and concerns the land of the covenantee could be regarded as other than a 'right' or 'advantage' which is 'appertaining' to the land. The dearth of reported decisions on this point should not deter the courts from applying the clear language of s 6(1) of the Conveyancing Act 1881 to circumstances that seem patently to invoke it.[4]

---

[1]   *Gaw v Coras Iompair Éireann* (1952) 89 ILTR 124. See para **[14.08]** ff especially **[14.11]**.
[2]   1 January 1882.
[3]   See para **[2.43]**.
[4]   See also *Corr v Bradshaw* (18 July 1967, unreported) SC.

The Property (Northern Ireland) Order 1997

[15.29] Article 34 of the Property (Northern Ireland) Order 1997, as has been shown,[1] introduced a new scheme for the enforcement of freehold covenants by and against the successors of the original covenantor and covenantee respectively.

---

[1]   See paras **[14.34]–[14.37]**.

[15.30] Part 11 of the 1997 Order provides specifically for the preservation of covenants in cases where the fee simple of property has been acquired through the redemption of the ground rent. Article 25(1) states that, in cases of unregistered land, once the certificate of redemption of the ground rent has been completed, and in cases of registered land, once the appropriate amendment has been made in the register, 'all covenants concerning the land by virtue of the rent-payer's fee farm grant or lease, or any superior fee farm grant or lease, or any collateral instrument, cease to have effect.' This provision, however, is stated to be '[E]xcept as provided by this Article', and Article 25(2) then proceeds to list a number of covenants which will 'continue to benefit or, as the case may be, burden the land' – these are, in effect, the same covenants as are stated to run with the land of the covenantee and against the land of the covenantor in Article 34.

[15.31] Article 26 of the 1997 Order sets out those by whom and against whom the preserved covenants are enforceable. In general terms, strictly landlord and tenant covenants (such as covenants as to title, covenants for quiet enjoyment and covenants in relation to past payment of rent)[1] are enforceable only against the party against whom they would have been enforceable prior to redemption, and not against that party's successors in title;[2] all other covenants, both positive and negative, are in the main enforceable by or against, as the case may be, all parties previously entitled to enforce such covenants, or to have such covenants enforced against them, and their successors.[3]

In the case of restrictive covenants 'for the protection of amenities or services',[4] once the freehold has been acquired through redemption of the ground rent in respect of at least one parcel of land, an estate scheme, whether or not it was deemed to exist previously, is taken as existing whenever 'all the persons holding parcels under dispositions in substantially similar terms from the same rent-owner, and the successors in title of those persons, are participants.'[5] All such covenants then become enforceable by and against the original rent-owner, and his successors, as long as they continue in the relation of rent-owner to any one participant,[6] and by and against all participants in the deemed estate scheme, regardless of whether or not any particular one of them has redeemed his ground rent and acquired the fee simple in his property.[7]

---

[1] Article 25(2)(a).
[2] Article 26(1).
[3] Article 26(2), (3), (4), (5) and (6).
[4] Article 25(2)(h).
[5] Article 26(6). A 'rent-owner' is effectively defined as a person entitled to receive the ground rent.
[6] Article 26(6)(a).
[7] Article 26(6)(b).

[15.32] Section 65 of the Conveyancing Act 1881 and s 11 of the Conveyancing Act 1882 are repealed by the Order and replaced by Article 35. This enables a lessee to enlarge his interest into a fee simple where the unexpired residue of the lease is more than 50 years, and if 'no rent is incident to the reversion', provided that the property held under lease is not used, or required to be used, wholly for business purposes. A business purpose can still arise even if there is obligatory or concessionary residence on part of the premises by a person in consequence of their employment or office. The Article does not apply if the lease has been created by way of mortgage. Upon enlargement, all covenants specified in Article 25 as continuing to apply in situations where the fee simple is acquired through the process of buying out a ground rent, continue to affect the fee simple estate into which the former leasehold is enlarged.

[15.33] The Order also prohibits the creation of a number of property entities, to which a ground rent or the equivalent of a ground rent formerly attached, and which were also often used as a device for carrying covenants: so that, both leases for lives, whether renewable forever or otherwise,[1] and also fee farm grants,[2] can now no longer be created. Likewise, notably except in the case of a mortgage, or where the property is a flat or held under an equity-sharing lease, a lease of a dwellinghouse for more than 50 years can no longer be granted.[3] The creation of a rentcharge, save as an annuity or on foot of a legal obligation, is also prohibited.[4]

---

[1] Articles 36 and 37.
[2] Article 28.
[3] Article 30.
[4] Article 29.

Chapter 16

The Enforceability of Restrictive Covenants

Introduction

[16.01] A restrictive covenant is one in which the covenantor agrees, either not to do, or to prevent from happening, something in relation to his own land with a view to benefiting the land of the covenantee. By its nature it involves land, both of the covenantor and the covenantee. Accordingly, a restrictive covenant bears close comparison to an easement, with the land of the covenantor constituted as a quasi-servient tenement and that of the covenantee a quasi-dominant tenement.

A restrictive covenant has been thus described:[1]

'It is not truly a right *in alieno solo*, as it operates merely so as to restrict the use that may be made of the servient tenement for the advantage of the dominant tenement. It does not directly affect or increase the use that may be made of the dominant tenement, nor does it permit the dominant owner to use the servient tenement in any manner; however, by restricting the use that may be made of the servient tenement, a covenant may considerably enhance the value of any estates or interests in the dominant tenement ... The advantages secured to a dominant tenement by an easement are usually more precise and substantial.'[2]

It is because the existence of such a covenant can significantly affect the value of the land meant to be benefited, that equity has intervened through its particular remedy of the injunction to ensure that breaches of covenant can be stopped in advance, rather than merely being compensated for after they have occurred. On account of this facility for equitable intervention, the principles underpinning the enforceability of restrictive covenants, by and against successors, have more to do with the doctrine of notice, and the character of the covenant being considered, rather than the technical legal issue of whether the covenant 'runs' with the land.

---

[1] Garner 'Restrictive Covenants Restated' (1962) 26 Conv 298.
[2] (1962) 26 Conv 298 at 305. See also Hayton 'Restrictive Covenants as Property Interests' (1971) 87 LQR 539.

The Burden and Successors of the Covenantor

[16.02] The principles governing the enforceability of restrictive covenants were first clearly articulated by Lord Cottenham LC in the leading case of *Tulk v Moxhay*,[1] explained as follows by Chatterton V-C in *Craig v Greer*:[2]

'The question was not whether the covenant ran with the land, but whether a party shall be permitted to use the land in a manner inconsistent with the contract entered into by his vendor, and with notice of which he purchased. [Lord Cottenham LC] observed that of course the price would be affected by the covenant, and that nothing could be more inequitable than that the original purchaser should be able to sell the property the next day for a greater price, in consideration of the assignee being allowed to escape from the liability which he had himself undertaken.'[3]

Craig v Greer concerned a covenant by a lessee with his lessor not to use any buildings erected on the demised premises other than as a dwellinghouse or tea-rooms. The plaintiff was a successor of the covenantee and the defendants included a number of sub-lessees of the covenantor. Claiming that the covenant had become otiose, the defendants purported to erect a large liquor store. Chatterton V-C was emphatic that it did not matter to the enforceability of the covenant whether it actually ran with the land or not. Instead, the question was governed by the equitable principle, that a person purchasing land, with notice of a covenant restricting its use in a particular way, will be restrained from using the land in a manner inconsistent with the covenant. This will be so regardless of whether the covenant is one which runs with the land. [4]

---

[1] *Tulk v Moxhay* (1848) 2 Phil 774. See also Robinson 'Restrictive Covenants' (1974) 38 Conv 90 at 91–92.

[2] *Craig v Greer* [1899] 1 IR 258.

[3] [1899] 1 IR 258 at 273. A further relevant factor is that the original covenantee, once he has parted with the land which the covenant was designed to benefit, would only be likely to secure nominal damages in an action taken for its breach: Denning LJ in *Smith and Snipes Hall Farm Ltd v River Douglas Catchment Board* [1949] 2 KB 500.

[4] [1899] 1 IR 258 at 272.

[16.03] The Vice-Chancellor drew support from the English case of *Hall v Ewin*,[1] in which Cotton LJ had applied the principle in *Tulk v Moxhay*[2] to a sub-tenant who, though not bound at law by a restrictive covenant, could be restrained in equity from acting in breach of the covenant if he had notice of it; similarly from the case of *Austerberry v Corporation of Oldham*,[3] in which Cotton LJ had laid down that where there was a restrictive covenant, the burden and benefit of which did not run at law, equity would prevent anybody who took the property with notice of that covenant from using it in a way inconsistent with the covenant. Chatterton V-C concluded that the principle in *Tulk v Moxhay*, summarised above, had been well established, but that it was confined to restrictive covenants, and could not apply in cases where the covenant involved works of repair or improvement, with the expenditure of money.[4]

---

[1] *Hall v Ewin* (1887) 37 ChD 74. A sub-lessee has neither privity of contract nor privity of estate with the head-lessor. See para **[15.03]**.

[2] *Tulk v Moxhay* (1848) 2 Phil 774.

[3] *Austerberry v Corporation of Oldham* (1885) 29 ChD 750.

[4] *Craig v Greer* [1899] 1 IR 258 at 274. In *Gaw v Coras Iompair Éireann* (1952) 89 ILTR 124, Dixon J, *obiter* at 136, without specifically referring to the case, endorsed the reasoning of Chatterton V-C in *Craig v Greer* [1899] 1 IR 258 when he interpreted the decision in *Austerberry v Corporation of Oldham* as being authority for the proposition that the principle in *Tulk v Moxhay* was not to be extended beyond restrictive covenants. 'The question of notice, of course, does not arise where the covenant does in fact run with the land. This limitation of the scope of *Tulk v Moxhay*, combined with the view – in line with the authorities – that the

burden of a covenant does not run with the land at law, except as between landlord and tenant, disposed of the plaintiff's claim in *Austerberry v Corporation of Oldham*' See also Murphy J in *Whelan v Cork Corpn* [1991] ILRM 19 at 26.

[16.04] The decision of Chatterton V-C, on the enforceability of the restrictive covenant, was upheld on appeal to the Court of Appeal. Fitzgibbon LJ observed that it made no difference to the prospect of being rendered liable to an injunction that the offending party was not the original covenantor, but a subsequent owner of the property who had taken it with express notice of the covenant.[1]

---

[1] *Craig v Greer* [1899] 1 IR 258 at 295.

Covenant must be intended to benefit land of the covenantee

[16.05] A restrictive covenant by definition limits in some respect the enjoyment of his land by the covenantor. However, in order for the burden of a restrictive covenant to be enforceable against an assignee of the covenantor, it must be established that it was intended to bind successors of the original covenantor and benefit successors of the original covenantee: in short, that the benefit of the covenant was not personal to the covenantee. This requirement is frequently expressed as being that the covenant must be intended to benefit land owned by the covenantee.

[16.06] In *Northern Ireland Carriers Ltd v Larne Harbour Ltd*[1] the plaintiff was the lessee, and the defendant its lessor, of lands at Larne harbour. The lease contained a covenant against assigning or sub-letting the premises (but not part of the premises) without the consent of the lessor and also a covenant against using the premises for anything other than the plaintiff's business of carriers and haulage contractors. The plaintiff wanted to sub-lease part of the site to the Department of Finance which intended to use it for weigh-bridge testing. The defendant was not agreeable to the proposed sub-letting, on account of the scarcity of land at the port of Larne and because the proposed use of the portion of the site being sub-let was not connected with normal port or dock activities.

---

[1] *Northern Ireland Carriers Ltd v Larne Harbour Ltd* [1981] NI 171.

[16.07] Murray J held that the covenants in issue were clearly intended to be personal only, a conclusion bolstered by the fact that the lessee had not purported to covenant on behalf of itself and its assigns.[1] As to whether the covenants in relation to user could be enforced against the proposed sub-lessee under the equitable doctrine of *Tulk v Moxhay*, Murray J, noting that there was neither privity of estate nor privity of contract between a lessor and a sub-lessee, observed:

> 'When the issue is whether the burden of a covenant runs in equity so as to bind a purchaser from the original covenantor, one of the questions which arises is whether the covenant was taken for the benefit of other land retained by the covenantee eg a no-building covenant taken by the covenantee to protect the view from his house ...'

'... a fundamental question which always arises in the *Tulk v Moxhay* context is whether the negative covenant in issue is (a) intended to run with the land so as to bind any person – whether subsequent purchaser or as in this case sub-lessee – into whose hands the land may come, or, alternatively (b) is a mere personal covenant which only binds the covenantor himself. The onus is on the person who alleges that the covenant was intended to run with the land to prove his allegation.'[2]

It is clear that the covenants were of a kind that, under other circumstances, might have been held as attaching to the land, but which, in the particular facts of *Northern Ireland Carriers Ltd v Larne Harbour Ltd*, were personal to the lessor and so immune from the application of the principle in *Tulk v Moxhay*.[3]

---

[1]   The importance attached by Murray J to the failure of the covenants in the lease to state that they bound the lessee and his assigns is inconsistent with the decision in *Holloway Brothers v Hill* [1902] 2 Ch 612, in which it had been held that the lessee of a person bound by a restrictive covenant could also be bound, regardless of whether assigns were mentioned in the original covenant. This case was cited with approval by Murphy J in *Whelan v Cork Corporation* [1991] ILRM 19. This discrepancy serves to emphasise the importance of the personal nature of the restrictive covenants in *Northern Ireland Carriers Ltd v Larne Harbour Ltd* [1981] NI 171 at 178 as found by Murray J.

[2]   [1981] NI 171 at 178.

[3]   *Tulk v Moxhay* (1848) 2 Phil 774.

[16.08] Where the covenantee is a mere licensee, and not the owner of any interest in land at all, the successor of the covenantor will not be liable on the covenant. In *David Allen and Sons Billposting Ltd v King*[1] the defendant, by written agreement, in July 1913, granted to the plaintiff a licence for a term of four years to erect film posters on the wall of premises at Phibsboro, Co Dublin. At the time of the agreement, the premises were about to be let to a picture house company then in the process of being formed. After a lease had been granted by the defendant to the newly formed Phibsboro Picture House Ltd, this company refused to allow the plaintiff access to the wall for the purpose of putting up the film posters pursuant to the licence agreement. In an action by the plaintiff for breach of the licence agreement, the defendant argued that, as the picture house company had taken the lease with notice of the licence agreement between the defendant and the plaintiff, it was affected by the plaintiff's rights and alone was liable to be sued.

The Court of King's Bench, and on further appeal in due course the Court of Appeal, and the House of Lords, all held that the agreement between the plaintiff and the defendant did not create any interest in land, with the result that the picture house company was not affected by notice such as would arise if there had been a restrictive covenant regarding an estate in land. As a result, the defendant remained liable to the plaintiff on an action for breach of contract.

Ronan LJ held that since there had been no dominant tenement there could not be an easement; and that, similarly, the burden of a restrictive covenant would not run, even though the assignee of the covenantor took with notice of the covenant, if the covenant did not touch and concern some land of the covenantee.[2]

1   *David Allen and Sons Billposting Ltd v King* [1915] 2 IR 213–249, 448–481.
2   [1915] 2 IR 448 at 461–462. Ronan LJ also cited in support, *Formby v Barker* [1903] 2 Ch 539; *In Re Nisbet and Pott's Contract* [1906] 1 Ch 386; *Millbourn v Lyons* [1914] 1 Ch 34 and *London County Council v Allen* [1914] 3 KB 642.

Covenant must be capable of binding party sought to be bound

[16.09] In order for the burden of a restrictive covenant to be enforceable against an assignee of the covenantor it must be one which, on its terms, is capable of binding the party sought to be bound. In *Williams and Co Ltd v LSD and Quinnsworth*[1] the first named defendant developed what became known as the Rathfarnham Shopping Centre and granted a lease of a shopping unit to the plaintiff. The lease contained a covenant by the lessor not to permit any other lessee to have a shopping area in the complex for the sale of food in excess of 1,300 square feet. Subsequently, the first named defendant granted a lease of a unit to the second named defendant in which there was a covenant by the second named defendant against having a total area for the sale of food in excess of 1,300 square feet. Notwithstanding this, the second named defendant also opened a supermarket in its shopping unit which comprised in excess of 1,300 square feet. The first named defendant did nothing about it.

After having rejected an argument that the only relevant area for the purpose of the covenant was the environs of the check-out where the purchase was actually completed, Pringle J concluded that both defendants were in breach of the relevant covenants in their respective leases. As between the plaintiff and the first named defendant, the obligation 'not to permit' had not been satisfied merely by the first named defendant's inserting a covenant into the lease to the second named defendant.[2]

1   *Williams and Co Ltd v LSD and Quinnsworth* (19 June 1970, unreported) HC.
2   The words 'not to permit', in the view of Pringle J, obliged the first named defendant 'to take all necessary steps in their power to prevent any lessee or tenant from having an area for the sale of food in excess of the area referred to.'

[16.10] Pringle J held that a claim by the plaintiff against the second named defendant on foot of its breach of covenant with the first named defendant would fail at common law because of the absence of privity of contract between the plaintiff and the second named defendant. He cited the principle in *Tulk v Moxhay*[1] thus:

> '... that a negative bargain, as for instance a covenant against a particular use of land retained on a sale or a lease of part of an estate, may be enforced by any person entitled in equity to the benefit of that bargain against any person bound in equity by notice of it, either express or to be imputed at the time of acquisition of his title.'[2]

According to Pringle J, it was clear that the covenant *did* restrict any party taking with notice of it, but, on its terms, could only apply to an assign of the lessor, not another lessee. The words 'not to permit' anticipated a successor of the lessor, an expression defined in the original lease as any party entitled to the reversion immediately expectant upon the term granted.

---

[1]   *Tulk v Moxhay* (1848) 2 Phil 774.

[2]   Quoted with approval by Murphy J in *Whelan v Cork Corpn* [1991] ILRM 19 at 23. This dictum has led Coughlan to question, in *Property Law* (2nd edn, 1998) Gill and Macmillan, p 285, whether in Ireland the emphasis is still more on notice of the restriction than the requirement for the covenant to benefit land of the covenantee. However, the dictum should be construed in the context of the facts to which it applied. Both in the *Williams* case (19 June 1970, unreported) HC and *Whelan v Cork Corpn* there was no issue over the benefiting of the land of the covenantee, so that the judge in neither case was obliged to address that requirement.

Equitable estoppel can both bind and loose

[16.11] In the same way as the equitable principle of notice governs the enforceability of a restrictive covenant, so too the equitable doctrine of estoppel can, on the one hand, affect the determination of who may be bound by a restrictive covenant and, on the other hand, in certain cases prevent a party entitled to enforce a covenant from enforcing it.

[16.12] In *Re Ashe and Hogan's Contract*[1] a vendor, who held under a 999-year lease of 1800 which contained covenants against alienation and against user as a licensed premises without the consent of the lessor, offered the premises at auction on the basis of title commencing with an assignment of 1839. At the time of auction the premises were being used as a public house without the consent of the lessor. The vendor made no specific reference to the covenants. Instead he maintained that an annual rent of £8, reducible to £4 if all covenants had been complied with, had been so reduced by the landlord. Upon the raising of requisitions on title by the purchaser, in relation to the reduced rent, the vendor refused to seek the landlord's consent to the assignment or to the use of the premises for licensed purposes. Instead, in replies to requisitions, the vendor sought to advance a possessory title on the basis of the Statute of Limitations. The question then arose whether the successful assertion of such a title would free the vendor from the covenants.

---

[1]   *Re Ashe and Hogan's Contract* [1920] 1 IR 159.

[16.13] O'Connor MR distinguished the decision of the English Court of Appeal in *Tichborne v Weir*[1] which had held that a lessor could not succeed in an action on a covenant to repair against a person who had acquired title to the lessee's estate by adverse possession, on the basis that the effect of adverse possession was not to transfer the ousted lessee's title, but to extinguish it. Instead, O'Connor MR followed the majority decision of the Irish Court of Appeal in *O'Connor v Foley*[2] which had held that the decision in *Tichborne v Weir* did not apply in circumstances where the adverse possessor had estopped himself from denying that he was an assignee. In *O'Connor v Foley* the occupier was held to be estopped from denying that he was the tenant after he had served a notice to fix a fair rent under the Land Purchase Acts. Fitzgibbon LJ had held that the principle enunciated in *Tichborne v Weir* was limited in its application to a personal covenant to repair and could not be extended so as to prevent the enforcement of a restrictive covenant. A covenant restricting the use of land is deemed to run with that land in equity, and binds all parties, even where the title is possessory, except a purchaser for value without notice.

---

1   *Tichborne v Weir* (1892) 67 LT 735.
2   *O'Connor v Foley* [1905] 1 IR 1, [1906] 1 IR 20.

[16.14] In *Re Ashe and Hogan's Contract*,[1] according to O'Connor MR an estoppel arose because the vendor had taken advantage of the facility to pay the reduced rent of £4 which was only properly applicable if the covenants had been observed. The Master of the Rolls stated that a person taking advantage of a clause in a lease and deriving benefit under it also had to accept the burdens. Hence, the vendor was unable to give a valid assignment to the purchaser without the consent of the lessor and would be estopped from endeavouring to disencumber himself of the covenants.[2]

---

1   *Re Ashe and Hogan's Contract* [1920] 1 IR 159.
2   O'Connor MR cited in support the judgment of Farwell J in *Re Nisbet and Potts' Contract* [1905] 1 Ch 391, in which Farwell J had held that the acquiring of title by adverse possession did not destroy the equitable right of persons entitled to prior restrictive covenants to enforce them against the land and, *a fortiori*, against the person in adverse possession of it. See also Bready 'Covenants Affecting Land' (1944) 6 NILQ 48 at 54; 'Restriction on Title – Squatter' (1932) 66 ILTSJ 93, where the effect of the caselaw above discussed is stated thus: '... the statutory 'extinguishment' of the title of the dispossessed owner of the land has not the effect of destroying the covenant, the equitable right of the covenantee not being in any way affected by the statute, and consequently the covenantee can enforce the covenant against the squatter, both before and after he has acquired his possessory title, and also against any subsequent owner of the land not being a *bona fide* purchaser for value without notice.'

[16.15] Article 34(9) of the Property (Northern Ireland) Order 1997, in relation to covenants stated to be enforceable under the article, includes in the definition of 'owner' a person who has been in adverse possession for sufficient time to dispossess the true owner under Article 26 of the Limitation (Northern Ireland) Order 1989, or a person who has been in adverse possession for a shorter time, provided in this latter case that the covenant is a restrictive covenant or relates to permission. Under Article 26(7) certain amenity covenants, which are restrictive in nature or relate to permission, can be enforced against the user or occupier of premises.

[16.16] In *Craig v Greer*[1] a successor of the covenantee sought to enforce against sub-lessees of the covenantor a covenant prohibiting the use of any buildings on the demised premises except as a dwellinghouse or tea-rooms. The defendants contended that the character of Belfast had been transformed between 1863, the date of a sub-lease through which the covenant was stated to bind them, and 1899, the date of the action. By 1899 the land affected by the covenant had become part of the municipal area of Belfast, where there had been significant building work undertaken and commercial development. Hence, it would be inequitable for the plaintiff to be permitted to enforce the covenant by way of injunction. Additionally, the defendants urged that the plaintiff herself had had constructed some shops on another part of her land and that this circumstance should estop her from enforcing the covenant.

On this latter point Chatterton V-C followed the decision of Lord Eldon in *Duke of Bedford v Trustees of the British Museum*[2] which, in the Vice-Chancellor's view, did not decide that contractual obligations disappeared as the circumstances changed; but that a person, who was otherwise entitled to the benefit of a restrictive covenant, may by his conduct or omissions put himself in such an altered relation to the person bound by it, as would make it unjust for him to seek to enforce the covenant by way of injunction.

Chatterton V-C concluded:

'The principle to be deduced from these authorities seems to me to be that in order to defeat the right of a person with whom a covenant has been entered into restricting the mode of user of lands sold or demised, it must be clearly established that there is a personal equity against him arising from his acts or conduct in sanctioning or knowingly permitting such a change in the character of the neighbourhood as to render it unjust in him to seek to enforce his covenant by injunction: a change resulting from causes independent of him will not have such an operation.'[3]

The changes taking place in that part of Belfast where the plaintiff's land was located were not the result of any act by the plaintiff, so that the mere fact that she had had constructed some small buildings now used as shops on part of her estate did not disentitle her to relief against the change of user proposed by the defendants in breach of the covenant.

---

1   *Craig v Greer* [1899] 1 IR 258.
2   *Duke of Bedford v Trustees of the British Museum* (1822) 2 Myl & K 552.
3   [1899] 1 IR 258 at 278–279.

[16.17] In the Court of Appeal Fitzgibbon LJ modified the approach adopted by Chatterton V-C: he declined to accept that in every case a covenantee, or covenantee's successor, should be free from equitable considerations merely because the change in the locality resulted from circumstances beyond her control or from building on lands which she did not own:

'The estoppel, where it exists, rests on personal conduct, and the acts which have been done upon her lands, though they have not originated the change, have at least adopted it, and have made a profit of it, and in that point of view might, in kind, suffice to make it inequitable for her to insist against another upon rights to which she herself has paid no regard.'[1]

However, in the view of Fitzgibbon LJ, the authorities did not support the defendants' contention that the covenant must be universally enforced on each occasion of breach if the covenantee or her successor were not to be estopped from seeking to enforce it. For example, said Fitzgibbon LJ, a breach of a covenant against building by the construction of a dwellinghouse might be ignored if the location of it did not cause annoyance to the covenantee; but that would not estop the covenantee from seeking an injunction against the construction of an offensive premises outside her own house. In the instant case, the injurious effect on the plaintiff's property by the proposed development of the defendants was far more significant than anything previously done by the plaintiff herself or her predecessors. Accordingly, the plaintiff was not estopped from seeking to enforce the covenant.

---

[1] *Craig v Greer* [1899] 1 IR 258 at 298.

The availability of an injunction

[16.18] A breach of restrictive covenant can be restrained by injunction. The general principle is that, provided there is no equity prevailing against the covenantee or his successor,[1] all that is necessary to be established is the fact of the breach:[2] a covenantee or his successor who holds the freehold interest in lands the subject of a leasehold covenant is not obliged to demonstrate any damage to the reversion if the breach continues.[3] The purpose of the injunction is principally to give effect to the agreement represented by the covenant, so that:

> '... all that a Court of Equity has to do is to say, by way of injunction, that which the parties have already said by way of covenant, that the thing shall not be done; and in such case the injunction does nothing more than give the sanction of the process of the Court to that which already is the contract between the parties.'[4]

An injunction is equally available to and against successors of the original contracting parties, provided that the successor to the covenantor has taken his land with notice of the covenant.[5]

---

[1] Such as laches, or acquiescence in certain actions taken to his detriment by the covenantor, which would make it inequitable for the covenantee or his successor to be able to enforce the covenant. See *The Dublin (South) City Market Co v McCabes Ltd* [1953] IR 283 at 315.

[2] Neither does the damage resulting from the breach have to be actual monetary loss, particularly if the covenant is against causing 'annoyance' or 'grievance', as opposed to 'nuisance' which is effectively a narrower prohibition. See *Tod-Heatly v Benham* (1888) 40 ChD 80; *The Dublin (South) City Market Co v McCabes Ltd* [1953] IR 283 at 312.

[3] [1953] IR 283 at 310.

[4] Lord Cairns in *Doherty v Allman* (1878) 3 App Cas 709 at 719–720, quoted by Budd J in *The Dublin (South) City Market Co v McCabes Ltd* [1953] IR 283 at 311.

[5] *Craig v Greer* [1899] 1 IR 258 at 295, per Fitzgibbon LJ.

[16.19] It is not a prerequisite that the granting of the injunction is a guarantee of resolving the problem thrown up by the breach of covenant. In *The Dublin (South) City Market Co v McCabes Ltd*, Budd J held that the guaranteed efficacy or otherwise of injunctive relief is not a compelling factor in deciding whether it should be granted or not.[1] However, it must at all times be remembered that an injunction is a discretionary equitable remedy, and that the likelihood of its being granted can never be assumed.[2]

---

[1] 'It does probably improve the chances of a plaintiff of obtaining relief by way of an injunction when he can show that there is a cheap and probably efficacious remedy for that of which he complains. If it were to be shown by the defendants that any remedy was impossible, then, no

doubt, great difficulties in granting an injunction might arise.' *The Dublin (South) City Market Co v McCabes Ltd* [1953] IR 283 at 317.

[2] See the concerns articulated in the Report of the Irish Republic's Law Reform Commission: *Land Law and Conveyancing Law: Positive Covenants Over Freehold Land and Other Proposals* (LRC70–2003) at 7 (para 1.08).

[16.20] Perhaps influenced by the urban expansion considerations adduced in *Craig v Greer*,[1] Article 45 of the Property (Northern Ireland) Order 1997 provides that eligibility to seek an injunction in the case of a breach, actual or anticipated, of the kind of covenants covered by the Order,[2] except in cases of injury to person or property, is limited to the extent to which the claimant 'is or may be materially prejudiced by the breach, or anticipated or threatened breach.'[3] In order to determine material prejudice, a court will have regard, both to the nature of the estate which enables the claiming party to enforce the benefit of the covenant and 'to the location of the land in which that estate subsists.'[4]

[1] *Craig v Greer* [1899] 1 IR 258.
[2] Freehold covenants in Article 34, see ch 14, para [14.34] and leasehold covenants continuing after purchase of the ground rent in Article 25. See para [15.303].
[3] Article 45(2).
[4] Article 45(3).

[16.21] Where a restrictive covenant is created in a lease from the covenantor to the covenantee, equity will intervene to prevent the covenantor using a subsequent freehold conveyance as a device to avoid compliance with the covenant. This is the effect of the judgment of Costello J in *Power Supermarkets Ltd t/a Quinnsworth and Quinnsworth Ltd v Crumlin Investments Ltd and Dunnes Stores (Crumlin) Ltd*.[1] In this the first named defendant was a commercial developer which had granted a lease of a unit in the Crumlin Shopping Centre to the plaintiff. The lease contained a covenant by the first named defendant that it would not grant any other lease allowing a lessee or sub-lessee to sell groceries in or over an area exceeding 3,000 square feet. Subsequently, the first named defendant got into financial difficulties and the Dunnes Stores Group, through one of its subsidiaries, purchased all its share capital and incorporated the second named defendant as a wholly owned subsidiary of one of the companies in the group. The newly incorporated second named defendant issued only two shares and took a freehold conveyance of one of the Crumlin Shopping Centre units comprising in excess of 3,000 square feet, for a consideration found by Costello J to be at an undervalue, which it then proceeded to use as a supermarket. Costello J concluded, from the evidence, that the second named defendant operated at the behest of the Dunne family whose principal purpose was to develop a supermarket in Crumlin and so attract custom to the Crumlin Shopping Centre, thereby enabling them charge higher rents on a rent review of the various trading units. The deed of conveyance from the first named defendant to the second named defendant had, neither been registered in the Registry of Deeds, nor contained any of the usual easements and covenants that would be necessary to make the shopping centre commercially viable.

---

[1] *Quinnsworth Ltd v Crumlin Investments Ltd and Dunnes Stores (Crumlin) Ltd* (22 June 1981, unreported) HC.

[16.22] The case argued by both defendants was that the restrictive covenant on its terms only applied to tenants and sub-tenants and could not prevent the lessor itself, or any assignee of the freehold interest, from selling groceries in an area exceeding 3,000 square feet.[1] Costello J, while acknowledging that the restrictive covenant had been poorly drafted, declined to hold with this narrow interpretation. Instead, he accepted the arguments of the plaintiff, that this was a case in which the corporate veil should be breached, so that the two defendants could be deemed to be a single trading entity, or, in the alternative, that this was a covenant which ran with the land and so would bind the second named defendant, even though the second named defendant was the assignee of the freehold interest.[2]

On the first point, Costello J decided that the commercial reality warranted breaching the corporate veil and holding that the two defendants were in effect a single trading entity. According to Costello J, the whole arrangement had been designed to promote the commercial plans of the Dunne family. To hold otherwise, said the judge, would be to enable the plaintiff's rights under the covenant to be defeated 'by the mere technical device of the creation of a company with a £2 issued share capital which had no real independent life of its own' and granting to it the fee simple of the relevant shopping centre unit.

---

[1] This was the argument that had commended itself to Pringle J in *Williams and Co Ltd v LSD and Quinnsworth*. See para **[16.09]**.

[2] Costello J seems not to have been concerned with the technical debate as to whether, on the one hand, the covenant was one which 'ran with the land', or, on the other hand, whether it attracted the application of the principle in *Tulk v Moxhay* (1848) 2 Phil 774.

[16.23] Costello J also held that the covenant was one which ran with the land and was enforceable by the plaintiff-covenantee against the second named defendant:

'The principle of equity which was developed in the [nineteenth] century is that the burden of restrictive covenants runs with the land to which it relates so as to bind successors in title of the original covenantor, except in the case of a *bona fide* purchaser without notice. The basis of this rule is that the covenant is concerned with preserving the value of the land retained by the covenantee. For it to apply there must be a clear intention that the burden is to run. ... Here, I think there can be little doubt that the parties to the lease intended that the lessor's covenant would run with the land. It is true that the lessor did not expressly covenant on behalf of its successors and assigns, but it could not have been intended that the day after the execution of the lease the lessor would have been at liberty to convey the fee simple of a unit in the shopping centre so as to permit a grantee of the fee simple to trade in a way forbidden to a lessee of the same unit. It is equally clear that the covenant is a restrictive one and that Dunnes Stores (Crumlin) had notice of it.'

Accordingly, Costello J granted an injunction restraining the breach of the covenant by the second named defendant.

The Benefit and Successors of the Covenantee

[16.24] In the particular case of restrictive covenants, the English courts have developed additional refinements to the covenant's touching and concerning the land of the covenantee in order for a successor of the covenantee to be able to sue on foot of the benefit of such a covenant. In the language which has developed, the covenant must either be 'annexed' to the land it is designed to benefit, or be expressly 'assigned' with the land to the successor of the covenantee, for the covenant to be enforceable.[1]

---

[1] See generally, Robinson 'Restrictive Covenants' (1974) 38 Conv 90 at 95–101.

Annexation

[16.25] In *Rogers v Hosegood*,[1] Farwell J, speaking of the running of the benefit of a restrictive covenant, observed:

> 'The accurate expression appears to me to be that the covenants are annexed to the land, and pass with it in much the same way as title deeds, which have been quaintly called the sinews of the land.'[2]

The question whether the original covenanting parties had intended that the benefit of a covenant was to be annexed to the lands depends on:

(i)   what might reasonably be inferred from the nature of the covenant itself;

(ii)   the language of the deed creating it;

(iii)   the surrounding circumstances.

---

[1] *Rogers v Hosegood* [1900] 2 Ch 388.
[2] [1900] 2 Ch 388 at 394.

[16.26] In *Rogers v Hosegood* the covenantor had covenanted in relation to the premises being demised to him by the covenantee, for himself and for anyone into whose hands they might pass, and the covenant had been stated to be for the benefit of the covenantees 'their heirs and assigns and others claiming under them to all or any of their lands adjoining or near to' the premises being demised. It was a significant factor in determining that the covenant had been intended to be annexed to the land that it was stated specifically as benefiting *other* land of the covenantee.[1] Such a covenant can be distinguished from that which featured in *Renals v Cowlishaw*,[2] where there had not been an express statement in the deed creating the covenant that it should enure for the benefit of each portion of the lands retained by the covenantee. Once the covenant has been annexed to the land, it is not necessary for a successor of the covenantee actually to have been aware of the existence of the covenant in order to be able to enforce it.[3] The judgment of Farwell J in *Rogers v Hosegood* was affirmed in the Court of Appeal, Collins LJ observing:

> '... when the benefit has been once clearly annexed to one piece of land, it passes by assignment of that land, and may be said to run with it, in contemplation as well of equity as of law, without proof of special bargain or representation on the assignment. In such a

case it runs, not because the conscience of either party is affected, but because the purchaser has bought something which inhered in or was annexed to the land bought.'[4]

---

[1] In *Reid v Bickerstaff* [1909] 2 Ch 305, Buckley LJ at 325, said of the covenant in *Rogers v Hosegood* [1900] 2 Ch 388: '... the deed expressed that the covenant was taken, not for the benefit of the vendors, but for the benefit of the other lands of the vendors.'
See also Lyall *Land Law in Ireland* (2nd edn, 2000) Sweet & Maxwell, p 699.

[2] *Renals v Cowlishaw* (1878) 9 ChD 130, in which Hall V-C stated that, in order for the successor of the covenantee to claim the benefit of the covenant, 'it must appear that the benefit of the covenant was part of the subject-matter of the purchase.'

[3] *Rogers v Hosegood* [1900] 2 Ch 388 at 398. See also Todd 'Annexation After *Federated Homes*' [1985] Conv 177 at 178–179, fn 13.

[4] [1900] 2 Ch 388 at 407.

[16.27] Accordingly, the following are the conditions under which alone a successor of a covenantee will be able to enforce the benefit of a restrictive covenant:

(a) he must be an express assignee of the covenant as opposed to an assignee of the land only; or,

(b) the covenant must be annexed to the land by being expressed to be for the benefit and protection of the particular land subsequently acquired by a successor of the covenantee; in such event, the benefit passes to the successor of the covenantee, regardless of whether he was aware of the existence of the covenant: this is because the restrictive covenant is akin to an easement, with the property of the covenantee, or his successor, deemed to be the equivalent of a dominant tenement; or,[1]

(c) if the covenant is not expressly annexed to the land of the covenantee by the deed creating the covenant, the covenantee himself, by subsequent deed, can annex the benefit of the covenant to the land which he continues to own.[2]

In the absence of an express assignment of the benefit of the covenant, or of an annexation of the benefit of the covenant to the land, either by the deed creating the covenant or by a later instrument under hand of the covenantee while he still owns the land, then the benefit of the covenant will not pass to a successor of the covenantee. In such circumstances, it is for the covenantee to enforce or to abstain from enforcing the restrictive covenant. Once the covenantee has disposed of all of the land intended to be benefited by the restrictive covenant, he will be unable to seek to enforce it, on the assumption that, if the land purported to be benefited by the covenant has been effectively disposed of, the covenantee will no longer require the benefit of the covenant.[3]

---

[1] *Reid v Bickerstaff* [1909] 2 Ch 305.

[2] [1909] 2 Ch 305 at 320.

[3] *Re Union of London and Smith's Bank Ltd's Conveyance* [1933] Ch 611, at pp 632–633, per Romer LJ; also *Smith and Snipes Hall Farm Ltd v River Douglas Catchment Board* [1949] 2 KB 500, per Denning LJ.

Disposal of part only of the land benefited by a covenant

[16.28] If the successor of the covenantee is the purchaser of part only of the land intended to be benefited by the covenant, then such successor cannot enforce the benefit of the covenant, on the basis of annexation, unless it can be shown that the benefit was intended to enure for each part of the land and not just for the entirety. If this intention can be demonstrated, the benefit of the covenant will run with the land and will pass to the purchaser of part of the land without being specifically mentioned.[1] The benefit of a covenant, in order to be validly assignable at law, must be assigned as a whole.[2] However, in *Re Union of London and Smith's Bank Ltd's Conveyance*, Romer LJ held that, even where the benefit of the covenant has not been annexed to all or any part of the lands of the covenantee, but to the entirety of the lands only, equity will permit the covenantee to assign the benefit of a covenant in successive pieces to the respective purchasers of each parcel of the lands affected by the covenant, provided that:–

(a)   the land must be capable of being benefited by the covenant;

(b)   the land must be certain or ascertainable;

(c)   the covenantee cannot enforce the benefit of the covenant after all the lands purported to be benefited by it have already been assigned.

The rationale behind the latter requirement is that, if the purpose of the covenant were to enable the covenantee to dispose of his land advantageously, that result would already have been obtained once the property had been disposed of; hence, there would be no need for equity further to protect the covenant. According to Romer LJ, even an express assignment of the covenant would be ineffective if the part of the property which the covenant was designed to benefit had previously been disposed of:

'The covenantee must, indeed, be at liberty to include in any sale of the retained property the right to enforce the covenants. He might not otherwise be able to dispose of such property to the best advantage, and the intention with which he obtained the covenant would be defeated. But if he has been able to sell any particular part of his property without assigning to the purchaser the benefit of the covenant, there seems no reason why he should at a later date and as an independent transaction be at liberty to confer upon the purchaser such benefit. To hold that he could do so would be to treat the covenant as having been obtained, not only for the purpose of enabling the covenantee to dispose of his land to the best advantage, but also for the purpose of enabling him to dispose of the benefit of the covenant to the best advantage.'[3]

Equity, therefore, will not permit a covenantee to assign the benefit of a restrictive covenant once it is no longer necessary for the benefit of the land which it was originally created to benefit.

---

[1]   *Re Union of London and Smith's Bank Ltd's Conveyance* [1933] Ch 611.
[2]   [1933] Ch 611 at 630; *Stilwell v Blackman* [1968] Ch 508 at 521. See para **[16.35]**.
[3]   [1933] Ch 611 at 632–633.

Whether annexation to the whole or any part

[16.29] In *Re Ballard's Conveyance*[1] Clauson J held that the principle of annexation was analogous to the old common law requirement, that for the benefit of a covenant to run, it must touch and concern the land of the covenantee. Hence, where the covenant is stated to run with the entirety, and not with the whole or any part, of the land retained by the covenantee, even a successor of the covenantee of the entire lands will be unable to enforce the benefit of the covenant where the overall area of the land is so large that the greater proportion of it does not stand to be affected by a breach of covenant. According to Clauson J, the principles articulated in *Rogers v Hosegood*[2] could not be interpreted as a proposition that, in such circumstances, the covenant might be severed and treated as annexed to only such part of the lands as it actually touches and concerns.

In *Re Ballard's Conveyance* the lands of the covenantee comprised 1,700 acres, and on the evidence it emerged that the greater proportion of them would be unaffected by a breach of covenant. This case was distinguished in *Marquess of Zetland v Driver*,[3] in which, although the area of the lands was also substantial, the covenant was deemed to be enforceable by a successor of the covenantee, because it had been expressed to be for the benefit of the whole or any part of the unsold property of the covenantee and not merely for the entirety of the lands owned by him.

[1]   *Re Ballard's Conveyance* [1937] Ch 473.
[2]   *Rogers v Hosegood* [1900] 2 Ch 388.
[3]   *Marquess of Zetland v Driver* [1939] Ch 1.

[16.30] *Federated Homes Ltd v Mill Lodge Properties Ltd*[1] can perhaps be construed as authority for a somewhat less restrictive and technical interpretation. In this Brightman LJ conceded that he had difficulty in accepting the idea that the benefit of a covenant could be annexed to the whole of the land but not to a part of it, unless the covenantee chose specifically to retain the benefit of the covenant under his own control, so that it would only pass with the lands if the covenantee himself chose to assign the benefit of it. According to Brightman LJ, the proper construction of an instrument creating a covenant was that it should be annexed to every part of the benefited land, unless the contrary clearly appears.[2] Manifestly, such a contrary intention would appear if the deed creating the covenant had specified that the benefit of it was not to pass unless it was expressly assigned.[3]

[1]   *Federated Homes Ltd v Mill Lodge Properties Ltd* [1980] 1 All ER 371.
[2]   [1980] 1 All ER 371 at 381.
[3]   *Roake v Chadha* [1983] 3 All ER 503.

[16.31] The difficulty of determining whether the benefit of a covenant has been annexed to the whole or any part of the lands affected, as opposed to the entirety of the lands, has been redressed, in Northern Ireland, by Article 34(5) of the Property (Northern Ireland) Order 1997 which provides, in relation to covenants specified in the article, that '... it is conclusively presumed that the benefit and burden of a covenant ... attach permanently to the whole and every part of the land of the covenantee and the covenantor respectively.'

Implied annexation

[16.32] Where the benefit of a restrictive covenant has not been expressly annexed to the land of the covenantee, the intention so to annex the benefit of the covenant must be determined from the deed creating the covenant when construed in the light of the surrounding circumstances, including any necessary implications in the deed which are warranted by the surrounding circumstances.[1] The absence of express words effecting annexation is not fatal. If, on the construction of the instrument creating the restrictive covenant, both the land meant to be benefited and an intention to benefit that land, as distinct from benefiting the covenantee personally, can be clearly established, then the benefit of the covenant will be annexed to that land and run with it, notwithstanding the absence of express words of annexation.[2]

---

[1]   *Sainsbury plc v Enfield London Borough Council* [1989] 1 WLR 590.
[2]   *Shropshire County Council v Edwards* (1982) 46 P & CR 270 at 277–278, per Judge Rubin; *Sainsbury plc v Enfield London Borough Council* [1989] 1 WLR 590 at 597, per Morritt J.

Covenant must have capacity actually to benefit covenantee's land

[16.33] There are many reasons, other than a desire to benefit the land currently owned by him, why a covenantee may take a covenant that seems to affect his land. It may be for his personal benefit only. The covenantee may wish to sell off the covenant, at his own time, to best advantage, in which case the covenant cannot be enforced by a successor or assign of the covenantee's land. The covenant might not be meant to benefit any lands currently owned by the covenantee, but to enhance the value of land he expects to acquire in the future.[1]

---

[1]   *Keates v Lyon* (1869) LR 4 Ch App 218, per Selwyn LJ.

[16.34] In relation to whether or not the covenant actually benefits the land purported to be benefited, the view of the party creating it should be regarded as *bona fide* unless there is manifest evidence to the contrary.[1] For example, a restrictive covenant will not be the less enforceable because there is other similar property in the area not subject to the same restrictions. Neither will the running of the benefit of the covenant be prevented merely because neighbouring landowners may also derive benefit from its enforcement.[2]

In *Lord Northbourne v Johnston and Son*,[3] Sargant J stated that, merely because a party arguing against the enforceability of a restrictive covenant urges that breach of the covenant would not damage the land still owned by the covenantee, is no reason why the covenant should not be enforced. Otherwise, there would be an onus on the covenantee to demonstrate that the covenant was intended to benefit each part of the estate that he happened to retain, and was, in fact still benefiting each such part, every time a challenge was mounted to the covenant.

If this requirement were to apply to a building development, according to Sargant J it would impose an impossible onus on the developer. The normal intention is for the covenantee-developer to benefit his retained land in a general way. It is not up to him to justify the ongoing benefit of the covenant each time a parcel of land is disposed of. The covenantee is entitled to assert that the purpose of the covenant was to protect his lands from acts 'likely to prove noxious or detrimental' to the property taken as a whole. The onus then shifts to the covenantor or his successor to show that the covenantee's remaining property either was not intended to be benefited by the covenant, or could not be affected by a breach of it.[4]

The reasoning of Sargant J was adopted by Brightman J in *Wrotham Park Estate Co Ltd v Parkside Homes Ltd*,[5] who stated that, between the extremes of cases where the covenant clearly is and clearly is not of benefit to a particular property, 'there is inevitably an area where the benefit to the estate is a matter of personal opinion, where responsible and reasonable persons can have divergent views sincerely and reasonably held.'[6] It is not for a court to determine which view is the correct one, but whether the view of the party seeking to enforce the covenant is one that could reasonably be held.

---

[1]   *Marten v Flight Refuelling Ltd* [1962] Ch 115, per Wilberforce J at p 316. See also *Earl of Leicester v Wells-next-the-sea Urban District Council* [1972] 3 All ER 77, in which a restrictive covenant affecting 19 acres out of a total estate of 32,000 acres was held to be enforceable by a successor of the original covenantee.

[2]   *Marquess of Zetland v Driver* [1939] Ch 1.

[3]   *Lord Northbourne v Johnston and Son* [1922] 2 Ch 309.

[4]   [1922] 2 Ch 309 at 318.

[5]   *Wrotham Park Estate Co Ltd v Parkside Homes Ltd* [1974] 1 WLR 798.

[6]   [1974] 1 WLR 798 at 808.

Annexation and assignment not mutually exclusive concepts

[16.35] It appears that annexation and assignment are not mutually exclusive concepts, but can apply in the alternative, depending on the proper construction of the instrument creating the covenant. In *Stilwell v Blackman*[1] lands had been conveyed to a purchaser subject to a covenant by the purchaser not to use a particular portion of them other than as a private garden or for keeping a limited number of hens. The covenant by the purchaser was stated to bind the lands being acquired by him, and subsequent purchasers of them, so as to benefit and protect the adjoining property of the vendor. The plaintiff was the assignee of the vendor-covenantee, under a conveyance that expressly assigned the benefit of the covenant. The defendant was the assignee of the covenantor. The plaintiff refused to waive the application of the covenant in favour of the defendant. The plaintiff then sold portion of her land, furthest away from the land of the defendant. The purchaser bought this land on trust for the defendant who later took a conveyance of it. By this stage the defendant had started parking derelict cars on his land. In an action by the plaintiff to enforce the covenant, the defendant sought to maintain that, as the benefit of the covenant had been annexed to the whole of the plaintiff's land, it was now no longer enforceable, because the plaintiff had sold off a portion of her lands only.

---

[1]   *Stilwell v Blackman* [1968] Ch 508.

[16.36] Ungoed Thomas J rejected the suggestion that the modes of passing the benefit of restrictive covenants were mutually exclusive: the effect of the case law on the running of the benefit of covenants was not to compartmentalise covenants in such as way as 'to put the equitable principles which govern the assignment of restrictive covenants into three or four completely separate strait jackets, in which each is a completely separate law to itself.'[1] These equitable principles were designed to give best effect to the intention of the parties in relation to the enjoyment of land, an objective which they achieved either through the covenant's being annexed to the land or being expressly assigned with it. Where the benefit of a covenant is capable of running with the land of the covenantee, it is a question of construction of the terms of the covenant whether the benefit is to pass automatically, by reason of its being annexed to the land, or whether it is to be expressly assigned, or whether either method of passing the benefit can be employed alternatively:

> '... whilst the passing of the benefit of a restrictive covenant by express assignment is permitted in accordance with equitable principles without any express provision between the original covenantor and the original covenantee for such assignment, an automatic assignment of the benefit by the passing of the covenantee's relevant land cannot operate, unless the benefit has been annexed to the land, and such annexation cannot be effective unless it is made positively.'[2]

In each case, said Ungoed Thomas J, it is a question of construction of the terms of the covenant whether the annexation of the benefit of the covenant to the covenantee's land precludes its being expressly assigned with part only of that land. It commended itself to sense that there should be a facility for automatic assignment of the benefit of the covenant if the land were being assigned as a whole, or as a unit; while express assignment might be required if part only were being transferred. This would enable the covenantee to transfer the benefit of the covenant on some dispositions, and not on other ones, while at the same time preserving the benefit of the covenant for such land as he retains.[3]

---

[1]   *Stilwell v Blackman* [1968] Ch 508 at 524.
[2]   [1968] Ch 508 at 525–526.
[3]   [1968] Ch 508 at 527–528. On the undesirable features of implied annexation as a legal doctrine, see Ryder 'Restrictive Covenants: The Problem of Implied Annexation' (1972) 36 Conv 20.

Other methods of assigning the benefit of a covenant

[16.37] In addition to annexation and assignment, the benefit of a restrictive covenant may also pass to a successor of the covenantee by devolution[1] or by operation of law.[2] In order for the benefit of a restrictive covenant to pass by way of assent, the assent must allude to it specifically. In the alternative, if the executors of the deceased covenantee hold the benefit of the covenant as trustees for the intended beneficiary, he will be entitled to the benefit of the restrictive covenant in equity.[3]

---

[1]   *Marten v Flight Refuelling Ltd* [1962] Ch 115.
[2]   *Earl of Leicester v Wells-next-the-sea Urban District Council* [1972] 3 All ER 77.

3 In *Earl of Leicester v Wells-next-the-sea Urban District Council* [1972] 3 All ER 77, the assent had only alluded to incorporeal hereditaments and not specifically to the restrictive covenant. In the opinion of Plowman J at 82, '[w]hether the benefit of a restrictive covenant can be described as an incorporeal hereditament is a very doubtful question.'

The view of the courts in Ireland

[16.38] Although the concepts of annexation and assignment have not been developed in Ireland, it is clear from the case of *Belmont Securities Ltd and Young v Crean and Tuite*[1] that a similar approach, if differently expressed, will be adopted by the Irish courts. For ease of understanding of this case, the respective roles of the parties to the dispute are set out graphically below.

Plaintiffs

Original covenantee	Lessees (grocery) of assignee of covenantee
Belmont Securities Ltd and Indemnity Investments Ltd	Kieran Young and Helen Young

Defendants

Original covenantor – freehold owner of newsagency	Lessees (newsagency) of covenantor
William Crean and Una Crean	John Tuite and Carmel Tuite

In 1980 the first and second named plaintiffs had developed a small shopping complex in Bray, Co Wicklow, comprising three units, which they intended to serve as a pharmacy, a newsagency and a grocery respectively. The object was to create different businesses which would not be in competition with each other. The first and second named plaintiffs granted each unit by way of freehold transfer. The purchasers of the newsagency, the first and second named defendants, entered into a covenant with the first and second named plaintiffs not to use the premises other than for the purposes of a newsagency. Despite this, from not long after the grant of the freehold transfer, the owners of the newsagency, the first and second named defendants, had used the premises partly as a grocery as an ancillary business to the newsagency. The third and fourth named defendants were the current lessees of this unit and had expended considerable money on the grocery aspect of the business in the belief that the covenant that the unit should be used only as a newsagency had become 'a dead letter'. The third and fourth named plaintiffs were the current lessees of the grocery unit and joined the first and second named plaintiffs, as the original covenantees, in an attempt to secure an injunction against the use of any part of the newsagency as a grocery. The original covenantees, having disposed of the three units by way of freehold transfer, had at the time of the action no interest at all in the shopping complex.

The third and fourth named defendants, the current lessees of the newsagency which had for some eight years been used partly as a grocery, contended that it would be inequitable and unconscionable to grant an injunction against them, especially as they had incurred expenditure in the belief that the covenant was moribund.

---

[1] *Belmont Securities Ltd and Young v Crean and Tuite* (17 June 1988, unreported) HC.

[16.39] O'Hanlon J observed that the creation of restrictive covenants binding on successors of the original covenanting parties was more difficult in freehold transactions than in leasehold ones, because in the case of leases the successors of the covenantee (where the covenantee is the lessor) retain an interest in the land through the reversion.[1] In freehold transactions, he held, there would have to be what had come to be known as a 'building scheme'. O'Hanlon cited, *verbatim*, the principles governing a building scheme, or a scheme of estate development, as these had been enunciated in 1909 by Cozens-Hardy MR in *Reid v Bickerstaff*:[2]

> 'What are some of the essentials of a building scheme? In my opinion there must be a defined area within which the scheme is operative. Reciprocity is the foundation of the idea of a scheme. A purchaser of one parcel cannot be subject to an implied obligation to purchasers of an undefined and unknown area. He must know both the extent of his burden and the extent of his benefit. Not only must the area be defined but the obligations to be imposed within that area must be defined ... A building scheme is not created by the mere fact that the owner of an estate sells it in lots and takes varying covenants from various purchasers. There must be notice to the various purchasers of what I may venture to call the local law imposed by the vendors upon a definite area. If on a sale of part of an estate the purchaser covenants with the vendor, his heirs and assigns, not to deal with the purchased property in a particular way, a subsequent purchaser of part of the estate does not take the benefit of the covenant unless (a) he is an express assignee of the covenant, as distinct from assignee of the land, or (b) the restrictive covenant is expressed to be for the benefit and protection of the particular parcel purchased by the subsequent purchaser ... Unless either (a) or (b) can be established, it remains for the vendor to enforce or abstain from enforcing the restrictive covenant.'

---

[1] One would have thought that the principal reason for the greater ease in enforcing covenants in leases, rather than among freeholders, was because of the provisions of ss 12 and 13 of Deasy's Act, see para **[15.12]**. Yet another illustration of the enduring proclivity of lawyers and judges to resort to the cold comforts of the common law in lieu of the facility afforded by statute?

[2] *Reid v Bickerstaff* [1909] 2 Ch 305 at 319–320.

[16.40] It should be noted, that in the lengthy passage quoted above, Cozens-Hardy MR was in fact addressing two separate issues: whether the ingredients existed for a 'building scheme', so that the restrictive covenant could be enforced in equity, by and against the various purchasers of the several plots and their successors; or whether, in the absence of such ingredients, the benefit of the covenant had been annexed to the lands of the covenantee. O'Hanlon J in his judgment in *Belmont Securities Ltd and Young v Crean and Tuite*[1] seems to regard the only relevant issue as being whether a 'building scheme' could be found to exist, even though the *dicta* he cites from Cozens-Hardy MR are equally applicable to annexation which O'Hanlon J addresses only indirectly.

[1]   *Belmont Securities Ltd and Young v Crean and Tuite* (17 June 1988, unreported) HC.

[16.41] In the judgment of O'Hanlon J, there was nothing to suggest that the third and fourth named plaintiffs, the current lessees of the grocery unit, were the express assignees of the benefit of the covenant that the newsagency unit should be used as a newsagency only. Neither had the covenant been stated to be for the benefit of the grocery unit. Hence, the covenant had neither been annexed to the grocery unit, nor had the benefit of it been assigned. Accordingly, the lessees of an assignee of the covenantee were unable to enforce the covenant against the lessees of the covenantor.

O'Hanlon J also held that, since the original covenantees could not be held to have had notice of the breach of the covenant in 1980, they were not estopped on their own account from invoking the covenant in the present proceedings. However, since they had not retained any ultimate interest in the lands affected by the breach of covenant, and as there was no proof of damage, O'Hanlon J declined to grant an injunction, instead awarding nominal damages of £5 to the first and second named plaintiffs and giving no order at all in favour of the third and fourth named plaintiffs.[1]

[1]   Coughlan in *Property Law* p 286 argues that, notwithstanding the failure by O'Hanlon J to find that a 'building scheme' existed, O'Hanlon J's holding that a restrictive covenant was in theory enforceable by a covenantee retaining no interest at all in the lands benefited by the covenant, and who had no contractual relationship with the successor of the covenantor, had to be effectively based upon an acceptance that a 'building scheme' existed. However, it must be recalled that the first and second named plaintiffs were the original covenantees, so that the primary issue under consideration, in relation to *those* plaintiffs, was whether the *burden* of the covenant could be enforced in equity under the principle of *Tulk v Moxhay* (1848) 2 Phil 774. The essence of a 'building scheme' is that *both* the burden *and* the benefit of restrictive covenants require to be mutually enforceable among a host of successors to the original covenanting parties, and O'Hanlon J's judgment was that the *benefit* did not run.

[16.42] Arguably, on the point that the covenantee had not retained any interest in land to be benefited by the covenant, O'Hanlon J could have disposed of the case in reliance on *London County Council v Allen*,[1] where the Court of Appeal had held that the benefit of a restrictive covenant could not be enforced, against a successor of the covenantor, if the covenantee owned no land capable of being benefited by the covenant; and on *Marquess of Zetland v Driver*,[2] where the Court of Appeal had held, that 'covenants can only be enforced so long as the covenantee or his successor in title retains some part of the lands for the benefit of which the covenant was imposed.'[3]

[1]   *London County Council v Allen* [1914] 3 KB 642.

[2]   *Marquess of Zetland v Driver* [1939] Ch 1.

[3]   [1939] Ch 1 at 8.

Whether there should be separate rules at law and in equity

[16.43] The concepts of annexation and assignment arise invariably in the context of restrictive covenants. The enforceability of restrictive covenants against successors of the original covenantor is a creation of equity. Annexation and assignment are likewise the offspring of equity and are regarded in the textbooks as applicable to restrictive covenants only. There is no indigenous jurisprudence regarding annexation and assignment in Ireland. Over a century and a quarter after the Supreme Court of Judicature (Ireland) Act 1877, it might reasonably be argued that the existence of separate rules of common law and equity in relation to the running of the benefit of different types of covenant does not commend itself to sense.

Moreover, there are pertinent judicial *dicta* to this effect. In the seminal case, relating to the annexation of restrictive covenants, of *Rogers v Hosegood*,[1] Farwell J, on the specific issue of the running of the benefit, observed:

'... in my opinion, there can be no difference between law and equity in construing such covenants with a view to seeing whether they do or do not run with the land. The same words in the same document must necessarily bear the same meaning in all the Courts. It is true that in many of the cases decided by the Court of Chancery expressions are found to the effect that the defendants are bound in equity, whether the covenants in strictness run with the land or not. But I think that such expressions are due to the reluctance that the Vice-Chancellors felt to express any opinion on points of common law, and ... I cannot see how such a covenant could run in equity if it did not run at law.'[2]

Similarly, in *Stilwell v Blackman*, Ungoed Thomas J stated:[3]

'... the burden of the covenant runs only in equity ... and although the benefit may run at law, yet the rules applicable to the benefit running are ... the same in law and in equity, except that equity, unlike law, does not require that the assignment of the benefit of the covenant be limited to an assignment of the whole of the covenantee's relevant land but permits separate assignments to assignees of part of that land.'

There is surely merit in urging that the rules governing the enforceability of the benefit of covenants, regardless of whether the covenant is positive or negative, should be uniform.

---

[1]   *Rogers v Hosegood* [1900] 2 Ch 388, see para **[16.25]** ff.
[2]   [1900] 2 Ch 388 at 397–398.
[3]   *Stilwell v Blackman* [1968] Ch 508 at 521.

[16.44] Ideally, the rules governing the running of the benefit of all covenants should be as follows:

(a)   the covenant must clearly benefit the land as opposed to just its owner;

(b)   the land intended to be benefited must be identified in the instrument creating the covenant;

(c)   the intention to benefit the land must be clear from the instrument creating the covenant;

(d)   such intention must also demonstrate whether the land is to be benefited only as an entirety, or whether each part separately disposed of by the covenantee is likewise meant to be benefited;

(e)   in cases of doubt or uncertainty, and in only those cases, the circumstances surrounding the execution of the instrument that created the covenant may be consulted as an aid to interpretation.

Chapter 17

Restrictive Covenants in Estate Schemes

Introduction

[17.01] A situation of potential complexity is presented, in an estate scheme or a scheme of development, by the need to include a range of restrictive covenants, which can be enforced among the first purchasers and the developer while the estate is in the process of development, and, in due course, by all purchasers and their successors by and against each other. Frequently, these estates comprise a considerable number of properties, with many of them interdependent, such as 'town houses' and apartments. The restrictive covenants sought to be enforced among the various owners and their successors most often conduce to preserving a measure of uniformity, or at least consistency, in estate structure. Hence, covenants in relation to user only as a private dwelling, the preservation of external colour schemes, the control of animals, avoidance of nuisance, collective utilisation either of television aerials or cable television as mutually exclusive alternatives, and common arrangements regarding the disposal of refuse are frequently employed. The provision of shared services, such as lighting, security, public insurance and parking, by a management company wholly controlled by the property owners is also often a feature. This can give rise to another set of covenants between the management company and the individual owners, in identical format for each premises, and reciprocally enforceable by all.

[17.02] In order for the successor of the covenantee to be able to enforce, and for the successor of the covenantor to be liable to, the type of covenants required in a residential estate, the purchaser of each newly developed plot would have to covenant directly with the vendor and with each previous purchaser. The benefit of such covenants could be enforced by previous purchasers under s 5 of the Real Property Act 1845, and by subsequent purchasers provided that the common vendor either expressly assigned or annexed the benefit of the covenant to each portion of the estate subsequently sold. Since each previous purchaser and each subsequent purchaser would ultimately have entered into similar covenants, they would each be liable to the burden of the covenants under the principle of *Tulk v Moxhay*[1] and each enabled to enforce them through annexation or assignment. It is clear that an infelicity in drafting, or the inadvertent exclusion at a later point in the development of one of the previous purchasers in a subsequent purchaser's deed of covenant, would result in a breach of the chain of enforceability.

Another possible device is for all of the purchasers to enter into mutual covenants with each other. However, this is more likely to arise where the lots are sold in their entirety at auction. If, as is more usual, they are sold by private treaty at different times, then the differing dates of the several sales would be likely to preclude, or at best render difficult, the establishing of a contract among all the purchasers. Especially would this be likely to arise where an earlier purchaser had died or had already sold on before a subsequent purchaser bought their plot from the original developer. '…it is unlikely that the prior and subsequent purchasers are ever brought into personal relationship, and yet the equity may exist between them.'[2]

It is clear that the conventional methods of enforcing covenants after the relevant properties have been disposed of by the original covenanting parties are scarcely adequate to the phenomenon of multiple holdings with comparable needs and obligations; and so equity has identified a number of necessary ingredients to simplify the process of enforcement.

---

1   *Tulk v Moxhay* (1848) 2 Phil 774.
2   *Elliston v Reacher* [1908] 2 Ch 374, at p 385, per Parker J. See, generally, Robinson 'Restrictive Covenants' (1974) 38 Conv 90 at 101–103.

Principles Governing the Enforceability of Estate Covenants

[17.03] The method by which equity has facilitated the mutual enforceability of restrictive covenants in an estate scheme, is to regard as enforceable, by and against all purchasers of property in the estate and their successors, covenants entered into by each purchaser with the vendor, at the time of the selling off of each site, that comply with certain conditions from which it can be inferred that the covenants are intended to be mutually enforceable among the purchasers and the developer and also among original and subsequent purchasers.

These conditions were first clearly articulated by Parker J in *Elliston v Reacher*:

(a)   **Common vendor** – that the party seeking to enforce the benefit of the covenant and the party against whom it is sought to be enforced must have derived title under a common vendor.

(b)   **Prior lotting** – that prior to selling the lands the developer must have laid out his estate, or at least a portion of it including the lands of the parties in dispute, for sale in lots, subject to restrictions which, though possibly varying to some degree, are consistent only with some general scheme of development.

(c)   **Benefit of all lots sold** – that the vendor must have intended these restrictions to benefit the lands sold, and that the restrictions *did* in fact benefit the lands sold, even if they also benefited other land retained by the vendor:

   (i)   the vendor's objective in imposing the restrictions is to be gleaned from the circumstances of each case, including the nature of the restrictions;

   (ii)   if the restrictions are generally calculated to enhance the values of the several lots sold, then it is a reasonable inference that the vendor intended the restrictions to benefit the lots, even though the value of other land retained by the vendor might have been similarly enhanced.

(d)   **Purchased on the basis of benefiting the estate** – that the parties in dispute, or their predecessors, had bought their respective lands from the common vendor on the basis that the restrictions were to enure for the benefit of all the lots in the scheme of development:

    (i)   if the first three ingredients have been established, and also that the purchasers were aware of them, then the fourth requirement can be readily inferred;

    (ii) once all four requirements have been established, then, regardless of the dates of the respective purchases, every purchaser is entitled in equity to enforce the restrictive covenants against every other purchaser, and liable to have the burden of the restrictive covenants enforced against them.[1]

  (e)   **Common area** – In *Reid v Bickerstaff*,[2] a further requirement was introduced – that the area of the scheme, within which the mutually enforceable covenants are to operate, must be defined. This was explained on the basis that there cannot be a reciprocity of obligation, which is the essence of the obligations imposed in a scheme of development, if a prospective purchaser is unaware either of the total area to be affected by the covenants or of the nature of the covenants being imposed upon him for the benefit of all purchasers. However, it is not necessary that all covenants are identical, since there can be different types and classes of property in different parts of the estate; even so, all the covenants must be consistent with the overall scheme of development.[3]

---

1   'It is, I think, enough to say, using Lord Macnaghten's words in *Spicer v Martin* (1888) 14 App Cas 12, that where the four points I have mentioned are established, the community of interest imports in equity the reciprocity of obligation which is in fact contemplated by each at the time of his own purchase.' *Elliston v Reacher* [1908] 2 Ch 374 at pp 384–385, per Parker J.

2   *Reid v Bickerstaff* [1909] 2 Ch 305.

3   At p 319, per Cozens-Hardy MR, at p 323, Buckley LJ; cited with approval by O'Hanlon J in *Belmont Securities Ltd and Young v Crean and Tuite* (17 June 1988, unreported) HC, see ch 16, para **[16.38]**, **[16.39]**.

Defined area

[17.04] In *Emile Elias and Co Ltd v Pine Groves Ltd*,[1] the purported development was sold off in five plots, of which the fifth plot did not appear in a map attached to the conveyances of the first three plots. The purchaser of the fourth plot was also the purchaser of the fifth plot. Lord Browne-Wilkinson, delivering the advice of the Privy Council, held that the area affected by the development had not been laid out with sufficient clarity when the development was established. It is not sufficient that the common vendor has himself defined the area. In order to create a valid building scheme, the purchasers of all the land within the area of the scheme must also know what that area is.[2]

---

1   *Emile Elias and Co Ltd v Pine Groves Ltd* [1993] 1 WLR 305.

2   [1993] 1 WLR 305 at 310.

A more flexible approach

[17.05] More recently, the courts have tended less to adhere to strict compliance with the rubrics enunciated by Parker J in *Elliston v Reacher*[1] and have striven more to infer an intention to create a scheme of mutually enforceable restrictive covenants in an estate scheme, even where certain of the traditional ingredients have been lacking.

---

1   *Elliston v Reacher* [1908] 2 Ch 374.

[17.06] In *Baxter v Four Oaks Properties Ltd*,[1] the development known as Four Oaks Estate had been sold off in plots in 1891 subject to covenants entered into by each purchaser which were stated to be for the benefit of all purchasers of properties on the estate and enforceable by anyone becoming entitled to any part of the estate. There was no evidence that the developer had laid out the estate in lots before selling it off and the plots sold were of various sizes. In a dispute over the enforceability of certain of the restrictive covenants by successors to the original purchasers, it was argued that the absence of 'antecedent lotting' was inconsistent with the principle underlying the enforceability of covenants in an estate scheme.

Cross J refused to accept this submission, observing:

'... for well over 100 years past where the owner of land deals with it on the footing of imposing restrictive obligations on the use of various parts of it as and when he sells them off for the common benefit of himself (in so far as he retains any land) and of the various purchasers *inter se* a court of equity has been prepared to give effect to this common intention notwithstanding any technical difficulties involved.'[2]

With the passing of time, stated Cross J, it had become apparent to the courts that there was no particular virtue in the execution of a deed of mutual covenant, except insofar as it evidenced the intention of the parties; and what came to be called 'building schemes' were enforced if it was manifest from them that the various purchasers were intended to have mutually enforceable rights, even though no attempt was made to bring them into contractual relations with each other.

After citing with approval the four-part test adumbrated by Parker J in *Elliston v Reacher*,[3] Cross J noted that *Elliston v Reacher* itself was not a case in which there was evidence of execution of a mutual covenant, but was authority for the proposition that one could infer from the surrounding circumstances the intention to establish a building scheme reciprocally enforceable by the several purchasers. Accordingly, the failure by the common vendor to lay out the estate in lots prior to the first sale was consistent with an argument against his having had the intention to establish an estate scheme, but did not establish that a scheme of development did not exist.

---

1   *Baxter v Four Oaks Properties Ltd* [1965] 1 Ch 816.
2   [1965] 1 Ch 816 at 825.
3   *Elliston v Reacher* [1908] 2 Ch 374.

[17.07] A similar approach was adopted by Stamp J in *Re Dolphin's Conveyance*,[1] in which, not only were all the plots not laid out as an estate prior to being sold in various stages between 1871 and 1877, but more than one vendor had been involved. Stamp J held, on the construction of the covenants in the deeds of conveyance – which had been stated to be for the benefit of all the owners of the plots comprising the estate – that they were intended to impose a local law for the benefit of all the owners of the plots making up the estate, despite the fact that the various purchasers had not covenanted with each other (so that it could not be held that there was a mutual covenant); nor had the vendors covenanted to enforce the restrictive covenants against subsequent purchasers, simply to impose the same covenants on them:

> 'To hold that only where you find the necessary concomitants of a building scheme or a deed of mutual covenant can you give effect to the common intention found in the conveyances themselves, would, in my judgment, be to ignore the wider principle on which the building scheme cases are founded ... where deeds of mutual covenant have fallen to be considered, effect has been given not to the deed of mutual covenant itself as such but to the intention evidenced by its existence.'[2]

Accordingly, the primary test is to look to the mutually agreed intention, as evidenced by the language in the deeds of sale. In *Re Dolphin's Conveyance* the conveyances executed by the original purchasers demonstrated a similar intention to a deed of mutual covenant. In neither event would all of the successive purchasers and persons claiming through them have been brought into direct contractual relationship with each other. But each was consistent with an intention to create an estate scheme, and in each case also the restrictive covenants were mutually enforceable by and against the successors to the original purchasers.

---

[1] *Re Dolphin's Conveyance* [1970] 1 Ch 654.
[2] [1970] 1 Ch 654 at 663.

[17.08] In *Brunner v Greenslade*[1] Megarry J rejected a suggestion that the principles in relation to the enforcement of restrictive covenants in an estate scheme must be founded on the law governing the running of covenants. If this were so, then the whole scheme would fail if any one purchaser were to buy a number of different plots. A common owner of several different plots cannot covenant with himself. However, if it turned out that covenants would be held unenforceable in relation to several plots owned by one purchaser, but would be both enforceable by and against that same purchaser in relation to other purchasers, 'then haphazard islands of partial immunity within the area of the scheme' would arise within the estate scheme which would defeat its entire purpose:

> 'Such immunities seem to me contrary to the whole basis of schemes of development, with their concept of a local law for the area of the scheme. If, then, the result of putting the basis of schemes of development upon a relentless application of the law governing covenants is to produce an unsatisfactory or unworkable result, some other basis must be sought.'[2]

The theoretical difficulties associated with the rules governing the running of covenants do not arise if the enforceability of restrictive covenants under a scheme of development is deemed to depend on an equity arising from the circumstances independently of contractual obligation. Neither does the difficulty, which would clearly exist in the case of an easement, of the possibility of unity of seisin destroying the enforceability of the restrictive covenants.[3]

---

[1] *Brunner v Greenslade* [1970] 3 WLR 891.
[2] [1970] 3 WLR 891 at 900.

[3] 'I accordingly think that I am fabricating no new equity, but merely emphasising an established equity. ... equity, in developing one of its doctrines, refuses to allow itself be fettered by the concept upon which the doctrine is based if to do so would make the doctrine unfair or unworkable. After all, it is of the essence of a doctrine of equity that it should be equitable, and, I may add, that it should work: equity, like nature, does nothing in vain. ... It may be, indeed, that this is one of those branches of equity which work best when explained least.' [1970] 3 WLR 891 at 902. See also *Texaco Antilles Ltd v Kernochan* [1973] AC 609.

Sub-purchasers within an estate scheme

[17.09] Where an estate has a principal scheme of development, and also a group of sub-purchasers within the principal scheme, the terms of the principal scheme are enforceable among the sub-purchasers provided that they do not seek to vary its terms.

[17.10] In *Brunner v Greenslade* a firm of builders, in 1928, bought a block of development land and covenanted with their vendors only to construct a certain number of dwellinghouses on the land bought. This covenant was expressed to be for the benefit of the vendors and of the present and future owners of the estate or any part of it. The builders divided the land into five plots, built one dwellinghouse on each of them, and then sold the plots off. Each purchaser entered into an indemnity covenant with the builders in relation to the builders' covenants in the 1928 conveyance. None of the several purchasers covenanted directly to observe the covenants in the 1928 conveyance. They each covenanted with the builders only to indemnify the builders against breach of covenant.

Megarry J distinguished, where there are two or more sub-lots in a scheme of development, between the existence of a sub-scheme, which usually involves some variation of the principal scheme for the purchasers of sub-lots, and the absence of a sub-scheme, in which case the question arises whether the terms of the original scheme are automatically enforceable by and against the purchasers of the sub-lots. According to Megarry J,[1] in order for a scheme of development to exist in the first place, there had to be a covenant establishing it, but it was not necessary for the sub-purchasers to enter into any covenant, in order for the original scheme of development to be enforceable by, against and among the sub-purchasers.

'What binds the sub-purchasers *inter se* is not any covenant of their own making (for there is none) but an equity independent of any contractual obligation entered into by them, and arising from the circumstances of the existence of the head scheme, the process of division into sub-lots and the disposal of those lots. If on the disposal the common intention was that the local law created by the head scheme should apply within the sub-area, then apply it would. It would be remarkable if the restrictions of the head scheme were to be reciprocally enforceable between the owner of a sub-lot and a plot elsewhere on the estate, however distant, and yet unenforceable as between neighbouring owners of sub-plots.'[2]

---

[1]   Following the decision of Simonds J in *Lawrence v South County Freeholds Ltd* [1939] Ch 656.
[2]   *Brunner v Greenslade* [1970] 3 WLR 891 at 899.

[17.11] However, the covenants in the scheme of development will cease to be enforceable among the sub-purchasers if the sub-purchasers enter into a new scheme of covenants with each other. In such event, as among the sub-purchasers, the new sub-scheme will supersede the principal scheme, so that 'there will be a new local law to replace the old.[1] Even so, the covenants in the head scheme will still be enforceable by and against the property owners in the sub-scheme in situations affecting property in the head scheme.

---

[1]   *Brunner v Greenslade* [1970] 3 WLR 891 at 902, per Megarry J.

Variation in covenants among similar estate properties

[17.12] A restrictive covenant will not be enforceable under a purported scheme of development if there is a significant variance among the covenants applicable to properties of a similar type. *Emile Elias and Co Ltd v Pine Groves Ltd*[1] came before the Judicial Committee of the Privy Council on appeal from the Court of Appeal in Trinidad and Tobago. Property owned by St Andrew's Golf Club in Trinidad had been sold in five plots in 1938. Each purchaser covenanted with the vendor company that they would only erect one dwellinghouse on their respective plots. The purchasers of plots 1, 4 and 5 entered into identical covenants. The purchasers of plots 2 and 3 entered into identical covenants with each other, but different in several respects from the covenants entered into by the purchasers of plots 1, 4 and 5.

Covenants by Owners of Plots 1, 4 and 5	Covenants by Owners of Plots 2 and 3
To construct one dwellinghouse only	To construct one dwellinghouse only
Not to discharge noxious or unsanitary matter into a drain being constructed	To construct and maintain grease traps at the outlet of all drains
	To use the one dwellinghouse as a private residence only
	Not to create a nuisance on the adjacent land

The plaintiff was the owner of the house on plot 3 who was endeavouring to prevent the defendant, the owner of the house on plot 1, from constructing a second house on his plot in breach of covenant. Lord Browne-Wilkinson noted that there had been neither privity of estate, nor privity of contract, nor a chain of assignments, nor appropriate words of annexation, so that the covenant against constructing any more than one dwellinghouse on the plot could be enforced, if at all, only on the basis that the covenants were mutually enforceable under a building scheme.

---

[1]   *Emile Elias and Co Ltd v Pine Groves Ltd* [1993] 1 WLR 305.

[17.13] Lord Browne-Wilkinson found that there was sufficient divergence between the covenants affecting the two groups of houses to prevent their being reciprocally enforceable among the purchasers or their successors:

'It is most improbable that a purchaser will have any intention to accept the burden of covenants affecting the land which he acquires being enforceable by other owners of the land in the scheme area unless he himself is to enjoy reciprocal rights over the lands of such other owners: the crucial element of reciprocity would be missing. That does not mean that all lots within the scheme must be subject to identical covenants. For example in a scheme of mixed residential and commercial development, the covenants will obviously vary according to the use intended to be made of each category of lot. But if, as in the present case, the lots are all of a similar nature and all intended for high class development consisting of one dwelling on a substantial plot, a disparity in the covenants imposed is a powerful indication that there was no intention to create reciprocally enforceable rights.'[1]

In particular, Lord Browne-Wilkinson felt that it was unlikely that the purchasers of plots 2 and 3 would have entered into obligations whereby the purchasers of plots 1 and 4 and 5 could prevent their taking lodgers, but without the same obligation operating in reverse: in short, there was an absence of an enforceable local law based on reciprocity.

It was also relevant that the covenants entered into by the purchasers had all been with the vendor company and were not stated in any case to be made with the owners of plots already sold by the common vendor. The common vendor as owner of the rest of the golf course, out of which the five plots had been carved, had a vested interest in securing covenants that would preserve the character of the land retained by it, regardless of any potential benefit accruing to the house owners. Hence, it had not been established that there was ever an intention to create mutually enforceable covenants among the purchasers or their successors as the owners of houses in a building estate.

---

[1]   *Emile Elias and Co Ltd v Pine Groves Ltd* [1993] 1 WLR 305 at 311.

In Ireland

[17.14] The principles governing schemes of development have not been considered to any significant extent in Ireland.[1] As has been shown, O'Hanlon J in *Belmont Securities Ltd and Young v Crean and Tuite*[2] quoted approvingly from the judgment of Cozens-Hardy MR in *Reid v Bickerstaff*,[3] in relation to the principles governing both schemes of development and annexation, while ostensibly purporting to rely on it in the former context only. Despite the continuing preponderance of leasehold titles in Ireland, particularly in relation to commercial property, there is no reason to suppose that the pervasive regime of equity now administered by the English courts, in the context of schemes of development, will not be followed in either part of the island.

---

[1]   *Elliston v Reacher* [1908] 2 Ch 374 was considered with approval by Kenny J in *Fitzpatrick v Clancy* (1965 unreported) HC, but an enforceable scheme of restrictive covenants was not found to exist.
[2]   *Belmont Securities Ltd and Young v Crean and Tuite* (17 June 1988, unreported) HC. See para **[16.38]** ff.
[3]   *Reid v Bickerstaff* [1909] 2 Ch 305.

[17.15] The Property (Northern Ireland) Order 1997 clarifies and codifies much of the law in relation to the enforceability of restrictive covenants in building estates. Among the covenants listed in Article 34 as enforceable among the owners of freehold estates are a number intended for the protection of amenities or services ('amenity covenants'), including:

(a)   covenants not to use property other than as a private dwelling;

(b)   covenants against creation of a nuisance;

(c)   covenants against interfering with facilities;

(d)   covenants prohibiting, restricting or regulating the erection of buildings or structures;

(e)   covenants relating to the planting, tending and removal of vegetation.[1]

---

[1]   Article 34(4)(e).

[17.16] An estate scheme, or scheme of development, in relation to freehold property, is deemed to arise, where:

(a)   the land is divided into two or more units, or 'parcels', by a developer, for the purpose of being conveyed to purchasers, in the article known as 'parcel owners';

(b)   there is an intention between the developer and the purchasers to create reciprocity of covenants;

(c)   this intention is shown expressly in the conveyances, or can be implied from the division of the land into parcels, the nature of the covenants contained in the conveyances, and 'the proximity of the relationship between parcel owners.'[1]

Where a development, as defined, arises, the covenants entered into between the parcel owners and the developer are deemed to have been made among the parcel owners themselves, to the extent that such covenants are capable of reciprocally benefiting and burdening the parcels in the estate.[2]

---

[1]   Article 34(7).
[2]   Article 34(6).

[17.17] Under Article 25 of the 1997 Order, which treats of the extinguishment of leasehold covenants following the acquisition of the freehold, the 'amenity covenants' listed above are among those specified as preserved.[1] Furthermore, any covenants formerly enforceable, by and against a lessee who acquires his freehold and others holding property in the same estate or building scheme, continue to be mutually enforceable after the acquisition of the freehold by any or all of the property owners under the scheme.[2] Such covenants are also enforceable among the successors to the participants in the building scheme.[3]

In a case where 'amenity covenants' apply, as soon as one house owner purchases the fee simple in the property, 'there is to be taken to subsist (if it does not subsist apart from this provision) a building scheme in respect of the land in which all the persons holding parcels under dispositions in substantially similar terms from the same rent-owner, and the successors in title of those persons, are participants ...'; so that the covenants are mutually enforceable by and against the former lessee and the other house owners, and amongst the various house owners and their successors, regardless of whether or not any more of the ground rents have been redeemed.[4]

---

1. Article 25(2)(h).
2. Article 25(2)(j).
3. Article 26(9).
4. Article 26(6).

Chapter 18

Extinguishment of Covenants

Statutory Removal of Covenants

Republic of Ireland

[18.01] There is no facility in the Republic of Ireland for the extinguishment of a covenant that has become moribund or which is no longer appropriate to the current use of the property it affects, except in cases where all parties entitled to enforce the covenant agree that it should be discharged or where it is incapable of being enforced.

[18.02] Under s 69(3) of the Registration of Title Act 1964, a covenant or condition which has been registered under s 69(1) may be modified or discharged by order of the court on proof to the satisfaction of the court:

   (a)   that the covenant or condition does not run with the land, or

   (b)   that it is not capable of being enforced against the owner of the land, or

   (c)   that the modification or discharge of the covenant would be beneficial to the persons principally interested in its enforcement.

A covenant that falls into one of the above categories may 'with the consent of all persons interested in the enforcement thereof be modified or discharged' by the Registrar of Titles without any court order being made.

However, this provision does not assist in cases where the covenant has become otiose or irrelevant but the party entitled to its enforcement is insisting either that it be complied with or that compensation be paid as a pre-condition to his agreeing to its discharge.[1] In such a situation one has to look to the principles of equity to seek to render the covenant unenforceable or have it extinguished by the acquisition of the fee simple under s 28 of the Landlord and Tenant (Ground Rents) (No 2) Act 1978.

---

[1]   See Lyall 'Freehold Covenants and What To Do With Them' (1991) 9 ILT (NS) 157; Wylie *Irish Land Law* (3rd edn, 1997) Butterworths, p 1014; Report of the Law Reform Commission: *Land Law and Conveyancing Law: Positive Covenants Over Freehold Land and other proposals* (LRC70–2003) pp 18–19, paras 1.18, 1.19.

Northern Ireland

[18.03] In Northern Ireland, s 48(1) of the Land Registration Act (Northern Ireland) 1970, as amended by Schedule 1 of the Property (Northern Ireland) Order 1978, provides that the Registrar of Titles may discharge or modify a covenant with the consent of the parties concerned, and that the court may discharge a covenant if satisfied that it does not run with the land or is not capable of being enforced against the owner of the land.

[18.04] The Property (Northern Ireland) Order 1978[1] also contains provision for the extinguishment of covenants, affecting either registered or unregistered land, by the Lands Tribunal, where the effect of such covenants is unreasonably to impede the enjoyment of land.[2] Article 5(1) provides:

> 'The Lands Tribunal, on the application of any person interested in land affected by an impediment, may make an order modifying, or wholly or partially extinguishing, the impediment on being satisfied that the impediment unreasonably impedes the enjoyment of the land or, if not modified or extinguished, would do so.'

Article 5(2) provides that no application can be made, except with the permission of the Lands Tribunal, in respect of an 'impediment' created by a lease that has run for less than 21 years.

An 'impediment' is defined as including easements, profits, restrictive covenants, and also positive covenants to carry out works on land, to permit works to be carried out on land, or to pay for, or contribute to payment for, works to be carried out on land.[3] The Lands Tribunal, upon application by a person interested in land, may by order determine whether such land is liable to any 'impediment', the nature and extent of such impediment and by whom it would be enforceable.[4] In determining whether to order that an impediment be modified or extinguished, the Lands Tribunal can take into account the purposes for which the impediment was created, any change in character of the neighbourhood in the meantime, the development trends in the neighbourhood as demonstrated by the granting or refusing of planning applications, the nature and extent of the practical benefit to the person intended to be benefited by the impediment[5] and, in cases where the impediment constitutes an obligation to execute works, or to contribute towards the cost of executing works, 'whether the obligation has become unduly onerous in comparison with the benefit to be derived from the works or the doing of that thing.'[6]

---

[1] 1978 No 459 (NI 4).

[2] For a detailed commentary on, and analysis of, the provisions of The Property (Northern Ireland) Order 1978, see Dawson 'Modification and Extinguishment of Land Obligations Under The Property (Northern Ireland) Order 1978' (1978) 29 NILQ 223; also Shaw 'Modification of Restrictive Covenants Under Statute' (1981) 32 NILQ 289.

[3] Article 3(1).

[4] Article 4(1).

[5] Article 5(5)(a), (b), (d) and (e).

[6] Article 5(5)(f).

[18.05] Where the Lands Tribunal makes an order modifying or extinguishing an impediment, it can substitute a new impediment in lieu of the one being modified or extinguished.[1] It can also direct the applicant to pay compensation to the party formerly benefited by the impediment so modified or extinguished.[2] A new impediment cannot be introduced without the agreement of the applicant, but the Lands Tribunal is empowered to refuse the original application where the applicant's agreement to the introduction of a new impediment in substitution for the one being extinguished is not forthcoming.[3]

Where court proceedings have been taken to establish or enforce an impediment, the court may refer any question to the Lands Tribunal, if satisfied that the circumstances are such that that question could have been disposed of by the Lands Tribunal had application been made to it.[4] In any such proceedings, the court can make an order modifying or extinguishing the impediment on the same terms as the Lands Tribunal could have done.[5] Any order in relation to the finding of the existence of an impediment not created by deed, or regarding the modification or extinguishment of an impediment, whether made by the Lands Tribunal or the court, is to be registered in the Land Registry or the Registry of Deeds, as appropriate.[6]

---

[1] Article 5(6)(a).
[2] Article 5(6)(b).
[3] Article 5(7).
[4] Article 6(1)(a).
[5] Article 6(2)(a).
[6] Article 8.

Equity

[18.06] As has been shown, in the Republic of Ireland the only freehold covenants which clearly can be enforced against successors of the covenantor are restrictive covenants, and these are enforceable in equity only.[1] The original covenantee will not be entitled to enforce the covenant against a successor of the covenantor if the original covenantee does not have an interest in any land capable of being benefited by the covenant,[2] or if they have parted with the ownership of the land intended to be benefited by the covenant.[3] A successor of the covenantee will not either be able to enforce the benefit of the covenant unless they retain some part of the lands intended to be benefited by the covenant.[4] Where the benefit of a restrictive covenant has not been annexed to all or any part of the land of the covenantee, neither the covenantee nor his successor will be able to assign the benefit of the covenant once they have already disposed of all or that part of the land which the covenant had purported to benefit.[5] Where at any particular time the covenantor or his successor can demonstrate that the estate of the covenantee then remaining either was not intended to be benefited by the covenant, or could not possibly be affected by a breach of it, a remedy for its breach will not be granted.[6]

---

[1] *Tulk v Moxhay* (1848) 2 Phil 774, as applied by Chatterton V-C in *Craig v Greer* [1899] 1 IR 258 at 272–273. See para **[16.02]**.
[2] *London County Council v Allen* [1914] 3 KB 642.
[3] *Smith and Snipes Hall Farm Ltd v River Douglas Catchment Board* [1949] 2 KB 500.
[4] *Marquess of Zetland v Driver* [1939] Ch 1.
[5] *Re Union of London and Smith's Bank Ltd's Conveyance* [1933] Ch 611.
[6] *Marten v Flight Refuelling Ltd* [1962] Ch 115; *Earl of Leicester v Wells-next-the-sea Urban District Council* [1972] 3 All ER 77; *Wrotham Park Estate Co Ltd v Parkside Homes Ltd* [1974] 1 WLR 798.

[18.07] A restrictive covenant can also be rendered unenforceable through the equitable doctrines of estoppel or laches which will result in the refusal of injunctive relief in appropriate cases. In *Belmont Securities Ltd and Young v Crean and Tuite*[1] the third and fourth named defendants had pleaded that it would be inequitable for the plaintiffs to enforce against them, as assignees of the original covenantor, a covenant restricting the use of the premises leased by them to the business of newsagency only, on the basis that they had expended considerable monies on the grocery aspect of their business in the genuine belief that the covenant had become moribund. O'Hanlon J concluded that the conditions necessary for the benefit of a restrictive covenant to run with a freehold property had not been satisfied.

---

[1]   *Belmont Securities Ltd and Young v Crean and Tuite* (17 June 1988, unreported) HC. See para **[16.38]**.

[18.08] In *Craig v Greer*[1] it had been contended, without success, by sub-lessees of the covenantor, that a successor of the covenantee was estopped from enforcing a covenant against the use of the demised premises other than as a dwellinghouse or tea-rooms on account of the construction by her of a number of shops elsewhere on her land. Here, both Chatterton V-C and the Court of Appeal had held that the plaintiff was not estopped from enforcing the covenant, by reason of the negligible impact of the building she had carried out on the change of character in commercial Belfast which had been central to the case urged by the defendants. Even so, the fact that a personal equity could have been applied against the successor of the covenantee was acknowledged.[2]

Under Article 5(5)(b) of the Property (Northern Ireland) Order 1978, any change in the character of the land or neighbourhood is a consideration which may be taken into account by the Lands Tribunal in determining whether a covenant should be modified or extinguished. Likewise, under Article 45(3) of the Property (Northern Ireland) Order 1997, the court must have regard to the nature of the estate and location of the land owned by a covenantee or his successor, before it can find that he has been so 'materially prejudiced' by any breach of covenant as to be entitled to relief.[3]

---

[1]   *Craig v Greer* [1899] 1 IR 258.
[2]   Particularly in the judgment of Fitzgibbon LJ at 298.
[3]   See para **[16.20]**.

Acquisition of the Freehold

[18.09] A covenant in a mesne lease, that an under-lease will be renewed for as often as, and to the extent that, the mesne lease is renewed, is extinguished if a purchaser of the mesne lease subsequently purchases the fee simple, on the basis that the fee simple in the hands of its vendor is not so liable.[1]

---

[1]   The so-called *toties quoties* covenant for renewal: *Kent v Stoney* (1859) 9 Ir Ch Rep 249, *Coey v Pascoe* [1899] 1 IR 125; 'The Right of a Covenantee for Renewal as Against a Reversioner' (1903) 37 ILTSJ 383.

[18.10] In Northern Ireland, Article 25[1] of the Property (Northern Ireland) Order 1997 provides that once the fee simple in a former leasehold has been acquired, through acquisition of the ground rent, all covenants concerning the land, other than those provided for specifically in Article 34[2] as binding successors to the covenanting parties in freehold estates, will cease to have effect.

---

[1]   See para **[15.30]**.
[2]   See para **[14.34]**.

[18.11] In the Republic of Ireland, s 28 of the Landlord and Tenant (Ground Rents) (No 2) Act 1978 provides for the automatic extinguishment of leasehold covenants on the acquisition by the holder of the land of the fee simple. Subsection (1) states:

> 'Where a person having an interest in land acquires the fee simple in the land, all covenants subject to which he held the land, other than a covenant specified in subsection (2), shall thereupon cease to have effect and no new covenant shall be created in conveying the fee simple.'

Subsection (2) preserves covenants affecting the amenities of land occupied by the immediate lessor, covenants relating to the statutory duty of such immediate lessor, covenants concerning a right of way over the land whose fee simple is being acquired, or concerning rights of drainage over other land, or rights 'necessary to secure or assist the development of other land'.[1]

---

[1]   The most significant category of covenants preserved are restrictive covenants facilitating the development of lands of third parties; see Lyall 'Freehold Covenants and What to Do with Them' (1991) 9 ILT (NS) 157 at 158–59.

[18.12] The pervasive effect of this section was demonstrated in *Whelan v Cork Corpn*[1] in which Murphy J[2] refused to allow an interpretation that would have had the effect of limiting the application of s 28 to covenants between the lessor and the lessee and not covenants in favour of third parties.

In 1908 the freehold owner of lands at Douglas Road, Cork granted a 99-year lease of them to a lessee. In 1937 the lessee granted a sub-lease of part of the lands, called Instow, in which the mesne lessee (the sub-lessor) covenanted not to erect on specified adjacent lands, also held by him under the lease of 1908, any construction beyond a height of 12 feet. This sub-lease was eventually assigned to the plaintiffs in 1989, subject to the rent, and subject to and with the benefit of the covenants.

In 1948 the mesne lessee under the 1908 lease granted a sub-lease of the adjacent lands that had been covered by the covenant in the earlier sub-lease of 1937 not to build anything in excess of 12 feet in height. This sub-lease contained a covenant by the sub-lessee to erect a dwellinghouse but not to erect any other property to a height of more than 12 feet. In due course the sub-lessee under the 1948 sub-lease built a dwellinghouse, known as the Cottage, Riverbank, in compliance with the covenant. In 1984 the sub-lessee's interest in the sub-lease of 1948 was assigned to the defendant, and in November 1989 the interest of the mesne lessee (or sub-lessor) in the leases of 1908 and 1948 was assigned to the defendant.

A week later, by conveyance dated 15 November 1989, the freehold in the lands known as the Cottage, Riverbank was conveyed to the defendant, subject to and with the benefit of the leases of 1908 and 1948, with the stated intention that the terms should merge in the freehold reversion and be extinguished by it. The proposal by the defendant local authority to carry out works which would result in erecting a construction of in excess of 12 feet in height led to an application for an injunction by the plaintiffs. While Murphy J held that the covenant not to construct to a height greater than 12 feet would have bound the defendants through the principle in *Tulk v Moxhay*,[4] a broadened definition of lessor, and also s 13 of Deasy's Act,[3] he accepted that the covenant had been extinguished by s 28 of the Landlord and Tenant (Ground Rents) (No 2) Act 1978, which provided for the extinguishment of *all* covenants subject to which the lessee had held the land.

---

[1]   *Whelan v Cork Corpn* [1991] ILRM 19.
[2]   And subsequently also the Supreme Court at [1994] 3 IR 367.
[3]   See para **[15.17]–[15.18]**.
[4]   *Tulk v Moxhay* (1848) 2 Phil 774.

[18.13] The plaintiffs contended that this section, in order to safeguard their constitutionally protected property rights, should be construed as confined to covenants between lessor and lessee and not include covenants affecting third parties. Murphy J held that this argument ran counter to the express words of the section, and was also inconsistent with the principles enunciated in *East Donegal Co-Operative v AG*[1] which provide for a presumption of constitutionality in the interpretation of legislation, subject to not flying in the face of the express words of the statute where they are clear and unambiguous.

> 'It is difficult to escape the wide net cast by the words 'all covenants' subject to which the land was held and any argument that the comprehensive expression should be limited to the relationship between the lessee and those entitled to the superior interests would be inconsistent with the subsequent provisions of the section which provide that certain covenants which do not cease to have effect may be enforced 'by any person aggrieved by breach of the covenant.' The Oireachtas clearly recognised that the covenants which were ceasing to have effect (subject to a very limited number of exceptions) included covenants for the benefit of a wide range of covenantees and not only the lessor or owner of a superior interest. In my view the Oireachtas has shown a clear and unambiguous intention to eliminate a wide range of covenants, including those for the benefit of third parties, where the fee simple is acquired under the provisions of the 1978 Act.'[2]

In relation to whether s 28 of the Landlord and Tenant (Ground Rents) (No 2) Act 1978 might be unconstitutional, through infringement of the property rights of citizens guaranteed under Article 40.3.2°, Murphy J said little, but tantalisingly. Submission from the Attorney-General would have to be heard before a definitive judicial pronouncement could be given. In the meantime a literal interpretation of s 28 would not 'necessarily render that section in conflict with the Constitution.' One possible argument which Murphy J suggested might lie with the Attorney-General was 'that the rights such as those enjoyed by the plaintiffs over the lands of others are now more effectively and more justly protected and vindicated under the Local Government (Planning and Development) Acts 1963 to 1982 and by the evolution and general acceptance of environmental planning which regulates property rights of this nature in accordance with the principles of social justice.'[3]

---

[1]   *East Donegal Co-Operative v AG* [1970] IR 317 at 341.
[2]   *Whelan v Cork Corpn* [1991] ILRM 19 at 27–28.
[3]   [1991] ILRM 19 at 28.

[18.14] This is an unfortunate pronouncement, since it confuses the public, social and environmental purpose of planning legislation with the purely proprietorial interests served by the legal and equitable principles that govern the running of covenants. The differences between planning control and the regulation of land usage by covenant are at least as significant, it is suggested, as their points of resemblance. Both have been thus tersely expressed:

> 'Restrictive covenants and planning are similar in that they both control land use: they are very dissimilar in that the control of one is based on the interests of the community, the control of the other is imposed by private individuals with no necessary regard for the community ... To this extent, then, planning and restrictive covenants are opposites, but the controls which they impose are cumulative. It ... is no defence to an action for breach of covenant that planning permission has been obtained.'[1]

The constitutional ramifications of the statutory extinguishment of the rights of covenantees and their successors need soon to be settled. One could only lament if the ultimate outcome were the submersion of the intricate jurisprudence regarding the running of covenants in the deep and muddied waters of local government planning control. It would be a sad day, one fears, for the preservation of property rights.

---

[1]   Mellows 'Planning and Restrictive Covenants' (1964) 28 Conv 190 at 191.

[18.15] As shown, in Northern Ireland, the Property Orders of 1978 and 1997, read together, provide comprehensively for the running of specified covenants, even after the enlargement of leaseholds into fees simple, while catering also for the extinguishment of covenants that unduly impede the enjoyment of land.

The law in the Republic of Ireland has considerable ground to catch up.

Chapter 19

Licences and How They Arise

Concept of a Licence

[19.01] Licences differ both from easements and covenants that run with land, by reason of the fact that they only involve lands of the licensor, and not lands of the licensee. In its simplest and most traditional form, a licence is merely a permission given by the licensor to the licensee to go on to the licensor's land for a purpose. This could be to admire a view or to pick daffodils. Ordinarily, such a licence does not warrant intervention from the courts. In conceptual terms, a licence is revoked once the permission is withdrawn. However, the question often arises whether a licensor is entitled to revoke a licence, or – put another way – whether, in the event that the licensor effectually revokes the licence, the licensee is entitled to redress; and whether, in appropriate circumstances, the licensee can seek to prevent the licensor from revoking the licence. This can occur, for example, where a licence is granted to enjoy the fruits of a profit à prendre, and the revocation of the licence means that ongoing access to the profit is denied.

[19.02] At one time the answer to these rudimentary questions depended on the nature of the instrument creating the licence and whether the licence was linked to a recognisable interest in land – such as a profit à prendre – or whether it merely conferred a contractual right between the two parties to the licence. The authority for this proposition derives from the English Court of Exchequer in *Wood v Leadbitter*,[1] where a ticket holder ejected from Doncaster Racecourse was held entitled to no redress. An interest in land had to be granted by deed. If the enjoyment was not granted by deed it could be revoked. According to Alderson B, a parol licence of something, which in order to be effective had to be granted by deed, was revocable; and, if revoked, conferred no rights at law on the licensee, other than perhaps for breach of contract. Hence, though the licensor might not have any *right* to revoke the licence, once he had exercised his capacity to do so, the former licensee became a trespasser and was liable to be evicted. In the eternal contest between might and right, the common law favoured might where a licence was revoked that had not been granted by deed.[2]

---

[1]   *Wood v Leadbitter* (1845) 13 M & W 838.

[2]   Except where the licensee had spent money on foot of it: *Blood v Keller* (1860) 11 ICLR 124. See para [19.11]. But see Lyall *Land Law in Ireland* (2nd edn, 2000) Sweet & Maxwell, p 512, in relation to the limited value of *Blood v Keller* as a precedent.

[19.03] The availability of equitable remedies in all courts since the Supreme Court of Judicature (Ireland) Act 1877 has modified the rigour of this approach. Equity takes

341

the view that the extent to which a licensor can revoke a licence with impunity is constrained by the terms of a contract, express or implied, which govern both the duration of the licence and the question of its revocability.

In *Hurst v Picture Theatres Ltd*,[1] in facts that broadly resembled those in *Wood v Leadbitter*,[2] a majority of the English Court of Appeal held that a man who had paid for a seat in a cinema to watch the screening of a film, when ejected in mid-performance on the mistaken basis that he had not paid, was entitled to damages for assault and false imprisonment. This was because there was an implied contractual term in the licence to watch the film that the licensee would be permitted to remain until the screening had ended. In theory, a breach of contract could have been restrained by an injunction. Hence, the licensee was not a trespasser after his licence was revoked, and accordingly was entitled to damages for being treated as one.

A similar approach was taken by the Irish Supreme Court in *Whipp v Mackey*,[3] where, although the licensee was in breach of his obligation to make periodic payments under the licence agreement, the proviso for termination in the event of non-payment of rent rendered the licence liable to equitable relief against forfeiture, which was granted.

---

1   *Hurst v Picture Theatres Ltd* [1915] 1 KB 1.
2   *Wood v Leadbitter* (1845) 13 M & W 838.
3   *Whipp v Mackey* [1927] IR 372, see para **[20.16]**; also 'When a Licence Is Revocable' (1915) 49 ILTSJ 33.

[19.04] The most contentious issues involving licences turn upon the subject matter of the licence itself and the terms or conditions in the agreement creating it: in other words, the purpose to be achieved for the licensee by the granting of the licence and the extent to which he is prejudiced by its infraction or revocation. Certain generic terms have emerged as the jurisprudence has developed, such as 'licence coupled with an interest' and 'contractual licence'; similarly the extent to which a licence is 'revocable' or 'irrevocable'. Arguably, these and kindred terms are qualifiers of convenience to determine whether, in the case of any particular licence, its infraction or revocation attracts legal or equitable redress. Though distinctive in sound and character, such terms are far from being so truly. Attempts to regard them as such can only augur additional confusion in an area of the law already deep in judge-made technicality and trammelled by historical complications.

[19.05] A palpable paradox of the tenuous nature of a licence is that, in many cases, the actual enjoyment by the licensee spawns an issue whether it confers merely a licence or, instead, a tenancy. In light of the wide gamut of statutory rights to which a tenancy is subject, and the resultant desire of parties in many cases to avoid its creation, the issue as to whether any particular agreement of which occupancy is a feature constitutes a licence or a lease is frequently fraught. It is strange, indeed, that a right, in theory the most ephemeral, can be argued as conferring an estate in land. The concomitant of occupancy, subject to detailed terms regarding duration and payment, doubtless at least in part accounts for what must justly be regarded as one of the law's most odd anomalies.

[19.06] Finally, a licence has also often been used, in recent times, as a kind of residual tag or badge to describe innovative equitable redress awarded by the courts. The principle is, that the court, frequently on the basis of an equitable estoppel applied against a party, either who has acted unconscionably or in whose favour it would be unconscionable to make an award, determines that a particular party should have a right, which, in the absence of clearer description, has been categorised as a licence. This licence, sometimes known as an 'estoppel licence', unlike other forms of licence, is not the product of agreement between the parties. It is a remedial device, created by equity, and is often associated with a constructive trust.

Definition and Characteristics of a Licence

General

[19.07] The traditional legal status of a licence is best summarised in the oft quoted description by Vaughan CJ in *Thomas v Sorrell*:[1]

'A dispensation or a licence properly passeth no interest, nor alters or transfers property in anything, but only makes an action lawful which, without it, had been unlawful.'

Similar language has been used in the Irish courts:

(a)   Madden J in *David Allen and Sons Billposting Ltd v King*:[2]

'a licence … renders lawful as against the licensor an act that would otherwise amount to an actionable act of trespass';

(b)   from a different perspective, but in similar terms, by Judge Shannon in Whyte v Sheehan and Sheehan:[3]

'If a person is not to have the exclusive possession of or sole dominion over the matter, then his limited right to use and enjoyment is a licence and merely affords an answer to a charge of trespass.'

---

[1]   *Thomas v Sorrell* (1674) Vaughan 330 at 351, cited with approval by Molony LJ in *David Allen and Sons Billposting Ltd v King* [1915] 2 IR 448 at 479. See also Hanbury 'Licences, A Jonah's Gourd' [1954] CLJ 201, [1955] CLJ 47.
[2]   *David Allen and Sons Billposting Ltd v King* [1915] 2 IR 213 at 244.
[3]   *Whyte v Sheehan and Sheehan* [1943] Ir Jur Rep 38 at 42.

[19.08] It is axiomatic that an interest so fleeting can normally be revoked by the simple fact of withdrawing the permission. Judge Deale in *Smith v Hogg*[1] stated:

'Ordinarily, though not invariably, a licence to use land is revocable at the will of the licensor and terminable with the death of either the licensor or the licensee.'[2]

But this can be varied by the terms of the contract creating the licence. In *Woods v Donnelly*,[3] Hutton J held that a licence to draw sand and gravel was valid for the lifetime of the licensee and was binding, during it, on a successor of the licensor.

---

[1]   *Smith v Hogg* [1953–1954] Ir Jur Rep 58 at 61. Judge Deale went on to hold that the grant of a burial plot in a graveyard by the parish priest who was the legal owner of the graveyard created an irrevocable licence in perpetuity: this was partly on the basis of the use to which the plot of ground was to be put and partly also because valuable consideration had been given for it. See

also Dowling 'Exclusive Rights of Burial' (1992) 43 NILQ 288 where it is suggested that a burial right is an exception to the normal principles governing contractual licences by being binding on a successor to the licensor. Since the burial right is intended to be perpetual, according to Dowling at 295, such a right is 'a unique species of incorporeal hereditament capable of existing in gross, which can be acquired by statute, grant or prescription.'

2   See also *Judge v Lowe* (1873) IR 7 CL 291. See paras **[5.36]–[5.38]**.
3   *Woods v Donnelly* [1982] NI 257.

[19.09] A licence which is linked to the enjoyment of a profit *à prendre*, sometimes described as a 'licence coupled with an interest', is inherently assignable and is also binding on successors of the licensor. Perhaps the more correct proposition is that the grant of a profit *à prendre*, being an interest in land, endures for as long as the profit either is capable of being enjoyed, or is permitted by the agreement granting it to be enjoyed, and the licence is carried forward by the durability of the profit. Both the profit, and the licence to access and secure the fruits of it, can be limited to the lifetime of one of the parties to the agreement[1] or to a term of years.[2] By its nature, a contractual licence, if unaccompanied by an interest in land, does not *itself* create such an interest, and so is not assignable.[3]

---

1   As in the case of *Woods v Donnelly* [1982] NI 257 – lifetime of licensee.
2   *Bayley v Marquis of Conyngham* (1863) 15 ICLR 406; see Wylie *Irish Land Law* (3rd edn, 1997) Butterworths, pp 1018–1019.
3   *David Allen and Sons Billposting Ltd v King* [1915] 2 IR 313, [1916] AC 54. See para **[20.11]**.

[19.10] Where a licensee has engaged in works on foot of the licence, he is entitled to reasonable notice of the termination of the licence in order to wind down his operation and remove any plant and equipment introduced by him onto the property of the licensor.[1] A licensee will be entitled to use reasonable force to remove from the land over which he has a licence anything that obstructs his enjoyment of it.[2]

---

1   Per McWilliam J in *Law and Fry v Murphy and Dooly* (12 April 1978, unreported) HC, following the cases of *Minister of Health v Belotti* [1944] 1 All ER 238 and *Winter Garden Theatre (London) Ltd v Millennium Productions Ltd* [1947] 2 All ER 331, 'from which it appears that no particular time is required to terminate a licence but that according to the circumstances of the particular case, a licensee will be allowed to remain in possession for a reasonable time after he has received notice of termination.'
2   Per Judge Deale in *Smith v Hogg* [1953–1954] Ir Jur Rep 58 at 61, by way of analogy with the principles governing interference with an easement, following Palles CB in *Jennings v McCarthy* (1908) 42 ILTR 217.

Acting on foot of a licence

[19.11] As long ago as 1860, the Irish Court of Exchequer, in *Blood v Keller*,[1] held that, where a licensee has incurred expense on foot of the licence, even if only a parol licence, it cannot be revoked without the licensor's making financial reparation to the licensee, so as to put him in the position he would have been in had he not acted on the licence.

The defendant erected a weir on that part of a river which flowed through his land. This raised the level of the river, with the result that that part of the river flowing through the plaintiff's land burst its banks. To the plaintiff's claim for damages, the defendant responded that he had constructed the weir under a parol licence from the plaintiff, in order to provide for a greater supply of water to a mill operated by him, and had, furthermore, expended £200 in improving the weir and providing additional machinery to work the increased water supply.

Fitzgerald B stated that:

' ... a parol licence given to do an act on the licensee's own land, which would, *prima facie*, be a lawful act independently of the licence, but which might, from circumstances, be attended with injurious consequences to the licensor, cannot be countermanded, if the act be done and completed and expense incurred on the part of the licensee; or that, at least, the licensor cannot insist on the removal of what has been done, without putting the licensee in *statu quo* as to the expenditure incurred.'[2]

---

[1]   *Blood v Keller* (1860) 11 ICLR 124. See also *Mulville v Fallon* (1872) IR 6 Eq 458; *Pullan v The Roughfort Bleaching and Dyeing Co (Ltd)* (1888) 21 LR Ir 73; also Lyall *Land Law In Ireland* pp 512, 534–535, Davis 'Abandonment of an Easement: Is It a Question of Intention Only?' [1995] Conv 291.

[2]   (1860) 11 ICLR 124 at 130.

Circumstances that Imply a Licence

[19.12] Normally a licence will come into existence through agreement between the parties. Sometimes, however, the precise nature of the agreement is difficult to identify and judicial pronouncement has been required to determine whether the relationship is that of licence or otherwise. A trespasser in a local authority house, who is allowed temporarily to remain there on the basis of periodic payments for 'use and occupation', has been held to be a bare licensee under a revocable licence.[1] However, where there is no contract between the parties any licence granted is revocable at will and does not constitute a contractual licence.[2]

A licence has also been deemed appropriate to describe the relationship between a former lessor and lessee in a case where the lessee remained in occupation paying a periodic sum as part of a 'tentative and interim arrangement' while a new tenancy agreement was being negotiated, albeit that negotiations ultimately broke down.[3]

In *Burrows v London Borough of Brent*,[4] the House of Lords devised the concept of a 'tolerated trespasser' to describe the status of a local authority tenant against whom the authority was forbearing to execute a possession order, obtained for non-payment of rent, pending compliance by the tenant with certain conditions. Inevitably, in such an inchoate relationship, the question of which, if any, terms from the former tenancy remain applicable, arises.[5] The concept has not been considered by the Irish courts. Indeed, apart from its alliterative ease of recall, the notion of 'tolerated trespasser' seems a highly dubious one. The traditional concepts of tenancy at will, or bare licence, are arguably preferable.

1 *Northern Ireland Housing Executive v McCann* [1979] NI 39.
2 *Northern Ireland Housing Executive v Duffin* [1985] NI 210.
3 *Irish Shell and BP Ltd v John Costello Ltd (No 2)* [1984] IR 511, per Henchy J at 517, who observed: '... if on a consideration of all the evidence in a particular case, it is shown that the payments made were not intended to be paid as rent, the presumption of a tenancy will be rebutted.' However, the significance of this dictum is vitiated by the fact that each of the three judges in the Supreme Court put a different interpretation on the status of the occupancy, in the particular facts of the case, following the termination of an earlier tenancy agreement: according to O'Higgins CJ the new arrangement was a tenancy at will, and according to McCarthy J it constituted a monthly tenancy; also *Bellew v Bellew* [1982] IR 447, in which the Supreme Court held that an occupancy entered into while negotiations for a tenancy were pursued constituted a licence, because the arrangements were between family members.
4 *Burrows v London Borough of Brent* [1996] 4 All ER 577.
5 See Cafferky 'Tolerated Trespass – What does this mean for the former Landlord and Tenant?' [1998] 62 Conv 39; Courtney 'Tolerated Trespass: *Burrows v London Borough of Brent*' (1999) 4 CPLJ 55.

[19.13] In *McGill v LS*[1] Gannon J held that the mutual convenience nature of the occupancy by a cohabiting couple would not give rise to a contractual licence by the owning partner in favour of the other after the relationship between them had ended.

The facts disclose a sorry tale of a long love languishing.

The plaintiff man and the defendant woman had met in 1963 while they were both employed by American radio companies in central Europe. They soon started to live together in the defendant's apartment in Munich. This continued until 1973. During the mid-1960s they used to holiday together in Ireland and while on holiday looked out for a house to purchase as their home. They found one in Co Cork in 1967, but it was in poor repair. The plaintiff bought it for £1,775. Over the next couple of years he also paid for renovations which came to nearly £10,000. The only contribution by the defendant was the sum of £1,000 for outbuildings which she described at the time as a gift to the plaintiff.

In 1973 American interest in broadcasting in central Europe was coming to an end and both the plaintiff and the defendant decided to settle down in the plaintiff's house in Co Cork. Not long afterwards the plaintiff went to America to cover the Watergate crisis and entered into a relationship with another woman there. In the meantime the defendant continued to live in the house in Co Cork. The plaintiff, believing his relationship with the defendant now to have concluded, sought an order for possession of the Co Cork property, which was granted in the Circuit Court.

---

1 *McGill v LS* [1979] IR 283.

[19.14] The defendant appealed to the High Court, claiming possession because:

(i) it had been the common intention of both parties that the premises should be acquired for their mutual benefit as a home, and that they should jointly have a beneficial interest in it;

(ii)   the defendant had contributed financially to assist the plaintiff in the purchase and refurbishment of the property;

(iii)   the plaintiff was estopped from denying possession to the defendant, having represented to her that she could live there, on foot of which she had given up her job in Germany and moved to Ireland.

The defendant asked that the plaintiff be deemed to have granted her 'leave or licence to have accommodation in the said premises to use or occupy the same as a home and to remain in possession of the same for so long as the defendant might wish or require.'[1] She further maintained that, since this leave or licence was coupled with an interest, it was irrevocable.

---

[1]   *McGill v LS* [1979] IR 283 at 286.

[19.15] In relation to the alleged existence of a contractual licence, the defendant sought to rely on the decision of the English Court of Appeal in *Tanner v Tanner*.[1] In this case, the parties had not been married; the property was in the name of the man, but the woman had contributed to the support of the household. The Court of Appeal, after the relationship had ended, held that there was an implied contractual licence in favour of the woman, to continue to reside in the house, which would persist for at least as long as the children of the relationship were attending school. According to Lord Denning MR, if the circumstances changed so that the accommodation was no longer reasonably required, then the licence might terminate.

Gannon J was unimpressed with this: the dates of commencement and termination of such an alleged licence would be impossible to reckon. Neither was the mutual convenience nature of the parties' joint occupancy consistent with a legally binding contractual relationship.

> 'The concept of a wavering licence terminable not at the will of the grantor but upon the possibility of changeable circumstances affecting the licensee ... is one which I find difficult to reconcile with the law. ... For so long as the domestic and personal relations between the parties remained stable it was unlikely that the licence would be terminated, but the evidence does not support a licence by implied contract which could continue against the will of the plaintiff or even beyond the period of their mutual association.'[2]

---

[1]   *Tanner v Tanner* [1975] 1 WLR 1346.

[2]   *McGill v LS* [1979] IR 283 at 293.

The Emergence of the Estoppel Licence

[19.16] In *John Cullen v Patrick Cullen and Martin Cullen*[1] Kenny J employed the principle of equitable estoppel to prevent the revocation of a facility to occupy, and so produced what has come to be known as an 'estoppel licence'. However, it is arguable that the true legal status of such ongoing occupancy is, not a licence in the conventional sense, but a judicially permitted possession (usually arising from an estoppel or a constructive trust), that more closely resembles a licence than any other enjoyment known to the law.[2] The facts in *Cullen v Cullen* are no less remarkable than the judgment.

---

[1]   *John Cullen v Patrick Cullen and Martin Cullen* [1962] IR 268.

[2]   For a discussion of the distinction between contractual and estoppel licences, see Wade 'Licences and Third Parties' (1952) 68 LQR 337; Briggs 'Licences: Back to Basics' [1981] Conv 212; Thompson 'Licences: Questioning the Basics' [1983] Conv 50; Briggs 'Contractual Licences: A Reply' [1983] Conv 285; Moriarty 'Licences and Land Law: Legal Principles and Public Policies' (1984) 100 LQR 376; Battersby 'Contractual and Estoppel Licences as Proprietary Interests in Land' [1991] Conv 36.

[19.17] The plaintiff at the time of the action was in his eightieth year. Married late in life, he had a successful boot, shoe and grocery business in Enniscorthy, Co Wexford. He had another business in nearby Adamstown where he also lived. The plaintiff and his wife had five children, two of whom were defendants in the action. He was a man of authoritarian cast, with strong views on the duty of his wife and children to obey him. His wife frequently sided with her sons against their father. This led him in turn to believe that they were robbing and cheating him. Occasionally, he turned some of them out of home.

The second defendant, Martin Cullen, had worked in the family business for several years, but in 1958 the plaintiff ended the arrangement and paid his son off. With this money Martin Cullen bought a farm at Adamstown. However, his father was unhappy with this, and so Martin Cullen continued to live in his parents' house. Early in 1959 Mrs Cullen engaged a mental specialist to attend her husband, who diagnosed that he was suffering from paranoia. In June that year efforts were made to have the plaintiff committed to a mental hospital. He escaped, but believing that, in law, he could at any time be arrested and recommitted, the plaintiff hid out in Dublin until January 1960, when he eventually returned to Adamstown.

While in Dublin, still believing that he could instantly be put back into a mental hospital, the plaintiff, through the intermediary of a priest, negotiated with his wife to hand over the family business and property at Adamstown to her, subject to her and the two defendants' confirming in writing that he was sane. This was all to avoid being returned to the mental hospital. The intermediary represented to Mrs Cullen that her husband intended to make over the business to her and encouraged her to put some of her own money into the running of it.

However, in September 1959 the plaintiff, through a solicitor, wrote to the two defendants, his sons, instructing them to vacate the house at Adamstown and to give up all connection with the family business. A similar letter issued to Mrs Cullen, telling her to cease involvement with the business and not to allow her adult sons reside in the house. In June 1960, the plaintiff instituted proceedings, seeking an injunction to restrain his sons from interfering with the business and from trespassing on his property.

[19.18] Kenny J held that children aged over 21 living in their parents' house are licensees only, and in the absence of any proprietary interest (which did not arise here), are liable to have that licence revoked. The solicitor's letter in this case effected such revocation.

A defence founded upon Mrs Cullen's having been told that the place was going to be made over to her, on the basis of which she had put money into the business and had employed the two defendants to assist her in running it, was held to fail, because the plaintiff's representations to his wife had been prompted entirely by his dread of going back to the mental hospital, and his anxiety to secure a written acknowledgment of his sanity from her so that he might remain at large.

In this context Kenny J considered the possible application of the then century-old case of *Dillwyn v Llewelyn*,[1] which he regarded as 'an authority for the proposition that a person claiming under a voluntary agreement will not be assisted by a court of equity but that the subsequent acts of the donor may give the donee a ground of claim which he did not acquire from the original gift.'[2]

In *Dillwyn v Llewelyn* a father had told his son that he would like the son to live near him and offered him a farm so that his son could build a house on it. The son spent considerable money building the house, but his father never handed over the farm. Lord Westbury held that the making of the promise to gift the lands, coupled with the knowledge that the plaintiff had incurred significant expense in constructing the house, conferred on the plaintiff an equity to call on those claiming through his father to complete the gift.

Kenny J drew attention to the discretionary character of the equity applied by Lord Westbury and felt that it was not appropriate to the facts before him. Mrs Cullen could easily have recouped from the profits of the business the money she had put into it. Furthermore, the plaintiff had only said he was going to make the business over to her, so that she would testify to his sanity and he retain his liberty: under these circumstances, according to Kenny J it would be grossly inequitable to compel the plaintiff to transfer his property to his wife.

---

[1]   *Dillwyn v Llewelyn* (1862) 4 DeGF & J 517.

[2]   *John Cullen v Patrick Cullen and Martin Cullen* [1962] IR 268 at 282.

[19.19] However – there was more. During the troubled year of 1959 Mrs Cullen had won a mobile home in a newspaper competition. She gave this as a present to her son, Martin, the second defendant. Martin offered it to his father, who refused it. Martin then decided to put the mobile home on his own farm at Adamstown, but, hearing that his father, the plaintiff, intended making over the Adamstown home place to his mother, allowed her to persuade him to locate the mobile home there. Mrs Cullen asked the mediating priest to secure her husband's permission to this proposal. The reply sent back was that, as John Cullen, the plaintiff, intended making over the Adamstown property to his wife, she could put the mobile home where she liked.

Accordingly, Martin installed the mobile home on his parents' Adamstown lands in the summer of 1959, incurring significant outlay in the laying of foundations and installation of a water supply.

[19.20] Having held that the children's licence to occupy their parents' house had been revoked by the plaintiff's solicitor's letter, it was inevitable that Kenny J should go on to deem them trespassers when they refused to leave. He declined to award the plaintiff an injunction, on the basis that the weighing of the balance of convenience became difficult when, as the judge put it, a touch disdainfully:

> '... the refusal of an injunction amounts to a denial of the plaintiff's right to decide who shall be on his property and the grant of an injunction is the intrusion by the Court into family and domestic relations which should be governed by affection, respect and the sense of moral obligation which all of us have and not by Court orders.'[1]

An injunction would, furthermore, leave Mrs Cullen defenceless against any erratic or violent behaviour by the plaintiff, would prevent her children from being able to visit their mother, and would also make eventual reconciliation with the aberrant plaintiff more difficult to effect. Even so, Kenny J awarded the plaintiff damages for the continuing trespass by the defendants, in the amount of £50 each.[2]

---

[1] *John Cullen v Patrick Cullen and Martin Cullen* [1962] IR 268 at 285.

[2] 'Relations between fathers and their sons should not be governed by the heavy artillery of Court orders, injunctions or the threat of committal to prison, but by respect, affection, honour and the feeling of moral obligation.' [1962] IR 268 at 290. Kenny J also quoted from the judgment of Buckley J in *Waterhouse v Waterhouse* (1893) 94 LT 133, in which Buckley J had similarly declined to grant an injunction in a case brought against a son by his father.

[19.21] Quite different considerations applied in the case of the mobile home erected on the Adamstown farm by Martin Cullen, the second defendant. Kenny J held that Martin Cullen would never have built where he did without his father's express permission, which he had clearly relied on. Kenny J also found that the plaintiff had been aware of this. He estimated that it would cost Martin Cullen significantly more than he had already spent to have the house removed, sited elsewhere and redecorated. It had been argued that the case of *Ramsden v Dyson*[1] was authority for compelling the plaintiff to transfer to Martin Cullen the site on which the house then stood. Kenny J did not think so:

> 'That case decides that if a stranger begins to build on land which he thinks is his and the real owner, seeing the mistake, abstains from correcting it and leaves him to continue, equity will not afterwards allow the real owner to assert his title to the land; but that if a stranger builds on land knowing it to be the property of another, equity will not prevent the real owner from claiming the lands afterwards.'[2]

According to Kenny J, *Ramsden v Dyson* did not apply because Martin Cullen knew that the site on which he had constructed the mobile home was part of his father's land. On the other hand, Kenny J held that the plaintiff was estopped by his conduct, in giving consent to the erection of the mobile home, which Martin Cullen had acted on, expending considerable time and money on the project, from asserting his title to the plot of land on which the house had been constructed.

> '[t]he plaintiff cannot withdraw the permission which he gave for the erection of the house on the lands at Adamstown and cannot now assert a title to the site on which the house stands or to the house. While the estoppel created by the plaintiff's conduct prevents him asserting a title to the site, it does not give Martin a right to require the plaintiff to transfer the site to him: if I had jurisdiction to make such an order I would do so, but I do not think I have.'[3]

---

1   *Ramsden v Dyson* (1866) LR 1 HL 129.
2   *John Cullen v Patrick Cullen and Martin Cullen* [1962] IR 268 at 291–292.
3   [1962] IR 268 at 292.

[19.22] The diffidence expressed by Kenny J in making an outright order transferring ownership has been overcome by the courts in more recent years. In *Smyth v Halpin*[1] Geoghegan J ordered the transfer of the fee simple remainder to an applicant who had taken a site and built an extension to an existing family home, on the basis of an assurance by his father, later dishonoured, that the family home would be his when his mother died. In *Norris and Norris v Walls*[2] Girvan J, following *Ramsden v Dyson*,[3] directed a transfer of the fee simple in a case where one party's mistake of title had been well known to the other, who had permitted the mistaken party to persist in their belief and carry out building works on foot of it. In the judgment of Girvan J, provided an equity had not been raised against the claiming party, and there were no countervailing legal prohibition, the court would protect the claiming party's legitimate expectation through such redress as, and to the extent that, it deemed appropriate.

---

1   *Smyth v Halpin* [1997] ILRM 38.
2   *Norris and Norris v Walls* [1997] NI 45.
3   *Ramsden v Dyson* (1866) LR 1 HL 129.

[19.23] In *Cullen v Cullen*[1] Kenny J concluded that neither the plaintiff, nor anyone claiming through him, could assert a title to the site, as a result of the estoppel that had been raised against the plaintiff, and that, on this basis, at the end of a 12-year period from the construction of the mobile home, Martin Cullen would be able to apply under s 52 of the Registration of Title (Ireland) Act 1891[2] to be registered as full owner of the site.

---

1   *John Cullen v Patrick Cullen and Martin Cullen* [1962] IR 268.
2   Now the Registration of Title Act 1964, s 49(2) of which states that '[w]here any person claims to have acquired a title by possession to registered land', they can apply to the Registrar of Titles to be registered as full owner, but that such registration shall be 'without prejudice to any right not extinguished by such possession.'

[19.24] Perhaps the most remarkable feature of *Cullen v Cullen*[1] is, not so much the employment by Kenny J of equitable estoppel to avoid unfairness, but his suggestion that the ultimate effect of it would be to enable the party whose occupancy was so protected to apply to be registered as full owner on the basis of, effectively, an adverse possession. It is difficult to understand how a possession could be 'adverse' when it had commenced by way of permission from the registered owner and was continued on foot of an order from the court once the registered owner's permission had been withdrawn.[2] From a different perspective, the decision in *Cullen v Cullen* is rather less remarkable:

the principle of equitable estoppel had been used to defeat an application for the equitable remedy of the injunction, the granting of which is by its nature discretionary.[3]

---

1   *John Cullen v Patrick Cullen and Martin Cullen* [1962] IR 268.
2   See also the views expressed in Wylie, *Irish Land Law* p 1024; Coughlan, *Property Law* (2nd edn, 1998) Gill and Macmillan, p 298.
3   The decision of Kenny J in *Cullen v Cullen* is of principal relevance in the context of proprietary estoppel, in which regard it influenced decisions in the later Irish cases of *McMahon v Kerry County Council* [1981] ILRM 419, per Finlay P and in *Re JR* [1993] ILRM 657 per Costello J, where, however, the issue of a licence did not arise. See discussion in Lyall *Land Law in Ireland* pp 543–549.

[19.25] The only licence found by Kenny J to have existed was the licence by the father to his two children to occupy the family home, a licence which the father then expressly revoked through a solicitor's letter. At no point did Kenny J describe the ongoing occupancy by Martin Cullen, that resulted from his refusal to award an injunction against him, as a licence. In the absence of any more appropriate designation, the term 'estoppel licence' can be applied. But this seems principally a label to be ascribed to an occupancy protected by the courts against the manifest wishes of the owner of property.

[19.26] Even so, it is difficult to understand how Kenny J could state, as he did, that neither the plaintiff '*nor any person claiming through him*' could ever assert title to the site occupied by Martin Cullen. A licence is inherently revocable by the licensor, in the absence of a contractual term, express or implied, which prohibits its revocation.[1] In this instance, the reluctant licensor would presumably continue to be estopped from revoking the alleged licence himself. However, the case of *David Allen and Sons Billposting Ltd v King*[2] affirms that a transfer by the licensor of the property subject to the licence does not, in the absence of express covenant by the licensor's assignee of the property, enable the licensee enforce the licence against him, even where the assignee takes the property with notice of the licence.[3] Neither will a covenant entered into by the licensor with his licensee, where the licence is not linked to an interest in land, be enforceable against a successor of the covenantor because the covenant does not 'touch and concern' any land of the covenantee.[4]

The better view is that, except where a licence has been granted for the purpose of enjoying a profit *à prendre* – the so-called 'licence coupled with an interest' – a licence cannot be assigned and will normally not be binding on any one other than the licensor. In cases where an estoppel licence is deemed to be binding against a third party, this is more likely to be because the original licensor is not the only party who can be estopped, rather than because the licence constitutes an interest in land.[5]

---

1   *Hurst v Picture Theatres Ltd* [1915] 1 KB 1. See also 'When A Licence Is Revocable' (1915) 49 ILTSJ 33, Walford 'The Nature and Effect of Licences' (1947) 11 Conv 178, Crane 'Licences and Successors in Title of the Licensor' (1952) 16 Conv 323, Wade 'Licences and Third Parties' (1952) 68 LQR 337, Hargreaves 'Licensed Possessors' (1953) 69 LQR 466. See para **[19.01]**.
2   *David Allen and Sons Billposting Ltd v King* [1915] 2 IR 213 (Court of King's Bench); [1915] 2 IR 448 (Court of Appeal); [1916] 2 AC 54. See para **[20.11]**.

3 This principle was affirmed by the English Court of Appeal in *Ashburn Anstalt v Arnold* [1989] 1 Ch 1, which expressly disapproved of an observation by Denning LJ in *Errington v Errington and Woods* [1952] 1 KB 290, that neither a licensor, nor anyone claiming through him other than a purchaser for value without notice, could disregard a licence created by contract. The court in *Ashburn Anstalt v Arnold* found other grounds to justify the actual decision in *Errington*. On the nature of an estoppel licence, and its contrast with a contractual licence, see Moriarty 'Licences and Land Law: Legal Principles and Public Policies' (1984) 100 LQR 376, Battersby 'Contractual and Estoppel Licences as Proprietary Interests in Land' [1991] Conv 36.

4 *David Allen and Sons Billposting Ltd v King* [1915] 2 IR 448, at 455, per Lord O'Brien LC, at 461–462, per Ronan LJ.

5 Todd 'Estoppel Licences and Third Party Rights' [1981] Conv 347 at 358: '… it may be the estoppel, rather than the licence, which affects the purchaser.' However, where the licence on its terms is to endure for the lifetime of the licensee, it can be enforced against a successor of the licensor: *Woods v Donnelly* [1982] NI 257. For rights of burial, see Dowling 'Exclusive Rights of Burial' (1992) 43 NILQ 288.

[19.27] It is difficult to see that *Cullen v Cullen*[1] has any profound precedent value in the domain of licences. In Ireland it represents the genesis of the 'estoppel licence'. But what really happened was that Kenny J employed an equitable estoppel so as to ensure that an ongoing judicially conferred right to occupy (best described, by default, as a 'licence') would eventually result in entitlement to registered ownership. At the risk of seeming sententious, one must also suggest that the extraordinary facts undergirding this case lie rooted in the social and historical milieu of the time when it was decided and are unlikely to recur in a *soi-disant* more sophisticated age.

---

1 *John Cullen v Patrick Cullen and Martin Cullen* [1962] IR 268.

Chapter 20

Devices for Protection of a Licence

Introduction

[20.01] The case of *Cullen v Cullen*[1] demonstrates how the courts, through the use of equitable estoppel, can fashion a judge-made licence to effect fairness *inter partes* and so indirectly produce a burgeoning proprietary right. The authorities considered in this chapter will show that the Irish courts have been no less vigilant in the protection of rights conferred by a licence made by the parties to it. This protection has been effected through a variety of legal devices, including:

(a)   the concept of a licence coupled with an interest;

(b)   the doctrine of non-derogation from grant;[2]

(c)   the application of implied contractual terms;

(d)   the equitable remedy of relief against forfeiture.

[1]   *John Cullen v Patrick Cullen and Martin Cullen* [1962] IR 268.
2   This has already been considered in the content of easements, in ch 2. See paras **[2.29]–[2.35]**.

Licence Coupled with an Interest

[20.02] A licence coupled with an interest arises when the right to be enjoyed on foot of a licence is not a mere privilege or entertainment, but an interest in land, most usually a profit *à prendre*. *Atkinson v King*[1] was such a case. It concerned a mining licence. The issue in contest involved, not so much the respective rights and duties of licensor and licensee to each other, but the liability of the licensor towards a neighbouring landowner for damage occasioned through the works of the licensee. The lands of the plaintiff and the defendant were adjacent, with a road running between them. The plaintiff was lessee of the surface only of his lands. The defendant was lessee of the entirety of his lands and also had a mining lease over the subterranean portion of the plaintiff's lands. The defendant purported to grant an exclusive mining licence, over both his own lands and that portion of the plaintiff's lands of which he had a mining lease, to one O'Neill.

The licence document is scarcely a demonstration model of comprehensive drafting:

'Mr James O'Neill,

'I agree to allow you to sink a pit for coal in Blackaville, at 1*s.* 6*d.* per ton, and not to allow anyone to sink on any coal you prove in the pit.—R. King.

Also an air-pit, and 100 yards in each square of the pit.'

The licensee, O'Neill, duly excavated for coal in a line that ran right beneath some houses built by the plaintiff, with the result that the houses collapsed. The plaintiff sued the defendant licensor for the damage done to his property, on the basis that the licensor, though he had not directed the licensee's mining operation, was aware that the work was injurious to the plaintiff's houses and had done nothing to stop it.

Accordingly, the issue to be decided was whether the licence granted by the defendant licensor was revocable. If it was, then the licensor remained in effective control of the property, and would be liable to the plaintiff for not having intervened. If the licence was not revocable, then there was nothing he could have done and he was not liable.

---

[1]   *Atkinson v King* (1877) IR 11 CL 536 (Court of Queen's Bench), (1878) 2 LR Ir 320 (CA).

[20.03] In the opinion of May CJ, this was clearly an irrevocable licence coupled with an interest. Nor did it resemble a case of a licence of lands subject to an already existing nuisance, in which case the licensor could not avoid liability merely by putting the lands out of his possession:

> 'But a licence under which it is contemplated that property of the licensor shall be taken and appropriated by the licensee, that is, what is termed coupled with an interest, is not revocable; and the reason is plain, otherwise the licensor, by revoking his licence, would derogate from the grant which is implied in the licence.'[1]

The licence given had been an exclusive one, and, since the licensee had undertaken considerable expenditure on foot of it, the proper construction was that the licence was to endure until all the coal had been exhausted.

---

[1]   *Atkinson v King* (1877) IR 11 CL 536 at 540.

[20.04] The Court of Appeal, by a majority, approved the decision of May CJ, for similar reasons. Even though only granted 'by a mere writing', this licence, in the view of Ball LC, was irrevocable because it was coupled with an interest and because the licensee had acted upon it, incurring expense. This was so, notwithstanding that an incorporeal hereditament could only be created by deed:

> 'The licence was one by its terms contemplating expensive works being carried on by the licensee, such as sinking a pit, and excavating under the surface; it was, at the time when the houses were approached, already a licence executed, the pit had been sunk and excavations made; coal had been found and the royalty for it regularly paid. Would it be consistent with justice to allow a party who had himself induced all this expense to nullify his own act and reap, it might be, himself the fruit of another's outlay? A case of licence unattended with expense or loss, as, for instance, to fish in a river, is altogether different; for there, if it be revoked, the licensee is merely left in the same position as if it had never been granted.'[1]

In the opinion both of Ball LC and Morris CJ, this licence was tantamount to a lease of the mining rights,[2] so that, being irrevocable, the licensor would have been unable to restrain the licensee upon discovering that damage was being done to the plaintiff's houses. According to the Lord Chancellor, the licensor could have no right to revoke the agreement until the coal had been exhausted. Nor had he any right to take action against the licensee for damage caused to the land of the plaintiff. Such a right was vested alone in the plaintiff, who might assign it, exercise it or ignore it, but the defendant had no right to interfere.

Deasy LJ expressed the view that, in all likelihood, the licensor could not have secured an injunction restraining the licensee from damaging the plaintiff's houses. Nor did his failure to seek one thereby make the licensee's acts his own. The licensee's activities had not been carried out on any land of which the licensor 'was in possession or of which he could have obtained the possession, and were being done under an irrevocable licence granted by him long previously for a valuable consideration.'[3]

---

1   *Atkinson v King* (1878) 2 LR Ir 320 at 335. Ball LC also expressed the view that this statement of principle was not affected by the judgment of Alderson B in *Wood v Leadbitter* (1845) 13 M & W 838. It is, however, more significantly, consistent with the judgment of Fitzgerald B in *Blood v Keller* (1860) 11 ICLR 124, see ch 19, para **[19.11]**.

2   A conclusion assisted by s 3 of the Landlord and Tenant Law Amendment, Ireland, Act 1860, which founds the relationship of landlord and tenant on contract, and also the case of *Bayley v Conyngham* (1863) 15 ICLR 242 which held that a mere writing, as opposed to a deed under seal, was adequate to create a letting of an incorporeal as well as of a corporeal hereditament.

3   (1878) 2 LR Ir 320 at 364–365.

[20.05] A vigorous and cogently reasoned dissenting judgment was delivered by Christian LJ.[1] In his view the original lease of 1632, which had excepted the minerals beneath the plaintiff's lands and reserved a right of access to them, had not created an absolute mining right, but one subject to the requirement that sufficient of the subjacent soil be left in order to continue to sustain the surface.[2]

---

1   The dissenting judgment of Christian LJ was preferred by Porter MR in the related case of *Stanley v Riky* (1892) 31 LR Ir 196 who nevertheless acknowledged that the majority judgment of the Court of Appeal was binding on him. It was also preferred by Hutton J in the case of *Woods v Donnelly* [1982] NI 257 who declined to follow the decision of the majority on the basis that he deemed it difficult to reconcile with the advice of the Privy Council (delivered by Lord Devlin) in *Australian Blue Metal Ltd v Hughes* [1963] AC 74 which, in the context of the revocation of a mining licence, Hutton J regarded as containing a correct statement of the law. See para **[20.20]** ff.

2   On this point Christian LJ discovered an analogy with easements of light cases, in particular, *Dent v Auction Mart Co* (1866) LR 2 Eq 238, in which it had been suggested, but not accepted by the court, that diminution in light could be compensated for by the person causing it by the putting up of bright tiles or mirrors so as to enhance the light remaining. In the same way as there could be no obligation on the part of the property owner diminishing his neighbour's light to preserve intact any such artificial enhancements in perpetuity, so too a person who through the exercise of a mining right removed the natural support to the land above could not compel the owner of that land to accept an artificial prop which, no matter how well constructed, would ultimately decay. See also *Mackey v Scottish Widows' Assurance Society* (1877) IR 11 Eq 541, see ch 7, para **[7.04]**, **[7.06]**–**[7.07]**.

[20.06] In relation to the tersely worded licence document, Christian LJ felt that this conferred a mere personal permission and was inherently revocable. The only commitment by the licensor was not to give a similar licence to any other party to work coal in any seam hit upon by the licensee. Other features supported this conclusion:

(i)   the licensor did not even undertake not to work the seam himself;

(ii)   there was no term mentioned in the document;

(iii)   there was no obligation on the licensee even to mine the coal, so that the licence could be abandoned by him at will;

(iv)   there was a total absence of precautionary clauses, such as restrictions on the mode of working, rights of re-entry, and forfeiture – a remarkable omission in a supposed grant of an irrevocable right.

According to Christian LJ, *prima facie* a licence which does not state a term is determinable at will and could in no way be construed as enduring until all the coal has been exhausted. Hence the writing created a mere revocable licence.

But even, continued Christian LJ, if this were a licence coupled with an interest, and thus irrevocable, on the authority of *Wood v Leadbitter*[1] it could only be irrevocable if granted by way of deed:

'In *Wood v Leadbitter* Alderson B, says: "Where there is a license by parol" – and the license in this case being by writing not under seal is just as much parol as if by word of mouth – "coupled with a parol grant, or pretended grant, of something which is incapable of being granted otherwise than by deed, there the license is a mere license, it is not an incident to a valid grant, and it is therefore revocable".'[2]

Similarly, if this were a licence coupled with an interest, the only ostensible interest was the defendant's entire lease. But the writing used between the defendant and O'Neill was not adequate to grant an assignment under s 9 of the Landlord and Tenant Law Amendment, Ireland, Act 1860. It would need to have been worded as an assignment. Neither could the document be construed as a sub-lease, as there were no words of demise, nor any term granted. Accordingly, there was no interest passed, and the document's '… legal category is that of a bare license without an interest, and consequently revocable.'[3]

---

[1]   *Wood v Leadbitter* (1845) 13 M & W 838.

[2]   *Atkinson v King* (1878) 2 LR Ir 320 at 350.

[3]   (1878) 2 LR Ir 320 at 350.

[20.07] The burden of the decision in *Atkinson v King*[1] fell to be reviewed in *Stanley v Riky*,[2] a case which also involved a mining licence, though expenditure by the licensee of a very different order. The defendant licensor was a life tenant of lands in Co Donegal. In January 1882 she entered into a three-year agreement with the plaintiff permitting him to mine a variety of iron extract known as 'bog ore', subject to a specified royalty, with provision for additional tonnage if the yield were to exceed a certain amount. There was an option for the licensee to extend the licence beyond the initial three-year term, subject to paying a revised royalty, but no further obligations. The licensor agreed to facilitate dealings between the licensee and the tenants occupying the lands on which the 'bog ore' was to be dug out.

Initially, the yield of 'bog ore' was modest, and then began to improve. The licence term was extended and the royalty revised. In 1891 the defendant licensor married. Her husband sought to terminate the mining licence and went on to the land to remove some of the ore himself. The plaintiff applied for an injunction.

---

[1] *Atkinson v King* (1878) 2 LR Ir 320 at 350.
[2] *Stanley v Riky* (1892) 31 LR Ir 196.

[20.08] Following the judgment of Ball LC in *Atkinson v King*,[1] Porter MR held that the initial three-year agreement of January 1882 was consistent with a lease of an incorporeal hereditament. Even if only a licence had been created, it was an irrevocable licence for the first three years, and also exclusive. It was exclusive because otherwise the licensee would be unable to pay the stipulated royalty. It was irrevocable because the licensee had acted upon it and incurred expense.

As in *Atkinson v King*, the issue of expenditure was crucial to determining the licensee's rights, but the level of expenditure in this case was considerably less and had primarily been incurred during the preliminary period of three years. Since 'bog ore' manifests typically in blocks close to the surface, the principal expenditure had been in stripping the soil, removing the ore, and negotiating market contacts.

In relation to the issue of expenditure generally, Porter MR observed:

> '... it is not to be expected that the exact cost of the preparatory operations can be ascertained, nor can it be said as a matter of law that any fixed amount of expenditure will render a license irrevocable, while a smaller sum would not have that effect'[2]

Even this rationalisation, however, left the difficulty that any expenditure incurred in getting at the bog ore originally had been a feature of the initial exclusive three-year agreement. But this had concluded and was not the subject of the current controversy. The Master of the Rolls conceded that it was incongruous that one part of an agreement should be construed as possibly creating a lease, while the remainder was a licence only. Yet there were significant differences between the two parts to the agreement. In the second part:

(a) the absence of any provision for a rent;

(b) the absence of any obligation on the licensees actually to work any ore;

(c) the absence of any requirement to pay a royalty;

meant that the relationship between the parties was of a different legal character from that in the earlier part. The second agreement could only be a licence. However, principally on account of the expense *already* incurred by the licensee, Porter MR held that the licence was to be irrevocable for the duration of the estate of the defendant licensor, but that it could not be an exclusive licence, since there was no actual obligation to work the ore.[3]

---

[1] *Atkinson v King* (1878) 2 LR Ir 320 at 350.
[2] *Stanley v Riky* (1892) 31 LR Ir 196 at 204.
[3] Porter MR was supported in this conclusion by a dictum in *Carr v Benson* (1868) LR 3 Ch App 524, to the effect that, where a licensee is under no obligation actually to work the lands, the

licensor cannot by the fact of having given the licence be prevented from giving as many more similar licences as he thinks fit, provided that he does not thereby defeat the known objects of the original licensee in taking the licence.

[20.09] The Court of Appeal found that the licence, after the preliminary three-year period when a rent had been reserved, was neither exclusive nor irrevocable. Walker C confirmed that, although a profit *à prendre* could only be created by deed, in a case where the licence has been granted by parol, and the licensee has incurred significant expenditure, the licensor will not be permitted to resile from it. However, in this case the licensee's expenditure in no way resembled that incurred by the licensee in *Atkinson v King*,[1] as the only real cost had been in employing estate tenants to lift the ore and cart it to the railway station.

In the opinion of Fitzgibbon and Barry LJJ, the licence agreement, insofar as it purported to confer an irrevocable licence on the licensee for the entirety of the life estate of licensor, would be unenforceable in equity as not properly reflecting the intention of the parties. In consequence, as there was no obligation under the later agreement on the licensee to work any ore, it was open to the licensor, through her husband, to revoke it.

---

[1] *Atkinson v King* (1878) 2 LR Ir 320 at 350.

Contractual Licence

[20.10] In 1915 the English Court of Appeal handed down the decision in *Hurst v Picture Theatres Ltd*[1] and added, in effect, an entire new concept to the vocabulary of licences over land. The court held that the owner of a cinema was liable in damages for assault to a ticket holder at a film screening whose licence to watch the film was revoked before the film had ended. In theory, the ticket holder could have sought an injunction to restrain revocation of his licence to view the film. This is because the licence carried with it an implied contractual term that it would not be revoked until the purpose for which it had been granted had been satisfied – in other words, until the ticket holder had watched the entire film.

In its introduction of the principles of contract law, bolstered by the availability of equitable remedies, to the revocation of a licence, the Court of Appeal delivered a resounding blow to the established orthodoxy of 'revocable' and 'irrevocable' licences and the cherished supremacy of a 'licence coupled with an interest'.

---

[1] *Hurst v Picture Theatres Ltd* [1915] 1 KB 1.

[20.11] By coincidence, in that same year of 1915, the Irish courts had to grapple with precisely the same issue – also in the context of the emergent world of 'moving pictures' – in *David Allen and Sons Billposting Ltd v King*.[1] Not surprisingly, since the decision in *Hurst v Picture Theatres Ltd*[2] was already to hand, certain of the judgments in *Allen v King* display a tortuous enthusiasm for efforts to marry the concepts of licence coupled with an interest, irrevocable licence, and a licence with an implied contractual term against revocation.

The defendant had granted to the plaintiff, for a four-year term, subject to a rent, in July 1913, a licence to erect film posters on the wall of premises at Phibsborough, Co Dublin. The terms of the licence were set out in a written agreement. At the same time the defendant licensor was treating for a lease of these premises to a picture house company then in the course of being formed. In August 1913 the defendant licensor entered into an agreement with the trustees of the picture house company, to grant it a lease of the premises, subject to the licence agreement of July 1913 with the plaintiff. In September 1913 the picture house company was incorporated and took a lease of the Phibsborough premises. The lease, unfortunately, made no reference to the licence agreement of July 1913. The picture house company then refused to allow the plaintiff licensee to put up film posters. The plaintiff sued the defendant for breach of contract. The defendant pleaded that the picture house company had taken its lease with notice of the plaintiff's licence, and being thereby affected by the plaintiff's rights, alone was liable in damages to the plaintiff.

---

[1]   *David Allen and Sons Billposting Ltd v King* [1915] 2 IR 213, 448, [1916] 2 AC 54.
[2]   *Hurst v Picture Theatres Ltd* 1 KB 1.

[20.12] Gibson J, at first instance, found that the licence agreement of July 1913 created a licence coupled with an interest. In his view, there was little difference between a licence to erect posters on the wall of a house, and a licence to enter that house to carry out works. In either case, there was a licence coupled with an interest, which was an assignable right. However, the contract remained intact between the licensor and the licensee, and the licensor was liable to the licensee for breach of it.

Despite finding a licence coupled with an interest, Gibson J had difficulty with the traditional concept of an 'irrevocable' licence:

> 'I consider that between an irrevocable licence, and a licence for withdrawal of which the licensor can be sued, there is no real distinction; either way there is a right of action with identical damages. If the revocation of the licence is lawful, no action can lie for revoking it. A contract not to revoke the licence makes the licence irrevocable, unless the contract must be under seal.'[1]

---

[1]   *David Allen and Sons Billposting Ltd v King* [1915] 2 IR 213 at 218.

[20.13] A majority of the Court of King's Bench, and on further appeals both the Court of Appeal and the House of Lords, held that there was not in this case a licence coupled with an interest, but that the licensor was liable to the licensee for breach of an implied term of the contract creating the licence, that he would remain in a position to enable the licensee to enjoy it for the full term of four years. It was for this reason, in the opinion of Dodd J, that the licence agreement had contained a promise by the licensor not to give any other parties the right to affix posters to the wall, and an undertaking by him, subject

361

to indemnity by the licensee, to take proceedings against anyone else purporting to affix posters.[1] Accordingly,

'[I]f a man who has given a licensee a right of entry, afterwards parts with the property so as to prevent him from carrying out his promise, he is answerable as for a breach of contract. But the breach is not that he parted with the property, but that he did not continue to give the permission.'[2]

In the view of Madden J, the licence was not coupled with an interest, but was supported by an implied contractual term against revocation, as in *Hurst v Picture Theatres Ltd*.[3] This protection derived either from the equitable principle that an injunction will restrain a party from breaching a contract given for valuable consideration or, alternatively, that a licence for a period certain is deemed to import an additional contract that the licence will not be revoked before the expiry of that period. Madden J stated that he would prefer the former approach, as it conformed to the principles established by the Supreme Court of Judicature (Ireland) Act 1877, whereas the latter necessitated the fiction of importing an additional contract which the parties at the time of the licence had not contemplated.

Dodd J, however, experienced little difficulty with the subtle relationship between revocation of licence and breach of contract:

'A man may contract to give a licence for a period of years. He is under a legal obligation to continue it for the period. It is not accurate to say he may revoke the licence. He may break his contract with such results as follow a breach of contract. He is answerable in damages once for all; just as in any other contract, say a contract of service for a definite period. The legal way of putting it is, not that he had revoked the licence, but that he has broken his contract.'[4]

---

1   This was on the basis of the alleged legal principle that a licensee, even in the case of a licence granted under seal, is precluded from suing on his own behalf for disturbance by a wrongdoer; a view accepted and repeated by Ronan LJ in the Court of Appeal: *David Allen and Sons Billposting Ltd v King* [1915] 2 IR 448 at 460; Molony LJ at p 479. Both cited in support the case of *Hill v Tupper* (1863) 2 H & C 121, which confirmed that the right of a licensee to go onto land for a particular purpose did not incorporate a right for him to sue in his own name for a violation of his right by a third party. However, see also *Littleton v McNamara* (1875) IR 9 CL 417, in which Lawson J held that a licensee whose licence had not been revoked had sufficient standing to maintain an action for trespass.

2   *David Allen and Sons Billposting Ltd v King* [1915] 2 IR 213 at 232.

3   *Hurst v Picture Theatres Ltd* [1915] 1 KB 1.

4   [1915] 2 IR 213 at 229.

[20.14] The Court of Appeal[1] concerned itself less with the debate regarding the application of *Hurst v Picture Theatres Ltd*.[2] The right granted by the defendant to the plaintiff could not be an easement, because there was no dominant tenement, and there cannot be an easement in gross; neither was it a lease because there was no possession; neither did it stand to be affected by the equitable principles that governed the running of restrictive covenants because there was no land of the covenantee. Accordingly, the right could only be a licence under a purely personal contract. As pithily put by Ronan LJ, 'It is all licence, and nothing but licence.' A licence for four years must mean a real valid continuing licence which implies that the licensor has the power to grant it and to continue it. Hence, an assignment of the subject matter of the licence is a breach of contract where the licence is for a definite period, as it puts it out of the power of the licensor to continue the licence.

In the House of Lords,[3] Lord Loreburn expressed the view, that if the agreement of July 1913 had granted a hereditament in the form of a lease, then the grantor's assignment of it would not have been a breach of contract because the grantee would have been bound. The licensor's liability to the licensee stemmed from the contract being personal to the two of them only, and not having created an interest in land.

---

[1] [1915] 2 IR 448.
[2] *Hurst v Picture Theatres Ltd* [1915] 1 KB 1.
[3] [1916] AC 53.

Equitable Relief Against Forfeiture

[20.15] In Ireland the case of *Allen v King*[1] established that the revocation of a licence by the licensor (albeit by an act not intended to have that effect) will result in the licensor being liable to the licensee in damages. This liability derives from an implied contractual term against revocation. The danger of the utilisation of implied contractual terms to ground a cause of action is the uncertainty to which this can lead as to precisely which circumstances will justify the revocation of a licence by the licensor, and whether there are any circumstances of revocation which will not render the licensor liable to the licensee in damages. A like peril arises through the potential availability to a licensee of equitable relief against forfeiture for non-payment of rent.

---

[1] *David Allen and Sons Billposting Ltd v King* [1915] 2 IR 213.

[20.16] This occurred in *Whipp v Mackey.*[1] In May 1919 a licensor, by agreement in writing but not under seal, granted to the defendant licensee the right to moor a number of underwater eel tanks against an island in the river Shannon, for 15 years, subject to a rent. The licence agreement provided, that in the event of breach by the defendant licensee, described as the 'tenant', the 'landlord' could determine the licence by giving one week's notice in writing. The agreement further provided that within one week after the determination of the agreement, whether by effluxion of time or otherwise, the tenant would remove the eel tanks and make good all damage to the soil, or in the alternative the landlord could remove them himself without notice to the tenant.

In September 1920 the licensor sold the island to the plaintiff, subject to the licence agreement with the defendant. At all stages throughout the subsequent proceedings the plaintiff acknowledged that he was bound by the agreement of May 1919 and effectively stood in the shoes of the original licensor.[2]

Throughout what later became known as the War of Independence and the Civil War, the defendant was denied access to his eel tanks by reason of the conflict raging in the country, and so did not pay rent, despite several demands for it from the plaintiff, latterly by solicitor's letter. The plaintiff then purported to determine the licence by giving one week's notice in writing in December 1923. In February 1924, the defendant tendered the arrears of rent, and refused to leave or to remove the eel tanks. The plaintiff sought an injunction.

---

[1] *Whipp v Mackey* [1927] IR 372.
[2] Accordingly, a large part of the complications arising in *David Allen and Sons Billposting Ltd v King* [1915] 2 IR 213 at 448, [1916] 2 AC 54 did not fall to be considered.

[20.17] The Supreme Court (overruling Meredith J in the High Court) held that, on a proper construction, the licence agreement provided for its forfeiture in the event of breach of condition through non-payment of rent by the licensee, and so could be terminated. The principal case for the plaintiff was that this was a mere personal licence, revocable in accordance with its terms, and that it had been validly revoked; while for the defendant it was urged that this was the grant of an easement, or at worst a licence coupled with an easement, in the form of a right of way.

In relation to the nature of the agreement, the Supreme Court found in favour of the plaintiff. According to Kennedy CJ, there could not be an easement, since there was no dominant tenement and there cannot be an easement in gross. Neither did the fact that 'rent' was spoken of, nor that the parties were described as 'landlord' and 'tenant', prevent the agreement having the character of a licence: the permission granted to use the eel tanks conferred a mere commercial advantage that was personal to the licensee. Accordingly, the licence was revocable in accordance with its terms. Kennedy CJ, citing the case of *Hurst v Picture Theatres Ltd*,[1] disposed thus of the ancient shibboleth of 'licence coupled with an interest':

> '[I]t is not necessary to decide whether the licence under the agreement is coupled with a grant, or with any interest which would differentiate it, as regards revocation, from a bare licence. Nor is it necessary to determine whether, when once the tanks had been placed in position, the licence became a licence coupled with an interest. The agreement contained a provision for its determination, involving revocation of the licence upon breach of any of the agreements comprised in it; whereof one was for payment of the yearly sum or rent on the specified gale days. A breach was, in fact, committed entitling the plaintiff in law to forfeit the defendant's rights under the agreement. It seems to me that the only real question in the case is whether the defendant is entitled to claim equitable relief from the consequences of his breach of the agreement.'[2]

In the opinion of Kennedy CJ, even though the contract was for a personal licence, the provision in it for termination for non-payment of rent rendered it liable to equitable relief against forfeiture. The forfeiture clause was in a sense no more than a security for the payment of the rent. There had been no suggestion that non-payment of rent could not be compensated for by the eventual payment of interest in addition. Noting the discretionary nature of equitable relief against forfeiture,[3] Kennedy CJ felt that it should be granted in this case, especially as the licensee had been forcibly denied access to his eel tanks in what were, effectively, war time conditions.

1 *Hurst v Picture Theatres Ltd* [1915] 1 KB 1.

2 *Whipp v Mackey* [1927] IR 372 at 382–383. Kennedy CJ went on to consider a number of cases which over three centuries had established the principle that equitable relief could be granted against forfeiture in situations where the only loss to the party having right at law was financial and could be remedied by payment of the sum owing and interest. In particular, he considered the case of *Hill v Barclay* (1810) 18 Ves 56, in which Lord Eldon had distinguished between breaches of covenants to pay rent and breaches of other covenants in relation to the availability of the equity, holding that the equitable remedy of relief against forfeiture was available in cases of non-payment of rent.

3 'Generally speaking, however, where the forfeiture is only for securing payment, and where there is no injury from the delay in payment, or only such injury that a payment of a sum for interest and – if needs be – costs will be a full compensation for it, the equitable relief will not be refused. Is there anything in the conduct of the defendant here which should make this case the exception? I think not. If there is no answer of a strictly acceptable kind in law to the failure to pay on the named day there is an explanation which would, I think, have fallen on receptive ears in Chancery in the days when equity afforded a refuge from the tyranny of law.' [1927] IR 372 at 385.

[20.18] Fitzgibbon J went so far as to state, that if the plaintiff had sought to remove the defendant licensee's tanks from their mooring at the bottom of the Shannon, in reliance upon the revocation of the licence:

> '... an injunction might have been granted to restrain him from doing so, notwithstanding the absence of any interest in land or rights in the nature of an easement, and the licensee would not have been told that his sole remedy was an action for damages for breach of contract.'[1]

According to Fitzgibbon J, this licence effectively included an agreement not to terminate it throughout its 15-year term, with the proviso for termination in the event of non-payment of rent added only as a kind of penalty clause. Equity would protect the rights of the defendant by preventing the revocation of the licence in breach of an agreement to continue it for 15 years.

According to Murnaghan J, this was an ideal case for the application of equitable relief against forfeiture, the underlying purpose of which is to prevent one party occasioning serious hardship to the other by relying on the stricture of a legal right, while still ensuring that the party with right at law is compensated. Murnaghan J described the agreement as creating 'a mere licence, with a contractual right that the licence would not be revoked during the period mentioned in the agreement.'[2]

1 *Whipp v Mackey* [1927] IR 372 at 388.

2 [1927] IR 372 at 390.

Principles for Protection of a Licence

[20.19] As has been shown, the rights of a licensee upon an attempted revocation of his licence can be protected by injunction, in cases both where there has been a licence coupled with an interest – such as, an easement or a profit *à prendre* – and also where there is a licence, not coupled with an interest, but subject to an implied contractual condition that it will not be revoked during the currency of its term.[1] In recent times, the distinction between the two types of licence has become blurred, the necessity that the licence carry with it an interest in land assuming diminished importance according as the principles of contract can be applied to invoke suitable redress where a licence has been wrongfully revoked.

---

[1]   This latter concept, now known as a 'contractual licence', has been given further judicial sanction by the decisions of the Court of Appeal (particularly the judgment of Lord Greene MR) and of the House of Lords in *Winter Garden Theatre (London) Ltd v Millennium Productions Ltd* [1946] 1 All ER 678 and [1948] AC 173 and in the judgment of Megarry J in *Hounslow London Borough Council v Twickenham Garden Developments Ltd* [1971] Ch 233.

[20.20] Of such a kind is *Woods v Donnelly*,[1] a decision of the High Court of Northern Ireland, where the licence was held, both to be coupled with an interest and, on a true construction of the agreement creating it, subject to a contractual term against revocation during the lifetime of the licensee.

In 1969 the father of the plaintiff agreed to grant a licence to the defendant to excavate and carry away sand and gravel from lands owned by him in Co Tyrone, subject to the payment of 1s. per ton. A licence agreement was never signed, until the licensor, in 1972, anxious to treat only with the licensee and not with his site manager, drew up a simple agreement that the licensee 'only ... is hereby authorised to draw Sand and Gravel ... [from the lands] ... for as long as he requires it on condition that the full and prompt payment for same be made each month at the stated price.' The agreement was signed by both parties.

The licensor died in 1979 and his lands passed to the plaintiff, his son. The plaintiff maintained that the licence had been revoked, either by the death of his father, the licensor, or by six weeks' written notice which he, the plaintiff, had given to the licensee in February 1980.

---

[1]   *Woods v Donnelly* [1982] NI 257.

[20.21] Hutton J acknowledged that the document signed by the parties, though imperfect, had been intended to create a contract between them in the form of a licence to excavate sand and gravel. On the nature of the actual interest enjoyed by a licensee under a mining licence, he considered the advice of the Privy Council in *Australian Blue Metal Ltd v Hughes*.[1] There were considerable points of resemblance between the licence agreements in each case. In each:

(a)   the licence had been for an unspecified term;

(b)   contained no provision as to termination;

(c)   nor any limit as to the quantity of materials to be mined;

(d)   nor did it specify whether or not the licence was to be exclusive.

Lord Devlin, in *Australian Blue Metal Ltd v Hughes*, speaking of the revocation of the licence, observed:

'When it is said that a licence coupled with an interest is irrevocable, what is meant is that the licensor cannot revoke such a licence if the licensee is thereby prevented from exploiting the interest that the licensor has granted to him. ... If what is conveyed is a right to mine for a certain quantity or for a certain period, then the licence is irrevocable until the interest has been determined, that is, until the certain quantity has been obtained or the certain period has run out.'[2]

Lord Devlin had held that the licence in *Australian Blue Metal Ltd v Hughes* was coupled with an interest. Hutton J held similarly in *Woods v Donnelly*, since the clear intention evinced by the language of the agreement was that the licensee was to have an exclusive right to draw sand and gravel for as long as he required it, but that the right could not pass to his personal representatives after the licensee's death.[3] It was not necessary for the licensee to have incurred any particular degree of expenditure in order for the licence to be found enforceable.[4] Neither was a deed necessary to grant a licence coupled with an interest, since equity would enforce a written agreement, though not under seal.[5]

---

[1] *Australian Blue Metal Ltd v Hughes* [1963] AC 74.

[2] [1963] AC 74 at 94, cited in *Woods v Donnelly* [1982] NI 257 at p 262.

[3] [1982] NI 257 at 263.

[4] Hutton J rejected the majority judgments in *Atkinson v King* (1878) LR 2 Ir 320, as being difficult to reconcile with the advice in *Australian Blue Metal Ltd v Hughes*.

[5] Relying upon *Frogley v Earl of Lovelace* (1859) John 333.

[20.22] The next question to be considered was whether the contract creating the licence provided for its revocation prior to the exhaustion of the right or during the lifetime of the licensee. Hutton J held that it did not. He quoted with approval from the judgment of Lord Greene MR in *Winter Garden Theatre (London) Ltd v Millennium Productions Ltd*:[1]

'A licence created by a contract is not an interest. It creates a contractual right to do certain things which otherwise would be a trespass. It seems to me that, in considering the nature of such a licence and the mutual rights and obligations which arise under it, the first thing to do is to construe the contract according to ordinary principles .... It seems to me quite inadmissible to say that the question whether a licence is revocable at all can be, so to speak, segregated and treated by itself, leaving only the other questions to be decided by reference to the true construction of the contract.'

Lord Greene MR had gone on to say that whereas, prior to the Judicature Acts the only remedy for the licensee might be damages at common law, now equity could intervene by injunction to stop the revocation, if there were a clause in the contract, express or implied, that prohibited it; or if it could not intervene in time to restrain the revocation, equity could prevent the licensor from subsequently acting upon it.

---

[1] *Winter Garden Theatre (London) Ltd v Millennium Productions Ltd* [1946] 1 All ER 678 at 680.

[20.23] In *Woods v Donnelly*[1] it had been argued that a licence could not be deemed to have been granted for the life of the licensee, because if the licensee discontinued the drawing out of sand and gravel, it would unduly tie up the property and prevent the licensor from getting any commercial return from it. Hutton J disposed of this by deciding that, if the need arose (which he did not believe it would, on the basis of the demonstrated activities of the licensee), a term could be implied into the licence agreement that the licensor could terminate it if the licensee did not excavate and take away sand and gravel on a continuous basis.[2]

---

[1]   *Woods v Donnelly* [1982] NI 257.

[2]   Hutton J stated: 'In my opinion the ordinary meaning of the words of a contract cannot be altered by one party pointing to some contingency which has not happened and which, at the time that the contract was made, was most unlikely to happen.' [1982] NI 257 at 267. In support of the possibility of implying a suitable term, Hutton J cited *Sharp v Wright* (1859) 28 Beav 150, in which it had been held that the contract as a matter of construction, obliged the licensee to start work immediately and proceed continuously throughout the term of the licence.

Conclusion

[20.24] It is clear from the decisions in *Allen v King*,[1] *Whipp v Mackey*[2] and *Woods v Donnelly*[3] that the remedy for revocation of a licence, whether directly caused by the licensor, or the inevitable indirect result of some act or default of his, lies in an action for breach, or threatened breach, of contract. The contractual term prohibiting the revocation may be express or implied from the surrounding circumstances. Appropriate redress includes damages at common law and the equitable remedies of injunction and (where it arises) relief against forfeiture. The question whether a licence is 'revocable' or 'irrevocable' is primarily a semantic one. A licence may be deemed 'revocable' because it is not a hereditament and so cannot be enforced other than between the original licensor and the original licensee. The same licence may be deemed 'irrevocable' because its revocation, in certain instances, can be restrained by injunction or compensated for by an award in damages. Similarly, a 'licence coupled with an interest' is liable to be terminated only in accordance with the provisions of the contract granting it. Where the contract is silent – and provided that the behaviour of the parties does not warrant the implication of a term for earlier revocation – there will be an implied term that the licence is irrevocable until the interest which it was granted to enjoy has been consumed or is no longer capable of being enjoyed.

---

[1]   *David Allen and Sons Billposting Ltd v King* [1915] 2 IR 213, 448, [1916] 2 AC 54.

[2]   *Whipp v Mackey* [1927] IR 372.

[3]   *Woods v Donnelly* [1982] NI 257.

[20.25] In *Jones v Jones*,[1] Girvan J applied the principles of a contractual licence to the case of a gift of a farm subject to a reserved right of residence in the farmhouse. In relation to the law governing the enforceability of licences generally, Girvan J observed:

'Licences may assume various forms and perform a multiplicity of purposes. The overlapping categories of licences recognised by the law include bare licences, contractual licences, equitable or irrevocable licences, licences based on proprietary estoppel and licences coupled with the grant of an interest. The precise proprietary context of each licence varies with the category concerned.'[2]

It seems, therefore, that only where there is no contractual right, express or implied, prohibiting a revocation of a licence, is a licence, in truth, a mere personal privilege. In such circumstance a licence can be peremptorily revoked, provided that there is enough time given to pack up and leave.

---

[1] *Jones v Jones* [2001] NI 244, see para **[22.21]** ff.
[2] [2001] NI 244 at 256.

Chapter 21

Whether a Licence or a Lease

Introduction

[21.01] In certain cases the question arises whether enjoyment of land, that involves actual occupation by the person designated as licensee, is properly described as a licence, or whether in effect a proprietary interest has been conferred. As a specific term of enjoyment and the payment of periodic remuneration are both features of a licence, the interest in land which most resembles this arrangement is a lease. A lease, however, is subject to statutory regulation governing the eligibility of a lessee to renew his lease,[1] and, in the case of residential lettings, to be furnished a rent book[2] and have the premises registered with the relevant housing authority.[3] A licence is immune from these arrangements. A lease is also assignable by both parties, whereas a licence, normally, is not – unless coupled with an easement or a profit *à prendre*. In consequence, parties (usually, but not invariably, potential lessors) who wish to ensure that a species of enjoyment of which possession is a feature do not accrue rights of renewal to the person in occupation, will endeavour to dress up an agreement that is in reality a lease as if it were a licence.

In many such situations, where the occupying party, despite the label put upon his or her enjoyment, seeks a renewal, which the landowner then refuses, the courts have had to adjudicate whether the alleged licence is in fact a lease, and thereby subject to the provisions of the Landlord and Tenant Acts.

---

[1] Landlord and Tenant (Amendment) Acts 1980–1994.

[2] Housing (Rent Book) Regulations 1993 (SI 146/1993).

[3] Housing (Registration of Rented Houses) Regulations 1996 (SI 30/1996).

[21.02] There would be no issue if the label ascribed by the parties to the relationship was conclusive of the matter. This is not so. As has been seen, in *Whipp v Mackey*[1] the parties to the agreement were described as 'landlord' and 'tenant' and the remuneration described as 'rent', but the right to affix eel tanks underwater to an island in the Shannon was found to be a licence only.

---

[1] *Whipp v Mackey* [1927] IR 372, see para **[20.16]**.

Intention of Parties as Embodied in Agreement Recording It – Exclusive Possession

[21.03] The principal method of determining, in any case, whether occupancy is consistent with either a licence or a lease is to look to the intention of the parties as evidenced in the agreement creating it, with particular reference to the extent to which the party in occupation has been given what is called 'exclusive possession'.[1] Where the possession is liable to be shared among a number, and any so-called licensee is obliged to seek an alternative sharer if one of those sharing vacates, then the agreement is likely to constitute a licence and not a lease or tenancy. If the grantor reserves a right at any time to share the occupation with the grantee, then the reasonable inference is that a licence only has been created.[2]

---

[1] It will be recalled, see para **[19.07]**, that a licence by definition merely enables the licensee do something which otherwise, as against the licensor, would have been a trespass. If the right granted enables the 'licensee' to claim exclusive possession against the whole world, including the 'licensor', then arguably the interest conferred is something larger than what is commonly understood by a licence. Molony LJ in *David Allen and Sons Billposting Ltd v King* [1915] 2 IR 448 at 479, had ruled out the possibility of the agreement in that case creating a lease because it had not granted exclusive possession.

[2] *AG Securities v Vaughan* and *Antoniades v Villiers*, respectively, [1990] AC 417. The appeals in both cases were heard together. In the latter case, the House of Lords found that there was a tenancy because the clauses inserted by the landlord, that otherwise would have been consistent with a licence, were deemed not to be genuine.

[21.04] The crucial importance of exclusive possession to the question whether a lease or a licence has been created was strongly stated by Judge Shannon in *Whyte v Sheehan*.[1] In October 1940, a company granted a weekly tenancy of a dwellinghouse in Dublin to the plaintiff for a rent of 8*s*. 8*d*. per week. The tenancy contained a covenant against assigning or sub-letting without the consent of the company. After the grant of his tenancy to the plaintiff, the company secretary agreed to let the house to one Richard Sheehan for a rent of 2*s*. 6*d*. a day, with a waiver of rent for several weeks provided that Richard Sheehan renovated the premises. In an attempt to avoid the application of the Increase of Rent Acts (by not granting an assignment of the tenancy), the company secretary insisted that Richard Sheehan sign a licence agreement with the plaintiff tenant.

The so-called licence agreement provided for the following:

(a)   that the licensee was a permissive occupant;

(b)   that the daily payment of 2*s*. 6*d*. was not a rent, nor to be construed as rent;

(c)   that the licensor made no warranty as to title, nor could be sued on foot of any defect in it;

(d)   that the licensee acknowledged that the licensor held under an agreement which prohibited assigning or sub-letting without the consent of the company.

The company secretary then insisted that Richard Sheehan obtain sureties. These were his father and brother, the defendants. When Richard Sheehan ceased paying his rent, the company, through the tenant, sued the sureties. The sureties contended that the surety agreement was invalid, as being based upon an arrangement that was not a genuine licence, but an attempted assignment of a tenancy – itself invalid, as the consent of the company to it, under the original tenancy agreement, had not been secured. Judge Shannon agreed with the defendants' contention that they could not be liable on their surety if the agreement between the principals were invalid.[2]

---

1   *Whyte v Sheehan* [1943] Ir Jur Rep 38.
2   '... the defendants guaranteed the performance and observance of the terms of a written document, and not the performance or observance of obligations which arose on the declaration that that agreement was null and void.'[1943] Ir Jur Rep 38 at 43.

[21.05] Furthermore, in the view of Judge Shannon, the entire arrangement culminating in the purported licence agreement, and associated sureties, was a stratagem devised by the company to avoid the application of the increase in rents legislation. He observed:

'Full regard must be paid to the words used, but terms of art cannot conceal or alter the truth, and no matter what words are used if it is clear from the document that it was intended to part with an estate in the property and to confer an exclusive right of occupation, so that the grantor had no right to come upon the premises without the consent of the occupier, a tenancy or demise is created although no words of letting are used, and although the remuneration is not spoken of as rent.'[1]

According to Judge Shannon, the agreement in *Whyte v Sheehan* was plainly designed to give exclusive possession to the deemed licensee as against everybody, including the tenant, his licensor, and so was not a licence proper, but a purported assignment of a tenancy.

---

1   *Whyte v Sheehan* [1943] Ir Jur Rep 38 at 41–42.

Limits on Scope of 'Exclusive Possession'

[21.06] Where the relationship between the parties is based on an 'arms' length' commercial transaction, it seems that the fact of exclusive possession is less conclusive of the relationship's legal character. In *Gatien Motor Co Ltd v Continental Oil*,[1] Kenny J stated that, in determining whether a person in possession of land holds under a lease or a licence, exclusive possession 'is undoubtedly a most important consideration but it is not decisive.' Whether the relationship between the parties is that of landlord and tenant, or otherwise, is a matter of law, to be decided, not merely by the label used by the parties to describe the relationship, but from '[A]ll the terms of the document and the circumstances in which it was entered into ...'[2]

In *Gatien Motor Co Ltd v Continental Oil* a lessee of commercial premises, following the expiry of one lease and before the commencement of another, entered into a caretaker's agreement for one week, during which he paid no rent. The purpose of this was to prevent his obtaining statutory rights to a further lease under the Landlord and Tenant Act 1931. In the opinion of Kenny J, notwithstanding that exclusive possession

373

continued to be a feature, the fact of the caretaker's agreement being entered into, together with the non-payment of rent, and 'all the surrounding circumstances' (one presumes that this alluded to the business relationship between the parties), warranted the conclusion that the possession on foot of the caretaker's agreement constituted a licence only.

Kenny J was sustained in his view by an earlier Supreme Court decision, *Davies v Hilliard*,[3] in which the defendant had signed a caretaker's agreement, paid six months' rent in advance, and gone into possession of two flats owned by the plaintiff, pending negotiations for a tenancy. When negotiations broke down, an order for possession was given to the plaintiff, on the basis that, despite the defendant's enjoying exclusive possession and having paid rent, his occupation was not on foot of a tenancy, but of a licence, as caretaker.

---

[1]   *Gatien Motor Co Ltd v Continental Oil* [1979] IR 406.
[2]   [1979] IR 406 at 420.
[3]   *Davies v Hilliard* (1965) 101 ILTR 50.

[21.07] In *Kenny Homes & Co Ltd v Leonard*,[1] it was held that the possession of a petrol station for over 20 years, as part of a licence agreement for the hiring of equipment, did not import exclusive possession for the purpose of claiming a tenancy. Even though the occupier of the premises was the sole key-holder, all the clauses in the agreement were consistent with a licence, and the agreement itself had provided that the occupier was a licensee. The fact that the occupier had not fully read the agreement which he signed, and later protested that he believed he was a tenant, did not convert the relationship to one of landlord and tenant.

---

[1]   *Kenny Homes & Co Ltd v Leonard* (11 December 1997, unreported) HC, Costello P; (18 June 1998, unreported) SC, Lynch J.

[21.08] Similarly, in a purely family or domestic arrangement, exclusive possession has been held to be consistent with a licence rather than a lease. In *Bellew v Bellew*[1] the occupation of Barmeath Castle in Co Louth by one of the Bellew family over a number of years, which included a right to farm the lands, started out on a permissive basis 'pending further negotiations.' These negotiations, which commenced in 1961, collapsed in 1963, after which the occupant remained in possession, eventually setting up a claim to ownership on the basis of adverse possession, under s 18 of the Statute of Limitations 1957. A majority of the Supreme Court held that possession during the negotiations, although exclusive, was on foot of a licence only,[2] following which the possession became adverse, and, after a further 12 years, extinguished the title of the tenant for life. Griffin J, delivering the judgment of the majority, observed:

> 'Although exclusive possession is an important consideration in determining whether the person in occupation is a licensee or a tenant, it is no longer a decisive factor; the transaction as a whole must be looked at to ascertain the intention of the parties.'[3]

Griffin J was supported by the observations of Denning LJ in *Facchini v Bryson*,[4] that where an occupier has been held to be a licensee, there has very often been a personal circumstance, such as a family arrangement, or an act of friendship or generosity, to negative the intention to create a tenancy.[5]

---

[1]   *Bellew v Bellew* [1982] IR 447.

[2]   O'Higgins CJ held that the possession was on foot of a tenancy at will, which, under s 17(1) of the Statute of Limitations 1957, is deemed to expire within one year of its commencement, unless earlier determined; he concurred with the view of the majority of the Supreme Court that possession thereafter became adverse.

[3]   [1982] IR 447 at 463.

[4]   *Facchini v Bryson* [1952] 1 TLR 1389.

[5]   Áine Ryall, in 'Lease or Licence? The Contemporary Significance of the Distinction' (2001) 6 CPLJ 56, suggests that the courts have failed to address the distinction between 'exclusive possession' and 'exclusive occupation', leaving 'exclusive possession' as a concept quite ill-defined: for example, a lodger of a room in a house owned and occupied by his landlord may be said to have 'exclusive occupation' of the room, but in no sense could be believed to be enjoying a tenancy.

Commercial Transactions

[21.09] In more complicated commercial transactions, frequently the entirety of the clauses in the parties' agreement have to be considered, so that a view can be arrived at by the court as to whether, on balance, the overall thrust of them is more consistent with a lease or a licence.

[21.10] This was the approach adopted by the Supreme Court in *Irish Shell and BP Ltd v John Costello Ltd (No 1)*.[1] The plaintiff was the owner of a garage site and petrol station at Roebuck Road, Dublin which, over several years and through a miscellany of oft-revised agreements, it had licensed to the defendant to facilitate the defendant's use of petrol pumps and ancillary equipment, hired by the plaintiff to the defendant, and the business connected with that equipment. When, in late 1974, the parties failed to reach consensus on the terms of a new agreement due to a wrangle over Sunday opening hours and the plaintiff sought possession, the issue fell to be considered whether the agreement created a licence or a lease.

The Supreme Court, by a majority (Kenny J dissenting), held that the successive agreements created a lease rather than a licence. In the opinion of Griffin J (with whose judgment O'Higgins CJ concurred), several features of the later agreements in particular were closely consistent with a lease. These included:

   (a)   the provision for quarterly payments;

   (b)   restrictions as to user;

   (c)   a prohibition on assignment;

   (d)   specific provision for access by the grantor;

   (e)   a right of re-entry for default in making quarterly payments;

   (f)   the reality that the grantee had exclusive possession.

In addition, the agreements entered into following the construction by the grantor of a garage workshop had deleted a number of clauses that would have been more appropriate to a licence than a lease, such as:

(i)   that nothing would be deemed to confer exclusive possession on the hirer or grantee;

(ii)   that nothing would be deemed to create the relationship of landlord and tenant;

(iii)   that nothing would be done to hinder the occupation of the grantor.

Despite the existence of certain personal stipulations, such as that the grantee would stock and sell only product manufactured by the grantor, in the opinion of Griffin J the real nature of the agreement was that the grantee operated a lock-up garage and service station, with workshop, on foot of a lease. The mere designation of an occupancy agreement as a licence was not definitive of its status. That depended on the nature of the transaction taken as a totality.[2] Griffin J quoted with approval the pronouncement of Lord Denning MR in *Shell-Mex v Manchester Garage*:[3]

> 'Broadly speaking, we have to see whether it is a personal privilege given to a person (in which case it is a licence), or whether it grants an interest in land (in which case it is a tenancy). At one time it used to be thought that exclusive possession was a decisive factor. But that is not so. It depends on broader considerations altogether. Primarily on whether it is personal in its nature or not.'[4]

---

[1]   *Irish Shell and BP Ltd v John Costello Ltd (No 1)* [1981] ILRM 66. See also Cooney 'Tenancy or Licence' (1982) 17 Ir Jur (NS) 121.

[2]   Citing *Addiscombe Garden Estates Ltd v Crabbe* [1958] 1 QB 513; *Gatien Motor Co v Continental Oil* [1979] IR 406.

[3]   *Shell-Mex v Manchester Garage* [1971] 1 WLR 612 at 615.

[4]   [1981] ILRM 66 at 70.

[21.11] Nor could the matter be regarded as settled by the absence of 'rent' necessary to bring the relationship within the definition of a lease or tenancy under s 3 of the Landlord and Tenant Law Amendment, Ireland, Act ('Deasy's Act') 1860: the reality of the case was that the periodic payments made by the grantee were, in fact, rent '... although cloaked under the guise or under the label of payment for the hire of equipment.'[1]

---

[1]   *Irish Shell and BP Ltd v John Costello Ltd (No 1)* [1981] ILRM 66 at 71. However, Kenny J dissented on the basis that the hiring agreement, which provided for a quarterly payment for the hire of the equipment and rendered the use of the filling station subject to the use of the equipment, was simply that and nothing more, and that the periodic payments for the hire of the equipment could not be construed as rent.

[21.12] The difficulties inherent in complex commercial agreements, from the perspective of whether they create a licence or a lease, were exemplified in a further decision of the Supreme Court involving the same parties, *Irish Shell and BP Ltd v John*

Costello Ltd (No 2).[1] This concerned the legal nature of ongoing agreed occupation by the grantee, following the expiry of the last written agreement between the parties, in July 1974. All three judges of the Supreme Court described the relationship differently.

---

[1]   *Irish Shell and BP Ltd v John Costello Ltd (No 2)* [1984] IR 511.

[21.13] According to O'Higgins CJ, the nature and terms of the agreed occupancy were the same as under the last written agreement, except that the tenancy, while negotiations were pending, was a tenancy at will. In the opinion of the Chief Justice, a tenancy at will, though somewhat outmoded as a concept, was the proper legal description of continued exclusive possession during a period of negotiation.[1] He was sustained in this view by the judgment of Scarman LJ in *Heslop v Burns,*[2] who had suggested that the principal continuing relevance of a tenancy at will was to protect an occupier of property pending negotiations for an interest in that property, such as prior to completion of a purchase or where a tenant overholds before the finalising of a new tenancy agreement: '... the tenancy at will is an apt legal mechanism to protect the occupier during such a period of transition; he is there and can keep out trespassers; he is there with the consent of the landlord and can keep out the landlord as long as that consent is maintained.'[3]

---

[1]   *Irish Shell and BP Ltd v John Costello Ltd (No 2)* [1984] IR 511 at 514–515.
[2]   *Heslop v Burns* [1974] 3 All ER 406.
[3]   *Heslop v Burns* [1974] 3 All ER 406 at 416, cited in [1984] IR 511 at 514–515. O'Higgins CJ had adopted similar reasoning in *Bellew v Bellew* [1982] IR 447 at 460. But see the House of Lords decision in *Burrows v London Borough of Brent* [1996] 4 All ER 577 and the emergence of the concept of 'tolerated trespasser'.

[21.14] In the view of Henchy J, the parties were now licensor and licensee only. Where a former tenant stays on and continues to make periodic payments, this is not always in the character of rent:

> 'The acceptance of the rent does not, of itself, create a new tenancy, but it is evidence from which a new tenancy may be presumed as being the intention of the parties. Thus, if on a consideration of all the evidence in a particular case, it is shown that the payments made were not intended to be paid as rent, or to be received as rent, the presumption of a tenancy will be rebutted. In all cases it is a question of what the parties intended, and it is not permissible to apply an objective test which would impute to the parties an intention which they never had.'[1]

The dissent of McCarthy J was largely based on the fact that nothing had really changed between the parties. In the same way as they had not formerly believed themselves to be landlord and tenant, so it was again, as the occupancy continued on similar terms. All that was different was that there was now no set term to the tenancy, which could be ended by the giving of a month's notice.

---

[1]   *Irish Shell and BP Ltd v John Costello Ltd (No 2)* [1984] IR 511 at 517.

[21.15] However, where the clear intention of the parties, as evidenced by the agreement taken as a whole, is to create a licence, this will not be denied merely because certain clauses, considered on their own, would sustain a relationship of landlord and tenant.

[21.16] In *Governors of National Maternity Hospital Dublin v McGouran*,[1] the defendant was given a licence to operate a shop and canteen in part of the plaintiff hospital. Although preliminary negotiations proceeded on the basis of a proposed 'lease' and a 'rent', the agreement ultimately executed was a licence, for a year, in respect both of the shop and the canteen, subject to what was termed a 'licence fee'. The licence term was later extended, and the fee increased, but no new agreement was entered into. Three years later, the plaintiff indicated that it wanted to put the franchises of the coffee shop and the shop out to tender. The defendant claimed that she was a tenant, with a statutory right to the renewal of her tenancy. The plaintiff then issued notice of termination of the licence.

In support of her claim, the defendant identified certain clauses in the agreement that were consistent with a tenancy and not a licence:

(i)   its being deemed to extend to her 'successors and assigns,' which would not be the case in a mere licence;

(ii)   the inclusion of a covenant prohibiting assignment, which is a standard landlord and tenant covenant;

(iii)   the inclusion of a full repairing covenant, which is also a standard landlord and tenant covenant;

(iv)   the obligation placed on the defendant occupier to pay rates;

(v)   the obligation placed on the defendant occupier to take out a public liability insurance based on her occupancy.

Morris J acknowledged that certain of the clauses in the agreement bore all the hallmarks of a lease, but added that any such inference was negatived by three particular clauses which made it clear that what was being granted was no more than a licence, with the defendant constituted as licensee:

(a)   a clause which stated that the agreement created a licence only, and not a lease, and that possession at all times remained in the hospital;[2]

(b)   a clause stating that the licence was non-exclusive, and that the licensee was entitled to use the premises in common with the licensor for the purposes of the two franchised businesses;

(c)   a clause providing that, on the giving of notice, the plaintiff could substitute alternative premises in the hospital for the businesses of the shop and the canteen respectively.

---

[1]   *Governors of National Maternity Hospital Dublin v McGouran* [1994] 1 ILRM 521.

[2]   This enabled Morris J to distinguish *Irish Shell and BP Ltd v John Costello (No 1)* [1981] ILRM 66, where the removal of a clause, from later agreements, that exclusive possession was

not being conferred on the grantee, enabled a majority of the Supreme Court to hold that a lease had been granted, and not a licence. See para **[21.10]**.

[21.17] Morris J noted that the defendant had, in fact, enjoyed exclusive possession of the two areas she occupied, by reason of being the sole key-holder, but held that the hospital continued to 'exercise dominion' through a variety of means:

    (a)   by requiring the defendant to provide a price list;

    (b)   by regulating the hours of opening;

    (c)   by the provision of safety catches to windows;

    (d)   by attaching supplementary fans to a smoke extractor unit which the defendant had installed.

Furthermore, the clause providing for the substitution of alternative premises by the plaintiff was not one which would be found in a lease. Nor was the significance of such a clause vitiated by the fact that, in practice, the hospital did not require to use the licensed area in common with their occupier.[1]

---

[1]   *Governors of National Maternity Hospital Dublin v McGouran* [1994] 1 ILRM 521 at 528.

[21.18] *Kenny Homes & Co Ltd v Leonard*[1] is a further example of a case in which the totality of the clauses in the agreement favoured a licence rather than a lease, notwithstanding that the defendant hirer of petrol equipment and a site for car-parking had possession for over 20 years. It had been agreed at the outset that the relationship of landlord and tenant would not be created. The possession was found not to be exclusive possession.[2] Even though the licensors did not have a set of duplicate keys to the site, it was held that they enjoyed contractual rights over the site which could be enforced at any time. It was a significant feature that the hiring and occupancy agreement did not contain clauses, seeking to restrict various acts by the licensee, which would only have been necessary to include if the occupier were a lessee. In this regard the case can be distinguished from *Irish Shell and BP Ltd v John Costello Ltd (No 1)*,[3] where the progressive elimination of what might be termed 'licence type' clauses enabled the court to hold that in fact a tenancy had been created. Nor could the occupier be heard to contend that he had not read the licence agreement initially, and had always acted under the assumption that he was a tenant.

---

[1]   *Kenny Homes & Co Ltd v Leonard* (11 December 1997, unreported) HC, Costello P, (18 June 1998, unreported) SC, Lynch J.

[2]   In 'The Lease/Licence Distinction' (2000) 5 Bar Review 332, Ruth Cannon contends that the caselaw in Ireland has now arrived at a point where the bare assertion, in an agreement involving occupancy, that exclusive possession is not intended to be created, is likely to result in a judicial finding that the resultant relationship is that of licensor and licensee, regardless of how the agreement is implemented in reality. It is difficult to deny the merit of this point of view, although, in the aftermath of the judgment of Peart J in *Smith v Coras Iompair Eireann* (9 October 2002, unreported) HC, this trend might be seen as in the process of reversal.

[3]   *Irish Shell and BP Ltd v John Costello Ltd (No 1)* [1981] ILRM 66. See para **[21.10]**.

[21.19] However, the decision of Peart J in *Smith v Coras Iompair Eireann*[1] represents a brave reassertion of the principles enunciated in *Irish Shell and BP Ltd v John Costello Ltd (No 1)*,[2] despite a clause in the agreement between the parties typically asserting that the contract did not create a tenancy and that the licensee was not entitled to possession. The purported licence was, in fact, of a shop unit under the arch of Tara Street railway station in Dublin. Peart J found:

(a)   that the applicant had, in effect, exclusive possession of the shop throughout the entire term of the agreement, and that this circumstance enabled the case to be distinguished from *Governors of National Maternity Hospital Dublin v McGouran*;[3]

(b)   that the respondent never entered the premises to inspect, clean, or to carry out repairs;

(c)   that the respondent did not have a key to the premises (this seems to have made little difference in *McGouran* or in *Kenny Homes & Co Ltd v Leonard*);[4]

(d)   that the respondent had no responsibility for the security of the premises;

(e)   that the applicant had invested significantly in the premises, including the payment of a substantial premium and heavy 'fitting out' costs; this factor enabled Peart J to hold that the agreement conferred far more than a mere personal privilege as contended for by the respondent.

In the opinion of Peart J, the entire agreement did not stand to be interpreted, in terms of the legal status of the party in possession on foot of it, by one clause only, the removal of which would have left the entirety of the remainder of the agreement consistent with a standard commercial tenancy. Notwithstanding that the contract had initially been offered as a licence, and that both parties had received legal advice in relation to it, the parties could not contract out of a tenancy agreement, merely by calling it a licence, when the provisions of the agreement, and the circumstances of possession, all tended to the conclusion that it *was* a tenancy.[5]

---

[1]   *Smith v Coras Iompair Éireann* (9 October 2002, unreported) HC.

[2]   *Irish Shell and BP Ltd v John Costello Ltd (No 1)* [1981] ILRM 66.

[3]   *Governors of National Maternity Hospital Dublin v McGouran* [1994] 1 ILRM 521. See para **[21.16]**.

[4]   *Kenny Homes & Co Ltd v Leonard* (11 December 1997, unreported) HC, Costello P, (18 June 1998, unreported) SC, Lynch J.

[5]   The judgment of Peart J is clearly more consistent with the view held by the English courts, that an agreement will be construed as a tenancy if that, in effect, is what it is, despite what it may be called, as exemplified in *Errington v Errington* [1952] KB 290 and *Street v Mountford* [1985] 1 AC 809.

Behaviour of the Parties and Background Circumstances

[21.20] As a general rule, the courts will strive to give effect to the intention of the parties, where these are *not* made clear in a written agreement, 'by examining the circumstances and conduct of each',[1] and will not seek to impose a landlord and tenant relationship merely because certain of the documents which changed hands could also be consistent with a tenancy.

Hence, the High Court of Northern Ireland declined to impute a tenancy in *Northern Ireland Housing Executive v McCann*[2] and *Northern Ireland Housing Executive v Duffin*.[3] In each case the housing executive, prior to seeking an ejectment order against a squatter on local authority property, had advised the squatter that he would be obliged to pay a certain sum of money for 'use and occupation'. In each case also the housing executive had sent to the squatter a 'rent book' to assist in the payment of the 'use and occupation' monies.

---

[1]   *Northern Ireland Housing Executive v Duffin* [1985] NI 210 at p 214, per Carswell J.
[2]   *Northern Ireland Housing Executive v McCann* [1979] NI 39.
[3]   [1985] NI 210.

[21.21] In *NIHE v McCann* Murray J held, citing the definition of 'rent' in s 1 of the Landlord and Tenant Law Amendment, Ireland, (Deasy's) Act 1860, that the requisite ingredients were not present for a tenancy in a situation where the periodic payment had not been intended as a rent. Against the background of the correspondence from the housing executive, it would be '… flying in the face of reality to say that there was an express or implied contract between the respondent and the appellant that the relation of landlord and tenant should exist between them.'[1] From the time the housing executive had written to the squatter until it moved to evict him, 'the appellant was in the house under a revocable licence – not a tenancy – from the respondent upon the basis that he would, while in occupation, have to pay the periodic sum demanded by the respondent as a charge for use and occupation.' Once the respondent moved to evict the appellant it clearly manifested an intention to revoke the licence.

In *NIHE v Duffin*, Carswell J stated that merely because money might be accepted by way of rent does not mean that the relationship of landlord and tenant exists. The use in the payment books of documents more appropriate to a tenancy could be argued as consistent with a tenancy, but it was also consistent with the adaptation of a rent payment book for tenants to cases of illegal occupancy.

> 'It is in my view necessary to look at all the facts, and to seek the true intention of the parties. One should not be over-astute to foist a tenancy upon the Executive as a consequence of its incautious use of documents if the facts of the case taken as a whole display a contrary intention.'[2]

---

[1]   *Northern Ireland Housing Executive v McCann* [1979] NI 39 at 43.
[2]   *Northern Ireland Housing Executive v Duffin* [1985] NI 210 at 214.

[21.22] The nature of the behaviour between the parties can, in an exceptional case, result in a finding by a court that an arrangement involving occupancy, described by the parties as a lease, creates no more than a licence. In *O'Siodhachain v O'Mahony*,[1] the plaintiffs had established a personal rapport with the defendants, through the proffering of quasi-legal and psychological advice. The plaintiffs had a terraced house in Co Cork, the defendants a 70 acre farm in Co Kerry. Discussions were broached about the possibility of an exchange of the respective properties. After all-night negotiations, a contract prepared by the plaintiffs, containing an agreement to exchange a substantial proportion of the defendants' farm, and also the farmhouse and outbuildings, for the plaintiffs' terraced house, was signed by both parties. This contract included a 15-year lease of the farmhouse to the plaintiffs. The plaintiffs moved into the farmhouse, but never paid any rent. Several subsequent attempts to enter into a new agreement for sale fell through. The defendants sought possession of the farmhouse.

Notwithstanding that the parties had characterised the plaintiffs' occupancy of the farmhouse as a lease, Kearns J deemed them to have a licence only:

(i) in the absence of any rent, or any periodic consideration in the nature of rent, the relationship could not be that of landlord and tenant;

(ii) there were no typical landlord and tenant covenants in the agreement;

(iii) there was clear undue influence operating from the plaintiffs upon the defendants. In consequence, the plaintiffs were held to have a licence only, which had been effectually terminated by the defendants' issuing of notice to quit.

---

[1]   *O'Siodhachain v O'Mahony* (31 October 2002, unreported) HC, Kearns J.

Unconcluded Negotiations

[21.23] As has been shown, a licence is consistent with the character of an occupancy while negotiations are in progress for an interest in land.[1]

In *Law and Fry v Murphy and Dooly*,[2] the predecessor of the plaintiffs had granted a licence to the defendants to excavate sand, gravel and stone. Negotiations ensued between the plaintiffs and the defendants for the grant of a lease for five years, but broke down. The court declined to hold that there was sufficient memorandum in writing to enforce an agreement, by reason of fundamental uncertainty over the area of the land involved and the commencement date for the lease. Nor could it be held that the plaintiffs were estopped from denying an agreement for lease, as the licensees had not in any way acted to their detriment in reliance on such presumed agreement, but had merely continued the business of excavation and removal of sand and gravel and stone on foot of their licence.

---

[1]   *Davies v Hilliard* (1965) 101 ILTR 50; *Bellew v Bellew* [1982] IR 447, see para **[21.08]**; but note the views of Scarman LJ in *Heslop v Burns* [1974] 3 All ER 406 and O'Higgins CJ in *Irish Shell and BP Ltd v John Costello Ltd (No 2)* [1984] IR 511, that a tenancy at will is the suitable legal status of agreed occupancy pending negotiations for a renewal of a lease.

[2]   *Law and Fry v Murphy and Dooly* (12 April 1978, unreported) HC.

[21.24] However, in *Texaco (Ireland) Ltd v Mark Murphy t/a Shannonway Service Station*,[1] Barron J found that there was an enforceable agreement for lease, even though its actual commencement date was uncertain. The defendant had been in occupation of a filling station, on foot of a succession of licence agreements, for 23 years, on the understanding that his lease was being prepared. The plaintiff's representative had never made it clear to him that it was not their policy to grant leases. According to Barron J, once the defendant went into possession and observed the terms of the licence, while repeatedly asking for his lease, this constituted the conclusion of the tenancy agreement. Barron J found that the defendant would not have gone into possession if he had believed he was not a tenant.

In the view of Barron J, the admission by the plaintiff that the defendant's lease was being prepared overrode the defendant's acknowledgement in the licence documents that his possession was as licensee only. Barron J cited in support the Supreme Court decision in *Irish Shell and BP Ltd v John Costello Ltd (No 1)*[2] and summarised his view of the law thus:

'Exclusive possession is still one of the important indicators that a tenancy and not a licence has been given. ... The normal implication from the granting of exclusive possession would be that a tenancy was being created. It is only where such exclusive possession is given as a personal privilege that no tenancy comes into being. If the grantor seeks to rely upon personal privilege, the onus is on him to establish that.'

Barron J furthermore declined to accept that the signing of each fresh licence agreement could be deemed to imply a surrender of each previous tenancy, as the occupier had always maintained that he had a tenancy, so that the grantor in consequence would not have been entitled to possession.

---

[1]   *Texaco (Ireland) Ltd v Mark Murphy t/a Shannonway Service Station* (17 July 1991, unreported) HC.
[2]   *Irish Shell and BP Ltd v John Costello Ltd (No 1)* [1981] ILRM 66.

[21.25] In conclusion, it must be acknowledged, that though a certain skein of consistency can be teased from the decisions, and cases can be clustered under headings as an aid to explanation, the actual application of the principles concerning 'whether a licence or a lease' remains confused. In some instances, individual isolated factors seem to have acquired pre-eminence, such as – the degree of control over the grantee's activity imposed by the grantor, the level of investment by the grantee, the extent to which the transaction was governed by personal relationship, the ease of adapting tenancy documents for licence purposes. Notwithstanding this, with a constant paramountcy attached to the ideal of 'exclusive possession', the tendency of the courts has been to seek the true relationship of the parties from their intentions as embodied in written form. Doubtless, those who draft such agreements take their cue from the enunciation of judges in decided cases. Even so, as shown frequently to have occurred, the adoption of mere cleverness to mask the true nature of the contract in dissembling language bids fair to fail, by being seen through by a judge and discounted.

Chapter 22

Rights of Residence

Introduction

[22.01] Rights of residence, though not unique to Ireland,[1] are commonly encountered in both jurisdictions on the island.[2] They broadly resemble licences and, indeed, are best regarded as a category of licence. Most often they take the form of a gift or bequest of a house or farm to a family member, subject to the right of another family member to continue to live there. In consequence, a right of residence frequently arises by way of reservation in a voluntary disposal of property, or as incident to a legacy otherwise unencumbered. Widows, unmarried children and relatives with a disability have featured as beneficiaries of a right of residence.[3] Sometimes the right of residence is linked to an auxiliary right to be supported and maintained by the person to whom the property has passed. It is only a right of residence that partakes of the attributes of a licence. Any right of maintenance, through the provision of clothing, food, produce or personal services,[4] is more akin to a positive covenant, the burden of which – at least insofar as concerns freehold land – does not run with the property so as to be enforceable against a subsequent owner of it.

---

[1] Their incidence in the Republic has lessened somewhat in recent years due to the provision by the Succession Act 1965 of a legal right share on the part of a non-owning spouse in the property of a deceased owning spouse; in particular, ss 56, 67 and 111. See also Coughlan 'Enforcing Rights of Residence' (1993) 11 ILT (NS) 168.

[2] 'The people of Ireland have always had a very keen, not to say punctilious, regard for family obligations and ties, and it is well known that such rights ... exist very extensively throughout the whole of Ireland.' *National Bank v Keegan* [1931] IR 344 at 347, per Johnston J. '... the granting and reserving of rights of residence is a common feature of Irish agricultural land transactions and is a tribute to the Irish sense of family obligation ...' *Jones v Jones* [2001] NI 244 at 247, per Girvan J.

[3] For example, *Kelaghan v Daly* [1913] 2 IR 328; *Lahiffe v Hecker* (28 April 1994, unreported) HC, Lynch J (unmarried daughter); *Johnston v Horace* [1993] ILRM 594 (disabled child).

[4] See Grattan 'Of Pin-Money and Paraphernalia, The Widow's Shilling and a Free Ride to Mass' in *One Hundred and Fifty Years of Irish Law* (eds, Dawson, Greer and Ingram, 1996) SLS Legal Publications (NI) and Sweet & Maxwell, pp 222–225.

[22.02] Rights of residence usually divide themselves into two categories:[1]

(a)   a general right of residence over the entirety of a property, often twinned with a charge for maintenance;

385

(b) a particular right of residence, 'created by reserving or giving the right to the exclusive use during life of a specified room or rooms in the dwellinghouse on the holding.'[2]

---

[1] Thus expressed by Kennedy CJ in *National Bank v Keegan* [1931] IR 344.
[2] [1931] IR 344 at 354.

Exclusive Rights of Residence in Unregistered Land

Republic of Ireland

[22.03] In *National Bank v Keegan*, a particular or exclusive right of residence, together with a right of maintenance, was given over two specific rooms in a house the title to which was freehold and unregistered. The right had been granted by an informal memorandum, rather than by deed or will. This was held, both by the High Court and a majority of the Supreme Court, to create an equitable life interest in the two designated rooms, and so had priority over an equitable mortgage through deposit of the title deeds. The mortgagee was found to be on notice of the right of residence.[1] According to Kennedy CJ, if the right had in fact been granted by deed or will, the donee would have had a life estate, so that the document actually executed by the property owner that created the right of residence was an executory agreement enforceable in equity.

The case can be criticised on the basis that its decision, in effect conferring on the beneficiary of the right of residence the powers of sale enjoyed by a tenant for life under the Settled Land Acts, seems ill to accord with the intention of the donor in granting the right of residence.[2] Furthermore, the document in question had not been under seal, and was unsupported by consideration.[3] The judgments seem also to ignore the fundamental principles that equity will not assist a volunteer,[4] and that an informal disposition of land will not be regarded as a declaration of trust.[5]

Even so, *National Bank v Keegan* remains authority, in the Republic of Ireland, for the proposition that an exclusive or particular right of residence over unregistered land creates, according to the nature and terms of the instrument establishing it, either a legal or an equitable life estate.

---

[1] See Johnston J [1931] IR 344 at 348, 350, Kennedy CJ at 355.
[2] See also, Wylie *Irish Land Law* (3rd edn, 1997) Butterworths, p 1026 and Lyall *Land Law in Ireland* (2nd edn, 2000) Sweet & Maxwell, p 527. However, see Coughlan, *Property Law* (2nd edn, 1998) Gill and Macmillan, p 300 where he observes, 'Although it may entail inconvenient consequences for others who have rights in the land, the view that an exclusive right of residence gives rise to a life estate is unproblematic as a matter of principle.' Except, perhaps, for the absence of reasoned legal analysis to sustain the proposition: *Re Walker's Application for Judicial Review* [1999] NI 84 at 90.
[3] Peel 'The Deserted Wife's Licence and Rights of Residence' (1964) 28 Conv 253 at 263–264.
[4] Harvey 'Irish Rights of Residence – The Anatomy of a Hermaphrodite' (1970) 21 NILQ 389 at 402.
[5] *Jones v Jones* [2001] NI 244 at 254, per Girvan J.

[22.04] This conclusion is, arguably, supported by s 40 of the Statute of Limitations 1957, which, in allowing a 12-year period within which to sue on foot of a lien for money's worth over land, likens such a lien to a right of residence or support, but *not* to 'an exclusive right of residence in or on a specified part of the land ...' The obvious legislative implication is that the grant of an exclusive right of residence creates *more* than a lien for money's worth. It should be noted that Article 40 of the Limitations (Northern Ireland) Order 1989 is in the same terms, but, in light of the decision of Girvan J in *Re Walker's Application for Judicial Review*,[1] it is suggested that diminished reliance can be placed upon the language of the Limitations Order in interpreting the legal status of an exclusive right of residence over unregistered land in Northern Ireland.

---

1   *Re Walker's Application for Judicial Review* [1999] NI 84, see para **[22.06]**.

[22.05] In *Atkins v Atkins*,[1] the right held to exist by the wife of a deceased testator is consistent with the majority decision of the Supreme Court in *National Bank v Keegan*.[2] A testator bequeathed property at Dunmanway, Co Cork:

> '... to the use of my wife Margaret during her widowhood and so long as she shall desire to reside therein and after her death, remarriage or her ceasing to reside therein to the use of my sons and nephews hereinafter named in the order for the estates and in manner following...'

Kenny J found that the wife had a life estate, under the Settled Land Acts, with full powers of sale and leasing, but that this determined once she ceased to reside in the property. From that time, the Statute of Limitations 1957 ran against her, in favour of a subsequently occupying party, and so extinguished the wife's title 12 years after she had left.[3]

Unlike in *National Bank v Keegan*, in *Atkins v Atkins* the right of residence was over the entire property: in this context, the finding of a life estate is arguably more defensible than in the case of an exclusive right to occupy a suite of rooms only, which has the effect of conferring different estates over different portions of the same property. Furthermore, since the occupier of the dedicated rooms would be deemed to have a life estate in those rooms only, they could, theoretically, be sold apart from the rest of the house.[4]

---

1   *Atkins v Atkins* [1976] ILRM 62.
2   *National Bank v Keegan* [1931] IR 344.
3   [1976] ILRM 62 at 65.
4   See Lyall *Land Law in Ireland* p 527.

Northern Ireland

[22.06] The proposition put in the preceding paragraph, that an exclusive right of residence over the entirety of an unregistered property is more consistent with a life estate, than an exclusive right over part only of such a property, can scarcely be sustained in Northern Ireland, in light of the decision of Girvan J in *Re Walker's Application for Judicial Review*.[1] A farmer, who owned a farm and farmhouse, decided to retire from farming, and gift his entire property to his son, subject to 'reserving' an exclusive right of residence in the farmhouse for himself and his wife, during the life of each of them, with the survivor to hold the property unto the use of the son in fee simple. The farmer then sought a grant from the housing executive to carry out repairs and renovations. On a form of application for a 'replacement grant', he certified that he had an owner's interest in the property. His solicitors later certified that the farmer and his wife were life tenants for the purpose of the Settled Land Acts 1882–1890. The housing executive contended that this was not the applicant's proper legal status.

According to Girvan J, the English case law prior to the Settled Land Acts had established that, depending on the purpose of the grant as demonstrated in the language used, a right of residence gave rise to no more than a licence, whereas a grant of use and occupation could confer a life estate. Girvan J found that the decision in *National Bank v Keegan*[2] (on which it seems the case for the applicant farmer primarily depended) had failed to demonstrate a legal basis for its assertion that an exclusive right of residence over unregistered land conferred a life estate, and so he elected not to follow it:

> 'Where a person grants or reserves an exclusive right of *residence* the right by definition is intended to be restricted to the very purpose of the grant or reservation. The grantee will fully appreciate that the right of residence does not, for example, envisage a right to use the premises for some non-residential purpose. Nor would the parties envisage the sale, letting or exchange of the property.'[3]

While a party enjoying an exclusive right of residence might be deemed to enjoy the powers of a tenant for life (regarding which, Girvan J suggested, there was considerable doubt), he or she could not be said to *be* a tenant for life. Accordingly, they did not have a freehold interest in possession, such as was required to support an application for a replacement grant. In addition, the right of residence, being created by way of purported reservation in a deed of gift, had not used appropriate words of limitation to grant an estate of any kind to the applicant farmer and his wife.[4]

---

[1]   *Re Walker's Application for Judicial Review* [1999] NI 84.
[2]   *National Bank v Keegan* [1931] IR 344.
[3]   [1999] NI 84 at 91.
[4]   [1999] NI 84 at 92.

[22.07] It is suggested that one of the principal distinguishing features between *Re Walker's Application for Judicial Review*[1] and *Atkins v Atkins*[2] (apart from the obvious circumstance of their being decisions of courts in different jurisdictions), is the fact that the disposition in *Atkins v Atkins* was by way of will, and seemed *intended* to grant a life interest, whereas the instrument in *Walker* was a purported reservation of a right of residence in a deed of gift, which, on its face, seemed designed to do no more than give an exclusive right to occupy to the farmer and his wife, and had failed to employ suitable words of limitation for the grant of a life estate.

---

[1]   *Re Walker's Application for Judicial Review* [1999] NI 84.
[2]   *Atkins v Atkins* [1976] ILRM 62.

General Rights of Residence

[22.08] The earliest known decision on general rights of residence, as they are termed, is *Ryan v Ryan*.[1] In this the testator bequeathed:

> 'I also order that my beloved wife shall have her diet and lodging in this my house of Owenduff as long as the lease of it will last, provided she will wish to remain in it with my aforesaid nephew Patrick Ryan: I also order that my wife shall get the bed and bedstead at present used by me, with bedclothes.'

After the death of the testator, his widow lived for a while in the house with the nephew, then left when he got married. Later she returned and required the nephew to provide board and lodging for her, in accordance with the will. He refused. The decision of Brady LC, and the language in which it was conveyed, have significantly affected both judicial and legislative attitudes to the subject ever since.

In the opinion of the Lord Chancellor, the widow was entitled to relief. An obligation had been created by the provisions of the will, which Brady LC declined to hold constituted a trust.[2] Even so, the obligation was such that a court of equity would enforce it, unless the widow by her conduct had induced a belief on the part of the nephew that she would not return, so causing him to alter his affairs after his marriage. This had not happened. The plaintiff's relief would be limited to the time following her demand for maintenance and support upon her return.

---

1   *Ryan v Ryan* (1848) 12 Ir Eq Rep 226. *Richardson v McCausland* (1817) Beat 457, which is sometimes referred to as the earliest case, seems more of an authority on the circumstances under which such a right can be deemed to be regarded as a lien affecting land. See *Kelaghan v Daly* [1913] 2 IR 328 at 330.

2   The general view is that, unless the terms of the instrument clearly establish it as such, the creation of a right of residence does not impose a trust: *Morice v Bishop of Durham* (1805) 10 Ves 522; *Leonard v Leonard* (1910) 44 ILTR 155; *Jones v Jones* [2001] NI 244 at 254; Peel 'The Deserted Wife's Licence and Rights of Residence' (1964) 28 Conv 253 at 260; Harvey 'Irish Rights of Residence – The Anatomy of a Hermaphrodite' (1970) 21 NILQ 389 at 412–413; Wylie *Irish Land Law* pp 1031–1032.

[22.09] The subsequent development of the idea that a general right of residence can somehow be compensated for in money terms, or substituted by a lien or an annuity, arguably has its genesis in the following observations by Brady LC:

> 'A difficulty is said to arise in carrying out a decree to enforce this gift. That may be so; but the difficulty is not insuperable .... If the Court cannot compel the maintenance bequeathed to be specifically provided, it can compel the payment of a proper sum to provide it. It would be very difficult to lay down a rule as to the quantity of diet the legatee should have, or the room in the house she should get; but it is perfectly plain she is entitled to have some diet and lodging, and there is no insuperable difficulty in enforcing that right. As to the past, there is nothing to be done but to ascertain a value in amount for it; as to the future, there is more doubt; but probably the best course will be to decree the plaintiff entitled in the words of the will, and leave her then to work out that declaration if she is dissatisfied with the way in which it is obeyed.'[1]

It should be noted that Brady LC seems to regard the right of residence and the right of maintenance as indistinguishable in terms of enforcement, a view which it is difficult to justify given the differing characters of the rights involved. However, the party against whom the covenant under the will was sought to be enforced was the original beneficiary, so that the question did not arise of the obligation to maintain passing to a subsequent owner of the property. This enables the decision of Brady LC to be justified with reference to the principle that a beneficiary cannot approbate and reprobate a legacy, but rather must accept it, if he is going to, subject to any conditions that attach to it.[2] It is manifest that Brady LC was also concerned, in so far as possible,[3] to give effect to the testator's stated intention, and encourage the continuance of the right of residence, without being specific as to the nature of the financial arrangements which could compensate for its loss, so that the property owner could not claim a right to 'redeem' the right of residence simply on the basis of paying over money.

---

[1] *Ryan v Ryan* (1848) 12 Ir Eq Rep 226 at 228. But see the criticisms of this judgment in *Jones v Jones* [2001] NI 244 at 252–253, per Girvan J.

[2] Harvey 'Irish Rights of Residence – The Anatomy of a Hermaphrodite' (1970) 21 NILQ 389 at 416–419, and the cases cited therein, especially *Re McMahon* [1901] 1 IR 489 and *Duffy v Duffy* [1920] 1 IR 132.

[3] In much the same way as was Lavan J in *Johnston v Horace* [1993] ILRM 594, see para **[22.24]**.

[22.10] *Kelaghan v Daly*[1] and *Re Shanahan*[2] are sometimes regarded, with doubtful justification, as supportive of the proposition that a general right of residence, and also a right of support, can be treated as akin to a lien over land. In *Kelaghan v Daly* a mother transferred farm lands to her son, who covenanted that:

> '... he the said Peter Kelaghan, his executors, administrators or assigns shall henceforth clothe, support, maintain, and keep the said Catherine Kelaghan [the donor, his mother] and her daughter Lizzie during their joint lives and the life of the survivor of them in a manner suitable to their condition in life; and will permit and suffer them to use, occupy and enjoy the dwellinghouse on the said farm in the same manner as they now occupy and enjoy the same.'

Subsequently, the mother died, the son got into financial difficulties, and a judgment mortgage was obtained against the lands. This culminated in a court order for sale. The court order stipulated that the lands should be sold subject to the covenant entered into by the son, since this had been the consideration for the transfer of the lands to him by his mother.[3] Boyd J, noting that it had been conceded that a vendor's lien applied insofar as concerned the right of residence, held that it was clearly the intention of the parties that the vendor's lien should also extend to the covenant for maintenance, as the support and maintenance could only be provided from the profits of the land.[4]

The decision is open to the criticism that a lien usually involves a specific sum and that such a right as arose in *Kelaghan v Daly* cannot easily be quantified in monetary terms.[5] Even so, it is difficult to see how *Kelaghan v Daly* can be construed as turning a vendor's lien into a device for enforcing the burden of a positive covenant against a subsequent owner of the land. From the slimly reported judgment, it appears that none of the cases concerning the running of covenants were either argued or considered,[6] and the case can instead be cited as illustrative of the more artificial method of maintaining the burden of a covenant through the use of an indemnity covenant, which in effect is what the subsequent purchaser entered into.[7] *Kelaghan v Daly* is of negligible value as a precedent.

---

1 *Kelaghan v Daly* [1913] 2 IR 328.
2 *Re Shanahan* [1919] IR 131.
3 In *Colreavy v Colreavy* [1940] IR 71 a covenant for maintenance was deemed to be valuable consideration.
4 Boyd J relied to a significant degree on the judgment of Lord Eldon LC in *Mackreth v Symmons* (1808) 15 Ves 329, that 'the lien exists unless an intention, and a manifest intention, that it shall not exist, appears' (at p 341) and that 'it depends upon the circumstances of each case, whether the Court is to infer that the lien was intended to be reserved, or that credit was given, and exclusively given, to the person from whom the other security was taken.' (at p 350).
5 Wylie *Irish Land Law* p 1028; see *Mackreth v Symmons* (1808) 15 Ves 329 at 343. On the other hand, Girvan J in *Jones v Jones* [2001] NI 244 at 253, did not believe that the facts in *Kelaghan v Daly* involved an unduly wide extension of the principle of an unpaid vendor's lien, as the covenant to provide accommodation and maintenance was part of the consideration for the transfer of the land.
6 With the exception of *Austerberry v Corporation of Oldham* (1885) 29 ChD 750 which was peremptorily distinguished.
7 Wylie *Irish Land Law* p 1004; Lyall *Land Law in Ireland* pp 686–687; Coughlan *Property Law* p 271.

[22.11] A similar verdict can be passed upon *Re Shanahan*.[1] The terms of a marriage settlement provided that a brother of the husband, in the event of the husband's predeceasing the wife, should have a right or residence on the farm. Both the husband and wife covenanted 'that they and each of them, their and each of their executors, administrators and assigns will support, clothe, and maintain the said Michael Shanahan in his present residence during his life in the same manner as he has hitherto been accustomed to ...' A further clause in the settlement provided for the payment of £15 per annum, on a quarterly basis, to Michael Shanahan in the event of disagreement and he being obliged to leave the lands. Some time following the death of the husband, Michael Shanahan left the farm and sought payment of the £15 per annum. In an application by the widow to have the monetary charge deleted from the folio, the Court of Appeal held that, since the right of residence was clearly a charge on the lands, the annuity, which was provided in lieu of the right of residence, was also a charge. Hence, this case is principally concerned with nothing more than a refusal by the court to accede to an application to delete a charge from the folio.

---

1 *Re Shanahan* [1919] IR 131.

[22.12] It is tempting to speculate that, were it not for the allusion to them, as alleged authorities for a broader proposition than they in fact establish, in *National Bank v*

Keegan,[1] both *Kelaghan v Daly*[2] and *Re Shanahan*[3] would be relegated to footnote status. As will be recalled, *National Bank v Keegan* was quite a different case altogether, featuring an exclusive right of residence to two rooms in an unregistered freehold property, coupled with a right of maintenance.

In *National Bank v Keegan* Johnston J, in the High Court, observed:

> 'It is well settled that a general right of residence and support in a house or upon a farm does not amount to an estate in the land, but is a mere charge in the nature of an annuity upon the premises in respect of which it exists, and when it becomes necessary to sell such property a Court of Equity has power and authority to ascertain the value of such charge, so that the purchaser may get the property discharged from the burden. This was decided in the case of *Kelaghan v Daly* and, later and more authoritatively, in *Re Shanahan*.'[4]

For the reasons already adduced, not least on account of their terse and strongly facts-focused judgments, *Kelaghan v Daly* and *Re Shanahan* are authorities for no such proposition. It could be argued that some support can be gleaned from *Ryan v Ryan*,[5] although, as has been shown, the judgment of Brady LC does not go quite so far as Johnston J in terms of its conclusions.

Unfortunately, the same theme was taken up by Kennedy CJ in the Supreme Court:

> 'The general right of residence charged on a holding is a right capable of being valued in moneys numbered at an annual sum, and of being represented by an annuity or money charge.'[6]

As a result, it would appear that the majority judgments in *National Bank v Keegan* are primarily responsible for the evolution of the modern view that a general right of residence is in the nature of a lien for money's worth.[7]

---

1   *National Bank v Keegan* [1931] IR 344.
2   *Kelaghan v Daly* [1913] 2 IR 328.
3   *Re Shanahan* [1919] IR 131.
4   [1931] IR 344 at 346.
5   *Ryan v Ryan* (1848) 12 Ir Eq Rep 226.
6   [1931] IR 344 at 354.
7   Peel 'The Deserted Wife's Licence and Rights of Residence' (1964) 28 Conv 253 at 265.

[22.13] If so, then demonstrably the dissenting judgment of Murnaghan J served to inspire subsequent legislative interventions treating of the matter. In the opinion of Murnaghan J, the agreement that created the right of residence, being informal, required to be interpreted in such a way as to carry out the intention of the parties, gleaned both from the document itself and the surrounding circumstances. If the words used were construed to create a life interest, then the aunt would have the right to let the rooms and 'introduce strangers into her nephew's dwellinghouse.'

According to Murnaghan J:

> '... the words meant a personal use, a personal right of residence in the dwellinghouse for which residence the aunt was assigned the exclusive use of the two rooms specified. A grant of the use of the premises may pass the estate in the lands, but the meaning of the word 'use' is flexible, and may be controlled by circumstances. It seems to me that the addition of the words 'with fuel and suitable support and maintenance' indicates that the

right of residence was a personal one, as it is, I think, admitted that no one was entitled to support and maintenance except Mary Keegan.'[1]

---

[1] [1931] IR 344 at 356.

[22.14] Against this background, it is now apt to consider the provisions of s 40 of the Statute of Limitations 1957 and of Article 40 of the Limitations (Northern Ireland) Order 1989:

'An action in respect of a right in the nature of a lien for money's worth in or over land for a limited period not exceeding life, such as a right of support or a right of residence, not being an exclusive right of residence in or on a specified part of the land, shall not be brought after the expiration of twelve years from the date on which the right of action accrued.'

From this one can infer that the intention of the legislature in each jurisdiction was to turn a right of residence, other than an exclusive right of residence, into the equivalent of a contract debt, albeit with a limitation period of 12 rather than 6 years. The actual character of the general right of residence is still not clearly defined, although the difficulty of quantifying it in money terms renders nugatory any purported analogies with liens, rentcharges or annuities. In terms of unregistered land, the most definitive judicial assessment remains that of Brady LC in *Ryan v Ryan*[1] over 150 years ago, to the effect that a general right of residence over unregistered land is a licence, revocable by the property owner on terms that financial reparation to the value of the right (whatever that may be and howsoever determined) is to be provided.

---

[1] *Ryan v Ryan* (1848) 12 Ir Eq Rep 226.

[22.15] In *Lahiffe v Hecker*,[1] Lynch J had to grapple with a general right of residence, in the context of a bequest of a house in Clontarf, Co Dublin, by their mother to a son and three daughters, with a proviso that the only unmarried daughter 'shall have a right of residence in the said house until she marries.' After the testator's death, the four children agreed to sever the joint tenancy, and so the house vested in them as tenants in common. The defendant unmarried daughter was the only one who lived in it. An issue arose when the defendant indicated that she was 'not anxious that keys of the property be floating around', and desired her sisters and brother to make special arrangements with her when they wished to visit the house.

Lynch J held that all four, as co-owners, were entitled to possession and occupation. Borrowing slightly from the language of Johnston J in *National Bank v Keegan*,[2] Lynch J held that the defendant's right of residence:

'... is in the nature of a charge affecting the interests of all parties in the property, and consequently the plaintiffs, while entitled to occupy the property if they so wish, by themselves and their reasonable invitees, such as spouses and children, would not be entitled so to overcrowd the property as to render the defendant's right of residence impossible or unduly incommodious.'

On the other hand, the defendant was not entitled to withhold the keys to the house from the plaintiffs, or to insist that they make advance arrangements with her if they required access. Even though the defendant, under a general right of residence, was not entitled to 'the exclusive use of any particular part of the house', Lynch J held that, in order for her practically to enjoy her general right of residence, she could choose one of three bedrooms for her own exclusive use. If the parties desired to sell the house, while the defendant's general right of residence was subsisting, it would be for the court to endeavour to value the right in a proportionate distribution of the proceeds of sale. Lynch J concluded that the holder of a general right of residence did not have any of the powers of a tenant for life.

It is suggested that the judgment of Lynch J, though offending against the principle of unity of possession by co-owners, represents a robust effort to apply a practical solution. Although categorising a general right of residence as 'in the nature of a charge', he seems sedulously to have avoided likening it to a lien or an annuity; the issue of its being quantified in money terms only arising if any one of the tenants in common, in exercise of his or her right to do so, purported to sell the house.

---

[1] *Lahiffe v Hecker* (28 April 1994, unreported) HC.
[2] *National Bank v Keegan* [1931] IR 344 at 346, see para **[22.03]**.

Registered Land

[22.16] As a result of the decision in *National Bank v Keegan*,[1] Land Registry practice, in the case of exclusive rights of residence in a room or rooms in registered property, used to be to open a separate folio for the relevant portion of the property and to register the person with the exclusive right as limited owner thereof.[2]

---

[1] *National Bank v Keegan* [1931] IR 344.
[2] It is difficult to dissent from the view of Peel in 'The Deserted Wife's Licence and Rights of Residence' (1964) 28 Conv 253 at 266: 'The inconvenience occasioned by this arrangement requires no emphasis.'

Republic of Ireland

[22.17] The need for this cumbrous procedure has now been removed by s 81 of the Registration of Title Act 1964, which provides:

> 'A right of residence in or on registered land, whether a general right of residence on the land or an exclusive right of residence in or on part of the land, shall be deemed to be personal to the person beneficially entitled thereto and to be a right in the nature of a lien for money's worth in or over the land and shall not operate to create any equitable estate in the land.'

Section 69(1) provides:

> 'There may be registered as affecting registered land any of the following burdens, namely, ...

(q) a right in the nature of a lien for money's worth in or over the property for a limited period not exceeding life, such as a right of support or a right of residence (whether an exclusive right of residence or not);'

The combination of these provisions leads one to conclude that the legislature was prepared to prefer, and partially adopt, the view of Murnaghan J in *National Bank v Keegan*[1] regarding the character of a right of residence, with a tincture from the judgment of Boyd J in *Kelaghan v Daly*[2] in relation to liens, while rejecting, insofar as it could be deemed to apply to registered land – the property in the case had been unregistered – the majority Supreme Court judgments in *National Bank v Keegan*.

---

[1] *National Bank v Keegan* [1931] IR 344.
[2] *Kelaghan v Daly* [1913] 2 IR 328.

[22.18] The Registration of Title Act 1964 avoids describing a right of residence in terms of its precise legal character. To call it 'a right in the nature of a lien' can arguably be construed as a mere hint to the judiciary as to how to deal with a dispute regarding a right of residence.[1] The only clear conclusion to be drawn from the Registration of Title Act 1964 is that a right of residence over registered land, whether general or exclusive, does not create an estate, either legal or equitable.[2] This effectively rules out any suggestion of a right of residence over registered land constituting a trust.[3] It appears, therefore, that the only category of legal entitlement with which a right of residence is consistent is a licence.

Even so, to describe a right of residence as a licence, notwithstanding the provisions of ss 69 and 81 of the Registration of Title Act 1964, begs the questions

(a) whether the right can be enforced against an owner of the property subsequent to the owner at the time the right was registered, and,

(b) whether the right of residence can be redeemed, at the insistence of either the owner of the right or the owner of the property.

The answer to the first question, it is suggested, depends on the principles of law that govern the running of covenants: a right of residence, by its definition, does not give rise to positive obligations, no more than did the covenant in *Tulk v Moxhay*[4] to keep the railing-surrounded garden 'in an open state, uncovered with any buildings, in a neat and ornamental order' create a positive obligation in that case. The answer to the second question is not clear: there is a danger one can push the analogy with liens too far and thereby ill serve the settlor's purpose in creating the right.[5]

---

[1] Lavan J in *Johnston v Horace* [1993] ILRM 594 at 600, observed that 'the objective valuation of the right of residence is the method signposted by the statute.' One cannot but concur, ruefully, with the waggish criticism by Harvey in 'Irish Rights of Residence – The Anatomy of a Hermaphrodite' (1970) 21 NILQ 389, regarding the marked differences between a conventional vendor's lien and a right of residence at 410–411, that 'to call the latter "a right in the nature of a lien" is little more helpful than calling a cat "an animal in the nature of a dog".'

[2] To this extent, as noted by Harvey, (1970) 21 NILQ 389 at 406, it is inconsistent, insofar as concerns registered land, with the Statute of Limitations 1957, s 40 of which defines 'a right in the nature of a lien for money's worth' as *not* including 'an exclusive right of residence.'

3   Wylie *Irish Land Law* pp 1031–1032.
4   *Tulk v Moxhay* (1848) 2 Ph 774 and see para **[22.28]** ff.
5   See *Johnston v Horace* [1993] ILRM 594. See para **[22.24]**.

Northern Ireland

[22.19] The Lowry Committee[1] was set up to consider the introduction of similar statutory changes regarding registered land in Northern Ireland. In relation to s 81 of the Registration of Title Act 1964, the Lowry Committee acknowledged that it was unsure whether this section enabled the owner of the land to 'buy out' the owner of the right of residence without their consent, and concluded that this was not something which ought to be possible, on the basis that it would ill accord with the intention of the original donor. At the same time, the Lowry Committee concluded that the right of residence, whether a general right or an exclusive right to reside on part of the land, should be made personal to the person beneficially entitled to the right and should not create a life estate: an *exclusive* right of residence over the *whole* of the property was deemed likely to have been intended to be a life estate by the donor or testator.[2]

---

1   Cmd 512, para 97, quoted in Harvey 'Irish Rights of Residence – The Anatomy of a Hermaphrodite' (1970) 21 NILQ 389 at 404–405.
2   In *Re Walker's Application for Judicial Review* [1999] NI 84, Girvan J had held that a reservation of an exclusive right of residence in a farmhouse had created a licence rather than a proprietary right. See para **[22.06]**. Accordingly, in *Jones v Jones* [2001] NI 244 at 255, Girvan J suggested that the observation by the Lowry Committee, that an exclusive right of residence over the entirety of a property was presumably intended to grant a life estate, must be regarded as open to question.

[22.20] Section 47 of the Land Registration Act (Northern Ireland) 1970 now provides:

'Where—

(a)   a right of residence in or on any registered land, whether a general right of residence in or on that land or an exclusive right of residence in or on part of that land; or

(b)   a right to use a specified part of that land in conjunction with a right of residence referred to in paragraph (a);

is granted by deed or will, such right shall be deemed to be personal to the person beneficially entitled thereto and the grant made by such deed or will shall not operate to confer any right of ownership in relation to the land upon such person, but registration of any such right as a Schedule 6 burden shall make it binding upon the registered owner of the land and his successors in title.'

It will be noted that the Northern Ireland provisions, unlike those in the Republic, state that a right of residence, once registered, is binding upon successors in title.[1]

---

1   However, both Harvey in 'Irish Rights of Residence – The Anatomy of a Hermaphrodite' (1970) 21 NILQ 389 at 410, and Wylie in *Irish Land Law* p 1028, noted that a lien is deemed

to be an 'incumbrance' within the meaning of the Conveyancing Act 1881, s 2(vii) and so runs with the land. However, this would only be enforceable if it took effect as a negative covenant.

[22.21] In *Jones v Jones*[1] Girvan J decided that a right of residence over registered land, where consideration has moved in order to create the right, can be construed as a species of contractual licence, whose terms, express or implied, will govern the extent to which the right can be interfered with by third parties, *including by the registered owner*. A farmer, desirous of retiring from agricultural life, made over his farming stock and equipment to his son. The son indicated that he was thinking of selling the stock and equipment unless the farm was transferred to him. Accordingly, the farmer agreed to transfer the farm to his son, subject to a right of residence in the farmhouse in favour of himself and his wife, for their respective lives. A covenant for support was later cancelled by agreement.

The following matters were also agreed:

(i)   the parents were to give vacant possession of all outhouses and buildings other than the farmhouse;

(ii)   the parents would keep their own fittings and furniture in the farmhouse;

(iii)   the father would pay contents insurance for the farmhouse, and also telephone and heating charges;

(iv)   the parents maintained the interior of the house, while the son looked after the exterior.

In 1997 the retired farmer died, and his wife (the plaintiff) remained on in the house on her own. Subsequently the mother (the plaintiff) developed serious health problems. She spent some time in hospital. Following her return home, in order to provide her needed medical care, her son, the registered owner (the first defendant), and his wife moved in with her. However, this proved too much for the son's wife, who had a nervous breakdown. It was agreed that the mother would go into residential care for a while. Throughout this time the son was reluctant to allow other people into the house without his permission. This became a source of anxiety to his mother, who disliked being in a nursing home, and wanted to return to her own home. Eventually, it was agreed that the mother should return home, but the son, arguing that the right of residence was exclusive to her, was unwilling to allow others to reside in the farmhouse with her. He thought it better that she remain in the nursing home. He refused to hand over the keys. At around the same time, he agreed to transfer the house to his own son, the grandson (the second defendant) and the grandson's wife (the third defendant). The grandson and his wife then moved into the house, and carried out improvements to the kitchen and bathroom, while leaving the mother's chairlift intact. They were prepared to share the house with the mother. The mother then instituted proceedings, claiming that she had an exclusive right of residence, or, in the alternative, that having regard to all the circumstances, she was entitled to *exclusivity* of residence.

Girvan J observed that the 'precise legal nature and incidents' of a right of residence were 'somewhat unclear and ill defined', and that an effort to elucidate them was not eased 'by the unsatisfactory way in which the law in this field has been analysed and developed heretofore.'[2]

Having considered the decisions of the Irish courts on rights of residence,[3] Girvan J concluded that they displayed:

> '... a somewhat incoherent and confused analysis of the rights of residence, with statements of principle arrived at by a flawed generalised interpretation of specific cases turning on their own terms and clauses in particular instruments.'[4]

In the opinion of Girvan J a right of residence was properly identified as a licence, and, in the instant case, since consideration had moved from the licensee on its creation, the right of residence was a contractual licence.

---

[1]   *Jones v Jones* [2001] NI 244.

[2]   [2001] NI 244 at 252.

[3]   [2001] NI 244. Between pp 252 and 255, Girvan J comprehensively considered the leading Irish authorities: *Ryan v Ryan* (1848) 12 Ir Eq 226; *Kelaghan v Daly* [1913] 2 IR 328; *Re Shanahan* [1919] 1 IR 131; *National Bank v Keegan* [1931] IR 344.

[4]   [2001] NI 244 at 256.

[22.22] Girvan J noted that the following principles in relation to contractual licences applied to the facts in *Jones v Jones*:

(a)   the willingness of the courts to protect a contractual licence by means of injunction or specific performance 'in effect confers on the licensee a quasi-proprietary interest in the land beyond a mere personal interest to use the land in common with others';[1]

(b)   the precise contractual rights conferred upon the licensee depended upon a construction of the agreement to create the right of residence, set in its proper context: the basic right was an irrevocable contractual licence to reside on the premises during the lifetime of the licensees; being a registered title, the right had been registered, and so was binding on successors in title;

(c)   in construing the nature and extent of the right, one has to look also at the factual context in which the agreement was made: this included the several commitments undertaken by the licensees, and the fact of their living on their own at the time;

(d)   a contractual licence can be subject to the interpolation of implied terms: in the instant case, having regard to the quality of the residence by the licensees at the time of the agreement, it was an implied term that the mother should not be obliged to share the occupation of the property with others whom she did not choose, who had entered the house without either her knowledge or approval; to hold otherwise would be to subject the mother '... to tensions and inconveniences inconsistent with the right to reside in the premises as contemplated at the time when the agreement was entered into.'[2]

Perhaps significantly, Girvan J declined to award an injunction, holding that the real problems disclosed by the case were not legal ones; that a return to the house on the mother's part would in no way resolve all her difficulties; and exculpating the son and his family from any dishonourable motives.

¹   *Jones v Jones* [2001] NI 244 at 257.
²   [2001] NI 244 at 258.

[22.23] The remarkable outcome of *Jones v Jones*¹ was that the holder of a right of residence, not stated by its nature to be exclusive, was held in fact to enjoy an exclusive right, even against intended transferees of the registered owner. This is at marked variance with *Lahiffe v Hecker*,² where one of four co-owners, with a general right of residence, was held entitled to the exclusive use of one bedroom only. However, the cases can be distinguished on the basis of the circumstances creating the right: in *Lahiffe* it was a bequest of the house to the brother and three sisters as co-owners, subject to a right of the unmarried sister to live there until she married; in *Jones*, the agreement setting up the right itself, and the background circumstances, led to the inference of exclusivity of occupation on the part of the owner of the right. The conclusion seems unavoidable that the precise conditions governing the enjoyment of the right of residence fall to be interpreted differently, depending on whether the right was granted by will or by deed. One can only subscribe to, and respectfully reiterate, the sage counsel imparted by Girvan J both in *Re Walker's Application for Judicial Review*³ and in *Jones v Jones*,⁴ that those responsible for the drafting of grants of rights of residence, whether by deed or will, ought to ensure to take appropriate care in the drafting, so that the intentions of the relevant parties are properly expressed in the right or interest which results.

¹   *Jones v Jones* [2001] NI 244.
²   *Lahiffe v Hecker* (28 April 1994, unreported) HC. See para **[22.15]**.
³   *Re Walker's Application for Judicial Review* [1999] NI 84 at 92.
⁴   [2001] NI 244 at 260.

Valuing a Right of Residence

[22.24] The question of whether a right of residence can be redeemed, on the basis of a money payment by the registered owner, and the measure by which such a right should be valued, arose for decision, in 1993, in the case of *Johnston v Horace*.¹

The facts are typical of their kind.² The testator was the registered owner of a cottage in Crumlin, Dublin. He bequeathed the cottage to a married daughter, subject to a right of residence in favour of another daughter (the plaintiff), a disabled son and the plaintiff's own daughter. The plaintiff's right of residence was registered as a burden on the folio at the time that her sister, the principal beneficiary, became registered as owner. In due course the registered owner died, having bequeathed the cottage to her son, the defendant, subject to her sister's right of residence. By this stage the testator's disabled son had already died and the plaintiff's daughter was living in her own house. Between 1986, when he inherited the property, and 1990 the defendant carried out a number of alterations and improvements. Following his engagement to be married, he sought either to be rid of the right of residence altogether or to sell the cottage outright to the plaintiff, his aunt.

Lavan J found that the defendant had 'engaged in a careful and sustained campaign to rid himself of his aunt.'[3] This took the form of general unpleasantness and concerted attempts to confine her to the use of her bedroom only. The plaintiff is finally leaving the house and moving in with her daughter was held by Lavan J, under the circumstances, not to have constituted an abandonment of the right of residence, since the cause of her leaving was the duress imposed on her by the defendant.

In relation to the principles governing abandonment, Lavan J stated:

'In my view the right granted is an unrestricted right. The right is not abandoned by an absence of a day, or a week, or indeed a number of years. The right cannot be varied to suit the whim of the owner. Its nature and context must be viewed by the court from the right granted in the ensuing conduct of all concerned ....

'The right may voluntarily be abandoned expressly and freely, or indeed by effluxion of time. However, a court would have to require strong cogent evidence from a party seeking to defeat such a right, whilst the right remains a burden on the folio and in the absence of express agreement parol or written to disclose an intention to abandon.'[4]

---

[1] *Johnston v Horace* [1993] ILRM 594.
[2] Except that on p 595 of the reported judgment, it is stated that the testator's will was dated 27 September 1961 and that the testator died on 2 January 1956. A curious state of affairs indeed, and hardly a tribute to the exactness of modern law reporting. However, since it is also stated that probate of the will was extracted on 27 September 1961, one hopes that the date of probate has been confused with the date of the will, and that the will was made by the testator some time prior to his death!
[3] [1993] ILRM 594 at 597.
[4] [1993] ILRM 594 at 600–601. This language is at variance with the notion that the right of residence could be unilaterally redeemed by the owner of the property selling it and compelling the owner of the right of residence to accept financial restitution.

[22.25] Lavan J granted an injunction restraining continued interference by the defendant with the plaintiff's right of residence, and ordered that she be given a key to the property. He also awarded damages in the amount of £7,500 for the interference by the defendant with the right of residence. In the course of his judgment Lavan J elaborated upon the methods of determining financial alternatives to the preservation of the right of residence. It is in the context of this analysis that the decision has attracted most academic commentary.[1] Unfortunately, much of this commentary, by reason of the wide-ranging and sometimes mutually inconsistent concerns identified by Lavan J, suffers from an inclination to replicate or paraphrase chunks of the judgment itself in an effort to explain it. The following principles were articulated in the course of the judgment:

(a)   because the right of residence is an ongoing one, its financial equivalent should be determined on a periodic basis, with reference to a month, a quarter, or a year;

(b)   the court should be able to embark upon a valuation of the right, either under its equitable jurisdiction, or at the behest of the parties;

(c)   in the absence of a market in rights of residence, the court should look at appropriate comparisons, such as;

the rental value of similar property elsewhere, bearing in mind that the plaintiff had not contributed to the cost of the refurbishments of the house where she lived, and allowing for the fact that her proportionate interest in the use and occupation of the cottage (one bedroom in a three-bedroom cottage) was one third;

or, the cost one would reasonably expect a residing relative to contribute in respect only of the right to reside, excluding other household expenses.

(d)   The measurement of the financial value of a right of residence should not stray into the realm of compensatory assessment;

(e)   the defendant's absence of means should be taken into account;

(f)   the defendant's conduct in intimidating the plaintiff out of the house was reprehensible;

(g)   a right of residence is a very significant right;

(h)   infringement of a right of residence is 'an act which warrants substantial damages in most cases.'[2]

On the facts before him, Lavan J expressed the view that a suggestion that the right of residence be valued was 'unreal'. Insofar as a valuation may have to be made in certain cases, that should be on the basis of a periodic sum,[3] which is not capitalised:

'It is only in circumstances where such periodic sums are not being paid or that the property is being disposed of that the lien becomes a lien secured or enforceable by way of additional security in the form of a capitalised sum if necessary. To capitalise the money's worth of the right is akin to giving the beneficiary the equivalent of the statutory rights of a tenant for life. To capitalise assumes the ability of the owner of the property to pay or raise a capital sum or in the alternative becomes punitive on the owner in that the cost of sale of the premises has to be borne and the additional cost of repurchasing another property at some later date.'[4]

---

[1] See Coughlan 'Enforcing Rights of Residence' (1993) 11 ILT (NS) 168; Coughlan *Property Law* pp 302–303; Lyall *Land Law in Ireland* pp 530–531; Wylie *Irish Land Law* pp 1029–1030.

[2] *Johnston v Horace* [1993] ILRM 594 at 601.

[3] However, Coughlan points out that, in the absence of specific statutory power, the court does not have an inherent jurisdiction to award damages on a periodic basis: 'Enforcing Rights of Residence' (1993) 11 ILT (NS) 168 at 169.

[4] [1993] ILRM 594 at 600.

[22.26] It is difficult to extrapolate clear conclusions from the judgment of Lavan J in *Johnston v Horace*.[1] In fairness to the judge, this is less a fault of the judgment, or its reasoning, than the confused sphere of the law with which it had to deal. In a similar fashion to Brady LC in *Ryan v Ryan*,[2] it seems as if Lavan J strove primarily to give effect to the testator's intention when he created the right of residence, by endeavouring to ensure its continuance despite the troubled relations between the owner of the property and the owner of the right. In this context, the judge's declining to capitalise the value of the right of residence arguably derived, not from disinclination or doubt, but from a knowledge that the result of this would be to terminate the right and worsen the circumstances of both parties: the plaintiff would have to find somewhere else to live, the defendant would have to sell the cottage, purchase another premises, incur the costs of both transactions and also pay an appropriate sum to the plaintiff in reparation for the lost right. Lavan J expressed his recognition of the fact that both parties were of limited means, and in the form of his order, effectively preserved the right of residence, satisfied the demands of fairness and also awarded to the plaintiff such compensation as was reasonably payable, given the limited means of the defendant – despite his reprehensible conduct.

Far less satisfactory is the wholly fortuitous circumstance of the property having been registered. The property was urban, in an old part of Dublin, and many such properties are still unregistered. The merits of the case, and the personal circumstances of the parties, would have been no different had the property been unregistered. Since, in such situation, the judge would not have had to consider s 81 of the Registration of Title Act 1964, would the result have been different? On the basis that a general right of residence over unregistered property is akin to a licence, and that the precepts limned in *National Bank v Keegan*[3] are broad enough to apply to a general right of residence, the outcome might well have been similar – though with fewer elaborations about liens and periodic payments. Even so, the mere prospect of possibly different decisions on the same facts, dependent only on whether the title is registered or unregistered, is disquieting.

---

[1]   *Johnston v Horace* [1993] ILRM 594 at 601.
[2]   *Ryan v Ryan* (1848) 12 Ir Eq Rep 226.
[3]   *National Bank v Keegan* [1931] IR 344 at p 346, per Johnston J, at p 354, per Kennedy CJ.

[22.27] In Northern Ireland, the decisions of Girvan J in *Re Walker's Application for Judicial Review*[1] and *Jones v Jones*,[2] taken together, may well be regarded as having brought a needed clarity to the legal status of exclusive rights of residence. In the Republic of Ireland, the courts are still burdened with the legacy of *National Bank v Keegan*.[3] It may be that legislation treating of all types of property is the only way to resolve the hiatus. By whatever method, certainty must be brought to the status of an exclusive right of residence over part of an unregistered property, since the current status, based on the majority judgments in *National Bank v Keegan*, that such a right comprises a life estate, can scarcely be sustained.

---

[1]   *Re Walker's Application for Judicial Review* [1999] NI 84, see para **[22.06]**.
[2]   *Jones v Jones* [2001] NI 244, see para **[22.21]**.
[3]   *National Bank v Keegan* [1931] IR 344, see para **[22.03]**.

Rights of Maintenance and Support

[22.28] Although rights of residence, maintenance and support are frequently encountered in combination, rights of maintenance and support are rights of quite a different kind, being more in the nature of positive covenants.[1] Furthermore, rights of maintenance and support are often contingent upon continuance of the right of residence and involve a personal relationship between the owner of the property and the owner of the right. For example, in *Ryan v Ryan*[2] it is clear that the right of maintenance and support was bound up with the widow's living in the house with the nephew: 'I also order that my beloved wife shall have her diet and lodging in this my house ... as long as the lease of it will last, provided she will wish to remain in it with my aforementioned nephew.' There is no suggestion in this bequest that the right of diet, whatever about the right of lodging, would enure should the nephew dispose of the house. Indeed, it is inferable from the judgment of Brady LC that the right of diet and lodging in favour of the widow was, in effect, a condition of the taking of the legacy by the nephew.

[1]   *Colreavy v Colreavy* [1940] IR 71.
[2]   *Ryan v Ryan* (1848) 12 Ir Eq Rep 226.

[22.29] In *National Bank v Keegan*,[1] a majority of the Supreme Court overruled the finding by Johnston J that the aunt was entitled to a charge upon the premises for fuel and suitable support and maintenance. According to Kennedy CJ:

> '... if she had called for a deed, she would not have been entitled under the terms of the agreement to ask for anything more than a covenant on the part of the defendant [the nephew] in respect of the fuel, support and maintenance which he agreed to give her, and she could not have required to have the benefits under the covenant charged on the house and premises.'[2]

This accords with the traditional view that the burden of a positive covenant is not capable of running against freehold land, as articulated by Dixon J in *Gaw v Coras Iompair Éireann*.[3]

[1]   *National Bank v Keegan* [1931] IR 344.
[2]   [1931] IR 344 at 354.
[3]   *Gaw v Coras Iompair Éireann* (1952) 89 ILTR 124 at 132, 135, 136. See para **[14.08]** ff.

[22.30] Furthermore, the mere fact that a right of support can be registered as a burden under s 69(1)(q) does not mean *per se* that it can be enforced against a subsequent owner of the land. The contrary, in effect, is specifically provided for by ss 3 or s 69(3) which states:

> 'Any covenant or condition registered under this section may be modified or discharged by order of the court on proof to the satisfaction of the court that the covenant or condition does not run with the land, or is not capable of being enforced against the owner of the land ...'[1]

The enforceability of a covenant to support or maintain against a subsequent owner of the land is subject to the general common law rules governing the running of positive covenants. Such a covenant, being innately personal in character, and not of a kind which concerns or benefits land, is not among those enforceable by and against the successors to the owners of property described in Article 34 of the Property (Northern Ireland) Order 1997.

Chapter 23

Conacre and Agistment

Introduction

[23.01] Conacre and agistment are agrarian rights in relation to land which demonstrate attributions of a licence. The essence of the right in each case is that permission is given to utilise land in a particular way, without creating an estate in it, and without (at least in theory) interfering with the overall right of the owner to possession. Conacre is a right to sow, cultivate and harvest crops on land owned by another. Agistment is a right to graze animals. It resembles the profit of pasture, but is more limited.[1] A profit *à prendre* must be granted by deed, but the creation of a right of conacre or agistment is invariably informal and most often by verbal agreement.[2] Rights of conacre and agistment are normally given for a fixed period of less than a year. The 'eleven month take' is frequently encountered.[3] However, these rights are often exercised on a more continuous basis,[4] which for the most part does not alter their status as licences.[5]

---

[1] See *Fletcher v Hackett* (1906) 40 ILTR 37; *O'Flaherty v Kelly* [1909] 1 IR 223, see para **[23.14]**. See para **[12.24]** ff.

[2] See Moore 'From Potatoes and Peasants to Quotas and Squires: The Endurability of Conacre from 1845 to 1995' in *One Hundred and Fifty Years of Irish Law* (eds, Dawson, Greer and Ingram, 1996) SLS Legal Publications (NI) and Sweet & Maxwell, p 204; also Doyle J in *Collins v O'Brien* [1981] ILRM 328 at 329: 'This is a difficult case to decide because there is no memorandum or note in writing relating to the transaction. A few words on a sheet of paper may have avoided litigation.'

[3] *O'Flaherty v Kelly* [1909] 1 IR 223 at 228, per Walker LC; *Crane v Naughten* [1912] 2 IR 318 at 325, per Gibson J; *Collins v O'Brien* [1981] ILRM 328 at 329, per Doyle J. But see *Fletcher v Hackett* (1906) 40 ILTR 37 where a 12-month letting was held to constitute an agistment.

[4] *Evans v Monagher* (1872) IR 6 CL 526; *Re Moore's Estate, Fitzpatrick v Behan* [1944] IR 295 (an agistment letting had continued for some fifty years, but did not constitute a tenancy); also, *Carson v Jeffers* [1961] IR 44.

[5] Not invariably so, however: *Irish Land Commission v Andrews* [1941] IR 79; *Crane v Naughton* [1912] 2 IR 318 (in which a six-month grazing contract was found to be 'a contract for exclusive grazing for a certain period' and thus to constitute a tenancy).

[23.02] Apart from their economic significance, as a method of facilitating those without means to cultivate land so as to produce food for themselves and their families, conacre and agistment also provided a device whereby tenants could permit others to use their lands without incurring penal rents through the breaching of covenants against sub-letting or parting with possession,[1] and without letting their land tenure fall below the minimum level necessary for voting rights.[2]

1   *Lord Westmeath v Hogg* (1840) 3 LR Ir 27; *Booth v McManus* (1861) 12 ICLR 418; *Irish Land Commission v Lawlor* [1944] Ir Jur Rep 55, although the Landlord and Tenant Law Amendment, Ireland, Act 1860, s 18 expressly differentiated between sub-letting and a letting in conacre.

2   *McKeowne v Bradford* (1862) 7 Ir Jur (NS) 169, 175.

Conacre – a Licence to Till

[23.03] Up to the middle years of the nineteenth century, the precise nature of a right of conacre was uncertain and variously described. Hence, in the view of Pennefather B in *Close v Brady*[1] a letting in conacre was merely a mode of tilling the land, with the rent forming part of the produce of the land, in lieu of the crop. In *Dease v O'Reilly*,[2] Crampton J observed (with a rich muddling of nomenclature) that a conacre agreement was not in the nature of a demise, 'but a sale of a profit to be derived from the land, a temporary easement, and not an estate in the land.'[3]

1   *Close v Brady* (1838–1839) Jon & Car 187.

2   *Dease v O'Reilly* (1845) 8 Ir LR 52.

3   (1845) 8 Ir LR 52 at 59.

Whether a right of possession

[23.04] The primary cause of controversy in the realm of conacre has been whether the granting of permission to sow and reap confers a legal right of possession on the party enjoying it.

In relation to possession, Crampton J observed in *Dease v O'Reilly*:

> 'There is not, in fact, any exclusive right to the party in the conacre holding – from the time of the contract until the potato planting begins, the possession remains with the landlord; and from that time, although a special possession for a particular purpose is with the conacre holder, the general possession remains with the landlord.'[1]

Crampton J also stated that any argument that the agreement constituted a letting encountered the difficulty that it was difficult to say when the letting should begin and when end; where lands are let in conacre to a number of different users, the potatoes tend to be planted and dug out at varying times depending on the needs and means of each particular conacre tenant.

1   *Dease v O'Reilly* (1845) 8 Ir LR 52 at 58–59.

[23.05] In *Lord Westmeath v Hogg*[1] the plaintiff landlord alleged that the defendant tenant was in breach of a covenant against sub-letting, so rendering him liable to a penal rent. The covenant against sub-letting had contained a specific proviso that the tenant 'shall continue to occupy the lands and premises'. In the submission of counsel for the landlord, the position was clear that:

'[T]he conacre tenant, therefore, having the exclusive possession of some part of the demised premises … there has been a manifest non-compliance with the terms of the proviso, and the lessor is entitled to demand the full rent reserved.'

Counsel for the tenant, on the other hand, borrowing from the language of Pennefather B in *Close v Brady*, variously described the conacre agreement as 'nothing more than a licence to sow the ground', 'nothing more than a tilling of land by an agent', an arrangement whereby the conacre tenant 'has not the soil, having nothing but a mere contract with the lessee, that if he sows he shall reap', and, succinctly, 'a license to till'. A further submission by counsel for the plaintiff landlord – to the effect that, since '[C]onacring was common in the country when the lease in question was drawn, and a covenant against it, under that name, is inserted in many of the leases', so the prohibition in the lease ought to have been more clearly expressed – was seized upon by the court. With deft equivocation, Doherty CJ held that 'we do not conceive that we are called upon, in the present instance, to decide, whether a letting of conacre generally is a letting within the meaning of the penal clauses of the sub-letting acts',[2] and hence gave judgment for the tenant.

Three years later, Lord Westmeath, the plaintiff, ruefully reported on the outcome of his case to the Devon Commission, established to examine the practice of land occupation in Ireland,[3] stating that 'the court above' had held against him on the basis that conacring was not sub-letting. With keen perspicacity, he added, '… in my judgment subletting is but letting to one, and conacre is letting to many.'[4]

---

[1] *Lord Westmeath v Hogg* (1840) 3 LR Ir 27.

[2] (1840) 3 LR Ir 27 at 31.

[3] Her Majesty's Commissioners of Inquiry into the State of the Law and Practice in relation to the Occupation of Land in Ireland.

[4] Witness No 1033, cited in Moore 'From Potatoes and Peasants to Quotas and Squires: The Endurability of Conacre from 1845 to 1995' in *One Hundred and Fifty Years of Irish Law* p 205.

[23.06] Twenty one years after the inconclusive decision in *Lord Westmeath v Hogg*,[1] the Court of Exchequer, in *Booth v McManus*,[2] explored the legal character of a conacre letting. Once again this was in the context of the provision for a penal rent in the case of infringement of a clause in a lease against sub-letting. The amount of land let out on conacre was in the order of 12 or 13 acres, but the tenant under the holding lease retained the key of the gate to the field. Fitzgerald B, who dissented on the law, summarised thus the facts, which are archetypical of their kind at the time:

'The portions of the premises so dedicated were strips of land in a field, of the gate of which the defendant kept the key, though the persons to whom conacre was given were allowed access to the respective strips at all times while their crops were in the ground. In these strips they sowed grain, they tended their growth, and they gathered them at maturity for their own benefit, for a pecuniary consideration then paid by them. The borders of the field about these strips were used by the defendant for her own purposes.'[3]

A witness for the defendant (the tenant under the lease) had stated that, in his own dealings with conacre, the landowner did not part with possession of the lands, but merely allowed the conacre tenant to use the land for the purpose of taking a crop. Furthermore, the conacre tenant was not allowed to remove the crop until he had paid for it, but, if the landowner injured the crop while it was in the ground, he would be liable to pay compensation to the conacre tenant.

The principal ground of the dissent by Fitzgerald B was that, notwithstanding that a conacre letting was not a sub-letting, the evidence showed that there was a giving of the use of the land by the lessee to another who, in turn, had a right to exclusive enjoyment of the crop while it was in the ground. Since this, in effect, involved a parting with the occupation by the lessee, it was in breach of covenant.

---

1   *Lord Westmeath v Hogg* (1840) 3 LR Ir 27.
2   *Booth v McManus* (1861) 12 ICLR 418.
3   (1861) 12 ICLR 418 at 432.

[23.07] Pigot CB held that a lessee who lets his land in conacre is still deemed to retain possession of it. The conacre holder has only a right to till the land, and an associated right of ingress and egress for that purpose. Accordingly, conacre '... is nothing more than a mode of tilling and farming the land.' He added:

> 'The dealing called conacre in this country is a very peculiar one. The person who takes the conacre has no absolute right in the crop. He has not a right to take the crop, with merely an obligation to pay for it as a debt. But the person who allows the land to be tilled retains the dominion over the crop, of holding it until the stipulated amount shall have been paid. He can prevent the conacre holder from removing the crop from the ground before payment. Can he have the power of thus preventing the removal of the crop, if he has not possession of the ground? Does not the right to obstruct and prevent the removal of the crop involve the right to the possession of the soil on which the crop rests? It seems to me that it does; and that the custom, which I believe is universal, by which the person who allows the crop to be tilled has the right of keeping the crop until he is paid, involves the right to keep possession of the ground, without which he could not exercise the right of detaining the crop until he is paid for it.'[1]

The judgment of Deasy B is to like effect. In his opinion, the legal character of conacre articulated by Pennefather B in *Close v Brady*[2] had received legislative recognition in s 18 of the Landlord and Tenant Law Amendment, Ireland, Act 1860 which expressly differentiated between sub-letting and a letting in conacre in the context of covenants prohibiting either. As had Doherty CJ in *Lord Westmeath v Hogg*,[3] so Deasy B took the view that, such was the unique character of conacre as a mode of dealing with land in Ireland, a covenant seeking to prohibit it ought to have done so expressly.[4]

---

1   *Booth v McManus* (1861) 12 ICLR 418 at 435–436.
2   *Close v Brady* (1838–1839) Jon & Car 187.
3   *Lord Westmeath v Hogg* (1840) 3 LR Ir 27.
4   'It was a mode of dealing with land perfectly well known, almost usual in Ireland. It had acquired a peculiar name, by which it was usually designated, and yet there is no mention of it, either in the reservation or the covenant ... I think that if the lessor meant to prohibit this mode of dealing with the land, he should have said so.' (1861) 12 ICLR 418 at 431.

[23.08] In *McKeowne v Bradford*[1] the legal status of conacre in relation to the possession of the lands fell again to be considered. The issue was that if the landowners, by letting their lands in conacre, were deemed to have parted with possession of them, they would lose their voting franchise. The nature of the agreement was found to be that the landowners

'... allotted and pointed out in some fields or parts of fields on their holdings, ploughed ridges or drills for persons who were either their own labourers, or other persons resident near them to whom they gave permission to plant potatoes, as conacre, as it is so called or known, and which potatoes were accordingly set or planted by said conacre holders with manure belonging to the appellants [landowners], and put by them on the land which was ploughed and prepared therefor by said appellants.'[2]

Other terms of the agreement included that the conacre holders were to pay for the crops either in money, or in labour as money's worth; those who supplied manure themselves were allowed to crop free of charge; the landowners undertook to protect the crops against trespass; the conacre tenants were to weed and tend the crops; there were no fences or divisions between the various parts of the fields let to different conacre tenants.

---

[1]   *McKeowne v Bradford* (1862) 7 Ir Jur (NS) 169.
[2]   (1862) 7 Ir Jur (NS) 169 at 176.

[23.09] By a majority of four to one,[1] the Court of Exchequer held that the landowners had not parted with occupation by entering into conacre lettings and so retained their franchise. One of the more remarkable features of the case was the cogency of the arguments put up by counsel opposing the landowners,[2] focusing primarily on the logical absurdity of the proposition that extensive lands could be let in conacre and it still be maintained that the owners remained in occupation:

'Would it not be a strong thing to say, that an owner of fifty acres of land might hand over all his land to conacre tenants, and yet be able to say that he remained in occupation?'[3]

In response to a query from Ball J, as to whether a conacre tenant had ever been rated as occupier of lands, counsel stated:

'No; but we will show, that if he continued to occupy the same land for two or three years, he might insist on being rated. Our proposition is, that the party who takes in conacre, acquires an intermediate occupational interest in the land while the crops are growing to maturity, and before they can be gathered.'

At one point, counsel sought to establish that a right of conacre gave the tenant a greater degree of exclusive possession than either an agistment or a profit of pasture:

'... the *status* of the conacre tenant towards the land is of a more exclusive character than that of a person who, for a time, takes the exclusive pasturage of the land; the conacre tenant's *status* is more exclusive, because the crop, his own property, is growing on the land. If the landlord entered and destroyed the crop, he would be a trespasser.'

The corollary was that the conacre tenant was an occupier for his own benefit, not a mere permissive occupier for the benefit of another. Since the conacre tenant had put his own seed in the ground, he had inevitably an interest in the land and should be enabled to bring an action in trespass for any infringement of it.

1   Deasy B, Fitzgerald J, O'Brien J, Ball J; Hayes J dissenting.
2   McDonagh QC and Chatterton QC (Lowry JC with them).
3   The submissions of counsel for the respondents appear at pp 178–179.

[23.10] These views commended themselves to Hayes J who delivered the sole dissenting judgment in the case. According to Hayes J, during the period that the conacre right was being exercised, it was the conacre tenant who exercised predominant control over the land.

> '... it is plain that in the absence of any stipulation to the contrary, the tenant is to be at liberty to put in his crop when and how he likes; and while it is in the ground he may cut, mow, reap, or dig it without any right of interference by the landowner; for the protection which the landowner is to contribute is for the tenant's benefit and may be dispensed with by him.'[1]

At a further point Hayes J urged:

> '... the conacre tenant is licensed to enter on the land, not merely for the purpose of cutting and carrying away the crop, but also for the purpose of planting and sowing, and even of renewing his crop if necessary, and managing it so as will best conduce to his profit. If this be so, how can it be said that it is not intended to exclude the landlord by this letting?'[2]

However, Ball J employed similar logic to arrive at the opposite conclusion. Since the permission given to a conacre tenant is to grow one particular type of crop only, his enjoyment cannot be tantamount to possession, as he would be liable in trespass to the landowner if he attempted to cultivate any other kind of crop.[3] Furthermore, since the landowners had covenanted to protect the crops from trespass, they would be unable, effectively, to do this if they ceased to occupy the lands.[4]

1   *McKeowne v Bradford* (1862) 7 Ir Jur (NS) 169 at 181.
2   (1862) 7 Ir Jur (NS) 169 at 182.
3   (1862) 7 Ir Jur (NS) 169 at 185.
4   (1862) 7 Ir Jur (NS) 169 at 186.

[23.11] Three of the judges, Fitzgerald J, O'Brien J and Ball J, were supported in their views, that the landowner in a conacre letting did not relinquish possession, by the decision in the sixteenth century case of *Hare v Celey*.[1] In this the plaintiff had given three of his neighbours, who joined him as co-plaintiffs, the right to plant seed on land owned by him; the arrangement was that the plaintiff should supply half the seed, the three neighbours the other half, and they should also manure the land; the three neighbours would then reap the crop and retain half of it, the other half going to the plaintiff. Before the crop came to maturity the defendant broke into the close and carried away the corn. In an action by Hare and the three neighbours for trespass, it was held that, though an action would have lain with Hare alone, the other three could not maintain an action of trespass *quare clausum frigit* because they did not have possession of the land. In the opinion of Ball J, the current case was even stronger, on its facts, than

Hare v Celey, in favour of holding that the conacre tenants did not enjoy possession, because the landowners were more remote from the activities of the conacre tenants. In *McKeowne v Bradford*[2] the landowners supplied no part of the seed, and no part of the produce became their property; they were to be remunerated either in money or money's worth; they had also covenanted to protect the crop from trespass, whereas Hare had entered into no such undertaking.[3]

---

[1] *Hare v Celey* (1589) L&T 526. 'It is an old case, but there are things in the world that are not the worse for being old.' (1862) 7 Ir Jur (NS) 175 at 185, per Ball J.

[2] *McKeowne v Bradford* (1862) 7 Ir Jur (NS) 169.

[3] (1862) 7 Ir Jur (NS) 175 at 185–186.

General rights of conacre tenants

[23.12] Although a conacre letting can be for a period of years, and a single short-term conacre letting can be often renewed, the conacre tenant has no right to do anything other than sow and cultivate crop. He does not have an auxiliary or an alternative right to meadow or pasture.[1] In the case of that part of the land let in conacre which is not tilled, the landowner 'would have been entitled to put his beasts upon so much of the land as was left in pasture; to cut hay upon the portions left uncropped; to let the pasture land for agistment; or to let, or sell the produce of, such portion as was meadow.'[2]

In *Roche v Fitzpatrick*[3] Fitzgerald J rejected the contention made on behalf of a landlord that, because ss 2 and 5 of the Land Law (Ireland) Act 1881 specifically provided that a letting in conacre for the purpose of growing potatoes and green crops is *not* deemed to be a sub-letting, a letting in conacre for the cultivation of corn *is* a sub-letting. Following *Booth v McManus*,[4] Fitzgerald J held that, notwithstanding a letting in conacre, the owner of the land continues to remain in occupation: this is not changed by the nature of the seed sown.

On the other hand, in *Irish Land Commission v Andrews*[5] the Land Commission was held entitled to re-possess land where the widow and administratrix of a statutory purchaser had contravened a clause in the purchase agreement, that the purchaser would not sub-let the land or part with possession, and would work the land to the satisfaction of the Land Commission. The widow had not lived on the lands but had entered an agreement with a neighbour that he would 'take the said land for tilling in bulk for four years', at a rent considerably in excess of the purchase annuity payable to the Land Commission. Even though the land had been worked to the satisfaction of the Land Commission, it was held that this arrangement was not a conacre agreement, but a letting of the land for a four-year term.

However, in *Irish Land Commission v Lawlor*[6] Judge Fawsitt noted that it was a common occurrence for farmers to require seasonal help in order to work their land, and that a conacre letting of portion of the lands purchased from the Land Commission was not an infraction of the terms of the purchase order, where the landowner retained at least some of the lands for personal cultivation. The obligation on the landowner, that the lands should be cultivated to the satisfaction of the Land Commission, did not import an additional obligation that the lands had to be cultivated by the statutory purchaser personally.

1   *Evans v Monagher* (1872) IR 6 CL 526.
2   (1872) IR 6 CL 526 at 530.
3   *Roche v Fitzpatrick* (1907) 41 ILTR 171.
4   *Booth v McManus* (1861) 12 ICLR 418.
5   *Irish Land Commission v Andrews* [1941] IR 79.
6   *Irish Land Commission v Lawlor* [1944] Ir Jur Rep 55.

[23.13] On the death of a tenant for life during a conacre letting, the conacre rent is payable to the life tenant's personal representatives up to the date of the life tenant's death, and thereafter to the remainderman. The remainderman is not bound to continue the conacre letting, but if he does so, either expressly or by implication based on acquiescence in its continuance, a new contract can be inferred from the date of the life tenant's death to the date on which the original conacre letting was to end.[1]

1   *Foster v Cunningham* [1956] NI 29.

Grazing Rights – Agistment

[23.14] Agistment is a right to graze animals on the lands of another. It has been held that a right to take land for grazing is not the same as a right to use the land for pasturing.[1] In *Fletcher v Hackett*[2] Gibson J held that there is a difference between letting the land for grazing and letting the grazing of the land: in the latter there is no change of possession of the land, only a grazing of the grass; in the former, there is a tenancy, and the relationship of landlord and tenant is created.

Similarly, in *O'Flaherty v Kelly*[3] Fitzgibbon LJ described an agistment contract as a 'grazing letting', which, he stated, 'did not mean, a letting of *land for grazing*; it meant the *hire of the grass* or "vesture" of the land. Such a hiring, in law, is an agistment contract and nothing more.'[4] According to Walker LC, the letting contract conferred 'only an exclusive right to graze, the breach of which would only give a right of action for breach of contract; and it is well settled that under such a contract no right to the soil, or right to the possession, passes.'[5]

Even though the owner of the animals did not remove his cattle for the one month of the year not covered by the agreement, and was subject to hardly any interference or supervision by the statutory tenant, the contract remained an agistment contract: a new contract was invariably negotiated, often at a different rent, prior to the fallow month. The fact that the grazing money was sought in advance, and that the statutory tenant paid the rates, was deemed to be consistent with an agistment letting.

1   *Mulligan v Adams* (1846) 8 Ir LR 132: '... he had no right to use it for any other purpose whatever; the plaintiff remained in possession of the land.'
2   *Fletcher v Hackett* (1906) 40 ILTR 37; see also *Crane v Naughten* [1912] 2 IR 318.
3   *O'Flaherty v Kelly* [1909] 1 IR 223.
4   [1909] 1 IR 223 at 229. Italics supplied by Fitzgibbon LJ. See also *Mogg v The Overseers of Yatton* (1880) 6 QBD 10. Those with the grazing rights had agreed to cut thistles and leave the

fences in good repair. A person with a mere agistment contract would neither have such a right nor assume such a responsibility.

5   [1909] 1 IR 223 at 228.

[23.15] The norm for an agistment letting is 11 months.[1] In *Fletcher v Hackett*[2] a contract of letting was found to be for agistment purposes, despite the fact that it was for a term of 12 (rather than 11) months and a house on the lands was continuously occupied by the cattle herd. Gibson J held that the intention of the parties was to create a legal relationship of a temporary character, and that possession of the lands did not pass. As in the case of a person holding under a conacre letting, a person holding under an agistment letting is deemed to have a 'special possession' of the lands, with an 'exclusive right' to graze.[3]

In *Re Moore's Estate; Fitzpatrick v Behan*[4] grazing rights had been enjoyed under an agistment contract for up to 50 years; this was still found not to create a tenancy. O'Byrne J stated that the owner of the cattle had never enjoyed possession, but had 'merely a licence to use the lands for the specific purposes set out in the several agreements.'[5]

---

1   *O'Flaherty v Kelly* [1909] 1 IR 223; *Crane v Naughten* [1912] 2 IR 318; *Carson v Jeffers* [1961] IR 44; *Collins v O'Brien* [1981] ILRM 328.
2   *Fletcher v Hackett* (1906) 40 ILTR 37.
3   *Winters v Owens* [1950] IR 225 at 229, per Lavery J.
4   *Re Moore's Estate; Fitzpatrick v Behan* [1944] IR 295.
5   [1944] IR 295 at 301.

[23.16] A person with grazing rights, even under a temporary agistment contract not for a fixed term, is entitled to reasonable notice of its termination so as to be able to remove his animals from the land.[1]

---

1   *Plunkett v Heeney* (1904) 4 NIJR 136.

Liability for damage

[23.17] The owner of land on which cattle are placed under an agistment contract owes a duty to the owner of the cattle to ensure that the cattle suffer no harm through any default of his. This includes a duty to pay the rates owing on the land so as to prevent the cattle from being seized. In a case where the landowner failed to pay the rates, he was held liable in damages to the tenant under the agistment contract to the amount of the market value of the cattle on the date they were seized.[1]

The owner of cattle, under an agistment contract, not having a right to possession, has no entitlement to erect fences between the area over which he has grazing and other of the landowner's land. Accordingly, if the cattle stray and cause damage to the landowner's vegetable garden, he has no cause of action against their owner, as it was for the landowner to have indicated where alone the cattle were to graze and to take steps to prevent their wandering anywhere else.[2]

[1]   *Acres v Maxwell* (1937) 71 ILTR 244.
[2]   *Hickey v Cosgrave* (1861) 6 Ir Jur (NS) 251.

[23.18] In *Winters v Owens*[1] Lavery J held that the owner of cattle grazing on lands, under a grazing agreement, was liable for damage that resulted from the escape of the cattle on to adjoining lands occupied under a conacre letting. This was despite the fact that under the grazing agreement the landowner had assumed responsibility for the herding of the cattle. Lavery J found that the obligation undertaken by the landowner to herd the cattle was as agent for the owner of the stock. Accordingly, the common law principle still applied, that the owner of an animal is bound to take steps to ensure that it does not stray upon the lands of a neighbour, and is liable in damages for the ordinary consequences of any trespass which occurs.[2]

This decision is at variance with that of Judge O'Briain, in the Circuit Court, in *Dalton v O'Sullivan*,[3] in which it was held that the owner of the cattle was not liable for damage done to a neighbouring landowner when they broke loose from the land where they were grazing. However, in *Dalton v O'Sullivan* the owner of the animals lived 100 miles away from where the cattle were agisted, whereas in *Winters v Owens* it was quite clear that he had, in effect, retained control of them. As Lavery J stated in *Winters v Owens*,[4] merely because in certain cases the owner of the land has been held liable, does not mean that there might not be other cases in which the owner of the stock will be held liable.

[1]   *Winters v Owens* [1950] IR 225.
[2]   [1950] IR 225 at 231; also, *Cox v Burbridge* (1863) 13 CB (NS) 430 at 438, per Williams J; *Menton v Brocklebank* [1923] 2 KB 212 at 233, per Atkins LJ.
[3]   *Dalton v O'Sullivan* [1947] Ir Jur Rep 25.
[4]   *Winters v Owens* [1950] IR 225 at 230; see also *Noonan v Hartnett* (1950) 84 ILTR 41.

Modern Developments: The Years after 1960

Republic of Ireland

[23.19] In the Republic of Ireland the law of conacre and agistment has not changed since 1861. Precisely 100 years after *Booth v McManus*,[1] the law was re-affirmed by the High Court in *Carson v Jeffers*.[2] The plaintiff owner of registered land in Co Meath had given to the defendant a letting that was a blend of conacre and agistment. The agreement provided for a letting over five separate periods, each of approximately 11 months; that the plaintiff landowner would assume responsibility for the discharge of all rates and drainage charges and would also indemnify the defendant for any loss of stock or crop that might result from court proceedings brought against him as registered owner of the lands.

Some years earlier the plaintiff had charged his lands with the payment of monies to a third party. When the plaintiff failed to pay, the third party instituted a mortgage suit and obtained an order for sale. The plaintiff now sought to deliver up possession and so determined the conacre and agistment letting. The defendant refused to leave. The plaintiff argued that it was an implied term of their agreement, since the defendant was well aware of the proceedings being brought against the plaintiff on foot of the registered charge, that in the event of his having to comply with a court order for sale, he would be entitled to determine the licence and obtain possession.

In relation to the nature of the right granted to the defendant, Budd J stated:

> 'Although the agreement is described as an agistment it is apparent from the terms of the agreement that the parties also intended it to be a grazing and conacre agreement ... The agreement is on the face of it an agistment letting, not creating any estate or interest in the land in the defendant. It is a licence to graze and conacre the lands only for the prescribed period of eleven months.'[3]

The defendant argued that, in effect, the plaintiff was not in possession of the lands, on foot of a '*de facto* or immediate right', and so was unable to sustain a claim for trespass. Budd J[4] refused to accept this argument, holding:

> 'The terms of the agreement in the present case actually state that the agreement is not to establish or constitute a tenancy of any nature. ... The agreement, moreover, provides for ... the usual 11 months and for a period of one month in between each letting during which the defendant was not to be entitled to graze or conacre the lands. The plaintiff was also, as is usual in agistment lettings, to pay the rates and annuity. The agreement is thus an ordinary agistment agreement, or licence to graze and conacre the lands, and I hold in law that the plaintiff did not by entering into this agreement part with possession of the lands.'[5]

---

[1]   *Booth v McManus* (1861) 12 ICLR 418.

[2]   *Carson v Jeffers* [1961] IR 44.

[3]   [1961] IR 44 at 47.

[4]   Citing as authority the cases of *Re Moore's Estate; Fitzpatrick v Behan* [1944] IR 295, *Mulligan v Adams* (1846) 8 Ir LR 132; *Booth v McManus* (1861) 12 ICLR 418.

[5]   [1961] IR 44 at 50–51.

Northern Ireland

[23.20] Recent judicial pronouncements in Northern Ireland have moved away from the notion that possession or occupation is deemed unequivocally to reside with the landowner.[1] *Maurice E Taylor (Merchants) Ltd v Commissioner of Valuation*[2] concerned the liability of a large potato producing company, which farmed in conacre approximately 100 hectares of land within a 20 mile radius of Draperstown, to be registered as rated occupier of a dressing shed and store used for the purpose of grading, bagging and labelling the potatoes. The plaintiff's annual turnover in terms of potatoes shipped was between 20,000 and 25,000 metric tonnes, of which about 3,000 metric tonnes were grown by it on the conacre lands. In order for the dressing shed and store to be omitted from the relevant valuation list, they had to be occupied together with agricultural land and used solely in connection with agricultural operations. Accordingly, the principal issue was whether the land enjoyed by the plaintiff in conacre was 'occupied' by it for rating purposes.

At the outset, it is clear that the economic conditions underpinning this conacre letting, and the contractual capacity of the parties, are at marked variance with those that prevailed throughout any part of the nineteenth century. This was a circumstance noted by Gibson LJ who delivered the principal judgment of the Court of Appeal, which contains a succinct and illuminating summary of both the nature of conacre in the nineteenth century and the social and economic environment that made it a necessity.[3] In the instant case, the landowner assumed no responsibility to maintain the fencing of the lands, and minor repair work would be carried out by the plaintiff company without recourse to the landlord.

---

[1]   Although it is clear from the terms of the will in *Re Steele* [1976] NI 66 that the traditional notion of conacre is still extant in Northern Ireland.

[2]   *Maurice E Taylor (Merchants) Ltd v Commissioner of Valuation* [1981] NI 236.

[3]   [1981] NI 236 at 243–244.

[23.21] Although holding that 'from the legal point of view the theory that a conacre agreement does not create a tenancy is so well established and embedded in our statute law that it cannot now be questioned',[1] Gibson LJ also decided that it was now no longer the law that only a lessee of land could be deemed to be in rated occupation. A conacre letting of 11 months in any one year was not 'too transient to permit the company being considered as in rateable occupation.' The fact that the occupier may be turned out at short notice did not deprive his occupancy of the character of permanence:

> 'The matter is to be looked at from the point of view of what period of occupation was contemplated at the outset rather than how long in fact the hereditament is occupied … The degree of permanence which is required for rateable occupation depends not merely on the length of actual occupation but also on the nature of the hereditament and of the occupation.'[2]

However, according to Gibson LJ, not only the law in terms of occupation for rating purposes, but even the character of conacre itself, had changed:

> 'The whole concept of conacre lettings has during the last 100 years undergone a radical change. … Nowadays it would be practically unknown for there to be a conacre letting of a small strip or area of ground having no obvious physical boundaries. The areas now correspond with the areas of fields or farms. The landowner no longer ploughs the land or provides the manure and he no longer reserves any right to exercise any control over or protection of the land, except in so far as the tenant may only grow one crop, is often obliged to fertilise the land and is required to vacate the land at the end of the term. The owner now merely has a claim in debt for the rent, and no longer has any lien or charge on the crop or right to prevent its removal. In perhaps most cases, as for example, where the farmer has retired or dies leaving a widow living in the house on the farm, the same land is let in conacre or agistment year after year, often to the same person, and in that case whether he vacates the land for a month is of little importance to the owner. In not a few cases, as, for example, where the owner is in America, the lettings are made for long periods, occasionally by a single contract to the same tenant, and apart from any special covenants in the agreement no rights are reserved or exercised by or on behalf of the owner of the land during the period of the conacre or agistment agreements.'[3]

In the opinion of Gibson LJ, the decisions of the Irish courts in the nineteenth century, that a conacre tenant was not in occupation of the land for rating, or other, purposes, have been overtaken by changes both in the nature of conacre lettings and the law in relation to rated occupation.[4] Gibson LJ furthermore held that the plaintiff had 'exclusive possession' of the various plots held by it under conacre and had the right to exclude all persons, adding:

> 'Whereas, in earlier days, the landowner retained paramount occupation of the land, it is now clear that if there is any question of paramount occupation, which would only arise in the case of some rather exceptional contract, it now resides in the tenant.'[5]

---

1   *Maurice E Taylor (Merchants) Ltd v Commissioner of Valuation* [1981] NI 236 at 245.
2   [1981] NI 236 at 246.
3   [1981] NI 236 at 244–245.
4   In this regard, one suspects that McDonagh QC and Chatterton QC, counsel opposing the landowners in *McKeowne v Bradford* (1862) 7 Ir Jur (NS) 169, 175, would have felt, 120 years later, 'vindicated'!
5   [1981] NI 236 at 245. It can be inferred that the 'paramount occupation' identified by Gibson LJ as residing in the conacre tenant is kindred to the 'special possession' spoken of by Crampton J in *Dease v O'Reilly* (1845) 8 LR Ir 52.

[23.22] The principles established in *Maurice E Taylor (Merchants) Ltd v Commissioner of Valuation* were followed by the Northern Ireland Court of Appeal, two years later, in the context of land occupied under an agistment letting, in *Northern Ireland Animal Embryo Transplant Ltd v Commissioners of Valuation*.[1] In this case the building sought to be rated was used for the artificial insemination of donor cows, whose fertilised embryos were extracted and then implanted in recipient cows. The surrounding lands were held under agistment for the purpose of feeding the donor cows prior to insemination and the recipient cows after insemination. Hay cropped on the land was also fed to the cattle while in the building. The Court of Appeal held that, notwithstanding that the plaintiff was deemed to be in actual occupation of the lands, in this case the use of the lands was subordinate to the use of the building which was not itself agricultural, and so the building was liable to be rated.

---

1   *Northern Ireland Animal Embryo Transplant Ltd v Commissioners of Valuation* [1983] NI 105.

[23.23] It remains to be seen whether the courts in the Republic of Ireland will take the same line, in relation to what might be termed the 'industry of agriculture' and the issue of rated occupation, as has been established by the Northern Ireland Court of Appeal. It is difficult to see any reason why not. On the other hand, with the increasing commercialisation of agrarian enterprise, and the disappearance from the Irish social scene of the landless rural labourer, it is hard to justify the continuance of the view, articulated by Gibson LJ in *Maurice E Taylor (Merchants) Ltd v Commissioner of Valuation*,[1] that the conacre contract's not creating the relationship of landlord and tenant 'is so well established ... that it cannot now be questioned.' There can be no sense in which the bare subsistence agrarian scenario that prevailed throughout the nineteenth century, and earlier, has any application at the dawn of the twenty first. Nor is the enterprise and investment which modern agriculture represents sensibly embodied in the fleeting device of a licence.

---

1   *Maurice E Taylor (Merchants) Ltd v Commissioner of Valuation* [1981] NI 236.

Index

All references are to *paragraph* numbers.

Profits à prendre (contd)
   corporeal right, as, **13**.08
   incorporeal right, as, **13**.09–**13**.13
   introduction, **13**.06–**13**.07
   lakes, in, **13**.14–**13**.17
   tidal waters, in, **13**.18–**13**.23
  grazing of cattle, etc.
   generally, **12**.24–**12**.30
   introduction, **11**.08
  introduction, **11**.01–**11**.02
  licences, and, **19**.09
  local customary rights, and
   generally, **11**.16–**11**.20
   introduction, **10**.20
  mining and quarrying, **13**.35–**13**.42
  pasturage
   generally, **12**.24–**12**.30
   introduction, **11**.08
  piscary, of
   access to rights, **13**.24–**13**.27
   corporeal right, as, **13**.08
   incorporeal right, as, **13**.09–**13**.13
   introduction, **13**.06–**13**.07
   lakes, in, **13**.14–**13**.17
   tidal waters, in, **13**.18–**13**.23
  pleasure and profit, for
   fishing, **13**.06–**13**.27
   mining and quarrying, **13**.35–**13**.42
   sporting rights, **13**.28–**13**.34
   tidal waters, **13**.01–**13**.05
  profits appurtenant
   meaning, **11**.09
   requirements, **11**.12–**11**.15
  sporting rights, **13**.28–**13**.34
  statutory prescription, and, **5**.02
  tidal waters, and, **13**.01–**13**.05
  turbary
   allocation, **12**.16–**12**.18
   characteristics, **12**.01–**12**.06
   choice, **12**.16–**12**.18
   drainage, **12**.13–**12**.15
   introduction, **11**.08
   rights of parties, **12**.19–**12**.20
   words of grant, **12**.07–**12**.12
  types, **11**.08–**11**.11

Profits appendant
  meaning, **11**.09
Profits appurtenant
  estovers
   generally, **12**.21–**12**.23
   introduction, **11**.08
  fishing rights, and, **13**.07
  meaning, **11**.09
  requirements, **11**.12–**11**.15
  turbary
   allocation, **12**.16–**12**.18
   characteristics, **12**.01–**12**.06
   choice, **12**.16–**12**.18
   drainage, **12**.13–**12**.15
   introduction, **11**.08
   rights of parties, **12**.19–**12**.20
   words of grant, **12**.07–**12**.12
Profits in gross
  fishing
   access to rights, **13**.24–**13**.27
   corporeal right, as, **13**.08
   incorporeal right, as, **13**.09–**13**.13
   introduction, **13**.06–**13**.07
   lakes, in, **13**.14–**13**.17
   tidal waters, in, **13**.18–**13**.23
  introduction, **11**.02
  meaning, **11**.09
  mining and quarrying, **13**.35–**13**.42
  sporting rights, **13**.28–**13**.34
Profits pour cause de vicinage
  meaning, **11**.09
Psychological effects
  rights of light, and, **7**.21–**7**.22
Public rights in tidal waters
  profits *à prendre*, and, **13**.01–**13**.05
Public rights of way
  abandonment, **10**.14–**10**.15
  access, **10**.12
  dedication, **10**.02–**10**.05
  demonstrable public user, **10**.06–**10**.10
  introduction, **10**.01
  maintenance by consent of owner, **10**.11
  obstruction, **10**.13
  termini, **10**.12